Belgium

routard

Managing editor: Liz Coghill
English translation: Tamsin Black
Editors: Clare Thomson, Timothy Wright
Proofreader: Hilary Hughes

Additional research and assistance:
Michael Hutchinson, Sofi Mogensen, Kate
Williams, Michael Summers
Index: Dorothy Frame

Series director: Philippe Gloaguen
Series creators: Philippe Gloaguen, Michel
Duval
Chief editor: Pierre Josse
Assistant chief editor: Benoît Lucchini
Coordination director: Florence
Charmetant

Editorial team: Yves Couprie, Olivier Page,
Véronique de Chardon, Amanda Keravel,
Isabelle Al Subaihi, Anne-Caroline Dumas,
Carole Bordes, Bénédicte Bazaille, André
Poncelet, Jérôme de Gubernatis, Marie
Burin des Roziers and Thierry Brouard.

Our guides provide independent advice. The authors and compilers do not accept any remuneration for the inclusion of addresses in this guide. Please note that we cannot accept any responsibility for any loss, injury or inconvenience sustained by anyone as a result of any information or advice contained in this guide.

Feedback
We have done our best to ensure the accuracy of the information contained in this guide. However, addresses, phone numbers, opening times etc. do invariably change from time to time, so if you find a discrepancy please do let us know and help us update the guides. As prices may change so may other circumstances – a restaurant may change hands or the standard of service at a hotel may deteriorate since our researchers made their visit. Again, we do our best to ensure information is accurate, but if you notice any discrepancy, please let us know. You can contact us at: hachetteuk@orionbooks.co.uk or write to us at Cassell & Co, address below.

Price guide
Because of rapid inflation in many countries, it is impossible to give an accurate indication of prices in hotels and restaurants. Prices can change enormously from one year to the next. As a result we have adopted a system of categories for the prices in the guides: 'Budget', 'Moderate', 'Chic' and 'Très Chic' (in the guides to France), otherwise 'Expensive' and 'Splash out' in the others.

First published in the United Kingdom in 2002 by Cassell & Co
© English Translation Cassell & Co 2002
© Hachette Livre (Hachette Tourisme) 2001
© Cartography Hachette Tourisme

Distributed in the United States of America by Sterling Publishing Co., Inc.
387 Park Avenue South, New York, NY 10016-8810.

A CIP catalogue for this book is available from the British Library.

ISBN 1 84202 022 6

Typeset at The Spartan Press Ltd, Lymington, Hants.
Printed and bound by Aubin, France. E-mail: sales@aubin-imprimeur.fr

Cover design by Emmanuel Le Vallois (Hachette Livre) and Paul Cooper.
Cover photo © Corbis/Michael Busselle. Back cover photo © The Travel Library/Stuart Black.

Cassell & Co, Wellington House, 125 Strand, London WC2R 0BB

Belgium

**The ultimate
food, drink and
accommodation guide**

HACHETTE

Contents

List of maps 8
Just exactly who or what is a
    Routard? 9

Map of Belgium 10
Symbols used in the guide 12

GETTING THERE 13

By Air 13
From Britain 13
From Ireland 15
From the United States 16
From Canada 18
From Australia and New Zealand 19
From South Africa 21
By Train 21
From Britain 21

By Sea 22
From Britain 22
From Ireland 23
By Car 24
From Britain 24
By Coach 24
From Britain 24
From Ireland 25

GENERAL INFORMATION 26

Accommodation 26
Budget 29
Climate and seasons 30
Communications 31
Conversion tables 32
Embassies 33
Entry formalities 34
Etiquette 35
Festivals and traditions 36
Health and insurance 39
Languages 40

Media 45
Money 46
Outdoor activities 47
Public holidays 48
Shopping 48
Smoking 49
Time 49
Tipping 50
Tourist offices 50
Transport 50
Useful websites 55

BACKGROUND 56

Vital statistics 56
History 56
Geography 66
Economy 67
Federalism 68
The Royal Family 70
Population 73

Human rights 73
Famous Belgians 75
Literature 79
Surrealism 80
Comic strips 80
Food and drink 81
Music 86

BRUSSELS 89

A short history 89
European institutions 93
Eurocrats 96
The Pentagon 96
Getting to Brussels 96
Useful information 100
Transport 109
Where to stay 110
Where to eat 117
Where to drink 125
Live music 131
Shows 131

Nightclubs 132
Shops 133
What to see 134
Within the Pentagon 135
    The Grand'Place ● The Îlot Sacré
    ● Sablon and Palais-Royal districts
    ● North of L'Îlot Sacré, the Old Port
    and the Béguinage ● The Marolles
    district
Walks outside the Pentagon 157
    Ixelles ● Saint-Gilles ● Bois de la
    Cambre ● The European district

● Northwest Brussels ● The Royal Estate at Laeken ● Heysel
The Main Museums 165
Musée Royaux des Beaux-Arts ● Musée des Instruments de Musique ● Le Centre belge de la bande dessinée ● Musée de la Dynastie ● Musée Horta
The Museums of the Parc du Cinquantenaire 171
Musées Royaux d'Art et d'Histoire ● Musée Royal de l'Armée et de l'Histoire militaire ● Autoworld
Other Museums 174
Musée Communal d'Ixelles

● Musée du Jouet ● Maison d'Érasme ● Musée Bruxellois de la Gueuze ● Musée du Costume et de la Dentelle ● Musée Constantin Meunier ● Musée Charlier ● Musée David et Alice Van Buuren ● Musée Antoine Wiertz ● Musée d'Art spontané ● Musée de l'Institut Royal des Sciences Naturelles
What to see around Brussels 177
Tervuren 177
Festivals and cultural events in Brussels 179
Flea markets 179
Leaving Brussels 180

FLANDERS 182

Flemish Brabant (Vlaams Brabant) 182
ZONIËNWOUD (FORÊT DE SOIGNES) 182
HALLE (HAL) 183
Huizingen 185
BEERSEL CASTLE 185
GAASBEEK CASTLE 186
NATIONALE PLANTENTUIN (NATIONAL BOTANIC GARDENS OF MEISE) 187
GRIMBERGEN 188
LEUVEN (LOUVAIN) 188
Heverlee, Park Abbey
DIEST 195
Aarschot ● Werchter ● Scherpenheuvel ● Averbode Abbey ●
ZOUTLEEUW (LÉAU) 200
TIENEN (TIRLEMONT) 202
Hoegaarden ● Landen
Province of Limburg 204
HASSELT 204
Bokrijk ● Beringen
Haspengouw 209
TONGEREN 210
The commandery of Alden Biesen ● Bilzen ● Borgloon
SINT TRUIDEN 215
The countryside around the Maas (Maasland) 217
Lanaken ● Rekem ● Maasmechelen ● Vucht ● Maaseik
North Limburg 221
Bree ● Bocholt ● Peer ● Lommel
Fourons/Voeren 223
Sint Pieters Voeren

The Province of Antwerp (Provincie Antwerpen) 224
ANTWERP (ANTWERPEN) 224
Cogels Osylei ● Silver Centre, Sterkshof provincial museum ● Linkeroever ● Openluchtmuseum voor Beeldhouwkunst St Middelheim Antwerpen ● The Port of Antwerp ● Lillo
MECHELEN (MALINES) 259
Dierenpark Planckendael
LIER 264
HERENTALS 266
GEEL 267
TURNHOUT 268
Hoogstraten
Walks in the Province of Antwerp 269
KEMPEN 269
KLEIN BRABANT 270
Breedonk fort
East Flanders (Oost Vlaanderen) 271
GHENT (GENT) 272
Ghent countryside: around the Leie 299
Duerle ● Sint-Martens Latem ● Deinze ● Ooidonk Castle ● Laarne Castle
Waasland 302
SINT NIKLAAS 302
Scheldt and Dender 304
GERAARDSBERGEN 304
NINOVE 305
AALST 306
DENDERMONDE 308
The Flemish Ardennes 309
OUDENAARDE (AUDENARDE) 309
RONSE (RENAIX) 213

The Province of Western Flanders (West-Flaanderen) 313
BRUGES (BRUGGE) 314
Around Bruges 350
DAMME 350
LISSEWEGE
ZEEBRUGGE 353
JABBEKE 354
OSTEND (OOSTENDE) 354
   Stene ● Raversijde Estate
The east coast, from Ostend to the Zwin 365
   De Haan ● Blankenberge ● Heist, Duinbergen, Albertstrand, Knokke-le-Zoute
HET ZOUTE 367

The west coast, from Ostend to De Panne 367
NIEUWPOORT 368
KOKSIJDE- OOSTDUINKERKE 368
DE PANNE 370
VEURNE 371
   Museum of Bakers and Confectioners
DIKSMUIDE 373
   The German cemetery of Praetbos-Vlasdo ● Lo ● Bachten de Kupe open-air museum ● Old Timer Museum Bossaert in Reninge
IEPER (YPRES) 377
   Hooge-Krater ● Langemark ● Poelkappelle ● Zillebeke ● Zonnebeke ● Wervik ● Poperinge
KORTRIJK 382
   Roeselaere

WALLONIA 386

Province of Walloon Brabant 386
WATERLOO 386
   Ittre
BRAINE-LE-CHÂTEAU 392
REBECQ 392
NIVELLES 393
VILLERS-LA-VILLE ABBEY 396
LOUVAIN-LA-NEUVE 398
WAVRE 399
   Domaine provincial Bois-des- Rêves ● Six Flags Belgium
CHÂTEAU DE RIXENSART 400
LAC DE GENVAL 400
   Domaine de la Hulpe
JODOIGNE 401
   Orp-le-Grand ● Folx-les-Caves ● Jauchelette ● Hélécine ● Chaumont-Gistoux ● Beauvechain ● Tourinnes-la-Grosse
The Province of Liège 404
LIÈGE 404
   La route du Feu ● Préhistosite et la grotte de Ramioul ● Manufacture de cristaux du Val-Saint-Lambert ● Herstal
Herve 440
BLEGNY MINE 440
   Mortier ● Dalhem
VISÉ 443
   Maastricht ● Aubel ● Herve ● Clermont-sur-Bewinne
SOIRON 445
   Soumagne ● Olne

THEUX 447
   Château de Franchimont ● Polleur ● Sart ● La Reid
VERVIERS 449
LIMBOURG 453
   Barrage and Lac de la Gileppe
EUPEN 454
   American cemetery of Henri-Chapelle
Hautes-Fagnes 457
CENTRE NATURE DE BOTRANGE 457
   Botrange
CHÂTEAU DE REINHARDSTEIN 458
   Robertville
MALMEDY 460
   Bütgenbach ● Hergesberg
SANKT VITH 464
   Burg-Reuland ● Our valley
STAVELOT 466
   Musée historique de Décembre 1944 in La Gleize ● Road from La Gleize to Spa ● Coo ● Ski resort at Mont des Brumes
SPA 471
South of Liège 474
   Harzé ● Grottes de Sougné-Remouchamps ● Aywaille ● Saint-Séverin-en-Condroz ● Jehay-Amay ● Jehay-Bodignée
HUY 476
   Amay ● Château de Modave ● Parc naturel des vallées de la Burdinale et de la Mehaigne

The Province of Luxembourg 480
LA ROCHE-EN-ARDENNE 480
Belvédère des Six-Ourthes in Nadrin
● Belvédère de Nisramont
VIELSALM 484
HOUFFALIZE 485
DURBUY 486
Église Saint-Martin in Tohogne
● Domaine de Hottemme in Barvaux
● Labyrinthus ● Grottes de Hotton
● Moulin à eau Faber
MARCHE-EN- FAMENNE 489
Église Saint-Étienne in Waha
FOURNEAU-SAINT-MICHEL 491
SAINT-HUBERT 492
Parc à gibier ● Centrale hydraulique
de Poix ● Redu
BASTOGNE 496
Ferme des Bisons in Foy-Recogne
ARLON 499
Marais de la Haute-Semois
The Gaume 501
VIRTON 501
TORGNY 502
Montquintin
ABBAYE D'ORVAL 504
Relais Romain de Chameleux ● The
Haute Semois
BOUILLON 506
Corbion ● Rochehaut ● Botassart
● Alle-sur-Semois ● Vresse-sur-
Semois ● Paliseul ● Neufchâteau
Province of Namur 512
NAMUR 512
Abbey of Floreffe
GEMBLOUX 527
Corroy-le-Château ● Galerie
Dieleman in Grand-Leez
ANDENNE 529
Vallée du Samson ● Goyet
THE MEUSE VALLEY 530
Château and gardens d'Annevoie-
Rouillon ● Château de Montaigle
● Sosoye ● Track cars of la
Molignée ● Abbaye de Maredsous
● Furnaux
Crupet Valley 533
CRUPET 533
SPONTIN 534
Château de Poilvache
BOUVIGNES-SUR-MEUSE 536
Château de Creve-Coeur
DINANT 537
Les rochers de Freyr ● Hastière-
par-Delà

CELLES 541
Château de Vêves ● Église de Foy-
Notre-Dame ● Parc naturel de
Furfooz
Southeast Namur 542
CINEY 542
Chevetogne
CHÂTEAU DE LAVAUX-SAINTE-
ANNE 543
GROTTES DE HAN 544
ROCHEFORT 545
Southwest Namur 547
OIGNIES-EN-THIÉRACHE 547
Viroinval, Vierves-sur-Viroin and
Dourbes ● Nismes
TREIGNES 548
Gambrinus Drivers Museum in
Romedenne
COUVIN 549
Hitler's Bunker ● Musée de la Vie
régionale in Cul-des-Sarts
● Walcourt
Province of Hainaut 551
CHIMAY 552
Étangs de Virelles ● Lacs de l'Eau
d'l leure
CHARLEROI 555
Mont-sur-Marchienne
● Marchienne-au-Pont ● Marcinelle
● Gozée ● Thuin ● Lobbes
BINCHE 563
Domaine and Musée royal de
Mariemont ● Canal du Centre
● Écomusée de Bois-du-Luc
● Château de Seneffe
MONS 568
Site archéologique industriel du
Grand-Hornu ● Maison de Van
Gogh in Cuesmes ● Marais de
Harchies-Pommeroeul ● Bernissart
SOIGNIES 577
Château d'Ecaussinnes-Lalaing
● Plan incliné de Ronquières
● Enghien ● Château du Roeulx
ATH 580
Château de Beloeil ● Château
d'Attre ● Parc Paradiso
● Archéosite d'Aubechies
LESSINES 583
Elezelles ● Écomusée du pays des
Collines in La Hamaide ● Brasserie
à vapeur Dits in Pipaix
TOURNAI 584
Mont Saint-Aubert ● Antoing
● Parc Naturel Transfrontalier du
Hainaut

INDEX 595

Map List

Antwerp 228–9
Belgium 10–11
Bruges 320–1
Brussels (Map I) 98–9
Brussels – North (Map II) 102–3
Brussels – South (Map III) 106–7
Brussels (Map IV) 159

Brussels 94–5
Ghent 276–7
Liège 408–9
Mons 571
Namur 516–7
Ostend 356–7
Tournai 587

Just Exactly Who or What is a Routard?

You are. Yes, you! The fact that you are reading this book means that you are a Routard. You are probably still none the wiser, so to explain we will take you back to the origin of the guides. Routard was the brainchild of a Frenchman named Philippe Gloaguen, who compiled the first guide some 25 years ago with his friend Michel Duval. They simply could not find the kind of guide book they wanted and so the solution was clear – they would just have to write it themselves. When it came to naming the guide, Philippe came up with the term Routard, which at the time did not exist as a bona fide word – at least, not in conventional dictionary terms. Today, if you look the word up in a French-English dictionary you will find that it means 'traveller' or 'globetrotter' – so there you have it, that's what you are!

From this humble beginning has grown a vast collection of some 100 titles to destinations all over the world. Routard is now the bestselling guide book series in France. The guides have been translated into five different languages, so keep an eye out for fellow Routard readers on your travels.

What exactly do the guides do?
The short answer is that they provide all the information you need to enable you to have a successful holiday or trip. Routards' great strength however, lies in their listings. The guides provide comprehensive listings for accommodation, eating and drinking – ranging from campsites and youth hostels through to four star hotels – and from bars, clubs and greasy spoons to tearooms, cafés and restaurants. Each entry is accompanied by a detailed and frank appraisal of the address, rather like a friend coming back from holiday who is recommending all the good places to go (or even the places to avoid!). The guides aim to help you find the best addresses and the best value for money within your price range, whilst giving you invaluable insider advice at the same time.

Anything else?
Routard also provides oceans of practical advice on how to get along in the country or city you are visiting plus an insight into the character and customs of the people. How do you negotiate your way around the transport system? Will you offend if you bare your knees in the temple? And so on. In addition, you will find plenty of sightseeing information, backed up by historical and cultural detail, interesting facts and figures, addresses and opening times. The humanitarian aspect is also of great importance, with the guides commenting freely and often pithily, and most titles contain a section on human rights.

Routard are truly useful guides that are convivial, irreverent, down-to-earth and honest. We very much hope you enjoy them and that they will serve you well during your stay.

Happy travelling.

Kortrijk (Courtrai)	Places covered in guide
Roeselaere	Addresses and places in the area
Mouscron	Locator only

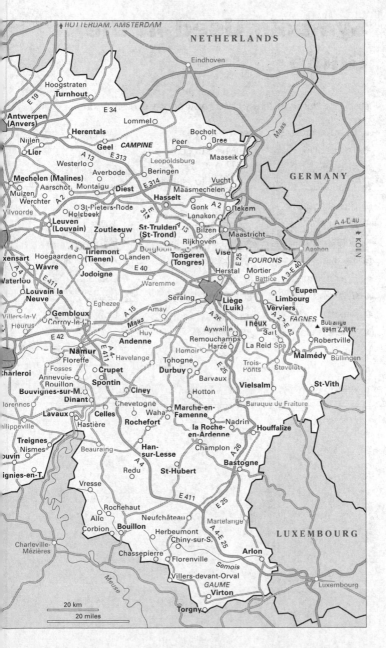

BELGIUM

Symbols Used in the Guide

Please note that not all the symbols below appear in every guide.

- Useful addresses
- Tourist office
- Post office
- Telephone
- Railway station
- Bus station
- Shared taxi
- Tram
- River transport
- Sea transport
- Airport
- Where to stay

- Where to eat
- Where to go for a drink
- Where to listen to music
- Where to go for an ice-cream
- To see
- Shopping
- 'Other'
- Parking
- Castle
- Ruins

- Diving site
- Shelter
- Camp site
- Peak
- Site
- Town
- Hill
- Abbey, chapel
- Lookout
- Beach
- Lighthouse

Getting There

By Air

FROM BRITAIN

British Airways, **bmi british midland**, **Sabena** and **Ryanair** and **Virgin Express** fly regularly to Brussels. British Airways flies non-stop from Birmingham, Manchester and Southampton, as well as from London Heathrow and Gatwick. Sabena flies direct from Edinburgh and Glasgow, Birmingham, Leeds/Bradford, Manchester and Heathrow. bmi british midland flies direct from Birmingham, East Midlands and Heathrow.

Flight time to Brussels is around one hour. Expect to pay at least £100 for a standard return, with higher prices for departures at weekends. Fares tend to increase for travel during the summer months or at Christmas. There are usually lots of good offers available on flights, particularly if you can be flexible about when you travel. Ryanair and Virgin Express often offer deals that bring the price of return tickets to under £60, so shop around.

Most flights arrive at Brussels National Airport, known almost universally as Zaventem. Zaventem is about 9 miles (14 kilometres) from Brussels city centre. Regular trains travel between the airport and Brussels Central Station from early morning until 11.45pm and there are additional bus and taxi services. Ryanair flights arrive at Brussels Charleroi Sud, which is a slightly longer journey to the city by bus or taxi.

Brussels is a popular destination, particularly for short breaks and package deals. Check the travel pages of the broadsheet newspapers for promotions, Teletext and websites such as www.cheapflights.com, www.expedia.com and www.lastminute.com for package and flight bargains. Always ensure that any travel agent or airline that you book with is insured by ABTA.

✪ bmi british midland: Donington Hall, Castle Donington, Derby DE74 2SB. ☎ (0870) 607 0555. Website: www.flybmi.com

✪ British Airways: Waterside, PO Box 365, Harmondsworth UB7 OGB. ☎ (0845) 773 3377. Website: www.britishairways.com

✪ Ryanair: Dublin Airport, County Dublin. ☎ (0870) 333 1231. Website: www.ryanair.com

✪ Sabena: Gemini House, Second Floor, West Block, 10–18 Putney Hill, London SW15 6AA. ☎ (020) 8780 1444. Website: www.sabena.com

✪ Virgin Express: Building 116, B-1820 Melsbroek Airport, Belgium. ☎ (020) 7744 0004. Website: www.virgin-express.com

✪ The Air Travel Advisory Bureau: Columbus House, 28 Charles Square, London N1 6HT. ☎ (020) 7635 5000. Website: www.atab.co.uk

TRAVEL AGENTS

■ **Airline Network**: (discount flights by phone only) ☎ (0870) 241 0019.

■ **Bridge the World**: (discount flights and packages) 47 Chalk Farm Road, London NW1 8AJ. ☎ (020) 7911 0900. Website: www.bridgetheworld.com

■ **Council Travel**: (discount flights) 28a Poland Street, London W1V 8AJ. ☎ (020) 7287 9410. Website: www.counciltravel.com

■ **Flightbookers**: (discount flights and packages) 177–178 Tottenham Court Road, London W1P OLX. ☎ (020) 7757 2444. Website: www.flight bookers.co.uk

■ **STA Travel**: (students and those under 26) 86 Old Brompton Road, London SW7 3LQ. ☎ (020) 7851 4132. Website: www.statravel.co.uk

■ **Thomas Cook**: (flights and packages) branches nationwide. ☎ (0990) 666 222. Website: www.thomascook.com

■ **Trailfinders**: (discounts and specialist itineraries) 42–50 Earl's Court Road, London W8 6FT. ☎ (020) 7938 3366. Website: www.trailfinders.com

■ **USIT Campus Travel**: (students and those under 26) 52 Grosvenor Gardens, London SW1 OAG. ☎ (0870) 240 1010. Website: www.usit campus.co.uk

Specialist Travel Agents

The following are just a selection of the companies in Britain who can arrange travel to Belgium.

■ **Bridge Travel**: (short breaks and self drive) Bridge House, 55–59 High Road, Broxbourne EN10 7ST. ☎ (0870) 727 5973. Website: www.bridge travel.co.uk

■ **Destinations Europe – Belgium**: 3 Orwell View Road, Shotley, Ipswich IP9 1RW. ☎ (01473) 787160. Website: www.heartofeurope.com/benelux

■ **Eurobreaks**: 10–18 Putney Hill, London SW15 2AX. ☎ (020) 8780 7700. Website: www.eurobreak.com

■ **Kirker Travel**: 3 New Concordia Wharf, Mill Street, London SE1 2BB. ☎ (020) 7231 3333.

■ **Leisure Direction**: (short breaks) Image House, Station Road, London N17 9LR. ☎ (0870) 442 9807. Website: www.leisuredirection.co.uk

■ **Motours Travel**: (self drive) Buckingham House, Longfield Road, Tunbridge Wells TN2 3DQ. ☎ (01892) 677777. Website: www.motours.co.uk

■ **Travelscene**: (short breaks and self drive) Travelscene House, 11–15 St Ann's Road, Harrow HA1 1LQ. ☎ (0870) 777 4445. Website: www.travel scene.co.uk

For a comprehensive list of tour operators and travel agents, contact:

■ **Tourism Flanders**: 31 Pepper Street, London E14 9RW. ☎ (020) 7867 0311 / 0891 887 799 (50p per minute). Email: office@flanders-tourism.org. Website: www.belgium-tourism.net

■ **Belgian Tourist Board**: (Brussels and Ardennes) 225 Marshall Wall, London E14 9FW. ☎ (020) 7531 0392. Email: info@belgium-tourism.org

FROM IRELAND

Aer Lingus flies three times daily from Dublin to Brussels Zaventem Airport, with connecting flights from Cork, Galway, Kerry, Shannon and Sligo. **Ryanair** flies from Shannon and Dublin to Brussels Charleroi Sud, which is a little further away from Brussels city centre. **Sabena** flies three times daily from Dublin to Brussels and once a day from Belfast to Brussels.

Prices for a standard return range from about IR£150 to IR£250, although promotions with airlines such as Ryanair can be as cheap as IR£70.

Ryanair, **British Airways** and **Aer Lingus** fly from cities in Ireland to London Heathrow and regional airports, from where travellers can fly to Brussels, travel by **Eurostar** from London Waterloo or arrange a package deal. For more details on flights and packages, see 'Getting there by air from Britain'.

⊕ **Aer Lingus**: 40–41 Upper O'Connell Street, Dublin 1. ☎ (01) 886 8888. Website: www.flyaerlingus.com

⊕ **British Airways**: 13 St Stephen's Green, Dublin 1. ☎ 1-800-626-747. For enquiries from Northern Ireland ☎ (0345) 222 111. Website: www.britishairways.com

⊕ **Ryanair**: Dublin Airport, Dublin. ☎ (01) 609 7881. Website: www.ryanair.com

⊕ **Sabena**: Dublin Airport, Main Terminal, Room 305, Dublin. ☎ (01) 808 7430. Website: www.sabena.com

TRAVEL AGENTS

■ **American Express Travel**: 116 Grafton Street, Dublin 2. ☎ (01) 677 2874.

■ **Budget Travel**: 134 Lower Baggot Street, Dublin 2. ☎ (01) 661 3122.

■ **Budget Travel Shops**: 63 Main Street, Finglas 11, Dublin. ☎ (01) 834 0637.

■ **Thomas Cook**: 118 Grafton Street, Dublin. ☎ (01) 677 1721. 11 Donegall Place, Belfast BT1 6ET. ☎ (01232) 554455. Website: www.thomascook.com

■ **Trailfinders**: 4–5 Dawson Street, Dublin 2. ☎ (01) 677 7888. Website: www.trailfinders.com

■ **USIT NOW**: 19–21 Aston Quay, O'Donnell Bridge, Dublin. ☎ (01) 602 1700. 13B Fountain Centre, College Street, Belfast BT61 6ET. ☎ (01232) 324 4073. Website: www.usitnow.ie

There is no branch of the Belgian Tourist Board in Ireland. Travellers should contact the UK office in London (see 'Travel agents in Britain').

FROM CANADA

Sabena flies from Montréal to Brussels and from Toronto to Brussels, usually via Boston. **Air Canada** flies regularly from Toronto and Montréal and **KLM** flies to Brussels from Toronto and Montréal, usually stopping in Amsterdam on the way.

There is less international competition on flights from Canada than from the United States. Fares to Brussels from Toronto start at around CAN$1000 in low season, rising to over CAN$1500 for July and August departures. Travellers from Canada might find cheaper flights to other European cities. The major international airlines fly at least daily to destinations such as Paris, Frankfurt, Amsterdam and London, from where there are frequent flights and trains to destinations in Belgium. Travelling first to the United States and then flying from a departure city such as New York or Boston to Belgium is also worth considering. For more details, *see* 'Getting there by air from the United States'.

Websites and the weekend travel sections of broadsheet newspapers are good hunting grounds for travel bargains.

✪**Air Canada**: 979 de Maisonneuve Boulevard West, Montréal H4A 3T2. ☎ 1-888-247-2262. Website: www.aircanada.ca

✪**British Airways**: 4120 Yonge Street, Suite 100, Toronto M2P 2B8. ☎ 1-800-AIRWAYS or 1-800-247-9297. Website: www.britishairways.com

✪**Canadian Airlines**: 165–168 Street South East, Calgary T2E 6J5. ☎ 1-800-466-7000. Website: www.cdnair.ca

✪**Northwest / KLM**: Toronto Pearson International Airport, Toronto. ☎ 1-800-374-7747. Website: www.nwa.com / www.klm.com

✪**Sabena**: 1253 McGill College Avenue, Suite 950, Montréal H3B 2Z7. ☎ 1-888-390-1223. Website: www.sabena.com

TRAVEL AGENTS

■ **Collacutt Travel**: (general travel services) The Bayview Village Centre, 2901 Bayview Avenue, Toronto M2K 1E6. ☎ 1-888-225-9811. Website: www.collacutt-travel.com

■ **New Frontiers / Nouvelles Frontières**: 1001 Sherbrook Street East, Suite 720, Montréal H21 1L3. ☎ (514) 526 8444.

■ **Sears Travel**: (general services. 81 offices throughout Canada). ☎ 1-888-884-2539. Website: www.sears.ca

■ **Travel Cuts**: (student travel organization. Branches countrywide) 187 College Street, Toronto M5T 1P7. ☎ (416) 979 2406 or 1-800-667-2887. Website: www.travelcuts.com

■ **Travel House**: (tours, packages, discount travel. Branches countrywide) 1491 Yonge Street, Suite 401, Toronto M4T 1ZR. ☎ (416) 925 6322. Website: www.travel-house.com

Many United States travel agents will also organize travel for Canadian travellers.

Specialist Travel Agents

The following are just a selection of the travel agents in Canada who can arrange travel to Belgium.

■ **Blue Marble Travel**: (bike tours to Belgium) 4 Woodvale Court, Cambridge, Ontario N1S 3Y2. ☎ (519) 624 2494. Website: www.bluemarble.org

■ **Butterfield and Robinson**: (general) 70 Bond Street, Toronto M5B 1X3. ☎ (416) 864 1354. Website: www.butterfieldandrobinson.com

■ **Contiki**: (tours for the under 35s) 355 Eglinton Avenue East, Toronto M4P 1M5. ☎ (416) 932 9449. Website: www.contiki.com

For a comprehensive list of tour operators and travel agents, contact:

■ **Belgian Tourist Office**: PO Box 760, Succursale, Montréal H4A 3S2. ☎ (514) 484 3594. Website: www.visitbelgium.com

FROM AUSTRALIA AND NEW ZEALAND

Major European airlines, such as **British Airways**, **Alitalia**, **KLM** and **Lauda Air**, fly to Brussels, usually via Asia and Europe. **Air New Zealand** and **Qantas** also fly to Brussels, also stopping in Asia and Europe on the way. Flight times to Brussels start at around 19 hours, but can increase to over 25 hours, depending on your departure airport and the number of stops on route.

Return fares to Brussels from Australia start at around AUD$1800 in low season on the cheapest airlines, rising to AUD$2500 in high season. Low season fares from New Zealand begin at NZ$2400 and increase to more than NZ$2800 in high season.

Travellers in search of a bargain might consider booking a flight to particularly competitive European destinations such as London or Amsterdam and travelling onwards to Belgium by plane or train. Most flights between Australia or New Zealand and Europe involve a stopover in an Asian city, which can be extended for a small charge.

The cheapest fares are frequently with Asian airlines such as **Garuda** or **Malaysia Airways**. **British Airways** and **Qantas** make the most frequent flights to Europe. For those with the time, round-the-world tickets offering up to six free stops are frequently only slightly more expensive than standard return fares.

➊ **Air New Zealand**: 5 Elizabeth Street, Sydney 2000. ☎ (02) 9937-5111. Air New Zealand House, 72 Oxford Terrace, Christchurch. ☎ 0800-737-000. Website: www.airnz.co.nz

➊ **British Airways**: Chifley Square, 70 Hunter Street, Sydney 2000. ☎ (02) 9258-3300. Auckland International Airport. ☎ (09) 356-8690. Website: www.britishairways.com

➊ **Cathay Pacific**: 3/F International Terminal, Sydney International Airport, Mascot, Sydney 2020. ☎ 13 26 27. Arthur Andersen Tower, 11th Floor, 205–209 Queen Street, PO Box 1313, Auckland. ☎ (09) 379-0861. Website: www.cathaypacific.com

✪ KLM / Alitalia: 115 Pitt Street, Level 13, Sydney 2000. ☎ (02) 9922-1555. Salvation Army Building, Second Floor, 369 Queen Street, Auckland 1. ☎ (09) 309-1782. Website: www.klm.com

✪ Lauda Air: 143 Macquarie Street, Level 11, Sydney 2000. ☎ (02) 9241-4277. Website: www.laudaair.com

✪ Lufthansa: 143 Macquarie Street, Level 12, Sydney 2000. ☎ (02) 9367-3861. 36 Kitchener Street, Auckland 1. ☎ (09) 303-1529. Website: www.lufthansa.com

✪ Malaysia Airlines: MAS, 16th Spring Street, Sydney 2000. ☎ (02) 913-2627. MAS, 12th Floor, The Swanson Centre, 12–26 Swanson Street, Auckland, PO Box 3729. Auckland. ☎ (09) 373-2741. Website: www.malaysiaairlines.com

✪ Qantas: Qantas Centre, 203 Coward Street, Mascot, Sydney 2020. ☎ 13 12 11 or (02) 9691-3636. 191 Queen Street, Auckland 1. ☎ (09) 357-8900 or 0800-808-967. Website: www.qantas.com

✪ Singapore Airlines: Singapore Airlines House, 17–19 Bridge Street, Sydney 2000. ☎ (02) 9350-0100. West Plaza Building, Tenth Floor, Corner Albert and Fanshawe Streets, Auckland 1. ☎ 0800-808-909. Website: www.singaporeair.com

TRAVEL AGENTS

■ **Flight Centres**: 33 Berry Street, Level 13, North Sydney 2060. ☎ (02) 924-2422. 205 Queen Street, Auckland 1. ☎ (09) 309-6171. ☎ 1-1300-131-600 for nearest branch.

■ **STA Travel**: 855 George Street, Sydney 2000. ☎ (02) 9212-1255 (72 branches). 90 Cashel Street, Christchurch, New Zealand. ☎ (03) 379-9098 (13 branches). For nearest branch ☎ 13 17 76. Website: www.statravel.com.au

■ **Thomas Cook**: 175 Pitt Street, Sydney 2000 ☎ 1-300-728-748 (branches nationwide) 96 Anzac Avenue, Auckland. ☎ 0800-500-600 (branches nationwide).

■ **Trailfinders**: 91 Elizabeth Street, Brisbane, Queensland 4000. ☎ (07) 3229-0887. Website: www.trailfinder.com/australia

Specialist Travel Agents

The following are just a selection of the travel agents in Australia and New Zealand who can arrange travel to Belgium.

■ **Adventure World**: 73 Walker Street, North Sydney. ☎ (02) 9956-7766. 101 Great South Road, Remuera, Auckland. ☎ (09) 524-5118. Website: www.adventureworld.net.au

■ **European Travel Office**: 133 Castlereagh Street, Sydney. ☎ (02) 9627-7727. 407 Great South Road, Penrose, Auckland. ☎ (09) 525-3074.

■ **KLM Vacations**: 456 Kent Street, Sydney. ☎ (02) 9285-6844. 326 Lambton Quay, Wellington. ☎ (04) 473-6427. Website: www.klm.com.au

There is no branch of the Belgian Tourist Office in Australia or New Zealand.

FROM SOUTH AFRICA

Sabena flies daily from Johannesburg to Brussels. **British Airways** and **South African Airways** fly frequently to Brussels from Johannesburg and Cape Town, usually stopping at a minimum of two destinations on the way. Standard return tickets should cost between ZAR3,300 and ZAR5,000, depending on the season.

➊ **British Airways**: Grovesnor Court, 195 Grovesnor Corner, Rosebank, Johannesburg 2196. ☎ 0860-011-747 or (011) 441-8600. Website: www.britishairways.com

➊ **Sabena**: 191 Jan Smuts Avenue, Second and Fourth Floors, Park Town North, Johannesburg. ☎ (011) 390-1586. Website: www.sabena.com

➊ **South African Airways**: Airways Park, Jones Road, Johannesburg International Airport, Johannesburg 1627. ☎ (011) 978-1763. Website: www.saa.co.za

TRAVEL AGENTS

■ **STA Travel**: Leslie Social Sciences Building, Level Three, University of Cape Town, Rondebosch 7700, Cape Town. ☎ (021) 685-1808. Website: www.statravel.co.za

■ **USIT Adventures**: Rondebosch Shopping Centre, Rondebosch Main Road, Rondebosch, Cape Town. ☎ (021) 685-2226. Website: www.usit-campus.co.uk

There is no branch of the Belgian Tourist Office in South Africa.

By Train

FROM BRITAIN

Eurostar

There are nine daily direct high-speed **Eurostar** trains between London Waterloo and Brussels Midi, with slightly fewer departures on Sundays. Journey time is 2 hours 40 minutes. Arrive at least 25 minutes before departure to be sure of your place.

Expect to pay from around £150–£300 for a standard return to Brussels from London Waterloo. Concessions are available for senior citizens and those under 26, and Eurostar frequently runs promotions through the broadsheet newspapers, their website and with travel agents.

Interrail

UK travellers can travel to Brussels by train on the **Interrail** system. Belgium is zoned with France, Luxembourg and the Netherlands. A full month of travel in Belgium, travelling via France, would cost from around £160 for those under 26. Pass holders are entitled to cheaper cross channel ferry tickets, but must pay hefty supplements if they wish to travel by Eurostar or high-speed trains such as the **Thalys** service. Contact travel agents such as STA and Campus for assistance in buying Interrail tickets (*see* 'Travel agents in Britain'). For further information on rail travel within Europe, contact **Rail Europe** or **International Rail**.

Brussels has three main railway stations – Nord/ Noord, Centrale/ Centraal and Midi/ Zuid.

🚄 **Eurostar**: (London Waterloo–Brussels Midi), Waterloo International Terminal, London, SE1 (Waterloo Tube). Also: Eurostar Ticket Office, 102–104 Victoria Street, London SW1 5JL. ☎ (0990) 186 186 (7am–10pm). Website: www.eurostar.co.uk

🚄 **Rail Europe**: Travel Centre, 179 Piccadilly, London W1J 9BA. ☎ (0870) 584 8848. Website: www.raileurope.co.uk

🚄 **Belgian National Railways**: (information only) Unit 200A, Blackfriars Boundary, 156 Blackfriars Road, London SE1 8EN. ☎ (020) 7593 2332. Website: www.b-rail.be

🚄 **International Rail**: Chase House, Gilbert Street, Ropley SO24 9BY. ☎ (01962) 773646. Email: info@international-rail.com. Website: www.international-rail.com

By Sea

FROM BRITAIN

Hoverspeed operates up to seven daily SeaCats between Dover and Ostend, with a crossing time of 2 hours. Prices for cars range from £150 to about £250 for a return ticket. Return fares for foot passengers cost from £30 return. Hoverspeed offers a linking service with trains from London Charing Cross to Brussels Central Station from around £65 return.

P&O North Sea Ferries travels from Hull to Zeebrugge in 13 hours, and Hull to Rotterdam in 18 hours. Rotterdam is about an hour's drive from northern Belgium. **Stena Line** sails from Harwich, in East Anglia, to Hook of Holland, which is about 2 hours' drive from the Belgian border, in under 6 hours. Prices start at £200 for a return ticket for a car and passengers.

Dover to Calais is the most popular route between Britain and Europe. Calais is 70 miles (110 kilometres) from Bruges and 125 miles (200 kilometres) from Brussels. **P&O Stena Line** sails from Dover to Calais in 75 minutes. **Sea France** and **Hoverspeed** sail regularly to Calais.

A wide range of discounts are available from all the ferry companies, including package deals, off-peak reductions, deals for five-day trips, and special prices for members of motoring organizations, or for booking well in advance.

Hoverspeed: International Hoverport, Marine Parade, Dover CT17 9TG. ☎ (0870) 240 8070. Website: www.hoverspeed.co.uk

P&O North Sea Ferries: King George Dock, Hedon Road, Hull HU9 5OA. ☎ (0870) 129 6002. Website: www.ponsf.com

P&O Stena Line: (Dover–Calais). Channel House, Channel View Road, Dover CT17 9TJ. ☎ (0870) 600 0600. Website: www.posl.com

Stena Line UK: Charter House, Park Street, Ashford TN24 8EX. ☎ (0870) 570 7070. Website: www.stenaline.co.uk

SeaFrance: Eastern Docks, Dover CT16 1JA. ☎ (0990) 711 711. Website: www.seafrance.com

FROM IRELAND

There are no direct ferries from Ireland to Belgian or Dutch ports. **Irish Ferries** runs a 'Landbridge' service in partnership with **P&O North Sea Ferries** which crosses first from Dublin to Holyhead, then you travel from Holyhead to Hull overland and finally catch the ferry from Hull to Zeebrugge or Rotterdam.

Most travellers who prefer not to fly usually travel from Ireland to Belgium via Britain, although it is possible, although inconvenient and expensive, to catch a ferry to Cherbourg, in France, and then drive from there to Belgium. **P&O Irish Sea Ferries** sail from Larne to Fleetwood and from Dublin to Liverpool. **Irish Ferries** and **Stena Line** sail from Dublin to Holyhead. The Dublin to Holyhead service connects with the direct **Virgin Trains** service to London Euston. The Stena Line service from Rosslare to Fishguard is useful for those taking a car.

For more information on routes to Belgium through the UK, see 'Getting to Belgium by sea from Britain' and 'Getting to Belgium by Train from Britain'.

Irish Ferries: (Dublin–Holyhead, Rosslare–Cherbourg) 2–4 Merrion Row, Dublin 2. ☎ (01) 638 3333. Enquiries from Northern Ireland: ☎ (01) 661 0511. Website: www.irishferries.ie

P&O Irish Sea Ferries: (Larne–Fleetwood, Dublin Port–Liverpool) Peninsula House, Wharf Road, Portsmouth PO2 8TA. ☎ (0870) 242 4777. Website: www.poirishsea.com

Stena Line: (Dublin Port–Holyhead, Rosslare–Fishguard) Charter House, Park Street, Ashford TN24 8EX. ☎ (01) 204 7700. Website: www.stenaline.co.uk

Those travelling from Ireland without a car can pick up a train service to the south of England from Liverpool or Holyhead in order to catch a ferry from Dover, or board a **Eurostar** service to Brussels at London Waterloo. Many foot passengers travel by ferry from Dublin to connect with a **Virgin Trains** service from Holyhead that reaches London Euston in 3 hours 30 minutes.

The Continental Rail Desk of **Iarnrodd Éireann** in Dublin can arrange journeys in Europe for you.

☎ **Iarnrodd Éireann**: (Continental Rail Desk) 35 Lower Abbey Street, Dublin 1. ☎ (01) 677 1871.

☎ **Virgin Trains**: (Holyhead–London Euston) ☎ (0345) 222 333. Website: www.virgintrains.co.uk

By Car

FROM BRITAIN

UK driving licences are valid in Belgium and you should contact the AA for advice on driving to Belgium. If you decide to take a car to Belgium, the alternative to the ferry is to cross beneath the channel by **Eurotunnel** train.

Eurotunnel trains transport cars and their passengers under the Channel to Calais Coquelles in about 35 minutes. Trains depart throughout the day and night, roughly every 30 minutes during the day and hourly at night.

Ferry services are normally cheaper, but Eurotunnel sometimes puts deals on its website or offers reductions through Sunday newspapers or travel agents, so look out for special offers.

Expect to pay at least £200 for a return ticket including a car and passengers. Advance booking can sometimes reduce prices and is recommended in high season. Arrive at least 25 minutes prior to departure to ensure that you aren't bumped onto the next available train (which can sometimes mean waiting for hours if the next few trains are full).

☎ **Eurotunnel**: (Folkestone–Calais), Customer Service Centre, Junction 12 of the M20, PO Box 300, Folkestone CT19 4DQ. ☎ (0870) 535 3535. 24-hour recorded information: ☎ (0891) 555 566. Website: www.eurotunnel.co.uk

■ **AA UK**: Norfolk House, Priestley Road, Basingstoke RG24 9NY. ☎ (0870) 500 600. Website: www.theaa.com

By Coach

FROM BRITAIN

Eurolines runs a combined coach/ferry service from London Victoria coach station (via Ramsgate and Ostend) to Antwerp, Bruges and Brussels, with linking services running to Ghent and Liège. The journey takes at least 8 hours. Return prices start at about £50 return and concessions are available.

Those travelling around Europe might consider the Eurolines Pass. Thirty days of unlimited travel between 30 European cities costs from £200, with concessions available. Contact Eurolines for more details.

CitySprint: Hoverspeed, International Hoverport, Marine Parade, Dover CT17 9TG. ☎ (01304) 240241. Website: www.hoverspeed.co.uk

Eurolines: (London Victoria–Antwerp, Bruges, Brussels), Eurolines Travel Shops, 52 Grosvenor Gardens, London SW1W OAG. (Victoria Tube). ☎ (0990) 143 219. Website: www.gobycoach.com

FROM IRELAND

The Irish bus service **Bus Éireann** (based in Dublin) runs regular buses from Dublin to London Victoria coach station. These services connect with **Eurolines** buses that leave London Victoria coach station for Belgium. There are regular direct buses from Dublin to Amsterdam and Rotterdam.

There is no direct service from Belfast to Brussels, or even Belfast to Paris. Your best bet is to travel first to London, and then board a coach bound for Brussels or other destinations in Belgium. Eurolines departs from Belfast to London Victoria twice a day. For more details, *see* 'Getting there by coach from Britain'.

Bus Éireann: Central Bus Station (Busaras), Store Street, Dublin 1. ☎ (01) 830 2222. Website: www.buseireann.ie

General Information

Belgium may not strike you as the world's most exciting holiday destination, but it has all the ingredients for a truly exotic trip, and if you only associate Belgium with chips, chocolates and beer, you're in for a big surprise. One of the most striking things about this small country is its cultural and geographical diversity. The land is mostly flat, but the people are anything but: Belgians are warm-hearted, humorous, modest and highly approachable. In fact, by the end of your visit, you'll wonder why you ever joked about famous Belgians.

Belgium has a lot to be proud of. For a start, there's a lot more to its wonderfully varied cuisine than mussels and chips. In its art galleries, you'll find a host of awe-inspiring Old Masters. The landscape isn't dramatic, and there aren't many beaches, but *le plat pays* is prime cycling territory, and you'll be amazed at the amount of history and culture that's packed into this small land: Gothic churches, Renaissance guildhouses, fascinating museums, flower and flea markets a-plenty and a wealth of festivals, carnivals and colourful processions. The Belgians have a seemingly inexhaustible capacity for feasting and carousing, whether it involves hurling oranges or onions, dancing through the streets or simply downing vast flagons of beer.

Politically, Belgium is a mind-bogglingly complicated place, with three official languages and three semi-autonomous Regions – Wallonia, Flanders and Brussels – as well as a national government. This clutch of administrations strikes compromise after compromise in an effort to solve problems peacefully and keep everyone happy, especially the increasing number of Flemish nationalists. As a result, respecting everyone's individuality while maintaining some kind of national identity is one of Belgium's strong points. Despite the calls for independence, the quarrels have rarely become too serious: Belgians have always preferred heated discussion to spilling blood, and people come from far and wide to study the mechanisms that maintain its precarious status quo.

Brussels, Flanders and Wallonia are three very separate worlds, and all three have something different to offer the visitor. As capital of Europe, Brussels is constantly in the news, although not always in a positive light. The historic Flemish towns of Bruges and Ghent are better known than those of Wallonia, but visitors to the French-speaking south will find themselves swept up in the giddy nightlife of Liège, or lulled by the deliciously soothing pace of life in the provinces. You won't have to look far for adventure, as there are new discoveries to be made around every corner.

ACCOMMODATION

There are campsites everywhere, especially on the coast and in the Ardennes. You'll also find youth hostels, family pensions, B&Bs and hotels to suit every taste and budget. That said, it's not always easy to find quality, comfort and affordability in one place, especially in Brussels, so make sure you book ahead. And be warned: the quaint and cosy hotels are often fully booked.

> **TIP** There are dramatic weekend reductions at some of the pricier hotels, which attract mostly business customers during the week. The midweek tariff may be cut by a third, or even halved, on weekends, so keep an eye out for special deals. You can always try negotiating when you book. Breakfast is almost always included, and is usually plentiful.

Price categories vary, and depend on area (historic centres are always more expensive) and time of year: the cheapest months (midweek) are January, February, July, August and December.

If you're looking for something more rural, try a 'country holiday', organized by Gîtes d'Étape or Amis de la Nature (in the Ardennes), or farm holidays, where you stay in a gîte.

B&Bs are becoming increasingly popular, especially in Flanders. You can ask about these at most tourist offices. They're state-controlled, and conform to fairly rigid standards. Even in the country, you're never too far from a town.

Taxistop can also help with finding accommodation (*see* 'Campsites, gîtes and B&Bs'), while the Trekkershutten chain (*see below*) provides simple overnight accommodation.

Tourism in Belgium is organized according to region, so you'll have to contact Flemish organizations to find out about Flanders and Walloon institutions for information about Wallonia. Both, however, cover Brussels, where roughly 80 per cent of the population is French-speaking. Tourist offices in Brussels can provide information about the whole country.

USEFUL ADDRESSES

🚩 **Tourist office** (**OPT** and **Toerisme Vlaanderen**): rue du Marché-aux-Herbes 61, Brussels 1000. ☎ (02) 504 0390. Fax: (02) 504 0270. Website: www.belgique-tourisme.net. A fantastic service, and they'll find another organization to help you if they can't do so themselves.

■ **Commissariat général au tourisme** (Wallonie): place de la Wallonie 1, bâtiment 3, Jambes 5100. ☎ (081) 33 31 11. Fax: (081) 33 40 33.

■ **Belgian Tourist Reservations**: boulevard Anspach 111, BP 4, Brussels 1000. ☎ (02) 513 7484. Fax: (02) 513 9277. No fee for bookings. If you're going to Flanders, there is a leaflet dedicated to staying in the Flanders region. You can also find out about weekend deals and discounted rail travel.

■ **Belsud** can book you into more than 1,000 furnished gîtes and farms, 450 rooms and 21 holiday villages: pick up a brochure at OPT. ☎ (02) 504 02 80. Fax: (02) 514 5335. Email: belsud@opt.be. Website: www.belgique-tourisme.net. Booking fee: 300BEF.

■ **Logis de Belgique**: rue de l'Église 15, La Roche-en-Ardenne 6980. ☎ (084) 412767. Fax: (084) 411142. Email: logis.be@skynet.be. Website: www.users.skynet.be. A network of 135 excellent, individual hotels in Belgium, especially Wallonia and the Grand Duchy of Luxembourg. They'll send you a guide on request (200BEF).

YOUTH HOSTELS

The good news is that there's usually no age limit for staying in a youth hostel in Belgium. Prices vary according to age: from three to 15, 100BEF; from 16 to 25, 350BEF; over 25, 475BEF.

For information and membership:

■ **Youth Hostels Association (LAJ)**: rue de la Sablonnière 28, Brussels 1000. ☎ (02) 219 5676. Fax: (02) 219 1451. Email: info@laj.be. Website: www.laj.be

■ **Vlaamse Jeugdherbergcentrale**: Van Stralenstraat 40, Antwerpen 2060. ☎ (03) 232 7218. Fax: (03) 231 8126. Email: info@vjh.be. Website: www.vjh.be. This is the main reservation point for Flemish youth hostels.

Joining the YHA in Britain

For information about joining before you leave, contact the **Youth Hostels Association (YHA)** for membership details and other information. An international YHA card costs £12 for adults for a year and is valid worldwide. The **International Youth Hostel Federation (IYHF)** will issue the card. They also produce guidebooks to hostels overseas and run an international booking network from the same number.

■ **YHA (Youth Hostels in England and Wales)**: Trevelyan House, Matlock, Derbyshire DE4 3YH. ☎ (0870) 870 8808. Fax: (01727) 844126. Email: customerservices@yha.org.uk. Website: www.yha.org.uk

■ **IYHF**: First Floor, Fountain House, Parkway, Welwyn Garden City, Herts AL1 6JH. ☎ (01707) 324170. Email: iyhf@iyhf.org. Website: www.iyhf.org

■ International booking site: www.hostelbooking.com

■ Irish website: www.irelandyha.org

■ Scottish website: www.syha.org.uk

CAMPSITES, GÎTES AND B&Bs

■ **Campsites**: there are around 350 sites in Belgium. Ask your tourist office for more information, or look at individual listings in the Guide.

■ **Gîtes d'étape**: Centre Belge du Tourisme des Jeunes, rue Montoyer 31, Brussels 1000. ☎ (02) 512 5447. Manages 27 sites in Brussels and Wallonia.

■ **Maisons des Amis de la Nature, Maison Verte**: rue des Frères-Descamps 94, Ath 7800. ☎ (068) 280909.

■ **Country tourism**: UTRA-UPA, chaussée de Namur 47, Gembloux 5030. ☎ (081) 600000. Fax: (081) 600446. Email: upa@win.be. FETOURAG, rue de la Science 30, Brussels 1040. ☎ (02) 230 4251. Email: alliance.agricold.belge@skynet.be

■ **ASBL Gîtes de Wallonie**: avenue du Prince-de-Liège 1, Namur 5100. ☎ (081) 311800. Fax: (081) 310200. Email: gitesdewallonie@skynet.be.

Website: www.gitesdewallonie.net. Country gîtes, 500 furnished homes and 250 B&B rooms.

■ **Taxistop** publishes the *Guide du logement chez l'habitant*, a guide to rooms in private homes. It can also arrange international house or apartment swaps, and co-ordinates Europewide offers and requests for seats in private cars (*see* 'Hitch-hiking' under 'Transport').

– Rue du Fossé-aux-Loups 28, Brussels 1000. ☎ (070) 222292. Fax: (02) 223 2232. Website: www.taxistop.be

– Onderbergen 5, Gent 9000. ☎ (09) 223 2310.

– Place de l'Université 41, Louvain-la-Neuve 1348. ☎ (010) 451414. Fax: (010) 455120.

TREKKERSHUTTEN

This is a new idea that you'll come across in Flanders. There are 280 Trekkershutten, mostly on cycling routes in the Kempen area. As the name suggests, they are cabins, 15 metres (50 feet) long and made of wood. Inside, you'll find four beds, four chairs, a table, an electric heater, two rings for cooking and a jerrycan of water. They're usually in campsites, so you can use the bathrooms there, and, if you pay a bit extra, you can use the pans and crockery as well. ☎ (014) 436111. Fax: (014) 428801.

BUDGET

In general, the cost of living in Belgium is quite high, although rents are much lower than in most cities. The restaurants seem expensive until you see the size of the portions. Clothes, books and newspapers are a bit pricey. Transport, however, is cheap.

HOTELS

Prices indicated are for two people.

– **Budget**: up to 1,800BEF (about £30).

– **Moderate**: up to 2,400BEF (about £40).

– **Expensive**: up to 3,600BEF (about £60).

– **Splash Out**: more than 3,600BEF (more than £60).

EATING OUT

Expect to pay 300–600BEF for a main course; unless you're a big eater, you won't need a starter. At lunch time, even in the more upmarket restaurants, you can usually get a filling *plat du jour* for 300–400BEF, but in the evening, a three-course meal in a good restaurant will set you back about 1,200BEF per person. If you're not careful, you can end up spending a lot on eating out.

CLIMATE AND SEASONS

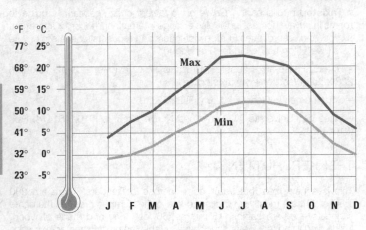

BELGIUM – Average Temperatures

Belgium's climate is similar to that of Britain: it's temperate, but it will probably rain at least once during your trip, so don't forget your waterproofs. You've probably heard talk of constant rain but, as always, that's pure exaggeration. Belgium has had some hot summers in recent years, but it doesn't experience the temperature extremes of landlocked European countries. In winter, conditions can be icy, with crisp, sunny days.

The most likely scenario is weather that's neither hot nor cold, with rain and sunny spells. One exception to this rule is the Ardennes plateau, where temperatures can be 5°C (10°F) lower than those on the milder coast. Fog frequently descends in the valleys.

Spring is the ideal time for walking by the canals of Bruges, or enjoying the blossoming cherry trees of Brussels. In summer, Belgian families jostle for space on the beaches in search of healthy North Sea air. Autumn, meanwhile, is perfect for a hike through the Ardennes forests, when the colours are magnificent and the wildlife is plentiful. The forest around Brussels is also spectacular at this time of year.

February sees the start of the carnival season, but watch out for fog and ice on the road.

– **Weather forecast** (Institut Royal Météorologique): ☎ (090) 027003.

COMMUNICATIONS

TELEPHONING

Dialling codes from Belgium: The code from outside Belgium is +32, followed by the number of the person/institution you are calling (without the zero; add this when dialling within the country).

Phoning within the country: the phone number system changed recently, and all landline numbers now consist of nine digits. Although the first two or three of these are the area code, they have been incorporated into the individual phone number. To phone within the same zone, you have to dial the whole number. There's no change if you're dialling from one zone to another.

Dialling codes from Belgium:

– To Great Britain: +44

– To Ireland: +353

– To the USA and Canada: +1

– To Australia: +61

– To New Zealand: +64

– To South Africa: +27

Phone booths: a few booths take coins (5BEF, 20BEF), but you're better off getting a phonecard. You can buy them at post offices or in shops displaying the little red icon in the window. Some phones also take credit cards.

Tariffs: you pay half price if you make a call between 6.30pm and 8am, on weekends or on public holidays.

USEFUL NUMBERS

■ **Ambulance and fire brigade**: ☎ 100.

■ **Police**: ☎ 101.

■ **Red Cross** (non-urgent medical advice): ☎ 105.

■ **Information**: ☎ 1307.

■ **International operator in Belgium**: ☎ 1324.

■ **International directory enquiries**: ☎ 1304.

POST

Post offices are open 9am–noon and 2.30–4pm, or 9am–5pm in major towns. On Saturday, they are open 9am–noon. One post office in Brussels is open continuously: 15 avenue Fonsny, near Gare du Midi. The current postage rate for a standard letter is 19BEF to the UK and Ireland, and 23BEF to the USA, Canada, Australia, New Zealand and South Africa.

CONVERSION TABLES

Men's sizes

Shirts

UK	USA	EUROPE
14	14	36
14¹/₂	14¹/₂	37
15	15	38
15¹/₂	15¹/₂	39
16	16	41
16¹/₂	16¹/₂	42
17	17	43
17¹/₂	17¹/₂	44
18	18	46

Suits

UK	USA	EUROPE
36	36	46
38	38	48
40	40	50
42	42	52
44	44	54
46	46	56

Shoes

UK	USA	EUROPE
8	9	42
9	10	43
10	11	44
11	12	46
12	13	47

Women's sizes

Shirts/dresses

UK	USA	EUROPE
8	6	36
10	8	38
12	10	40
14	12	42
16	14	44
18	16	46
20	18	48

Sweaters

UK	USA	EUROPE
8	6	44
10	8	46
12	10	48
14	12	50
16	14	52
18	16	54
20	18	56

Shoes

UK	USA	EUROPE
3	5	36
4	6	37
5	7	38
6	8	39
7	9	40
8	10	42

Temperature

- To convert °C to °F, multiply by 1.8 and add 32.
- To convert °F to °C, subtract 32 and multiply by 5/9 (0.55). 0°C=32°F

US weights and measures

1 centimetre	0.39 inches	1 inch	2.54 centimetres
1 metre	3.28 feet	1 foot	0.30 metres
1 metre	1.09 yards	1 yard	0.91 metres
1 kilometre	0.62 miles	1 mile	1.61 kilometres
1 hectare	2.47 acres	1 acre	0.40 hectares
1 litre	1.76 pints	1 pint	0.57 litres
1 litre	0.26 gallons	1 gallon	3.79 litres
1 gram	0.035 ounces	1 ounce	28.35 grams
1 kilogram	2.2 pounds	1 pound	0.45 kilograms

EMBASSIES

EMBASSIES IN BELGIUM

Great Britain: Rue d'Arlon 85, 1040 Brussels. Metro: Maelbeek. Open: Mon–Fri 9.30am–5.30pm. ☎ +32 2 287 6211. Fax: +32 2 287 6360. Website: www.british-embassy.be

Ireland: Rue Froissart 89–93, 1040 Brussels. Metro: Schuman. Open: Mon–Fri 10am–1.30pm. ☎ +32 2 230 5337. Fax: +32 2 230 5312.

USA: Boulevard du Régent 27, 1000 Brussels. Metro: Arts-Loi. Open: Mon–Fri 1.30–4.30pm. ☎ +32 2 508 2111. Fax: +32 2 511 2725. Website: www.usinfo.be

Canada: Avenue de Tervueren 2, 1040 Brussels. Metro: Mérode. Open: Mon–Fri 9am–noon, 2–4.30pm. ☎ +32 2 741 0611. Fax: +32 2 741 0643. Email: bru@bru02.x400.gc.ca

Australia: Rue Guimard 6–8, 1040 Brussels. Metro: Arts-Loi. Open: Mon–Fri 9am–5.30pm. ☎ +32 2 286 0500. Fax: +32 2 230 6802. Email: austemb.brussels@dfat.gov.au. Website: www.austemb.be

New Zealand: Boulevard de Régent 47–48, 1000 Brussels. Metro: Arts-Loi or Madou. Open: Mon–Fri 9am–1pm, 2–3.30pm. For other inquiries, call for an appointment. ☎ +32 2 512 1040. Fax: +32 2 513 4856.

South Africa: 5th floor, rue de la Loi 28, 1000 Brussels. Metro: Arts-Loi. Open: Mon–Fri 9am–noon. ☎ +32 2 285 4400. Fax: +32 2 285 4402. Website: www.ambassade.net/southafrica

BELGIAN EMBASSIES ABROAD

Great Britain: 103–105 Eaton Square, London SW1W 9AB. Open: Mon–Fri 8.30am–5.30pm (except public holidays). ☎ +44 20 7470 3700. Fax: +44 20 7259 6213. Website: www.belgium-embassy.co.uk

Ireland: Shrewsbury House, 2 Shrewsbury Road, Ballsbridge, Dublin 4. ☎ +353 1 269 2082, 1588 or 9403. Fax: +353 1 283 8488.

USA: 3330 Garfield Street NW, Washington DC 20008. Open: Mon–Fri 9am–4.30pm. ☎ (202) 333 6900. Fax: (202) 333 3079. For details of the 28 honorary consulates dotted around the country, visit: www.diplobel.org

Canada: 80 Elgin St, 4th Floor, Ottawa, Ontario K1P 1B7. ☎ +1 613 236 7267, 68 or 69. Fax: +1 613 236 7882. Open: Mon–Fri.

Australia: 19 Arkana Street, Yarralumla, Canberra, ACT 2600. ☎ +61 2 62 73 25 01 or 02. Fax: +61 2 62 73 33 92.

New Zealand: Willis Coroon House, 12th Floor, 1–3 Willeston St, Wellington. (Mailing address: PO Box 3379, Wellington.) ☎ +64 4 472 9558 or 59. Fax: +64 4 471 2764.

South Africa: 625 Leyds Street, Muckleneuk, 0002 Pretoria. ☎ +27 12 44 32 01. Fax: +27 12 44 32 16.

ENTRY FORMALITIES

PASSPORTS AND VISAS

EU citizens can enter Belgium with an official identity card (British citizens must take a passport) and can usually stay for up to three months. No visa or return ticket is required.

Non-EU citizens must have a passport valid for at least three months after the period of intended stay. Travellers from the USA, Canada, Australia and New Zealand do not need a visa for a stay of up to three months, but must be in possession of a return ticket.

In addition to a valid passport and a return airline ticket, South African visitors will also need to present a visa, whether travelling to Belgium for business or personal reasons. Only Schengen visas are issued (short-stay tourist or business visa for up to 90 days); your stay should not exceed 90 days in a six-month period. You will need to apply for a visa through a Belgian consulate general in Johannesburg or Cape Town.

Cost of visas in Belgian francs with current rand (ZAR) equivalents:

Transit visa: 400BEF (ZAR 60)

Maximum 30-day stay: 900BEF (ZAR 136)

Maximum 90-day stay: 1200BEF (ZAR 180)

For visa requirements regarding working or living in Belgium, contact your local embassy.

CUSTOMS AND DUTY-FREE

No matter where you are travelling from, the importing of narcotics, copyright infringements, fakes and counterfeit goods is strictly prohibited for anyone travelling to Belgium. Firearms and ammunition are also forbidden unless accompanied by specific authorization from the appropriate ministry in Brussels.

When returning to the UK, obscene material and offensive weapons are prohibited in addition to those items listed by Belgian customs.

UK (EU) citizens: any goods that are for personal use are free from both Belgian and UK customs duty. To meet the criteria of 'personal use' there is a set of guidelines that are used by all EU customs officers. These allow up to 800 cigarettes, 200 cigars or 1kg of loose tobacco, 10 litres of spirits, 20 litres of fortified wine, 90 litres of wine and 110 litres of beer. Despite the liberalized restrictions on importing and exporting tobacco and alcohol, the removal of duty-free allowances for EU visitors means that prices in Belgium now include duty, which cannot be recuperated.

Belgium is a signatory of the Schengen agreement, so European Union citizens no longer have to pass through customs on arrival in the country. However, the UK did not sign this agreement and as a consequence has maintained inter-EU immigration control. When returning to the UK those with nothing to declare should use the 'Green Channel' and those with goods in excess of their allowance should use the 'Red Channel', both marked clearly after passport control. At many ports there is also a separate 'Blue Channel' for EU residents who can simply wave their passport at an immigration officer.

For further information and clarification, in the UK contact the Excise and Inland Customs Advice Centre ☎ (020) 7202 4227, or visit their website at www.hmce.gov.uk. The UK Customs Office ☎ (020) 7919 6700 publishes a leaflet called *A Guide for Travellers*, detailing regulations and duty-free allowances.

Non-EU citizens: the limitations on import and export outside the EU are far more stringent than within it, but visitors from outside the EU may take home goods including gifts and souvenirs free of duty up to the limit of £145. For items worth more than the limit of £145, you will have to pay charges on the full value, not just on the value above £145. In addition you may leave Belgium with 200 cigarettes, 50 cigars or 250g of smoking tobacco, 2 litres of still table wine, 1 litre of spirits, 2 litres of fortified wine and 60g of perfume. Those under 17 may not export tobacco or alcohol from Belgium.

For more information, the US Customs Service (PO Box 7407, Washington, DC 20044; ☎ (202) 927-5580) publishes a free leaflet entitled *Know Before You Go*.

ETIQUETTE

Languages: Rather than commit the *faux pas* of talking French to a Dutch-speaker, it's better to say immediately that you don't speak Flemish, and simply speak English, which most people will be able to deal with.

Meeting people: In Wallonia and Brussels, young people or friends greet members of the opposite sex with one or three kisses on the cheek, but never with two. They're a bit less demonstrative in Flanders.

Don't turn up late for appointments, although arriving 15 minutes late will be tolerated. If you're invited for coffee, you should turn up at 4.30pm. Business relationships tend to be non-hierarchical, so simplicity is the key to all your professional dealings. You won't be considered dull-witted if you hesitate and demonstrate a British politeness and courtesy.

In conversation: Don't play devil's advocate. Consensus of opinion is the preferred position in Belgian conversation, and taking the opposite tack is not necessarily seen as a sign of intelligence. In Liège, joviality is much appreciated, and a dash of mockery won't go amiss. Whatever your feelings about monarchies, don't make fun of the Belgian royal family; disrespect is generally considered bad taste.

And finally: Only country bumpkins (and tourists!) stroll about in shorts on Brussels' Grand'Place, so if you don't want to stand out . . .

FESTIVALS AND TRADITIONS

Belgium is a country where individualism has become an institution, and processions, parades, carnivals, religious festivals, fêtes and jamborees dedicated to local saints and historic events take place throughout the year. Tradition and festivals are taken very seriously and each village and region will have its rituals and customs; indeed, the many festivals give the locals a chance to celebrate their regional identity with appropriate pomp and merriment.

In contrast to many of its European neighbours, Belgium's folklore forms a vibrant part of the nation's life. And the events aren't particularly commercial, either; indeed, it's their authenticity that makes them so attractive. They are also unbelievably varied, so it's impossible to describe every one in detail.

Carnivals

Carnival is part of the country's cultural heritage. The pulsating rhythm of traditional clog dances, hammering the ground, was thought to encourage seeds to fertilize, while some sociologists believe the masks symbolize the faces of dead ancestors, who must be placated by the harvesting of crops. Carnival means total abandon and release from the pressures of law and religion; it's the last chance to party before Lent.

In Wallonia, 17 towns celebrate Mardi Gras (Shrove Tuesday) with a carnival. Tradition dictates a costume code that is rigorously followed, down to the last accessory, and the festivities attract vast, enthusiastic crowds who follow the show.

There are three sorts of carnival:

– those in the Rhine tradition, in the eastern cantons (Eupen)

– those in the Walloon tradition (Binche, Malmédy)

– mid-Lent carnivals (Fosses-la-Ville, Stavelot).

Any of these carnivals, but especially the one in Binche, make for an unforgettable experience. To find out when they take place, pick up a brochure listing the year's carnivals from the tourist office.

Giants

The giants of Belgian folklore grew out of an oral tradition of tales of myth and battle. Their first appearance seems to have been in the 15th century. Biblical figures jostle with profane characters and fight symbolic battles, or marry amid scenes of great jubilation. Creating a giant character for a carnival is not always easy – they can be the size of a small house.

Processions

With a patron saint for every village, there's plenty of opportunity to wheel out local relics that commemorate a plague epidemic or a vow made by a knight returning from the Holy Land. These relics are often paraded through the surrounding countryside.

In the old days, period-costume pageants were used to enlighten illiterate peasants. In similar fashion to the Mystery plays performed on church squares in Britain, every procession tableau illustrated a historical event. The most famous is the lavish procession of the Holy Blood, which takes place in Bruges on Ascension Day. It's a solemn, mystical affair that celebrates the homecoming of Thierry of Alsace from the Second Crusade in 1150.

– In **Veurne** at the end of July, and in Lessines on Good Friday, hooded penitents parade through the streets to the eerie sound of muffled drum beats. It's a macabre, haunting event, similar to the procession that takes place in Seville during Holy Week.

– In **Mechelen** at the end of April, you can catch up with the time-honoured Hanswijck procession in honour of the Virgin Mary; in mid-September, Tournai is the backdrop for the Quatre Cortèges ('four processions'), which thank the Virgin for saving the town from the plague.

– In **Mons** on Trinity Sunday, the Car d'Or (Golden Chariot) procession bears the reliquary of St Waudru up to the collegiate church; the day winds up with a mock fight between St George and the Dragon, first staged in medieval times. Traditionally, spectators steal hairs from the dragon's tail, as they're supposed to bring you good luck.

– The Ommegang ('going around') is a secular festival that takes place in **Brussels** on the first Tuesday and Thursday of July. It's a joyous commemoration of the procession that paraded through the streets in 1549 in honour of Charles V, the Holy Roman Emperor, and winds up in the evening on the Grand'Place. A spectacular event with fantastic costumes, it attracts hordes of tourists from Belgium and beyond, so book a seat well in advance (TIB: ☎ (02) 513 8940).

Every three years in August, **Bruges** hosts a canal-side night-time procession, the Reiefest. The next one is scheduled for 2004. Check the website for more information: www.reiefest.be. Every five years, the city stages the procession of the Arbre d'Or (Golden Tree), which celebrates the wedding of Charles the Bold and Margaret of York. More than 2,000 people take part. The next one takes place during Bruges' stint as European Cultural Capital, in 2002, and is scheduled for August 31 and September 1.

– **South of Charleroi**, almost every village has a relic to parade through its streets. Since the Napoleonic era, soldiers and officers in period dress have joined the procession. Uniformed grenadiers and light infantrymen march around, fully armed, stopping off at bars and taverns, where they fire their guns into the air. The best of these displays are at Gerpinnes, during the March of Ste Rolende at Pentecost, and at Ham-sur-Heure, on the first Sunday after 15 August, during the March of St Roch. Other August marches take place in Thuin, Florennes, Nalinnes, Thy-le-Château, Fosses-la-Ville, Walcourt and a host of other villages. Every seven years, the Saint-

Feuillien procession parades through Fosses-la-Ville; the next is scheduled for 2005.

Other Local Events

A few other events not to be missed if you're passing that way:

– In May, the planting of the Meiboom (maypole) in Hasselt, Genk and Tongeren. Brussels hosts its own version – in August.

– A Witches' Procession is held in Beselare, near Ypres, on the last Sunday of July; Vielsalm holds a witches' sabbath (the witches are called *macrâles*) during the Fête des Myrtilles (Bilberry Festival), on 20 July. Finally, witches dance with werewolves before being tried and burned at the stake in Ellezelles every June 25.

– If you're looking for a soulmate, you should go to the famous Goûter Matrimonial d'Ecaussines Lalaing (marriage breakfast of Ecaussines Lalaing) on Pentecost Monday. Pay a nominal fee, find your suitor and head for the 'bridge of sighs' or the nearby 'lovers' arbour'.

– Péket, or gin, flows freely in the Liège district of Outremeuse on Assumption Day, 15 August. Visitors can join the three-day binge.

– In Arlon at the end of May, there's a steady flow of white wine laced with cognac for the festival of *Maitrank* (May drink), while beer-drinkers should head for the Brueghelian festival of Wingene, where ale is quaffed by the gallon (last Sunday of August in even years).

– The French-speaking community holds its main festivals in Namur. Even experienced French-speakers may have trouble following the language in the Wallonian Contest of Lies, but you can still enjoy the epic jousts and party atmosphere.

– Lenten fires are lit in Bouge, near Namur, to celebrate the return of light. A vast log is lit above the cliffs that overhang the Meuse, while the village of Tiff elects its Carnival Prince.

All Creatures Great and Small

– The Procession of Cats takes place in Ypres every three years on the second Sunday in May (the next is scheduled for 2003). In the Middle Ages, the unfortunate felines were hurled from the belfry. You'll be relieved to hear that toy cats are used today.

– In times gone by, the Antwerp polders, Hainaut and the Lower Maas all held a ritualistic decapitation of a live goose that was strung up by its neck. A speaking contest was held to elect the 'king' of this event. This practice still goes on, but with a dead goose.

– Cock-fighting was once popular in and around Liège (the cockerel appears on the Walloon flag, its foot raised in a gesture of defiance). The bouts were the object of outrageous bets, and are now illegal. Today, people bet on how many times the cock will crow in an hour.

– Belgium's favourite bird, bizarrely is the carrier pigeon. This national sport is called *colombophilie*, and some of the pigeons used are very valuable. They're lovingly raised, then released a long distance from the dovecote. Pigeons are competitive, and usually (but not always) find their way back to their beloved owners, who bet on the length of the return journey.

Sports Events

– In Brabant and Hainaut, there's a '*balle-pelote*' championship, a traditional ball game where opposing teams meet on specially marked 'pitches' in the roads and public squares.

Also in Brabant, you'll often see an archery competition at one of the village fêtes with targets over 20 metres (65 feet) high. Guilds in Flanders still organize regular crossbow and arquebus contests.

Puppet Theatres

– In Brussels, the Toone Theatre continues a tradition of classic drama, with shows such as *The Three Musketeers*, *El Cid*, *The Four Sons Aymon* and *The Passion of Christ*, all peppered with local dialect.

– In Liège, you can meet Tchantchès, the affable drinker, who'll tell you the story of the Nativity or legends from the era of Charlemagne.

St Nicolas

Belgian children look forward to 6 December, when, if they're lucky, they are showered with toys, for this, according to tradition, is the festival of the patron saint of children. Seated on a throne with his right-hand man, *le père Fouettard*, he hands out sweets to children who have been good. He is much more important than Father Christmas for Belgian children, although most of them receive yet more presents on 25 December.

HEALTH AND INSURANCE

> **TIP** In an emergency, call ☎ 100 for an ambulance or the fire brigade. For the police call ☎ 101.
>
> (*See also* 'A few useful numbers' *under* 'Communications').

Belgium has an excellent public health service, and standards of care are among the best in the world. For minor ailments, go in the first instance to a pharmacy (look out for the green cross), where highly qualified pharmacists should be able to give you advice. Many medicines are available over the counter in Belgium. There are no compulsory inoculations for visitors to Belgium.

Hospitalized visitors will be expected to make immediate payment for any treatment – indeed, the blunt approach to money may come as a shock to British patients used to the NHS but hospital staff will help with arrangements with insurance companies. British and Irish citizens should apply for an E111 form, available at the local post office, before leaving home. This covers most, but not all, medical costs, although it excludes dental treatment or calling a doctor out to see you.

Statistically speaking, you are far more likely to encounter accidents or fall victim to some form of crime when abroad than at home, so you are strongly advised to take out private insurance as well. It is available through credit-card companies, travel agents and student and senior-affiliated organizations (such as STA and SAGA). Insurance may be included in the price of your ticket or package, or you may be covered by your credit-card company (particularly American Express) if your ticket was purchased using that card.

Citizens of South Africa, USA, Canada, Australia and New Zealand require full private medical insurance.

Take details of any medication you are using, as this will help a doctor to assess your situation and prescribe the correct treatment. A lot of brand names are different when abroad, so ask a pharmacist for the nearest local equivalent.

LANGUAGES

A word of warning: even if you remember your school French, don't try a 'Belgian' accent, for there are many Belgian accents and you'll never fool a local. But make an effort to pronounce the names of French and Flemish places and people accurately. It's not just a question of being respectful; it'll make life much easier.

DUTCH AND FLEMISH

Dutch and its dialects, described as Flemish, are spoken by 20 million Europeans in the Low Countries and in Belgium. The dialects grew out of the German spoken by invaders who spread across western Europe after the fall of the Roman Empire. The language evolved over the centuries, eventually developing into the Scandinavian languages, High German, Luxembourgish, English, Low German and Dutch.

Official Dutch (known as ABN, or Algemeen Beschaafd Nederlands) is taught in schools in Belgium and the Netherlands. This is the language that unites the main dialects: Dutch, in the central Low Countries; Saxon, to the north of Arnhem; Limburg dialects (there are two, those of Hasselt and Maastricht); the Brabant dialects of Ghent, Brussels, Antwerp and Noord-Brabant; and the Flemish dialects of Western Flanders and Zeeland.

You can't really talk of a homogenous Dutch in the Low Countries, nor can you talk of a homogenous Flemish for Dutch-speakers in Belgium. A Flemish-speaker uses a dialect at home that is quite different from what children learn at school, and totally different from the language he hears on TV. The differences, of course, give rise to all sorts of jokes between the Dutch and Flemings, just as the French and French-speaking Walloons poke fun at each other.

Almost everyone in the main Flemish towns speaks excellent English, but any effort to utter a few words of Flemish will be much appreciated.

– **Dutch, and how to pronounce it**: Dutch is pronounced like English, with the accent falling on the first syllable, except where the word has a prefix, such as *be-*, *ge-*, *er-*, *her-*, *ont-* or *ver-*. In this case, the accent falls on the following syllable.

Numbers

one	*een* (ayn)
two	*twee* (tway)
three	*drie* (dree)
four	*vier* (fear)
five	*vijf* (fayf)
six	*zes* (zayss)
seven	*zeven* (sayven)
eight	*acht* (ahght – a guttural sound, similar to the German)
nine	*negen* (nayghen)
ten	*tien* (tin)
eleven	*elf* (elf)
twelve	*twaalf* (twarlf)
thirteen	*dertien* (dairtin)
fourteen	*veertien* (vairtin)
twenty	*twintig* (twintigh)
thirty	*dertig* (dairtigh)
forty	*veertig* (vairtigh)
one hundred	*honderd* (honndert)

Travel

plane	*vliegtuig* (vleagtowgh)
boat	*boot* (boat)
port	*haven* (harven)
train	*trein* (train)
station	*station* (stassion)
quay	*perron* (perron)
car	*auto* (owto)
bus	*bus* (beuss)
bike	*fiets* (feats)
left	*links* (links)
right	*rechts* (raihghts – the guttural sound again)

Hotels

hotel	*hotel* (otel)
room	*kamer* (karmer)
youth hostel	*jeugdherberg* (yeughd-hair-bairgh)
bed	*bed* (baitt)
key	*sleutel* (slirtel)

bathroom	*badkamer* (bad-karmer)
to sleep	*slapen* (slarpen)
price	*prijs* (prayss)
B&B room	*gastenkamer* (ghass-ten-karmer)

Meals

restaurant	*restaurant* (like the French)
table	*tafel* (tar-fel)
to eat	*eten* (ay-ten)
to drink	*drinken* (drin-ken)
wine	*wijn* (wayn)
beer	*bier* (beer)
water	*water* (wa-ter)
bread	*brood* (broat)
coffee	*koffie* (koffee)
tea	*thee* (tay)
milk	*melk* (maylk)
meat	*vlees* (vlayss)
vegetables	*groenten* (groon-ten)

Out and About

street	*straat* (strart)
avenue	*laan* (lahn)
square	*plein* (playn)
market	*markt*
dyke	*dijk* (dayk)
beach	*strand* (strant)
church	*kerk* (kairk)
castle	*kasteel* (cass-tayl)
bridge	*brug* (brugh)
town hall	*stadhuis* (stad-howss)
museum	*museum* (mu-se-om)
closed	*gesloten* (ge-slo-ten)
forbidden	*verboden* (ver-bo-den)

Meeting People

yes	*ja* (yar)
no	*neen* (nayn)
where?	*waar*? (much like the English)
how?	*hoe*? (hoo)
how many?	*hoeveel*? (hoo-fayl)
too expensive	*te duur* (te dooer)
thank you (polite form)	*dank U* (as it looks)
thank you (familiar)	*dank je* (dank yer)
hello (familiar)	*dag!* (dagh)
good morning	*goedemorgen* (goo-de-morghen)
good evening	*goedenavond* (goo-de-na-vond)
goodbye	*tot ziens* (tott-zeenss)

today	*vandaag* (van-dargh)
tomorrow (also morning)	*morgen* (mor-ghen)
yesterday	*gisteren* (hghis-te-ren)
please (polite)	*alstublieft* (alss-tu-bleaft)
please (familiar)	*alsjeblieft* (alss-yer-bleaft)

If you bother to say a few words following the phonetic instructions, your efforts will be met with smiles of delight.

BELGIAN FRENCH

If you speak any French, you'll be fine in French-speaking Belgium, although there are some local peculiarities.

Counting in Belgian French is much easier than in France. Instead of the complicated 70 (*soixante-dix*) and 90 (*quatre-vingt-dix*), in Belgium, you can simply say '*septante*' and '*nonante*'.

These linguistic peculiarities are, in fact, more logical in terms of the Latin origins of the language, and bring it closer to other Romance languages, such as Spanish, which uses '*setenta*', '*ochenta*' and '*noventa*' (70, 80 and 90), or Italian, where the same numbers are '*settenta*', '*ottanta*' and '*novanta*'.

Below is a comparison of Belgian French and 'French' French terms (with the English translation); the list provides some (not all) of the picturesque aspects of the language.

Belgian French Peculiarities

English	Belgian	French
affectionate	*amitieux*	*affectueux*
bread roll	*pistolet*	*petit pain*
carpet	*tapis plain*	*moquette*
chicory	*chicon*	*endive*
door handle	*clenche*	*poignée de porte*
dustbin	*bac à ordures*	*poubelle*
folder, file	*farde*	*chemise, dossier*
French stick	*pain français*	*baguette*
handbag	*sacoche*	*sac à main*
he's helpful	*il n'est pas contraire*	*il est accommodant*
to indicate (in a car)	*renseigner*	*indiquer, signaler*
to manage, work out	*tirer son plan*	*se débrouiller*
mess, chaos	*brol*	*désordre*
newspaper stand	*aubette*	*kiosque à journaux*
OK?	*ça va?*	*d'accord?*
pedestrianized area	*piétonner*	*rue commerçante réservée aux piétons*
pensioner	*pensionné*	*retraité*
to phone	*sonner*	*téléphoner*
plate of chips	*friture*	*baraque à frites*
postcard	*carte-vue*	*carte postale*
to queue	*faire la file*	*faire la queue*

rubbish dump	*dépôt d'immondices*	*décharge*
see you soon	*à tantôt*	*à tout à l'heure*
seriously	*pour du bon*	*sérieusement*
to shine	*blinquer*	*reluire*
spare time	*fourche*	*temps libre*
studio flat	*flat*	*studio*
sweets	*boules*	*bonbons*
tip	*dringuelle*	*pourboire*
well-built	*castaud*	*costaud*
wise	*brave*	*sage*
woodland path	*drève*	*allée forestière*

Just to confuse you, you'll need to unlearn the French meal times you learnt so studiously at school, or you could find yourself wondering why the Belgians eat lunch first thing in the morning and turn up to an invitation to *dîner* six hours too late. *Déjeuner* in Belgium is breakfast (*petit déjeuner* across the border), *dîner* is lunch and *souper* is supper – almost like English. Still more confusing, if someone answers a question with '*oué sans doute?*', this means 'no', whereas if they say '*non peut-être?*', they mean 'yes'.

BRUXELLOIS

Brussels is officially a bilingual city, with more than 80 per cent of the population claiming to speak French, but Brussels also has its own patois.

The city has Flemish roots (a continuing source of contention today), but has been shaped by other cultures, too, including that of the Spanish occupiers in the 16th century. A distinct dialect called *Vloms* survives in some districts of Brussels, where it is spoken by older residents and even has its own literature. You can hear it at the Toone puppet theatre (*see* the chapter on Brussels).

The list of Bruxellois insults is particularly rich, and bears witness to the city's cultural heritage; many are closer to English than French. If you're keen to follow a conversation in a local café *(caberdouche* or *stamineî*), here are a few invectives worthy of Captain Haddock (the French-language versions of Tintin are riddled with Bruxellois words):

smeerlap (smayr-lap)	bastard
snotnuis (snot-nows)	snotty-nosed
dikkenek (dicken-naik)	conceited
froecheleir (frooshe-lair)	shark; groper
ettefretter (aite-frai-tter)	worrier
broebeleir (broobe-lair)	stammerer, someone who's not with it
puuteleir (poo-te-lair)	groper
klachkop (klashe-kop)	bald
schieve architek (skieve arshitaik)	idiot

This last insult, (literally, 'twisted architect') comes from the Marolles district, which was partially knocked down to make way for the Palais de Justice; the inhabitants have never forgiven the architect responsible, Joseph Poelaert.

You're now fully equipped to take on an evening in Brussels; nobody will be able to *enquiquiner* you (make fun of you) nor make you swallow *zieverderâ* and *carabistouilles en stoemelinks* (gossip and tall stories).

WALLOON

Walloon has been least influenced by French, as it is the northernmost part of francophone Europe. It has also retained a number of Latin characteristics.

The 'Enry 'Igginses among you will notice that the Walloons drag out their words a bit, and hang on the vowel sounds. Some nasal vowels are much more distinguishable than they are in French.

Walloon is a living language, and its literature has been evolving since the 16th century, especially in the fields of drama and poetry. A literary society set up in 1856 listed the vocabulary, and this inventory shows that the language is much richer than other French dialects.

There are three Walloon dialects: eastern Walloon, spoken around Liège and in the north of the province of Luxembourg; central Walloon, spoken in Walloon Brabant, Namur and the Ardennes; and west Walloon, spoken in Hainaut.

Other dialects used in Wallonia include the French dialects of Picardie (spoken around Tournai), Lorraine (spoken in Gaume) and Champagne (spoken south of the province of Namur); Luxembourgish (spoken around Arlon); and German, which is spoken in the cantons of Sankt Vith and Eupen.

GENERAL INFORMATION

A Few Walloon Words

berdeller	to grumble
bouquette	pancake
canada	potato (in Namur)
capon	mischievous
chipoter	to dither
crompîre	potato (in Liège)
djâle	devil
djauser	to speak
dringuelle	tip
fristouiller	to cook
huche	door
il fait douf	it's hot
péket	gin
rawette	supplement, extra
tiès	head
wachotte	washing

MEDIA

TV

If your hotel room is equipped with a TV, you'll soon find that you have a choice of 30 or more stations thanks to cable TV. Access to such a large choice of images and information is taken for granted in Belgium, where there are 15 French-language stations and most viewers have access to BBC1 and 2, MTV and CNN. Belgians are small-screen junkies, which helps to explain why the streets tend to be rather deserted in the evening. Competition between stations is intense, with everyone fighting for advertising revenue and market share.

THE PRESS

The press has always been more or less linked to dominant political parties, or to the Roman Catholic Church. In a small country where many people don't bother to buy a daily paper, newspapers find it hard to make ends meet, and many rely on regional editions grouped together under holding companies.

For French-speakers, Brussels offers *Le Soir* and *La Libre Belgique* (a Catholic paper) with listings supplements on Wednesday. Tabloid papers include *La Dernière Heure* and *La Lanterne*. In Liège, there's *La Meuse*; in Namur, Luxembourg and Walloon Brabant, you'll come across *Vers l'avenir*; while Tournai brings out *Le Courrier de l'Escaut*. These are the main dailies. The only widespread weekly paper is *Le Vif/L'Express*, which shares some of its content with the French weekly *L'Express*, though *Le Soir illustré* also has its followers.

The most common Flemish dailies are *De Standaard*, with political leaders that have quite a dominant influence on Flemish opinion, *Het Nieuwsblad*, *Het Volk*, *Het Laatste Nieuws*, *Gazet van Antwerpen* and the left-wing *De Morgen*.

English-speakers, meanwhile, can get most English and American national papers on the date of publication (*The Times* is particularly current, as its European edition is printed in Charleroi), as well as the *International Herald Tribune*. You can catch up with Belgian news and culture thanks to the weekly *The Bulletin*.

MONEY

THE EURO

TIP Euro coins and notes are due to be introduced in January 2002 and the euro will be the sole currency in Belgium from 28 February 2002. At the time of writing we were unable to include the equivalent euro prices alongside prices in Belgian francs, however those readers familiar with the Belgian franc should find the franc prices a useful guide.

To convert Belgian franc prices into euros, divide the amount in francs by 40.34; so for example, 1,000BEF = 24.79€. The official euro/franc conversion rate has been fixed at 40.34 Belgian francs to one euro. The euro/£ conversion rate stands at about 63 pence to one euro. Check the currency website **www.oanda.com** for up-to-date Sterling/euro conversion rates.

1 euro = 40.34BEF
1 euro = circa 63 pence

BANKS AND BUREAUX DE CHANGE

Banks are open from Monday to Thursday, 9am–3.30pm. Some close for lunch. Closing time is later on Friday, sometimes as late as 7pm. A few are open on Saturday morning.

When changing money in Belgium, it's better to use banks than bureaux de change (especially in tourist hot spots). Commission varies, so check the boards before your transaction. You shouldn't have any problem changing travellers' cheques.

CREDIT CARDS AND ATMS/CASHPOINTS

There's a network of cash machines (called Mister Cash and Bancontact) that allows you to draw money using your bank or credit card. Cash machines display the logos of the cards they accept around the edge: look out for Maestro, Cirrus or the name of your credit-card provider.

Note that, over long holiday weekends, some cash machines run out of notes, so stock up in advance.

Lost or Stolen Cards

If your card is lost or stolen, cancel it as soon as possible by calling your card provider in your own country; make sure you have the 24-hour contact number with you. Visa and Barclaycard holders can phone the UK from Belgium for assistance:

Barclaycard (24-hour) ☎ + 44 1604 234234.

Visa (24-hour) ☎ + 44 1383 621166.

OUTDOOR ACTIVITIES

Flat Flanders is the ideal place for a cycling holiday. The coast, with its vast expanse of beaches near De Panne, offers sailboarding and seaside watersports.

Horse-riders should head for the Kempen region. Watersports are available on the lakes of the lowlands, while the Ardennes rivers attract canoeing enthusiasts and fishing fanatics in summer.

There's no shortage of caves for speleology addicts.

Long-distance footpaths are signposted for hardened walkers, and there are climbing opportunities next to the River Meuse.

Some useful addresses for nature-lovers, walkers and cyclists:

■ **Europ'Aventures**: Sprimont 41, Sainte-Ode 6641. ☎ (061) 688611. Tour operator specializing in hiking and trekking on foot, horse, bike and mountain bike. Many activities are centred in the Transardennes and the Transgaume. For maps and guides, contact Maison de la Randonnée c/o Sprimont (address above)

■ **Association Belge des Sentiers de Grande Randonnée**: BP 10, Liège 4000. The association will point you in the direction of 3,500 kilometres (2,200 miles) of signposted walks in the south of the country. It also publishes guides that describe the routes, and can suggest cycle routes along country roads and canal and riverside paths. Publications are available from: Auberges de jeunesse ASBL, rue de la Sablonnière 28, Brussels 1000. ☎ (02) 219 5676.

■ **Grote Routepaden**: Van Stralenstraat 40, Antwerpen 2060. ☎ 03 232 7218. This organization provides information about 2,500 kilometres (1,500 miles) of Flemish footpaths (guides in Dutch). It also organizes walking holidays, where your baggage is carried for you, and can suggest cycle routes with guides and maps (e.g., Vlaanderen Route, 700 kilometres/440 miles).

■ **Réserves naturelles et ornithologiques de Belgique**: rue Royale Sainte-Marie 105, Brussels 1030. ☎ (02) 245 5500.

■ **Equi-Info-Développement**: rue A.-Fossant 20, Lasne 1380. ☎ (02) 633 1887. Everything you could ever want to know about equestrianism in Belgium.

PUBLIC HOLIDAYS

1 January, Easter Monday, 1 May, Ascension Day, Pentecost Monday, 21 July (national holiday), 15 August, 1 November, 11 November, 25 December. 'Community festivals' may mean services don't function. In Flanders, this falls on 11 July; the French-speaking community celebrates on 27 September.

SHOPPING

Most shops open at about 9am or 10am and close at about 6pm or 7pm. Big stores are often open until 8pm, and until 9pm on Friday. Everything closes on Sunday, although in the cities, 'night shops' are open round the clock for basic items, munchies and drink. There are lots of Belgian 'specialities' that you might like to take home as souvenirs, including:

FOOD

Chocolates (pralines) keep for a week in a cool place.

Marzipan comes in every imaginable shape.

Babeluttes are hard butter sweets.

The most popular sweet snacks are *couques* (pastries), *speculoos* (cinnamon biscuits), macaroons and *pain à la grecque*.

Cheese fans should try *herve*, a runny and decidedly fragrant cheese, or one of the soft abbey cheeses.

Don't forget to sample the famous smoked sausages of the Ardennes region.

DRINK

If you can carry it, buy a crate of Belgian beer and glasses to go with it. Try *gueuze* beer and *péket* (gin).

BOOKS

Comic strips, what else? Fans and collectors will find the choice bewildering. In Brussels, there's an area around chaussée de Wavre that's devoted to the comic strip (*see* 'Brussels').

GADGETS

A mass of objects, souvenirs and accessories bear the blue and gold of the European Union flag.

CRAFTS

– **Lace**: a Belgian speciality. You can choose from Brussels, Bruges and Mechelen lace, and find out everything you could possibly want to know about this industry, which provided the income for more than 15 per cent of Brusselers in the 18th century.

– **Tapestry**: destined for decorative use, tapestry reached the height of its glory in the 15th and 16th centuries. Today you'll find a variety of pieces in all the tourist shops.

– **Glass and crystal**: Val Saint-Lambert, near Liège, is the country's most famous producer of glass and crystal.

– Other Walloon specialities: copperware; pewterware (at Huy); ceramics and pottery (La Louvière) and porcelain (Tournai).

– If you know what you're looking for, Belgium can be an antiques-hunter's paradise.

SMOKING

Smoking is forbidden in all public places. In restaurants, smokers and non-smokers are divided.

TIME

Belgium is one hour ahead of GMT (Greenwich Mean Time) and changes its clocks in spring and autumn. In Belgium, as in France, 'am' and 'pm' are not used – the 24-hour clock is widely applied.

TIPPING

In cafés and restaurants, prices include service, but it's always a good idea to round up the bill.

At the cinema, you must give 20BEF to the usherette who gives you your programme. And, in cinemas, bars and restaurants, leave 10BEF (sometimes 15BEF) for the toilet attendant, known locally as Madame Pipi.

TOURIST OFFICES

BELGIAN TOURIST OFFICES ABROAD

Britain

■ **Tourism Flanders**: 31 Pepper Street, London E14 9RW. ☎ (020) 7867 0311/0891 887 799 (50p per minute). Fax (020) 7458 0045. Email: office@flanders-tourism.org. Website: www.belgium-tourism.net

■ **Belgian Tourist Board**: (Brussels and Ardennes) 225 Marshall Wall, London E14 9FW. ☎ (020) 7531 0392. Fax (020) 7531 0393. Email: info@belgium-tourism.org

Ireland

There is no Belgian tourist office in Ireland, so you should contact the branch in Britain.

United States

■ **Belgian Tourist Office**: 780 Third Avenue, Suite 1501, New York, New York 10017. ☎ (212) 758 8130. Fax (212) 355 7675. Email:info@visitbelgium.com. Website: www.visitbelgium.com

Canada

■ **Belgian Tourist Office**: PO Box 760, Succursale, Montréal H4A 3S2. ☎ (514) 484 3594. Fax (514) 489 8965. Website: www.visitbelgium.com

■ **Wallonie-Brussels Tourist Office** : 43 rue de Buade, Bureau 525, Quebec Ville G1R 4AZ. ☎ (418) 692 4939. Fax (418) 692 4974.

There is no branch of the Belgian Tourist Office in Australia, New Zealand or South Africa.

TRANSPORT

Given Belgium's diminutive size, the density of its road network and the fact that motorways are free, driving is an attractive option for getting about. Parking, however, can be very expensive and the rush-hour traffic jams are a nightmare. Fortunately, there are other ways to get around.

CAR HIRE

If you're coming from Britain, Ireland, the USA or Canada, you'll only need a domestic driving licence to be able to drive in Belgium (a valid USA driver's licence is accepted for stays of less than 90 days). Australian, New Zealand and South African drivers, however, must apply for an international permit before departing.

Car-hire desks at Brussels national airport are located in the arrivals hall, and are open 6.30am–11pm.

National/Alamo: ☎ +32 2 753 2060

Avis: ☎ +32 2 720 0944

Budget Rent-a-Car: ☎ +32 2 753 2170

Europcar: ☎ +32 2 721 0592

Hertz: ☎ +32 2 720 6044

If you want some information on car hire before leaving America, call the numbers below. For guaranteed US$ rate, reserve in the USA. Minimum driving age is 25.

Avis: ☎ 1 800 331 1084

Alamo: ☎ 1 800 522 9696

Auto Europe: ☎ 1 888 223 5555

Budget: ☎ 1 800 472 3325

Europe by Car: ☎ 1 800 223 1516

EuroDollar: ☎ 1 800 800 6000

Hertz: ☎ 1 800 654 3001

Kemwell: ☎ 1 800 678 0678

Driving

The official speed limits are: motorways, 120kph (72mph); main roads, 90kph (54mph); built-up areas, 50kph (30mph).

Seatbelts are compulsory everywhere, including in the back seats, and the local gendarmerie carry out random checks on Friday and Saturday nights. This is as much to punish alcohol abuse (you're over the limit with more than 0.5g/l of alcohol in your blood; the equivalent of a glass of wine) as to track down drug use at the wheel. It's no laughing matter: on-the-spot action by police can lead to you losing your licence or having your car clamped. Judging by the pile-ups when everyone comes out of the clubs on a Saturday evening, these measures are wholly justified.

Motorways

When astronauts return to earth with stories of what they could see from outer space, they never fail to describe the twinkling of the world's cities in the night, including a curious shining web in a corner of western Europe –

Belgium's well-lit motorways. Every evening, thousands of sodium lamps illuminate the roads of one of the tightest communication networks in the world.

When you're in Brussels, the most far-flung points of the country are never more than two hours' drive away. The only excuse for turning up late to an appointment is if you don't pay enough attention to the place-name changes as you pass from one linguistic area to another. Knowing the French and Dutch names of your destination can save you a lot of hassle. Some places are known in English by their Flemish name, some by their French, and sometimes by a third, Anglicized name. Here are the main ones to look out for.

French	Dutch	English
Anvers	Antwerpen	Antwerp
Braine-le-Comte	'S Gravenbrakel	
Bruges	Brugge	
Bruxelles	Brussel	Brussels
Courtrai	Kortrijk	
Furnes	Veurne	
Gand	Gent	Ghent
Grammont	Geraardsbergen	
Jodoigne	Geldenaken	
Liège	Luik	
Louvain	Leuven	
Malines	Mechelen	
Mons	Bergen	
Namur	Namen	
Ostende	Oostende	Ostend
Renaix	Ronse	
Soignies	Zinnik	
Tirlemont	Tienen	
Tournai	Doornik	

This schizophrenia creeps across the border, too: you may come across Parijs for Paris, Rijsel for Lille and Aix-la-Chapelle for Aachen, or find that the rivers Escaut and Meuse (in French) become Scheldt and Maas (in Flemish). Finally, Uitrit is not the most commonly signposted town in Belgium; it's the Dutch for exit.

Belgian motorways, unlike the French *péages* and German Autobahns, are free.

HITCH-HIKING

No real problems here, but it's illegal to hitch-hike on motorways and sliproads. Stand by the signposts with a piece of card stating where you're going.

> **TIP** Between April and October, you can get an update on the latest offers and requests for lifts advertised by Taxistop on the French-language Radio 21; this system enables private individuals to offer seats in their cars to destinations in Belgium and Europe, while others use Taxistop to request lifts to their chosen destination. The basic rate is 1BEF per kilometre for the driver, and 0.30BEF per kilometre for Taxistop, with a minimum cost of 250BEF and a maximum of 800BEF. Call ☎ (070) 222292 for more information, or check their website www.taxistop.be. You can request or offer lift-shares directly. Don't forget that you have to supply a phone number they can call you back on.

BICYCLES

Flanders is a cyclists' heaven, with cycle routes and even cyclist-only signs. Although the flat terrain makes for relatively easy going, you may have to struggle against the wind, which can whip across the flatlands. An ideal place to hire a bike or mountain bike is at a railway station, where you'll pay roughly 325BEF a day (half-day 225BEF), plus a deposit. You can also get combined rail-cycle tickets. Alternatively, the local tourist office can tell you where you can hire bikes – pick up a brochure for details.

TRAINS

There are two sorts of line: the IC (Intercity, serving major cities, as it suggests), and IR (Interregion, serving the smaller towns). The linchpin of the network is Brussels, but you don't always have to change trains, as the city is crossed by a six-way junction that links Gare du Midi to Gare du Nord via Gare Centrale (a short walk from the Grand'Place). Belgian trains are fast, frequent and cheap, especially if you take advantage of the special deals listed below:

– day-return tickets (North Sea and the Ardennes).

– tickets that also get you into sporting events, exhibitions, concerts and carnivals.

– weekend tickets (for a maximum of four days).

– Multipass (for groups of three to five people).

– Go-Pass (for under-26s): 10 journeys for 1,390BEF; it lasts for up to six months and can be used by your friends.

– Golden Railpass: same idea, but for six journeys, and for the over-60s accompanied by children between six and 12.

– B-Tourrail: five days, not necessarily consecutive, over one month for less than 400BEF per day, for any journey within Belgium.

If you haven't bought your ticket before you board the train, you'll be liable for a 50BEF supplement if you find the ticket inspector before he finds you. Otherwise, you'll have to pay a fine. And you can't break your journey to have a look at a town and continue later on.

– Railway information: ☎ (02) 555 2525.

Eurostar in Belgium

Eurostar tickets can be bought from the three Brussels stations, as well as from the stations at Bruges, Brussels National Airport 'Zaventem' and Brussels Airport Charleroi Sud.

🚆 **Eurostar**: Bruxelles Midi Eurostar Office, Bruxelles Midi, Bruxelles. ☎ (02) 528 2828. E-bookings: http://tickets.b-rail.be. Website: www.eurostar.be

Thalys Train

Also known as the 'Red Train', the high-speed Thalys train is provided by the Belgian, French, Dutch and German railways. Thalys links Brussels directly to Paris, Cologne, Düsseldorf, Amsterdam and other cities in Europe including Geneva and Marseilles.

Thalys tickets can be bought from booking offices in Brussels Nord/Noord, Central/Centraal or Midi/Zuid. Alternatively, contact Thalys direct by telephone or via the website. In order to make bookings before you leave Britain, contact **International Rail** or **Rail Europe** by phone, post or via the website. The Rail Europe booking office in Piccadilly is particularly convenient for personal bookings if you live in or near London. Interrail passes are not valid for travel on Thalys services unless you pay a supplementary fee.

🚆 **Thalys Train**: Bruxelles Midi Railtour Office, Bruxelles Midi, Bruxelles. ☎ (070) 667 788. Website: www.thalys.com/www.b-rail.be

🚆 **Belgian National Railways**: (information only) Unit 200A, Blackfriars Boundary, 156 Blackfriars Road, London SE1 8EN. ☎ (020) 7592 2332. Website: www.b-rail.be

🚆 **International Rail**: Chase House, Gilbert Street, Ropley SO24 0BY. ☎ (01962) 773646. Email: info@international-rail.co.uk. Website: www.international-rail.com

🚆 **Rail Europe**: Travel Centre, 179 Piccadilly, London W1J 9BA. ☎ (0870) 584 8848. Website: www.raileurope.co.uk

BUSES

On the stretches of Belgium not covered by the rail network, there are bus links between rail routes. The bus companies operating in Flanders (De Lijn) and Wallonia (TEC) are separate, but the timetable is organized so that, in theory, you shouldn't lose too much time hanging around at bus stops. The timetable is included in the SNCB/NMBS rail timetable.

The major conurbations have their own networks of buses and trams (one tram line runs along the coast). Brussels, Antwerp and Charleroi also have metro systems and underground trams. Brussels has its own transport company, STIB/MIVB. Many hotel package deals include tram, train or bus tickets.

BOATS

Why not take advantage of the network of navigable rivers and canals to sightsee by water? It's not the speediest method, especially as you'll have to negotiate frequent locks, but it's definitely the most attractive. You'll find plenty of day-long (or less) tourist cruises: along the Meuse around Namur, or the Lower Maas (in the direction of Maastricht); on the Albert canal around the port of Antwerp and in the estuary of the Escaut/Scheldt; on the Escaut/Scheldt between Tournai and Ghent, and on the canals in the centre of Belgium. You can also go by water individually or in groups: buy a seven-day cruising ticket from Antwerp via Brussels, Ronquières, La Louvière, Mons or Ghent.

– Information: Heilig Hartlaan 30, Aalst 9300. ☎ (053) 779286.

USEFUL WEBSITES

Travellers will find many websites devoted to Belgium and all things Belgian on the net. The following are just a selection of the best available.

www.visitbelgium.com – official site of the Belgium Tourist Office in the Americas. This useful and interesting site is full of helpful suggestions for travel in Belgium. **www.belgium-tourism.net** is the official site for European branches of the Belgian Tourist Office and has some useful links. **www.brussels.org** is a useful listings site. **www.expatriate-online.com** is aimed at foreigners living or planning to live in Belgium, but also contains useful information for long-stay travellers. There are plenty of sites devoted to European politics – try **www.eurobru.com** or **www.europa.eu.int** if you're interested. The official government site for Belgium is **www.belgium.fgov.be**. Tintin fans should check out **www.tintin.com** for the latest on the little blond explorer, and motor enthusiasts will enjoy **www.auto world.be**

Background

VITAL STATISTICS

- **Area**: 30,513 square kilometres, or 11,787 square miles.

- **Capital**: Brussels.

- **Population**: just over 10.2 million.

- **Population density**: 332 inhabitants per square kilometre (860 per square mile), making Belgium one of the most densely populated areas of Europe, with 97 per cent living in towns. Annual growth rate: 0.3 per cent.

- **Main cities**: Brussels (960,000 inhabitants), Antwerp (465,000), Ghent (230,000), Charleroi (209,000), Liège (200,000), Bruges (116,000), Namur (104,000).

- **Government**: constitutional and parliamentary monarchy.

- **Head of state**: King Albert II.

- **Prime minister**: Guy Verhofstadt (Flemish Liberal).

- **Administrative divisions**: three Regions (Brussels-Capital, Flanders and Wallonia) and 10 Provinces.

- **Linguistic communities**: Flemish, French-speaking and German-speaking.

- **Official languages**: French, Dutch and German.

- **Maximum height above sea level**: 694 metres (2,276 feet).

HISTORY

The area that we call Belgium has been densely inhabited since neolithic times, and right up until the second half of the 20th century, its history has been a succession of invasions and changing frontiers.

AVÉ CAESAR!

'Of all the Gauls, the Belgians are the bravest warriors!' Every schoolbook in the kingdom quotes the fulsome praise offered to the students' forbears by Julius Caesar. On his departure, Caesar bequeathed his adversaries four centuries of Roman administration and prosperity. Roman rule in Gaul gave the Belgians secure frontiers to keep out the Germans, and an early communications network, with straight Roman roads running from Boulogne to Cologne and from Reims to Trier. Towns such as Arlon, Tongeren and Tournai developed at the crossroads of these major thoroughfares. Economic development was largely centred on the *villae*, and traditional farming and market gardening methods became increasingly dependent on the metalworking industry. Imperial civil servants, soldiers and traders made Latin the *lingua franca*, and the Celts had no choice but to learn it.

Christianity came to the area in the third century, with the foundation of the abbey at Tongeren.

THE INVADERS

Since time immemorial, the plains of northern Europe have been a busy highway, and with the first cracks in the Roman Empire, the eastern peoples began to head southwest. The Vandals, Swabians, Saxons and Frisians were content to pass through, but the Franks stopped and set up home. Merovia founded the dynasty that bears his name; Childeric had his remains interred in Tournai; and his son, the leader of the Clovis tribe, united the Franks after 30 years of conquests. He chose Paris as his capital, starting the trend for Belgian emigration to France.

These were turbulent times, but they gave the land that would one day become Belgium lasting links with the Salien Franks, in the north, and the Ripuanian Franks, in the south. The former gave the inhabitants their Germanic idiom, while the latter reinforced their Roman roots with the development of monastic orders. The language was repeatedly modified over the next few centuries, and philologists claim that one can identify populations by the names they gave themselves: from Scotland to Istria, you find, on the Germanic side of the linguistic line, the people called simply 'the people' – Diets, Deutsch, Teutsch; on the other side, the name for the people is 'the foreigners' – Gauls, Gallo, Welsh and Walloons.

When the Church arrived to civilize these barbarous tribes, a wave of holiness engulfed Francia. The basilicas and collegiate churches were named after their founding missionaries: Remacle (in Stavelot), Vincent (Soignies), Lambert (Liège), Hubert and Waudru (Mons), Gertrude (Nivelles). The successors of the Frankish kings, meanwhile, had entrusted the administration of their lands to the palace mayors, and they had some trouble with the mayors of Herstal and Landen, the first rumblings of the troublesome Liégeois. The most energetic of these was Charles, of the Hesbaye family, who, armed with a hammer, gave chase to the Turks at Poitiers in 732.

In 800, Charlemagne (the Liégeois say he was born in nearby Jupille), was crowned Emperor in Rome by the Pope. He chose Aachen as his capital, and during his lifetime, the Carolingian empire stretched from the Elbe to the Pyrenees, and from the North Sea to Abruzzi.

DIVISION OF LANDS

In 843, the Treaty of Verdun split the hard-won conquests of Charlemagne between his three sons: Charles the Bald, King of France, inherited land to the west of the river Scheldt/Escaut; Louis inherited the area to the east of the Rhine, later to become the Holy Roman Empire; and the middle domains that stretched from Holland to Italy fell to Lothair. On Lothair's death, his short-lived realm was broken up into Italy, Burgundy and Lotharingia. Paradoxically, German-speaking Flanders was a vassal state to the King of France, while the Emperor of Germany became the liege lord of the lands that were home to a Latin-based language. Liège, whose bishop, Notger, was raised to the rank of prince, benefited from a relatively independent statute: combined with growing prosperity, it earned the city the nickname of 'Athens of the North'.

WEALTH AND THE FEUDAL SYSTEM

The marauding Vikings sailed up the rivers in their ships, pillaging and terrifying the local populations. Territories were carved up and power was dispersed, leaving the covetous and ambitious to grasp what they could by force of arms, alliances or treachery; quarrels and looting were the order of the day. The strongest eventually seized power, and bigger entities were formed, including the county of Flanders, where merchant cities with English contacts grew rich from weaving and selling cloth, using sea routes to trade with the Baltic and the Gulf of Gascony. Bruges, Ghent and Ieper flourished (the architectural traces of their golden age still stand), Brabant became a duchy centred on the House of Leuven, and Brussels and Mechelen emerged as prosperous cities. Godefroid de Bouillon set off at the head of a 100,000-strong army in the direction of Palestine, with the intention of capturing the Holy Lands. He was proclaimed King of Jerusalem, and was buried in the city's Holy Sepulchre.

With the warrior chiefs absent on their crusades against the infidels, new social classes began to develop in the towns. The guilds took over where serfdom left off, and merchants and artisans began to obtain real privileges from their overlords. Belfries symbolized the liberties obtained via town charters, and the autonomy of the communes became a fixture that has lasted right down to the present day. The merchant towns strengthened their independence in 1302, when beneath the walls of Kortrijk, they inflicted a stinging defeat on the French knights who had come to wreak vengeance for the massacre of the royal garrison. Six centuries after the event, 11 July 1302 is still commemorated with a Flemish festival; the 700th anniversary, in 2002, will be a huge event.

THE BURGUNDIANS

In 1369, Margaret of Maele, daughter of the last Count of Flanders, married Philip the Bold, Duke of Burgundy. Their union brought together for the first time the regions making up what we now call Belgium, and gave birth to a political entity called the Low Countries, with Brussels as its capital. Their son, Philip the Good, Grand Duke of the West, maintained a constant policy of centralization and unification, which brought prosperity to the towns, but left the surrounding countryside ravaged by famine and war. The principality of Liège was sacked in a succession of bloody revolts.

Intellectual and cultural life, however, flourished. The University of Leuven was founded, and Antwerp replaced Bruges as Europe's most important port as the latter's river silted up, inhibiting access to the sea. This was the heyday of the Gothic style, and the development of a new technique for painting in oil saw the rise of artists like the Van Eyck brothers, Hans Memling, Rogier Van der Weyden, Huge Van der Goes and Dirk Bouts, who are collectively known by the misleading name of 'Flemish Primitives'.

LIFE AS PART OF THE SPANISH EMPIRE

Thanks to Marie of Burgundy's marriage to Maximilian of Austria, the 17 'united provinces' of Burgundy passed, on the death of Charles the Bold in 1477, to Habsburg Austria. The Habsburg heir, Philip the Fair, married a Spanish princess, Joanna the Mad, and their son, Charles V, who was born in Ghent in 1500, reigned over Flanders and Spain as well as the new Spanish territories in South America. Before abdicating in 1555, he bequeathed to the Low Countries a statute called the Circle of Burgundy, which sought to prevent the disintegration of the 17 provinces.

The Spanish colonial empire brought vast riches to the area, and a new age of discovery and desire for knowledge dawned. The philosophy of Erasmus, the maps of Mercator and Ortelius, Vesalius's study of anatomy and discoveries in the fields of astronomy and botany reached a wide audience thanks to the invention of the printing press, and prepared the way for humanism. The new religious ideas of Martin Luther, however, disturbed the unity of the 17 provinces. In an effort to quell the spread of Luther's ideas, Charles V imposed the Inquisition, paving the way for the troubled times ahead.

There was nothing very cheering about Philip II, Charles V's son and successor, whose answer to the tenets of the Reformation was bloody repression. The struggle for political liberty went hand in hand with the desire for religious tolerance, and followers of the Reformation sacked and desecrated many of the region's finest churches. The reaction was brutal: Philip II put the Duke of Alba at the head of an arrogant army, and the provinces of the south were set alight amid much loss of life. Attempts at conciliation failed dismally. Holland and Zeeland won their independence under the colours of William of Orange, and a highly skilled band of artisans and burghers fled north, taking with them the secrets of their trade and considerable amounts of money. The Flemish workers preferred exile in England, while the Walloons emigrated as far as the New World, where they put down roots in 1624 in a village on the edge of an island called Manhattan. The Protestant Liégeois, protected by their principality, where they had been spared (they sold arms indiscriminately to both camps), left the plains of the Meuse for Sweden, where they took their metal-working skills. The frame of present-day Belgium took shape with the partition of the 17 provinces: the north became the Union of Utrecht, then the United Provinces of the Netherlands, while the south, the Confederation of Arras, was destined to become the Catholic Low Countries.

Under the rule of Archduke Albert and his wife, Isabella (daughter of Philip II), a truce was finally agreed. The Church took advantage of this state of affairs to re-establish Catholicism with a vengeance. The Jesuits created 34 colleges, Rubens founded his school and became a roving ambassador, and baroque art emerged as an expression of a new faith that combined exuberant worship with superfluous triumphalism.

BELGIUM, BATTLEFIELD OF EUROPE

Albert and Isabella died without issue, and while the 17th century was known in the Low Countries as the Golden Age and in France as the Grand Siècle, Belgium hit an all-time low. The estuary of the Scheldt was closed to the Antwerpers, while Spain let the French have Artois, part of Flanders and Hainaut.

Louis XIV's marshals, Condé and Turenne, galloped onto Belgium's plains to add a few glorious pages to the French history books, with disastrous results for the Belgians. There followed the War of Devolution, the War of Holland, the War of the League of Augsburg and the War of the Spanish Succession, with a whole litany of battles involving France, Spain, the Low Countries and England.

The low point was the bombardment of Brussels in 1695 by the Villeroy, who was acting on the orders of the Sun King (even Napoleon referred to it as a 'meaningless act of barbarity'). There was, however, a silver lining: the magnificent Grand'Place was built over the ruins of the city centre.

THE AUSTRIANS

Once again, with no heir on the Spanish side, the Low Countries fell to the Austrian Habsburgs under the Treaty of Utrecht in 1713. Under Charles of Lorraine, the country sank into a soothing, economically stagnant provincialism. The decline was intellectual, too: Voltaire, passing through Brussels, described it as a place where 'ignorance has set in and imagination has been eclipsed'. The only notable event was the fire of 1731 at the Palace of the Dukes of Burgundy (supposedly caused during the making of the royal jam, which bubbled over).

From his Viennese capital, Joseph II attempted a few reforms, but his well-meaning attempts to reorganize the administration brought discontent, then out-and-out revolt from a people whose roots were steeped in Catholicism and individuality. Indignation reached its peak when he decreed that all fêtes and fairs had to take place on the same day. In 1789, lawyers and local politicians deprived of their powers by the Austrians staged rebellions in Brussels (where the conservative spirit was strong) and Liège (where they hoped to imitate the French Revolution). General confusion followed, and resulted in the short-lived constitution of the United Belgian States. Brabant and Liégeois patriots buried their differences and for the first time sported the same national colours: black, red and yellow.

THE FRENCH

Meanwhile, in Paris, things were taking a more radical turn, and the young French Republic found itself obliged to strengthen its borders. The result was the unceremonious annexation of Belgium, which was split into *départements* named after the country's rivers.

The principles of the French Revolution were rigorously applied: young men were forced to join the army, church possessions were seized and artistic treasures found their way to Paris. Nevertheless, there were a few positive changes: the Scheldt was reopened, Antwerp was modernized and Belgian traders and industrialists congratulated themselves on the new opportunities presented by the French market. The last traces of feudalism disappeared with the arrival of a *code civil* and legal and administrative structures that reflected the Age of Reason. Many Belgians took part in Napoleon's campaigns, and to this day, in the Entre-Sambre-et-Meuse district, there are costume parades in memory of the imperial era. Napoleon was finally defeated at Waterloo, south of Brussels, where 48,000 soldiers were killed. There were Belgians in both camps.

THE DUTCH

At the Congress of Vienna in 1815, the powers of the Holy Alliance asked William of Orange to form the realm of the Low Countries. It was doomed from the start. The Belgians were Catholic, the Dutch Protestant; the towns in the south were industrial, those in the north were mercantile; Dutch rule displeased the Frenchified Flemish elite. Faced with a common enemy, the outraged Belgians gathered outside Brussels's opera house, La Monnaie, in August 1830 and staged a revolt. The Dutch were routed on 27 September and independence was, at last, declared.

INDEPENDENT BELGIUM

A national congress voted in the constitution, and the young state won the approval of France and England. A constitutional monarchy was adopted, and the Belgians looked around for a king. First on their list was the Duke of Nemours, the son of King Louis-Philippe of France. Fearing the English, the Duke declined. Next, the Belgians approached Leopold of Saxe-Coburg, the widower of the heir to the English throne. On his gracious acceptance, Leopold I became King of the Belgians and was sworn in on 21 July, 1831. William of Orange, however, had not quite given up, and sent in his troops. Prompted by the great powers, France came to the help of the youthful Belgium, and the Dutch were sent packing, though not without compensation in the form of territory. A skilful diplomat, Leopold I married Louise-Marie d'Orléans, Louis-Philippe's daughter. Luxembourg was divided between Belgium and a new state, the Grand Duchy, which was economically part of Prussia.

In the decades that followed, the two main bourgeois parties, the Catholics and the Liberals, transformed Belgium into a vast, hyperefficient producer. It was the age of industrialization, cheap labour and, thanks to the new railways, free trade between nations. Capitalism triumphed, and Belgium was able to reap the benefits. Or, at least, the ruling classes were.

While politicians squabbled about education and military service, the biggest problem facing the young nation was the poverty in the industrial areas and in rural Flanders. Striking labourers were repressed by the army, and the Church unhelpfully preached submission to the ruling classes. Mutual societies were formed, with the help of some enlightened members of the middle classes, and these became Belgium's Labour party in 1885. The right to strike was recognized, universal male suffrage was acquired in 1892, women and children were offered social protection and Sunday was voted as a day of rest. The national Flemish movement claimed recognition of its cultural and linguistic identity, and in 1898 Dutch was given the status of an official language, alongside French.

As the enterprising middle classes sought to extend their wealth, Belgian capital was invested further and further afield. Tramways were exported to Odessa, railways were shipped to Beijing, factories were built in Asia and an entire town was founded in Egypt.

The new king, Leopold II, nurtured visions of grandeur for a country that 'thought small and criticized everything'. After abortive initiatives in Brazil and Guatemala, he financed an exploratory expedition to one of the last undiscovered areas of the world. The expedition (led by H.M. Stanley, of Livingstone fame) planted the Belgian flag on a vast area of central Africa and called it the Independent State of the Congo. Exploration of the 'Dark Continent' had been under the pretext of fighting the slave trade, and Leopold's management of 'human resources' was deplored even at the time (Conrad's *Heart of Darkness* was inspired by the Belgian Congo), but on his death in 1909, he bequeathed a magnificently wealthy colony to Belgium: 80 times the size of his own country and stuffed with silver, gold, copper and diamonds.

Brussels became the artistic centre of the avant-garde, and took to its bosom a string of modern masters who had not been accepted by the Paris salons. Two groups, Les Vingt (written 'Les XX') and the Libre Esthétique, became melting pots for the latest trends in art, literature and music.

SURVIVING TWO WORLD WARS

With the outbreak of war in August 1914, Belgian neutrality was violated because it refused to respond to a German ultimatum and allow the Kaiser's army access through the country. So began another invasion of the land . . . Albert I became a legendary *roi chevalier*, clinging desperately to a little strip of waterlogged land by the river IJzer. The king and his wife spared no expense in their endeavour to maintain independence and keep suffering to a minimum.

After the war, the Treaty of Versailles gave Belgium the German-speaking cantons of Eupen and Malmédy, and the League of Nations placed the former German Rwanda-Burundi colony under Belgian supervision. Belgium's participation in the war on the side of the Allies finally ended Belgian neutrality, and in 1920, Belgian troops occupied the industrial region of the Ruhr alongside the French.

In 1922, the Belgian-Luxembourg Economic Union was created, prefiguring the Benelux and the various European unions. Ghent University became Flemish-speaking, and the country's centenary was celebrated with a World Fair in Liège and Antwerp.

As the clouds gathered over Europe in 1936, Leopold III and his government declared neutrality, in imitation of the events in 1914. This time, however, with no ultimatum, the Wehrmacht entered Belgium on 10 May, 1940. War was no longer fought in the trenches, and, despite the efforts of Britain and France, who leapt to defend Belgium's violated neutrality, the battle was won in 18 days. Hundreds of thousands of civilians took to the roads in a bid to escape the bombs of the Stukas. Massively outnumbered, the Belgians soon began to fall back and then, on May 28, Leopold III capitulated, bringing down on his head the wrath of the French. The Germans took just three weeks to get to Paris.

Belgium was occupied by the Nazis until September 1944. In a gesture that was more than just symbolic, it left the Congo's mineral resources at the disposal of the Allies. Uranium from Katanga went into the first atomic bomb.

After a final bloody episode, the Battle of the Ardennes, the Belgians could celebrate their liberation; but the monarchy had been badly damaged by Leopold III's controversial actions at the beginning of the war. Fearing civil war, he stepped down in favour of his son, Baudouin in 1951 (*see* 'Royal family').

POST-WAR PROSPERITY

In the post-war years, Belgium enjoyed a spectacular economic recovery. Industry had not been killed off altogether, and monetary reform kept inflation firmly under control. While business at the port of Antwerp was in full swing, with shipments of Congo minerals arriving every day, American dollars from the Marshall Plan flowed into the country. In 1957, the Treaty of Rome opened the way to an immense manufacturing market, and Brussels became the seat of the European Economic Community and the European Atomic Energy Commission. The World Fair of 1958 drew thousands of visitors to the foot of the Atomium.

The 1960s opened with the Congo establishing its independence under chaotic circumstances. At home, political and linguistic squabbles resumed, and degenerated into communal battles. Flanders and Wallonia experienced wildly fluctuating fortunes. In the south, the bottom fell out of the coal and steel markets; in the north, industry became heavily trade-based.

The world was astonished at the grief that united the whole country on the death of King Baudouin on 31 July, 1993. But, in a country where differences are far more obvious than common goals, the royal family has been a much-needed focal point for patriots.

BELGIUM TODAY

In August 1996, two missing girls were rescued from the basement of a convicted rapist, Marc Dutroux, after months of torment. Dutroux was soon linked to the killing and sexual abuse of at least four other girls, possibly as part of an organised international paedophile ring. The brutality of his actions, and the police incompetence that had allowed someone with a history of sexual crime to be in a position to carry out further crimes, shook Belgium to its core, and the nation was forced to confront the problems at the heart of its system. In October 1996, following the discovery of another paedophile killing (unrelated, it soon emerged), 300,000 people took to the streets of Brussels in a march to express their indignation. The extent of public feeling forced the government to set up a parliamentary commission to investigate the failings of the police's inquiries. It found that the various police forces involved in the case had been more concerned with fighting a turf war than effectively fighting crime.

After more than a year of often surreal revelations, the commission published a report that damned the police and the justice system. The document brought to light a dysfunctional legal system that paid no heed to the voices of the victims, although it stopped short of suggesting that rogue policemen were involved in organized crime. To cap it all, Marc Dutroux escaped from custody one afternoon, following another bungling performance by policemen; his liberty lasted only three hours, but it was enough to make the minister of justice, the minister of the interior and the chief of police resign. Dutroux is currently awaiting trial.

Abroad, following the overthrow of President Mobuto in May 1997, Zaïre changed its name to the Democratic Republic of Congo; sadly, the new government made little real effort to improve democracy.

Early in 1998, the venerable Société Générale, a pillar of the Belgian economy since Dutch rule in 1815, was taken over by the French giant Suez-Lyonnaise des Eaux. Petrofina, another of the country's economic giants, was taken over by Total, while the Dutch assumed control of banking groups and insurance companies. The jewels in the crown of Belgian capitalism had been auctioned off. As if this wasn't enough, cases of corruption, organized crime and tax fraud came to light, plunging the population, apparently deprived of any trustworthy institutions, into gloom.

The 1999 election was overshadowed by the dioxin crisis, in which contaminated vegetable oils were placed in animal feed, raising fears about the health of thousands of people, and costing an estimated 40 billion BEF. The coalition parties in government at the time, the Christian Socialists and Socialists, took a hammering at the polls. The Greens, on the other hand, saw huge gains in both Flanders and Wallonia, and were able to take their place in the 'Rainbow coalition' put together by the country's new political top dogs, the centre-right Liberals. More worryingly, the far-right Flemish nationalist party, the Vlaams Blok, won 30 per cent of the vote in Antwerp and Mechelen.

Even now, the government is wrestling with the same problems: linguistic squabbling, the far-right Flemish calls for independence, the inadequacies of the legal system and how to deal with the growing tide of asylum-seekers. Still, there is a bit of good news: Philippe, the heir to the Belgian throne, and his wife, the radiant Mathilde, had their first baby in October 2001. Baby Elisabeth is the first female heir to the Belgian throne. And at Wimbledon 2001, 19-year-old tennis ace Justine Henin made it to the women's final to prove that Belgium is emerging as a worldwide tennis power: she and fellow teenager Kim Clijsters are both in the world Top 10. Watch this space . . .

MAIN HISTORICAL EVENTS

– **57 BC**: Gaulish war.

– **AD 255**: Frankish invasion.

– **481**: Clovis leaves his bishopric in Tournai and settles in Paris.

– **720**: Pepin the Quick deposes Childeric III and takes the crown of France.

– **800**: Charlemagne is crowned Emperor by the Pope.

– **843**: Treaty of Verdun. The Carolingian empire is split three ways; Flanders falls to the King of France.

– **980**: Notger becomes prince-bishop of Liège, now part of the Holy Roman Empire.

– **1099**: Jerusalem is captured by the crusaders of Godefroid de Bouillon.

– **1300**: annexation of Flanders by Philip the Fair.

– **1302**: Battle of the Golden Spurs; Flemish peasants rout French knights.

– **1337**: Hundred Years War; the people of Ghent revolt.

– **1384**: Philip the Bold, Duke of Burgundy, inherits Flanders and extends his domination over the Low Countries.

– **1468**: Charles the Bold destroys Liège and annexes the principality.

– **1477**: Marie of Burgundy inherits the Burgundian possessions; her marriage to Maximilian of Austria means Austria is now in control of the Low Countries.

– **1500**: birth in Ghent of Charles, son of Philip the Fair and Joanna the Mad; as Charles V, he reigns over the Habsburg empire of Spain from 1519 to 1555.

– **1576**: 'Pacification of Ghent' liberates the Spanish Low Countries from the oppressive control of Philip II; foundation of the Calvinist United Provinces. By 1579, the Spanish had regained control of most of what is now Belgium.

– **1598**: beginning of the reign of Archduke Albert and his wife Isabel.

– **1648**: Treaty of Münster, which cuts off the Catholic Low Countries; the Dutch close the Scheldt.

– **1695**: bombardment of Brussels on the orders of Louis XIV.

– **1713**: Treaty of Utrecht. The Low Countries become Austrian again; Charles of Lorraine becomes governor in 1744.

– **1780**: Emperor Joseph II imposes reforms that are not popular with the Belgians. They revolt in 1789 and throw off Austrian rule.

– **1795**: annexation of the Austrian Low Countries by the Republican French.

– **1815**: Congress of Vienna brings Belgium and Holland together; William of Orange becomes King of the Low Countries.

– **1830**: Brussels revolts; the Dutch are driven out.

– **1831**: Belgian independence is recognized; Leopold I is made King.

– **1865**: beginning of the reign of Leopold II, who bequeathes the Congo to Belgium in 1909.

– **1914**: beginning of the Great War. Belgium takes part, siding with the Allies; Albert I resists on the other side of the IJzer.

– **1934**: accidental death of Albert I; Leopold III becomes king.

BACKGROUND

- **1940**: the Germans invade Belgium. Leopold III capitulates after 18 days of fighting; the country is occupied until 1944.

- **1951**: Leopold III abdicates in favour of his son, Baudouin.

- **1959**: Brussels becomes the seat of the EEC.

- **1980**: regionalization is established.

- **1993**: death of Baudouin; his brother, Albert II, succeeds him.

- **1994**: the constitution is changed, and Belgium becomes a federal state made up of Communities and Regions.

- **1996**: Belgium is shaken by revelations about paedophilia.

- **1998**: Belgium fulfils the criteria for joining the European single currency.

- **1999**: Belgium wins its first Palme d'Or at Cannes for *Rosetta*, an uncompromising social drama by the Dardenne brothers.

- **2000**: Brussels is Cultural Capital of Europe, and several major buildings get a much-needed makeover.

GEOGRAPHY

Belgium is divided into three distinct geographical regions. From the 70-kilometre (45-mile) coast, the land rises gradually to the east, culminating in the plateau des Fagnes at 694 metres (2,276 feet) above sea level – so it's not as flat as you might have thought. Two rivers, the Escaut/Scheldt and the Meuse/Maas, run through the country en route to the North Sea.

LOWER BELGIUM

This area consists of a straight coastline with long, sandy beaches and dunes that have resulted in a depressing string of tourist developments. The hinterland is made up of fertile polders that are below sea level and are surrounded by a protective network of dykes and canals. A small coastal river, the IJzer, forms part of this network.

Lower Belgium stretches into the vast plain of Flanders, rising to 100 metres (330 feet) above sea level, then continues into the Kempen, a sandy wasteland of ponds and marshes where nothing but scrub and pine trees grow. Seams of coal were once mined here.

The clay plains of the Scheldt basin are uniformly flat, with the river meandering in large loops through the countryside. Between the Leie and the Dender, gently rolling hills rise to 150 metres (nearly 500 feet). This area is called the Flemish Ardennes. The plain is a built-up area roughly the same size as Flanders, comprising Kortrijk, Ghent, Brussels, Leuven and Antwerp. The ancient ground can be dug with ease, and has led to quarrying in western Hainaut. The Forêt de Soignes/Zonienwoud, once part of the vast charcoal forests exploited by the Romans, lies south of Brussels and marks the start of middle Belgium.

MIDDLE BELGIUM

Between 100 and 300 metres (330 and 1,000 feet) above sea level, this area consists largely of fertile plateaux used for crops and livestock. Vineyards and pastureland are the norm in the east. A coal seam that crosses the area from Mons to Liège was responsible for the region's intensive industrialization.

UPPER BELGIUM

This area corresponds to the Ardennes (400–600 metres/1,300–2,000 feet), and is a continuation of the German Eifel, a high, rocky plateau consisting of impermeable rock, with folds running from east to west; these stopped the German tanks getting through in 1940 and 1944.

The narrow, winding valleys of the Semois, Ourthe and Amblève rivers cross the thickly wooded hills of the Ardennes. Caves are common, but people are few and far between.

Above 500 metres (1,650 feet), the land becomes increasingly inhospitable, with the marshy peat bogs and conifers of the Hautes Fagnes recalling the landscape of northern Scandinavia.

La Gaume, part of the Lorraine region, lies south of the Ardennes, and is characterized by tiled roofs and a vine-friendly microclimate.

BACKGROUND

ECONOMY

Belgium's livelihood depends on economic exchange with its European neighbours. Since time immemorial, raw materials (with the exception of coal) have been imported and released on to the domestic market or re-exported as finished products.

With one of the densest communication networks in the world (including roads, railways, canals and rivers), Belgium is well placed for the rapid exchange of goods. Antwerp is the largest port in Europe after Rotterdam, and each year tens of millions of tonnes of merchandise pass through it to the hinterland, and to Germany, France, Switzerland and Italy, while supertankers arrive and depart from the port at Zeebrugge. Most energy still comes from nuclear power.

Less than three per cent of the population works in agriculture, producing mainly wheat, sugar beet and potatoes. Livestock consists mostly of cattle and, increasingly, pigs.

WALLONIA

The exploitation of the Walloon coalfields ended in the 1970s, along with those of Limburg. The steel industry, founded in the 19th century in the valley created by the Sambre and Meuse rivers, brought prosperity to the region, but has been hit hard by the decline of Europe's manufacturing industries. The workforce, historically highly organized in Belgium, has fought to maintain the benefits acquired via continual struggle over the decades, but the unions have been unable to prevent mass redundancies at unprofitable factories. Faced with the collapse of traditional industries, a dramatic population decrease and rocketing unemployment figures, Wallonia is trying to promote medium-sized businesses, with an emphasis on new technologies such as aeronautics, computers, biotechnology, telecommunications and food processing.

FLANDERS

Flanders has fared rather better than its French-speaking neighbour: with no natural resources of its own, it has always relied on processing industries. Traditionally, its main industry was textiles: in the Middle Ages, English cloth was woven by Flemish workmen. Linen, hemp and wool brought affluence to Flanders in bygone days. Today, a flourishing synthetic-materials industry stretches from Kortrijk to Ghent. In the years following the World War II, foreign capital (mainly American) poured in, attracted by the skilled and stable workforce. Petrochemicals, heavy chemicals, mechanical construction, processing of minerals from the Congo, electronics and cars (although there's no Belgian marque, Belgium is the biggest manufacturer of cars per capita in the world) are the most dynamic sectors of Flemish industry, while Antwerp's diamond trade represents 7 per cent of Belgian exports. Traditionally Catholic, Flanders has experienced a demographic growth that far exceeds the national average, and its population now accounts for 58 per cent of Belgians.

BRUSSELS

As in all the industrialized countries, the white-collar sector accounts for the greatest part of GDP (Gross Domestic Product). Brussels has become a city of service industries from which primary industries have all but disappeared. It relies instead on trade, banking, tourism, insurance, transport and jobs that feed off the presence of European and international organizations.

FEDERALISM

Although Belgium is made up of different components, the country had unified institutions until the 1970s. Since then, a succession of constitutional reforms have been adopted to create a federal structure. Here's a brief outline of the country's unusual and highly complex administrative institutions, which frequently confuse even the most up-to-date Belgians.

The first clause in the current constitution says that Belgium is a federal state consisting of three linguistic Communities (Flemish, French-speaking and German-speaking) and three geographical Regions (Flanders, Wallonia and Brussels).

On the federal level, executive power is exercised by the king and the federal government in areas of national importance, such as foreign affairs, the law, finance, defence, internal affairs and social welfare. Legislative powers fall to the King, the Council of Representatives and the Senate, where laws are voted in. Each community is responsible for cultural affairs, tourism, health and social affairs.

On the Regional level, a system of local government deals with areas concerning each Region, such as housing, employment, the environment, economic development, transport, agriculture, trade and international co-operation. The Regions have the power to sign agreements with other countries.

Belgium is also divided into 10 provinces, the origins of which go back to the French *départements* of 1795.

The **Walloon Region** (with 3.2 million inhabitants) includes the provinces of Hainaut, Namur, Liège (which is also home to the 66,000-strong German-speaking community), Luxembourg and the new province of Walloon Brabant. Namur is the Regional capital. The French-speaking community consists of the population of the Walloon Region and the French-speaking inhabitants of the Brussels Region.

The **Flemish Region**, which has a population of 5.8 million, is also made up of five provinces: West Flanders, East Flanders, Antwerp, Limburg and the new province of Flemish Brabant. The Flemish community consists of the population of the Flemish Region and the Dutch-speaking inhabitants of the Brussels Region.

The **Brussels Region** consists of 19 communes. There are officially two languages in the capital, Dutch and French. As well as being the federal capital of the whole country, Brussels is also the capital of the Flemish Region, and is surrounded by the province of Flemish Brabant.

Belgium's 589 communes are the country's political and administrative basis. They have extensive powers, which date back to the Middle Ages. Although they are all in single-language areas (except those in Brussels), those on the Walloon-Flemish borders are special cases: citizens in the communes can choose to deal with officials in Dutch or French.

These 'facility' communes are the battlegrounds for the whole linguistic squabble: the affluent communes outside Brussels, for example, are in Flemish territory but are inhabited by a French-speaking majority.

The Flemish Region has spent years trying to abolish its linguistic privileges, arguing that the 'facility' concept was only supposed to be a temporary measure to help newcomers who hadn't yet mastered Dutch. There's a lot of disagreement about this, with the most determined opponents using the issue to destabilize the federal government.

For the most part, however, the different administrations avoid treading on one another's toes, and while the system isn't perfect, it does give the different communities some freedom to manage their own future. Whether that freedom is enough for all parties, only time will tell.

THE ROYAL FAMILY

When Albert II took the constitutional oath on 8 August, 1993, as successor to his brother, Baudouin, he became the sixth King of the Belgians since 1831.

At the beginning of the third millennium, the presence of a royal family seems like an anachronism to some, and many people see it as nothing more than material for the gossip columns in the popular press. Nevertheless, nearly half the countries in the EU have a monarchy, and it can be seen as a stabilizing factor that guarantees the principles of democracy.

This is particularly true of Belgium, where an elected head of state could pose serious problems. Over the years, the Belgians have come to be happy with this system, and their king plays a more active role than first appearances suggest.

The constitution of 1831, which defined the sovereign's role, limited his powers to the legal and executive domains. Although all acts passed by parliament need the king's signature, they also require the signature of a minister. This helps to explain why the public gestures of the king and his family can look like mere formalities: the king doesn't give interviews or press conferences; if he bends the rules ever so slightly, there is an immediate outcry and his neutrality is questioned.

From the wings, however, he wields discreet yet considerable influence: he has private meetings with economists and politicians, making him the best-informed man in the country, and he has unquestionable moral authority. Traditionally, what happens during an audience with one of the Royal Family is kept secret. Bending the rules would effectively be to expose the crown.

As in all families, the Saxe-Coburg dynasty has not been devoid of drama, but it has successfully steered clear of the kind of unfortunate scandals associated with the Windsors or Grimaldis; were anything of the kind to be uncovered, their response would most certainly be: 'No comment'.

Here are potted histories of the six kings of the Belgians:

LEOPOLD I (1790–1865)

When the Belgians offered the Duke of Saxony the crown in 1831, he graciously accepted, although he had turned down a similar offer from the Greeks, newly freed from the Ottoman yoke. His first task was to face the wrath of the Dutch, who were none too pleased by the loss of their southern provinces. In the brief battle that followed, he pulled off a diplomatic *tour de force*, averting both Prussian expansionism and French hopes of annexing Belgium. He took the further step of allying his country with France by marrying Louise-Marie d'Orléans, daughter of Louis-Philippe. He distinguished himself as a skilled diplomat and peace maker, and when he died in 1865, he left a country that was firmly on the road to prosperity.

LEOPOLD II (1835–1909)

A more dominant personality than his father, whom he succeeded in 1865, Leopold II was much more readily criticized by his subjects. A man of vision and high ambitions, he dreamt up giant projects with consummate ease, filling some politicians with apprehension. At home, his wings were clipped by the intricacies of the constitution, so he looked abroad to construct a personal empire that might satisfy his ambitions: the Belgian Congo, whose resources and people he exploited in brutal fashion for 25 years. He used the links of a privileged cousinhood (Queen Victoria in Britain and the Kaiser in Prussia) to assert Belgium's place in Europe. Fearing the outbreak of war in Europe, he used his influence to build up as strong an army as the size of his country allowed.

Leopold II was a lover of the arts and life in all its forms, and his amorous escapades made him the talk of the Belle Époque. Ostend owes its popularity to him, much as Brighton does to the Prince Regent, while Brussels has him to thank for many of its monuments and prestigious boulevards. In old age, Leopold II became bitter and cynical, disappointed by the absence of a male heir (his only son had died aged 10).

BACKGROUND

ALBERT I (1875–1934)

The second son of Leopold II's brother, Philippe, Albert I came to the throne as a result of the early death of his brother, Baudouin. He succeeded his uncle in 1909, and, together with his wife, Elisabeth of Bavaria, he is best remembered for his tenacious struggle to hold on to a tiny strip of land when the Germans invaded in 1914 (*see* 'History'). His brave conduct in support of the Allies during the war won him the nickname of 'Roi Chevalier' (the Cavalier King). An accomplished sportsman, Albert loved to go on solitary rock-climbing expeditions. During one of these excursions, he suffered a fatal fall on the crumbling rocks of Marche-les-Dames, near Namur. His widow outlived him by 30 years, devoting herself to the arts and establishing the country's prestigious classical-music contest, the Queen Elisabeth Competition for young singers, pianists and violinists.

LEOPOLD III (1901–83)

Leopold, who found himself suddenly on the throne after his father's unexpected death while climbing, was destined for a troubled reign. A year after his succession in 1934, he was responsible for a road accident in which his beautiful Swedish wife, Astrid, died, much to the horror of the Belgian population. In the face of rising hostilities in Europe, he fought for Belgian neutrality, and in May 1940, he capitulated unconditionally to the Germans, without consulting the Allies and against the wishes of his own government, which continued the fight in exile in London.

Leopold's meeting with Hitler and marriage to Liliane Baels in 1941 provoked widespread disapproval. In 1944, the Germans deported the whole of the royal family, and it was left to his brother, Charles (who had joined the resistance), to act as regent until a referendum in 1950 (carried, but not very convincingly) allowed him to return to his country. Of his 17 years on the throne, Leopold III had spent four as a prisoner in his own palace at Laeken, one in Germany while he waited for the war to end and six as an exile in Switzerland. Faced with angry outbursts from his indignant subjects, he chose, as a gesture of goodwill, to abdicate in favour of his son, Baudouin, in 1951. He devoted the rest of his life to travels in distant countries and to the study of ethnology.

BAUDOUIN I (1930–93)

History was not kind to the fifth King of the Belgians. At the age of five, he lost his mother, while war cut short a carefree youth and deprived him of contact with the country over which he was called to reign. He ascended the throne when he came of age, and had to carry the burden of resentment against his father on his youthful shoulders. Ill at ease and shy by nature, he was rumoured to belong to a religious order to which his fervent piety predisposed him. He married Doña Fabiola di Mora y Aragón in 1960, and although they had no children, the presence of a queen by his side allowed Baudouin to fulfil his duties with exemplary devotion.

During his 42 years on the throne, Baudouin became the personification of political consciousness in Belgium, and a venerable authority on the international level. One episode stands out: in 1990, his staunch Catholic beliefs prevented him from signing a law to decriminalize abortion. In a legal and constitutional volte-face, Baudouin left the throne for 36 hours while parliament voted and promulgated the law under the signature of the prime minister. This step was highly controversial, but typical of a man to whom principles were of paramount importance.

Baudouin died after a heart attack while holidaying in Spain. The grief and public outpouring of emotion at his funeral proved that the Belgians were still attached to the concept of the monarchy. One important change in the constitution during Baudouin's reign deserves mention: women were allowed to ascend to the throne.

ALBERT II (1934–)

It came as a big surprise to see Baudouin's brother crowned at the age of 59, since everyone had expected the succession to pass to his eldest son, Philippe. Nevertheless, the considerable experience he brought as head of the foreign-trade office, and the advantage of a beautiful and popular queen, the Italian-born Paola, gave the feeling of continuity that Belgium needed at a time when it was steering a difficult course towards constitutional reform. Albert (whose health is now uncertain) and Paola have three children: Philippe, Astrid, married to the Archduke Lorenz of Austria (they have four children), and Laurent, an ecologically minded animal-lover who's refreshingly unroyal. Only weeks after the world learnt of the existence in London of Delphine, a previously hidden half-sister (the result of an extramarital affair), 39-year-old Philippe married Mathilde, a vibrant blue-blooded local girl. Their first child, a daughter named Elisabeth, was born in October 2001, and royalists must be hoping she's the first of several.

POPULATION

In this small country, there are 10.2 million people. This makes Belgium one of the most densely populated countries in the world. Almost all live in the cities, and a good proportion commute daily from one town to another for work.

The main conurbations – Antwerp, Ghent, Mons, Charleroi and Namur – are no more than 30 minutes' train ride from Brussels (Liège and Bruges are an hour away) – hence the huge daily migration. In the 1970s, most families just wanted to find a pleasant area of countryside to settle in. Towns, as a result, are fairly deserted in the evening, and such is the extent of development along the communication routes that it is virtually impossible to tell when you have left one town and entered another. Everything runs into everything else: fields, houses, canals, motorways, industrial estates, housing estates, chimneys, belfries, tunnels and viaducts.

Fifty-eight per cent of the population lives in Flanders, with 32 per cent in Wallonia and the remaining 10 per cent in Brussels.

It's impossible to talk of typically Belgian physical characteristics. Given the many nationalities who have passed through this land, the population is shaped by a substantial pool of genes. There are, however, some recent contributions to the population that can be identified. According to the statistics, the 200,000 Italians constitute the largest group of the country's 900,000 foreign nationals. Most came to Belgium in the post-war years to work in the mines. Second- and third-generation immigrants are now completely integrated, and there are people of Italian origin in positions of responsibility in business and government.

In second place are the Moroccans (130,000), more recent immigrants, whose concentration in ghetto areas has led to tension. Young North Africans stand little chance of getting on in the professional world, and this, combined with efforts by the forces of law and order to 'control' them, has created some explosive situations that far-right politicians have exploited for their own ends.

The Turkish population, based in Brussels and the Kempen (Campine), stands at about 70,000. Together with the French and Dutch, the European contingent, in addition to the 15,000 civil servants working in Brussels' EU institutions, is made up of communities from Spain (47,000), Germany (33,000), Britain (26,000) and Portugal (25,000). Surprisingly, the Congo and central Africa account for only 20,000 inhabitants.

About 450,000 Belgians live outside their native country.

HUMAN RIGHTS

Belgium's human-rights record is among the best of any state. Its democratic tradition is so tightly enmeshed in Belgian life, that an attempt to isolate human rights issues for discussion in a guidebook is a near impossibility, so this is a brief overview.

Belgium was an early signatory to the European Convention on Human Rights, and has also ratified most of the other major human-rights treaties and co-operates with the organizations that monitor and enforce them. Domestically, the constitution protects human rights, and the political and legal systems take the issues seriously. Belgium's proactive concern with human-rights issues is illustrated by the recent convictions in Brussels of four Rwandans who were involved in the 1994 genocide, a legal first.

However, there are a few human-rights issues that give cause for concern. For some time now the legal system hasn't been as efficient as previously, and there are often lengthy delays before court proceedings begin. Concerns regarding the often excessive length of pre-trial detention, and the failure to separate remand prisoners from convicted prisoners are a direct result of the rather glacial pace of Belgian legal proceedings, which the government has attempted to improve with limited success. The United Nations raised the issue of alleged police brutality towards suspects being held in custody, and in particular the secrecy surrounding official investigations into these claims. Strikes by members of the prison service have brought attention to the extent of the appalling conditions in overcrowded prisons while people await trial. The suicide rate behind bars is one of the highest in Europe, and drug abusers don't always get the necessary medical treatment.

It's a sad fact that in a country that's recognized for its hospitality, temporary lodgings assigned to foreigners (often asylum seekers from African countries) waiting to receive their papers, are more like prison camps, and international human-rights groups have suggested that asylum-seekers are often repatriated irrespective of their having a convincing case to remain in Belgium, sometimes at risk to their lives. The UN also questioned the treatment of asylum-seekers during repatriation, including the death of a Nigerian national as a result of having a cushion placed over her face. However, it would be fair to point out that, compared with other developed nations, these are isolated events.

Recent cases of paedophilia have drawn attention to the crucial question of helping and listening to the victims. There's a growing demand among the public, unhappy about the weaknesses of enquiries into unresolved crimes, to allow public access to the files.

With regard to voting, observers often note with astonishment that it is in fact obligatory in Belgium (what's more, you get fined for *not* voting) but the Belgians don't appear to have a problem with this, and so far it has not sparked off any internal debate.

To Find Out More, Contact:

Liberty (independent human-rights organization): 21 Tabard Street, London SE1 4LA. ☎ (020) 7403 3888. Website: www.liberty-human-rights.org.uk. Email: info@liberty-human-rights.org.uk

Amnesty International: 99–119 Rosebery Avenue, London EC1R 4RE. ☎ (020) 7814 6200. Email: information@amnesty.org.uk. Website: www. amnesty.org.uk

FAMOUS BELGIANS

Although you can't really talk about 'Belgians' before 1830, the year they gained independence, anyone born or who was active on what is now Belgian soil should be counted as Belgian.

– **Brel, Jacques** (1929–78): you can't get more Belgian than Brel, with his cheek, his mockery of the clergy and the bourgeoisie, his tales of women's infidelity, his abuse of anti-Flemings and his passion for Flanders. *Le grand Jacques* was Belgium's best *chansonnier*, and one of the few Belgians in popular music to have influenced the outside world. Songs like *Amsterdam* are classics by any standard.

– **Brueghel, Pieter 'the Elder'** (1528–69): the Flemish painter from Brabant who fell in love with Alpine scenery during his travels in France and Italy, and used the mountains to form the background of his rural peasant scenes. Once settled in Antwerp, he became acquainted with many of the great figures of the Reformation, among them Erasmus, Ortelius and the progressive publisher Christopher Plantin. He regularly disguised himself as a peasant in order to take part in village fairs, and used biblical allegory in his rural scenes to denounce the harsh measures of the Spanish regime. After some trouble with the Inquisition, he moved to Brussels, where his sons were born: Pieter (the Younger) and Jan (nicknamed 'Velvet' because of his delicate representations of flowers and genre scenes). Pieter the Elder was buried in the church of Notre-Dame de la Chapelle. He was one of the world's greatest painters, so don't leave Brussels without seeing the collection of his works at the Fine Arts Museum, especially *The Fall of Icarus*, *The Census at Bethlehem* and *The Fall of the Rebel Angels*.

– **Charlemagne** (742–814): the French and Germans have some claim to this bearded emperor, but he's first and foremost a Walloon hero. He invented school, turned the Merovingian inheritance into a European empire and was both a successful conqueror and a visionary legislator.

– **Claus, Hugo** (1929–): Belgium's most famous Dutch-speaking writer. He's seen by many people as Nobel Prize material (the only Belgian to win a Nobel Prize for Literature was Maurice Maeterlinck, in 1911). A poet, dramatist and novelist, Claus has also tried his hand at film production, and was once the lover of Sylvia Kristel, star of the 1970s erotic movie *Emmanuelle*.

– **Delvaux, Paul** (1897–1994): weird, naked women drift between ancient ruins in Delvaux's paintings, accompanied by skeletons and railway carriages against a backdrop of provincial stations. His erotic dreamworld places him among the Surrealists. At the Venice Biennale in 1948, the Vatican recommended that priests abstain from visiting the Belgian Pavilion, where Delvaux's works were on show. At Saint-Idesbald, on the coast, you can visit the Fondation Paul Delvaux. He also produced casino frescoes at Ostend, Chaudfontaine and Knokke.

– **Ensor, James** (1860–1949): his father was English, but Ensor lived in Ostend and became one of the most significant painters of the late 19th and early 20th centuries. His style anticipated Expressionism, but he took his inspiration from the macabre and satirical themes (carnival masks, for example) that heralded Surrealism. His portrait adorns the 100BEF note.

– **Franck, César** (1822–90): a composer and organist from Liège, Franck became a French citizen by working in Paris. A self-effacing character, he was not adequately recognized until late in his career. At a time when musical life swore by opera, his non-operatic works were unusual, and he won renown as an innovator with his symphonic poems and their intensely lyrical musical line. The admiration he won from his friends and disciples, including Liszt, Saint-Saëns and Fauré is proof of his brilliance.

– **Hergé** (1907–83): when Georges Rémi, the creator of Tintin, died on 4 February, 1983, he was mourned across the world. His importance in the development of the comic strip is unparalleled. The fluidity of his drawings was to influence a generation of artists in the *ligne claire* (clear line) school, while his stories won renown for their inspirational narrative technique (Rémi's pen name, by the way, came from reversing his initials).

– **Horta, Victor** (1861–1947): architect and undisputed master of art nouveau. With the building of the Tassel town house in 1893, Horta brought the art-nouveau style to Belgium, and introduced an entirely new concept of architecture: the straight lines of neo-Classicism gave way to designs inspired by nature, light entered through stained glass decorated with floral motifs, and, thanks to new techniques in industrial building, brick, glass and wrought iron were used in delightfully inventive ways. Horta's concern for detail led him to design every decorative element, and he established a philosophy of life based on harmony, elegance and ingenuity. Horta's face now graces the 2,000BEF note, a belated tribute to a genius whose legacy Brussels's authorities have shamefully neglected.

– **Ickx, Jacky** (1945–): Belgium's most famous racing driver. He'll always be remembered for his victory in the 24-hour Le Mans race, where he voluntarily started at the back, believing this to be the safest place on the grid. He won at Le Mans six times, took part in 116 Formula 1 Grand Prix, of which he won 18, and came second twice in the Formula 1 championship. Now over 55, he continues to take part in his favourite race, the Paris–Dakar rally.

– **Magritte, René** (1898–1967): '*Ceci n'est pas une pipe*' (this is not a pipe), wrote the high priest of Belgian Surrealism in 1929, beneath a realistic representation of a pipe. Magritte's provocative wit shines through in unexpected, disturbing associations, where ordinary domestic objects are set against a strange background and the whole composition has an absurd title. A glass of water placed on an umbrella becomes *Les Vacances d'Hegel* (Hegel's Holiday). These juxtapositions shook his contemporaries' ideas and provided a wealth of material for the advertising world, in which he worked as a means of earning a crust. The Modern Art Museum in Brussels has the largest collection of his works in the world. The centenary of his birth in 1998 was celebrated with a huge and highly successful exhibition, while a youthful portrait of him graces the 500BEF note.

– **Mercator** (1512–94): the most famous cartographer of the 16th century. Mercator was a real Renaissance man: theologian, philosopher, mathematician and astronomer. He altered irrevocably mankind's vision of the planet: most of the maps used today are based on his projections, and it's thanks to him that ships were able to navigate through unknown waters with the aid of reliable charts. He was also the first to use the word 'atlas' to signify a collection of maps, and published his own *Atlas Minor*, the first of its kind, in a user-friendly pocket edition.

– Merckx, Eddy (1945–): nicknamed 'Cannibal' because of his insatiable appetite for victory, Eddy Merckx is widely regarded as the greatest cyclist of all time, and is even a candidate for sportsperson of the 20th century. A list of his successes would take up several pages; suffice to say that he won the Tour de France and the Giro d'Italia five times each, and clocked up 525 race victories in his career. Following retirement from racing, he now devotes all his time to his bike business and to his son Axel, who is also a cyclist.

– Michaux, Henri (1899-1984): originally from Namur, but naturalized in France, the Surrealists inspired Michaux to write poetry. He brought back extensive diaries from his travels in Asia and South America, including a pioneering journey to Kathmandu. His experiments with mescalin took his poetry to new extremes, and his work defies categorization. Michaux refused all honours, although his drawings won a prize at the Venice Biennale.

– Rubens, Pieter Paul (1577–1640): born in exile in Germany, where his Calvinist father had sought refuge, he didn't reach Antwerp until he was 12 years old. He attended classes there before spending eight years in Italy, where he studied the great masters of the Renaissance: Tintoretto, Titian, Veronese, and Caravaggio. After returning to the Low Countries, he found favour with Archduke Albert and his wife, Isabella, and was able to establish his famous studio. He was something of a celebrity in his day, and was helped by numerous collaborators, including Van Dyck and Jan Brueghel. Combining ambassadorial missions with artistic activity, he travelled to Holland, Madrid and London. A visit to his house in Antwerp, where the great minds of his age once gathered, is essential.

– Sax, Adolphe (1814–94): in 1994, Dinant had hoped to celebrate the centenary of the death of its most famous native by welcoming the world's most famous amateur saxophonist, Bill Clinton. Sadly, a packed schedule prevented the President from paying his respects. Sax began his career working in his father's workshop, and soon created innovative instruments made from copper that he called *saxhorn*, *saxtuba* and *saxtromba*. But it was only when he set himself up in Paris that he became famous. The sounds produced by these instruments were particularly suited to military bands, and Berlioz, Bizet and Verdi composed pieces using the saxophone. It was only after his death, however, with the arrival of jazz, that the instrument assumed its rightful place in the musical mainstream. As a posthumous tribute, his face adorns the 200BEF note.

– Scifo, Enzo (1966–): the shining light of Belgian football was born to Italian parents near La Louvière, and by the age of 18 was playing for the national side, the Red Devils. He was a key member of the side that reached the semi-finals of the 1986 World Cup – Belgium's finest footballing hour – and played for Anderlecht, Milan, Bordeaux, Auxerre, Turin and Monaco before becoming manager of Charleroi. The only disappointment in his glittering career was Belgium's lacklustre performance in the 1998 World Cup, which saw him leave international football on a very low note.

– Simenon, Georges (1903–1989): known as 'petit Georges', Simenon was as popular as he was prolific: he wrote 300 books, including 80 Maigret books, 1,000 short stories and countless articles, and sales of his books hover around the 600 million mark, with translations in 47 languages. His appetite for women is also legendary – he was rumoured to have 'known' no less than 10,000.

– **Van Dam, José** (1940–): one of the world's best-loved singers, Van Dam is a bass-baritone who appears regularly at international festivals and at the world's top opera houses. He's also starred in several films, including Gérard Corbiau's *The Music Master* and Joseph Losey's *Don Giovanni*.

– **Van Dormael, Jaco** (1957–): a director whose first full-length film, *Toto le Héros*, won the Caméra d'Or at the 1991 Cannes Film Festival. In 1996, Daniel Auteuil and Pascal Duquenne won best performance prizes for his next feature, the drama *Le Huitième Jour*. His work has helped to put French-speaking Belgian films firmly on the map, paving the way for *Rosetta*, by Luc and Jean-Pierre Dardenne, winner of the Palme d'Or at Cannes in 1999.

– **Van Eyck, Jan** and **Hubert** (end 14th to beginning 15th century): the two brothers are indistinguishable; indeed, some experts are not convinced that Hubert existed at all. They are the most important members of the 'Flemish Primitive' school, along with Rogier van der Weyden and Hans Memling. Working in Ghent and Bruges, they made a decisive break with medieval art. Jan and/or Hubert Van Eyck perfected the process of oil painting, bringing to it an unprecedented luminosity, naturalism and concern for detail. His/their masterpiece is *The Adoration of the Holy Lamb*, which you can see in Ghent; the Groeninge Museum, in Bruges, also holds incomparable examples of Flemish Primitive painting.

– **Vésale, André (Vesalius)** (1514–64): born in Brussels, Vesalius studied medicine in Leuven, then Paris, where his passion for anatomy led him to take down hanged men from the gibbet for dissection and research – a crime punishable by death. In Padua, he published his treatises on anatomy, richly illustrated with engravings. His methods of observation and dissection established him as one of the fathers of modern medicine.

IMAGINARY HEROES

– **Lucky Luke**: the 'poor lonesome cowboy' who 'shoots faster than his own shadow', and rides off into the sunset on his faithful horse, Jolly Jumper. Morris, his creator, spent six months in the States in 1948 to accumulate the material he needed to create this parody of Westerns. Terence Stamp adapted the cartoon Lucky Luke for the cinema.

– **Hercule Poirot**: what made Agatha Christie choose Belgium as the birthplace of her perspicacious sleuth? In 1916, the young author settled in Torquay, Devon, to write her first novel, and found herself among a number of Belgian refugees who had fled war-torn Europe. She decided to make her hero an agent from the Belgian criminal investigation department. Poirot is an Anglophobe with pretentious Continental mannerisms who waxes his moustache, sports polished shoes and drinks chocolate at five o'clock.

– **The Smurfs (Schtroumpfs)**: the Smurfs made their first appearance in a Johan and Peewit story in *Le Journal de Spirou* on October 23, 1958. Their creator, Pierre Culliford, better known as Peyo, had previously had a number of jobs as an Illustrator but the introduction of the Smurfs into *Spirou* would change his life. The Smurfs are all identical, with the exception of Papa Smurf, who is several hundred years old, and they provide the opportunity for gentle satire on human faults in a utopian cartoon world where the only wicked characters are a cack-handed magician, Gargamel, and his two-faced cat, Azrael. The Smurfs captured the imagination of the Americans, who made them global stars through a series of Hanna Barbera cartoons. Peyo, who died in 1992, became one of the wealthiest men in Belgium.

– **Tintin**: the very symbol of the Franco-Belgian comic strip, the intrepid boy reporter, aided and abetted by his dog, Snowy, has had a vast cult following since 1929. Although he is the righter of wrongs *par excellence*, Tintin is sometimes criticized for lacking a personality. The series owes its success, however, to the characters who surround him: the foul-tempered Captain Haddock ('Blistering barnacles!'), the distracted, naive Professor Calculus, the ridiculously determined Thomson and Thompson, the unthinkingly negligent Castafiore and Snowy the faithful mutt. Hergé's 23 Tintin books have been the subject of scholarly theses, and given rise to commercial outlets devoted to Tintin memorabilia. He's been translated into 51 languages, and estimates put sales of books at more than 200 million copies.

LITERATURE

It's hardly surprising that a country with two main languages has two distinct literatures. The distinction, however, has not always been so obvious or straightforward. Although no Walloon has ever written in Flemish, many dyed-in-the-wool Flemings have used French, once the only official tongue, as a literary language. It was not until the end of the 19th century, and the emergence of nationalism and the 'Flemingization' of the University of Ghent in 1930, that Flemish was officially recognized.

FLEMISH LITERATURE

Although the printing press was developed at the University of Leuven and in Bruges, Antwerp and Brussels, the language of the scholarly world was Latin. With few exceptions (Simon Stévin used Flemish for his works on algebra and optics), Flemish was not favoured by the great men of learning. Following Belgian independence, a new interest in intellectual and national themes inspired some young members of the middle classes to point to the rich heritage of the Flemings and call for Dutch to be given cultural parity.

The most famous modern Flemish writer is Hugo Claus, Belgium's pre-eminent living author in either language: his masterpiece, *The Sorrow of Belgium* is widely available in English.

BELGIAN LITERATURE IN FRENCH

From the Middle Ages to 1830, it's not easy to distinguish between French-language works produced in Belgium and those produced in France. After Belgian independence, though, a distinctively 'Belgian' canon began to take shape. Paradoxically, born-and-bred Flemings, writing in French, were the first to gain critical recognition. Charles de Coster (born in Germany to a Flemish father and Walloon mother), Nobel Prize-winner Maurice Maeterlinck and Georges Rodenbach were among those who established Belgian writing.

They were followed by Charles Plisner (the first non-French winner of the prestigious Prix Goncourt), the Surrealists Marcel Mariën and Louis Scutenaire, and Henri Michaux and Marcel Moreau, who don't fit neatly into any category.

Leading contemporary authors include the novelists Jacqueline Harpman and Pierre Mertens (both winners of the prestigious Prix Médicis) and Amélie Nothomb. Marguerite Yourcenar was born in Brussels to a Belgian mother, but became French before she took American nationality. Popular Belgian authors who you will probably find in translation include Georges Simenon, Henri Vernes and Thomas Owen.

SURREALISM

Since the Middle Ages, this flat land has churned out generations of artists and writers keen to produce an offbeat vision of reality. From the fantastical allegories of Brueghel, which provided the inspiration for Bosch, down to the novelists and poets of the Surrealist movement, Belgium has been fertile ground for a seemingly endless stream of illustrations of the weird and wonderful. The list is long: the languour and mysticism of the Symbolists; the masks and skeletons of Ensor; the railway nightmares of Paul Delvaux; Magritte and his bowler hats; the waking dreams of film director André Delvaux; and the wisdom of Hergé's madmen. You'd be forgiven for thinking that weirdness is part of the national character.

COMIC STRIPS

The comic strip evolved and flourished principally in Belgium. Sometimes dubbed the 'ninth art', it's particularly popular in Belgium and France, but its most famous characters are stars worldwide.

You can gain valuable, or at least amusing, insights into the Belgian character from comic strips. The Tintin albums are all available in English, and in *Asterix in Belgium*, drawn by Uderzo and told by the inimitable Goscinny, you'll get a fanciful version of how the famous *frites* evolved.

You'll find fine examples of this very Belgian art in the most unexpected of places, including restaurants, the Brussels Metro and Brussels's Centre Belge de la Bande Dessinée. But what is the history of the comic strip?

THE BELGIAN BOY SCOUT

Georges Remi (1907–1983), better known as **Hergé**, was the creator of Tintin. Born in Etterbeek, Hergé loved cartoons from an early age – the only thing that would keep him quiet as a boy was a piece of paper and a pencil to draw with. Most of the inspiration for his early cartoons came from the time he spent travelling round Europe with the Belgian boy scouts and his first series, 'The Adventures of Totor' (1926–1930), was published in the monthly publication *Le Boy-Scout Belge*.

The young Hergé started work as an illustrator for the daily paper *Le Vingtième Siècle* (The 20th Century) in 1927. When the editor decided to expand the newspaper and include a children's supplement – *Le Petit Vingtième* – he entrusted the illustrations to Hergé. On 10 January, 1929, Tintin, a reporter for the *Petit Vingtième*, appeared on the scene in his first adventure, which took him to the Soviet Union. The tone was anti-Communist, in keeping with the prevailing spirit of the time, and the drawing was clumsy, but Tintin had been born.

In later years, Tintin went off to the Congo, America, Egypt and then the Indies. The plots were always routine (punch-ups and chases), but by the time he got to *The Blue Lotus*, the author went to the trouble of researching the background from a young Chinese student, who taught him the importance of telling his young readers the truth.

Tintin was published by the well-established publisher Casterman, and this assured the books a wide readership. The formula for children's Thursday supplements caught on, and in 1938, a printer in Charleroi, Jean Dupuis, started the magazine *Spirou*. The foundations for the Belgian comic strip were now firmly in place.

After World War II, the unemployed Hergé took up a suggestion that he should start a weekly magazine bearing the name of his hero, Tintin. *Le Journal de Tintin* and its main competitor, *Spirou*, monopolized the comic-strip market and still do even today. In the playground, children still define themselves as *Spirou* or *Tintin* supporters.

BACKGROUND

FOOD AND DRINK

From the countless depictions of banquets, weddings and village fêtes, and the wide range of still lifes with tempting arrays of food and drink, it is clear that the Belgians have long been interested in food.

As you wander around the historic city centres, you'll notice that the street names recall the produce sold in the markets: in Brussels alone, you'll find rue Chair-et-Pain (meat and bread), rue des Poissonniers (fishmongers), rue Marché-aux-Fromages (cheese market), rue des Harengs (herrings), rue des Bouchers (butchers) and many more.

To reduce the pleasures of eating to the ubiquitous '*moules-frites*' (mussels and chips) is a bit like saying the Italians only eat spaghetti bolognaise or the French only eat frogs' legs. Belgian food rivals that of France, and you'll eat well wherever you go. There's always a wide choice of dishes and prices, and helpings are usually generous. You'll be more than satisfied by a single course, and you shouldn't feel you have to have a three-course meal every time you sit down to eat.

Breakfast

Try *couques* (brioches), *cramique* (bread with dried fruit), *craquelin* (the same, but with sugar instead of raisins), bread and butter sprinkled with *sirop de Liège*, all with black or white coffee.

Starters

Anguilles au vert (eels in a herb sauce)

Asperges à la flamande (asparagus with hard-boiled egg and melted butter)

Croquette de crevettes (prawn croquettes)

Filet d'Anvers (smoked horsemeat)

Flamiche (hot cheese quiche from Namur)

Fondue au parmesan (parmesan croquettes)

Jambon d'Ardennes (smoked Ardennes ham)

Jets de houblon sauce mousseline (hop shoots in a mousseline sauce – available in March)

Moules à l'escargot (mussels with garlic)

Terrine de gibier aux champignons (game pâté with mushrooms)

Tomate-crevettes (tomatoes stuffed with prawns)

Fish

Filets de sole à l'ostendaise (sole in a seafood sauce)

Lotte aux poireaux (monkfish with leeks)

Moules parquées (raw mussels – they're always fresh)

Poisson à l'escavèche (fish in a vinegar marinade)

Waterzooî (fish cooked in a tangy soup of vegetables and cream: a Belgian classic)

Meat

Carbonades flamandes (a Flemish speciality: beef braised in beer)

Choesels au madère (only for the courageous: it's sometimes been identified as bulls' testicles, while others have said it is just offal)

Coucou de Malines (chicken in the pot)

Faisan à la brabançonne (pheasant with braised chicory)

Lapin à la bière (rabbit stew in beer)

Oie à l'instar de Visé (goose in a mustard sauce)

Oiseaux sans tête (rolled veal with currants)

Rognons de veau à la liégeoise (veal kidneys with juniper berries)

Waterzooî gantois (chicken in vegetable soup)

Single Dishes (Enough for a Meal)

Boudin-compote-purée (black and white sausages, like black pudding)

Chicons au gratin (chicory with ham in a béchamel sauce)

Filet américain (like steak tartare, and always comes with chips)

Hochepot or *hutsepot* (casserole of meat and vegetables)

Salade liégeoise (salad of potatoes, beans and pieces of bacon laced with vinegar)

Stoemp (good, filling fare of sausages and sauerkraut)

Tarte al djote (warm quiche with spicy cheese and chard – a speciality of Nivelles)

Cheese

Athough you may not be familiar with Belgian cheeses, make sure you sample a few during your stay – they are much better than you might expect.

Soft cheeses
Creamy, full-fat cheeses go well with a salad or a crusty baguette, washed down with good wine or beer. Look out for Bouquet des Moines, Herve doux, Fleur des Fagnes, Madreret, Paillardin, Vieil Aubel, Trou d'Sottai and the not-to-be-missed Remoudou Herve, one of the world's finest, most flavoursome and most odoriferous cheeses.

Semi-soft cheeses
These come in a huge variety of shapes and flavours, and many of them are made in monasteries. They melt in the mouth and should, of course, be tried with their corresponding beer: Orval, Postel, Val Dieu, Maredsous, Corsendonck, Westmalle, Floreffe or Affligem, Chimay (both plain and beer-flavoured versions), Damme, Loo, Passendaele, Dom Tobias, Rubens, Père Joseph, Val de Salm or Watou.

Hard cheeses
These are best left to age for the full flavour to emerge. They include: Vieux Bruges, Vieux Chimay, Beauvoorde, Fagnar, Oude Postel, Sezoen or Ambiorix.

Blue cheeses
Blue cheese is formed by the addition of bacteria to the curds at the point at which they are shaped. They have a strong, unique flavour. Bleu de Franchimont, Château d'Arville and Pas de Bleu are the best known.

Cakes, Sweets and Biscuits

Cakes and pastries abound, so you're spoilt for choice. Some of the most typical cakes are listed below:

Pain à la grecque is a Brussels speciality: a hard biscuit with crystallized sugar.

Speculoos are rich, hard cinnamon biscuits, cut into all shapes and sizes but often in the form of saints and religious figures.

Couques de Dinant are hard honey biscuits cooked in wooden moulds.

Gozettes are similar to apple turnovers.

Babeluttes are hard butter sweets.

Marzipan comes in the shape of pigs or fruits.

Frites

The origins of the Belgian *frite* are shrouded in mystery. Sir Walter Raleigh is credited with discovering the potato, while the first recorded chip stand was on Paris's Pont-Neuf. But, since independence, the Belgians have certainly made up for lost time.

In 1857, the Belgian paper *Courrier de Verviers* wrote about a man named Fritz, who owned a fairground *friterie*. Leopold II was reputedly a *frite* fan, and Belgian chips are unquestionably the best in the world. The secret? They're cooked twice. The recipe is as follows: take a good-quality spud (the Belgian *bintje* is best), cut it into 1cm lengths, fry for 5–7 minutes in oil heated to 160°C (320°F), leave to cool for a few minutes, then plunge the chips into the same oil, which should now be at 180°C (356°F); finally, tip them into a twist of paper to soak up the excess fat, then add salt and mayonnaise or pickle. Alternatively, just head for the nearest *friture/frituur*.

Chocolate

Until a short time ago, two things struck the unsuspecting traveller who stepped off the train at Brussels's Gare du Midi: the sight of huge replicas of Tintin and Snowy revolving on top of the offices of Editions du Lombard, and the teasing waft of chocolate. Côte d'Or (the one with the elephant) had a factory right next to the station. Now, however, the Swiss brand Suchard has bought up Côte d'Or, and the old premises have been pulled down.

The French claim to be the world's finest *chocolatiers*, but don't believe them for a second. From sweet white chocolate to dark, bitter chocolate with a high cocoa content, from fruit fondants to hazelnuts, the Belgians have turned chocolate into an art form. The high point is the famous praline, which you'll find on every street corner under brand names like Leonidas, Neuhaus, Godiva, Corn and Daskalidès. Whatever your favourite brand, buy a *ballotin* of pralines before you leave – and maybe a few for your friends as well.

Beer

Each year, the average Belgian consumes 150 litres (30 gallons) of beer, holding his or her own with Europe's other great beer-drinkers, the Czechs, Germans and Danes. On the facade of the Maison des Brasseurs, on Brussels' Grand'Place, you'll see the words: 'It is by the grace of Saint Arnould and the expertise of mankind that Heaven and Earth spawned that divine drink, beer.'

You will soon discover that beer flows freely wherever you go: before lunch, on the café terraces, with the family, recovering after a football match, watching TV, during meetings, before, during and after meals – it's not uncommon to down a pint after a substantial meal that's already been washed down with plenty of wine. It doesn't matter how elegant the setting: nobody will look down on you for ordering a beer with your meal instead of wine.

The production process

Barley is the starting point. The grain is soaked in water to encourage germination, and the result is dried (*touraillé*) and reduced to flour. The malt is then finely milled and turned into a sugary juice (*wort*). Brewing turns the barley starch into maltose sugar, and when the wort has been brought to boiling point, hops are added: the quantity determines how bitter or sweet the beer will eventually taste.

The wort is then placed in great vats for several days, as the yeast transforms the sugar into alcohol and carbonic acid. Fermentation takes place at the top or bottom of the vat, or occurs spontaneously. In the most common beer, **pils** (Stella, Maes, Jupiler), fermentation and maturation occur at the bottom of the vat over a 7–10 day period. The resulting beer is pale and light.

When fermentation occurs at the top, the yeast rises to the surface of the vat. There are several varieties:

Red beers (*bruin bier* in Flemish) are produced by mixing ordinary beers with beer that has been in an oak barrel for 10 months. Their bittersweet, fruity flavour makes them ideal for the addition of grenadine – try it with a Rodenbach.

White beers are made from a wheat and barley base. They are also called *bières troublés* ('murky beers') because they're unfiltered. These pale, sweetish beers are especially refreshing on a hot summer day. If you find them too sweet, just add lemon.

Brown beers are highly aromatic, initially dry on the palate, but very mild, if not in alcohol content.

Trappist beers

The jewels in Belgium's brewing crown are the Trappist beers, which have been much imitated down the years: they now bear the legend 'Authentic Trappist Product' to distinguish them from their inferiors. The monks no longer brew the ales, but they have passed on (or sold) their secret recipes without compromising the quality. You should be able to tell a Trappist brown or pale beer (Orval, Chimay, Rochefort, Westmalle, Westvleteren), from 'abbey beers' – Leffe, Grimbergen, Affligem, Maredsous, Saint-Feuillen – which are at best tenuously related to any religious tradition. Though some of them are pretty good.

Trappist beers are usually thickish, strong and full of flavour: needless to say, it would be unthinkable to drink them out of anything other than the appropriate chalice.

Beers that undergo spontaneous fermentation are peculiar to Belgium, and are only brewed around Brussels. There's no yeast involved, but the beer is exposed to the fresh air in great barrels called *foudres*; the wort slowly becomes beer under the action of unique microbiotic fermenting agents (*Bretanomyces bruxellensis*) that are present in the Brussels air. You can drink the resulting *lambic*, but it is usually left to mature in oak barrels and then in bottles, where it referments and creates *gueuze*. *Gueuze* is a mixture of several lambics of different ages, which have been bottled to eliminate the sugar. It is frothy and sparkling, and if you find it too bitter, you can always add sugar or grenadine. *Kriek* is a lambic beer with added cherries. It has a pleasant reddish colour and a refreshing fruity flavour.

Beer glasses
Before you begin, you need to know that each beer has its own glass. Pale beer, which is at its best between 4°C (39°F) and 6°C (43°F), should be drunk from tall glasses with a stem. Dark beers require a pot-bellied glass, and should be served between 10°C (50°F) and 12°C (54°F). Some beers have special glasses, such as Kwak, which is supported by its own spectacular wooden stand, although these may owe more to marketing than necessity. Unsurprisingly, the glasses, which usually bear the arms of the brewer, are desirable collectors' items: indeed, the landlord of the Dulle Griet, in Ghent, demands a shoe as a deposit from his customers. Judging by the plethora of footwear adorning the walls of his establishment, it hasn't deterred everyone from taking home a souvenir glass.

MUSIC

CLASSICAL

Although Belgium isn't well known for its composers it has produced a number of remarkable musicians and has a rich musical heritage dating back to the Renaissance. During the second half of the 15th century, before Belgium was an independent country, the Franco-Flemish school of composers were particularly influential in Europe. Amongst them Johannes Ockeghem, born in East Flanders, and Josquin des Prez, born in the Duchy of Burgundy in modern-day Belgium, contributed a significant number of polyphonic choral compositions to the church music of the period. Later on, in the 16th century, Mons-born Orlandus Lassus was to become one of the most important composers of the Renaissance and a seminal figure of the Franco-Flemish school, composing a considerable amount of church music including over seventy settings of the Mass. The 18th century marked the emergence of several significant opera composers, including Antoine Gresnick and André Grétry who produced over 50 popular comic operas. Post-independence saw the success of one of the greatest musical figures ever to have come out of the country, César Franck. As well as writing large-scale sacred choral works he excelled in the field of instrumental writing, with many symphonic, chamber and keyboard compositions, influencing future generations of musicians including French composers Vincent D'Indy and Henri Duparc and the Belgian composer Guillaume Lekeu. Other composers including Paul Gilson and Jean Absil have also won international acclaim whilst Henri Pousseur and Pierre Bartholomée have made significant contributions in the field of contemporary music.

Belgium has also had its fair share of talented performers: Eugène Ysaÿe and Arthur Grumiaux were both legendary violinists and the bass-baritone José Van Dam is among the world's finest singers and performers. Belgian conductors Philippe Herreweghe and Sigiswald Kuijken have also made their mark by bringing early music to new audiences.

POPULAR MUSIC

Belgian *chansonniers* are legion, the most famous of all being Jacques Brel. Other notable performers include Salvatore Adamo, originally of Italian descent, Annie Cordy, Jules Beaucarne, Paul Louka, Plastic Bertrand (whose smash hit 'Ça plane pour moi' brought him instant fame in Europe and America), Pierre Rapsat, Victor Lazlo and female artist Maurane. On the Flemish side, Arno is one of the most popular singers, combining American blues and funk with French and Belgian *chansons*, while one-time Elvis impersonator, Helmut Lotti, became the nation's favourite in the late 1990s with his ghastly crooned versions of classical favourites. More recently, hip Flemish bands dEUS and Soulwax have established an international cult following with their own brand of rock and punk-pop, while Front 242 and the Utah Saints have made their mark on the dance and techno scenes with their electronic sampling.

JAZZ

The Belgian jazz world has also produced some great names. Belgian-born Gypsy guitarist Django Reinhardt, who made his name in France, is one of the most influential jazz musicians of all time. Developing his own unique style of playing following a fire that severely damaged two of the fingers on his left hand, he helped bring about a new era in European jazz through his innovative work with French jazz violinist Stéphane Grapelli and the quintet of the Hot Club de France. Other notable jazz musicians include harmonica player, guitarist and whistler Toots Thielemans and guitarist Philip Catherine, both of whom were influenced by Django Reinhardt, pianist Charles Loos, vibraphonist Sadi who recorded with Django Reinhardt and saxophonist Steve Houben.

FOLK MUSIC

Belgium has an unusual mix of traditional music on offer ranging from traditional Flemish and Walloon songs and dance tunes to the more experimental fusions arising out of Belgium's Congolese population. Much of the traditional music of Belgium has been kept alive as a result of the efforts of folksong collectors at the beginning of the twentieth century. Key figures of the folk revival in the 1960s, such as the talented singer Wannes Van de Velde and dance-tune collector Hubert Boone and his traditional ensemble the Brabants Volksorkest, have since helped to promote traditional music within their own country as well as abroad. Similarly, in the 1980s, folk-rock band Kadril successfully brought traditional Belgian music to a new audience at a time when folk music was quickly becoming unfashionable. However, a change of direction came with the emergence of 'world music' in the 1980s and 1990s when Western musicians began experimenting with musicians from other countries, notably Africa. Before long, Belgium's African community was making an impact on the global music scene. Zap Mama, comprising five female a cappella singers from mixed ethnic backgrounds, have been the most successful 'fusion' group to come out of Belgium, producing a unique blend of musical styles. Other worthy musicians include the Rwandan singer Cécile Kayirebwa (a Belgian resident) and the eclectic group Tango al Sur which play a mix of Argentinean tangos and their own Flemish and Dutch compositions.

Brussels

Arriving in Brussels can sometimes be a bit of a shock to the visitor. Despite being the capital of Belgium, it's surprisingly modest and, at first glance, bewilderingly incoherent. Don't however, be taken in by first apperances. The baroque buildings of the Grand'Place and the medieval streets that surround it will make you feel as if you've travelled back through the centuries, but around the corner you'll find demolition sites and traffic-choked main roads, the results of bad town planning and more than a century of intense urban development. And even when you think you've got to grips with the place, you'll come across things that'll make you see the city in a whole new light.

Brussels may not be the most beautiful city in Europe, but it's surprisingly easy to enjoy it and even get addicted to it. Now famed as the 'capital of Europe', it's been under the cosh of most of Europe's empires – the Spanish, the Austrians, the French, the Dutch and the Nazis have all sunk their claws into the capital over the past 500 years. Small wonder the locals are so fond of the place – and so critical of the way it has been run.

As well as being the capital of Belgium, Brussels is the capital of Dutch-speaking Flanders, a tough role to live with when 80 per cent of the population are Francophones. But you'd be wrong to dismiss it as a French-speaking island marooned in Flemish territory. The *bruxellois* refer to themselves as *zinneke* (mongrel, or bastard), and are proud of their mixed-up past and self-mocking humour, known as *zwanze* – good-humoured cheek that's most at home in a *caberdouche* (local café). Once you've been on the receiving end of this *zwanze*, you won't be surprised to hear that this is the spiritual home of *bande dessinée* (comic strip), which the Belgians call the 'ninth art' – or that the locals love their beer, which they've been brewing to perfection for thousands of years.

If the Grand'Place is the Brussels you're looking for, then you may be in for a disappointing stay. But arrive with an open mind and go beyond the glittering guildhouses to discover the 'real Brussels' – the earthy Marolles district on a Sunday morning, the art-nouveau treasures of Ixelles, the hidden squares and parks, and the cosy local bars – and you might just enjoy yourself more than you thought possible.

A Short History

The Middle Ages

In 979, the city's foundations were laid by Charles of Lower Lotharingia, who built a 'castrum', or little fortress, in the marshes in a curve of the River Senne. Bruocsella ('marsh settlement') soon became Brussels. The town already had its saint, Gudule, whose relics are dutifully preserved to this day. In 1041, the counts of Leuven, later to become the dukes of Brabant, erected a chapel on the Coudenberg ('cold mountain'), which is now the site of place Royale. At the beginning of the 12th century, the fledging town was surrounded by ramparts, traces of which can still be seen today.

Brussels developed steadily under the management of the dukes of Brabant and a benevolent middle class. Seven rich families shared power, each choosing an alderman to create the town's judiciary. As the population expanded, the town spread outside its walls, occupying the area that's now known as the Pentagon. By the 14th century, local craftsmen had established guilds, and their desire for more say in the running of the city's affairs led them to rebel and take control of Brussels. Although order soon returned, the guilds had shown their might, and their power that was to grow unchecked during the next centuries. For two months in the 14th century, the town was occupied by the troops of the Count of Flanders: Everard 't Serclaes, a local alderman, came to the rescue, but was murdered by his enemies in 1388; you can see his bas-relief on an arcade off the Grand'Place (the locals rub his elbow for good luck). The 14th century also saw a flourishing of the arts and crafts, especially in the fields of lace, cloth and sculpture.

From the Burgundians to the Habsburgs

By the early 15th century, Brussels had acquired a constitution that put the nobility and the craftsmen on an equal footing. As a result of shrewd marriage alliances, the Dukes of Burgundy, the successors of the Dukes of Brabant, absorbed a large part of the Low Countries into their territory, and moved their court from Dijon to Brussels. The city reaped the benefits, most obviously on the artistic front (jewellery, sculpture and tapestry), with the construction of the town hall and the carving of several fine altarpieces. Rogier de la Pasture, better known as Roger van der Weyden, became Brussels' official painter.

There were new alliances and shifts in power – when Marie of Burgundy (the daughter of Charles the Bold) married Maximilian of Austria, she created a dynastical link with the Habsburgs, as a result of which the young Charles V found himself in 1516 in charge of domains in Spain, the Low Countries and later Germany. He entered the town to have himself crowned with pomp and circumstance aplenty. In 1549, there was a procession (*ommegang*) in his honour, which is re-created every year on the Grand'Place. But a new period of turbulence was to follow when Philip II succeeded Charles V in 1555. The country said goodbye to a golden age and entered a period of sorrow and decline that lasted nearly two centuries.

The Protestant Dutch ruler, William of Orange, opposed Philip II's oppressive Catholic regime, and Brussels was caught in the crossfire. The Inquisition came to town, bringing terror in its wake: popular feeling is captured in Brueghel's paintings, which denounced the 'Spanish occupation', especially the heavy taxes. The inevitable happened: the people closed ranks and revolted, their rage reaching its zenith on June 5, 1568 when the Duke of Alba, Philip II's hatchet man, had the Counts of Egmont and Hoorn beheaded on the square in front of the Grand'Place. A plaque on a pillar of the Maison du Roi commemorates their deaths.

Until the end of the 16th century, the non-Dutch parts of the Low Countries were going nowhere. However, the creation of the Willebroek canal gave Brussels a link to the sea via the River Scheldt. The northwest quarter of the town became a port, and several quays were constructed. Philip II's daughter, the Archduchess Isabella, and her husband, Albert, took the reins in Spain in 1598, but were ready for a reconciliation with the rebellious Low Countries, leaving Brussels to enjoy a period of relative calm.

But not for long. France was on the rampage in Europe. To counter Louis XIV's constant warmongering, the Dutch and English sent defensive flotillas into the ports of the Channel. On the pretext that they were bombarding the ports, Louis ordered his forces to fight fire with fire, and the result was the bombardment of Brussels in 1695. The city centre was destroyed, and 4,000 houses were reduced to ashes. But it took just four years for a shiny new Grand'Place to emerged from the rubble, stunning the whole of Europe.

In 1715, under the terms of the treaty of Utrecht, the Austrians took over. As with the Spanish, the early years of their domination were fraught with problems. When the citizens rebelled against Joseph II, for example, he retaliated by lopping off the head of the leader of the professional classes, François Anneessens. Charles of Lorraine, who governed the Low Countries between 1744 and 1780, was the only one of the dynasty to bring any lustre to Brussels, adorning it with numerous classical monuments in the French style. Place Royale, the church of Saint Jacques-sur-Coudenberg and the surrounding roads were the first large-scale architectural projects in the city, with artists from several countries involved in their construction.

A cultural rebirth

Following the French Revolution, Brussels was downgraded to *département* capital, a humiliating status that came to an abrupt end in 1815, when the British and Germans defeated Napoleon at nearby Waterloo. Brussels was held in higher regard by its new ruler, the Dutch king William I, but Belgium was not content simply to be part of the United Kingdom of the Netherlands.

In 1830, following religious, linguistic and political problems as well as widespread famine, the people revolted. The revolution began in Brussels on the nights of 24 and 25 August, and quickly reached the provinces. Belgium gained her independence, and the town became the capital of the new country, which gained international recognition in 1831. Reflecting the new mood of independence, a canal was dug from Brussels to Charleroi, and the Free University of Brussels was founded.

Industrialization gave Brussels a new lease of life. New districts were developed according to a radical, and often controversial, urbanization scheme, and works of gigantic proportions were undertaken. Prompted by Leopold I and especially Leopold II, the 19th century saw the building of the Galeries Saint-Hubert, the burial of the River Senne and the construction of the Palais de Justice and the Parc du Cinquantenaire. Victor Horta introduced art nouveau in the late 19th century, and a host of other architects adopted the style, with spectacular results for those who could afford to pay for such houses. Brussels was experiencing a cultural rebirth that drew favourable comparisons with Paris.

The 20th century

Leopold II's dream was to establish Belgium as a European imperial power on a par with France or Germany, with the riches of the Congo at its disposal. To this end, he exploited his central African dominion in brutal fashion between 1885 and 1908, when international concern about the ruthlessness of his regime led the Belgian state to wrest control of the Congo from the king. Leopold II died in 1909, disillusioned by what he saw as the small-mindedness of his subjects, and it took just five years for his delusions of grandeur to go up in smoke.

In 1914, the Germans violated Belgium's neutral status and swept across the country's western border. The new king, Albert, did his best to resist, but was powerless in the face of superior military might. The French and British rallied to little Belgium's aid, but they too failed to halt the Kaiser's forces, and by the end of August, Brussels was in German hands. The king and his shattered army clung onto a strip of land around De Panne, which became the de facto capital.

The citizens of Brussels saw their property seized and their factories plundered, while many were deported to labour camps in Germany or to the front; thousands of people fled the city to join their king in virtual exile. The city remained in German hands until the Armistice of November 1918.

Brussels' recovery was aided by a programme of reparations from Germany, while it was allowed to forego its neutrality and sign a defence pact with France. Things took a sharp turn for the worse in the 1930s, however, as the Depression wiped out foreign trade, the much-loved King Albert died in a climbing accident and, most ominously of all, the Nazis made it increasingly plain that they planned to make Europe their own.

The Germans attacked Belgium on 10 May, 1940, and took Brussels within a fortnight. By May 28, the new king, Leopold III, had surrendered to the Germans – to the disgust of his critics, who say he endangered the Allies' retreat to Dunkirk by giving up too soon.

Leopold and his family were confined to the Royal Palace in Laeken, to the north of the city, while the citizens of Brussels endured another four years of German rule, this time far more brutal than the first. Despite the dangers involved in breaking Nazi laws, Belgium kept up an active resistance throughout the war, and many families in Brussels' working-class Marolles neighbourhood risked their lives by sheltering Jews.

The city was freed on September 3 1944, and was at least spared the bloodshed of the battle for the Ardennes. Leopold II, meanwhile, was deported to Austria, where he remained until 1950. His return from exile caused such controversy that he was forced to abdicate.

Brussels today

After 1945, construction continued at a cracking pace. Highways were built, trunk roads were widened and old districts were pulled down to make way for office blocks. These projects met with little official opposition. The disruption in the city meant the bruxellois left for the suburbs in droves, leaving the way clear for speculators of every genre.

At the 1958 World Fair, the star attraction was the Atomium – a huge model of an iron molecule that towers over the Heysel area, northwest of the city – although the network of tunnels and mini highways constructed for the event are perhaps a more lasting legacy. In 1967, the area to the north of the city felt the shock of pneumatic drills as Brussels acquired its own World Trade Centre.

In 1969, after the destruction of the Maison du Peuple, perhaps Victor Horta's finest art-nouveau building, frustrated locals formed committees and societies to defend the town against the schemes of property developers, and offered alternative plans with an emphasis on restoration rather than wholesale destruction. They've won their share of battles to save certain buildings, but the scale of the task facing them can be seen in the so-called 'European quarter', centred on rue de la Loi and Rond-Point Schuman, where redevelopment has meant cumbersome buildings to accommodate Europe's 'technostructure'. Even in the centre of town, it's no surprise to see medieval buildings next door to concrete monstrosities or building sites.

Brussels' architecture isn't the only thing that's radically changing. While it remains the unchallenged capital of Europe, its status as capital of Belgium is up in the air as the Flemish make increasingly powerful bids for independence. Since 1989, the country has been run on a federal basis, with three Regions – Brussels (the *commune* of Brussels and 18 others within the conurbation), Flanders and Wallonia – each with its own government and a degree of political independence, as well as three linguistic Communities (French, Dutch and the smaller German-speaking group, most of whom live in the extreme east of Belgium). Many Flemings believe that this compromise does not go far enough, but the sticking point is this: Brussels, the capital of Flanders, is a largely French-speaking city, and is unlikely to welcome any change in its status as a national, rather than regional, capital. Pushing the federalist logic to its conclusion, some politicians have proposed that Brussels should become an international district, like Washington, D.C. But this risks depriving it for ever of what remains of its identity, and depriving its population of the right to govern itself.

Brussels is also the seat of NATO, the European Commission and the European Parliament. The *bruxellois* are all too aware that Europe is crucial to them, but worry that their city and its architecture are paying a heavy price.

European Institutions

Following years of rivalry with Strasbourg and Luxembourg, Brussels can finally claim the title of undisputed Capital of Europe. The most important EU institutions are here: the Commission, the Council of Ministers and the European Parliament (which holds its parliamentary commissions here, although the monthly plenary sessions, controversially, take place in Strasbourg).

Alongside the institutions are a swarm of pressure groups, whose frenetic lobbying activities show just how important the EU has become. With more than 500 consultancies in Brussels, it's second only to Washington, D.C. as the lobbying capital of the world.

Although the Council of Europe is in Strasbourg, the European Court of Justice is in Luxembourg and the Central European Bank is in Frankfurt, Brussels is at the heart of the EU's decision-making process, and it is here that the future of Europe will be decided.

The Commission: the European Commission is headed by 19 commissioners and one president, drawn from the 15 countries in the Union, and is no stranger to scandal, with its members frequently accused of incompetence and mishandling funds. When it's not diddling the continent's taxpayers, the Commission makes sure European treaties are carried out, offers proposals

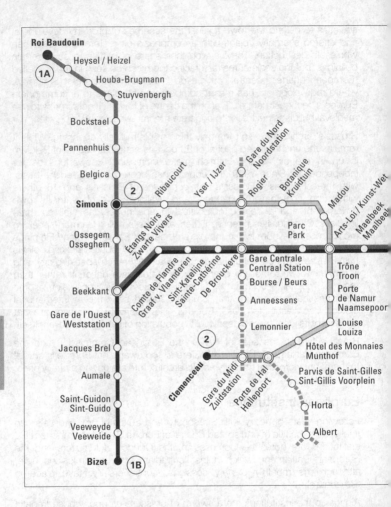

for the Union's future development and tries to reconcile the (often very different) views of the member states. It acts as a kind of administrative policeman, especially in the delicate area of the single currency. Although its members are not elected – as anyone who reads the British tabloid press will know – it's obliged to submit its annual accounts for approval by the European Parliament. In 1999, the fear that the Parliament would refuse to endorse a report led Jacques Santer and his Commission to resign en masse.

The Council of Ministers: consisting of an army of 2,000 civil servants, is the council that votes on European directives. Each of the Union countries takes a turn at heading it, with two countries presiding over it each year. The

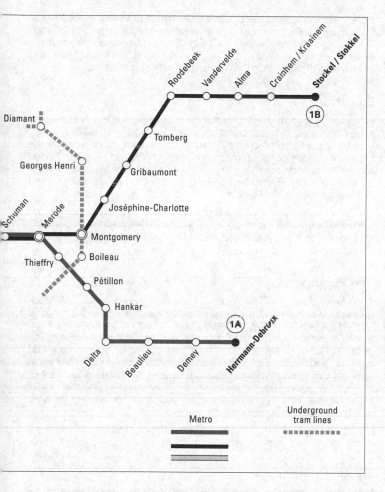

Diamant
Georges Henri
Schuman
Merode
Thieffry
Montgomery
Boileau
Pétillon
Hankar
Joséphine-Charlotte
Gribaumont
Tomberg
Roodebeek
Vandervelde
Alma
Crainhem / Kraainem
Stockel / Stokkel
1B
Delta
Beaulieu
Demey
Herrmann-Debroux
1A

Metro

Underground
tram lines

BRUSSELS

BRUSSELS – METRO

headquarters has its offices in the architectural mammoth called the Justus Lipsius, but the ministers hold council regularly in the country of the current president, and it is the job of the presidents to organize the six-monthly European summit of the heads of state which ends their turn in presidency.

The European Parliament: the Parliament has 626 members, elected by the citizens of Europe, and hosts parliamentary commissions for three weeks each month before traipsing off to Strasbourg for the monthly voting session. The Parliament's Brussels headquarters is known as 'Caprice des Dieux' (literally 'whim of the gods', because of its similarity in shape to the cheese of the same name). It amends and ratifies the Commission's proposals, and shares decision-making power with the Council of Ministers, although most EU-watchers believe it could do with a rather greater share of the latter. Basically, the Council is where reps of the EU member states veto anything they don't think will play at home: it's non-elected, unaccountable, and much less high-profile than the Commission, which gets all the flak.

Eurocrats

Eurocrats (i.e. people working for the EU institutions) are blamed for all the evils of the capital: rising rents and house prices, traffic jams, building works, the cost of eating out. The locals grumble that they receive grossly inflated salaries, pay little or no tax and send their children to specially funded schools. What they don't tell you is that the presence of these parasites is worth 200 billion BEF each year – 12 per cent of the region's GDP – and indirectly generates 30,000 jobs.

The Eurocrats themselves are generally fairly content in Brussels, although many find it provincial and most can't stand the bureaucracy. They also think the centre is grubby, preferring to live in rather soulless Euro-ghettoes to the east of the city.

The Pentagon

Don't waste your time looking for a European branch of the CIA headquarters. The Pentagon is the name given to the centre of Brussels, which is shaped like, well, a pentagon. Its boundaries are the wide boulevards and tunnels that make a sort of ring road around the city. These follow the outline of the old, and chiefly demolished, second city wall: you'll see the odd remnant, such as the Porte de Hal on boulevard de Waterloo, standing in splendid but slightly bewildered isolation between the office blocks. Confusingly for the visitor, these boulevards have different names on either side of the street: they fall within Brussels commune on the inner side, but the outer side is within a different commune.

GETTING TO BRUSSELS

By Air

If you come by plane, you'll arrive at Brussels National Airport (Zaventem), 15 kilometres (9 miles) northeast of the city centre. A shuttle service links the airport to Gare du Nord and Gare Centrale. The journey takes about 20 minutes, and trains leave every 30 minutes from 5.30am to 11.45pm. Tickets cost 90BEF.

A taxi into town costs 1,000BEF – so let the train take the strain.

By Train

The Eurostar is a great way to get to Brussels from London, and if you're travelling around the Continent, you can reach the city by Thalys from Amsterdam, Paris, Cologne and Aachen. The old-fashioned Gare du Midi has been adapted to receive high-speed trains, including the Eurostar, for which a special terminal was built. It is undergoing a much-needed facelift, but the area around the station is notorious as a haunt of muggers and should be avoided if at all possible. If you are heading for the city centre (the Pentagon), you can take a high-speed train towards Amsterdam and get out at Gare du Nord. Most domestic trains stop at Gare Centrale, a five-minute walk from the Grand'Place.

Arriving at the Gare du Midi

To get to Gare Centrale, head for platforms 9 to 18.

On the concourse, you'll find telephones and automatic left-luggage pigeon-holes (make sure you've got 5, 20 and 50BEF coins). You can also hand your luggage in over the counter to an assistant between 4am and 2am. This office also sells phonecards (200BEF).

At the end of this concourse is a little **TIB** (Tourist Office) kiosk, where you can get basic information. The interactive terminal is user-friendly, but has limited information, especially on hotels. It's better to ask the assistant. Open weekdays 8.30am–12.30pm and 1.30am–5.30pm, weekends 9am–noon and 1am–6pm.

On the main concourse, heading towards Avenue Fonsny, you'll find a range of shops and services (including car hire) and the **Travel Centre**, where you can buy tickets for domestic and international journeys (you can expect to wait in line for a long time).

If you continue along the first concourse, you'll see a walkway leading to the outside, where you can pick up the bus or tram. Line No. 3 will take you into the centre of town (a single ticket costs 50BEF, and is valid for one hour regardless of how many changes you make).

To the right of this walkway is a bureau de change, but don't use it unless you have to, as rates and commission are appalling. Better to use an automatic cash machine that takes credit cards or bank cards linked to

BRUSSELS

■ **Useful addresses**

🚃 Gare du Nord
🚃 Gare Centrale
🚃 Gare du Midi
🚃 Gare du quartier Léopold

🛏 **Where to stay**

21 Hôtel Lloyd George

★ **What to see**

108 Serres Royales
109 Pavillon Chinois and Tour Japonaise
110 Atomium
111 Musées Royaux d'Art et d'Histoire

112 Musée royal de l'Armée et de l'Histoire Militaire
113 Autoworld
114 Musée Communal d'Ixelles
115 Musée Bruxellois de la Gueuze
116 Musée Constantin Meunier
117 Musée Antoine Wiertz
118 Musée de l'Institut Royal des Sciences Naturelles
119 Hôtel Stoclet
120 Musée du Transport Urbain Bruxellois
121 Squares Marie-Louise et Ambiorix
122 Musée David et Alice Van Buuren
126 Musée René Magritte

BRUSSELS

BRUSSELS NATIONAL AIRPORT

LIÈGE, A 3 E 40

A 3 E 40

Avenue Leopold III

Bd A. Reyers

Bd G. Wahis

Louvain

Rogier

Lambermont

Chaussée

SCHAERBEEK

Avenue

SAINT-JOSSE-
TEN-NOODE

Vilvorde

Vilvorde

avenue de

PONT VAN PRAET

Château Royal

Domaine Royal
de Laeken

Chaussée

★ 109
★ 108
Av.

Parc de
Laeken

Av. du Parc Royal

Av. de la Reine

PL J. DE TROOZ

Allée Verte

Q. de Willebroeck

BRUSSELS

Gare
du Nord

See map II

ANTWERP A 12

★ T10

Heysel

Av. H. de Strooper

de Wand

Emile Bockstael

Smet

de

Boulevard

LAEKEN

126 ★

Boulevard Léopold II

KOEKELBERG

Basilique
du Sacré-Cœur

Bd de Ninove

MOLENBEEK-SAINT-JEAN

NORTH

GHENT, BRUGES, OSTEND, E 40, A 10

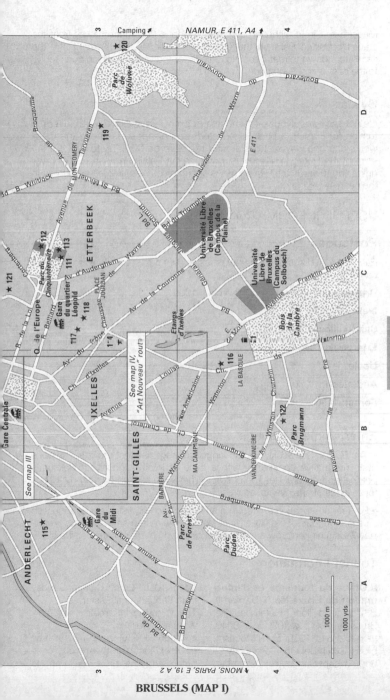

BRUSSELS

Maestro or Cirrus, although the nearest one is 200 metres away from the station on place Bara. At the end of the walkway, on the right, are the escalators down to metro line No. 2 (look for the M sign), which goes round to the east of the Pentagon.

By Car

It's not easy once you've left the ring at exit 17 (marked 'Centre', after the turning for Forest): a badly signposted road disappears among the road-works and one-way systems around the Gare du Midi. Try to pick out the spire of the Hôtel de Ville or the dome of the Palais de Justice, which will guide you towards the Pentagon. As soon as you're there, leave your car in the nearest car park.

USEFUL INFORMATION

Postcodes

Each of the 19 Brussels *communes* has its own postcode. Here are the most useful ones:

Brussels (the Pentagon and environs): 1000

Ixelles: 1050

Saint-Gilles: 1060

Etterbeek: 1040

Uccle: 1180

Anderlecht: 1070

Forest: 1190

Entertainment Listings

– *The Bulletin* is a weekly English-language magazine that provides the city's huge non-native community with a mine of information about Belgium's political and cultural life. The pull-out *What's On* section has handy listings for all kinds of arts events, again in English.

– For French-speakers, *Kiosque* is an erratic monthly listings magazine with a useful roundup of the city's more fashionable restaurants and bars. *Tenue de Ville* is a higher-brow arts mag that gives you more of a feel for the city.

Tourist Information

🛈 **Office du tourisme et d'infor-mation de Bruxelles (TIB**, map II, B3): ground floor, Hôtel de Ville, Brussels 1000. ☎ (02) 513 8940. Fax: (02) 514 4538. Email: tourism. brussels@tib.be. Open every day 9–6pm; except Sundays in December: open 10am–2pm. Closed Sunday from January until Easter.
The following information and services are available:
● Reservation of hotel rooms (free service): just tell them your price range and the area you want to

stay in, and they'll find you something suitable. Youth hostellers can find out which hostels have beds available. Several of the posher hotels slash their prices at the weekend, so ask about this as well.

● Advance booking for shows in town: ☎ (02) 513 8220.
● One-day travelcards: 130BEF.

■ **Useful addresses**

🛈 Office du tourisme et
d'information de Bruxelles (TIB),
OPT et Toerisme Vlaanderen
✉ Main post office

♔ **Where to stay**

5 Hôtel Atlas
6 Hôtel Arenberg
9 Hôtel La Légende
10 Centre Vincent-Van-Gogh
CHAB
11 Youth Hostel Jacques-Brel
13 Espace du Marais – Sleep Well
15 Hôtel des Éperonniers
16 Pacific Sleeping
18 Hôtels La Tasse d'Argent et
Madou
19 Résidence Les Écrins
22 Hôtel Noga
23 Hôtel Welcome
24 Hôtel Opéra
25 Auberge Saint-Michel
26 Hôtel La Madeleine
29 Hôtel Le Dixseptième

✕ **Where to eat**

32 La Galettière
35 Bij den Boer
36 Le Pré Salé
37 Le Falstaff
38 't Kelderke
41 Le Petit Boxeur
42 Chez Jean
43 Hémisphères
44 In 't Spinnekopke
46 Chez Vincent
47 L'École Buissonnière
49 La Roue d'Or
50 Waka Moon Dibi-Groove Café
51 Halloween
53 Chez Henri

58 L'Achepot

🍸 **Bars, cafés, clubs**

61 À la Mort Subite
62 Goupil le Fol
63 Le Java
64 L'Archiduc
65 Poechenellekelder
67 Le Métropole
68 Le Cercueil
69 Chez Toone
71 Au Soleil
72 H2O
73 Le Travers
76 La Tentation
78 La Rose
79 L'Acrobate
80 Le Magasin 4
82 L'Espérance
83 À la Bécasse
84 À l'Image Notre-Dame
87 De Ultieme Hallucinatie
88 Loplop Café

★ **What to see**

90 Hôtel de Ville
91 Maison du Roi et Musée de la
Ville
92 Galeries Saint-Hubert
93 Manneken-Pis
97 Église de la Madeleine
98 Église Sainte-Catherine
99 Église Saint-Jean-Baptiste-du-
Béguinage
100 Place des Martyrs
102 Centre Belge de la Bande
Dessinée
104 Musée du Costume et de la
Dentelle
105 Église Saint-Nicolas
107 Anciens bassins
125 Album

BRUSSELS

BRUSSELS

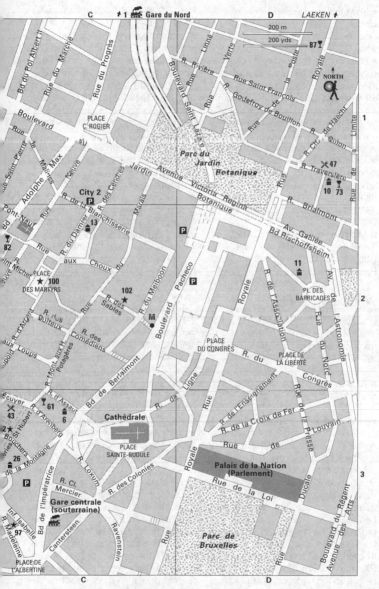

BRUSSELS – NORTH (MAP II)

• Information booklet *Bruxelles-Guide et Plan:* 70BEF. Excellent and useful information about Brussels.

• Map of the town centre *(Brussel Cityscape en 3D)* showing all the monuments. Great value.

• Brochures on the rest of Belgium.

• The Tourist Passport (300BEF): this gets you into museums at a reduced rate, and gives you a travelcard for two days. It's only available to those spending three or more days in town, but it's sometimes bundled in a weekend special deal.

• Weekly schedule of cultural events in the city.

🅗 **Maison du tourisme OPT et Toerisme Vlaanderen** (map II, B3): rue du Marché-aux-Herbes 63, Brussels 1000. ☎ (02) 504 0390.

Fax: (02) 504 0270. Website: www.opt.be. For Flanders: www.visitflanders.com. In July and August, open 9am–7pm, closed 1–2pm on Sunday; in May, June, September and October, open 9am–6pm, closed 1–2pm at the weekend; otherwise 9am–6pm, Sunday 9am–1pm. Same free services as the TIB, but covers the whole of Belgium, including Brussels.

■ **BTR**: telephone bookings for hotel rooms. ☎ (02) 513 7484. Fax: (02) 513 9277.

■ **Album** (map II, A2-3, **125**): rue des Chartreux 25, Brussels 1000. ☎ (02) 511-90-55. Open 1–7pm. Closed Tuesday. This little museum (*see* 'What to see') is also a mine of information on how to get the most out of your stay in Brussels and discover its best-kept secrets.

Walks and Tours

Brussels can be a puzzling city, and it's not immediately obvious where its attractions lie. Fortunately, it's blessed with several commendable tour companies whose programmes are worlds away from the usual tourist tat.

■ **ARAU**: boulevard Adolphe-Max 55, Brussels 1000. ☎ (02) 219 3345. Fax: (02) 219 8675. The Workshop for Research and Urban Action is a committee of residents set up in 1969 to deal with Brussels' urbanization problems. The organization offers alternative plans for urban redevelopment, and suggests institutional or administrative reforms to increase the control residents have over construction projects. The organization played an important part in the process that led to the creation of the region Brussels-Capital. They also arrange delightful themed coach tours (*see* 'What to see').

■ A number of other organizations offer some great themed walks:

• **Le Bus Bavard**: rue des Thuyas 12, Brussels 1170. ☎ (02) 673

1835. Fax: (02) 675 1967. 'Our groups are not herds and our guides are not parrots': that's the appealing claim of this association, which offers original tours on weekends between March and October. Themes include cemeteries, Anderlecht, Schaerbeek, the Marolles, taverns, the Senne, Brussels' women, art nouveau, comic-strip Brussels, Brussels and Paris, the baroque and so on. Brussels Down the Ages, which takes just over 2 hours, is an excellent introduction to the centre. The tours start at 10am every day between 15 June and 15 September at the entrance to the Galeries Saint-Hubert (map II, C3).

• **Arcadia**: rue du Métal 38, Brussels 1060. ☎ (02) 534 3819. Fax: (02) 534 6073. Free for children under 12. Guided tours of Brussels by district every Sunday, with an emphasis on art and architecture. Tours include a lecture by an art historian.

● **Itinéraires**: rue Hôtel-des-Monnales 157, Brussels 1060. ☎ (02) 534 3000. Fax: (02) 534 0214. Website: www.itineraires.be. Themed tours on subjects including literary cabarets, Hercule Poirot in Brussels, Surrealism, witchcraft and astrology.

● **La Fonderie**: rue Ransfort 27, Brussels 1080. ☎ (02) 410 1080. Individual walks in summer; groups only in winter. Tour topics include: the Grand'Place as seen by the working classes, pralines, from *gueuze* to pils, working Brussels, Brussels on the sea and many more.

● **Provélo**: rue de Londres 15, Brussels 1050. ☎ (02) 502 7355. Fax: (02) 502 8641. Website: www.users.skynet.be/provelo
Three-hour guided tours by bike, every Sunday in summer: the Pentagon, the mysteries of green Brussels, cafés, comic strips, etc. Bike-hire available.

● **Cap Vélo**: chaussée de Wavre 1782, Brussels 1160. ☎ (02) 660 9562 (evenings and weekends). Themed cycle tours.

Embassies

■ **GB**: rue Joseph II 28. ☎ (02) 217 9000.
■ **USA**: boulevard du Régent 27, 1000. ☎ (02) 513 3830.
■ **Ireland**: rue Froissart 89. ☎ (02) 230 5337.

■ **Australia**: rue Guimard 6-8. ☎ (02) 286 0500.
■ **New Zealand**: boulevard du Régent 47-48. ☎ (02) 513 3830.
■ **Canada**: avenue de Tervueren 2, 1040. ☎ (02) 741 0611.

BRUSSELS

🛏 Where to stay	
7	Hôtel La Grande Cloche
8	Résidence Galia
12	Youth Hostel Bruegel
17	Duke of Windsor
20	Hôtel Les Bluets
27	Hôtel Ustel

✕ Where to eat	
30	Athènes
33	Le Pain Quotidien
34	Les Brassins
39	La Grande Porte
40	Indigo
45	Stekerlapatte
48	L'Ultime Atome
52	Le Bermuchet
55	Le Volle Gas
56	Bleu de Toi
57	Le Bazaar
59	La Tour d'y Voir

🍷 Bars, cafés, clubs	
60	La Fleur en Papier Doré
66	Le Cercle
70	À Malte
74	Le Grain d'Orge
75	Chicon Masqué
77	La Samaritaine
81	New Tom-Tom Alive
85	Le Perroquet
86	Chez Richard

★ What to see	
94	Église de la Chapelle
95	Église Notre-Dame-du-Sablon
96	Palais des Beaux-Arts
101	Musées Royaux des Beaux-Arts
103	Musée de la Dynastie
106	Hôtel Ravenstein
123	Musée des instruments de Musique
124	Fondation Jacques-Brel

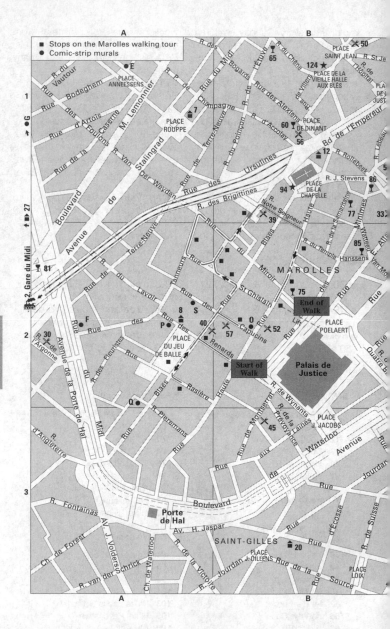

Stops on the Marolles walking tour
Comic-strip murals

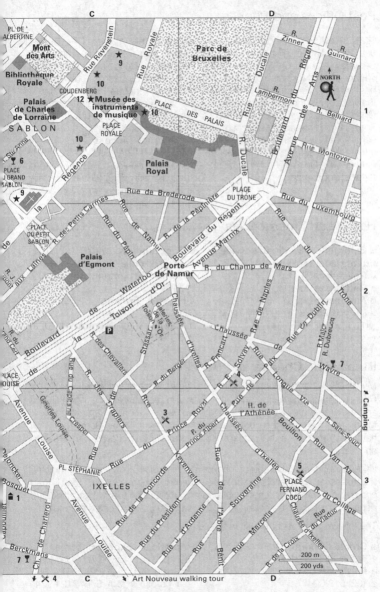

BRUSSELS

Post Offices and Phones

✉ **Post offices**: Monday to Friday 9am–5pm. Some open later and on Saturday morning.
• Place de la Monnaie (map II, B2) has the most central post office, on the first floor of the shopping centre. Open Monday to Saturday 8am–8pm. For financial transactions, 9am–9pm July and August.
• Gare du Midi (map I, A3): avenue Fonsny 15. Open round the clock for post and stamps.

■ **Telephone** (map II, C3): Belgacom, boulevard de l'Impératrice 17 (near Gare Centrale). Open 8am–10pm. Pay by cash, credit card or travellers' cheque. Phone booths that take cards are located throughout the city. You can buy cards at newspaper kiosks.
■ **Internet access**: easyEverything, place de Brouckère 9-13, 1000 Brussels. Access from 100BEF, with 450 terminals available. For more inormation, visit www.easyeverything.com

Health and Emergencies

■ **Emergency medical services, fire brigade**: ☎ 100.
■ **Police**: ☎ 101.
■ **Red Cross**: ☎ 105.
■ **Ambulance**: ☎ (02) 649 1122.
■ **Duty doctors**: ☎ (02) 479 1818 or (02) 648 8000.

■ **Duty dentists**: ☎ (02) 426 1026 or (02) 428 5888.
■ **Hôpital Brugmann**: ☎ (02) 477 2111.
■ **Hôpital Érasme**: ☎ (02) 555 3111.
■ **Poison help centre**: ☎ (070) 245245.

Bureaux de Change and Banks

Most banks change money. There's no commission, but rates can vary. The Change Points, Exchange and other kiosks in the centre don't open till late and their rates are usually extortionate, so use them only in an emergency. Most of the banks in the centre are open Monday to Friday 9am–4pm, and have cash machines that accept Visa cards and bank cards with Maestro and Cirrus.

If you're not careful, bureau de change agents will slip you a map of the city, regardless of whether you want one, during your transaction. They'll then charge you 75BEF for what would cost you 20BEF in the tourist office. It's illegal, and it should be stamped out, so write to us if you catch them at it.

The following is a list of banks in the centre:

■ **Crédit Général**: Grand'Place 5, 1000. ☎ (02) 547 1601.
■ **Fortis**: rue de la Colline 12, 1000. ☎ (02) 513 0247.
■ **CGER/ASLK**: rue du Fossé-aux-Loups 48, 1000. ☎ (02) 228 6111.
■ **BBL**: boulevard Anspach 2, 1000. ☎ (02) 218 1100.
■ Major credit-card agencies:

• **American Express**, bureau de change and travellers' cheques, place Louise 2. ☎ (02) 676 2424. Lost cards: ☎ (02) 676 2121 (24-hour).
• **Eurocard and Visa** (Bank Card Cy), boulevard Jacqmain 159, 1210. ☎ (02) 205 8111. Lost or stolen cards: ☎ (070) 344344 (24-hour).

TRANSPORT

– **On foot**: within the Pentagon, your best bet is to do your sightseeing on foot.

– **Metro**, **bus**, **tram**: there's an excellent public-transport network, with tickets valid for all types of journey. It's run by STIB: ☎ (02) 515 2000. In general, public transport operates from 6am to midnight. The TIB has a helpful map showing all the different lines. Metro stations are marked by a big 'M' sign.

● Travelcards for one, five or 10 journeys: each journey must take no more than one hour, but may include different means of transport, including the train (within the appropriate zone and a two-hour time limit). A single ticket is 50BEF; at 350BEF, the 10-journey card is a worthwhile investment, though the five-trip ticket is less competitive.

● One-day travelcard: unlimited travel on all public transport for 130BEF.

● Buy your ticket on the tram or bus, at main stations or from newspaper kiosks.

– The three main stations are Gare du Midi (map I, A3), Gare Centrale (map I, B3) and Gare du Nord (map I, B2).

Most of Brussels' stations have been decorated by Belgian artists. In the course of your visit, you'll see works by Pol Bury and Paul Delvaux at Bourse, Pierre Alechinsky and Christian Dotremont at Anneessens and Jacques Moeschal at Gare du Midi. Hergé appears at Stockel, while Montgomery is decorated by Pol Mara, Jean-Michel Folon and Jo Delahaut. You can pick up a brochure at the tourist office, or at Porte de Namur station, for a full list of the artists who contributed to this delightful project.

– **Taxis**: Londoners will be horrified by most cabbies' inability to find their way around. Unless you're on one of the main boulevards or at a taxi rank, don't count on flagging one down. Cab companies include: ATR, ☎ (02) 647 2222; Autolux, ☎ (02) 411 1221; Taxis Verts, ☎ (02) 349 4949. Don't tip, as service is included.

> **TIP** STIB has come up with a novel way for night-owls to get around. On your outward journey, buy a STIB-TAXIS ticket for 60BEF; when you come back (after a night's clubbing, for example), present it to the taxi driver, who will give you a reduction of 80BEF per ticket on the price of the taxi journey. It's a great idea if there are three or four of you, but if the fare is less than the total discount, you won't be reimbursed. In other words, don't push your luck.

– **By car**: a bit of a nightmare in a city with so many high-speed roads, tunnels, passages and one-way streets. Without a good map – the TIB can provide one – you're likely to get totally lost. In any case, Brussels is not a city that lends itself to sightseeing by car, so the best thing to do is to find a car park (they close at 1am) and explore the Pentagon on foot. Should you decide to park on the streets, be sure you don't obstruct a garage or park anywhere with a towing sign: the local police will take great pleasure in having your car towed away – even if it's not impeding the traffic. Retrieving it is an expensive business, and the fees are doubled at the weekend and at night. If you do run into trouble, go to the main police office on rue Marché-au-Charbon (map II, B3). ☎ (02) 517 9611.

You don't have to pay on Sundays and between 6pm and 9am. Public car parks have automatic machines where you pay on collecting your car. These accept coins, notes and credit cards.

● Outside the Pentagon, driving is much easier, although you should watch out for no-parking signs.

● Don't leave valuables in your car; some areas are notorious for break-ins.

WHERE TO STAY

A bed for the night doesn't come cheap in Brussels, the world's third-busiest conference city. Of its 18,000 hotel beds, many are in half-empty deluxe establishments or overpriced two-star hotels, and there's not a lot in between. Good one-star hotels are hard to come by, unless you're prepared to stay away from the action. On the other hand, there are several smaller establishments offering rooms that are more like family pensions than hotels proper. The warm atmosphere and low prices make these an attractive option. And don't dismiss the luxury and medium-priced hotels, as they often do 'weekend' and 'holiday-season' deals. Don't be shy about bargaining over the phone before you book. For example, the Métropole, on place de Brouckère, cuts its prices by at least 50 per cent at the weekend, and throws in breakfast as well.

If you're on a backpacker's budget, you'll find Brussels very much to your liking: there are five youth hostels or associated organizations near the centre, all comfortable and as cheap as you could hope for.

B&Bs

♠ **Bed and Brussels**: rue Kindermans 9, Brussels 1050. ☎ (02) 646 0737. Fax: (02) 644 0114. Email: BnBru@ibm.net. Website: www.bnb-brussels.be. A competent and efficient organization that represents 104 addresses in the capital. Doubles are 1,470–2,730BEF, with discounts for children under 12 and for stays of more than seven nights. Some places add 20 per cent for a single-night stay. Rooms in houses or apartments, with private or shared bathroom, start at 850BEF per person, Call between 9am and 6pm to book. If you get an answerphone, leave a message, and a fax number if you have one. Lifts from the station or airport can also be arranged.

♠ **Windrose**: avenue Brugmann 11, Brussels 1060. ☎ (02) 534 7191. Fax: (02) 534 7192. Email: windrose@skynet.be. A booking centre for rooms in a private home – anything from a room in town to a chic villa in the leafy suburbs or even a country château – for one or several nights, by the week or for longer periods. Prices from 1,000BEF to 1,350BEF per person, with doubles 1,600–2,200BEF. Special deals for long stays and for students.

♠ **Taxistop**: rue du Fossé-aux-Loups 28, Brussels 1000. ☎ (02) 223 2310. Fax: (02) 223 2232.

Website: www.taxistop.be. A booking centre for B&Bs, with 40-odd Brussels addresses available.

Campsites

⌂ **Bruxelles-Europe à ciel ouvert** (map I, C3): chaussée de Wavre 203, Brussels 1050. ☎ (02) 640 7967. Fax: (02) 648 2453. Open July and August only. Between the *quartier* Léopold and place Jourdan (bus Nos. 34 and 80 pass it). Two-person tent site: 600BEF. Tents only on this campsite, a stone's throw from the European institutions. It's next to a church with a garden, bang in the middle of a housing estate, but there's not much in the way of infrastructure. It's a bit on the spartan side, but it's perfect if location is more important than comfort, and handy if the youth hostels are full.

⌂ **Camping Wezembeek** (off map I, beyond D3): Warandeberg 52, Wezembeek-Oppem 1970, 10 kilometres (6 miles) east of the centre. ☎ (02) 782 1082. Take metro 1B towards Stockel, get off at Kraainem, then take the No. 30 bus (runs till 9pm; no Sunday service) and get out at Sint-Pieterplein; the campsite is a few minutes' walk from the church. It's family-oriented, surrounded by countryside and well equipped, although there's a bit of noise from the airport.

☆ Budget Youth Hostels

⌂ **Espace du Marais – Sleep Well** (map II, C2, **13**): rue du Damier 23, Brussels 1000, near rue Neuve and the City 2 shopping centre. ☎ (02) 218 5050. Fax: (02) 218 1313. Email: info@sleepwell.be. Metro: Rogier. Overnight stays 330–695BEF. It looks like a hotel, smells like a hotel and is run like a hotel, but offers the tariffs and services of a youth hostel without demanding a member's card. In the entrance hall,

adorned with plants and banners in the colours of the Belgian provinces, and decorated with a comic-strip fresco by Johan de Moor, you're greeted by a clone of the Manneken-Pis. Reception is open 24 hours a day, you'll get a magnetic card instead of a room key and facilities include a TV room with a billiard table, leather seats and a frieze of the Ommegang, a bar offering speciality beers and local culinary delights, a left-luggage area, a lift, and, on the first floor, a patio with a glass ceiling. There's a light and airy dining room, a buffet and a cybercafé; you can even change money here. The 170 beds are housed in functional rooms that sleep two, three, four or six, and the state of the shared bathrooms is beyond reproach, no matter how busy things get. In fact, there's only one backpacking feature here: in July and August, the main function room becomes a dormitory, with several dozen mattresses on the floor. Reservations are taken over the phone or by fax, and sheet rental is available if you don't have a sleeping bag. The staff, meanwhile, are hugely dedicated, and organize activities on some evenings. The hostel publishes a guide, *Brusswell*, with plenty of tips and discount coupons, while Gustave, a wonderful old chap who's retired and is a fount of knowledge and juicy stories, takes guided tours around the city every morning at 10am.

⌂ **Centre Vincent-Van-Gogh CHAB** (map II, D1, **10**): rue Traversière 8, Brussels 1210, just outside the Pentagon, near the Parc du Jardin Botanique. ☎ (02) 217 0158. Fax: (02) 219 7995. Website: www.ping.be/chab. Metro: Madou or Botanique; bus No. 61 from Gare du Nord and Nos. 65 or 66 from Gare Centrale. Overnight stays 550–585BEF, including breakfast; 10 per cent discount if you have an international student card, FITO or YMCA card. Eurocheques and credit cards accepted. This isn't an official youth hostel, but it's an essential address for backpackers in Brussels: bohemian, hip and, with 210 beds, the largest such establishment for young people in Belgium. It's divided into two sections on either side of the street, in a quiet area that hots up a bit at night. There's no curfew, and entry is by swipe card. Rooms sleep two, three or four (with showers and private loos), and there are dormitories with anything from six to 15 beds. Facilities include a kitchen, a pleasant veranda with wicker chairs in the common room, a gently splashing fountain, a tiny garden, a left-luggage room (free) and a cybercafé, as well as a billiard table, a phone booth that takes coins and a washing machine. Sheet hire is available, and you can get a hot meal in the evening. As if that wasn't enough, the staff are extremely friendly.

🛏 **Youth Hostel-Gîte d'Etape Jacques-Brel** (map II, D2, **11**): rue de la Sablonnière 30, Brussels 1000, northeast of the centre, about 15 minutes' walk from the Grand'Place. ☎ (02) 218 0187. Fax: (02) 217 2005. Website: brussels.brel@laj.be. Closed the second fortnight in December. Metro: Botanique or Madou. Overnight stays 420–800BEF; doubles 585BEF. Sheet hire 125BEF. One of the new generation of youth hostels, this spotless, purpose-built place, run by a dynamic and chatty team, has 175 beds in rooms that sleep between one and 14 people, with showers. Rooms in a new wing are almost luxurious: there's a great pad for eight with a mezzanine, as well as a room for two with a kitchenette. Reception is open until 1am, but you can come and go as you please thanks to the entry code. Among the hostel's many assets are a

bureau de change, washing machines, table-tennis and billiard tables. You won't go hungry, either: copious breakfasts are served in a railway-style café with benches, you can ask for a packed lunch, and, from 7pm to midnight, cheap meals are available. There's always something going on in the bar, and on Thursday evenings in July and August, the hostel puts on a free concert with a barbecue. This place is great.

🛏 **Youth Hostel Bruegel** (map III, B1, **12**): rue du Saint-Esprit 2, Brussels 1000, a 10-minute walk from Gare du Midi and Gare Centrale. ☎ (02) 511 0436. Fax: (02) 512 0711. Overnight stays 420–800BEF, including breakfast; more for non-members. Closed for cleaning 10am–2pm. Reception is open 7.30am–1am; curfew at 1am. Just behind the Église de la Chapelle, right in the heart of town, this place is ideal for exploring Brussels, but it isn't exactly a bundle of laughs. The staff are rather lugubrious, and the 45 rooms, with 134 beds in all, are uninspiring. If you're around between 6.30pm and 7pm, you can get a cheap meal; otherwise, there's not much else to say: sheet hire is available, there's an extortionate bureau de change and bicycles and motorbikes can be locked away at night.

🛏 **Youth Hostel 'de Bruxelles' Génération Europe**: rue de l'Éléphant 4, Brussels 1080, in a dull district north of the centre. ☎ (02) 410 3858. Fax: (02) 410 3905. Email: brussels.europe@laj.be. Reception 7–10am and 2pm–1am. No curfew. Overnight stays 420–695BEF, including breakfast. Closed first two weeks in January. Metro: Comte-de-Flandre. This peaceful, pleasant modern building is home to a functional, clean and soulless hostel. There are 162 beds in bright, clean, well-equipped and comfortable rooms that sleep two, four, six or eight, all with toilets and showers. Facilities on offer to guests include sheet hire, washing machines, a car park, a cafeteria, a terrace, a mini football ground and a garden, while the bar has a good choice of Belgian beers. A good fallback if you can't get into one of the more central hostels.

☆ Budget

♠ **Hôtel des Éperonniers** (map II, B3, **15**): rue des Éperonniers 1, Brussels 1000, a 30-second walk from the Grand'Place. ☎ (02) 513 5366. Fax: (02) 511 3230. Doubles 1,800–2,550BEF. This is a classic hang-out for students, backpackers and those of modest means, with the relaxed, anything-goes atmosphere as big a draw as the low prices. With rooms for one to six, this little hotel is perfectly comfortable: the carpet has seen better days, and the paint's a bit grubby, but the rooms are light and pleasant, and the large ones, including No. 18, which has a mezzanine (sleeps six), will delight your average bunch of students. Rooms with showers and/or toilets are more expensive. There's no restaurant, but there are several hundred eating options on your doorstep.

♠ **Duke of Windsor** (map III, C3, **17**): rue Capouillet 4, Brussels 1060. ☎ (02) 539 1819. Metro: Louise. Doubles with baths from 2,250BEF, including breakfast. No smoking. No credit cards. This cosy, welcoming place in a brick house is a real find. The flamboyant Madame Amanda Daenen runs her five rooms with a personal touch that seems to have gone out of fashion. It's a bit like visiting a great-aunt, so if you want to be well received, make sure you stick to the rules: stay at least two nights, phone a few weeks ahead to book, confirm your intentions in writing, and get there before 6pm on

weekends. In return, you'll get a big room with comfy chairs, a bathroom and breakfast (with fresh bread) in a carefully decorated room. You won't get better value for money in the Louise district.

♠ **Résidence Les Écrins** (map II, B2, **19**): rue du Rouleau 15, Brussels 1000, a stone's throw from Église Sainte-Catherine. ☎ (02) 219 3657. Fax: (02) 223 5740. Metro: Sainte-Catherine. Doubles from 1,800BEF (with sink) to 2,900BEF (toilet and bath), including breakfast. This well-kept hotel, in a quiet street near the delightful old harbour, has prettily refurbished rooms of wildly different sizes (take a look at several when you arrive). The two most expensive rooms are suites. Whatever you choose, this place adheres to the best traditions of hospitality, with friendly hosts and a pleasant atmosphere.

♠ **Hôtel Lloyd George** (map I, C4, **21**): avenue Lloyd George 12, Brussels 1000, on a quiet street opposite the Bois de la Cambre. ☎ (02) 648 3072. Fax: (02) 646 5361. Tram No. 93. Doubles with sink from 1,750BEF. An old-fashioned but good-value hotel in a characterful brick house with a bow window. The huge rooms for four, with bath and toilet, are a real bargain, although rooms with showers are less appealing. The restaurant on the ground floor attracts an artsy clientele who crowd the terrace in summer.

♠ **Résidence Galia** (map III, A2, **8**): place du Jeu de Balle 15, Brussels 1000, five minutes from Gare du Midi. ☎ (02) 502 4243. Fax: (02) 502 7619. Website: www.hotel.galia.com. Doubles 1,900–2,500BEF, with discounts at weekends. Metro: Porte de Hal; bus No. 48. Antiques-lovers will love this place, as they'll be woken by the sounds of the Marolles's legendary flea market at the crack of dawn, and can stagger out in search of the best bargains. Otherwise, the hotel offers small but pretty rooms, all well equipped and soundproof. The service is professional and straightforward: breakfast is not included, but it's worth paying extra to join the antiques dealers and get a slice of Brussels' real life.

â Hôtel La Grande Cloche (map III, A1, **7**): place Rouppe 10, Brussels 1000, halfway between Gare du Midi and the Grand'Place. ☎ (02) 512 6140. Fax: (02) 512 6591. Website: www.hotelgrandecloche.com.
Metro: Anneessens. Doubles 2,450–2,950BEF, including breakfast. The town house where Verlaine once shot Rimbaud in a fit of jealousy is now a rather spruce-looking hotel with views of old Brussels on the reception walls. It's not exactly irresistible, and the functional rooms are on the small side, but it's quiet, in a good area not far from the action, and has parking on the square.

☆☆ Moderate

â Hôtel Noga (map II, B2, **22**): rue du Béguinage 38, Brussels 1000, on a quiet road near the old docks. ☎ (02) 218 6763. Fax: (02) 218 1603. Email: info@nogahotel.com. Metro: De Brouckère or Sainte-Catherine. Doubles 2,600–3,300BEF, including breakfast. In a district with ghostly lighting after dark, this aristocrat among hotels offers a pleasant welcome and a sociable reception area and lounge. The bar is full of *Titanic* memorabilia – the ship, not the film – and other unusual touches include a telephone kiosk, a billiard room and a selection of games and comic strips on the piano, all for the use of guests. As you mount the stairs, a pageant of Belgian kings and queens looks down upon you, and, throughout the hotel, the walls have been recently stencilled in bright colours. The good-sized rooms for two,

three or four people are all different, but all have comfy beds, showers and toilets, hairdryers, TV and phone. There's also a secure car park (extra charge). The best value for money in this category.

â Hôtel Les Bluets (map III, B3, **20**): rue Berckmans 124, Brussels 1060, not far from Porte Louise and avenue Louise. ☎ (02) 534 3983. Fax: (02) 543 0970. Email: bluets @eudoramail.com. Metro: Hôtel-des-Monnaies. Doubles 2,000–2,650BEF, including breakfast. No smoking. You get a good sense of the place from the exterior: flowers at every window, and glazed tiles around the door. The couple who run this establishment have developed their house with a good deal of taste, choosing each object with loving care. The result is splendid, if a bit chocolate-box; you can almost hear the sound of music floating in the air. The cheapest rooms are those with shower only, and rooms for three people are also good value. At breakfast, everyone sits around one big table. A very good place to unwind, although everything feels a little too well drilled.

â Hôtel Opéra (map II, B3, **24**): rue Grétry 53, on a shop-lined street near the Bourse and La Monnaie. ☎ (02) 219 4343. Fax: (02) 219 1720. Doubles 3,150BEF. This friendly place has 50 newly decorated rooms, with bright, if unspectacular, décor and internet connections and safes as standard. If you're looking for peace and quiet, ask for a room at the back; if you need room to breathe, get one of the triple rooms. It's fairly comfortable, not bad value, and you'll get fresh croissants for breakfast. Not the most charming hotel in the capital, but handy if you can't find a room anyone else.

â Hôtel La Vieille Lanterne (map II, B3, opposite **93**): rue des Grands-Carmes 29, Brussels 1000, opposite the Manneken-Pis. ☎ (02) 512 7494. Fax: (02) 512 1397. Doubles 2,500BEF; breakfast 150BEF, and you can have it in bed for a small fee. This tiny place in a Renaissance house above a souvenir shop is more of a B&B than a real hotel, There are six clean, small rooms, two upstairs, with renovated furniture. It's a lively area, so expect plenty of noise throughout the night.

☆☆☆ Expensive

🛏 **Hôtel Welcome** (map II, B2, **23**): rue du Peuplier 5, Brussels 1000. ☎ (02) 219 9546. Fax: (02) 217 1887. Email: @hotelwelcome.com. Metro: Sainte-Cathérine. Doubles 2,600–3,600BEF; breakfast 300BEF. With 10 good-sized rooms, it may not be the smallest hotel in Brussels, as it claims, but the Welcome is certainly the best-loved in the area around place Sainte-Cathérine. The friendly couple who run the place will make you feel instantly at home, and will do everything in their power to make you comfortable. The service is beyond reproach, and it's a very pleasant place to stay. Guests get a small discount at La Truite d'Argent, the rather fine fish restaurant on the ground floor (set menus from 1,100BEF).

🛏 **Auberge Saint-Michel** (map II, B3, **25**): Grand'Place 15, Brussels 1000. ☎ (02) 511 0956. Fax: (02) 511 4600. Doubles from 5,100BEF, with huge reductions at the weekend. This is the only hotel on the Grand'Place, in the Maison de la Fortune, and it's only worth staying if you can get a room with a view of the square. These are big, airy and exceptionally clean, with toilets and showers, and the evening light show bathes the rooms in the most amazing colours. The Saint-Michel has more to offer than its views, though; after a much-needed face-lift, it's now a hotel to be reckoned with.

There's a car park two minutes' walk away.

🛏 **Hôtel La Légende** (map II, B3, **9**): rue du Lombard 35, Brussels 1000, between the Grand'Place and the Manneken-Pis. ☎ (02) 512 8290. Fax: (02) 512 3493. Email: hotel.lalegende@hotmail.com Metro: Bourse. Doubles 2,850–3,600BEF, with good weekend reductions from December to mid-January and in July and August. If location is your priority, you could do a lot worse than this hotel. The modern, functional rooms are decked out in bright colours, with light-wood floors, panelling and double-glazing, and prices are more than reasonable, especially given the location. There's also a suite for four with a put-me-up bed. Light floods into the breakfast room overlooking the courtyard, which has a pleasant garden.

🛏 **Hôtel Arenberg** (map II, C3, **6**): rue d'Assaut 15, Brussels 1000, near the Centre Belge de la Bande Dessinée. ☎ (02) 501 1616. Fax: (02) 501 1818. Metro: Gare Centrale. Doubles 4,500BEF, with big discounts at weekends; breakfast 750BEF. The 'weekend special' includes meals and free entry to the Centre Belge de la Bande Dessinée. This large four-star hotel attracts a business clientele during the week, but completely changes its character at the weekend. The clean, functional rooms have showers or bathrooms, and many can be converted into family rooms with put-me-up beds. Kids will love the décor, which is inspired by French and Belgian comic strips: a splendid rocket from the adventures of detective duo Blake and Mortimer stands in the entrance hall, and the bar carries on the cartoon theme; the rooms and hallways are decorated with pictures, lithographs and book covers; and information for guests is given in speech bubbles.

Guests can use the hotel's gym, and if you opt for breakfast, you'll find the buffet well stocked. Even if you're not staying, pop in at lunch time to see the décor and enjoy a good-value *plat du jour*.

🛏 **Hôtel La Madeleine** (map II, C3, **26**): rue de la Montagne 22, Brussels 1000, on a delightful little square just off the Grand'Place. Metro: Gare Centrale. ☎ (02) 513 2973. Fax: (02) 502 1350. Doubles 2,595–3,495BEF, including breakfast. This tiny hotel with a charming Renaissance facade somehow manages to cram in 53 rooms of all sizes, including some triples, with a range of facilities that reflects the range of prices. The service is routine, and the rooms are pretty nondescript, but they're comfortable, and the central location makes this a good option.

🛏 **De Boeck's Hôtel** (map IV, A1, **28**): rue Veydt 40, Brussels 1050, in a residential area near avenue Louise. ☎ (02) 537 4033. Fax: (02) 534 4037. Trams Nos. 91 and 92. Doubles 1,600–3,600BEF, with weekend discounts. Metro: Louise. The place exudes character and a sense of nobility, with the fine staircase, great hall and huge, if somewhat faded, rooms evoking former opulence. The quiet rooms in the rear section, called the 'Villa', have been completely refurbished, and would grace a deluxe hotel. Those at the front are pretty good, too: backpackers may baulk at the prices, but those in search of creature comforts will want for nothing, and there are several rooms for three or four. There's a wide choice of facilities in the rooms, which explains the differing prices: make sure you specify your requirements when you book. Breakfast is a little institutional.

🛏 **Hôtel Sema** (map II, B3, next to **68**): rue des Harengs 6-8, Brussels 1000, on a narrow street that leads onto the Grand'Place. ☎ (02) 514 0760. Fax: (02) 548 9039. Metro: Gare-Centrale. Doubles, 5,000BEF, including breakfast; 3,750BEF at the weekend. The Sema is a former town house that's been turned into a very comfortable hotel with sober, Scandinavian-style décor. The 10 rooms have all mod cons, including marble bathrooms, and a 1900s look; there's also a suite with its own terrace. It's good value for money, but light sleepers should give it a miss: the hotel is next to a nightclub, and the walls are not particularly soundproof.

🛏 **Hôtel Atlas** (map II, A2, **5**): rue du Vieux-Marché-aux-Grains 30, Brussels 1000, in the trendy district around rue Antoine-Dansaert. ☎ (02) 502 6006. Fax: (02) 502 6935. Metro: Sainte-Cathérine. Doubles 4,950BEF, with 30–40 per cent discounts at weekends. This business hotel has 88 modern, comfortable, light and airy rooms, all decorated in beige and blue, with modern but characterless paintings on the walls. The quietest rooms are at the back. The breakfast room, in the basement, includes a section of the original town walls. The Atlas won't take your breath away, but it's useful if you can't find anything cheaper.

🛏 **Hôtel Ustel** (off map III beyond A1-2, **27**): square de l'Aviation 6-8, Brussels 1070, five minutes' walk from Gare du Midi. ☎ (02) 520 6053. Fax: (02) 520 3328. Email: hotel.ustel@ping.be. Metro: Gare du Midi. Doubles 4,300BEF, including breakfast, with discounts at weekends and every day in July and August. This business hotel is handy for Eurostar travellers, but the area, dominated by the six-lane boulevard du Midi, is rather off-putting, making it a fallback rather than a first choice. The rooms are slightly shabby, but offer all mod cons, and there's a courtyard garden. The hotel sometimes hosts exhibitions of engravings of old Brussels, and there's a rather expensive restaurant, La Grande Écluse, in a wonderful 19th-century industrial building (three-course set menu 750BEF).

☆☆☆☆ Splash Out

⚱ **Hôtel Le Dixseptième** (map II, C3, **29**): rue de la Madeleine 25, Brussels 1000, a stone's throw from the Grand'Place. ☎ (02) 502 5744. Fax: (02) 502 6424. Metro: Gare Centrale. Doubles from 6,600BEF, with discounts at week-

ends. One of the few truly delightful hotels in the Belgian capital. The muffled elegance, warm welcome and excellent service befit the former residence of a Spanish ambassador. The entrance hall is sumptuous, and the 12 comfortable suites are beautifully furnished, with reproductions of Old Masters on the walls; some have balconies and views of the spire of the Hôtel de Ville. There's an interior courtyard, and it's extremely quiet for a city centre hotel.

WHERE TO EAT

Brussels has thousands of excellent eateries, from no-nonsense brasseries to palaces of *haute cuisine*. You'll eat well almost everywhere you go: listings have been limited to the Pentagon and the main tourist attractions, as that's where you'll be spending most of your time, but Ixelles, Saint-Gilles, Saint-Josse, Schaerbeek and Uccle are all happy hunting grounds for the gourmets among you.

Brussels is famous as a gastronomic paradise, but you don't have to splash out to get great grub. The roads leading off the Grand'Place are crammed with ghastly snack bars, but there are plenty of little cafés and restaurants offering simple, tasty food that'll set you up for a strenuous afternoon of sightseeing. Even the best restaurants usually offer a cheap lunch-time *plat du jour*, and you won't go hungry if you order just one course: in fact, portions are so big that you'll be hard put to finish it.

The sweet-toothed should make a beeline for Brussels' *boulangeries* and *pâtisseries*, where they'll find plenty of tempting local goodies. Try the buttery *speculoos* biscuits and *cramique*, with raisins, or pop into the legendary Dandoy (on rue du Beurre, near the Grand'Place, for *pain à la grecque*.

Whelks

If you're keen to sample the local snacks, they don't come more local than *caricoles*: tubs of whelks sold at temporary stalls, which should be eaten with a glass of white wine. It's a quintessential, if fast-fading Brussels experience, even if they do come from Brittany. There are always stalls on place de la Chapelle (at the edge of the Sablon and Marolles districts) and, on weekends, at the corner of rue Haute and rue des Renards.

Chips (*frites*)

Although it's famous as the national dish, the Belgians don't eat chips all the time! Still, they're proud of their *frites* (*fritkotten* in Dutch), and there's always a queue at the best of them. You can choose from a score of sauces, but mayonnaise is the classic accompaniment.

✕ **Maison Antoine** (map I, C3): place Jourdan, near the Parc du Cinquantenaire. Open 11.30am–1am (to 2am on Saturday and Sunday). The Belgian press makes this out to be the ultimate *friture*, while *The New York Times* heralded its chips as 'the best *frites* in the world'. You get the usual cornet of chips wrapped in three thicknesses of paper and smothered in sauce, although a sign of this place's success is that it occupies a fixed stall rather than the traditional van. Apart from chips, Antoine serves kebabs, *fricandelles* (sausages fried in oil) and the ultimate fast food, the *mitraillette*: a baguette stuffed with meat, lettuce, tomatoes, a choice of sauces and, needless to say, chips. The same menu as a million other chip shops, then, but here everything is homemade.

☆ Budget

As well as cafeterias and cheap snack bars, Brussels has an abundance of Greek and Turkish kebab shops, which offer a range of filled pittas. Rue du Marché-aux-Fromages (map II, B3), near the Grand'Place, is lined with takeaway joints: while it won't get your taste buds tingling, the fare on offer should line the most demanding of stomachs.

✕ **Fin de Siècle** (map II, between A2-A3 and B2-B3): rue des Chartreux 9, Brussels 1000. ☎ (02) 513 5123. Open every day except Monday, from 4.30pm. Main courses 300–450BEF. Meals 6pm–1am. Next door to Le Greenwich, a chess bar frequented by René Magritte, this great restaurant has a basic décor that's considerably enhanced by some beautiful art-nouveau glass. It's a bit noisy when it's crowded, but the atmosphere is typical of a *stamcafé* (a bar with its own bunch of regulars). Beer is cheap, and you can sip a glass while you read the papers or sample one of the daily specials, which are chalked up on the blackboard. The food is homely – large portions of stuffed chicory, rabbit cooked in beer and a few Mediterranean and Far Eastern dishes, followed by a choice of simple desserts. The wine list is well balanced, and the hot chocolate is without peer. Impish waitresses pirouette between the tables as they serve locals trendsters and tourists exploring this up-and-coming district.

✕ **Arteaspoon**: 32 rue des Chartreux. ☎ (02) 513 5117. Open Monday to Friday 11.30am–6pm, Saturday noon–7pm. You can feast your eyes as well as your stomach at this art gallery-cum-snack bar. The gallery hosts temporary exhibitions, while the snacks include sandwiches with an inventive selection of fillings, soup of the day, tapas, the pizza-like *pissaladière*, tajines and guacamole. On fine days, you can sit outdoors.

✕ **Mokafé** (map II, C3): in the Galeries Saint-Hubert, Brussels 1000. ☎ (02) 511 7870. Open 8am–midnight. Main courses 200–300BEF. This popular café-brasserie, in the first covered arcade in Europe, was once a coffee grinder's. The décor is not especially distinctive, but this extraordinary place has survived all manner of fads while remaining true to itself. The regulars are old ladies in mink coats and harassed local workers, but you'll see plenty of tourists slouched in wicker chairs on the terrace, soaking up the atmosphere of days gone by or tucking into pasta or a salad. On the first and third Monday of each month, there's a 'philosophers' café' at 8pm, although you'll need a good com-

mand of French if you want to split
hairs about Socrates or Hegel.

✗ **La Galettière** (map II, B3, **32**):
rue des Pierres 53, Brussels 1000,
just behind the Hôtel de Ville. ☎ (02)
512 8480. Closed Tuesday and
Sunday. This delightful little place
serves mouthwatering Breton
crêpes with Quebecois flavourings
in a fairy-tale setting. A sweet or
savoury crêpe costs about 200BEF,
but you won't be able to resist
having more than one. To drink, try
a bowl of cider or a Canadian
beer (some of which are peat-
smoked, like whiskey). The service
is frank and direct, in a lumber-
jack sort of way, but that doesn't
deter the locals from queueing for a
table.

✗ **Le Pain Quotidien** (map III, B1
53): rue des Sablons 11, Brussels
1000; rue Antoine-Dansaert 16 (map
II, B2); and branches across the
capital. ☎ (02) 513 5154. Open from
7.30am (Sunday 8am) to 7.30pm.
With branches across Europe and
even in New York, Le Pain Quotidien
is something of a Belgian success
story. It started out as a bakery
making traditional loaves, with three
types of bread, pastries and tarts,
and has remained more or less faithful to its original formula. You can buy
freshly baked bread, croissants or
takeaway sandwiches, or take your
place at the long table, where you sit
cheek by jowl with the other customers and eat a salad or a freshly
prepared sandwich of fromage
blanc, beef and basil or Bayonne
ham. Unfortunately, breakfast is
rather disappointing, and the popularity of the place has rather dimmed
its charm, with a scrum of figure-
fixated women congregating there
for lunch. If you can keep hunger at
bay, it's more relaxed after 3pm.

✗ **Athènes** (map III, A2, **10**): rue
d'Argonne 22, Brussels 1000, near
Gare du Midi. ☎ (02) 538 2113.
Open 11am–midnight. Closed Mon-

day. *Plat du jour* 220BEF. If it's
quantity, not quality, you're after,
this is the best address in town,
and it's always crowded, especially
after the Sunday-morning Midi market. Once you've secured a table,
venture into the kitchen to choose
your meal from the pans bubbling
gently on the hob. The Mediterranean cuisine isn't especially refined,
but it does the job nicely. On the
same street, you'll find L'Athanas
(closed Tuesday), which has the
same menu.

✗ **L'École Buissonnière** (map II,
D1, **47**): rue Traversière 13, Brussels
1210, northeast of the centre.
☎ (02) 217 0165. Open noon–
2.30pm and 6–10.30pm. Closed
Saturday and Sunday. *Plat du jour*
350BEF. It's well worth making a
detour to this establishment if you're
looking for good food at bargain
prices. For 600BEF, you can get a
starter, a main course and a dessert
– all prepared with panache, especially the puddings – and drinks as
well. A few well-chosen wines are
suggested on the menu. The simple
décor is light and alluring, and the
service is professional and disar-
mingly friendly. If you're really
strapped for cash, try the lunchtime omelettes, salads and pasta.

✗ **L'Ultime Atome** (map III, D2,
48): rue Saint-Boniface 14, Brussels
1050. ☎ (02) 511 1367. Open 9am–
12.30am (11am–2am at the weekend). *Plat du jour* 350BEF. One of
Brussels' liveliest restaurants, this
huge yellow room with panelling,
worn parquet flooring and a fan is
popular with students and families
alike. You can get a late breakfast,
sample one of the tasty daily specials, pop in for a late-night snack or
just have a drink and watch the
world go by. The food is always
good, and there's a wide choice of
beers as well.

✗ **Hémisphères** (map II, C3, **43**):
rue de l'Écuyer 65, Brussels 1000,

near the Galeries Saint-Hubert. ☎ (02) 513 9370. Open 11am–10.30pm, Saturday 6pm–midnight. Closed Sunday. Main courses about 300BEF. The décor at this restaurant-cum-cultural centre is a cheerfully Arabic affair, with low sofas, Moroccan lamps, drapes, big tables with coloured candle-holders, pictures straight out of a harem, and photos and portraits of late-19th-century bedouins. The food has a North African flavour, including tajines and couscous as well as Lebanese mezze, Chinese noodles and Balkan yoghurt, and you can wash it down with a slightly dodgy organic wine or an *infusion* (herb or fruit tea). Unfortunately, the food is on the bland side, and the service is a bit erratic. Still, the restaurant's profits go to needy children, and the multicultural atmosphere and excellent music make up for the kitchen's shortcomings. There are concerts on Friday evenings.

✕ **Waka Moon Dibi-Groove Café** (map II, B3, **50**): rue des Éperonniers 60, Brussels 1000. ☎ (02) 502 1032. Closed Monday. Main courses 450BEF. Run by a Senegalese woman from the Ardennes, this place has a bit of a colonial feel. There are mountains of fruit in the window, so it's no surprise that excellent fruit juices, tropical cocktails or caipirinhas are among the specialities. The décor is Flanders meets Africa, with 17th-century chairs covered in fake zebra skin, but the cooking is mainly Congolese: grilled chicken wings, fried bananas, tilapia and chicken *moambé*, a peanut sauce with palm oil. For dessert, there's ice cream or sorbet.

☆☆ Moderate

✕ **'t Kelderke** (map II, B3, **38**): Grand'Place 15, Brussels 1000. ☎ (02) 513 7344. Open noon–2am.

Closed mid-June to mid-July. Full meals about 1,000BEF; *plat du jour* 295BEF (Monday to Friday until 3pm only). Mind your head as you climb down the narrow stairway into the beautiful vaulted cellar of the biggest house on the Grand'Place. Given the location, the setting and cuisine are surprisingly authentic, which explains why so many local business types pop in at lunch time to wolf down unfussy *plats du jour* such as beef braised in beer and traditional Belgian black pudding. The main menu is 100 per cent Belgian: prawn croquettes, *stoemp* (mash) with sausage, rabbit cooked in *gueuze* beer and Belgian waffles. It's not *haute cuisine*, but it's tasty enough, and you can do a lot worse for more money in this area.

✕ **Bij den Boer** (map II, A2, **35**): quai aux Briques 60, Brussels 1000. ☎ (02) 512 6122. Open noon–3pm and 6–11pm. Closed Sunday and public holidays. *Plat du jour* 250BEF; four-course set menu 750BEF. Fish restaurants abound on the pretty quai aux Briques, but most are expensive, average, or both. The exception is this timeless café-restaurant, with a blue-tiled facade and white-haired regulars. There are few frills and even fewer pretensions, but it has bags of character, and the jolly service and delicious fish dishes have been drawing the locals here for decades. The poached cod, fried plaice and sole are fresh and simply served, and you'll get excellent mussels in season.

✕ **Le Volle Gas** (map III, D3, **55**): place Fernand-Cocq 21, Brussels 1050. ☎ (02) 502 8917. Open for lunch and dinner (until 1am). Closed Sunday lunch time. Main courses 350–500BEF; full meal about 900BEF. A classic Brussels bistro with a cheerful atmosphere, especially on a Saturday evening, when it lives up to its name: 'Full throttle'.

The retro décor includes benches, marble-topped tables, enamel plaques, old advertisements and a pretty tiled stove, while the menu offers a host of Belgian specialities: s*toemp*, black pudding, veal brains, *ballekes à la marollienne* (meatballs) and steak tartare prepared before your eyes. In summer, you can sit outside and admire Ixelles town hall, once the home of the singer La Malibran.

✗ **La Grande Porte** (map III, B1, **39**): rue Notre-Seigneur 9, Brussels 1000. ☎ (02) 512 8998. Open for lunch and dinner (until 2am, or 3am on Saturday). Closed Saturday lunchtime and Sunday. Main courses 400BEF; full meal about 900BEF. It's not exactly off the tourist trail, but this is a classic Marolles establishment, and remains as warm and welcoming as ever. The plain walls, painted wooden plates, pianola, lanterns and mirrors with sculpted frames are quintessentially Brussels, as is the cuisine: *ballekes à la marollienne* (meatballs with tomato), endives *au gratin*, *stoemp* of the day (vegetable mash with sausage). It's at its most atmospheric in the evening, when everyone stays around till late, sometimes very late, over La Grande Porte's deservedly famous onion soup.

✗ **Indigo** (map III, A-B2, **40**): rue Blaes 160, Brussels 1000. ☎ (02) 511 3897. Open 10am–3pm on weekdays and 9.30am–4pm at the weekend. Closed Monday and Tuesday. With wonderful, brightly coloured bric-à-brac everywhere, Indigo is more like an antiques shop than a restaurant, with plain tables, garden chairs, plenty of candles and a tiny balcony at the top. Jazz plays gently in the background as you tuck into a tasty tart (285–310BEF), a salad or the soup of the day, followed by homemade *pâtisserie*.

There's a special 'flea-market brunch' on Sunday.

✗ **Le Bazaar** (map III, B2, **57**): rue des Capucins 63, Brussels 1000. ☎ (02) 511 2600. Open 7.30pm–1am. Closed Monday. Brunch on Sunday. Full meal about 800BEF. Bazaar calls itself 'a centre where the arts and cultural traditions of Brussels' different communities meet', which sounds like a recipe for disaster. Fortunately, it lives up to the description. The setting is an old warehouse hung with drapes, lit with old glass lamps and furnished with a mixture of Afghan chairs, stuffing-less sofas and animal skins. There's even a hot-air balloon above the bar. The daily specials mix southeast Asian cuisine and Mediterranean flavours, and the music, which could be anything from Dixieland to Arab melodies, burbles unobtrusively in the background. There are regular live bands, and you can sit out on the roof terrace on fine summer evenings. It attracts a hip crowd, especially for the members-only club nights (Thursday, Friday and Saturday), but it's not at all precious.

✗ **Chez Jean** (map II, B3, **42**): rue des Chapeliers 6, Brussels 1000, just off the Grand'Place. ☎ (02) 511 9815. Open noon–2.30pm and 7–10pm. Closed Sundays, Mondays and in June. *Plat du jour* 325BEF. This wonderfully old-fashioned restaurant has been unostentatiously ticking over for several decades, based on nothing more than good, solid food and the personal touch. Chez Jean's owners know better than to tamper with a winning formula, whether it's the worn benches, the waitresses' dated uniforms or the traditional cuisine: *carbonade flamande* (braised beef stew), mussels, rabbit in cherry beer and chicken *waterzooi* (creamy chicken stew with vegetables). The plates are heaped, the cooking is good and wholesome, and there are two cheap four-course menus. No wonder it's so popular with the locals, and with those tourists lucky enough to have found it.

✕ **L'Achepot** (map II, B2, **58**): place Sainte-Catherine 1, Brussels 1000. ☎ (02) 511 6221. Closed Sundays. *Plat du jour* 295BEF. Credit cards not accepted. The café décor evokes the Brussels of yesteryear, complete with little bistro tables, benches that'll numb your bum and a sloping floor. As for the nosh, you have to like your offal. The blackboard sets the tone, with tempting suggestions like solid black pudding, *stoemp* with bacon, grilled *andouillette* (tripe sausages) or ox kidneys. If you can't stomach any of that, try the fish of the day. It can get a bit cramped at times, but there's a good-sized terrace in summer.

✕ **Les Brassins** (map III, C3, **34**): rue Keyenveld 36, Brussels 1050. ☎ (02) 512 6999. Open Monday to Friday 5pm–2am. Closed in August. Set menu 360BEF. A café-restaurant in a quiet corner of central Ixelles, where the glossy walls are decorated with enamelled plaques. Les Brassins attracts a young crowd who seem to be sold on the copious portions of tasty Belgian cuisine, cooked by the owner herself. Either that, or it's the nonstop 1970s music.

✕ **Halloween** (map II, B3, **51**): rue des Grands-Carmes 10, Brussels 1000, not far from the Manneken-Pis. ☎ (02) 514 1256. Open noon–2.30pm, and 7–11.30pm (until 3am on Friday and Saturday). Closed Monday lunchtime and Sunday. Main courses 500–600BEF. Vampires and bats greet you at the entrance, the candlestick holders are skulls, and the waiters are dressed as monks: this is a devilishly weird restaurant, but it's original and far less gimmicky than you might

fear. The three rooms are always packed: unsurprising given the low prices, especially at lunch time, when there's a two-course *plat du jour*. The menu is laced with over-the-top black humour: 'massacre of cellular tissues' is steak tartare, 'slab of tombstone' is thickly cut steak and summer-fruit bavarois becomes 'the perfect haemoglobin'. Unfortunately, success has made the staff a bit complacent, and the service isn't as friendly as it used to be. It's also dead slow, so skip it if you're pressed for time. You can book the crypt for parties (up to six people); if it's someone's birthday, let them know when you book and they'll give you a little present.

✕ **Chez Agnès** (map III, B2, opposite **85**): rue Charles-Hanssens 5, Brussels 1000, near the Sablon. ☎ (02) 502 0680. Open noon until the evening. Main courses 500BEF. This intimate café has wonderful décor inspired by Jules Verne, with *trompe l'oeil* paintings, bookshelves filled with the great man's works and 1930s lights. The tiny tables are crammed together so that as many people as possible can enjoy the simple but inventive cuisine – salads, pasta, shrimp croquettes, pittas and the like. The desserts are truly excellent, and in fine weather, you can nurse a beer on the terrace.

☆☆☆ Expensive

✕ **Stekerlapatte** (map III, B3, **45**): rue des Prêtres 4, Brussels 1000, behind the Palais de Justice. ☎ (02) 512 8681. Open 7pm–1am. Closed Monday. Full meal about 1,100BEF; *plat du jour* 400BEF. In the heart of the Marolles, this authentic-looking bistro attracts a good cross section of the capital's citizens: youngish Eurocrats, locals and bourgeois folk from the Sablon jostle to be served by smiling waitresses who weave between the tables and run from one room to the other, laden with plates of steaming veal kidneys, *ballekes*, steak, shrimp croquettes and eels in green sauce. You'll be won over by the friendliness and warmth of this popular place, but be warned that one course will be more than enough for most appetites.

✕ **Chez Henri** (map II, A2, **53**): rue de Flandre 113, Brussels 1000. ☎ (02) 219 6415. Open for lunch and dinner (until midnight). Full meal about 1,500BEF. The panelling on the walls is worthy of an Ardennes chalet, and there's an outside counter where you can buy chips. But don't be deceived: the décor may be banal, but this place is always heaving, even on weekdays. The reason is obvious once you've tried the food: Chez Henri imports *kouroush* caviar from Iran, and has been dishing up eels, mussels, oysters and lobster since 1922. Everything is fresh and simple, and the wine list is impeccable. It's not cheap, but you can stick to a bowl of mussels and a beer without incurring the waitresses' wrath.

✕ **Chez Vincent** (map II, B3, **46**): rue des Dominicains 8-10, Brussels 1000. ☎ (02) 511 2303. Open for lunch and dinner (until 11.30pm; 10.30pm on Sunday). Closed beginning of January and beginning of August. Three-course set lunch 675BEF (until 2.45pm); otherwise about 1000BEF. It may be pricey and a little bit touristy, but eating here is an experience everyone should have once, if only to admire the magnificent art-nouveau décor. You have to cross the kitchens to get to the dining room, and the walls and ceiling are covered in tiles depicting land- and seascapes; at the back, fishermen fight the stormy seas. Even the waiters are decked out in nautical gear. The menu is carnivore heaven, with excellent beef in beer, chicken dishes and splendid steaks, and the service is

excellent. Unfortunately, the prices on the wall date from 1912.

✕ **Le Bermuchet** (map III, B2, **52**): rue Haute 198, Brussels 1000. ☎ (02) 513 8882. Open for lunch and dinner (until midnight). Closed Saturday lunchtime and Sunday evening. Full meal about 800BEF; *plat du jour* 295BEF, with a lunch menu at 495BEF. This old café in the Marolles has been transformed into a hip restaurant, although the stencils on the wall, the squeaky flooring, the candles and the chairs hanging from the ceiling are rough-edged enough for would-be bohemian Sablon types to feel at home. As for the cuisine, it's good, reliable and unpretentious, with a strong French influence and plenty of vegetarian options. Service is friendly, and the house wine is a rather cheeky Chilean.

✕ **In 't Spinnekopke** (map II, A3, **44**): place du Jardin-aux-Fleurs 1, Brussels 1000. ☎ (02) 511 8695. Open for lunch and dinner, noon–3pm and 6–11pm (midnight on Friday and Saturday). Closed Sunday and holidays. Full meal about 1,200BEF; *plat du jour* 295BEF. In a delightful flowery house, the 'Little Spider's Head' has been serving good Belgian cuisine and excellent beers since the 18th century. The *plats du jour* are a godsend for those on a low budget: beef or rabbit in *gueuze* beer, *waterzooî* (fish cooked with vegetables in a creamy sauce), chicken *Spinnekopke* and many more. The menu is in French, but you're likely to hear your fellow diners chatting away in the local dialect. If you can, sit in the downstairs dining room; it's like being in your great-aunt's front room, old-fashioned and unapologetically bourgeois. In fine weather, the terrace has a nice, villagey feel.

✕ **La Taverne du Passage** (map II, C3): galerie de la Reine 30, Brussels 1000. ☎ (02) 512 3731. Open every day noon–midnight continuously. Closed Wednesday and Thursday in June and July. Full meal about 850BEF, excluding drinks; *plat du jour* 395BEF. An art-deco masterpiece that dates from 1928, this Brussels institution is the last word in after-theatre eating. The slightly affected, retro style is perfect for the regulars: portly gentlemen and ladies with bouffant hairdos that the wheezing air conditioning can't displace. Menu staples include *toasts aux oeufs de mulet* (mullet eggs on toast), shrimp croquettes, sauerkraut and steak tartare. Even the house wine is classy, although the chips are frozen, which rather lowers the tone. Nonetheless, this place is well worth putting on your Sunday best for.

✕ **Le Pré Salé** (map II, A2, **36**): rue de Flandre 22, Brussels 1000. ☎ (02) 513 4323. Closed Monday and in June. Set menu 995BEF; *plat du jour* 295–400BEF. You can't get more local than this old butcher's shop with tiling, benches, and an open-plan kitchen. The menu sticks to the classics – shrimp croquettes, Flemish-style rabbit and great mussels in season. On Friday evenings and the first Saturday in every month, the staff put on an outrageous mime show, during which the waiters sing along to a pre-recorded tape. It's an absolute scream. Book a table in advance if you want to see the show.

☆☆☆☆ Splash Out

✕ **La Roue d'Or** (map II, B3, **49**): rue des Chapeliers 26, Brussels 1000, just off the Grand'Place. ☎ (02) 514 2554. Open every day from noon to 12.30am. Closed mid-July to mid-August. Starters 400BEF, main dishes 650BEF; *plat du jour* 395BEF. Booking recommended. This 1900s-style brasserie, with Magritte-inspired murals, old-fashioned lamps, bevelled mirrors

and a wonderful silver sideboard, is a favourite haunt of the local movers and shakers, but the atmosphere's pleasantly relaxed, with staff who keep smiling when they're working at top speed. The accomplished Franco-Belgian fare fits the setting, with generous helpings of *andouillette*, cod steaks, grilled sole in an olive-oil purée, steak, *stoemp* with sausage, stuffed leg of rabbit or chicken *waterzooï*.

✕ **Le Petit Boxeur** (map II, B3, **41**): rue Borgval 3, Brussels 1000, between the Bourse and place Saint-Géry. ☎ (02) 511 4000. Open from Tuesday to Saturday from 8pm. Full meal more than 1,500BEF. It's easy to miss this discreet little restaurant, as a gold velvet curtain hides the entrance. Inside, you'll find a refined décor inspired by the Ancient World. The short menu is constantly changing, as the mission here is to offer astonishingly inventive *haute cuisine*, with the pleasure of sharing new discoveries as important as the ringing of the till. If you fancy yourself as a gourmet, you'll come away well satisfied. Past triumphs include caviar pâté, vegetable *tartare*, squid lasagne, sea bass on a bed of lentils and a fabulous *osso buco*. For dessert, meanwhile, the ladlesful of *mousse au chocolat* are indescribably good. The wine list lives up to the restaurant's ambitions.

✕ **Bleu de Toi** (map III, B1, **56**): rue des Alexiens 73, Brussels 1000. ☎ (02) 502 4371. Open noon–2pm, and 7.30–11pm (to midnight on Friday and Saturday). Closed Saturday lunchtime and Sunday. Full meal about 1,200BEF; two-course lunch 395BEF. This cosy little place is perfect for an intimate tête-à-tête. The ground floor has exposed brickwork and an open fire, while the first floor is decorated with *trompe l'oeils*. There's also a marvellous little balcony. House specials include *bintje* potatoes with all sorts of stuffings, and half or whole lobsters in all sorts of sauces.

✗ **Amadeus** (map IV, A1, **54**): rue Veydt 13, Brussels 1050; in Ixelles, on the art-nouveau circuit. ☎ (02) 538 3427. Open noon–3pm and 6pm–1am. Closed Monday and Saturday lunchtime. Full meals 1,000BEF, excluding drinks; weekday set lunch 475BEF; Sunday brunch 650BEF. This outrageously baroque establishment looks like a mystical palace. You start in a little garden, then pass under the glass roof, into an electric-blue area that's guarded by impassive stone statues. Continue through the bar, with its olive-green tiles, to the dining area, decked out in black and decorated with facades of miniature houses, lit up to look like a display of Chinese lanterns. The atmosphere is fantastic, but the brasserie-style fare is surprisingly down to earth: caramelized spare ribs, beef *carpaccio* and salmon steaks in honey and lime. More style than substance, then, but there's a good choice of beers and the wine cellar is one of the best in town.

✗ **La Tour d'y Voir** (map III, B1, **59**): place du Grand Sablon 8-9, Brussels 1000. ☎ (02) 511 4043. Closed Monday and from mid-July to mid-August. Full meal 1,500BEF; lunch-time menu 695BEF. Booking recommended. Even by Brussels standards, the setting is spectacular: a 14th-century chapel on the first floor of a Sablon gallery, transformed into a gastronomic temple. The service is charming, and the inventive French-inspired cuisine uses wonderfully fresh ingredients. For 1,000BEF, including wine, the three-course 'surprise menu' gives the chef the chance to bring his talent to bear on the finest market produce. The price of the deluxe five-course menu (1,700BEF in the evening) slumps by 1,000BEF at lunchtime. Amen to that.

✗ **Le Stekerlapatte**, **In 't Spinnekopke**, **La Taverne du Passage** and **Chez Vincent** (grilled meat a speciality here), described in the cheaper categories, also offer the possibility of a posh meal in the evening.

WHERE TO DRINK

If you're looking for crazy, crazy nights, then Brussels doesn't pack the same punch as the fleshpots of Antwerp, Liège or Ghent. But there are few cities in the world with so many convivial watering holes in such a small space, and an extended session in the city centre is one of Brussels' greatest pleasures. For starters, there's an all-hours drinking culture – you'll often see older workers having a beer for breakfast, while in summer, bar terraces across the city are buzzing well into the wee small hours. On top of that, the quality of most Belgian beers means that boozing isn't a means to an end, but an experience to be savoured. And whatever your preferred environment – from period pieces to posing paradises – you'll be able to find something that fits the bill.

Some of the bars in the city centre, especially on the Grand'Place, are squarely aimed at tourists, but there are plenty of locals-only joints where you can get a sense of how the locals live it up. The expat communities tend to congregate at the city's 15-odd Irish bars, although younger Euro types mix with fashionable Flemings in the trendy bars of Rue Dansaert and the Saint-Géry district. If you're not sure which of the bars below will suit you, however, your best bet is to crawl the centre until you find somewhere comfortable, then stay there until they kick you out.

A few of these beer and *zwanze* temples are on a guided walk organized by the **Bus Bavard** (*see* 'Useful addresses and information'). This offers you three hours of drinking and discovery, in the company of voluble and passionate guides – with two drinks thrown in for good measure.

♟ **Le Cirio** (map II, B3): rue de la Bourse 18-20, Brussels 1000, opposite the Bourse. ☎ (02) 512 1395. Open until 1am. Belle Époque Brussels has largely faded from view, but this fantastic local institution remains pretty much as it was in the capital's heyday – indeed the 80-something customers, who come with their dogs, may well have experienced the era. The eclectic style is here in all its artificial splendour, with stucco painted to resemble Cordoba leather, dark glass and polished brasses. It's worth visiting the loos just to see the porcelain.

✕ **Le Falstaff** (map II, B3, **37**): rue Henri-Maus 17-23, Brussels 1000, opposite the Bourse. ☎ (02) 511 9877. Open 8am–3am. Shock waves ran through the capital a few years back when this legendary brasserie, a deserved fixture on the city's tourist trail, fell into deep financial trouble. It was snapped up by a French group Monte-Cristo, whose plans to create an on-site salsa bar provoked howls of protest. Fortunately, they've left the art-nouveau décor intact: mirrors with bevelled edges, ceilings decorated with embossed paper, paste-glass chandeliers and wonderful stained glass at the back, depicting the Fat Knight downing a cup of sack. The place was designed in 1903 by a disciple of Victor Horta, and despite the new owners, not much has changed: the pricey food is not as good as it used to be, and the Cuban music in the background is pleasant but inappropriate, but it still has a fantastic heated terrace in winter and a wonderful range of beers. One thing that could do with changing is the patronizing service.

♟ **À la Bécasse** (map II, B3, **83**): rue Tabora 11, Brussels 1000. ☎ (02) 511 0006. Open until 1am (to 2am on Friday and Saturday). 'Bécasse' means woodcock, and the pavement outside this place bears an image of the bird. At the end of a passage, you'll find this archetypal Brussels tavern. Once the haunt of the author Guy de Maupassant, it has a lively, rustic feel and offers a good range of local beers – *lambic*, Blanche de Bruxelles and *gueuze* – as well as simple yet marvellously tasty food: it's great for a lunchtime snack. It's a bit of a tourist trap, though and the waiters can be a bit snooty.

♟ **À l'Imaige de Notre-Dame** (map II, B3, **84**): impasse des Cadeaux 3, Brussels 1000, tucked away off rue du Marché-aux-Herbes. ☎ (02) 219 4249. Open noon–1am or later, depending on customers. This friendly old bar, with heavy beams and pewter tankards on display, is great for a pit stop as you pound the pavements of the Îlot Sacré. The house speciality is spaghetti bolognaise, which comes in gargantuan heaps and will set you back a mere 210BEF. On the beer front, try the draught Bourgogne des Flandres, a rare find in the capital.

♟ **À la Mort Subite** (map II, C3, **61**): rue Montagne-aux-Herbes-Potagères 7, Brussels 1000. ☎ (02) 513 1318. Open 10am–3am. If you're looking for the definitive *kaberdouch* (old café), this is the place to come. It's the only place in town to get proper Mort Subite ('Sudden Death', named after a card game) *lambic* beers; the bottles on sale elsewhere are a pale imitation of the real thing. The café itself is a cheerful mix of *passé* gilt, mirrors and moleskin benches, fluted pilasters and brusque waitresses: a veritable temple to Brusselsness. Tourists and expats love it – indeed, many come for the privilege of being insulted by the staff – but it still has a coterie of regulars who turn up with the regularity of clockwork for a *kriek* or *faro* beer to wash down *fromage blanc* on toast or an omelette.

♥ Poechenellekelder (map II, B3, **65**): rue du Chêne 5, Brussels 1000, opposite the Mannekon Pis. ☎ (02) 511 9262. Open 11am–midnight (to 2am on Friday and Saturday). If you can get through the throng of tourists, you'll find this a rather more appealing homage to Brussels' folklore than the micturating midget. Puppets from all the local legends hang from the ceiling, and the engravings and paintings on the wall create a cheerful atmosphere. Guest beers are marked up on the blackboard, while the authentic snacks include *potte kees*, *kip-kap* and *tête pressée*, all served on toast (if you need to ask what they are, you're not going to like them). Unfortunately, the service is slow, going on non-existent, and the dinky terrace is always heaving.

♥ Chez Richard (map III, B1, **86**): rue des Minimes 2, at the corner of place du Grand-Sablon, Brussels 1000. ☎ (02) 512 1406. Open every day from 7am until the last customer leaves. A proper Brussels café, packed with regulars, and a favourite with dealers from the Sablon's Sunday antiques market. It's a tiny place with no pretensions, and about as authentically Brussels as you can get. The lunchtime set menu (290BEF) offers lamb's tongue, *carbonade flamande* (braised beef in beer) and other hearty fare – perfect if you've been traipsing about the Marolles all morning, or if you need to stoke up for a night on the tiles.

♥ Le Perroquet (map III, B2, **85**): rue Watteau 31, Brussels 1000,

between the Sablon and the Marolles. ☎ (02) 512 9922. Open 10am–1.30am. This café's main asset is its wonderful art-nouveau décor, in which iron, glass and ceramics create curling, interweaving patterns with no straight lines or corners, but it's also a good spot for a cheap snack, with a choice of rather tasty filled pittas, light salads and homemade *pâtisseries*. There's outside seating on sunny days, when the youngish crowd are often as appealing as the setting.

♥ Le Chapeau d'As (map II, B3, near **49**): rue des Chapeliers 36, Brussels 1000, a stone's throw from the Grand'Place. ☎ (02) 511 2708. In this traditional Brussels *stamcafé*, part of La Roue d'Or (*see* 'Where to eat'), the murals offer an aesthetically pleasing explanation of the street's former function: hatmaking. At the little tables, you can sip one of the unusual bottled beers, such as Kapittel, brewed in Watou, or Abbaye de la Moinette, or tuck into spaghetti, quiche, lasagne and chilli con carne, none of which will worry your wallet.

♥ La Tentation (map II, B2, **76**): rue de Laeken 28, Brussels 1000, not far from place de Brouckère. ☎ (02) 223 2275. Open 11am–11pm. Closed Sunday evening and Monday. This splendid former material shop, with exposed brickwork, beams and a monumental staircase with a wrought-iron balustrade, now houses the Galician cultural centre in Brussels. Part of it is devoted to exhibitions reflecting the Spanish region's rich heritage, but the part you really need to know about is the roomy bar, which is decorated in Celtic motifs. If *tinto* is your thing, you can drink your fill while nibbling the excellent tapas. If you want a full meal, the upstairs restaurant offers delicious Iberian specialities: Serrano ham, grilled meat and fish in white wine (full meal 1,000BEF). On

BRUSSELS

Friday, the café hosts performances of Celtic folk music, although you'll need a membership card to get in. Whenever you go, though, this place is great.

♥ De Ultieme Hallucinatie (map II, D1, **87**): rue Royale 316, Brussels 1210. ☎ (02) 217 0614. Open 11am–2am. The Ultimate Hallucination is a pretty good description of this bar-restaurant's flamboyant art-nouveau interior. The restaurant is rather expensive, so walk on by to the café-brasserie, in what was once the garden: the rockery, wrought-iron bar and flowery stained glass are reminders of its former function. The wooden seating recalls old railway carriages, but it helps to split the café into pleasantly intimate compartments, and there's a very pleasant terrace. It's a Flemish bastion, from the landlord to the waiters, so order in English unless your Dutch is up to scratch. You can get decent snacks and full meals, but the main draw is the timeless atmosphere. Make sure you peek into the restaurant as you leave for a glimpse of art nouveau at its purest.

♥ La Fleur en Papier Doré (map III, B1, **60**): rue des Alexiens 55, Brussels 1000, near the Église de la Chapelle. ☎ (02) 511 1659. Open every day 11am–1am. The Gilded Paper Flower is somewhat surreal, with three rooms decorated in the ghostly tones of an engraving and the sayings of famous authors and Dadaists adorning the walls, but it's been blooming since 1846. The art dealer who opened the café would probably never have guessed that it would become a Brussels institution. When the Surrealists held sway, poets, writers and painters came here to show off their works and have them criticized or praised. A notice on the facade describes the café as an 'Estaminet folklorique', and in its own way, it lives up to this claim. On the bottom of your beer glass, you'll find the following thought-provoking phrase: '*Tout homme a droit à 24h de liberté par jour!*' ('Every man has the right to 24 hours' freedom a day.')

♥ Goupil le Fol (map II, B3, **62**): rue de la Violette 22, Brussels 1000. ☎ (02) 511 1396. Open 7pm–6am. This unusual café is the perfect place for a quiet chat in the muted company of a good French *chansonnier*. It's a pleasantly crazy place, with books scattered everywhere, LPs sprouting from the ceiling and yellowing engravings, with pictures of Belgium's sovereigns keeping a watchful eye on proceedings. The ground floor is fun, but hopeless romantics and young lovers should head for the dimly lit first floor, where the comfy, worn-out armchairs and sofas give it a den-like air that's perfect for late-night intimacies. Fruit wines and non-alcoholic cocktails are among the house specialities, while famous clients include Prince Philippe, the heir to the Belgian throne, and his cousin Felipe, son of King Juan Carlos of Spain.

♥ Chez Moeder Lambic (map I, B3): rue de Savoie 68, Brussels 1060, just behind Saint-Gilles town hall. ☎ (02) 539 1419. Open 4pm–2am or later. A beer-lovers' paradise, with a selection of brews that knows no equal in Brussels. It's tiny, hot as an oven and full of regulars, and the menu offers more than 1,000 beers (although not all are available at any one time). The walls are covered in dusty old empty bottles, and high-spirited students bawl at each other across the grubby, old wooden tables. In summer, the pavement tables are a good bet. If you're on your own, why not brush up on your *bande dessinée* by browsing one of the well-thumbed comic strips?

♥ Le Java (map II, A-B3, **63**): on the corner of rue Saint-Géry and rue de la Grande-Île, Brussels 1000. ☎ (02)

512 3716. Open 8pm–3.30am. Closed Sunday. Launched by the Belgian singer Arno and his Flemish mates, Le Java is a meeting point for Dutch- and French-speakers, In fact, this Gaudí-esque bar attracts a whole cross section of society from pinstripe-suited men to skinheads. It's a bit of a sardine tin, so the terrace is unsurprisingly popular in summer.

♀ L'Archiduc (map II, B2-3, **64**): rue Antoine Dansaert 6, Brussels 1000. ☎ (02) 512 0652. Open 4pm–4am. Night time is the right time to visit this splendid art-deco speakeasy, which has been a magnet for local jazz buffs since 1937. Upstairs or down, you can soak up the atmosphere with a highball in your hand, nod your head in appreciation of the music and observe the trendy thirty-somethings who frequent this place. There are informal concerts by big-name artists on Sunday afternoons.

♀ Au Soleil (map II, B3, **71**): rue Marché-au-Charbon 86, Brussels 1000. ☎ (02) 512 3430. On fine days, a fashionably bohemian crowd flocks to the terrace of this former men's outfitters to sample the excellent beers listed on the slate board above the bar or snack on the good-value sandwiches, soups and chilli. Unfortunately, the terrace is out of bounds after midnight. If you can't get in, rue Marché-au-Charbon has plenty of good late-night options.

♀ H2O (map II, B3, **72**): rue du Marché-au-Charbon 27, Brussels 1000. ☎ (02) 512 3843. Open 7pm–2am. This cosy bar, with heavy drapes, baroque, vaguely astrological décor, candles and relaxing classical music, is perfect for a romantic evening gazing into your beloved's eyes. If you want to make a meal of it, you can feast on tagliatelle, salads and fruit cocktails.

♀ Loplop Café (map II, B3, **88**): rue de l'Écuyer 29, Brussels 1000.

☎ (02) 512 1889. A rough and ready caff that draws a young, international crowd, especially on Friday and Saturday nights, when there are rock and jazz gigs. For the rest of the week, a piano provides the requisite atmosphere. Clients stand about in the street holding their glasses of Guinness, while inside the atmosphere is one of benevolent chaos.

♀ Le Métropole (map II, B2, **67**): place de Brouckère 31, Brussels 1000. ☎ (02) 219 2384. Open every day 9am–1am (to 2am on Friday and Saturday). In summer, this place has one of the most popular terraces in town. Painted old ladies sit in wicker chairs to take the sun or shelter in the shade, nibble a cake and sip a cup of tea, their serenity interrupted from time to time by the odd impertinent youngster. What's weird is that they prefer a view of a heavily redeveloped square to the café's flamboyant interior: the high, cubic room is like something out of a Cecil B DeMille spectacular, with gilt columns, heavyweight chandeliers, marble walls and outsize mirrors. It's Belle Époque gone crazy, but the Chesterfield sofas are comfortable, the waiters are nicer than they first appear and the whole place has a pleasant air of Brussels past.

♀ L'Espérance (map II, C2, **82**): rue du Finistère 1-3, 1000 Brussels, just off Rue Neuve. ☎ (02) 217 3247. Open Monday to Friday. One of the city's best-kept secrets, this art-deco masterpiece was once a hotel-cum-brothel, and is a popular backdrop for film-makers. Stained-glass images of African lakes run down the side, and the low benches, sofas, panelling and lighting are all in authentic deco style, right down to the worked wood of the pot-plant holders and radiator covers. Even the loos have the right tone. Excellent beers and '*half en*

BRUSSELS

half (champagne and white wine) at a price to match any in town.

Le Cercueil (map II, B3, **68**): rue des Harengs 10, Brussels 1000, on the right-hand side of the Maison du Roi, off the Grand'Place. ☎ (02) 512 3077. Open until 2am (to 5am on Friday and Saturday). The Coffin has been lubricating its customers since the 1930s with 'devil's sperm', 'devil's spit' and other 'cadaver's secretions' (they're cocktails, in case you were wondering). Decorated with funerary wreaths and coffin covers, bathed in a lugubrious dim light and macabre humour, this ridiculous café still draws a slightly tipsy crowd of riotous students, kitsch-loving Japanese tourists and young girls who sip the aforementioned drinks without so much as a second thought. That said, you'd have to be in grave need of a drink to come here as it's a bit of a tourist trap.

Chez Toone (map II, B3, **69**): Impasse Schuddeveld, Brussels 1000, a cul-de-sac off Petite Rue des Bouchers. ☎ (02) 511 7137. Open noon–midnight. Although you'll probably be more interested in the famous Théâtre de Toone (*see* 'What to see: L'Îlot Sacré'), it's worth taking a look at this charming historic café, a slice of genuine Brussels among the raft of ripoff restaurants in the area.

À Malte (map III, C3, **70**): rue Berckmans 30, Brussels 1060. ☎ (02) 537 0991. Open from 10am to dawn. Closed Saturday lunch time. This trendy, yuppie bar in the Louise district serves breakfast and snacks for 400–500BEF – less than you'd expect, but it's the decadent atmosphere, not the food, that's the main draw here. The décor is striking – a Venetian chandelier lights a kitsch counter decorated with an eclectic collection of flea-market finds – and you can slump in the armchairs sipping wine or a herbal tea. In fine weather, you can have

brunch in the sunny courtyard at the back.

Zebra (map II, B3): place Saint-Géry 35, Brussels 1000, on the corner of rue Orts and place Saint-Géry. ☎ (02) 511 0901. Open noon–2am. This friendly, candle-lit bar with exposed brickwork is the best of the several bars on place Saint-Géry, with jazzy tunes and a laid-back, fashionable crowd. It can get a bit crowded, but overhead fans keep the air fairly smoke-free and there's a vast terrace that spills out onto the square. In winter, you can huddle inside, have tea, cocktails or fresh fruit juices and warm your stomach with quiche, pasta or toasted sandwiches.

Mappa Mundo (map II, B3, opposite Zebra): rue du Pont de la Carpe 2, Brussels 1000. ☎ (02) 514 3555. This huge bar is only three years old, but the mock-Oirish interior has the worn, homely feel of a joint that's been here for decades. If you don't fancy the heated terrace, head inside to the magnificent ground-floor bar, or take the winding staircase to the upstairs area to join a trendy crowd who probably wouldn't be seen dead in a real Irish bar. With exposed brickwork and snapshots of people's travels on the walls, it's like a local pub run by a landlord with a bad case of wanderlust, with beers from all manner of distant places, and a menu inspired by most of the world's great cuisines. It's always busy, but the staff are unfailingly polite, which helps the atmosphere no end. If you can't find a table, try the Roi des Belges, Mappa Mundo's sister bar, across the road.

Le Chicon Masqué (map III, B2, **75**): rue de l'Épée 18, Brussels 1000, in the shadow of the Palais de Justice. ☎ (02) 503 3034. A cosy regulars' café, with Modernist murals on the walls and legendary locals immortalized in the frieze around the bar, which looks a bit like a cabaret artist's dressing room. If you're in luck, there'll be a guitarist or pianist performing when you get there. If not, the excellent beers and local dishes are ample compensation.

LIVE MUSIC

♪ **Le Travers** (map II, D1, **73**): rue Traversière 11, Brussels 1210. ☎ (02) 217 6058. Closed Sunday. Metro: Botanique. Admission 300–600BEF. Free entry on Monday. This tiny bar is without doubt the best jazz venue in Brussels, with a roster of big-name musicians from Belgium and beyond. The Belgian guitarist Philip Catherine is a regular.
♪ **Le Grain d'Orge** (map III, D2, **74**): chaussée de Wavre 142, Brussels 1050, in Ixelles. ☎ (02) 511 2647. This venue calls itself a 'bistr'ock', which is a pretty good description. It's ludicrously small, and everything takes place in a corridor, but the music is of a high standard, with excellent rock groups on Friday evening and bluesier bands at other times. It's always crammed with pretend Hell's Angels, complete with rings and beards. Happy hour 7–8pm.

♪ **Marcus Mingus Jazz Spot** (map II, B3): impasse de la Fidélité 10, Brussels 1000, off rue des Bouchers. ☎ (02) 502 0297. Open from 8.30pm; concerts start at 10pm. Closed Monday. Entry fee 300BEF at the weekend. The décor at this jazz joint is nothing to write home about, but it has good bands and you don't have to have a goatee to fit in.
♪ **Sounds Jazz Club** (map III, D3): rue de la Tulipe 28, Brussels 1050, near place Fernand-Cocq. ☎ (02) 512 9250. Open 11.30am–4am (to 7am on Saturday). Closed Sunday. Concerts start at 10pm. Despite the name, this place has an eclectic programme that covers rock and blues as well as jazz. The blues concerts are particularly good. Light meals are available, although, like the drinks, they're expensive.

SHOWS

– **Chez Toone** (map II, B3, **69**): impasse Schuddeveld, a cul-de-sac off Petite-rue-des-Bouchers, Brussels 1000. ☎ (02) 511 7137. *See* 'What to see: L'Îlot Sacré' for details of this wonderful little puppet theatre.
– **Ancienne Belgique** (map II, B3): boulevard Anspach 110, Brussels 1000. ☎ (02) 548 2424. Despite the name, this is a Flemish-run concert venue – more importantly, it's a wonderful mid-size venue whose acoustics were vastly improved by a renovation in the mid-1990s. The big names in indie, postrock, folk and world music all come here on their European tours. Cafeteria open

until midnight every day except Monday.
– **Les Halles de Schaerbeek** (map I, B2): rue Royale Sainte Marie, 1210 Brussels. ☎ (02) 218 2107. Trams Nos. 92, 93, 94. This former covered market, with splendid steel arches, is a fine example of the industrial architecture of 19th-century Brussels. These days, Les Halles hosts rock and world-music concerts as well as dance and theatre performances.
– **Beursschouwburg** (map II, B3): rue Orts 22-28, Brussels 1000, not far from the Bourse. ☎ (02) 513 8290. Open Thursday to Saturday, 7.30pm–4am. Referred to locally as

the Beurs, this post-Gothic warehouse is the Flemish community's flagship cultural centre, although it's popular with trendsters from both sides of the linguistic divide. The main building hosts avant-garde exhibitions, plays and concerts, while there's a cavernous café with an irresistible mixture of cool sounds and cheap beer.

– **Le Cercle** (map III, C1, **66**): rue Sainte-Anne 20-22, Brussels 1000. ☎ (02) 514 0353. Near the smart-set bars of the Sablon district, this bar organizes a host of cultural events between September and June, with an emphasis on up-and-coming talents. Broadly speaking, it's a theatre-café on Monday, an artsy cabaret on Tuesday, a jazz hangout on Wednesday, a 'world music' venue on Thursday, a Latin dancehall on Friday, a disco inferno on Saturday and a centre for philosophical debate on Sunday afternoon. Something for everyone, in other words. Entry fees vary, but are rarely extortionate. Drinks are a trifle expensive, although not by Sablon standards.

– **La Samaritaine** (map III, B1, **77**): rue de la Samaritaine 16, Brussels 1000. ☎ (02) 511 3395. Open from 7.30pm. Closed Sunday, Monday and from the beginning of July to mid-August. Shows start at 8.30pm. Reasonable entry fee, with student reductions. For the past decade, this delightful little theatre-café has been a cultural oasis in an area on the outskirts of the Marolles. It's run with energy and good humour, and the programme features everything from *chanson* to theatre, mime and one-(wo)man comedy shows.

NIGHTCLUBS

Brussels isn't great for 24-hour party people. It's buzzing on Thursday, Friday and Saturday, but at other times, there's not much going on, and what there is won't set your pulse racing.

– **New Tom-Tom Alive** (map III, A2, **81**): place de la Constitution 5, Brussels 1000, near Gare du Midi. ☎ (02) 525 1055. Open 6pm–midnight. Admission free. During the week, this place is a tapas bar, but, come Thursday, the tables are pushed aside and the atmosphere hots up as *salseros* dance the night away to the sensuous rhythms of the Brazilian samba. The Anglo-Saxon evenings on Friday and Saturday are rather more restrained. On Sunday afternoons, there are Latin tea dances (from 5pm).

– **La Rose** (map II, B2, **78**): rue des Poissonniers 21, Brussels 1000, near the Bourse. ☎ (02) 513 4325. Open Wednesday, Friday, Saturday and Sunday from 7pm until dawn. The Rose is a kind of *café-dansant*, frequented by the thirty- and forty-somethings as well as the more mature. Secretaries come in pleated skirts with their girlfriends to jive, waltz, do the paso doble and slow-dance. Teenagers come in droves to find out what clubbing was like before disco and strobe lighting. You can even hear yourself speak. It's hopelessly dated, but that hasn't affected its popularity at all. Sunday afternoon's the time for tea dances, with a live orchestra.

– **L'Acrobate** (map II, B3, **79**): rue Borgval 14, Brussels 1000. ☎ (02) 513 7308. Open Tuesday to Sunday, 11pm–5am. At last, a real club, in a hall with a long counter and a dancefloor at one end. There's a modern, young, colourful and relaxed atmosphere, and everything's easy on the eye. You can see your friends, you can hear each other, and the toilet attendant's only 20, which makes a change. Remember to tip the bouncer as you leave: this is true at all Brussels' clubs.

– **Magasin 4** (map II, B1, **80**): rue du Magasin 4, Brussels 1000. ☎ (02) 223 3474. Open Friday and Saturday from 10pm until dawn. This cavernous brick warehouse is decorated with all manner of bits and pieces – old tyres, cinema seats, swings – and attracts a grungy crowd who shuffle about to industrial, alt-rock, reggae and hip-hop tunes. Fun, if you like that sort of thing.

– **Le Mirano Continental** (map I, C2): chaussée de Louvain 38, Brussels 1210. ☎ (02) 218 5772. Open every Saturday from 11pm. Themed evenings on the first Friday in the month. Admission: 300BEF, or 500BEF including a drink. The venue of choice for the capital's beautiful people, with a door policy that favours catwalk models and dedicated followers of fashion. If you can get in, the place looks like an old cinema, the tunes are housey and the clubbers are advertising creatives, PRs and media types.

– **Chez Johnny** (map I, C2): chaussée de Louvain 24, Brussels 1000. ☎ (02) 227 3939. Open Friday and Saturday from 11pm. Admission: 150BEF. Near the Mirano, but worlds away in terms of attitude, Chez Johnny draws a mixed crowd who come for the wild 1970s atmosphere – ultra-kitsch, but with tongue firmly in cheek. Revellers sweat it out in figure-hugging garb to the music of French *chansonniers*.

– **Fuse** (map III, A2): rue Blaes 208. ☎ (02) 511 9789. Email: info@ fuse.be. Open Saturday from 10pm. Admission: 300BEF. One of the best clubs in the Benelux, with world-class guest DJs and a decent roster of local talents. It's techno on the ground floor, house on the first floor and experimental music on the second floor. Le Fuse undergoes a metamorphosis on the first and last Sundays of the month, when it hosts **La Démence**, the capital's best gay night.

SHOPS

🔒 **Pierre's Délices & Caprices** (map II, B3, near **32**): rue des Pierres 49-51, Brussels 1000, near the Hôtel de Ville. ☎ (02) 512 1451. This tiny shop is run by a young Swiss gentleman who knows everything you could possibly want to know about brewing. As well as collectors' glasses, he sells a few rare beers at decent prices; some that are really surprising, including Liefmans Goudenband, which you should heat in a bain-marie. He also sells gin and runs a B&B with a few sensibly priced rooms, although they tend to get booked up.

🔒 **Elvis Pompilio** (map II, B3): rue du Lombard 18, Brussels 1000.

☎ (02) 511 1180. Elvis Pompilio is to the hat what Jean-Paul Gaultier is to the kilt or the Breton sweater, and the mad milliner's flagship store sells way-out nightcaps, mantillas, top hats and Basque berets. Like the headgear, the prices are crazy.

🔒 **La Vaisselle au Kilo** (map III, C1): rue Bodenbroek 8, Brussels 1000, off the Sablon. ☎ (02) 513 4984. Phone for opening hours. A tried-and-tested concept: crockery sold by weight. There's a wide range of high-quality tableware and glasses, and the prices are extremely reasonable.

🔒 **Rosalie Pompon** (map III, B1): rue Lebeau 65, Brussels 1000, between the Sablon and the city centre. ☎ (02) 512 3593. The clocks, furniture, jewellery, lamps and bathroom accessories on sale here have been designed by someone with a fertile imagination, a good sense of humour and a deep love of animals.

🔒 **Papier d'Antan** (map III, B1): rue de l'Hôpital 19, Brussels 1000. ☎ (02) 511 2470. The place to come for retro postcards, chocolate wrappings, enamelled plates, advertising labels for Dubonnet and Thermolactyl and tourist maps from the early days of the car.

🔒 **Palais des Cotillons** (map II, B3): rue du Lombard 66, Brussels 1000. ☎ (02) 512 2320. Jokes and tricks are big business in Brussels, and this is an essential stop-off if you're in need of fancy dress. Un-

surprisingly, it's heaving at Halloween. Costume hire available.

🔒 **Passage 125 Blaes** (map III, B2): rue Blaes 125, Brussels 1000, near the flea market. ☎ (02) 503 1027. Antiques-lovers will love this huge market, with 30 antiques stalls on three levels covering nearly 1,000 square metres (11,000 square feet).

🔒 **Stijl Men & Women** (map II, A2): rue Antoine-Dansaert 74, Brussels 1000. ☎ (02) 512 0313. If you want Antwerp fashions but don't have time for a trip to the town itself, rue Dansaert is the place to go. Stijl was the first of several shops on the street to showcase the creations of the country's avant-garde designers, and it's the blueprint for all the others: a 19th-century town house offering cutting-edge clothes in a minimalist setting.

WHAT TO SEE

– **Guided tours with ARAU**: boulevard Adolphe-Max 55, Brussels 1000. ☎ (02) 219 3345. Fax: (02) 219 8675. ARAU (Atelier de Recherche et d'Actions Urbaines; *see* 'Addresses and useful information') is a pressure group, not a tour operator, but it offers excellent coach tours on a variety of themes, including alternative Brussels, art-nouveau Brussels, 1930s Brussels, squares, parks, gardens and housing estates, life in Brussels and the Grand'Place. Price: 600BEF, 300BEF if you're under 26. Tickets available from the TIB, the Post Office and the FNAC in City 2. Tours are run between March and November, usually on Saturday or Sunday morning, and leave from place de Brouckère (Hôtel Métropole). The tours are worth every penny, as you'll get a passionate guide and a real insight into the city. As well as showing you the beauties of Brussels, ARAU tours highlight past mistakes, present threats and possible solutions for the future. You can also get a brochure and a map with two walks that take you past some of the best art-nouveau facades in central Brussels 'from sgraffiti to the magnificent renovated window of an old department store built by Victor Horta'. If you're an art-nouveau fan, there's an excellent book called *Bruxelles Art Nouveau* (published by AAM).

– There are other pleasant themed walks organized by other associations. See 'Useful Addresses and Information'.

Within the Pentagon

THE GRAND'PLACE (map II, B3)

The best time to get your first glimpse of the Grand'Place is at dusk. As you emerge from one of the small cobbled streets that lead onto the square, you'll be dazzled by the ornate gilded gables and the dramatic, beautifully illuminated spire of the Hôtel de Ville. If you visit in the morning, you'll be distracted by less romantic things, like the delivery vans that crowd the square and the surrounding streets.

Many writers have been seduced by the beauty of the Grand'Place, describing it as 'the most beautiful place on earth' (Victor Hugo) or 'the richest theatre in the world' (Jean Cocteau). The most striking thing about it is its architectural harmony: the whole square was built in one go following Louis XIV's bombardment of Brussels in 1695, which left only a portion of the Hôtel de Ville standing. Undaunted, the city's stalwart burghers rebuilt everything in just four years, a fact their modern-day descendants are justifiably proud of.

The square has been home to a market since the 11th century, when it was surrounded by marshes – the city's name comes from the Dutch word *broekzele*, which means 'dwellings around the marshes'. The city's emblem is an iris, one of the few flowers that can grow in water, against a blue background, which symbolizes the water of the marshes. The square was a political forum as much as a trading centre, and was used for celebrations, festivals and public executions. In the 13th century, wooden houses were built for wealthy merchants, and the guilds also set up shop here. The Hôtel de Ville, erected in the 15th century, was a suitably elaborate illustration of secular power. The first Ommegang, a sumptuous pageant held in honour of Charles V, was held in 1549, and the Counts of Egmont and Hoorn were beheaded on the Grand'Place in 1568. After the senseless French bombardment of 1695, the citizens of Brussels decided to give their square a more coherent look, and invited architects to submit their plans to a judge. The result was healthy competition among the guilds, who strove to outdo each other with the beauty and elegance of their designs.

Today, the car-free Grand'Place, with its gold trimmings and wealth of decoration, is an architectural gem and one of Europe's most famous squares. Every facade is worth studying closely, and it retains at least a hint of its original function thanks to the daily flower market and Sunday bird market – and the numerous events, from opera to ice-skating, that take place there. Every two years, the square is covered with an extravagant carpet of petals (*see* 'Events in the Grand'Place').

Several artists were involved in the square's post-bombardment reconstruction. Some travelled to Italy to study new trends that they could apply to the Grand'Place. The Renaissance-inspired designs were so rich that the overall look – apart from the Gothic Hôtel de Ville – was dubbed 'Flemish baroque'. Take a closer look, and you'll see how every building wavers, often almost imperceptibly, between the Renaissance and the baroque, and how the careful blending of the two styles has resulted in a unique architectural hybrid. The artists obeyed certain Classical rules (the columns, for example, are Doric on the first level, Ionic on the second and Corinthian on the third), but otherwise let their imaginations roam free as they incorporated the symbols of the different guilds into their work. Sometimes, it's easy to see which house belonged to which guild; at others, you'll have to work it out. You can hire an audio guide to the Grand'Place at the tourist office.

★ The **Hôtel de Ville** (map II, B3, **90**) is the main focus of the Grand'Place. Built in pure flamboyant Gothic style (Charles the Bold laid the first stone in 1444), it was to be even more magnificent than its counterpart in Bruges. The tower was the only part of the building to survive the French bombardment, but the rest was reconstructed according to the original plans. The left-hand wing is not as long as the one on the right because rue Tète d'Or stood in its way.

The 91-metre (300-foot) tower is unashamedly elegant, with turrets, pinnacles, corbelled balconies and Flamboyant Gothic windows make it a masterpiece of secular Gothic architecture. It's topped by a slender spire and the figure of Saint Michael, patron saint of the city.

Take a closer look and you'll see that the porch is out of kilter with the tower: the architect, so the story goes, was so devastated when he realized his mistake that he threw himself from the tower.

The ground-floor arcades were originally occupied by tradesmen's stalls. The sculptures of dukes and duchesses above them were added in the 19th century.

Take a look at the capitals of the three columns in front of the tourist office, beneath the right wing of the Hôtel de Ville. They are reminders of the three taverns that once stood here. The first capital (on the left) represents the word Scupstoel (spade and chair): the sculptors represented the word literally, and chose to depict men digging a pile of chairs. The second capital, which shows monks drinking, was straightforward, as it represents a tavern called Papen Kelder (Monks' Cellar). But the third tavern, De Moer, proved rather more complicated. Some claimed it was a reference to the Moors, and, sure enough, there's a series of characters sporting turbans. Others reckoned it meant 'mother', so the other side of the capital shows a mother beside a cradle. Such is the way of the famous Belgian compromise.

In the main courtyard (open continuously) are two splendid stone fountains that represent the Meuse and Scheldt rivers.

Tours
The Hôtel de Ville is open for guided tours on certain days and at certain times, mainly 20 July–15 August, with seven visits a day on Tuesday and Thursday, and four visits on Wednesday and Sunday. For the rest of the year, there are two visits on Tuesday and one on Wednesday and Sunday. The one-hour tour takes you through a host of reception rooms, salons and galleries, up the main staircase and through corridors and antechambers. Every room is hung with paintings, filled with busts and decorated with Gothic panelling and spectacular tapestries. Much of this valuable ornamentation dates from the 18th century. The finest items on display include Vanderborght tapestries, paintings of old Brussels, romantic rustic scenes in the antechamber, the tapestries in the Gothic room (well, neo-Gothic: it was refurbished in 1868) and, in the marriage chamber, allegorical paintings and a ceiling decorated with the coats of arms of the various guilds.

★ The **Maison du Roi** (map II, B3, **91**), opposite the Hôtel de Ville, was built in Late Gothic style at the beginning of the 16th century. Despite its name, the Maison du Roi was actually a bread market, and no king ever lived there. It has served as the home of the Duke of Brabant, a tax office, a court and even a prison (the Counts of Egmont and Hoorn spent their last night there on 4 June, 1568). The structure you see today is a splendid example of neo-Gothic architecture, built to the original designs, with elegant flying buttresses, a loggia and a balcony. The doorway is framed by statues of Marie of Burgundy and Charles V. The building houses a fascinating museum, the **Musée de la Ville de Bruxelles**, which offers an invaluable explanation of the development of the city.

The Musée de la Ville de Bruxelles

Open 10am–12.30pm and 1.30–5pm (to 4pm in winter); Saturday and Sunday, 10am–1pm. Closed Friday and public holidays. ☎ (02) 279 4358. Tickets: 80BEF. Every aspect of the city's history is represented here, but what really draws the crowds, depressingly, are the costumes of the Manneken-Pis.

– The ground-floor exhibits include carved capitals, baroque statues, 17th-century bas-reliefs and Brussels porcelain. There's also a beautiful altarpiece depicting the Nativity. The splendid collection of tapestries includes *Wedding Procession*, attributed to Pieter Brueghel the Elder (1567), and *Spear Hunt*, in sumptuous shades of blue. You can also see some fine silverware.

– The first-floor display traces the history of Brussels. You can see a model of the first walled town, and engravings and old maps from previous centuries. Take a look at the beautiful map of the *Ville de Bruxelles à l'usage des habitants et des étrangers* ('Map of Brussels for inhabitants and foreigners') and the extraordinary gouache for a project to build a bridge linking boulevard Anspach with rue Royale. It remained on the drawing board, as did plans for a funicular railway to join the upper and lower parts of the city. You can also see engravings of the gardens of the Cinquantenaire and the river Senne, which was buried in the 19th century, and an impressive painting of the 1695 bombardment.

– The second floor houses engravings and portraits of local personalities, as well as items relating to local crafts.

– On the top floor, you'll find the extraordinary wardrobe of the Manneken-Pis: hundreds of tailor-made costumes from all over the world. They are shown by theme (sport, for example, or the professions, or traditional costumes). Among the less explicable costumes are those of an anaes-thetist, a station manager and Dracula. The central case contains a photo-graph of Maurice Chevalier standing next to the wee lad.

★ Start your tour of the guildhouses on the west (left-hand) side, to the right of the Hôtel de Ville.

– **La maison du Renard** once housed the haberdashers' guild, as you'll have guessed from the bas-reliefs on the facade. A statue of Justice wearing a blindfold evokes the honesty of the trade. She is flanked by four statues symbolizing the four continents then known to exist: the haberdashers traded with all of them.

– **Le Cornet** was once the house of the boatmen. The style is Italian-Flemish, and the gable is in the shape of a ship's stern. Four angels blow the winds from the four points of the compass, while on the third level, you'll see a panoply of sea symbols and the arms of the Spanish kingdom at the top. There's a balustrade in the form of a landing stage lower down.

– **La Louve**, the house of the guild of archers, has a bas-relief depicting a she-wolf suckling Romulus and Remus. It's in the Classical style, with pilasters and allegorical representations of Truth, Falsehood, Peace and Discord. Higher up, you can make out the medallions of the Roman emperors. The gilt phoenix at the top is a reminder that the house was reborn from the ashes.

– **Le Sac** takes its name from the bas-relief above the door. Even by Grand'Place standards, it's an ornate affair, with garlands, shells, balustrades and torch-holders around the top.

– **La Brouette** was the chandlers' guild. Two delightful wheelbarrows frame the doorway of the rigorously Classical facade.

– You'll recognize **Le Roy d'Espagne**, the bakers' guildhouse, from its cupola. The facade is Classical, with a bust of the bakers' patron, Saint Aubert, above the door, and the titular King of Spain in the centre. There's a gilt allegory of Renown on top. The building now houses a café with the best terrace on the square. If it's cold, you can enjoy the view from the comfort of the first floor.

– A series of less interesting houses lines the north side (to the left of the Maison du Roi). The facades of **La Maison du Paon** (with a bas-relief of a peacock) and the house of **L'Heaume** are both decorated with scenes of children.

– Another row of houses occupies the northeast side. **La Chambrette de l'Amman** was once the home of a magistrate who acted for the Duke of Brabant. You can see his coat of arms on the facade.

– **Le Pigeon** once housed the guild of painters. Victor Hugo lived here in exile in 1852. The facade is as Classical as they come, with only a Venetian window on the first floor to lighten the austere effect.

– **La Chaloupe d'Or** (an excellent bar) and **La Taupe** (The Mole) were once owned by the tailors' guild. A bust of an unhappy-looking Sainte Barbe looks down from the comparatively dull Mole, but if she gets you down, cheer yourself up with some chocs from the Godiva on the ground floor.

– The most imposing collection of guilds was housed on the south side of the Grand'Place, where six of them shared the **Maison des Ducs de Brabant**. Busts of four dukes and duchesses adorn the Italian-Flemish facade, which is decorated with pilasters in 18-carat gold leaf. At the top, you can see an allegory of Plenty, a balustrade and several torch-holders. There are three porches, which served two guilds apiece. You can tell them apart by the bas-reliefs above each door: an exchange, tools for the house of sculptors and masons, a pewter pot for the carpenters, a windmill and a watermill for the millers, Fortune for the tanners, and a hermit for . . . well, nobody really knows.

– The first house on the southwest side, **Mont-Thabor**, was a private house.

– **Musée du Cacao et du Chocolat:** 13 Grand'Place, on the ground floor, off a corridor with splendid Portuguese tiling. Open 10am–5pm. Closed Monday. Admission: 200BEF. This small museum explains how the cocoa bean arrived in the western world, and the passion it inspired. There's a strong emphasis on the economic implications of the 'tropical' product trade for both north and south hemispheres. You can watch a video, read the explanatory panels, watch pralines being made and taste some chocolate. The setting is fantastic, but it's a bit pricey, free choco notwithstanding.

– **La Rose** belonged to the Van der Rosen family. There's a blooming rose in a vase at the window.

– **La maison des Brasseurs** (Brewers' House) is decorated with bas-reliefs depicting the harvesting of hops. At the top, there's a statue of Charles of Lorraine, a reminder of the Austrian occupation. The building houses the small **Musée de la Brasserie**, in the cellars (open 10am–5pm; admission 100BEF; ☎ (02) 511 4987). The museum's collection includes displays of tools and items used to make barrels, as well as 17th- and 18th-century machines, but you'll probably find the reconstruction of an 18th-century tavern more entertaining. If you're interested in modern brewing techniques, there's a high-tech display of them at the back of the museum, put together by the Confederation of Belgian Brewers, a guild that still has real clout. An educational, interactive video answers any questions you might have about the world of brewing, although you might want to rein in your inquisitive streak when you remember that you'll get a free beer after the tour.

– **Le Cygne** is a handsome, Louis XIV-style building that once housed the butchers' guild. In the 19th century, the Swan was a workers' café, frequented by Karl Marx, when he was writing the *Communist Manifesto*; in the 20th century, it was a key venue for power-lunching corporate monsters. Above the building, look out for the allegories of Plenty, Agriculture and the art of being a butcher.

– The last house, **L'Étoile**, is less ornate than its neighbours, but it's worth a look because it has an arcade instead of a porch. Look out for the fine art-nouveau bas relief below the arcade.

– Just off the square by L'Étoile, you can see a bronze statue of **Everard 't Serclaes** on his deathbed. A local hero who liberated Brussels in the 14th century, Everard was murdered by the Count of Flanders; the locals avenged his death by attacking the home of the assassins. To sustain themselves, they took dozens of chickens with them, earning the nickname '*kieken-fretters*', or 'chicken-eaters'.

– **Events in the Grand'Place:** the bird market takes place on Sunday mornings, and there's a *son et lumière* every evening in summer, with the Hôtel de Ville as the star of the show, and some rather pompous piped music.

In early July, the Grand'Place hosts the Ommegang (*see* 'Festivals') and in mid-August in even years, there's an elaborately patterned carpet of begonias (about 750,000), which is best viewed from the balcony of the Hôtel de Ville. The Christmas market, with stalls from the EU countries, takes place in early December.

THE ÎLOT SACRÉ (map II, B3)

North of the Grand'Place, you'll find a labyrinth of narrow, winding streets and alleyways known as the Îlot Sacré. There are plenty of handsome facades here, although they often house tacky, tourist-trap restaurants. Take a look at the evocative street names as you stroll through the area: rue au Beurre (Butter Street), rue des Harengs (Herring Street), rue des Bouchers (Butcher's Street), rue du Marché-aux-Fromages (Cheese Market Street). If you're determined to eat here, do some research before you plunge in, or plump for the reputable restaurants, such as Chez Léon (for mussels) or Aux Armes de Bruxelles (for atmosphere and classic Belgian food).

★ Start your tour of the Îlot Sacré at **Place d'Espagne**, which is also known as **Place de l'Agora**. From the Grand'Place, take rue de la Colline (there's a Tintin shop on the left); on the right, you'll see a delightful little square that hosts a craft market on weekends. Most of the houses still have their original baroque features, although three have been rebuilt in a tacky neo-Renaissance style. There's a sculpture of Don Quixote and Sancho Panza on the esplanade leading to Gare Centrale: the ornate fountain in the centre features an eye-catching bronze statue of Charles Buls, a 19th-century burgomaster. His moustache is ostentatiously waxed, and he is accompanied by a pampered-looking pooch. Rue de la Montagne, which leads off the square, is lined with attractively gabled houses made of alternating brick and stone. Most of them have recently been restored.

★ **Galeries Saint-Hubert** (map II, C3, **92**): off rue du Marché-aux-Herbes. This impressive neoclassical structure was designed in the 1840s, and housed Europe's first indoor shopping centre. Marble pilasters, bow windows and a series of sculpted busts create a successful, if mildly monotonous, ensemble, elegantly filled with tea rooms, cafés, upmarket bookshops and chic boutiques. The upper floors are private residences. The mall's most famous customer was the poet Paul Verlaine, who bought a pistol here before his failed attempt to shoot his fellow poet and lover, Rimbaud, on the Grand'Place. In 1896, the arcades provided the backdrop for the first film shot by the Lumière brothers. Chocoholics, meanwhile, will be thrilled to hear that the praline was invented in the Neuhaus shop here.

★ **Cathédrale Saint-Michel** (map II, C3): open 8am–6pm. After 20 years of nonstop building works, the cathedral is in tip-top condition. Since the 12th century it's been dedicated to Sainte Gudule as well as Saint Michael: Gudule, a local lass, earned her sainthood in the time of Charlemagne, when she defied the Devil. Old Nick got his revenge in 1961, when the city authorities celebrated the church's ascension to cathedral status by cutting Gudule out of its official name.

This beautiful hilltop structure is surrounded by ugly buildings that cut it off from the rest of the city: a real shame, as it's a rare example of a religious building that has benefitted from being built in several styles: Romanesque, Early Gothic, Late Gothic and baroque. The twin 15th-century towers show Gothic Brabant influence.

Inside, you'll be struck by the vast, high and elegantly proportioned nave, which is separated from the north and south aisles by heavy columns lined with 12 huge baroque statues of the apostles. The 14th-century pillars on the south side are very different to those on the north side, which were built a century later. The capitals of these huge columns, typical of the Brabant Gothic style, are decorated with cabbage leaves, while the elegant triforium depicts the narrative of Adam and Eve. The choir, the oldest section, is early Gothic, while the chevet displays a Romanesque influence. The Chapel of the Holy Sacrament houses a finely carved oak altar in Late Gothic style.

The stained glass, most of which dates from the 16th century, is the work of the master glazier of Margaret of Austria's court. The windows in the chapel of the Holy Sacrament tell the story of the theft of the Host and the 'miracle' (*see below*). If you turn your back to the altar and look above the organ loft, you'll see a beautiful stained-glass version of the Last Judgment, all blues, greens and golds. The stained-glass windows in the transept are equally splendid: on one side are Charles V and Isabel of Portugal, while Louis II, King of Hungary, is the star of the south transept. Before you leave, take a look at the baroque Chapel of the Virgin Mary and the 18th-century confessionals in the side chapels.

In the crypt, you can see the remains of the Romanesque church that once stood here.

– The Miracle of the Holy Sacrament: several windows and paintings in the cathedral depict episodes from the 'miracle of the Blessed Sacrament', when Jews were said to have stolen the sacred host. Blood poured from the sacrament – constituting the 'miracle' – and the alleged thieves were caught and burned at the stake. Their guilt was never proved, and the fact that the miracle occurred at the height of a plague outbreak may have something to do with that, but the event gave rise to a legend, and many an artist has made it the subject of a tapestry or stained-glass windows. Many of these works were given to the cathedral in the 16th century by Charles V, and the miracle was celebrated for years to come in the shape of an annual procession, the Procession of the Blessed Sacrament. A plaque questioning the truth of the story was finally unveiled in 1977, and hangs on the wall of the Chapel of the Blessed Sacrament.

★ Make your way back to the fringes of the Grand'Place via **rue des Bouchers** (map II, B-C3), a crammed collection of touristy restaurants that specialize in unremarkable cuisine, overhasty service and inflated prices. The crowds of undemanding tourists don't seem to mind, perhaps because they don't know where else to go. In the evening, especially during high season, half of the city's tourist population pours into this street. Crossed by the handsome galleries, it isn't devoid of charm, although the outdoor table awnings and ubiquitous neon lighting block any view of the street's attractive gables.

– To your right, take Petite-rue-des-Bouchers, a narrower version of the street with which it shares a name. At the end of impasse Schuddeveld, a cul-de-sac on the left-hand side, you'll find a Brussels institution: the tiny **Théâtre de Toone** (map II, B3, **69**). ☎ (02) 511 7137 or (02) 513 5486. There are daily shows at 8.30pm; admission 400BEF, with discounts for students. This sophisticated puppet theatre was established in 1830 – for adults, not children – by Antoine Genty (its name means Antoine in local dialect). A number of stalwarts have continued the tradition, and the place is run today by José Géal, who's known as Toone VII. He is responsible for a repertoire of 33 humorous, often savagely satirical, puppet shows performed by marionettes on rods, not strings.

The original role of the puppeteer was to inform people about real events, not just to entertain. At the end of the 19th century, Brussels was home to 45 puppet theatres; this proud establishment is the sole survivor, but it maintains its predecessors' traditions.

Today, you can see a variety of traditional dramas riddled with contemporary comments and jibes, including *The Hunchback of Notre Dame*, *The Three Musketeers* and even versions of *Macbeth* and *Othello*. For each production, puppeteers manipulate the puppets while Toone VII provides the voices. Shows are usually in French, but are peppered with *vloms*, a Brussels dialect. If you sit at the front, you can see the energetic puppeteers at work.

During the interval, you can visit a small museum with a collection of the theatre's 19th-century puppets. Some characters have heads made of chalk and a paste mixture, while those who get involved in fights have tougher wooden heads; their bodies are made of straw-stuffed card and the oldest have glass eyes. Woltje, a playful star character who brings the action to a close, appears in every show. Some people even maintain that Woltje was the inspiration for Tintin, although there's not much evidence to support this claim.

On the ground floor, there's an atmospheric old tavern where you can sample traditional Belgian beers; if you can't make it to a show, this is a good way to sample this slice of authentic Brussels.

★ **Église Saint-Nicolas** (map II, B3, **105**): this pretty little church is the only one in the city that's still surrounded by houses. The reconstructed facade is rather ugly, but you'll get a fairy-tale view of the church from rue au Beurre. There's been a church on this site for nearly 1,000 years, although nothing remains of its earliest days. Inside, the nave and choir are not straight; instead, they respect the course of an ancient stream that the workmen left alone during construction. Take a look at the Shrine of the Martyrs of Gorcum, a fine piece of 19th-century work, the Romanesque fragments and the *Virgin with Sleeping Child*, a painting attributed to Rubens. The third pillar in the left-hand aisle has a French cannonball lodged in it, a souvenir of the 1695 bombardment. Before this attack, the church had an enormous belfry, which you can still make out in old engravings. It was never rebuilt.

★ **La Bourse** (map II, B3), the city's stock exchange, is a perfect example of complacent 19th-century neo-Classicism, a squat, supremely smug structure that's benefitted enormously from a recent clean-up. The young Rodin helped to sculpt the pediment frieze.

On the right of the Bourse as you walk down from the Grand'Place, you'll see traces of a 13th-century seminary and the tombs of the Dukes of Brabant through a set of large windows. If your curiosity is piqued, the site is home to a museum, **Bruxella 1238** (guided tours every Monday, Tuesday, Thursday and Friday at 10.15am, 11.15am, 1.45pm and 3.15pm; meet outside the Maison du Roi, on the Grand'Place. Admission: 80BEF).

If art nouveau is more your thing, pop into the **Falstaff**, on the other side of the Bourse; this cavernous tavern has a sumptuous interior with fabulous sculpted wood (*see* 'Where to drink').

★ From here, stroll down boulevard Anspach to see the **Pathé Palace** cinema (No. 85), built in 1913 and topped by a crowing cockerel. The architecture is clearly influenced by the Viennese Secession movement.

★ There's a small museum, **Scientastic**, in the basement of the Bourse metro station. ☎ (02) 646 8915. Open weekends, public holidays and during the school holidays, 2–5.30pm. Admission: 160BEF, with discounts for children and senior citizens. Scientists, teachers and animators explain the laws of physics in a reassuringly basic manner, while the 70 interactive experiences based on the five senses are great entertainment, if fiendishly difficult to explain to streetwise kids. A strong point is the false lift that disorients your senses, and the 'impossible box', inspired by M.C. Escher's mind-bending drawings. It's a good place to take the kids if they're bored with old buildings, and a godsend if it's raining.

★ On the other side of boulevard Anspach is **place Saint-Géry** (map II, A3-B3), the historic heart of the city. It was here, in the marshes of the Senne Valley, that the first fortified 'castrum' was built in the 10th century, and the city's first houses appeared. All that's left from those days is the bed of the river Senne, which was filled in during the 19th century for hygienic reasons (and, cynics might say, to make room for several huge boulevards). You can still see a trickle of the old Senne if you enter a courtyard off rue de la Grande-Île, in a collection of old, prettily renovated houses (the gate is locked at nightfall). It's a timeless setting: against the backdrop of the bell tower of the Riches-Claires convent, below a stone staircase, runs, or rather stagnates, the little stream of water that once made Brussels rich.

In the middle of the square is the **Halles Saint-Géry**, a glass, brick and iron building constructed in 1881. It's now home to a museum that explores the city's history and present-day culture. ☎ (02) 502 4424. Open 10am–7pm, weekends 2–5pm. Closed Monday and in January. Admission: 100BEF. There are two sections: in the first-floor galleries, there's a short audiovisual presentation, after which you can follow the history of Brussels' urban development between the bombardment of 1695 and the Belle Époque. It's well done, with clear commentary panels, good illustrations and attractive presentation. The ground floor is devoted to temporary exhibitions, most of which are about architecture and town planning, although you might find your attention wandering to the brasserie's pavement terrace.

On one side of the square, you'll see a building site with a line of facades in front: the houses they once belonged to have been knocked down by developers. Local pressure groups have covered the gutted remnants of the buildings with cheerful multicoloured murals.

Despite years of doom and neglect, an attractive district is emerging on this side of boulevard Anspach, with cafés, restaurants and chic boutiques, often opened by young Flemings. The centrepiece is the once rundown rue Dansaert, which is now awash with high-fashion shops stocking ultratrendy togs by the likes of Ann Demeulemeester and Dries Van Noten. Slightly cosier is nearby rue des Chartreux, which has been given a total face-lift in recent years and is now home to several hospitable cafés and an interesting little museum.

★ **Album** (map II, A3, **125**): rue des Chartreux 25. ☎ (02) 511 9055. Open 1–7pm. Closed Tuesday. Admission: 50–200BEF, depending on how long you spend inside. Housed in a 17th-century building that's been lovingly refurbished by a young Frenchman and his Belgian wife, Album's ambitious mission is to tell the story of Europe; not the Europe of Maastricht and mismanaged money, but a Europe based on the things its nations have had in common since the Dark Ages. Album has an interactive museum experience, Europe Zig-Zag, as well as an information centre.

The main display is a mixture of commentary panels, video screens, random objects and tables highlighting entertaining comparisons between the different European countries. There are several themes: Roman Europe (a frontier-free area with a single currency), Europe of the conquerors (Charlemagne, Charles V, Napoleon, Stalin, Hitler); artists and great minds (Leonardo da Vinci, Gutenberg, Erasmus, Mozart, Karl Marx, the Beatles); contemporary Europe (football and the 2CV); Tintin's Europe; and, as a concession to the EU, political Europe (how the institutions work and so on). Overall, it's an intelligent and witty place. Don't leave without taking a look at the splendid renovation of the houses round the back.

Head back towards the Grand'Place via rue des Riches-Claires, crossing boulevard Anspach, and you'll reach a maze of medieval streets known as the quartier Saint-Jacques, centred around the baroque church of Notre-Dame-du-Bon-Secours. The lively rue Marché-au-Charbon was once the pilgrims' road, guiding the pious to Santiago de Compostela. You can still see scallop shells, the badge of this pilgrimage, on the facade of the church.

SABLON AND PALAIS-ROYAL DISTRICTS (map II, B-C3 and map III, B-C1)

From the Grand'Place, take rue Charles-Buls. A plaque at the corner of rue des Brasseurs reminds you that this is where Verlaine shot Rimbaud with the revolver he had purchased in the Galeries Saint-Hubert (*see above*).

The **Musée du Costume et de la Dentelle** (*see* 'Museums') is on rue de la Violette (on the left-hand side). At the corner of rue de l'Étuve and rue du Chêne, beyond rue du Lombard, you'll see the world's most famous midget. At least, you will if you can get through the crowds.

★ The **Manneken-Pis** (map II, B3, **93**) is a national monument, and Belgium's most popular postcard image. He's also honoured by a variety of interesting souvenir corkscrews. The urinating little boy is only 55.5cm (22in) tall, but his spray is surprisingly far-reaching. He was sculpted by Jérôme Duquesnoy in 1619, although a stone fountain, the Fountain of Little Julian, has been on the site since the 14th century, and women are believed to have collected water here. He's a symbol of irreverence and independence of spirit (how many men, after all, pee with their back to the wall?). He's also the proud owner of a huge wardrobe, examples of which are on display in the Maison du Roi (on the Grand'Place). His first costume was gifted by Maximilian of Bavaria in 1698, and visiting dignitaries have followed suit ever since. You'll probably find the whole thing rather silly, but he does at least have an appealingly mischievous smile.

For a frivolous monument, the Manneken-Pis has had a tough life. Louis XV's armies lopped off an arm, even though the French king had presented the statue with a splendid costume. In 1817, he was smashed into pieces by a former convict who wanted to avenge himself on the city authorities; he was publicly branded and banged up for 20 years, while a copy of the Manneken was installed in its rightful place. Since then, he's been the target of regular abuse from the local youth, and was stolen by students from Antwerp in 1963. But he's still smiling, and still peeing, to the bemusement of thousands of tourists from around the world. For special occasions, the Manneken has an official dresser, Jacques Stroobants, who regularly changes his clothes. The ladder he uses stands to the right of the fountain.

Since 1985, the little boy has had a companion, Jeanneke-Pis, In a cul-de-sac off rue des Bouchers. Purists don't think much of her, since she was created by a local restaurateur to boost business. But she's starting to attract her share of tourists . . .

★ **From Manneken-Pis to place du Grand-Sablon:** follow rue du Chêne, past the fine 17th-century house at No. 27, until you come to the charming place de la Vieille-Halle-aux-Blés, with crumbling gables and romantic facades. Once the site of a noisy coaching inn, it is now almost eerily silent. The fountain in the centre, which depicts two feasting peasants, may be a reference to the square's name: Old Cornmarket. Look towards rue du Lombard, and you'll see the Parliament of the Brussels Region, a glass fish bowl that tops the Classical structure of the old Provincial Palace. In a city scarred by architectural blunders, this stands out as an altogether successful project. The politicians can enjoy a fine view of the city's spires, blocks and towers from the balcony that overlooks the road.

★ **An evening with Jacques Brel**: Fondation Jacques-Brel, place de la Vieille-Halle-aux-Blés 11 (map III, B1, **124**). ☎ (02) 511 1020. From May to the beginning of November, open Tuesday to Sunday 11am–6pm; for the rest of the year, closed Sunday. Tickets: 200BEF, with discounts for senior citizens, under-20s and groups. Visits last about 35 minutes

This small, wonderfully atmospheric exhibition, created by the Fondation Brel (run by the legendary *chansonnier*'s daughter, France), plunges you into the world of the 1950s, where you're invited to follow *le grand Jacques* on one of his provincial tours. The scene is set by a ticket seller who stands at the reception of the Hôtel du Centre, a modest hotel that could be anywhere in Belgium or France. Brel has just checked in, along with his backing orchestra. His raincoat, suitcase and guitar case lie in the corner of the room. An old TV shows news from the 1950s, and there are magazines from the period on the table. A lift takes you up to the artist's seedy dressing room. You can see his shoes and smoking jacket in one corner. An actor who plays Brel sits at a table in front of the mirror and talks to visitors about his life as a performer. The table is scattered with Brel's personal belongings: a diary, photos for autographs, the scribbled draft of a song, Eau Sauvage, a watch, razor and a bottle of Scotch, an ashtray overflowing with Gitanes butts and the pills he used to take to relieve the stage fright he suffered before every concert. An accordion plays the opening phrases of *Amsterdam* while, backstage in the dusty Théâtre Municipal, visitors hear a recital of the song and watch silhouettes of Brel in performance.

After the show, you walk down a corridor that leads to a station buffet, a place that often features in Brel's songs, and was only too familiar to the nomadic singer and his friends. They sat in any number of railway restaurants discussing love, friendship and women, or swearing drunkenly that tomorrow would be a better day, and that they would one day leave for sunnier climes. Press the beer mats and you can hear Brel's character-istically blunt answers to a host of questions. Brel buffs can test their knowledge in a computer quiz about his life and career, or ask the jukebox to play their favourite Brel song. Photographs pinned to the wall show images taken during the singer's 45 tours, including less familiar ones of him sporting a moustache. Meanwhile, the barman serves the last round, a train whistles in the distance and the next thing you know, day breaks and you're back outside on the shining cobbles of downtown Brussels.

– Take a detour via rue de Villers, where you can see fragments of the 13th-century wall that once ringed the city; it now stands in front of a miserable wasteland. To the left is a handsomely restored house with a porch, above which you can see a cannonball in the wall – another reminder of 1695.

Continue until you come to place de Dinant, where the historic centre comes to an abrupt end and you're confronted instead by the ugly boulevard de l'Empereur, which runs above the underground railway linking Gare du Midi and Gare Centrale. The **tour Anneessens**, another fragment of the city's inner wall, stands on the other side of the boulevard.

★ **Église de la Chapelle** (map III, B1, **94**): open 10am–5pm in summer and noon–4pm in winter. This church, which lies on the frontier between the Sablon and Marolles districts, was built in the 11th century outside the first city wall. It has been altered on several occasions, but is a fine example of Brabant Gothic, recognizable thanks to its chunky, square tower. To the left of the porch, there's an underground medieval cemetery, while the Holy Trinity above the entrance was sculpted by Constantin Meunier. Inside, you can see a memorial to Pieter Brueghel the Elder in the fourth side-aisle chapel on your right. The painter once lived in the Marolles, on nearby rue Haute. Take a look at the baroque pulpit, which is decorated with exotic trees and palms, and symbolizes Elijah in the desert.

Before you leave, walk around the church to the rounded chevet at the far end; it's a perfect example of the transition between the Romanesque and Gothic styles.

★ **Rue de Rollebeek**: built on the bed of an old tributary of the Senne, this delightful, car-free cobbled street is lined with beautiful houses, most of which house antiques shops and restaurants. There are two identical brick houses at No. 7, both with attractive gabling.

★ **Place du Grand-Sablon** (map III, B-C1): this upmarket rectangular square, lined with historic houses, expensive antiques shops and smart restaurants has a discreetly wealthy atmosphere, and is a suitably classy home for the chocolatier and cake-maker Wittamer (favoured by the Belgian royals). The area was once sandy marshland (hence the name Sablon, or sand), and later became the site of a cemetery. It wasn't until the 18th century that wealthy burghers decided to make their homes here. Today, the square is a lively place, especially on Saturday (all day) and Sunday morning, when it hosts an expensive antiques market. The fountain in the centre was funded by a Scotsman who sought refuge in Brussels in the 18th century, when he was living in exile.

A small museum, the **Musée des Postes et Télécommunications**, is at No. 40. Open 10am–4.30pm. Closed Monday and Sunday. Admission: free.

★ **Église Notre-Dame-du-Sablon** (map III, C1, **95**): open 9am–5.30pm. Closed Sunday morning. This former oratory was converted into a large church following the exploits of Beatrice Soetkens, who heard voices telling her to steal a statue of the Virgin Mary from Antwerp cathedral and take it to Brussels. In 1348, she did precisely that, escaping from Antwerp in a boat. The crossbowmen's guild took Beatrice under their protection, and turned the oratory into a church and a destination for pilgrims. The statue has not survived the centuries, but the legend also gave rise to an annual procession that later became the Ommegang (*see* 'Festivals').

The church has an elegant Flamboyant Gothic facade with a rose window, while the tower is in Brabant Gothic style. A parrot is fixed to the top of the tower during the city's annual crossbow contest. In 1615, Archduke Albert, who was suffering from gout, was unable to participate, so his wife stood in and won (nobody knows which skill or diplomacy was the true winner). Traditionally, royal weddings are held here, and the church was also popular with the guilds, including the arquebusiers, archers and fencers as well as the crossbowmen, who came here to worship their patron saints. Enter the church through the south transept.

The handsome Brabant Gothic interior has capitals ornamented with curling cabbage leaves. These support the 12 apostles. There's a fine blind triforium, and the vaulting over the nave is marked by ogive windows. The rather heavy baroque pulpit is adorned with representations of the four Evangelists: a bull (Luke), a lion (Mark), an angel (Matthew) and an eagle (John). You can see a copy of the statue of the Virgin Mary on the left of the choir, above a sculpture describing the story of Beatrice's escape. In the north transept, you'll find the chapel of the Tour and Taxis family, who served Charles V and were responsible for the postal service.

The choir is a masterpiece, with beautiful columns, marked ribbing and stunning stained-glass windows.

★ **Place du Petit-Sablon** (map III, C2): in contrast to the Grand-Sablon with its central car park, the Petit-Sablon is a green oasis, a formal garden fringed with columns surmounted by bronze statues representing the guilds. Each column is decorated with a different geometric design, while each section of the fence between the columns is ornamented in individual style.

This exquisite square was laid out in the 19th century as a nostalgic homage to the 16th century, a period plagued by religious conflicts and iconoclasts. Statues of the counts of Egmont and Hoorn, who were beheaded on the Grand'Place in 1568, dominate the upper part of the park, above the fountain, while there are stone statues of humanists, scholars and map-makers, including Gerhardus Mercator and Abraham Ortelius. The Egmont Palace, where the Foreign Affairs Ministry hosts receptions, stands behind the garden. As you leave this peaceful place, turn left and walk along rue de la Régence, a broad road built in the 19th century, until you reach the Palais de Justice.

★ **Palais de Justice** (map III, B2): it may be the seat of Belgium's highest court, but this colossal structure is first and foremost the fruit of Leopold II's delusions of grandeur. The king found a willing accomplice in Joseph Poelaert, the architect responsible for this monstrosity, which has a surface area of 26,000 square metres (280,000 square feet), 4,000 square metres bigger than St Peter's, in Rome. When it was opened in 1883, amidst predictable pomp and ceremony, it was the biggest building in Europe. Léopold, who was hell-bent on establishing Brussels as a rival to Paris, wanted the building to symbolize his vision for the city: the result was a bizarre architectural melting pot of neo-Classicism and Syro-Babylonianism, with the odd nod to styles such as Gothic.

Some architecture buffs will argue that this is a neglected masterpiece of eclecticism: judge for yourself, but remember as you do that the Palais de Justice was built on the back of human suffering. A large portion of the Marolles was bulldozed to make way for this Palace of Justice, leaving thousands homeless and earning Poelaert the undying hatred of Brussels' working classes.

Take a look at the 40-metre-high porch, which is utterly out of proportion to the rather silly-looking cupola that surmounts it. During World War II, the Nazis set fire to the cupola after discovering that a band of locals had stolen bottles of wine and champagne that the Germans had stored in the Palace of Justice cellars. There are numerous statues symbolizing Justice in all its forms, but we'll spare you the soporific details. To the left, under the gigantic porch, you'll see a collection of flowers and photographs that commemorate the victims of the paedophile cases that rocked Belgium in the mid-1990s (*see* 'History').

The Palais de Justice marks the beginning of the avenue Louise district, which in turn links the centre with the Bois de la Cambre, further south. The area around avenue Louise, boulevard de Waterloo, avenue de la Toison-d'Or and place Stéphanie is home to the chic boutiques of Armani, MaxMara, Gucci et al. Several shopping centres and arcades, some rather down at heel, lie between avenue Louise and porte de Namur.

★ **Place Royale** (map III, C1): this rather uninspiring neoclassical complex stands at the top of the Coudenberg ('cold mountain'), near the fine arts museums. You could be in almost any pompous 18th-century square in France, which is hardly surprising since French architects were responsible for their construction. The place was commissioned by Charles of Lorraine, governor of the Low Countries, when the region was under Austrian rule. A statue of the crusader Godefroid de Bouillon, the first king of Jerusalem, stands in the centre, on the spot once dominated by a statue of Charles of Lorraine, who was dethroned during the French Revolution. The church of Saint-Jacques-sur-Coudenberg, a rather intimidating Classical structure, was built here when the palace of the Dukes of Burgundy burnt down in 1731. Several kings have been crowned there.

Recent archaeological digs have unearthed the remnants of the **Magna Aula**, the ceremonial hall of the Dukes of Brabant, where Charles V abdicated in 1550. Together with the underground **rue Isabelle**, these remains could form a major tourist attraction.

The place des Palais was developed alongside the place Royale. The frosty Classical-style Royal Palace overlooks a vast esplanade opposite the French-style Parc de Bruxelles. If you ever happen to be flying over the city in a private plane, you'll see that the park is laid out to represent Masonic signs.

The **Palais de la Nation**, which houses the parliament, stands opposite the Royal Palace on the other side of the park. To the left of it, you can see the headquarters of a venerable Belgian business institution, **Société Générale**, now owned by the French company Suez-Générale des Eaux. This collection of buildings was the first of Brussels' endless urban developments.

The pediment of the Royal Palace is decorated with a frieze symbolizing Belgium and its two main rivers, the Meuse and the Scheldt. The palace is open to the public in August and the first half of September (9.30am–3.30pm; closed Monday). You can visit the gallery, the Throne Room and the Empire Room, where you'll find the usual luxurious assortment of gold and massive chandeliers.

On the right is the **Musée de la Dynastie** (*see* 'Museums').

★ If you're determined to see the whole of this area, turn down rue Royale, past the Parc de Bruxelles and rue de la Loi, until you get to the place du Congrès (map II, D2), where you'll see a tall **column** with a statue of Leopold I, first King of the Belgians, on top. This monument commemorates the promulgation, after independence, of the first Belgian constitution by the Congrès National of 1831. Behind it lies a soulless, windswept wilderness of office blocks, complete with a giant concrete terrace and hanging gardens that are at the mercy of the savage winds.

★ **Le Jardin Botanique** (map II, D1). the enormous glasshouses of the botanical gardens, which stand at the end of rue Royale, level with the porte de Schaerbeek, have been transformed into the French-speaking community's main cultural centre, with auditoriums for drama and music as well as exhibition spaces. Much of the original garden disappeared to make way for the Nord-Midi railway junction. But the complex is beautifully illuminated at night, and it's still home to some fine trees and sculptures, including pieces by Constantin Meunier and Charles Van der Stappen.

You can now return to the place Royale circuit.

★ Take rue de la Montagne-de-la-Cour, which leads down from place Royale. On your right, you'll see the magnificent iron and-glass **Old England** building (map III, C1, **123**), one of the city's finest art-nouveau structures. Once a department store, it was designed by the architect Paul Saintenoy, and has a majestic turret into which daylight streams through spectacular oriel windows. Since June 2000, this building has been home to the **Musée des instruments de Musique** (*see* 'Museums'). The airy top-floor restaurant has a terrace with superb views of the city.

To your left, overlooking the wonderful skylight of the Musée d'Art Moderne, you can see the elegant Classical facade of the **Palais de Charles de Lorraine**. The recently refurbished rooms now house displays of decorative art from the Age of Enlightenment, including crockery, sculptures, tapestries and engravings. Slightly further down the hill, you'll see a monumental steel sculpture, The Whirling Ear, by the American Alexander Calder; in true Brussels style, it was erected last year – replacing a car park – after spending 40 years gathering dust in the Fine Arts Museum's vaults.

★ **Hôtel Ravenstein** (map III, C1, **106**): this building on the corner of rue Ravenstein, with a handsome, finely worked facade, is all that remains of the 15th century, when the Dukes of Burgundy held sway.

★ **Palais des Beaux-Arts** (map III, C1, **96**): this art-deco complex on the corner of rues Ravenstein and Baron-Horta, a late work by Victor Horta, is one of Belgium's best venues for classical music, and is home to the Rideau theatre company. It also hosts excellent temporary exhibitions and the annual Queen Elisabeth Music Festival, one of Europe's most important. Next door, on rue Baron-Horta, you'll find the **Musée du Cinéma** and the **Royal Film Archives**.

This district has been transformed by the construction of the railway junction linking Gare du Nord with Gare du Midi. The project took nearly 50 years to finish, and the modern Mont des Arts was constructed after its completion, in the 1960s. There's a monumental clock with automatic chimes beneath the arcade. Every 15 minutes, it rings out alternate French and Dutch songs. Walk through the gardens of the Mont des Arts, and you'll see what looks like a bunker, but is in fact the **Bibliothèque royale** (Royal Library). A fine Gothic chapel has been incorporated into the modern building. This is also the site of the **Musée du Livre et de l'Imprimerie**. Statues of Albert I (on horseback) and his wife, Queen Elisabeth, stand on either side of boulevard de l'Empereur.

★ **L'église de la Madeleine** (map II, C3, **97**): rue de la Madeleine. This is a small Gothic church with a baroque doorway. A tiny chapel was tacked on to the left-hand side in 1958 after the area was redeveloped, to uncommonly successful effect.

You have now reached the end of the second walk.

NORTH OF L'ÎLOT SACRÉ, THE OLD PORT AND THE BÉGUINAGE
The area northwest of the Pentagon lay on the old trade route that connected Flanders with the Rhine, and was a key port on the canal network. When the original port became too small, a new port was built further north. Today, the Metro passes under quai au Bois-à-Brûler, where Brussels' first docks once stood. If old photographs are anything to go by, the area has definitely seen better days, for the old waterway, now filled in, brought a certain cachet to this part of Brussels. Still, this is a pleasant, quiet place that's well worth exploring, and a whole range of curiosities awaits those who venture beyond place de Brouckère.

From the Grand'Place, take rue au Beurre and turn right into rue des Fripiers, then head for place de la Monnaie.

★ **Théâtre royal de la Monnaie** (map II, B2): rebuilt in the middle of the 19th century by Joseph Poelaert (of the unforgettable Palais de Justice) and substantially renovated in the 1980s, Brussels' opera house has little to recommend it architecturally, but it's an essential stop for visitors because of its role in the fight for Belgian independence. In 1830, the audience watching Auber's opera *La Muette de Portici* were stirred to action by the words of the lead tenor: 'Sacred love of my country, give us pride and courage. To my country I owe my life; it owes me freedom.' The audience poured onto the square, and the Belgian Revolution was born. More recently, the Monnaie has established a formidable reputation thanks to its artistic director, Antonio

Pappano, who's taking over from Bernard Haitink at the Royal Opera House, Covent Garden, in 2002.

Rue Neuve, which leads off this square, is a lively, tacky, pedestrianized street full of high-street shops. It's pretty much deserted at night.

★ **Place de Brouckère** (map II, B2): at the turn of the last century, this glamorous square was the favourite hangout of the Brussels bourgeoisie. It's now full of ugly office blocks, and all that remains of its heyday is the Hôtel Métropole, with a Statue of Liberty at the top and a splendid Belle Époque café (*see* 'Where to drink').

★ **Église Sainte-Catherine** (map II, B2, **98**): as you head for the old docks, glance up at this church, another Poelaert project. His design lacks flair and character, and the church looks as if it's been built by a steamroller. Behind the church, you can see the Tour Noire (Black Tower), a rare remnant of the 13th-century city wall, which is now surrounded by a salmon-pink Novotel.

★ **The old docks** (map II, B1, **107**): this area was once a harbour, accessible by canal. The quays have long since been filled in, but the streets are still named after the products that were traded here: quai aux Briques (brick), quai au Bois-à-Brûler (firewood); and further north, quai aux Pierres-de-Taille (stone) and quai au Foin (hay). Today, fish restaurants line the docks.

– Place Sainte-Catherine and rues Sainte-Catherine and Vieux-Marché-aux-Grains, together with the surrounding streets, are home to a host of fascinating **gables** that date from the 17th to the 19th centuries. Perhaps the finest is the corner building at the end of quai aux Briques, the Cheval Marin: once the harbour master's house, it's a priceless example of Flemish Renaissance architecture.

★ **Maison de la Bellone** (map II, A2): rue de Flandre 46. Open Tuesday to Friday, 10am–6pm. Closed July. Admission: free. At the end of a passage-way off this busy street, the Maison de la Bellone has one of the city's finest facades (it was designed by Jean Cosyn, the brains behind the Grand'Place). The house is a splendid blend of French Classicism and Flemish baroque. Protected by a translucent roof, the building is now used for exhibitions, plays, dance and poetry events.

★ The best and worst of Brussels sit cheek by jowl in a working-class area between place du Marché-aux-Porcs and place du Nouveau-Marché-aux-Grains. On rue Rempart-des-Moines (which leads off rue de Flandre), the **impasse de la Cigogne** (map II, A2), with its pretty baroque porch, is a typical example of the *impasses* (cul-de-sacs) that were dotted across the city in the 19th century. The dim yellow lighting lends the area a somewhat ghostly feel after dark.

★ **Église Saint-Jean-Baptiste-du-Béguinage** (map II, B2, **99**): place du Béguinage. Open Tuesday to Friday, 10am–5pm. This is Brussels' most elegant example of Flemish baroque, with a balanced facade consisting of three separate registers, shaped like a cross in accordance with Italian tradition. Whilst the exterior is baroque, the interior, which has outstanding fluted vaulting, is Gothic.

The long, white Classical facade of the nearby **Hospice Pachéco**, which has somehow survived demolition, adds to the peaceful atmosphere.

★ **Koninklijke Vlaamse Schouwburg**, rue de Laeken 146 (map II, B1): the Royal Flemish Theatre is a hybrid, pagoda-like structure, built in the 19th century using the materials that were fashionable at the time, in particular wrought iron. The facade is faux-Renaissance, while the side walls are swollen with crescent-shaped balconies and linked by stairways that make it look a bit like a pyramid. The theatre was founded by a militant Flemish worker, and was a huge success: today, it's one of the Flemish community's flagship cultural spaces.

On rue de Laeken, between rue du Pont-Neuf and rue du Cirque, there's an interesting restored building that retains the style of the typical 19th-century Brussels house. Boulevard Jacqmain, on the other hand, is one of the most glaring examples of *bruxellization*.

Cross boulevard Adolphe-Max, barge your way onto rue Neuve and you'll come across a ghastly concrete block that houses the Inno department store. This architectural aberration replaced a Horta building that burned down in 1967, claiming 350 lives. Opposite, and a slightly forlorn sight amid all the neon, is the baroque Église de Notre-Dame-du-Finistère. Stroll down rue Neuve towards place de la Monnaie and you'll see the odd survivors of a bygone era, such as the broad Spanish house with stepped gabling and, hidden away behind the shopfront of a high-street clothes store, the art-deco Métropole cinema, which is vaguely reminiscent of an old steamship. It's also worth popping into the passage du Nord, a kind of mini Galeries Saint-Hubert, with an elegant glass ceiling.

★ **Place des Martyrs** (map II, C2, **100**): Brussels' most beautiful neo-classical square is named after the patriots who lost their lives in the struggle to liberate Belgium. Despite its symbolic importance, it was left to rot by developers before residential flats and government offices moved in. In the centre is a tomb, with a memorial to those who fought in the Belgian Revolution. On the right, you can see an interesting art-nouveau-style statue of the heroes of independence.

★ **Le Centre belge de la bande dessinée**, rue des Sables 20 (map II, C2, **102**): a homage to cartoons of all kinds, housed in a former department store designed by Victor Horta (*see* 'Museums'). This is the end of this circuit.

Comic-strip murals
If you're inspired by your visit to the Centre belge de la bande dessinée, you should look out for the comic-strip murals that have sprung up all over the city. There's no special itinerary, because the walls in question are all over the Pentagon: instead, look for the capital letters A-S on maps II and III, which mark the murals that you'll come across during your walks through Brussels. They're listed below (the name in brackets at the end of each description is the publisher).

A. **Le Passage** (map II, B3): rue Marché-au-Charbon, opposite the police station. This side gable by François Schuiten is a tribute to 'Brüsel', from the *Cités obscures* series (Casterman).

B. **Broussaille** (map II, B3): rue Marché-au-Charbon, level with the Plattesteen café. Frank Pé's work looks a bit like the cover of a guide (Dupuis).

C. **Victor Sackville** (map II, B3): rue Marché-au-Charbon and rue du Lombard. Francis Carin's spy, in the service of the king of England during the Belle Époque (Lombard).

D. **Ric Hochet** (map II, B3): rue du Bon-Secours, between rue du Marché-au-Charbon and boulevard Anspach. The raincoat-clad detective gets on with his acrobatic antics under the watchful eye of Commissaire Bourdon and his niece. The artist, Tibet, lived in this neighbourhood after leaving his native Marseille (Lombard).

E. **Isabelle** (map III, A1): on the corner of place Anneessens and rue de la Verdure. Will's sorceress, Calendula, shows off her charms and an imaginary world that takes us beyond the destruction of Brussels' apartment blocks (Dupuis).

F. **Le Chat** (map III, A2): boulevard du Midi. Garfield's lookalike appears in the Saturday supplement of the newspaper *Le Soir*, and is the creation of Philippe Geluck. Here, he looks astonished by the number of trains coming and going at Gare du Midi (Casterman).

G. **La Marque Jaune** (off map III, beyond A1): rue du Petit-Rempart, near porte d'Anderlecht. A homage to Edgar Jacobs's legendary Blake and Mortimer, in the shadow of a sinister symbol (Blake et Mortimer).

H. **Lucky Luke** (map II, A3): rue de la Buanderie. The fastest cowboy in the West and the criminal exploits of his incorrigible cousins, the Daltons (Lucky Productions).

I. **Yslaire** (map II, A3, next to **125**): rue des Chartreux (Glénat and Delcourt).

J. **Néron** (map II, A3): place Saint-Géry. The most popular Flemish cartoon hero, drawn by Marc Sleen, is full of optimism and common sense (Standaard).

K. **Cubitus** (map II, A2): rue de Flandre 109. Dupa's sweet old seadog, Sémaphore, has found his natural home (Lombard).

L. **Bob et Bobette** (map II, B1): on the corner of rue de Laeken and rue du Canal. The Flemish public's best-loved tribe, all here, as they should be, next to the Royal Flemish Theatre (Standaard).

M. **Gaston Lagaffe** (map II, C2): boulevard Pachéco, near the Centre belge de la bande déssinée. André Franquin's quintessential antihero appears with his laughing gull and piratical cat, this time in 3-D (Dupuis).

N. **Olivier Rameau** (map II, B3): rue du Chêne, a stone's throw from the Manneken-Pis. Dany's triumphant tribute to Disneyworld, from the country of Rêverose (Dreamland), arrived here thanks to a special request from the firework-seller next door (P&T Production).

O. **Quick et Flupke** (map III, B2): rue Haute. The *ketjes* of Brussels deal with Agent 15 in the heart of the Marolles. A homage to Hergé (Casterman).

P. **Boule et Bill** (map III, A2): rue du Chevreuil. Right by the flea market, this is a delightful evocation of life in this neighbourhood. Roba's comic-strip facades is one of the most successful in town (Dargaud).

Q. **Jojo** (map III, A3): rue Pieremans 43. André Geerts's affectionate vision of a little boy's domestic universe, complete with mum and best friend (Dupuis).

R. **Cori le Moussaillon** (map II, A3): rue des Fabriques. The great period of 'ocean-going beggars' opposing the Spanish Armada, as seen by Bob de Moor, one of the pillars of the Belgian school (Casterman).

S. **Blondin et Cirage** (map III, A2): rue des Capucins. A tribute to the hilarious multiethnic duo created in 1939 by Joseph Gillain, aka Jijé (Dupuis).

– **Fresque Bruxelles** (map II, C2, **13**): in the foyer of the Sleep Well (*see* 'Where to stay'). Johan de Moor's humorous fresco features some of Brussels' most familiar images: Woltje, Agent 15, Le Chat, the Atomium, Magritte and Brel's favourite tram, No. 33, taking Madeleine to eat chips at Eugène's.

– After your tour of the Centre belge de la bande dessinée, return to the centre via rue du Marais and rue Montagne-aux-Herbes-Potagères. Pause at the corner of rue du Fossé-aux-Loups to admire the impressive building that houses the CGER/ASLK bank; the curves soften the harshness of the bronze plaques that cover the facade. Take a look, too, at the structure opposite, built in ocean-liner style. Next door, you'll see the Radisson SAS Hotel, built more recently in a moderately convincing neo-art-deco style. A piece of the medieval city wall, which was destined for demolition, is now on show in the hotel's cavernous foyer. It's a weird combination, but at least it's still there.

THE MAROLLES DISTRICT (map III, A-B2)
The Marolles, a neighbourhood long associated with *zwanze* (cheek) and revolt, embodies the true spirit of Brussels, although it's beginning to show signs of gentrification. It's not exactly pretty, but it's a fascinating place that you should explore at a leisurely pace, paying as much attention to the sounds and smells of the district as its sights.

Short history
In the 13th century, the Marolles lay outside the city walls and was home to a 'marginal' population of peasants who had to leave the city proper when bells sounded the evening curfew. During this period, the Marolles was a centre of religion, care for the sick and justice: Notre-Dame-de-la-Chapelle became an important place of worship, the neighbourhood harboured a hospice for lepers – and was also home to the Galgenberg ('gallows hill'), which stood on the site of the Palais de Justice. The Jews accused of the sacrament were burnt on this wretched spot.

From the Middle Ages to the 19th century
During the Middle Ages, the Marolles was chiefly inhabited by clothiers and tanners, who were not allowed to practise their mucky trades in the centre of town. The Minimes Brotherhood, a religious community from Anderlecht, also settled here, to tend to the city's poor. When the second city wall was erected, in the 15th century, the Marolles became part of the expanded city centre, and the standard of living in the area improved, although the Bowendael district remained one of the city's most shunned. Residents frequently demanded that gates be erected at the end of the streets with the worst reputations, supposedly to stop prostitution spreading from there to

the rest of the neighbourhood. The Marolles acquired its name until the 17th century, when the Apostolline Sisters of the Miriam Colentes community moved in (Marolles is a corruption of 'Miriam Colentes'). In the 19th century, the proletariat suffered appalling deprivation, and quality of life in the area sank to an all-time low. At the time, there were some 40,000 inhabitants, around four times the number of people who live in the area today, and landlords frequently crowded several families into one tiny apartment.

The first stone of the city's megalomaniacal Palais de Justice was laid in 1866. It took 17 years to complete, and required the wholesale demolition of a huge residential area in the Marolles. From that time on, the palace has cast a long shadow over the neighbourhood. The Marolles was fertile ground for the spread of socialist ideals; towards the end of the 19th century, the Belgian Workers' Party commissioned Victor Horta to build the Maison du Peuple in rue Joseph-Stevens. It was regarded as the art-nouveau guru's masterpiece, but that didn't stop it being knocked down in 1965, despite protests by the world's leading architects, to make way for an ugly office block. You can now see rescued fragments of the original in Antwerp, where they have been controversially incorporated into a café, the Horta Huis.

'Sanitization' and the 19th century

A host of urban-development ideas were bandied about during the 19th century, including 'sanitization', which ostensibly meant improving basic standards of living. In 1913, the construction of the first blocks of flats in the Marolles, predecessors of the modern housing estate, reduced yet another area to rubble. Howling gales blew along the passages between the sterile blocks, and the inhabitants felt increasingly isolated and alienated.

During World War II, the Marolles became the centre for a thriving black market. Many of the district's traditionally anti-authoritarian inhabitants went out of their way to protect Jews in the neighbourhood, and the SS carried out regular raids here.

In the 1950s, the influence of the Modernist architect Le Corbusier spread to the area, and a whole host of 'neighbourhood associations' were formed, including the Brigittines, la Querelle and Les Radis. In 1969, the associations joined forces to oppose a mad plan to enlarge the Palais de Justice. They founded the Comité Général d'action des Marolles (Marolles General Council for Action) and, after a vigorous campaign, managed to scotch the expansion plan. They also lobbied for several rehabilitation projects to be launched in the neighbourhood, with an emphasis on respecting the history and architecture of the Marolles. King Baudouin and King Albert II even laid the foundation stones for some of the buildings that were constructed as a result of the council's triumph over the state.

Today, the Marolles is still inhabited by immigrants (from Spain and, more recently, from Turkey and Morocco), while on some street corners, you can hear the old Brabant dialect, Brusseleir, a fantastically mixed up language peppered with Walloon, Spanish and Yiddish words. Thanks to the local *bloedpanch* confraternity, there are white street signs in the local dialect, as well as the usual blue signs in French and Flemish.

While it remains a bastion of Brussels' traditions, the Marolles is fast developing a trendy side. Rue Blaes is now home to several excellent antiques shops, fashionable eateries and bars. Many people welcome the odd sign of gentrification, believing that the neighbourhood's character is not under threat. The district is usually pretty peaceful, but it bursts into action on Sunday morning, when the biggest flea market is held. It's still a very authentic event, so try not to miss it.

A walk through the Marolles

The whole area (map III, A-B2) is organized around two parallel one-way thoroughfares: rue Haute and rue Blaes. Rue Blaes leads into place du Jeu de Balle, the site of the daily flea market. If you like the weird and apparently inconsequential things that explain why certain people love a certain neighbourhood, this is the tour for you; don't bother with it if you're only interested in ticking off the sights.

★ Start at the corner of **rue Haute** and rue des Renards, where there's a *caricoles* (whelk) seller on weekends. It's a Brussels speciality, although the tradition is dying out.

★ Walk down **rue des Renards**, where you can still see some of the original facades and several small, modest dwellings. There are several good antiques shops here.

★ **Place du Jeu de Balle** (on your left): every morning, come rain come shine, from 8am to 1pm, you'll find the flea market in full swing. Sunday is the biggest day, but the pros come at the crack of dawn on weekdays, when the real bargains are to be had.

The square was designed in the mid-19th century, at the same time as rue Blaes, when there was a drive to clean the Marolles up. It was originally intended for pelota-playing, but in 1873, it was designated a *marché au carreau*: this meant that traders could only operate from stalls, and could only sell second-hand items. New merchandise was forbidden. Today, you can browse through a miscellany of paintings, books, tables, chairs, telephones, lamps, cutlery, shoes, wine-glasses, comic strips and, well, pretty much anything.

On the rue Blaes side of the market square, an old fire station has been converted into flats, with antiques dealers occupying the ground-floor stands. When you're all browsed out, wind down with a beer – and some live music on Sunday – at **La Brocante** (rue Blaes 170, on the corner of rue des Renards). Chris, the percussionist, and Ray, who plays the accordion, perform simple, popular music, and their concerts are popular with inveterate drinkers and stray tourists – but don't stay all day or you'll never see the rest of the area.

★ Trace your steps back to **rue de la Rasière**. At the beginning of the street, to your right, you'll see the first social-housing estate, which was erected in the early 20th century and is now a listed building. It's built of alternating brown and yellow bricks, with recesses in the facades and covered walkways linking each block.

★ Return to rue Blaes and take a left onto rue Ghislain. There's a kindergarten school at No. 40, built in pure art-nouveau style by Victor Horta.

★ At rue de Nancy 18, you'll see a late-19th-century institutional building with the **sgraffito** inscription 'Hygiène-Sécurité' in the centre. Sgraffito is a decorative technique that consists of applying several colours, then removing parts of the outer layers of the material that have been applied. This, as you've probably guessed, is where the policy of 'sanitization' was overseen. The art-nouveau building at No. 6 used to be a doctor's house: it's less florid than many examples of the style, but the tendency towards asymmetry is pretty pronounced.

★ Rue des Tanneurs 60, a little further on, was once home to the **Palais du Vin**, as you can see from the clusters of grapes that decorate the broad pediment. The upper part is ornamented with sgraffiti images of the coats of arms of Europe's wine-producing regions.

★ Turn right into rue du Miroir, then left down rue des Visitandines, where you can see an example of 1960s architectural blundering. The tiny **Église des Brigittines**, however, is a perfect example of Brabant baroque, with alternating layers of brick and stone. Today, it's a theatre.

★ Turn right into rue Notre-Seigneur; if you're feeling peckish, you can dine at La Grande Porte, a popular Marollien restaurant that's something of an institution (*see* 'Where to eat'). If not, take a look at the baroque doorway next door, then head back up the street and turn right into **rue Haute**. There's some fine old gabling at No. 118, and Pieter Brueghel the Elder lived in the brick house at No. 132. Café Ploegman, at No. 148, is one of the neighbourhood's oldest taverns; it serves draught *faro* beer, and local children come here to sing songs at Epiphany (6 January). No. 164, which was built under Spanish rule, is known as the Spanish House.

You can wend your way back to place du Grand-Sablon by turning left onto rue des Minimes and taking one of the new hydraulic lifts up the 17-metre (56-foot) slope that leads to place Poelaert. It's similar to the lifts connecting the lower and upper parts of Lisbon, which is where the Belgians got the idea. A metal walkway provides a spectacular panorama over the city.

★ If you're interested, head south to **porte de Hal**, a remnant of the second city wall, which is medieval in origin but was largely rebuilt in neo-Gothic style in the late 19th century.

Walks Outside the Pentagon

IXELLES (map I, B3)

This lively commune with a socially and ethnically diverse population lies southeast of the Pentagon. Like most of the city's communes, it has its own distinct character. It is bisected by avenue Louise, which is lined with comfortable dwellings and luxury boutiques: the street is actually under the jurisdiction of Brussels commune, but you don't need to worry about the reasons. The area around chaussée de Wavre (near porte de Namur), in particular the Galerie d'Ixelles, is home to a well-integrated Congolese community; it's nicknamed Matongé, in memory of a district of Kinshasa, in what is now the Democratic Republic of Congo.

Chaussée d'Ixelles leads all the way down to place Flagey, where you can see the wonderful Maison de la Radio Belge, a fine example of art-deco architecture whose ship-shaped design earned it the nickname *Le Paquebot* ('Steamship'). Abandoned for many years while pressure groups and developers squabbled over its future, the building has been renovated, not redeveloped, and its future appears secure. The area on the chaussée d'Ixelles side of the square is home to a Portuguese community.

Further south you can stroll around the romantic, willow-swept Etangs (ponds), and admire the desirable turn-of-the-last-century houses that overlook the water. There used to be seven ponds stretching along the Maelbeek valley, all segments of the old canals, but only two survive. Continue south to the Abbaye de la Cambre, which is worth exploring although little of the original building remains. The monastery was destroyed during the religious conflicts that erupted after the Reformation. It was rebuilt in the 17th and 18th centuries.

Ixelles is home to the highest concentration of art-nouveau buildings in the capital, and some of the finest examples of the style. Enthusiasts can take an art-nouveau walk round some of the most beautiful facades.

What is art nouveau?

Art nouveau describes a movement that flourished 1895 and 1905, and affected architecture and the decorative arts throughout Europe. There were several terms for the new style: Liberty (after the London store) in Italy, Arte Jóven in Spain, Jugendstil in Germany and eastern Europe, and Secession in Austria. In Britain, it was represented by the Arts and Crafts movement, while in Belgium, it was also described as 'Ligne Coup de Fouet' (Whiplash Style), a reference to the use of swirling organic patterns, inspired by plant stalks and flowers.

The common characteristic linking these different trends was the desire to break away from the eclecticism that dominated the 19th century.

Art-nouveau designers tried to harmonize the structure of their buildings with the decorative features and furniture inside, from the masonry and shape of the windows down to the door handles and details of the interior flooring. Everyday objects were invested with a new importance and dignity as designers went out of their way to reinvent utilitarian objects. Although this highly personal approach was the antithesis of mass production, art-nouveau artists exploited the technical potential of new materials, especially iron, glass and cement.

The movement aimed to create an aesthetic utopia accessible to all, where the beauty of nature was seamlessly linked to daily life, but art nouveau was essentially a middle- and upper-class movement – nobody else could afford the precious woods or the delicate stained-glass and wrought-iron work, which only specialized craftsmen could carry out. Indeed, art nouveau's popularity owes much to the emergence of a thriving business class, who wished to reaffirm their success and to emphasize how different they were to the landed gentry.

In Belgium, the trail-blazer for the art-nouveau movement was the architect Victor Horta, supported by his disciples Paul Hankar, Gustave Strauven and Ernest Blérot. Henry van de Velde, who devoted himself to transferring the style's theories to the applied arts, designed brocades and tapestries, while the socially progressive Gustave Serrurier-Bovy applied the new aesthetic to wallpaper and stained glass, and produced rather sober, functional furniture that people could assemble themselves.

BRUSSELS (MAP IV)

🛏 Where to stay	✕ Where to eat
28 De Boeck's Hôtel	**54** Amadeus

As time went on, art nouveau lost its force and became ridiculously overelaborate, finally acquiring the dishonourable nickname of Style Nouille ('noodle style'). This helps to explains why some of the finest examples in Brussels were demolished.

Art-nouveau walking tour (map IV)
This tour lasts between one and two hours, and takes you through the winding streets of Saint-Gilles and Ixelles in search of the city's finest art-nouveau facades. This attractive, mainly residential district is where Victor Horta set the agenda for the new architectural style, and where his successors, Octave Van Rysselberghe, Paul Hankar and Henry van de Velde, designed a handful of outstanding dwellings. The best time to follow this walk is just after lunch, as it ends with a visit to the Musée Horta, which is open 2–5.30pm (closed Monday and public holidays; *see* 'Museums').

The tour begins at Rond Point, on avenue Louise, which you can reach on tram Nos. 93 or 94. Jump off at Abbaye.

★ **Avenue Louise 346**: this Horta-designed house is a relatively late work and has a slightly stiff air. The facade isn't especially interesting, but the courtyard terrace of the café at No. 344 offers fine views of the back of the building, in particular the elegantly proportioned, curvaceous double window.

From here, walk down rue du Lac:

★ **No. 6** is a house with an artist's studio. All the elements of art nouveau are here: the bow window on the second floor, the curved door that's not flush with the rest of the house and the windows decorated with plant motifs. Follow avenue Général-de-Gaulle, and enjoy a peaceful stroll by the delightful ponds of Ixelles.

★ **No. 36**, La Cascade, is a streamlined, cruise-liner version of art deco. Turn right, away from the ponds, onto rue Vilain-XIIII and take a look at the very different houses at Nos. 7, 9 and 11. Next, turn right onto Avenue Louise, an artery where most of its old buildings have been destroyed to make way for modernity. Once lined with large, elegant town houses, it is one of the city's main thoroughfares, running from the centre of town to the Bois de la Cambre, the manicured prelude to the Forêt de Soignes.

★ **Hôtel Solvay**, avenue Louise 224: this is one of Horta's finest works. He built it for the nephew of a chemical industry magnate and, unusually for an art-nouveau building, it's perfectly symmetrical. Horta's obsession with detail is reflected in the ends of the pipes, the curving line of the windows and the absence of harsh angles. Now cross avenue Louise and turn left.

★ **Hôtel Tassel** (rue Paul-Janson 6): built by Horta in 1893, this showpiece of art nouveau was the first building to combine new materials in such an extravagant fashion. Iron and stone are decoratively blended, while iron is also is used in part of the building's structure.

★ Turn right into **rue de Livourne**. The architect Octave Van Rysselberghe built, and lived in, the austere building at No. 83. It's a typical example of late art nouveau. You can still see the curving lines, but it has lost the plant motifs that characterized many of the earlier works.

★ A the corner of rue de Livourne and rue Florence, at No. 13, you'll see the **Hôtel Otlet**, another work by Van Rysselberghe. Turn left onto rue Veydt, then left onto **rue Faider**, and pause to gawp at the splendid gilt sgraffiti on the house at No. 83, at the intersection with rue Janson.

Go back to rue Veydt, then onto **rue Defacqz**. No. 48 is a fine example of Paul Hankar's work, with rounded windows and sgraffiti. No. 71, where Hankar once lived, has an extraordinary stone base. The building lightens considerably as your eye travels upwards towards the Japanese-inspired sgraffiti, with animal and plant motifs. Turn left onto rue Simonis, then right onto rue du Bailli. At the corner of the square, in front of the Église de la Trinité, complete with baroque facade, take a look at the curving lines of the corner house, which is covered in polished brick and decorated with images of darting swallows. The **Passiflore** tea-room, on the ground floor, is a good place to stop for a drink and a cake or two. Once you're suitably reinforced, circle the right side of the church until you come to rue Africaine.

★ **Rue Africaine 92** shows the influence of the Viennese Secession style, especially in the rounded windows, which are bordered by intricate stone-work and wrought iron.

★ The **Hôtel Hannon**, one of the city's finest examples of art nouveau, is on the corner of avenue Brugmann and avenue de la Jonction. It's now home to Contretype, an exhibition area devoted to photographs: ☎ (02) 538 4220.

Open 1–6pm. Closed Monday. There's an admission fee, even if you just want to see the interior. The gallery houses works by contemporary Belgian and foreign photographers, a fitting tribute to the building's original owner, the industrialist Edouard Hannon, who was a fanatical snapper. In 1902, Hannon enlisted the services of the architect Jules Brunfaut, who had no experience of art nouveau, but created one of the movement's master-pieces. Outside, there's a remarkable mixture of brick and stone, while the corner balcony seems to open like a flower. A little winter garden in a bow window completes the picture. Inside, you can admire the magnificent staircase, decorated with a frieze incorporating an allegory on the theme of poetry and music. Note the plant mosaic on the floor and the corner piece covered in friezes depicting women.

You leave via the back of the house and enter avenue Brugmann, which becomes chaussée de Charleroi as you head back towards the city centre. Turn right onto rue Américaine, where this walk ends.

★ **Musée Horta**: rue Américaine 23. See 'Museums'.

♼ **Tea for Two** (map IV, A2): chaussée de Waterloo 394. ☎ (02) 538 3896. Open 11am–7pm. Closed Monday. A short walk from the Musée Horta, this delightful tea-room offers teas from all over the world, with light meals at lunchtime. You can sit outside in fine weather.

SAINT-GILLES (map I, B3)
The liveliest part of this commune is wedged between porte de Hal and place Louise. It consists of a pleasant network of quiet, increasingly trendy streets. The bohemian atmosphere has made this commune popular with artists, while the atmospheric town-hall square and the cafés and shops on the surrounding streets make this a great place to hang out.

Art nouveau diehards should cast an eye over rue Van der Schrick (map III, A3), between avenue Volders and chaussée de Waterloo, where the architect Ernest Blérot built a collection of outstanding buildings (Nos. 1 to 25) at the turn of the last century. They are all based on the same design, but with a subtly different use of decorative elements.

BOIS DE LA CAMBRE (map I, C4)
The avenue Louise comes to a majestic end (tram Nos. 23, 90, 93) at the Bois de la Cambre, a 124-hectare (310-acre) 'pleasure wood' that was designed and landscaped for Sunday walks, with paths planted with flowers, lakes, ponds for fishing and several wooded walks. The area was originally part of the Forêt de Soignes, but was snapped up by Brussels commune, and landscaped, in the 19th century. The forest itself is a splendid 4,000-hectare (10,000-acre) beech forest, which was once three times as big and belonged to the crown. It has been lovingly maintained since the days of Charles V, with slender beeches regularly planted to preserve the dense, uniform appearance. The Brabant-style neo-Renaissance buildings of the Université Libre de Bruxelles, the city's French-speaking university, are at the edge of the bois de la Cambre.

THE EUROPEAN DISTRICT (map I, C3)
Whatever you make of this area – and parts of it are truly ghastly – the home of the Eurocrats is a vital part of modern Brussels, and merits at least a brief

visit just to see what it's like. The main focus is the hideous rue de la Loi, which leads to rond-point Robert-Schuman. It's drafty, miserable, traffic-heavy street that's lined with office blocks. And it's best avoided if you're feeling down. The building that represents Europe with a capital 'E' is the cross-shaped Berlaymont, or 'Berlaymonstre' to the locals. Originally constructed as the headquarters of the European Union Commission. The Commission building was succeeded by the new European Parliament, nicknamed 'Caprice des Dieux' ('Whim of the Gods) because its elongated oval shape resembles the French cheese of that name, and also because it cost so much. Most of the buildings wedged between rue de la Loi and rue Belliard house political institutions of one sort or another, including the home of the EU's Council of Ministers, the tedious Justus Lipsius building.

Despite the dedicated lobbying of neighbourhood action groups, the whole of Europe is here, and nowhere else. Local associations want the institutions to be properly integrated into local life; instead, they appear to have taken over local life.

– A little to the south of the station, in the Léopold quarter, comic-strip fans can lose themselves in a dozen second-hand bookshops devoted to their obsession, all of them on chaussée de Wavre (map I, C3), between rue du Trône and rue Goffart. If you're in search of bargains or rare classics, you might be in luck.

★ The **squares Marie-Louise** and **Ambiorix** (map I, C3, **121**), to the north of rond-point Schuman, are at the heart of a 19th-century residential neighbourhood that provides a pleasant backdrop for a brief stroll. There are several Horta buildings on Avenue Palmerston, which links the two squares, including the stunning **Hôtel Van Eetvelde** at No. 4. One of Belgium's, if not the world's, frilliest examples of art nouveau is the **Hôtel Saint-Cyr**, at square Ambiorix 11, built in 1903 by Gustave Strauven. There's plenty to look at on every floor, but the highlight is the circular window on the top floor, where iron, glass, wood and brick are used to create a crazed design of extravagantly curling lines.

NORTHWEST BRUSSELS (map 1, A1-2)

★ **Koekelberg Basilica** (map I, A2). Metro: Simonis. This vast, indigestible neo-Byzantine pile was commissioned by Leopold II to mark the 75th anniversary of Belgium's independence. The original project never got off the drawing board, and a new one eventually took off in 1926 – and was completed in 1969. Not much of note came out of all those years of building, except the awe-inspiring dimensions of the place and a few modern windows. You can visit the cupola, from where there are panoramic views.

★ **Musée Renée Magritte** (map I, A1, **126**): rue Essegem 135, Brussels 1090. Metro: Belgica. ☎ (02) 428 2626. Open Wednesday to Sunday, 10am–6pm. Admission: 240BEF, with discounts for under-23s. There's a maximum of 20 visitors at one time, so booking is advisable. Located in Jette commune, this new museum opened in June 1999 in the modest suburban house where René Magritte lived between 1930 and 1954. The painter's Surrealist world has been faithfully reconstructed on the ground floor. At first sight, it's nothing special – but that's the point. The décor is painted in Magritte's favourite colours, while his paintings are hung next to pieces of furniture you'll recognize from his works of art – the wood stove, for example, the mantelpiece, the bath and the piano. The second floor houses an exhibition of paintings by Magritte's followers and members of the Belgian Surrealist movement, as well as a display of 400 rare objects and documents, including a telegram of condolence sent by King Baudouin and Queen Fabiola to Magritte's widow, Georgette, when the artist died.

THE ROYAL ESTATE AT LAEKEN (map I, B1)

This vast area on the city's northern fringes consists of parks, wooded areas and lakes, all carefully landscaped in the English style. The 18th-century royal palace, once home to the Austrian governors and briefly possessed by Napoleon, who acquired it in 1804, stands in the middle of the estate. It became a royal palace when Leopold I was crowned King of the Belgians. In the western section, you can see a beautiful 18th-century pavilion a Flemish neo-Gothic monument to Leopold I and the remarkable **Royal Greenhouse** (map I, B1, **108**). This spectacular glass-and-iron structure consists of a series of different-shaped glass domes that match together. It was designed by the architect Alphonse Balat and his pupil, Victor Horta himself. The elegant main rotunda is the masterpiece among the many masterpieces here. You can catch a glimpse of it from avenue du Parc-Royal, but for a few days at the end of April and the beginning of May, the glasshouses are open to the public. ☎ (02) 513 8940. Trams Nos. 19 and 23 will take you there. Entry is free except in the evening, when you pay 100BEF to see them illuminated. Whenever you go, be prepared for a long wait to get in and, given the crowds inside, for a rather cramped exploration of the superb collection of tropical plants.

★ The **Église Notre-Dame de Laeken** stands at the southern end of the estate. It was built by Joseph 'Palais de Justice' Poelaert at the request of Leopold I's queen, Louise-Marie, and he came up with a rather heavy structure that's best described as Poelaert Gothic. You can visit the royal crypt and the cemetery behind the church, where you'll find a copy of Rodin's *Thinker*.

★ **Pavillon Chinois** and **Tour Japonaise** (map I, B1, **109**): avenue Van-Praet 44, north of the royal estate. Trams Nos. 23, 52 and 92. ☎ (02) 268 1608. These wonderfully incongruous structures ended up here thanks to a whim of – you've guessed it – Leopold II. You can buy a combined ticket for both attractions for 120BEF; free every first Wednesday of the month. Both are closed on Monday.

– **Pavillon Chinois**: open 10am–4.45pm. It looks Chinese, but it's the work of a French architect. Inside, you'll find a mad mix of Louis XIV- and Louis XVI-style furnishings, with gilt and mirrors, as well as Chinese ornamentation. There are some fine collections of porcelain and silverware.

–**Tour Japonaise**: open 10am–5pm. The pagoda was presented at the 1900 World Fair in Paris. Leopold II saw it, took a fancy to it and had the whole thing taken down and reassembled on its present site. The impressive wooden structure houses a display of traditional Japanese military costumes and weaponry.

HEYSEL (map I, A1)

The stadium and exhibition halls of Heysel are situated near the royal estate. For many non-Belgians, the name is inextricably linked to the collapse of part of the football stadium in 1985, following a fight between fans of Liverpool and Juventus: 40 people died, and the resulting inquiry found that many of these deaths could have been prevented. The stadium has been renovated and renamed the Stade Roi-Baudouin (King Baudouin Stadium).

There's more to Heysel than football, however: it's also home to a vast complex of cultural, sporting and commercial facilities. There's a huge exhibition centre, a recreation complex (Bruparck), a giant cinema complex (Kinepolis), a planetarium and the Atomium, which is the main draw for tourists.

Before hunting out the Atomium, take a look at the enormous art-deco exhibition area, built in the 1930s, with giant statues gracing the skyline. The Atomium, which dominates the skyline, is right behind you.

★ **Atomium** (map I, B1, **110**): boulevard du Centenaire. ☎ (02) 474 8977. Metro: Heysel. From April to August, open 9am–8pm; otherwise 10am–6pm. Admission: 200BEF or on a combined ticket for Bruparck. This molecule of iron has been magnified 165 billion times. As a rough comparison, the book you're holding would be 330 million kilometres (200 million miles) high at the same scale. The highest of the nine spheres is 102 metres (330 feet) high, and has excellent views of the city and a fair chunk of Belgium. This amazing structure was built for the 1958 World Fair, and was due to be demolished shortly afterwards, but it's grown to be one of the city's best-loved monuments. You can take a lift up to the highest sphere, admire the view, then descend via escalators that link the spheres, pausing in each for a giggle at the antiquated displays.

★ **Bruparck**: right next to the Atomium, this huge recreation park is home to several attractions, including **Océade**, which has several scary-looking water slides. Entry fees are a bit steep, but a combined ticket will get you into Mini-Europe as well.

★ **Mini-Europe**: ☎ (02) 478 0550. Website: www.minieurope.com. In summer, open 9.30am–7pm; otherwise 9.30am–5pm. Closed January, February and March. From mid-July to mid-August, there's a fireworks display on Saturday at 10.30pm. Admission: 420BEF, with discounts for senior citizens and children under 12.

Crowds flock to Mini-Europe, a three-hectare (7.5-acre) site dotted with 350 scale models of the famous sights in 70 EU towns. It sounds pretty impressive, if a bit tacky, but the detail is remarkable. Most of the models are made of resin or polyester on a scale of 1:25 – the Eiffel Tower, for example, is 12 metres (nearly 40 feet) high – but some, such as the marble Leaning Tower of Pisa and the French-stone Château de Chenonceaux, are made from more extravagant materials. The average cost of each model was almost £50,000 and some took two years to build. The replica of Paris's Arc de Triomphe lists the 600 generals from the Napoleonic era and the 150 military victories; Big Ben chimes the hour; Vesuvius erupts; the 6,000 hand-painted spectators in Seville's bullring shout '*Olé*'; the Kinderdijk windmills dry out a tiny polder; and a Finn plunges into a lake on her way out of a sauna. Mini-Europe is constantly updating, too, with interactive CDs and teaching manuals for schoolchildren, who are wild about the place. Only in Brussels could you find an attraction so faithful to the expansive spirit of

Europe, although you fear for the model-makers when 12 more countries join up.

Next door, you can visit **Kinepolis**, a vast cinema complex with 27 screens, one of which is a dizzying 600 square metres (nearly 6,500 square feet). It's run by a family-owned Belgian company whose expertise in multiplex building puts the Americans to shame: its Decatron arm built the world's largest cinema, in Madrid. ☎ (02) 478 0450.

The Main Museums

★ **Musées Royaux des Beaux-Arts** (map III, C1, **101**): entry via 3 rue de la Régence. Trams Nos. 92, 93, 94. ☎ (02) 508 3211. Website: www.fine-arts museum.be. Open 10am–5pm. Closed Monday and public holidays. NB: some rooms close for an hour at lunchtime, so plan your visit around that. Admission: 150BFF, with discounts for students and senior citizens. Free for under 13s.

Two top-class museums for the price of one: the Fine Arts Museum and the Modern Art Museum both offer a comprehensive overview of Belgian artists as well as international names. The **Musée d'Art Ancien** (Fine Arts Museum) deals with painting and sculpture from the 15th to the 18th centuries, while the **Musée d'Art Moderne** concentrates on the 19th and 20th centuries, and also houses ambitious temporary exhibitions, such as the retrospectives devoted to Paul Delvaux in 1997, Magritte in 1998 and James Ensor in 1999.

There are several themed routes through the museum, and you can also tour the rooms with an audio guide. The cafeteria on the lower ground floor is nothing special, but the well-stocked gallery shop on the ground floor is definitely worth a visit.

The following guide is a brief resumé of the highlights:

Musée d'Art Ancien
The main hall contains some fine statues and a few bizarre, gigantic paintings.

– **Flemish Primitives** (blue route, rooms 10–45): the museum's pride and joy. The work of these painters shows an almost obsessive preoccupation with detail and realism, and the quality of the oils they used was such that you can still appreciate the colours centuries on.

● In Room 11, *The Annunciation*, by the Master of Flémalle, has an astonishingly detailed background. This room also contains Rogier Van der Weyden's moving 15th-century *Pietà*.

● Room 13 houses *The Judgment of Emperor Otto*, a magnificent 15th-century diptych by Dirk Bouts, with superbly detailed clothes and facial expressions.

● In Room 14, the highlight is *The Martyrdom of Saint Sebastian*, by Hans Memling.

● Room 15 has a rare portrait of Philip the Fair, son of Marie of Burgundy and father of Charles V. You can see a portrait of Charles's mother, Joanna the Mad, in Room 16.

• In Room 17, there's a copy of *The Temptation of Saint Anthony*, a triptych by Hieronymus Bosch (the original is in Lisbon). The hideous hybrid monsters and humans are a feature of Bosch's work. Note the concern for detail and heavy symbolism.

• Room 18 is devoted to German art, with Lucas Cranach the Elder's *Venus and Love* perhaps the highlight. This style of painting was highly criticized by Luther: the hat places the naked Eve in the ranks of the nobility, and it was her social status that shocked Cranach's contemporaries.

• Rooms 21–33 are devoted to 16th-century Flemish art. Room 22 contains a poignant painting called *Girl with Dead Bird*. In the same room, Quentin Metsys's *Virgin and Child* is a tender reflection on maternal love.

• In Room 29, look out for Lucas Gassel's *Copper Mine*, one of the earliest artistic representations of the industrial world.

• Whatever you do, don't miss Room 31, where you'll find the museum's Brueghels. In Pieter Brueghel the Elder's *The Fall of the Rebel Angels*, which is clearly influenced by Bosch, a seething mass of monsters plagues the angels. You could spend hours identifying the horrors depicted here, and the painting contains symbols that have still not been fully understood. The perpetual movement of the piece heralds the baroque style. In the same room, *The Census at Bethlehem,* again by Brueghel the Elder, shifts a biblical myth to a Flemish village, with peasants and children sledging on pigs' jaws; the figure taking money has been interpreted as a veiled critique of the Spanish regime and its heavy taxes. An identical painting by the less talented Pieter Brueghel the Younger hangs in the same room. Best of all is the famous *Fall of Icarus*, whose message is that life goes on: the dramatic death of Icarus, who was vain enough to think that he could fly to the sun, is reduced to a tiny splash in an uncaring sea.

On the stairway leading upstairs, you'll see the vast, anachronistic *Panorama of Brussels in the 17th century* by Jean-Baptiste Bonnecroy, which gives you some idea of how the city looked before the French bombardment of 1695. You can still see the belfry, which was pulverized by cannon fire, as well as the palace of the Dukes of Burgundy, which burned down in 1731.

– The 17th and 18th centuries (brown route)

• The main draw of Rooms 50–61 is the extensive collection of works by Rubens: one contains his smaller works, the other his altarpieces. The portrait of Hélène Fourment, Rubens's wife, is still in the style of the Flemish School, with great attention given to her expression. The study of *Four Negroes' Heads*, however, is thoroughly baroque: the emphasis is on movement, great rolls of drapery and mythological themes.

• Room 54 has large still lifes in the 17th-century Flemish style, and works by Jan 'Velvet' Brueghel, Pieter's other son, who specialized in painting flowers.

• In Room 56, there's a copy of *The Nightwatchman and his Wife,* by Quentin Metsys. The original is in the Louvre.

• Room 57 is dedicated to the three great Antwerp painters: Rubens, Van Dyck and Jacob Jordaens.

- The Dutch art section contains works by Frans Hals and Rembrandt; in the French section, Chardin is the best of the bunch.

Return to the entrance hall and take the escalator to the lower ground floor.

- Room 62 contains some fabulous Rubens paintings, including *The Ascent to Calvary* and *The Assumption*, complete with twisting angels and skilful depictions of the play of light.

– **The 19th century** (yellow route, bottom to top)

- Level -2 has neoclassical works by Ingres, Navez and Jacques-Louis David, who lived as an exile in Brussels. *Death of Marat* is one of his finest works. The Romantic school is represented by Géricault, Delacroix and the Belgians Wappers and Gallait, who specialized in historic paintings that glorify patriotic feeling and the new Belgian state. The deranged Antoine Wiertz has his own museum elsewhere in Brussels, but you can get the idea from his *Beautiful Rosine*, which depicts a naked and knowingly bashful girl confronted with a skeleton.

- Level -1 is devoted to Realism, with highlights including Gustave Courbet's *Paysage à Ornans* and *Chien à la mouche*, a masterpiece of tension and intensity by Alfred Stevens, an acute observer of nature who was also the darling of Parisian ladies. Hippolyte Boulenger represents the Tervuren school of landscape artists.

- On Level 1, you'll find examples of Social Realism, whose exponents tried to represent the everyday lives of labourers and craftsmen. There were plenty of Social Realists in Belgium, where workers' movements were particularly active in the late 19th century. Eugène Laermans (*La Flânerie au village* and *L'Ivrogne*), anticipated Expressionism with his *Drapeau rouge* and *Un Soir de Grève*. Constantin Meunier is best known for his sculpture, represented here by the poignant *Mineur*. Léon Frédéric's monumental *Marchands de craie* is a stark depiction of abject poverty.

Impressionism caught on in Belgium after 1883, with the formation of two artistic schools, Les XX (The Twenty), followed by Libre Esthétique (Free Aesthetic). Théo Van Rysselberghe's *Arab Fantasy* shows the influence of the French Orientalists, while his portrait of Madame Charles Maus is strikingly innovative. Henry van de Velde's Pointillist *Ravaudeuse* is reminiscent of works by Seurat.

- The Symbolists hold sway on Level 2. In Belgium, this movement was eagerly embraced as one that opposed middle-class life and attempted to express the soul's elevation to higher planes by searching for the deeper truths that lie behind appearances. It also offered artists a chance to do a bit of meaningful soft porn. Fernand Khnopff is the most important exponent of this movement in Belgium, and his *Memories of Lawn Tennis* evokes a strange and dusky world on the fringes of an uneasy, waking dream. It is in fact his sister, painted from different angles. Look, too, at the *Portrait of Mademoiselle Van der Echt*, wide-eyed and smooth of feature. The dream world of William de Gouve de Nucques's *Peacocks* anticipates Surrealism.

Level 2 also contains examples of Luminism and neo-Impressionism, which sought to 'dematerialize' the subject by focusing on the play of light. Emile Claus is the best of the artists on show.

• Level 3's highlight is the collection of works by James Ensor, the precursor of Flemish Expressionism, in which bright colours appear to have been flung against the canvas to almost crude effect, such is the force of the painter's emotions. *Scandalized Masks*, a striking example of his work, uses the theme of carnival to denounce society's hypocrisy. *Le Petit Lampiste*, an earlier work, is more in the style of Social Realism. Level 3 also has some fine examples of pre-, neo- and post-Impressionism, with paintings by Monet, Seurat, Signac, Gauguin and Bonnard. Rik Wouters and the sculptors Georges Minne and Gustave Van de Woestijn represent the Expressionist movement.

Le Musée d'Art Moderne

The 20th-century collection is housed in a striking subterranean spiral structure that opened in the 1980s. It's organized around a vast light well, with paintings displayed on seemingly endless levels. Its open-plan layout, while pleasant, makes it difficult to suggest a coherent tour.

• On Levels 2 and 3, you'll be greeted by Pol Bury's amusing kinetic works, including *Vibratile* and *Erectile*, and touching work by a local artist, Jephan de Villiers. *Canticle to the memory of a tree* evokes the secret and mystical life of a tree in the Forêt de Soignes. There are also several witty works by Vic Gentils, made of salvaged bits and pieces from pianos and furniture.

• Level 4 begins with Brabant Fauvism, notably Rick Wouters's *The Flautist*, which shows the influence of Cézanne. Léon Spilliaert's intense, almost monochrome landscapes verge on the abstract. The Flemish Expressionists are out in force on this level, with several works by Constant Permeke, including *The Fiancés* and *The Potato Eater*. Permeke was particularly attached to Flemish traditions, and produced dark, hulking works. This level is also home to works by Gustave de Smet and Frits Van den Berghe.

• Level 5 is devoted to the Belgian Surrealist Paul Delvaux, famous for spooky trains, skeletons and large-breasted, large-eyed, naked women who look curiously out of place in their settings. *Evening Train*, *The Public Voice* and *Pygmalion* are all striking examples of his work.

• Level 6 is the Modern Art Museum's main earner, with the world's largest collection of works by René Magritte. The paintings on display, many of which are universally familiar, include *Empire of Light* and *Man from the Sea*. Works by Dali, Ernst and De Chirico complete the section. You can also see paintings by the CoBrA movement, launched by Christian Dotremont and Joseph Noiret in 1948. The name reflects the movement's cosmopolitan composition: it was founded by artists from Copenhagen (Co), Brussels (Br) and Amsterdam (A). Karel Appel and Asger Jorn were at the forefront, and a few of their works are on show. alongside an extensive collection of calligraphy and graphic art by the Belgian CoBrA artist Pierre Alechinsky.

• On Levels 7 and 8, things start to get downright weird, with works by the Zero movement and some photographic installations. In the deepest circle, where light no longer penetrates, you'll find wild works by contemporary Belgian artists, including the multitalented Jan Fabre.

★ **Musée des Instruments de Musique** (plan III, C1, **123**): Rue Montagne de la Cour. Metro: Gare Centrale. ☎ (02) 545 0130. Open Tuesday to Friday

9.30am 5pm; weekends 9.30am–5.30pm; to 8pm on Thursday. Closed Monday and public holidays. Admission: 150BEF, with discounts for under-26s and senior citizens.

After a long struggle, MIM has moved from its cramped quarters in the Sablon to the splendid iron and glass Old England building and the Hôtel Barré-Guimard, next door.

The museum provides an ideal, highly aesthetic setting for the 1,500 rare instruments in the museum's collection, not least because there's three times as much room. Visitors borrow infrared headphones that allow them to stand next to some of the (often very beautiful) instruments and listen to the music that was played on them. Displays are devoted to different countries and historical periods, and you can tune into sounds as disparate as those of the Peking Opera, the Binche carnival, Indonesian gamelan orchestras and modern-day synthesizers. It's well organized and altogether an excellent museum.

The MIM also organizes children's events and concerts on Thursday evenings in the intimate auditorium; the latter focus on rare restored or reconstructed instruments. Don't miss the panoramic view over the city from the restaurant's terrace.

★ **Le Centre belge de la Bande dessinée** (map II, C2, **102**): rue des Sables 20. Metro: Botanique. ☎ (02) 219 1980. Open from 10am–6pm. Closed Monday. Entry: 250BEF; reductions for students, children and senior citizens. Tintin and co have made a sizeable contribution to the Belgian economy, so they deserve a decent museum. And what a museum it is. A fine example of art nouveau, this former department store was built by Victor Horta for a wealthy textile wholesaler in 1905. The availability of cast iron made it possible to create hitherto unheard-of architectural structures that wedded iron with glass. Horta designed everything, right down to the door handles and the lighting. He even created a subtly curving facade to make the whole thing look bigger than it really is. Inside, there's a vast foyer with a superbly uplifting glass ceiling and a monumental staircase, decorated with a balustrade of wrought-iron plant motifs. The shop closed its doors in 1970, and the building was abandoned. It fell into neglect, attracting squatters who trashed much of the treasure inside, and it was not until 1983 that renovation work breathed new life into this masterpiece of art nouveau. When you enter, pause to admire the foyer, the statue of Tintin and Snowy and the immense windows.

● On the ground floor, you'll find the best-stocked comic-strip shop in the world, as well as a reading room where you can work your way through more than 24,000 titles in 10 languages (open Tuesday, Wednesday and Thursday, noon–5pm, Friday noon–6pm and Saturday 10am–6pm). The Espace Horta has an interesting display of drawings that explains the background to art nouveau. There's also a reasonably priced and highly atmospheric brasserie-restaurant.

● As you ascend the monumental staircase, you'll see a bust of the first astronaut, Tintin, sculpted in 1952 by Nat Neujean. It used to be in Hergé's office.

● On the mezzanine, two permanent exhibitions trace the evolution of the comic strip and the animated cartoon. Each phase is minutely analysed, with the drafts, storyboards, artists' materials and plates. All the plates were in

30x40cm format, and were reduced at a later stage to conserve the level of detail. Every three months, there's a display of one artist's original plates. You can also see films in the project room. Every style of drawing is represented and amply illustrated, so you can follow the history of the cartoon film from the magic lantern to the present day. Visitors can gawp at the first animated drawing, *Gertie the Dinosaur* (1914), followed by *Snow White* (1937). You can also find out about animation techniques, including mixing, voiceovers and sound effects.

● On the first floor, you'll find temporary exhibitions devoted to various comic-strip artists, and, at the back, the Musée de l'Imaginaire, which focuses on the masters of the art: first the Belgians, then non-Belgian artists whose work was published in Belgium. It's divided into two sections: before and after 1960. Each artist is represented by the world of his star character. Hergé, unsurprisingly, takes centre stage, with original editions of *Tintin*, portraits of the boy reporter and of Captain Haddock, and a replica of the wooden statue in *The Broken Ear*.

★ **Musée de la Dynastie** (map III, C1, **103**): place des Palais 7, in the right-hand wing of the Palais Royal. ☎ (02) 502 2541. Trams Nos. 92, 93, 94. Open 10am–6pm. Closed Monday and public holidays. Admission: 250BEF, with (small) discounts for students and senior citizens. Audio guides available in several languages. Up-to-date interactive displays guide you through the history of the Belgian monarchy, from Leopold I to Albert II. A lift takes you up to the second floor, where you're treated to a short film about the Belgian Revolution, narrated in French, Dutch and German (Belgium's three official languages).

The chronologically arranged exhibition continues with a host of documents and objects associated with the royal family, including the solemn oath taken by Leopold I when he was crowned king and a series of family portraits. A collection of plans and models evokes the bombastic architectural dreams of Leopold II, while the staunchness of Albert I and his wife, Elisabeth, during World War I is touchingly re-created.

The tragedies of Leopold III's life are retold, from the car crash that killed his beautiful wife, Astrid, to a typed version of his interview with Hitler, revealing the king's powerlessness in the face of Nazi cynicism.

The presentation of King Baudouin is something of a hagiography: you can see his toys and schoolbooks displayed around a model of the games pavilion in the gardens of Laeken, while one room runs a continuous film of the funeral of Baudouin in August 1993. Finally, a multimedia display in the form of a TV studio shows the present king, Albert II, surrounded by the rest of the royal family as they go about their business.

It's interesting enough in a *Hello!* sort of way, but it's really too expensive – especially since it used to be free.

★ **Musée Horta** (map IV, end of the art nouveau route): rue Américaine 25. Trams Nos. 91 and 92. ☎ (02) 543 0490. Email: musee.horta@horta.iris-net.be. Open 2–5.30pm. Closed Monday and public holidays. Admission: 200BEF at the weekend, 150BEF on weekdays, with discounts for students. As well as extra cost, the weekend means long queues, as only a limited number of visitors are allowed in at a time.

The former residence and workshop of Belgium's most famous architect is a fine illustration of his belief that business and pleasure (in aesthetic terms, at any rate) should mix. It's an uncompromising project, and was considered something of an oddity at the time.

The moderately elaborate exterior, ornamented with ochre-coloured iron-work and rounded, stained-glass windows, doesn't prepare you for the flamboyance of the interior, where the focal points are the stairway and the decorative skylight, through which light streams into the house. The most striking thing, apart from its supreme beauty and the fact that it was entirely designed by Horta (right down to the hinges), is the way the rooms are connected: they're all on different levels, with a short flight of steps leading up or down to them, and there's a wonderful sense of space.

Take a good look at the curvy banister that starts low and increases with height to provide greater protection as you climb up. The staircase narrows towards the top, creating a conical effect that allows more light to flood in. The detail throughout is remarkable: in the drawing room on the right, for example, the banister provides an elbow rest for the sofa, while the polished brick and mosaic floor in the dining room becomes parquet flooring underneath the table, providing a warmer base for feet.

You can see examples of Horta's furniture in the small drawing room, and drawings and models of his work in the study. His bedroom is on the first floor, and visitors are told on which side of the bed he slept (the garden side). The architect even designed a cupboard with a chamber pot for nocturnal use. At the very top of the stairs, two facing mirrors create endless reflections, adding to the overall feeling of space.

The Museums of the Parc du Cinquantenaire (map I, C3)

This impressive, 30-hectare (75-acre) park, east of the European district, was commissioned in 1880 by Leopold II to celebrate the 50th anniversary of Belgian independence. The focal point is the monumental, neoclassical triumphal arch, built by the French architect Charles Girault in the early 20th century. On top is a bronze statue representing Brabant. The arch stands at the centre of a vast semicircle of colonnades, which are decorated with mosaics in honour of Belgium. Two vast structures, originally built in the late 19th century now house the Musées Royaux d'Art et d'Histoire, the Musée Royal de l'Armée and Autoworld.

The park is surrounded by splendid houses in a variety of styles, most of which were built at the beginning of the 20th century. One of the most interesting is the Maison Cauchie, which has fantastic pre-Raphaelite sgraffiti (rue des Francs 5). In the park itself, take a look at the Pavillon des Passions Humaines, one of Victor Horta's first creations (1889). It was designed to house a work representing the human passions: the sculptor was Jef Lambeaux, and his depiction was so passionate that it scandalized public opinion. The building was swiftly locked up, and remains closed to this day, although it will be opened on request (information from the Tourist Office).

★ **Musées Royaux d'Art et d'Histoire** (Musée du Cinquantenaire; map I, C3, **111**): Parc du Cinquantenaire 10. Metro: Merode or Schuman. ☎ (02) 741 7331. Website: www.kmkg-mrah.be. Open from 9.30am (from 10am on

Saturday, Sunday and public holidays) to 5pm. Closed Monday. Admission: 150BEF, with discounts for students and senior citizens. Free entry every first Wednesday afternoon of the month.

This vast repository has 140 display rooms containing examples of art from all the world's civilizations (except Central Africa, which has its own museums; *see below*). A visit will take you at least half a day, even if you skate through. In fact, it's so big that many of the rooms are closed, and can only be seen if you ask at reception.

The museum is divided into four main blocks: the ancient world, non-European civilizations, Belgian archaeology and European decorative arts. That said, for reasons of space, there are some exceptions which disrupt this neat ordering of the world. When you enter, for example, you walk straight into *God of Thon*, a rare statue brought back from Easter Island, pass a selection of carriages and then find yourself in a reconstruction of Wolfers's jewellery shop (art nouveau again).

The top floor of the **Ancient World** section is devoted to Egypt. The other levels, in descending order, include Greece, Rome and, finally, the Near East, where you can see a huge 5th–6th-century hunting mosaic that once graced the ceremonial hall of the Roman governor of Apamaea, in Syria.

The rooms devoted to the **decorative arts** feature a selection of tapestries and triptychs, of which, the gruesome highlight is the *Martydom of St George*, wherein the saint is burned, whipped, hanged by his feet, quartered and finally beheaded. Collections of old and new glass, costumes, porcelain and lace are also on display in this rich section.

The **national archaeology** section has been superbly renovated, and is now intelligently laid out. Highlights include a room devoted to the life of the first Belgians, a reconstruction of a Merovingian necropolis, where a glass walkway takes you over the tombs, and the dimly lit Treasure Room (it's the last one, and has different opening hours to the rest of the museum: 10am–noon and 1–4pm). Laid out like a crypt, it contains some splendid pieces of Romanesque and Mosan religious art, including an ivory relic shaped like a Romanesque basilica and a reliquary attributed to the jeweller Hugo d'Oignies. Precious medieval objects in metal, wood and ivory sit alongside more recent works in the collections of porcelain, silverware, textiles, tapestries, copperwork, tapestries and textiles. The most spectacular object is the reliquary of Pope Alexander I, which consists of a Classical bronze head on a brass and silver-gilt pedestal, decorated with saints and the virtues, and encrusted with enamels, rock crystal and other precious stones.

Pick up the museum brochure (it's free), which will help you navigate your way through this enormous place and guide you to the unmissable treasures on show. You can read it over a cup of coffee in the pleasant museum cafeteria.

★ **Musée Royal de l'Armée et de l'Histoire Militaire** (map I, C3, **112**): Parc du Cinquantenaire 3. ☎ (02) 737 7811. Website: www. klm-mra.be. Open 9am–noon and 1–4.30pm. Closed Monday. Admission: free. This museum, which offers you an overview of war and the myriad ways of inflicting death, is another monster – perhaps the biggest museum of its kind in the world. If 18th-century swords, World War II tanks and fighter planes are your kind of thing, you'll be in hog heaven. If not, you'll find that the collections are impressive, but that the presentation is rambling and often poorly explained.

Here's an overview of the main sections:

The Austrian occupation of the Low Countries (1713–1792) and the Brabant Revolution (1789–1790) are illustrated by a host of weapons, swords and portraits. A section devoted to the French period of Belgian history (1792–1815) includes souvenirs from Waterloo, mainly medals and the like. The Weapons and Armour Room contains splendid collections of swords, daggers, crossbows, spears and halberds that date from the 10th to the 18th centuries. If you're looking for an overview of Belgian history, head straight for the Historic Room, where paintings, objects, documents, uniforms and armour illustrate war-related aspects of the country's past.

The **Musée de la Résistance**, in the Bordiau room, was opened in 1998. Unlike much of the museum, the presentation is high-tech, with CD-Roms, films and sound effects evoking life under the Germans. Visitors can also see reconstructions of a shop belonging to a persecuted Jewish cobbler, a collaborator's bookshop selling Nazi publications and a grocer's shop with shelves depleted by rationing.

The Tanks section, arranged according to country and period, has several World War II machines, and is a rather chilling experience. But the most awe-inspiring collection is on show in the vast, iron-and-glass central hall, where you can gawp at more than 130 planes. The display traces the history of aviation from the hot air balloon to the jet plane: the first old crate from World War I; splendid biplanes with wooden propellers; the Fokker of Manfred von Richthoffen, The Red Baron; airship pods; a De Havilland Mosquito of 1945; the Fairchild C119, which could carry 50 paratroopers; American fighters from the 1950s and 1960s; a McDonnell Douglas F-4 Phantom used during the Gulf War; and even a Sabena airliner. It's incredible to find so much under one roof – and it's all free.

Finally, a winding staircase from the entrance hall leads to two vaulted rooms that house private collections of Napoleonic objects. Pause to enjoy the panoramic view of avenue de Tervueren and rue de la Loi from the 70-metre (220-feet) high terraces that overlook the arcades.

★ **Autoworld** (map I, C3, **113**): also in the Park du Cinquantenaire. ☎ (02) 736 4165. Website: www.autoworld.be. Open 10am–6pm (to 5pm in winter). Admission: 200BEF, with discounts for students and senior citizens. Audio guides available. This extraordinary private museum houses hundreds of vehicles, beginning with the earliest versions of the car. The well-organized collection has been assembled in a vast, hangar-like building in the south wing of the Cinquantenaire, and contains some rare vintage items in mint condition. You can see a fantastic array of vehicles, including Léon Bollé's 1896 'voiturette', the Aster tricycle of 1899, a 1904 Oldsmobile, with a handle instead of a steering wheel, the first mobile home, a 1911 Rolls-Royce, Kennedy's 1956 Cadillac, the 2CV and several more recent models. The mezzanine is used to display less glamorous cars, some of which would have been driven by our grandparents, parents or even elder siblings, while there's a section devoted to unusual vehicles from around the world. If you like old cars, you won't be disappointed.

Other Museums

★ **Musée Communal d'Ixelles** (map I, C3, **114**): rue Jean-Van-Volsem 71, Brussels 1050. ☎ (02) 515 6122. Email: musee.ixelles@skynet.be. Bus No. 71. Open 1–6.30pm, weekends 10am–5pm. Closed Monday and public holidays. Admission: free, except for temporary exhibitions. This former abattoir has been converted into a modest but delightful exhibition space dedicated to 19th- and 20th-century painting, and also hosts excellent temporary exhibitions. Among the treasures in the permanent collection are 30 of the 32 posters designed by Toulouse-Lautrec, part of a 1,000-strong collection of lithographs that are shown in rotation, wonderful old advertisements by the likes of Mucha, Toulouse-Lautrec and Magritte, a drawing by Dürer, several Flemish paintings and 18th-century views of Brussels. The core of the collection, though, spans the late 18th and early 19th centuries, with Impressionist and neo-Impressionist paintings by Maurice Denis and Théo Van Rysselberghe (*Tea in the Garden*) and a Rik Wouters sculpture, *The Mad Virgin*. Brabant Fauvism and Expressionism are represented by Constant Permeke, while Jan Toorop's *Woman with Parasol* is a fine example of Belgian Impressionism.

This museum is well worth a visit, and will certainly whet your appetite for the Belgian holdings at the Modern Art Museum.

★ **Musée du Jouet** (map II, D2): rue de l'Association 24, Brussels 1000. ☎ (02) 219 6168. Open 10am–12.30pm and 2–6pm. Admission: 100BEF. Housed in a mansion in the northeast of the Pentagon, the Toy Museum is a nostalgic homage to childhood before the computer game. You can study old dolls, parlour games, shops, robots, models and electric trains, and you can even touch the less fragile items on display. There's a games library, and a puppet show takes place every third Tuesday in the month.

★ **Maison d'Érasme**: rue du Chapitre 31, Brussels 1070. ☎ (02) 521 1383. Website: www.ciger.be/erasmus. Metro: Saint-Guidon. Open 10am–noon and 2–5pm. Closed Tuesday and Friday. Admission: 50BEF. Guided tour on request. If you're a fan of Erasmus's *In Praise of Folly*, it's worth trekking out to Anderlecht, a rundown district that was once a thriving industrial neighbourhood, thanks in part to the canals that slice through it. It's now best known for its football team, but it was once home to the humanist Didier Erasmus, who lived here for five months in 1521. The well-proportioned red-brick building he stayed in, with a small, peaceful garden, was built in 1515 and converted into a museum in the 1930s. The great man's office contains a cast of his head and a letter to a friend in Latin. A selection of books, expurgated by the censors (you can see their pen marks and white paper stickers) is on show in the white room on the first floor, while this beautifully restored residence also houses a collection of furniture, books, engravings and paintings from the 15th and 16th centuries.

The highlights, however, are two engravings by Albrecht Dürer and a 1480 triptych by Hieronymous Bosch. The left-hand panel of the triptych, the *Adoration of the Magi*, once depicted St Jerome, but a century after it was painted, the curate of the collegiate church of Saint-Pierre-and-Guidon, where the painting was stored, decided to swap the saints. A few brush strokes later, Jerome had become Saint Peter, guardian of the keys to Paradise.

If you have time, visit the neighbouring **Béguinage**, near the collegiate church. This delightful collection of houses, the earliest of which dates from the 13th century, is arranged around a fountain and garden. The Béguinage is also home to a museum devoted to the history of Anderlecht. Opening hours are the same as for the Maison d'Erasme.

★ **Musée Bruxellois de la Gueuze** (map I, A3, **115**): rue Gheude 56, Brussels 1070. ☎ (02) 521 4928. Metro: Gare du Midi. Open 8.30am–5pm, Saturday 10am–5pm. Closed Sunday and public holidays. Admission: 100BEF, including a tasting session. The Cantillon brewery is the last of the city's *lambic*-makers to use traditional 19th-century techniques. Four generations have brewed beer here, and before you wander round the brewery itself, a family member will treat you to an impassioned, introductory talk about why Cantillon is so special.

The unique thing about the brewing process is that the wort is 'fermented' by the outside air. In other words, the beer depends on spontaneous fermentation, which is how beer was produced 6,000 years ago by the Sumerians. Babylonia had 150 breweries, and the Egyptians, Romans and Gauls knew of this miraculous process, although they were unable to explain it. Nowadays, fermenting agents are scientifically prepared in the laboratory and added artificially, except at Cantillon, where they have conserved the magic. Brewing takes place between October and the end of March, when the wort can cool naturally and the conditions for fermentation are ideal; in summer, the hot weather means spontaneous fermentation could be a health risk.

The resulting beer is called *lambic* (two thirds barley, one third wheat), and forms the starting point for several other beers: *gueuze* (a blend of young and old *lambics* refermenting together in a corked bottle), *kriek* (with cherries), *framboise* (with raspberries) and *faro* (with caramel).

Upstairs, you can see the huge, shallow copper vat where inoculation takes place. The barrel room, which is vaguely reminiscent of a wine cellar, is packed with tuns and 650-litre (130-gallon) barrels, filled to the brim and left open for three days to allow for overflow. Before you leave, you can sit in the tavern area, where you can sample these highly distinctive beers and mourn the collapse of family breweries. If you're there in mid-August, ask about the *lambic* festival in the town of Lembeek, south of the city.

★ **Musée du Costume et de la Dentelle** (map II, B3, **104**): rue de la Violette 6, Brussels 1000. ☎ (02) 512 7709. Open 10am–12.30pm and 1.30–5pm (to 4pm in winter), weekends and public holidays 2–4.30pm. Closed Wednesday. Admission: 100BEF. This little museum, devoted to the art of lace-making, is housed in two handsome, step-gabled brick houses. Lace-making was one of the oldest and most popular crafts in the Low Countries, and here you'll see some of its finest examples, exhibited by theme.

★ **Musée Constantin Meunier** (map I, B4, **116**): rue de l'Abbaye 59, Brussels 1050. ☎ (02) 648 4449. Bus Nos. 38 and 60. Open from Tuesday to Friday, 10am–noon and 1–5pm, and one weekend in two (phone to check). Admission: free. Constantin Meunier (1831–1905) was a Social Realist, who painted, sculpted and drew the everyday life of the workers as he saw it going on around him, and you can't help but be impressed by his ability to turn the act of labour into something beautiful. Perhaps surprisingly, he was not an active champion of the people's cause, which was very fashionable at the time, but tried to depict the condition of 'labouring man', the hero of many of his painting and sculptures, including *Homme qui boit* (Drinking Man) and *Retour des mineurs* (Miners' Homecoming). There's also a fine series of drawings inspired by workers and artisans. The largest works are on display at the back, in Meunier's studio: the refined, powerful *Débardeur* (Docker) and *Semeur* (Sower), and *Maternité* (Motherhood), a touching blend of simplicity and pride. The subjects' facial expressions are curiously peaceful, as though the characters have transcended the grind of their daily lives.

★ **Musée Charlier** (off map II, beyond D3): avenue des Arts 16, Brussels 1210. ☎ (02) 218 5382. Metro: Madou. Open Monday 10am–5pm, Tuesday to Thursday 1.30–5pm and Friday 1.30–4.30pm. Closed at weekends. Admission: 100BEF. This old family mansion, decorated by Horta, belonged to Guillaume Charlier, an academic sculptor with a mildly socialist streak. He had the good fortune to meet the philanthropist Henri Van Cutsem, an enlightened art-lover who provided Charlier with the means to live an untroubled life of comfort, and made him his heir. After his death, the house became the property of the commune of Saint-Josse, which converted it into a museum. The result is a beautiful, two-storey house that gives you some idea of the affluence of the city's bourgeoisie at the turn of the last century. Sumptuously furnished with 18th-century French furniture, it has plenty of treasures for visitors to admire: a Chinese Room, tapestries from Brussels and Oudenaarde, glassware, porcelain, silverware and, most importantly, a fine collection of Belgian paintings and sculptures. These include minor works by James Ensor, Xavier Mellery, Fernand Khnopff, Alfred Stevens and Hippolyte Boulenger, as well as striking Realist works by Eugène Laermans and a neglected painter called Léon Pion, who used charcoal to create almost photographic black-and-white landscapes. There's also an amusing, chubby-cheeked child's head, sculpted by Rik Wouters. The museum also organizes classical and jazz concerts (phone for a programme of events).

★ **Musée David et Alice Van Buuren** (map I, B4, **122**): avenue Léo-Errera 41, Brussels 1180. ☎ (02) 343 4851. Trams Nos. 23 and 90. Open Sunday 1–6pm and Monday 2–6pm (except in July). Admission: 300BEF. It's a shame this superb museum and art-deco home in leafy southern Brussels, built for a Dutch banker and collector, doesn't have more generous opening hours. There's a fine selection of paintings from the 16th to the 20th centuries, all hung in delightful art-deco rooms decorated with original furniture and carpets: highlights include a *Fall of Icarus* attributed to Brueghel, and paintings by Fantin-Latour, Ensor, Wouters, Van Gogh and Van de Woestyne. The museum's magnificent gardens, which include a maze, are open to the public every afternoon (admission: 100BEF).

★ **Musée Antoine Wiertz** (map I, C3, **117**): rue Vautier 62, between Etterbeek and Ixelles. ☎ (02) 648 1718. Bus Nos. 34, 59, 80. Open Tuesday to Friday 10am–noon and 1–5pm, and one weekend in two. Closed Monday and public holidays. Admission: free. Antoine Wiertz was a real eccentric. Born at the beginning of the 19th century, he thought he was the new Rubens or Michelangelo, but was not the talented artist he liked to think he was. Perhaps, deep down, he knew this, as he was canny enough to strike a cunning deal with the Belgian government: the state gave him a villa-cum-studio (today's museum) and was promised his paintings when he died. Rather than relying on his art to earn his keep, he became an 'artist and civil servant' who paid for his lodgings with his paintings – which are overwhelming in size, but not in quality. *Miroir du diable* (Devil's Mirror), *Baigneuses et satyres* (Bathers and satyrs), or *Laotitia Bonaparte dans son cercueil* (Laetitia Bonaparte in her coffin) are entertaining in a kitsch kind of way, but that's about the best you can say. In the studio, gigantic baroque-style works modelled on Rubens are nothing like as good as the works of the Flemish master.

★ **Musée d'Art spontané** (map I, A2): boulevard Léopold II 51, Brussels 1080. ☎ (02) 426 8404. Open 1–5pm. Closed Sunday and Monday. This former printing press hosts temporary exhibitions of 'spontaneous art'; work by untrained artists that falls somewhere between naïve art and art brut. Its rawness is sometimes shocking, but its directness makes a refreshing change.

★ **Musée de l'Institut Royal des Sciences Naturelles** (map I, C3, **118**): chaussée de Wavre 260. ☎ (02) 627 4238. Website: www.kbinirsnb.be. Bus Nos. 34, 59, 80. Open 9.30am–4.45pm (10am–6pm on Sunday). Closed Monday and public holidays. Admission: 150BEF. The city's natural history museum is located in an ugly modern building; you'll recognize it by the life-size model of a dinosaur outside the front entrance. It's not the best of museums, unless you're a fan of stuffed animals, but there are two outstanding displays: a room filled with fossil iguanadons, discovered in a Belgian coalmine in 1891, and a collection of frighteningly hairy trapdoor spiders. Otherwise, the museum consists of dioramas of Belgian fauna, dull explanatory panels, laughable animated plastic dinosaurs and a collection of shells and stones. It's in the throes of modernization, and frankly can only get better.

– The **Musée du Transport Urbain Bruxellois** is dealt in the Tervuren section below, as it's on the way.

– As you probably guessed, there are dozens of other museums in Brussels. The Tourist Office can provide you with a comprehensive list.

WHAT TO SEE AROUND BRUSSELS

TERVUREN

Tervuren, in Flemish Brabant province, is 13 kilometres (eight miles) southeast of Brussels. From Parc du Cinquantenaire, follow avenue de Tervueren, a long boulevard constructed in the 19th century. The town is famous for its enormous museum, the Musée Royal de l'Afrique Centrale, but there are a couple of interesting sights before you arrive.

★ **Palais Stoclet** (map I, D3, **119**): avenue de Tervueren 275, Brussels. Metro: Montgomery. Tram Nos. 39 and 44. This fine building, an example of the Viennese Secession style, is closed to the public, but it's well worth seeing the amazing, marble-ornamented exterior. Unlike traditional art-nouveau façades, it has sharp angles and broken lines that end in a tiered tower surrounded by bronze sculptures.

★ **Musée du Transport Urbain Bruxellois** (map I, D3, **120**): avenue de Tervueren 364, Woluwe-Saint-Lambert 1150. ☎ (02) 515 3108. Tram Nos. 39 and 44. From the last Saturday in March until the first Sunday in October, open weekends and public holidays, 1.30–7pm. Admission: 80BEF; 150BEF including a return ticket to Tervuren. Discounts for children. Free the first Wednesday afternoon of each month. The main attraction of this museum, apart from the beautifully presented collections, is that you can take a trip on a vintage tram from the museum to the Parc du Cinquantenaire, or from the museum to the Forêt de Soignes. The second option is better, as you can get off at the Musée Royal de l'Afrique Centrale, take a look around, and return on the same vintage tram. Trams leave about once an hour on Saturday, and every 40 minutes on Sunday, and the journey to Tervuren takes about 25 minutes.

The Transport Museum is a vast transport depot, which is still partly in use, but also houses a fantastic array of vintage trams and buses that were once used in the commune of Brussels. These include early horse-drawn trams, which were affectionately known as *moteurs à crottin* ('dung-powered motors'), steam trams and a fine selection of buses, the first of which came into service in 1923. The collection of trams from 1900 to 1950 shows its evolution from the first delightful vehicles with open platforms and pretty seats, to more comfortable, uglier models.

Among the more unusual vehicles are a 1904 American snow-sweeper and a 'stroller' (an open carriage for use in summer). The striped 4CV at the entrance, meanwhile is an old service vehicle. You can visit the café at the back of the museum before boarding your vintage tram, accompanied by staff in period uniforms.

★ **Musée Royal de l'Afrique Centrale**: Leuvensesteenweg 13, Tervuren 3080. ☎ (02) 769 5211. Website: www.africamuseum.be. Tram No. 44. Open 10am–5pm (to 6pm at weekends). Closed Monday. Admission: 80BEF. This incredible museum is housed in a bombastic neoclassical building in the middle of a beautiful park. It was built in the late 19th century by the French architect Charles Girault, on the orders of Leopold II, who wanted a repository for the spoils of the Belgian Congo. The colony was Leopold's private property until 1908, when the international outcry over the ruthlessness of the regime in the Congo became so strident that the state took over its administration. The Congo remained under Belgian rule until 1960.

The sheer scale of the collections is impressive: only 800 of the 250,000 items in stock are on permanent display, but the reserves are used to mount lavish temporary exhibitions. The museum adopts an impressive multi-disciplinary approach, with sections on ethnography, archaeology, war, agriculture, music and weapons – all displayed in large, rather dreary-looking glass cases – and dioramas showing the flora and fauna of the region. The centre of the first room on the left is taken up by a vast canoe, 22.5 metres (74 feet) long, while your tour ends with huge diagrams showing the topography of mountains and details of agricultural and forest economies. In between, the highlight is the tomb of Kisalieh, with a skeleton decked out in finery and surrounded by earthenware pots.

With its lack of explanatory notes, this museum is a bit antiquated, but it does give you some idea of Belgium's involvement in Central Africa. The horrors of the early days of colonization, however, are swept under the carpet, although there's a selection of Belgian colonial art. When you're done, you can ponder the folly of Empire in the pleasant cafeteria.

Now that you're here, you might as well carry on towards Waterloo (*see* 'Walloon Brabant').

FESTIVALS AND CULTURAL EVENTS IN BRUSSELS

– **January**: Car Fair, every even year; Brussels International Film Festival (in the second fortnight).

– **February**: International Festival of Animated Film; Antiques Dealers' Fair; Book Fair.

– **March**: International Festival of Fantasy Film; Ars Musica (new music).

– **April**: seasonal opening of the Royal Greenhouses in Laeken (end April/beginning May); Iris Festival (27 April), the Brussels Region's official celebration.

– **May and June**: KunstenFESTIVALdesArts (avant-garde plays, concerts, dance and opera); Queen Elisabeth Competition (an annual event, alternating between piano, violin and singing, with a year off after each cycle); Jazz Marathon (last weekend in May), when Brussels rallies round podiums set up throughout the city, then heads off to a host of bar gigs; Couleur Café (last weekend of June), a vibrant world-music festival.

– **July**: drive-in cinema with giant open-air screen in the Parc du Cinquantenaire (July and August, weekend evenings); Ommegang (end June/early July) , a centuries-old historical procession that winds up at the Grand'Place; Festival de l'Eté, Brussels' summer music festival, with concerts in some unusual venues; National Day (21 July); Dimanches de la Bois de la Cambre (July and August), Sunday-morning classical and jazz concerts in prime picnic territory; Brosella Festival (free folk and jazz at the Heysel, second weekend).

– **August**: planting of the 'Meiboom' (May Tree), a traditional folkloric festival; carpet of flowers on the Grand'Place (even years); Midi Fair, a huge funfair around Gare du Midi.

– **September**: Les Nuits Botanique, a 10-day festival of rock, chanson and world music at Le Botanique; Festival of Flanders (big-name classical concerts); Îlot Sacré festival; Brueghel festivals.

– **October and November**: Audi Jazz Festival (which attracts international artists, though purists deplore its definition of jazz).

– **December:** Christmas Market and skating on the Grand'Place.

FLEA MARKETS

– **Brussels commune**: place du Jeu de Balle, every morning 7am–2pm; place du Grand-Sablon (upmarket antiques market) all day Saturday and Sunday morning.

– **Auderghem commune**: flea markets between 7am and 1pm. First Sunday of the month, place Pinoy; third Sunday, boulevard du Souverain/GB; fourth Sunday, viaduc Herrmann-Debroux.

– **Forest commune**: place Saint-Denis, Sunday 8am–1pm.

– **Schaerbeek commune**: place Dailly, first Saturday of the month, all day.

– **Woluwe-Saint-Lambert commune**: place Saint-Lambert, first Sunday of the month, morning only.

– **Anderlecht commune**: Westland Shopping Centre, Sunday 8am–1pm.

– **Koekelberg commune**: place Simonis, second Saturday of the month, morning only.

– **Midi Market:** every Sunday morning, around Gare du Midi. A huge, noisy market selling exotic produce from North Africa, Italy and Turkey, as well as plants, kitchen equipment and clothes.

LEAVING BRUSSELS

Hitch-hiking

– **Heading for Paris**: get onto the E19 Brussels–Mons at exit 13 (Drogenbos). Take bus No. 50 at Gare du Midi and get out at the Maxi GB stop in Drogenbos. Stand at the traffic lights. A lot of traffic goes on to the motorway.

– Heading for **Liège** and **Germany**: metro line No. 5, get off at Diamant. The sliproad onto the E40 towards Liège is nearby.

– Heading for **Antwerp** and **Holland**: take tram No. 52 from Gare du Nord or Gare du Midi, and get off at the Japanese Tower, in Laeken. There, traffic heads towards A12 motorway.

– Heading for **Ghent** and **Ostend**: from Gare du Midi, take tram No. 82 to avenue Charles-Quint, and the Maxi GB at Berchem Sainte-Agathe. The E40 motorway goes off to your left.

– Heading for **Namur** and **Luxembourg**: take Metro No. 1 (Hermann-Debroux terminus) and get off at Delta, where you'll find the start of the E411.

By Train

🚆 There are four stations in Brussels: Gare du Nord (map I, B2), Gare Centrale (map I, B3), Gare du Midi (map I, A3) and Gare Léopold (map I, C3).

Thanks to the Nord-Midi junction, the stations are all connected. So, for example, if you want the Eurostar to London, which leaves from Gare du Midi, you can get a connecting train at Gare du Nord.

Where to get your train to leave Brussels

– **For Antwerp and Amsterdam**: Midi, Centrale, Nord.

– **For Ghent, Bruges and Ostend**: Nord, Centrale, Midi.

– **For Liège and Cologne**: Midi, Centrale, Nord.

– **For Namur and Dinant**: Midi, Centrale, Nord, Quartier Léopold.

– **For Mons**: Nord, Centrale, Midi.

– **For Nivelles and Charleroi**: Nord, Centrale, Midi.

  For Namur and Luxembourg: Midi, Centrale, Nord, Quartier Léopold

– **For Paris**: Midi.

– **For London and Kent (Eurostar)**: Midi.

By Coach

■ **Eurolines**: Eurolines-Europabus, Coach Station CCN, Gare du Nord. ☎ (02) 203 0707 or (02) 274 1350. Tickets from L'Épervier, place de Brouckère 50, Brussels 1000. ☎ (02) 217 0025. Fax: (02) 217 3192.

– For buses to **Walloon Brabant**: TEC, ☎ (010) 480404.

– For buses to **Flemish Brabant**: De Lijn, ☎ (02) 526 2811.

Flanders

Flemish Brabant (Vlaams Brabant)

On 1 January 1995, Belgium added a 10th province to the nine it had consisted of since 1830 – Brabant. It didn't matter whether it was Flemish or Walloon, because the dictates of federalism meant bilingual Brabant would have to be subdivided anyway. Brussels, Brabant's capital since time immemorial, became a Region in its own right, but was limited to the 19 *communes* of the metropolis. Once again, a common heritage was carved up: Leuven became the capital of Flemish Brabant (geographically, Brussels is surrounded by this area), while Wavre became the capital of Walloon Brabant (beating Nivelles to the title). The boundary between these two new entities, respecting the 'linguistic boundary' agreed in 1963, was sealed for ever.

From a historical and geographical perspective, this decision seems rather arbitrary. For one thing, there's no natural boundary along the dividing line; it separates two villages, for example, that are not in the least bit different. In any case, history tells us that, in its day, Brabant was one of the most powerful duchies in the Low Countries, its territory stretching all the way to Holland, taking in Breda, Antwerp, Mechelen, Brussels and Leuven.

It may be a treacherous thing to do, but one cannot help wondering how this will affect the heir to the throne, who has taken the title of 'Duke of Brabant' since Leopold I's day? Will he be Walloon or Flemish? No doubt a third way will be decided upon, so as not to upset anyone.

ZONIËNWOUD (FORÊT DE SOIGNES)

Glorified in the memoirs of August Rodin, Brussels's 'green lungs' provide the city with 4,300 hectares (10,750 acres) of greenery. Surrounded by pretty villages, the forest spans all three administrative Regions. Filled with majestic beech trees, their slender trunks rising like columns, the forest is often described as a living cathedral. The present forest is all that remains of the great charcoal woods that stretched from Leuven to Halle, right up to the edge of the Sambre, in Charlemagne's day.

A succession of kings used to hunt here, and the forest was also a vital source of firewood, charcoal and iron ore. It's often depicted in hunting tapestries, known as 'Maximilian tapestries'. More recently, the construction of abbeys and holiday castles altered the appearance of this vast area. Under the Austrians, a huge number of trees were felled for timber, and thousands of fast-growing beeches were planted, giving the forest its present appearance. Charles de Lorraine had straight paths (*drèves*) built throughout so aristocratic ladies could follow the hunts. In the 19th century, Société Générale, a holding company, acquired 11,000 hectares (27,500 acres) and sold them off in successive lots, which led to deforestation as the plots were converted for agricultural use. Since then, despite the construction of major roads and the ferocious appetite of developers, environmental-protection organizations have worked to maintain the forest as a natural sanctuary. Recent storms have brought down many 100-year-old beeches, and other species are now being planted, including the sturdier oak.

Animals, including fallow and roe deer, foxes, badgers, falcons, kestrels and sparrowhawks, thrive in this habitat. Some of the most beautiful spots, many of which lie on the edge of the forest, are listed below:

★ In the far west, near Tervuren, is an **arboretum**, part of the Bois des Capucins, where woods that flourish in temperate climates have been planted. Here, you can see species that grow on the Pacific coast, such as the douglas pine and sequoia.

★ **Jesus-Eik**, at the end of the E411, is the perfect spot for a Sunday stroll and a snack, which you can wash down with a russet Rodenbach while admiring the picturesque baroque church across the street.

★ The villages of **Hoeilaart** and **Overijse** are famous for the cultivation of grapes in greenhouses. A little museum dedicated to vine-growing explains how this tradition started: Justus Lipsiusplein 9, Overijse. Open from April to the end of October, 9am–noon and 1–4.30pm on weekdays, 2–6pm on Sunday. Admission free. The Festival of the Grape, in late August/early September, provokes considerable celebrations.

★ The Rouge-Cloître priory, on the edge of Auderghem and therefore still within the Brussels region, is a delightful rosary of ponds surrounding the 14th-century Augustinian convent where the painter Hugo Van der Goes worked. It's an ideal starting point for pleasant forest walks. For information, contact the Forest information centre: ☎ (02) 660 6417.

★ **Groenendael**: a fairy-tale 18th-century castle in the heart of the forest, not far from the racecourse, and part of the old priory, with its chain of little ponds.

★ **La Hulpe and le parc Solvay**: *see* 'Walloon Brabant'.

HALLE (HAL)   33,000 inhabitants

The best time to visit this overgrown village is on a Sunday during Pentecost, when Halle hosts the famous procession of the Holy Virgin. It's because of her, or rather a small statue of her, that pilgrims have been flocking to the town since 1267. An added bonus, at the time, was the 40-days' indulgence you were granted if you took part in the procession. The tradition continues to this day. The nearby woods provide excellent walking terrain, especially at the end of April, when the ground is covered with a dazzling carpet of bluebells.

FLEMISH BRABANT

WHERE TO EAT IN THE COUNTRYSIDE

☆☆ **Moderate**

✗ **Het Kriekske**: Kapittel 10, Hallebos, Halle 1500. ☎ (02) 380 1421. Closed Monday and Tuesday. Take Nijvelsesteenweg and cross the bridge over the E19 motorway, then turn right. Expect to pay between 550 and 1000BEF for a good meal. Set in the rolling hills of the Pajottenland, on the Bruegel Trail, Het Kriekske ('Little Cherry'), is a red-brick smallholding in the middle of nowhere that treats walkers to generous pieces of red meat, *salade liégoise*, eels in herb sauce, rabbit stewed in cherry beer or bowls of steaming mussels. For pudding, or afternoon tea, try a delicious apple, cherry or cheese tart, which you can linger over on the terrace.

WHAT TO SEE

★ The **Onze Lieve Vrouwebasiliek**: open 9am–6pm. A splendid example of Brabant Gothic, originally named after Saint Martin: the saint was usurped when the Countess of Hainaut bestowed a miracle-working Madonna on the basilica. Despite the rather depressing appearance of this edifice, there are several notable details: a complete series of apostles in the niches of the triforium (the gallery above the arcades of the nave); superb stained-glass windows, some entertaining votive tableaux; a Renaissance alabaster tabernacle in the chapel of Trazegnies; and, in the narrow ambulatory, a document that confers on the visitor the right to obtain a full indulgence. A French dauphin (Joachim, son of Louis XI) is buried in the Chapel of Our Lady. A 15th-century figure of Christ on a polychrome wooden cross hangs in the vault. Outside, head for the splendid south door, with its wrought-iron plant clusters, where there's a highly stylized Madonna (typical of the work of Claus Sluter, sculptor to the Dukes of Burgundy) accompanied by angelic musicians and the three kings. The head of each nail is in the form of a human face, and the baptistery is topped by an unusual, apple-shaped dome.

The treasury in the crypt is only open to the public on Ascension Day, at Pentecost or on the first Sunday in September. Admission: 30BEF

★ The **Stadhuis**, housed in a fine Renaissance building, is the place to go for tourist information. Statues by Jérôme Duquesnoy stand in the niches of the facade.

WHERE TO STAY IN THE AREA

☆ **Budget**

⬩ **Youth Hostel 't Golvende Brabant**: in the provincial estate. Torleylaan 1654. ☎ and fax: (02) 383 0026. De Lijn buses run from Brussels on weekdays only. Prices start from 245BEF, including breakfast. Open mid-February to end November. The cheapest overnight stopover anywhere in Belgium, with 58 beds and five family rooms. A youth hostellers' haven. The provincial estate is an area of outstanding natural beauty and only a short trip from Brussels. Breakfast aside, meals are not provided. Bike-hire available.

⬩ **Camping** possible in the same complex.

WHAT TO SEE IN THE AREA

★ **Huizingen**: the estate of an old castle, with gardens, boating, a garden for the blind, an adventure playground for kids, mini golf, the whole caboodle. Open year-round, 9am–sunset. Admission: 100BEF.

BEERSEL CASTLE

A few miles south of Brussels: if you're in a car, take the E19 towards Mons, then the Beersel exit. It's well signposted. From 1 March to 15 November, open Tuesday to Sunday, 10am–noon and 2–6pm; weekends only in winter. Closed January. Admission: 100BEF. Free tour. Bucolic and delightful. There's a small adventure playground, with ducks and chickens roaming around nearby.

A stunning fortified 16th-century castle, which was altered at the end of the following century after being partially destroyed, this is one of Belgium's few surviving examples of medieval military architecture. Surrounded by marshland and water, it was an important defensive post for the city. Particularly impressive are the three chubby towers, which are linked by a covered walkway. Inside, the gable-decorated towers are curiously flat. The pointed slate roofs were added in the 18th century, by which time the castle was no longer the proud fortress of bygone days. Still, you can see examples of just about every item of defensive architecture – crenellations, arrow slits, drawbridge, watchtower – and ponder how molten lead would have been poured down from above.

The castle rooms are empty and not particularly well maintained. But it's fun to wander around the towers, discovering how the castle would have operated. It is actually made up of three separate parts, all rather small, and you can see how they've been built onto one another, giving the building its strange appearance. Don't miss the vault in the third tower and the ground-floor trial room, where you will find a peculiar, minuscule hidey-hole with a grating in the wall, and a gruesome instrument of torture. The victim would be laid out on this cross so that the torturer could get a better grip while breaking his legs. Best not ponder the details if you're squeamish.

WHERE TO STAY AND EAT

☆☆ Moderate

⬧ ✕ **Hôtel-restaurant du Centre**: Steenweg naar Ukkel 11, Beersel 1650. ☎ (02) 331 0615. Fax: (02) 378 3461. Doubles 1,600–2,500BEF. A stone's throw from Brussels, this is a good base for a visit to Bruegel country, with a family atmosphere and regional specialities in the restaurant. There are a few cheaper rooms with no shower.

GAASBEEK CASTLE

Gaasbeek is bang in the middle of the Pajottenland, which was given its name in the 19th century by a slightly barking lawyer. The name stuck, finally becoming part of the language. The landscape and villages of this region are most famously depicted in the paintings of Pieter Brueghel the Elder.

The castle is 15 kilometres (about 10 miles) southwest of Brussels: open from 1 April to 31 October, every day except Monday and Friday, 10am–5pm; in July and August, it also opens on Monday. The last tour leaves at 5pm, but the park is open until 9pm. Admission: 150BEF, with student discounts. ☎ (02) 531 0130. If you come by bus (De Lijn), take line LK, which leaves from the Gare du Midi in Brussels.

Originally built in the 13th century, the present castle is in fact a vast neo-fortress, created in the 19th century, when it was completely rebuilt after centuries of fire, war and neglect. It belonged in the 14th century to the Lord of Gaasbeek, the man behind the assassination of Everaert 't Serclaes, a famous Brusseler. Eager to avenge the murder, the *bruxellois* besieged the castle and destroyed it. The Count of Egmont lived here for several years, although his tenure came to a abrupt end when he was beheaded in Brussels in 1569. The last recorded owner was the Marquis of Arconati, who lived there until the beginning of the 20th century.

Tour of the Castle

It may look like a giant cake, but the castle has a fantastic location. It's set in 40 hectares (100 acres) of parkland, part of which is landscaped in the French style. It also houses some priceless *objets d'art*, bequeathed to the state by the Marquis on his death.

There are 45-minute tours every 20 minutes. Don't expect the guides to offer any information, however; they're just there to make sure you don't pinch anything. They're not very approachable, and heaven forbid that you should ask any questions.

If you're into stately homes, you can buy a brochure about the 16 rooms laid out for your enjoyment. Otherwise, you can wander around admiring the furniture, paintings and tapestries that decorate the walls, all dating from the 15th to the 18th century. At the risk of boring you with an exhaustive description of every detail, here are the highlights: the Flemish Renaissance furniture in rooms one and two, the neo-Gothic knights' room and a portrait of Erasmus above the mantelpiece in the library.

The four magnificent 16th-century Brussels tapestries in the archive room are the focal point of the tour. You can also see Rubens's marriage contract and will in the display cabinet.

Next up are several bedrooms. There are fine, Flemish-style sculptures from the 15th and 16th centuries in the Count of Egmont's bedroom. The museum room is jam-packed with beautiful *objets d'art*, including a Gothic chest, a Neo-Renaissance fireplace and multicoloured panelling. The tour continues through several rooms until you get to the kitchens. Above the fireplace is the cryptic family motto: *Tout à temps* ('All in time'). While you're musing over its meaning, survey the fine paintings in the last bedrooms, among them a *Tower of Babel* and a *grisaille* of the Count of Hoorn, Egmont's fellow decapitee, defending his case. In the Infanta's room, not surprisingly, there's a painting of the Infanta Isabella. There's a lot to digest, so a stroll in the park afterwards is definitely in order.

★ Also worth a visit in Gaasbeek is the local-history museum, in the old presbytery. Open April to end October, weekends only, 10am–4pm.

WHERE TO EAT IN THE AREA

✕ ❢ **Oud Gaasbeek**: Kasteelstraat 37, Lennik 1750; near the car park. ☎ (02) 532 5692. Open from March to October. A traditional little white farmhouse offering the ubiquitous toast cooked over an open fire and served with *fromage blanc*, radishes and chives. Washed down, of course, with cherry beer (*kriek*).

NATIONALE PLANTENTUIN (NATIONAL BOTANIC GARDENS OF MEISE)

These wonderful botanic gardens are in the splendid Bouchout estate, a beautifully maintained park covering 93 hectares (over 220 acres). A must for lovers of flower gardens, exotic plants and ancient trees, as it's one of Europe's best-stocked gardens. The locals come here *en famille* for their Sunday constitutional.

And it's not just a beauty spot: it's also a research centre, where rare and impressive species are protected. Besides the superb greenhouses, which take up more than a hectare (a couple of acres) of land and contain plants from all five continents, there's an orangery, a castle and a herbarium. You'll find every type of tropical and subtropical plant here.

✕ There's a little **cafeteria** near the castle where you can sit outside after your walk.

GETTING THERE

The Nationale Plantentuin, about 1.5km (1 mile) from the village of Meise, is easily accessible from Brussels, which is 15 km (9 miles) to the north.

– **By car**: take the Ring, then the A12 towards Antwerp, then the exit for Meise. Follow the signposts.

– **By bus**: SNCV company, take line L from the Gare du Nord in Brussels. Get off at the stop Nationale Plantentuin. ☎ (02) 269 3905.

THE TOUR

You can visit the park free of charge every day, 9am–6.30pm (until sunset in winter). The greenhouses are open from Easter to mid-November, Monday to Thursday and Saturday 1–4pm, Sunday and public holidays 1–5.30pm; in winter from Monday to Thursday 1–3.30pm. Admission: 120BEF; student discounts. Maps are available at the entrance.

GRIMBERGEN

A stone's throw from Meise: follow the directions given above for the botanical gardens. There's not much to say about this tiny village on the edge of Brussels, but it does have a baroque church, which is something of a rarity in Belgium.

WHAT TO SEE

★ **The Abbey Church**, on the village square. The original medieval abbey has been replaced by an unfinished 17th-century church with an odd-looking facade. When the Norbertine abbey was destroyed, a church was built in its place, but there weren't enough funds to complete it. The dimensions and odd proportions are the most striking thing about the interior, in the form of a Roman cross: there's a tiny nave and a disproportionately large choir and high cupola. But the main point of the visit is to see the baroque decoration: four open confessionals, ornamented with remarkably graceful, life-size wooden sculptures of saints. Note their wonderfully expressive faces. The misericords, by the same sculptor, are equally noteworthy. Finally, if the sacristy is open, take a look at its fine wooden panelling.

★ **Museum Voor de Oudere Technieke**: Guldendal 20, Grimbergen 1850. ☎ (02) 269 6771. De Lijn buses run from Brussels's Gare du Nord. Open from April to the beginning of October, Saturday, Sunday and public holidays 2–6pm. Admission: 90BEF. This little museum comprises three buildings a kilometre apart. The first is housed in a fine 17th-century edifice, where you can see craft objects from bygone centuries. The other two parts, Liermolen and Tommenmolen, are working watermills that offer abbey beer tasting in the mill taverns.

LEUVEN (LOUVAIN)　　　86,000 inhabitants

About 25 kilometres (15 miles) east of Brussels, Leuven has all the trappings of a large, affluent Flemish town, with none of the developments that have scarred the nearby capital. During term-time, the terraces are awash with students, and the Oude Markt and the town in general get caught up in the rhythm of the academic year. Despite the bustle, there's a calm, settled feel to Leuven, and it's unlikely to change. Following the fierce language riots of the 1960s, the prestigious Catholic University of Leuven was split, with the French-speaking students carted off to a brand-new university, Louvain-la-Neuve. Sometimes, it seems French-speakers get a bit ostracized, but this doesn't seem to pose too much of a problem. The cafés hum, but the liveliness never gets out of hand, and the little River Dijl flows peacefully by. Visitors will appreciate the flamboyant Stadhuis, the city's architectural cohesion and the fact that Leuven doesn't look like a museum town – oh yes, and Britain's favourite beer, Stella Artois, is brewed here.

A Short History

Although a Norman fortress was established here in the ninth century, Leuven didn't really take off until the 11th century, when Lambert I ('the Bearded') built a castle here. Another two centuries were to pass before the town became a major centre with its own town wall, growing rich from the cultivation of cereal crops and the manufacture of cloth. After a series of bloody uprisings in the 14th century, Leuven lost out to Brussels, which became the capital of Brabant. The city's second golden age was based on the cultivation of learning. Leuven acquired its Stadhuis in the 15th century, during the Burgundian occupation, and became a university town whose reputation soon spread throughout Europe; Erasmus taught here. The town is still known for its intellectual excellence, despite the separation of Dutch and French-speaking students in 1968. Indeed, Leuven has wended its student way down the centuries without too many mishaps befalling it. It survived a fire started by the Germans in 1914, which ravaged the university library, and the terrible bombardments of 1944. Builders repeatedly rebuilt what was destroyed, sticking as closely as possible to the original plans.

USEFUL INFORMATION AND ADDRESSES

Postcode: 3000.
🏠 **Tourist office**: Stadhuis, Grote Markt. ☎ (016) 211539. Fax: (016) 211549. Email: toerisme@leuven.be. Open Monday to Friday 9am–5pm and Saturday 10am–5pm; also open on Sundays and public holidays from 1 March to 31 October. You can pick up an excellent city guidebook, and buy combined tickets to the parish museum and Sint

Pieterskerk: 200BEF. A list of B&Bs is also available.
✉ **Post office**: Smolderplein 1. Open Monday to Friday 9am–6pm, Saturday 9am–noon.
🚂 **Station**: Martelarenplein. ☎ (016) 221321. Trains to and from Brussels every hour from 6am to 10pm.
■ **Bike hire**: at the station. ☎ (016) 221321. Open every day 7am–9pm. Cheaper if you come by train.

WHERE TO STAY

☆–☆☆ Budget–Moderate

⚓ **Industrie**: Martelarenplein 7. ☎ (016) 221349. Fax: (016) 208285. Two steps from the station. Doubles 2,000BEF. A recently renovated hotel offering good value for money. The spotless rooms have showers and toilets. There's a large dining room on the ground floor, where indoor plants fill the gaps left by customers whose absence is hard to understand given the temptation of the inexpensive daily special.
⚓ **Professor**: Naamsestraat 20. ☎ (016) 201414. Fax: (016) 291-416. Doubles 2,600BEF. Housed in

a fine old building opposite the Gothic cloth market, this hotel proves that you don't have to pay through the nose for comfortable, airy rooms, bathrooms with windows and a central location. Eight rooms in all, and there's a café on the ground floor with pleasant service. A good bet if you're not too broke.
⚓ **Jackson's Hotel**: Brusselsestraat 110-112, five minutes from the Grote Markt. ☎ (016) 202492. Fax: (016) 231329. Doubles 2,950BEF, including breakfast. The landlords are charming, and usually put up

businessmen during the week. They reduce prices on Friday and Saturday nights to make the place pay. So, for a reasonable price, you can enjoy modern comfort, free breakfast and rococo-style decoration, complete with red velvet and murals. Just one thing: doors close at 11pm. Free parking on weekends at the hospital across the street.

WHERE TO EAT

There are plenty of restaurants in the pedestrianized centre, but there's not much on offer besides pizzerias, Mexican and Chinese eateries, and 'authentic' places aimed at the better-off tourist. Better to head for one of the many cafés (see the list below) offering decent snacks. Often a safe bet if you don't want to part with a month's salary.

⊡ Budget

✕ **De Lange Trappen**: Mathys de Layens Plein. ☎ (016) 223777. Open every day except Sunday, noon–2am or later; food served until 11pm. Overlooked by the impassive facade of the collegiate church, this old café has retained its stained glass, and its new owners have exercised tasteful restraint and turned it into a charming place, with collections of mirrors, alarm clocks, spectacles and old framed photographs. There's a designer bar, and the lamps are stunning. As for atmosphere, people stay till late, even if it means spilling out onto the terrace or going upstairs to the function room. Tempting snacks on toast, pasta or a daily special. Helpings are generous and the food is always good.

✕ **De Blauwe Schuit**: Vismarkt 16. ☎ (016) 220570. Open every day noon–1am. You can't miss this large building at the back of the market square. Inside, it has two-tone vaulting and a pleasant atmosphere. The ventilation's good, but whenever the sun's out, everyone heads outdoors to sit under the trees in a vast enclosed terrace, one of the best in town. Tasty snacks include toasted sandwiches, omelettes, pasta, chili con carne and soup of the day.

⊡⊡ Moderate

✕ **De Nachtuil**: Krakenstraat 8. ☎ (016) 220259. Open every day 6pm–4am. Full meal 750 BEF. The restaurant's name ('The Night Owl') is a reference to the hours it keeps, as well as to its owl-like landlord. It's in a little street off the Oude Markt. Ravenous night owls can tuck into fresh, unpretentious Belgian fare, including tasty meat dishes and generous portions of good home cooking. The restaurant has three dining areas, one of which is upstairs. The décor is unremarkable, but there's a pleasant, cosy atmosphere.

⊡⊡⊡ Expensive

✕ **De Blauwe Zon**: Tiensestraat 28. ☎ (016) 226880. Open for lunch from noon and for dinner from 6.30pm; closed Saturday lunchtime and Sunday. A stylish restaurant with a large dining area and a mezzanine. The student clientèle seems at home with the prices. The inventive menu includes crayfish tartare with cucumber sauce and eel and crayfish hotpot. Vegetarians will appreciate the delicious vegetable casseroles cooked with seasonal greens. Excellent wines for which you pay by the centimetre (they tot up consumption by measuring it, instead of giving you a 25cl or 50cl carafe), including Rueda, a famous Spanish white.

WHERE TO GO FOR A DRINK

Leuven is a beer and student town par excellence, so there's no shortage of watering holes. In the evening, the Oude Markt overflows with the swelling ranks of noisy, cheerful café-crawlers. Around the square, the most popular taverns (apart from De Giraf – *see below*) are Bierkelder, Het Grote Genoegen, Charlatan, Nota Bene and Oase. If you want to wind up the night with a dance, head for Danceria Rumba, open every night. It's on Kiekensstraat, just off the Oude Markt.

❢ Herberg Huisbrouwerij Domus: Tiensestraat 8. Open every day. The Domus brewery, which takes up the entire corner of a cobbled street and has a courtyard terrace, is a Leuven institution. The décor's a bit folksy-touristy, almost Bavarian, but take a good look round and wander upstairs to admire the brickwork, exposed beams and antiques. Two speciality beers are highly recommended from a list of beers that's as big as the Yellow Pages: Bink, from the Kerkom brewery in Sint-Truiden, and the fearsome Chouffe at 8%. Or try one of the seasonal beers brewed on the premises. Light meals available.

❢ Café in 't Onderwoud: Grote Markt 13. Open every day from 10am–midnight. Closed for two weeks in September. Leuven's biggest, and most essential, café is a splendid Belle Époque establishment dating from 1896, with mirrors, stained glass with floral motifs, allegorical frescoes and embossed gilt wallpaper. Note the decorative details of the mural panelling and bar.

❢ Tavern Erasmus: Tiensestraat 96 (at the corner of Kardinal Mercierplein). Open every day from 9am–4pm. This large café in a white-washed house does justice to the great humanist it's named after. Portraits of Erasmus and a fresco of the great man teaching decorate the walls of this pleasant, rustic venue, where customers huddle round the little tables and wrought-iron stove, sipping barley beer or eating excellent waffles. In summer, they crowd onto the terrace, which is a short distance from the centre and just off the tourist track. It's a shame the food (except the desserts) is so mediocre.

❢ De Giraf: Oude Markt 38. Open every day from 11am–6am or later. Of all the cafés on this square, De Giraf deserves a special mention because of its plain wooden décor, which makes it look a bit like a log cabin, because of the giraffe's head, and because it's open all night.

❢ De Blauwe Kater: Hallengang 1 (off Naamsestraat). Open every day from 8pm–2am. Tucked away at the end of an alleyway, the 'Blue Cat' has live jazz and blues. Concerts are free and usually take place on Wednesdays and Thursdays between October and May, although you can also hear live music here in summer, when the mass exodus of students can make Leuven a very sleepy place. It's a cosy bar, ideal for a chat by candlelight.

❢ Den Clijne Tafel: Naamsestraat 47. Open 11am–1am. The panelling of this café, established in 1675, has been well polished by the passage of time. Light meals, mostly salads and toasted sandwiches. Below, in the **Brunch Inn**, there's a vaulted cellar where you can sit long into the night and almost imagine that you're in a monastery.

FLEMISH BRABANT

WHAT TO SEE

★ **Grote Markt**: unlike most of Belgium's town and village squares, Leuven's central square is not a separate entity, but merges with the surrounding sites. Squeezed between the Stadhuis and Sint Pieterskerk (which was, until the 1940s, fringed with houses), its cafés feel a little cramped, and it's hard to find a good spot from which to admire the flamboyant facade of the Stadhuis. A Gothic building, rebuilt according to original plans in 1921, stands left of the Tafelronde, or Round Table, which makes the square and its gabled houses architecturally coherent.

★ **Sint Pieterskerk**: Grote Markt. Open Tuesday to Saturday 10am–5pm, also Monday 10am–5pm between mid-March and mid-October. Closed to the public on Sunday morning. Building began in the 15th century, on the site of a Norman church. The architect Mathys de Layens was involved in the construction, which continued for several dozen years. The ground was particularly unstable and caved in a number of times, so, in the 17th century, they gave up trying to build the 165-metre (545ft) tower. Although the exterior is nothing to write home about, the proportions of this masterpiece of Brabant Gothic are striking, in particular its high vaulted roof. Panels obscure part of the luxurious nave. In the choir is a 15th-century Sedes Sapientiae, the emblem of the University, which is a copy of a 12th-century version. Note also the Edelheere triptych, commissioned by the family of that name; it's a smaller version of Rogier Van der Weyden's *Descent from the Cross*, which once hung in this church but is now in Madrid's Prado. Also on display here are two triptychs by Dirk Bouts, a Flemish Primitive painter born in Haarlem, who trained at Van der Weyden's school in Brussels. He became Leuven's official painter in 1468 and died there seven years later. One of his sons, Albrecht, became moderately famous in his own right. Bouts's chef d'oeuvre, *The Last Supper*, on show here, was painted between 1464 and 1468. Bouts's depiction of himself, wearing a red cap, is in the central panel, to the right of a radiant Christ. His other triptych represents the *Martyrdom of St Erasmus*, in which an apparently unflinching saint looks on as his torturers wind his innards round a winch. Note too an especially moving 13th-century Norman head of Christ, a seated figure of Christ in multicoloured wood that was miraculously saved from fire in 1914, and several other religious treasures. Don't leave the church without taking a look at the impressive baptismal fonts, with their ironwork lids, the 15th-century rood screen and the exuberant baroque pulpit, dedicated to St Norbert, who was struck by lightning while out riding. This huge chunk of wood, with its flamboyant plants and flowers dripping on to the carved animals and people below, is the fantastical creation of the 18th-century sculptor Jacques Berger. The 48-bell carillon plays every Saturday between 3pm and 4pm.

★ **Stadhuis**: Grote Markt. ☎ (016) 152539. Guided tours: Monday to Friday, 11am–3pm, Saturday and Sunday at 3pm; weekends only from November to late February. The meeting point is at the main entrance, or in the small garden to the left of the building. Admission: 50BEF. Tours last for about 45 minutes.

The town hall's wonderfully elaborate facade, designed by Mathieu de Layens, is *the* reason to visit Leuven. Built in the 15th century during the reign of Philip the Good, Duke of Burgundy, it rises resplendent beneath six octagonal turrets. The vertical lines, hardly broken by a host of niches, rise to a three-level pitched roof with dormer windows. In the 19th century, following a recommendation from Victor Hugo, who travelled extensively in Belgium, a statue was placed in each niche. As a result, more than 200 stone characters took their place in the facade. A belfry was to have topped the Stadhuis, but the instability of the ground beneath prevented it being built.

The tour starts with a visit to the 'room of lost steps', adorned with sculptures by Constantin Meunier and Jef Lambeaux, and a statue of Margaret, a mythical Leuven figure whose body is buried in Sint Pieterskerk. She is reputed to have floated miraculously down the river Dijl to the town after bandits had raped and murdered her (a contemporary work in Tiensestraat tells the story). Visitors are then shown other rooms in a variety of styles, including a stunning Gothic vault and the register room, where the town silver is kept behind a heavy door. There's a fine oak ceiling on the first floor.

★ **Naamsesstraat**: this road, on the right of the Stadhuis, leads south to the Groot Begijnhof (Beguine convent), and its buildings provide an overview of the styles and history of the town. On the left stands the baroque Drapers' Deanery, built in 1680, almost opposite their exchange, and now part of the university. The Gothic exchange dates from the end of the 14th century, and was rebuilt after the 1914 fire. A little farther along, on the left, stands Sint Michielskerk, of which only one baroque facade survived the bombardments of 1944.

Take the first street on the left, Berriotstraat, which passes the Sint-Donatus Park, where you can see a few traces of the city's 12th-century ramparts. Now turn back towards Naamsesstraat, looking out for the King's College (No. 59), the rococo facade of the Premonstratensian College (No. 61) and Arras College (No. 63). All three date from the 18th century. At No. 69, there's a Gothic brick facade with decorated gabling that belongs to the 15th-century Huis van 't Sestich. The 16th-century Renaissance-style building opposite is Van Dale College. Turn right onto Karmelietenberg, by the neo-Gothic American College, to get to the Begijnhof.

★ **Groot Begijnhof**: open early March to late October 11am–3pm. Admission: 50 BEF. Belgium's largest *begijnhof* was built in the 13th century, when there was not enough convent accommodation to house the enormous number of women and children who were widowed and orphaned as a result of the Crusades. Eventually, the women won the right to set up a religious community in exchange for a promise of chastity and observance of religious duties, but without having to take nuns' vows. The Beguines, as they were called, were responsible for the education of girls and care of the sick. Most of the 72 half-timbered houses around the church of St John the Baptist date from the 17th century. It's a calm, fairy-tale collection of buildings, with two slivers of the River Dijl flowing through. Stroll along the small cobbled streets, admiring the pretty springs, bridges and fountains, the statues that adorn the niches of the facades and the sparrows hopping on the lawns. The wonderfully romantic Groot Begijnhof has traded asceticism for academia; the university snapped up the properties in 1962, and these desirable residences now house staff, and the students, all no doubt very grateful for the peace and quiet. There's only one Beguine left. The complex is a UNESCO World Heritage Site.

FLEMISH BRABANT

★ **Museum Vander Kelen-Mertens**: Savoyestraat 6 (entry also through the garden of the Tourist Office). ☎ (016) 226906.

Open Tuesday to Saturday 10am–5pm, Sunday 2–5pm. Closed from mid-December to mid-January. This 16th-century college was once the home of Burgomaster Vander Kelen-Mertens. His son donated the house to the town, and it became a museum. The rooms are laid out in different styles, according to the taste of the Burgomaster: baroque, Renaissance, rococo and 18th-century. The Flemish painting and sculpture rooms (19th-century) contain works by Constantin Meunier and Jef Lambeaux, including a fountain with swans, from which wine flowed on festive days given by the burgomaster. This, of course, was long before public funds were abused . . .

Objects from tombs dating from the time of Charlemagne and a few vestiges of Brabant prehistory are on display on the lower ground floor.

The first floor, which contains objects temporarily housed here while works are carried out on Sint Pieterskerk, is the most interesting. Among the highlights are the 14th- and 15th-century multicoloured wooden statues, among them a particularly moving *Pietà*. Paintings by local artists, including Rogier Van der Weyden and Quentin Metsys, complete this fine collection. Note too, the 16th-century triptych. Two other sections are devoted to porcelain and stained-glass windows.

★ If you're not in a hurry, visit the **Klein Begijnhof**, on the street of that name. This street leads to the Gothic Sint Gertrudiskerk, which overlooks a delightful tributary of the river Dijl. Take a look at the University Library on Herbert Hooverplein, rebuilt according to the original plans by an American architect after World War II, and at the bizarre bronze hot-air balloon on the square, and you'll really be able to say you've seen Leuven.

Of Special Interest

– **Marktrock**: open-air rock festival, mid-August.

WHERE TO STAY IN THE AREA

⌂ **Campsite Ter Munck**: Campingweg, Egenhove 3000, southwest of Leuven. ☎ (016) 238668. There's room for 50 tents.

WHAT TO SEE IN THE AREA

★ **Heverlee, Park Abbey**: Abdijdreef 7. ☎ (016) 403640. Open Sunday at 4pm and by appointment. Admission: 100BEF. Just as you're leaving town, by the Park gateway; leave the boulevards that ring the town when you get to the Philips factory, then take the first left after the railway bridge. If you can't make it on a Sunday, or if you haven't booked in advance, you can go for a stroll and admire the abbey buildings. Stone lions sit above the doorways that divide the courtyards, where chickens and turkeys cluck and gobble. If you do visit this impressive complex of buildings, founded in the 12th century and rebuilt in the 16th and 17th centuries, you'll only see a limited number of rooms, but you will get a peek into the splendidly stocked library.

DIEST   22,000 inhabitants

Off the tourist track on the road to Limburg, Diest is a little-known town that's worth spending a few hours exploring. It's a 20-minute drive from Leuven via the A2 motorway. The town is hemmed in by a curve of the Demer river. Apart from its fascinating monuments, it's also the home of the deliciously smooth, pale Gildenbier.

A Short History

In 1229, the city received its charter from Duke Henri I of Brabant. Its textile trade brought it considerable wealth, particularly in the 15th century, when it belonged to the Orange family, along with Breda, in the Low Countries, Dillenburg, in Germany, and Orange, in France. The most famous member of this dynasty was William of Nassau, also known as William the Silent, who led the revolt against the Spanish in the 16th century. His eldest son is buried in the Sint Sulpitiuskerk. Thanks to this connection, Queen Beatrix, the current Dutch monarch, is known as *Vrouw van Diest* (Lady of Diest). Diest saw action in 1830, during the battle for the independence of the young Belgian nation, when the Dutch were the enemy. Diest was a fortress town, and was hemmed in by a ring of forts, which prevented its expansion.

USEFUL ADDRESSES

Postcode: 3290.
🛈 Tourist Office: Stadhuis, Grote Markt 1. ☎ (013) 312121. Open Monday to Friday, 10am–noon and 1–5pm; also weekends from May to mid-September. The staff will fall over themselves to help you.

🚂 Station: to the north of the town (a kilometre from the Grote Markt); links to Leuven, Hasselt, Antwerp and Liège.
■ Bike hire: Halve Maan Leopold-vest. ☎ (013) 311528. From May to late September.

WHERE TO STAY

It's unlikely that you'll decide to spend the night in Diest, delightful though it is, but should you decide to prolong your stay after an evening meal, here are a couple of suggestions, one of them a real gem.

☆ Budget

🛏 Youth Hostel Den Drossard: Sint Janstraat 2A. ☎ and fax: (013) 313721. Closed mid-November to mid-February. Basic rate per night: 420BEF. In all, 68 beds. Like all Belgian youth hostels, it's spotless and offers sheet hire, packed lunches and bike hire.

☆☆ Moderate

🛏 Hotel Fransche Croon: Leuven-sestraat 26-28 (first road on the right as you leave the Grote Markt, facing away from the Stadhuis). ☎ (013) 314540. Fax: (013) 333159. Email: de.fransche.croon@skynet.be. Closed end of December. Doubles 3,800BEF, with a 10 per cent mid-week discount. The great thing about three-star hotels in provincial towns is the price:quality ratio. This listed building continues to offer the kind of relaxed hospitality that characterized it in the 19th century, when it was a coaching inn, with a welcoming atmosphere, all mod cons and 23 spacious but cosy rooms with plenty of character. The breakfast room has beautiful furniture, and to top it all, there's an *haute cuisine* restaurant (closed Saturday evening) offering business menus and a daily special: à la carte, expect to pay about 1,000BEF. A must, if only for the fun of it.

WHERE TO EAT

There are plenty of tavern-restaurants around the Grote Markt, but none are much to write home about.

☆☆ Moderate

✕ **Cafeteria-Tea-Room 't Dambord**: Ketelstraat 30 (on the corner of Schotelstraat, in the pedestrianized road to the right of Sint Sulpitiuskerk). Closed Tuesday evenings, Wednesday and November. Located in a half-timbered, 15th-century house. Good for a snack or for lunch. On the menu: steak or rabbit in beer, and a daily special with dessert and coffee at competitive prices.

✕ **Gasthof 1618**: in the Begijnhof (right at the back, on the left). ☎ (013) 333240. Set menus 595–695BEF. A splendid old-world tavern, serving fast food but also offering a menu with a historic flavour (try the 'little Beguine's little rabbit') and mouthwatering crêpes.

WHERE TO GO FOR A DRINK

Diest doesn't exactly whoop it up of an evening, but a few cafés provide local atmosphere.

♟ **Bij de Baas**: Grote Markt, 14. Closed Wednesday evening and Thursday. A fine selection of beer is on offer in this funny little inn. Drink up while you listen to 1950s crooners, and don't forget to try the frothy, dark brown Gildenbier before you leave.

WHAT TO SEE

Any tour of Diest should begin at the Grote Markt, with its handsome 17th- and 18th-century houses. Two buildings stand out:

★ **Stadhuis**: a neoclassical facade houses the tourist information office and, in the basement (Gothic and Norman), the Stedelijk Museum (town museum). Open every day 10am–noon and 1–5pm. Admission: 50BEF. The vaulted cellars contain a well-arranged display of armour, statues of saints from the Begijnhof, religious treasures that used to belong to the guilds, porcelain, sculpted furniture, arms – and a spring that proves the place was once a brewery. You can even see the brewer's tools. The focal point of the museum is *The Last Judgement,* an anonymous 15th-century painting on wood that shows the gruesome fate of the damned.

★ **Sint Sulpitiuskerk**: from May to the end of August, open 2–5pm. Admission charges for the choir and treasury. Combined tickets available for the regional museum: 80BEF. Building took place between 1321 and 1354 in two materials – dark sandstone and white stone from France – in a style called Demer Valley Gothic. The apse and the tower were never finished. The 43 bells hang in a bell tower that's revered by locals, who call it 'the mustard pot'. In the 15th-century choir, the stalls are decorated with wry misericords illustrating the seven deadly sins. The treasury houses several fine precious religious objects (admission: 50BEF).

★ Just off the Grote Markt as you head towards the Refugiestraat, at the edge of the river's oxbow lake, you'll come to the refuges of the abbeys of **Tongerlo** (by Spijker, 16th-century) and of Averbode (15th-century), to which undesirable monks were sent. What, one wonders, had they been up to?

★ As you come back towards Sint Sulpitiuskerk and go round it, you'll come across the cloth hall, now called Lakenhal, which is used for functions. It was built in the local rust coloured stone (hardened lumps of sand, proof that the place was under sea seven million years ago). The 15th-century cannon is called Holle Griet ('Angry Margaret').

★ Head for the pedestrianized area at the back of the cloth hall; if you cross it via Koestraat, you'll end up on a square that marks the entrance to the Warandestatspark. Opposite the entrance is the impressive house of Nassau, where the Prince of Orange stayed. From here, stroll back down Guido Gezellestraat and take a look at the baroque facade of Sint Barbarakerk, founded by the Augustinians, and the wood and clay corbels of the half-timbered houses. Follow the shop-lined Koning Albertstraat to Begijnhofstraat (about 10 minutes on foot) and the Begijnhof.

★ **The Begijnhof** in Diest, founded in 1253, is now a UNESCO World Heritage Site and one of the best maintained in the former Low Countries. The Dutch inscription over the magnificent baroque door reads: 'Come into my garden, my sister and my bride'. Christ's 'brides', who once numbered as many as 400, have not lived here since 1928. The buildings now belong to the town, which uses them for exhibitions and cultural activities. The small houses provide accommodation for families in need and also house some artists' workshops. You can get some idea of Beguine life by visiting the Engelconvent Museum, on the street of that name, (open Saturday and Sunday, 2–5.30pm), which has a typical array of furniture and objects from a Beguine house.

The church at its heart is a perfect illustration of the modesty of Beguine women: the materials are of poor quality and the design is austere. It's not easy to visit, unless you sneak in with the faithful during Mass. There's a workshop where you can see lace-makers at work: Infirmeriestraat 5. Open weekends only, 2.30–6pm.

The Begijnhof is lit by candles on the first Sunday in September from 7pm.

★ **A walk round the ramparts** (via the Léopoldvest): built after Belgian independence together with the Schaffensepoort (a fortified narrow way across the two arms of the River Demer) and the **Lindenmolen**, a traditional windmill.

★ **Ezeldijkmolen** (mill of the Princes of Orange): 16th-century. Makes a pretty picture with the weeping willow and the canal. Access via Schaffen-straat.

★ **Birthplace of St Jan Berchmans** (No. 24 in the road of the same name): local saint, born in 1599 and the patron of youth organizations.

In the Area

Diest is part of Hageland, a region in the eastern part of Flemish Brabant. Diest, Aarschot, Zoutleeuw and Tienen form the angles of a trapezium in the hills between Antwerp Campine and Limburg Campine, a landscape rich in Norman remains that the Belgian writer Ernest Claes used as the setting for his novels. Claes is buried in the nearby cemetery of the Abbey of Averbode.

AARSCHOT

Fate has not been kind to Aarschot. The town has a rich heritage and was once a ducal seat, but it was pillaged by the Austrians, the Burgundians and the Spanish, then demolished by the two world wars. Today, its market gardens produce the country's finest asparagus.

WHAT TO SEE

★ **Onze Lieve Vrouwkerk**: dates back to the 14th and 15th centuries. The 85-metre (281ft) tower is an odd mix of colours (sandstone and limestone), but the spire, with its onion dome and bell tower, is rather elegant. The interior, with a wrought-iron chandelier attributed to Quentin Metsys and moralizing misericords in the choir stalls, is worth a quick look.

★ **The old Begijnhof**: opposite the church. Shamefully bombarded during the two world wars, only the oldest part remains. No. 25 houses the **Museum voor Heemkunde en folklore**. Open Tuesday to Friday 9am–noon and 1.30pm–4.30pm, Saturday 9am–4pm and Sunday 9am–noon. Admission: 40BEF. Devoted to folklore and daily life, the museum focuses on religious history, crafts and the manufacture of local brown beer.

★ **The Dukes' Mills**: rebuilding works have brought to light the 16th-century mills that also operated as locks and toll booth, enabling the town to tax boatmen.

★ The **main square** had to be rebuilt after 1945. The **Tower of Saint Roch** is all that remains of the 13th-century town hall.

★ The **Tower of Orléans**, on the Kouterberg, south of town, offers fine views of the region. An orientation table helps you identify the towers (ask for the key at the tourist office, situated at the foot of the Saint Roch tower; open Monday to Friday 9am–noon and 1–5pm).

– On **15 August**, the town is plunged into darkness and thousands of candles are placed in the windows, in memory of a plague outbreak that struck the inhabitants at the end of the 17th century.

– **Cheese market** 10am–6pm on the fourth Sunday in May.

WERCHTER (NORTH OF LEUVEN)

– On the first Sunday in July, Werchter hosts the country's biggest **rock festival**.

HOLSBEEK

★ **Horst castle**: Sint-Pieters-Rode. ☎ (016) 623345. Open weekends 1–6pm and Wednesday and Friday outside term time. Admission: 100BEF. About 15 kilometres (10 miles) from Leuven, on the way to Holsbeek. Set in a private, 250-hectare (600-acre) park with a massive keep and odd-looking tower dominating the moat, this wonderfully solid castle was built in the 13th and 15th centuries. Climb the bizarre tower, visit the knights' room and take a look at the frescoes in the chapel. Pause for coffee in the courtyard or go for a stroll in the surrounding countryside. Note that the café serves the one and only Hageland wine, the grapes for which are grown in the vineyards of Houweart. In 1975, a grand total of four bottles were produced; in 1995, the harvest resulted in a whopping 60,000.

SCHERPENHEUVEL

A detour to Scherpenheuvel en route between Aarschot and Diest is essential if you want to see just how kitsch religious tourism can be.

In 1609, in good Counter-Reformation spirit, Archduke Albert and his wife Isabella decided to build a town dedicated to the worship of Mary. As a result, pilgrims invaded the place, travelling along the seven carefully constructed roads that converge on the seven-sided sanctuary, which is topped with the first baroque dome built in the territory now known as Belgium. Designed by Wencelas Cobergher, there's something vaguely Roman about it, despite the modest dimensions. Inside, look out for a figure of Christ sculpted by François Duquesnoy (son of Jérôme, of Manneken-Pis fame) and a fascinating wood and marble tree above the altar. It's supposed to have been inspired by a sacred oak – could this be an ancient druid site?

Between May and August, the faithful arrive by the coachload, and rush to follow the route of the Cross marked out around the sanctuary before casting coins at the foot of the altar, then piling into the souvenir shops that line the roads. Then, at last, they flop in the outdoor cafés and stoke up on waffles and beer.

A huge candle-lit procession takes place on the first Sunday after All Saints to thank the Virgin for deliverance from the plague in 1629.

AVERBODE ABBEY

North of Diest, at the point where three provinces meet, the Premonstratensian order, whose patron saint was St Norbert, founded the Averbode Abbey (1134). The main attraction is the majestic baroque church, built in 1672. The facade is particularly elegant. Open 9am–12.30pm and 1.30–5pm. You can admire the five altars and baroque stalls, as well as the paintings by Theodoor Verhaegen. You can only visit the monastic buildings beyond the cobbled courtyard on special request.

Ernest Claes's grave is in the little cemetery that lies between the nave of the church and the street.

ZOUTLEEUW (LEAU) — 8,000 inhabitants

Take the road from Tienen to Sint-Truiden and head for Zoutleeuw. It's hard to believe that half a century back, this sleepy, overgrown village, one of the seven towns of Brabant, was a flourishing centre that prospered thanks to the cloth trade. Traces of its bygone wealth have, miraculously, survived, which is why it's worth stopping off here.

A Short History

Zoutleeuw's prosperity, which made it rich enough to build eight convents and three ramparts, came about because of the town's strategic position on the River Gette, which made it accessible by boat and made it the frontier town for the Duchy of Brabant. Zoutleeuw endured its fair share of the turbulence that plagued the region, and saw many an army march beneath its walls. During the Wars of Religion, hordes of Protestant iconoclasts descended on the town, but its walls were enough to deter the assailants, who went elsewhere to indulge their favourite pastimes of pillaging and destroying religious treasures. So, Sint Leonarduskerk managed, for the first time, to hold onto its riches. The strategically desirable church was later captured by Louis XIV, then fell into neglect. When the armies of the French Revolution arrived, the local canons sensibly pledged allegiance to the Republican power, and thereby saved their church a second time. Thanks to them, you can see what a fine church looked like in the Middle Ages: this is the only known example in Belgium.

USEFUL ADDRESSES

🛈 **Tourist office**: Grote Markt. ☎ (011) 781288. In the cloth hall, to the right of the Stadhuis.

■ **Bike hire**: Het Vinne, Ossenwegstraat 70. ☎ (011) 781819. Several itineraries provided.

WHERE TO STAY

☆☆ Moderate

🛏 **Hotel Arconaty**: Sint Truidensesteenweg 61, Linter 3350. ☎ and fax: (016) 788502. On the Tienen-Sint-Truiden road, six kilometres (3.5 miles) from Zoutleeuw. Doubles 1,000–1,350BEF. A big, seaside-style villa with a family atmosphere and basic levels of comfort. Half-board available. A good starting point for exploring the area. Helpful tips for cyclists and bike hire available.

WHERE TO EAT

✗ The Grote Markt has three or four taverns, should you feel peckish during the two hours it takes to visit Zoutleeuw. The **Pintelier** tavern serves pancakes and waffles.

WHAT TO SEE

★ **Sint Leonarduskerk**: Open Tuesday to Sunday 2–5pm from Easter to late September; weekends only in October. Closed November to March. Admission: 40BEF. Part Romanesque, part Gothic, the church was built between the 13th and 15th centuries, and is dedicated to a doctor saint. A fussy bell tower above the nave houses a 49-bell carillon that plays every 15 minutes.

The church is an impressive museum of religious art, and is well worth a visit. As you enter, look up towards the nave, where you'll see the *Marianum* (1533), a double-sided, multicoloured image of the Virgin; she looks somewhat amused, though only from one side. She is cradling the infant Jesus, holding a rosary and crushing a dragon that looks like a piece of Nepalese statuary. Angels wearing dresses strew a garland of flowers around her. To the left of the transept is a huge stone tabernacle, an amazingly elaborate, lace-like piece of carved stone. It was commissioned in 1551 by a pair of local philanthropists, who asked the Antwerp sculptor Cornelis 'Floris' de Vriendt to undertake the work. He made it in his workshop and sent it by boat to Zoutleeuw. The tower of the Holy Sacrament is 18 metres (nearly 60ft) high, and its nine levels are home to no less than 200 statuettes. You can see traces of Gothic flamboyance here, although Floris spent a fair amount of time in Rome and introduced the Italian Renaissance style as well. The scenes are all biblical (if he's in the mood, the curate at the entrance will be happy to fill you in, but don't forget to drop a coin or two in the chest to help with restoration).

At the top of the first floor, there's a truly unusual image of Christ: a pelican ripping open its chest to feed its offspring.

The second-largest Easter candelabrum in Europe, completed in 1483, hangs at the entrance to the ambulatory (which takes you round behind the choir). Europe's biggest, incidentally, is in England's Durham Cathedral. This one consists of six bronze branches and weighs 950kg (2090lb). The upper part shows Mary Magdalene and John at the foot of the Cross. There are several other fine artefacts in the church, notably a painting of *Three Weeping Women* (1504), a *Pietà* from the 15th century; a fresco of the Last Judgment (1490), a superb lectern in the shape of an eagle (note the knot in the dragon's tail) and the religious treasures on display in the chapel.

★ **Stadhuis**: A Gothic building with Renaissance ornamentation, built during the reign of Charles V. A fine flight of steps, decorated with the arms of the House of Burgundy and the Holy Roman Empire, leads up to it. The building also boasts a huge art-nouveau mural and a panelled great council room with a monumental fireplace on the first floor.

★ The **cloth hall**: next door to the Stadhuis. Built in the 14th century, it abuts part of the old ramparts.

★ The **pump** on the square is a copy of one built in 1762. The original was destroyed in 1944 by an American tank, which lost its way in fog.

– **Pentecost Monday**: procession of Saint Leonard, fancy-dress floats.

FLEMISH BRABANT

TIENEN (TIRLEMONT)   32,000 inhabitants

Tienen is on the Brussels–Liège road, and is surrounded by a sea of sugar beet. It is the centre of the sugar industry for East Brabant. Originally dependent on the textile industry, Tienen was demolished in 1635 by the French and Dutch, who were busy besieging the Spanish, and again by a bombardment in 1944, which left 650 houses in ruins

USEFUL ADDRESS

🖬 Tourist office: Grote Markt 4. ☎ (016) 805686. Bike hire available at reasonable prices. Booking advised. You can also book to visit a sugar refinery.

WHERE TO STAY

☆ Budget

♠ Youth hostel Het Sporthuis: Kabeekvest 93, Tienen 3300. ☎ (016) 821460. Fax: (016) 822-796. Basic rate per night: 420BEF. Book in before 7pm. Twelve beds available.

☆☆☆ Expensive

♠ Hotel Le Nouveau Monde: Vierde Lancierslaan 75-77, Tienen 3300. ☎ (016) 814321. A fine 19th-century building with 12 rooms (half have baths, half showers) near the station. Business clientèle. Restaurant on the ground floor.

WHAT TO SEE

★ **Onze-Lieve-Vrouw-ten-Poel**: this Brabant Gothic edifice on the vast Grote Markt (constructed on the site of a dried-out marsh) boasts a beautiful French-style triple porch, above which is the onion-dome bell tower. There are some fine sculpted characters in the niches, which have finely carved pedestals. As soon as you enter the church, you'll soon notice that there's something missing: the nave was never finished. The attractive confessional boxes provide some compensation.

★ To the right of the square, facing away to the church, is the **Stedelijke Museum Het Toreke**. Open 10am–5pm. Closed Monday. Admission: 100BEF. The building was a prison until 1975, but is now used to display Gallo-Roman objects, crafts and religious art. Themed exhibitions on festivals, religion and work tell the entire history of the Hageland.

★ **The church of Saint-Germanus**: at the heart of the old part of the village, near the animal market (Veemarkt). Closed Tuesday morning. This church is the result of a sanctuary founded by the Abbey of Saint-Germain-des-Prés, in Paris. In the 12th century, it was a Romanesque basilica. You can see the alterations that have been made over the centuries, throwing everything out of alignment: the choir isn't at the end of the nave, while the transept is out of proportion. On Wednesdays in July and August, there's a carillon concert at 8pm.

On the right, facing away from the porch, in the Wolmarkt, are two handsome **Renaissance houses** (Nos. 19 and 21).

– **Suikerrock**: last weekend in July at 4pm. Annual rock festival that gets better each year. Check out www.suikerrock.be

– Every Monday at Easter, after 10 o'clock Mass, the village of **Hakendover**, near Tienen, hosts an equestrian procession in memory of a legend described in a 1432 manuscript: in about 630, an angel showed three young virgins, who wanted to build a church, a spot that had miraculously escaped the rigours of winter. Only 12 masons were allowed to work on it, the 13th being no less than the Holy Saviour himself. Two bishops came to bless the place, but were struck blind by the wrath of God, who was annoyed to see them consecrate a place dedicated to Him – and built by His own hand! They had to pray for a long time before their sight was restored. Thousands of pilgrims come here to commemorate the event.

WHAT TO SEE IN THE AREA

HOEGAARDEN

Traditionally a brewing area known for its 'white' (i.e. unfiltered) beer, Hoegaarden is a delightful agricultural village that lies in the shadow of Sint Gordon church, with its impressive square tower. There's a wonderful pavilion on the village square.

★ If you want a peaceful stroll, try the **Vlaamse Toontuinen**: Houtmarkt 1. ☎ (016) 767843. Open all year except January from 10am to sunset. Admission: 175BEF; a bit pricy, but discounts are available. Four hectares (10 acres) of land have been laid out at the back of the chapterhouse. The result is an oasis of verdant landscape, with winding paths leading to beautifully landscaped plantations. Horticultural boffins can pick up an informative leaflet that tells you all about the place. The last garden is dedicated to the memory of King Baudouin. Stop at the outdoor café for refreshments.

★ Finally, don't miss **'t Nieuwhuis**, a tavern/museum dedicated to beer and folklore: Ourystraat 2. Open Monday to Saturday 10am–6pm.

LANDEN

An ancient Merovingian centre. A railway junction links the town to Brussels and Liège.

★ **Rufferdinge Watermills**: Molenberg 2. One of the province's top cultural and tourist spots, with a small agricultural museum and a perfectly preserved grinding mechanism. Apart from the food at the local tavern, the main attraction here is that you can cycle among the orchards of the surrounding countryside. Bike hire and reservation: ☎ (011) 883468. Available from Easter to late September.

FLEMISH BRABANT

Province of Limburg

Limburg is one of the least-known Belgian provinces, perhaps because it lacks a city of the stature of Bruges or Antwerp to pull in the crowds. It's well worth making the effort to visit, however, as you'll be pleasantly surprised.

The region is enjoying something of an economic renaissance. Once dependent on the coal industry, Limburg has become a hot spot for SMFs: small- and medium-sized firms. It's well placed to benefit from Europe's growing economic ties, lying as it does at a major western European crossroads – between the Netherlands, the Ruhr, the Rhine and Liège, and the rivers Maas and Scheldt – and it has taken full advantage of its location.

The province owes its name to the old county, then a duchy, of Limburg. The duchy covered the southern part of what is now the Netherlands, a region situated around the north-south axis of the Lower Maas, with Maastricht as its principal town. Belgian independence sealed the division of this area. Historical links with the inhabitants of what is now Dutch Limburg make this region very different from the rest of Flanders. Indeed, someone from the Belgian coast would have trouble understanding the Flemish dialect spoken in these parts.

So, what does Limburg have to offer? The towns are compact but not too provincial, with plenty of cultural and historical attractions, while the country-side, which consists mainly of the Kempen heathlands, remains unspoiled. This makes Limburg a surprisingly rural province despite its highly developed industries. And the locals are fun-loving and hospitable by nature.

The local tourist office produces a range of rather brash leaflets, advertising year-round trips and holidays. The Belgian Royal Meteorological Office points to statistics indicating that Limburg gets more sunshine than any other part of the county.

WHERE TO STAY IN THE PROVINCE

There are 40 farm holidays listed in the Provincial Tourism brochure. For information: ☎ (011) 237980. Fax: (011) 237993.

HASSELT   67,000 inhabitants

Hasselt's central position makes it an ideal base for exploring the region. The capital of Limburg and, after Antwerp, Belgium's most fashion-conscious city, its lively atmosphere and attractive architecture will soon dispel any doubts you had about coming here. A flight of stone steps symbolizing liberty dates from the days when Hasselt was part of the principality of Liège, but most of the city's attractions are thoroughly modern: luxury shops, designer boutiques and trendy cafés and restaurants. Some of the facades have been decorated with comic-strip murals, as in Brussels. The only bum note is struck by the administrative centre, which is a concrete catastrophe. At night, during term-time, a few thousand students liven up the streets.

PROVINCE OF LIMBURG

Hasselt is also at the forefront of Flanders's pro-cycling and -pedestrian movements, with several very welcome initiatives for non-drivers. The inner ring, once an express route for motorists, has been transformed by an eight-metre (26-foot) tree-lined pedestrian walkway. A 'park and ride' system allows visitors to leave their cars at Grenlandshallen and take public transport (bus H3) to the town centre, and free bike hire is available.

USEFUL INFORMATION AND ADDRESSES

Postcode: 3500.
🄷 Tourist Office: Stadhuis, Lombardstraat 3. ☎ (011) 239540. Fax: (011) 225742. Combined tickets to several museums are on sale here.

🄷 Provincial Tourist Office: Universiteitlaan, 1. ☎ (011) 237450. Fax: (011) 237466.
🚃 Railway station: to the west of town, on the edge of the inner ring. There are frequent services to Liège, Antwerp and Brussels.

WHERE TO STAY

🖈 Budget

🛏 Hotel De Nieuwe Schoofs: Stationplein 7. ☎ (011) 223188. Fax: (011) 223166. Near the station. Double rooms 1,700BEF–2,000BEF. An unpretentious hotel with a family atmosphere, although not very central. There are 14 rooms above a bar.

while it's worth checking out the daily special in the restaurant-tavern.
🛏 Hotel Pax: Grote Markt 16. (011) 223875. Fax: (011) 242137. Double rooms 2,500BEF. This central hotel has nine rooms above a lively restaurant, and the price is about right for what you get.

🖈🖈 Moderate

🛏 Hotel Century: Leopoldsplein 1. ☎ (011) 224799. Fax: (011) 231824. On the fringes of the pedestrianized zone. Double rooms 2,800BEF. A good-value hotel/restaurant/bar. The rooms are airy, if functional, and have been recently done up,

🖈🖈🖈 Expensive

🛏 Hotel Portmans: Minderbroedersstraat 12–14. ☎ (011) 263280. Fax: (011) 263281. Double rooms 3,400BEF. An elegant new hotel with all mod cons, right in the heart of town. Offers special dinner-and-accommodation deals.

WHERE TO EAT

The most interesting place for eating and drinking is the Zuivelmarkt ('dairy market'), which runs from Sint Quintuskathedraal to the Begijnhof.

🖈🖈 Moderate

✕ Brasserie De Groene Hendrick: Zuivelmarkt 25. Food served from 11am to 11pm. A wonderful old brick building with a coaching entrance, a paved courtyard and a

terrace. There's a mural featuring Thomas Edison and Count Zeppelin, and an 18-metre (59-foot) bar. The menu is long on drinks, but also features tasty snacks. There's a patio garden if the sun's out.

✗ **Bistro de Karakol**: Zuivelmarkt 16. ☎ (011) 227878. Open noon–2pm and 6–11pm. Expect to pay 750BEF for a meal. Closed Monday. A blue- and white-painted house with a snail on its sign. The menu majors in fish and grilled meat.

✗ **Brasserie Le Montmartre:** Walputstraat 17. Open 9am–10pm (later at the weekend). Closed Wednesday. This is a charming place behind the Stadhuis, with live jazz and blues on two Saturdays each month. Prices are low, and the house wine is excellent.

☆☆☆ Expensive

✗ **Martenshuys**: Zuivelmarkt 18. ☎ (011) 229656. This classy restaurant-café with a fine pale-yellow Classical facade is run by the Martens brewery, based in Bocholt and best known for the crisp, blond Sezoens brew. You can sample the brewery's products in the café area, which has a wonderfully ornate bar, or tuck into good salads and slightly pricey steaks in the main restaurant. Try the fish *brochette*. Live jazz concerts take place on the first Thursday of the month between November and April.

WHERE TO GO FOR A DRINK

♙ **'t Stokerijke**: Hemelrijk 3 (parallel with the Zuivelmarkt, behind the cathedral). The landlord, Johan, is a Brusseler who fell in love with a Limburg lass. He tends to wax lyrical on the subject of gin, which is a speciality here, and claims to have visited every *witteke* outlet in Belgium. Whatever the truth, his bar's a delightful, friendly place, with a fantastic jukebox.

♙ **La Belle Époque**: Kortstraat, between Grote Markt and Vismarkt. Closed Sunday. A pretty, Viennese-style tea-room with a light-green facade, where you can indulge your sweet tooth with cakes and pastries galore.

♙ **Café De Egel**: Zuivelmarkt 64. Open till 1am. Closed Wednesday. A tiny café with a hedgehog adorning the entrance and a warm, vaguely Irish feel.

WHAT TO SEE

You'll spy several unusual statues as you wander about town, including a strikingly realistic young couple sitting on a bench, slap bang in the middle of the Grote Markt. Behind it stands De Sweert, a chemist's on the ground floor of a half-timbered Renaissance house.

★ **The two main churches**: one of these (**Sint Quintus**) is technically a cathedral. It's slightly underwhelming, although the gargoyles are great. Inside, take a look at the polychrome 16th-century statues. The bell tower, which resembles an upside-down trumpet, houses the carillon and a small museum, open in the tourist season.

The other church, **Onze Lieve Vrouwekerk**, on Kappellestraat, houses the Virga Jesse, a statue that's wheeled out every seven years for a procession. It's part of a festival to commemorate the miracle of the Herkenrode sacrament, which supposedly bled when it was touched by a sacrilegious hand in 1317. You'll have to wait till 2003 to attend the next one.

PROVINCE OF LIMBURG

★ **Begijnhof**: at the end of Zuivelmarkt. The former Beguine complex, which was bombed during the last war, now houses contemporary-art exhibitions. Open Tuesday to Saturday, 10am–5pm (to 2pm on Sunday).

★ **Nationaal Jenevermuseum**: Witte Nonnenstraat 19. Behind the Begijnhof. ☎ (011) 241144. Open 10am–5pm; 1–5pm at the weekend from November to the end of March. Closed Monday and in January. Admission: 90BEF, including gin-tasting.

The museum is housed in a distillery, where you can watch the process of making gin, a malt wine concocted from barley and rye, from start to finish. There's a room with a steam distillery in operation. The most interesting part (because it's less technical) concerns the marketing of the product at the turn of the last century. A host of bottles, glasses and labels are on display. A poster depicting Leopold II shows how the king's name was used to laud the merits of one firm. Finally, there's a section on alcoholism at that time, with a moralizing poster offering a million Belgian francs to anyone who can prove that alcohol makes you strong, increases the appetite, sharpens the mind and is good for both our moral and physical health. It's worth getting someone to translate the sufferings that the boozers (*zatlappen*) experienced. Don't forget to sample the local white gin (it's 40 per cent proof) in the bar before you leave. Or, if you can't handle the hard stuff, try Saint-Lambert, a 22 per cent proof tipple made of herbs and blackcurrant.

If you're not averse to a tot or two of mothers' ruin, the best time to visit Hasselt is during the annual gin festival on 10–15 October. During the festival, café waiters take part in races to prove their dexterity.

★ **Stedelijk Modemuseum**: Gasthuisstraat 11. ☎ (011) 239621. Open 10am–5pm from Tuesday to Friday and 1–5pm at the weekend; from April to October, also Saturday and Sunday mornings. Closed Monday. Admission: 90BEF. The story of fashion from the 18th century to today, covering designers, photographers and jewellers. There are regular temporary exhibitions.

★ **Museum Stellingwerff-Waerdenhof**: Maastrichterstraat 85. ☎ (011) 241070. Open 10am–5pm from Tuesday to Friday and 1–5pm at the weekend; from April to the end of October, also Saturday and Sunday mornings. Admission: 90BEF. The collection focuses on the history of Hasselt and the old county of Loon. You can marvel at the world's oldest monstrance (1286) and a delightful display of art-nouveau ceramics, then sample the local *speculoos* biscuits and Limburg's finest beers in the café.

★ **Japanese Gardens**: Kapermolenpark, to the Northeast of town, between the inner and outer rings. Open from early April to the end of October from 10am to 5pm on Tuesday to Friday, and 2–6pm at the weekend. Admission: 100BEF, with reductions for young people and senior citizens. Hasselt is twinned with the Japanese town of Itami, which gave the town this wonderful 2.5-hectare (6.25-acre) garden, based on the 1,000-year-old principles of Saku-ki. It's a stunning, subtle garden, full of water features and small paths edged with rocks. In spring, the blossoming cherry trees and irises are delightful, and best admired from the tea house or the house of ceremonies. In return, incidentally, Hasselt gave the Japanese town a carillon.

PROVINCE OF LIMBURG

FESTIVAL

– **Pukkelpop**: top-drawer indie rock and dance music. End of August.

BOKRIJK

GETTING THERE

– **By car**: take the E314 (Park Midden Limburg exit).
– **By train**: hourly service from Brussels to Genk.
– **By bus**: from Genk and Hasselt stations (No. 46).

WHERE TO STAY

☆ Budget

⬥ **Youth hostel De Roerdomp:** Broekrakelaan 30, Genk 3600. ☎ (089) 356220. Fax: (089) 303980. Five kilometres (three miles) from Bokrijk station; take bus No. 46. Basic rate per night: 420BEF. Open from March to beginning of November. Right next to the Domein Bokrijk, and surrounded by beautiful woodland, this hostel has 112 beds and three five-bed studio flats for families. Groups are especially welcome. Bike hire available.

⬥ **Holiday Centre De Borgraaf**: Borgravevijverstraat 5, Genk 3600. ☎ (011) 226932. Fax: 011234365. Three kilometres (one mile) from the centre of Hasselt, surrounded by forest and not far from Bokrijk. Young people and families welcome. Bike hire available.

⬥ **Bokrijk Gasthof**: Hasseltweg 475, Genk 3600. ☎ (011) 229556. Double rooms from 1,950BEF. Not far from the Domein Bokrijk, this small hotel-restaurant has 15 rooms offering all mod cons at keen prices.

WHAT TO SEE

★ **Provinciaal Openlucht Museum, Bokrijk**

To the northeast of Hasselt, near Genk, a centre for the car industry. ☎ (011) 224575. Open Easter to end September, 10am–6pm. Guided tours.

★ Once owned by the abbey of Herkenrode, the wooded, 550-hectare (1,375-acre) **Bokrijk estate**, comprising a park and a museum, is one of the most popular tourist attractions in eastern Belgium, and with good reason.

– **The park**: admission free. Children will love the huge play area, and the estate's other charms include a rose garden, a nature reserve, ponds, a splendid arboretum and a little train that takes you round the grounds. The only drawback is that it's heaving with families at the weekend.

– **The open-air museum**: open from the end of March to the end of September. Admission: 200BEF; more at the weekend and on public holidays. Discounts for children under 15 and senior citizens. Covering 90 hectares (225 acres), this is a masterly reconstruction of rural life in Flanders. There's even a small 16th-century cityscape. It's a huge space, so you won't have to fight your way through any crowds, but be prepared for a lot of walking. As you wander from farm to hamlet, barn to country school, windmill to blacksmith's forge, and from the chapel to the inn, you'll get a glimpse of a way of life that's long since been abandoned. Sheep and cows graze in the pastures, chickens cluck in the yards, the miller grinds his corn, the craftsmen go about their business in period costume, and you can sip a *gueuze* beer and eat bread and cheese on the village square, where chicken thieves sit in the stocks.

Despite the occasional inauthentic touch, this is the thinking man's answer to tourism, and it's a fashionable destination for northern Europeans. You'll need a good few hours to really get to grips with the place.

BERINGEN

Beringen is two kilometres (one mile) from the E313 (exit 26), in the heart of the industrial landscape near the Albert Canal and northwest of the abandoned coal mines of the Kempen. You can still see traces of the area's industrial heritage – pit towers and chimneys, workers' villages (now inhabited by Turks) and the houses of the engineers and managers – but the best way to find out what it was like in its heyday is to visit the local museum.

★ **Museum Van de Kempische Steenkoolmijnen** (Museum of the Kempen Coal Mines): Koolmijnlaan 201. ☎ (011) 422001. Open Saturday noon–4pm and Sunday 10am–4pm. Admission: 100BEF. Located in a vast brick building, the museum uses a film narrated by miners to trace the story of the coal industry, from the geology of the area to the discovery of seams, the digging of galleries and the excavation of coal, and the work and welfare of the miner. The basement has been laid out to resemble a coal mine. The last wagon left Beringen in 1989, by which time the mine had produced 79 million tons of coal. Buildings in the mining area (Elsden, Waterschei, Winterslag and Zwartberg) have been reinforced: they were in danger of collapsing due to the underground tunnels that had been dug underneath them.

Haspengouw

Tongeren is the main town in the southern part of the province of Limburg, which stretches between Sint Truiden and the left bank of the Maas, opposite Maastricht. An agricultural region, it's often described as Belgium's garden, especially around Sint Truiden, where apples, pears, cherries and strawberries are grown in vast quantities.

USEFUL ADDRESS

🛈 **Haspengouw tourist office**: Van Leeuwenstraat 23, Borgloon 3840. ☎ (011) 685859.

PROVINCE OF LIMBURG

TONGEREN   30,000 inhabitants

Along with Tournai, Tongeren is Belgium's oldest town, founded on the site of a Roman crossroads. It was the country's first bishopric, and is now home to several tourist attractions, including an innovative Gallo-Roman museum, the stunning basilica and some Roman fortifications. An excellent antiques market takes place every Sunday on Leopoldwal and Veemarkt.

A short history

In his *Commentaries*, Julius Caesar refers to the camp of Atuatuca, near which Ambiorix, a Gaulish chieftain, defeated his legions. This victory was in vain, however, as Tongeren became a Roman settlement on the Bavai–Cologne road. A double wall ringed the town, and sections of it can still be seen today. With the fall of the Roman empire, Tongeren was besieged by the Salian Franks, Attila the Hun and the Vikings before becoming a vassal town of the principality of Liège. In the 17th century, Tongeren was destroyed by the forces of Louis XIV, and it became part of Limburg after Napoleon's defeat in 1815.

GETTING THERE

– **By car**: you can get to Tongeren from the Brussels–Liège motorway (exit 30) or the Antwerp–Liège motorway (exit 32).

– **By train**: the railway station is on the far side of the ring road, east of the town. Trains run from Liège and Hasselt.

USEFUL ADDRESSES AND INFORMATION

Postcode: 3700.
🖬 **Tourist office**: Stadhuisplein 9. ☎ (012) 390271. Open 8am–noon and 1–4.30pm; on Saturday and Sunday, open 9.30am–5pm from April to the end of September, otherwise 10am–4pm. You can pick up a brochure with details of country walks.

WHERE TO STAY

☆ Budget

⚑ **Youth hostel Begijnhof**: Sint Ursulastraat 1. ☎ (012) 391370. Fax: (012) 391348. Basic rate per night: 420BEF. Next to the Begijnhof, this excellent, ultramodern hostel has 78 beds, mostly in dormitories sleeping four to eight people. Meals start at 270BEF, and you can stay on a half- or full-board basis. Bike hire available. If only they were all this good . . .

☆☆ Moderate

There isn't much on offer here, but there are a couple of hotels if you're desperate.

⚑ **Hotel-restaurant Lido**: Grote Markt 19. ☎ (012) 231948. Double rooms 2,000BEF. The staff are reserved, and the five rooms are rather old-fashioned side.

⚑ **De Dubbelmolen**: Tweemolenstraat 38, in Nerem, a couple of miles east of Tongeren. ☎ (012) 261132.

Double rooms 1,800BEF. Breakfast 200BEF. An old watermill that's been converted into *gîtes* for two to six people, complete with private bath-

rooms and living rooms. There's also a pretty, private courtyard. Ideal for families or small groups. Half- and full-board available.

WHERE TO EAT

You have to look hard to find anything out of the ordinary here, but this is a reasonably cheap option.

✗ **De Pelgrim**: Brouwerstraat 9 (next to the church as you head for the Begijnhof). ☎ (012) 238322. Closed Monday and Tuesday lunchtime. Main dishes about 300BEF. Food is available till midnight, but the café is open until 2am. An old cottage with a pleasant atmosphere and wooden tables. In summer, you can sit outside in wicker chairs. Try the delicious *boerenomlet* (country omelette), spare ribs, open sandwiches and apple tart. The cooking is simple, and the toilets are suitably rustic.

WHAT TO SEE

★ **Ambiorix**, to whom the Belgians owe their reputation as the 'bravest people in the whole of Gaul', dominates a dolmen in the middle of the Grote Markt, his eyes fixed on the splendid tower of Onze Lieve Vrouwebasiliek. Take the walkway named after the basilica, which is marked with bronze-coloured bricks and signposts, and head straight there.

★ **Onze Lieve Vrouwebasiliek**: open 9am–noon and 1.30–5.30pm. The first thing that strikes you about the basilica is its symmetry. It's one of the most beautiful Gothic buildings in Belgium, despite the fact that it lacks a bell tower.

As you'd expect of a fourth-century building, the basilica has quite a history. The oldest stone cathedral on this side of the Alps, it's said to have been founded by St Servatius, who was then in charge of the bishopric. The oldest parts of the foundations date back to Roman times. In the 12th century, a Romanesque church, together with a surrounding wall and four corner towers, replaced the original chapel. Work on the present structure began after the church was destroyed during a siege in 1213. It took three centuries to complete, which means that it's a perfect example of how the Gothic style evolved. First came the choir, then the nave, the transept, the aisle chapels, the porch and finally the tower. The church was badly damaged by fire when Louis XIV's troops traipsed through town, but was sensitively restored in the late 18th century. The interior, with its majestic, unfussy austerity, is equally impressive. The organ pipes are being renovated.

In the left transept is the celebrated 15th-century statue of the Our Lady of Tongeren. Every seven years, a festival commemorates the cathedral's acquisition of the statue: the next one's due in 2002, when half a million spectators are expected to turn up. Behind the altar, you can see ropes that reputedly bound two locals held captive in the Holy Land. According to legend, their fervent prayers to the Madonna were answered in spectacular style one morning, when they were 'teleported' from Palestine to the middle of the cathedral.

– **The treasury**: admission costs 80BEF From April to the end of September, open every day except Monday, 10am–noon and 1.30–5pm; otherwise by appointment only. This is one of the most richly endowed treasuries in the country, with more than 100 items. The stars of the show are a sixth-century Merovingian gold buckle, set with gemstones and enamel, a reliquary shrine decorated with ivory from the ninth century and an eleventh-century Romanesque wooden head of Christ.

Before you leave, take a look at the horseshoe-shaped cloister, where gravestones lean against the walls. This is all that remains of the old monastery, and its simplicity is humbling.

– Between May and July, the basilica hosts **classical concerts** as part of the Festival of Flanders. For details, call Basilica Concerten: ☎ (012) 235719.

– Below the cathedral on the right, archaeological digs have uncovered the remains of the second- and third-century Roman town, as well as a section of the fourth-century town wall.

★ **Stadhuis**: a smaller version of the one in Liège, and a fine example of neoclassicism. It now houses a particularly friendly tourist office.

★ **Gallo-Roman Museum**: Kielenstraat 15. ☎ (012) 233914. A bizarre, sombre avant-garde structure behind the basilica. Open 9am–5pm, weekends 10am–6pm. Closed Monday. Admission: 200BEF; discounts for families, students and senior citizens. Any preconceptions you have about endless displays of broken pots and spear tips will be blown away by this high-tech multimedia venue, built six years ago for a whopping 353 million BEF. Instead of thrusting history upon you, the museum's displays encourage you to explore your own past, while the layout resembles an archaeological cross section of the town. Even the designer cafeteria has an interactive edge.

You start on the lower ground floor, a vaulted space that resembles an amphitheatre. Using audiovisual effects by the film director Stijn Coninx (best known for the Oscar-nominated *Daens*), this section takes a look at objects drawn from various civilizations, and invites you to consider how what the archaeologists of the future will make of our own. Perhaps the most curious artefact is the dodecahedron, a 12-sided object that looks a bit like a deflated mini football with little balls at each corner. Many of these things have been discovered in the area, and they date more or less from the end of the Roman era, but nobody knows what they were used for – in religious ceremonies, as a weapon, in the kitchen? – or are we looking at the Roman version of the Rubik's cube? We'll never know, but it's fun trying to puzzle it out.

The more traditional collections – pots et al – are arranged as though they've just been unearthed on a dig, so you get an idea of the kick felt by archaeologists when they make an important find. You can even do a bit of on-the-spot analysis to work out the objects' age. The final section, meanwhile, offers a short film in which a father tells his daughter about the Roman-Gaulish war. You then see them cycling around the Tongeren countryside in search of Roman remains. The only drawback is that everything's in Dutch, which is a shame given the museum's obvious international appeal.

★ **Begijnhof**: a fine collection of prettily restored cottages with a 13th-century Gothic church. It's a peaceful haven, filled with statues of the Virgin Mary, the silence broken only by the cooing of pigeons. You can also wander into the church of Sint Katharina.

★ The **medieval ramparts** run along Leopoldval, heading towards the railway station. There's a military museum in the sturdy, square tower of the Moerenpoort (open by appointment only: ask at the tourist office).

★ The **Roman walls** lie to the west of the town, beyond the ring road. In the second century, they used to be 4.5 kilometres (2.5 miles) long. Only one kilometre remains, but a few sections are an impressive four metres (13 feet) high.

FESTIVALS IN AND AROUND TONGEREN

Festival of Our Lady of Tongeren: held every seven years. Don't miss the next one in 2002 (*see* 'Onze Lieve Vrouwebasiliek' *above*).

– **Sint Evermarus games**: held on 1 May in **Rutten**, these games commemorate an eighth-century Frisian martyr who met his maker in a local wood together with seven of his companions after returning from a pilgrimage to Santiago de Compostela. Their bodies were left out in the open until they were discovered and buried by a certain Pepin de Herstal. Two centuries later, the vicar of Rutten had a recurring dream that led him to have them exhumed, only to discover that the bodies were still intact. A chapel was erected on the spot where they were buried, and numerous miracles were reported. Since time immemorial, the legend of Sint Evermarus has been the subject of a Mystery play; afterwards, everyone sits down for a slice of tart and a glass of beer.

Around Tongeren

THE COMMANDERY OF ALDEN-BIESEN

In Bilzen-Rijkhoven, Kasteelstraat 6. Take exit 31 on the E313, 10 kilometres (six miles) from Tongeren. ☎ (089) 519393. Fax: (089) 417033. Email: info@alden-biesen.be. Website: www.alden-biesen.be. Open 10am–6pm daily; closed for two weeks at Christmas. Admission: free, although there are charges for temporary exhibitions and the gardens.

– Bike hire is available in the regional **tourist office** at the entrance of the commandery: ☎ (089) 411944. There are signposted routes for cyclists.

– There's a **visitors' centre** at the old main gate, and a local flora and fauna museum (open from Easter to the end of September, 10am–6pm. Admission: 80BEF).

The Alden-Biesen commandery is an impressive fortified complex that makes up Belgium's biggest castle. In the Middle Ages, it was at the centre of a settlement of Teutonic knights.

PROVINCE OF
LIMBURG

A Short History

Merchants from Bremen and Lübeck set up this order of warrior monks to care for the sick and wounded in the Holy Land. It had its heyday after the Third Crusade, when it owned territory across Europe. In the 13th century, the Teutonic Order conquered the Baltic coast and founded its own state, the Ordeland, with Marienburg (now in Poland) as the capital city. Its power peaked in the 14th century, when it had 363 commanderies, stretching from northern Germany to Sicily. Initially a hospital, the Alden-Beisen commandery later became a residence for the Order, which lost all its possessions after the French Revolution, when 1,800 hectares (4,500 acres) of land were sold off in Limburg alone. Following a fire in 1971, the Belgian state and the province of Limburg took over and renovated the complex.

WHAT TO SEE

The building is now used for meetings, conferences and seminars, as well as exhibitions on historical subjects. Most of it is open to the public. At the entrance, there's a permanent exhibition about the history of the building and a cafeteria. The main buildings date from the 16th century, with the exception of the magnificent 17th-century baroque church. The rest of the complex includes a square castle, a farm, a hospital, an orangery and a pilgrim's house. The surrounding moats, orchards and parks, one English-style, the other French-style, make it well worth taking a walk through the grounds.

BILZEN

A delightful little town with a dinky town hall in front of the church.

BORGLOON

Take a short detour to the former capital of the old county of Looz (off the N79 between Tongeren and Sint Truiden), and you'll see some fine buildings surrounded by rolling hills planted with orchards. In April, there's a Festival of Flowers.

WHERE TO STAY AND EAT

📦 ✕ **Het Klaphuis**: Kortestraat 2, Borgloon, opposite the Stadhuis. ☎ (012) 747325. Fax: (012) 369938. Email: sarto@skynet.be. Double rooms 2,500BEF. The hotel has eight, well-equipped modern rooms and a good restaurant with outdoor seating (closed Wednesday), which offers *haute cuisine* in high season. If your budget won't stretch to fine dining, the daily special offers good quality at 375BEF. Or just pop in for a teatime crêpe or ice-cream.

WHAT TO SEE

Wander through the medieval streets of the Speelhof, beside the hill where the Gravensteen (Castle of the Counts) was built. Take a look at the 11th-century Romanesque **Sint Odulfuskerk**, the **Stadhuis**, with its handsome arcades and tower, a fine example of Mosan (i.e. from the Maas area) Renaissance architecture, and the former **canon's house**.

The Cistercian convent of Mariënhof: North of Borgloon. Open Mondays to Fridays from 10–11.30am, and 2–5pm. Its main point of interest is the reliquary of St Odile (1292), the oldest surviving painting on canvas in the Low Countries, albeit one stuck onto a wooden panel. The nuns serve sandwiches and delicious homemade fruit tarts.

SINT TRUIDEN	**37,000 inhabitants**

Sint Truiden is the other main town in the Haspengouw region. An important agricultural centre, it's also home to some impressive monuments. It's best to visit in spring, when the apple trees groan with fragrant blossom.

GETTING THERE

– **By car**: 15 kilometres (9 miles) from exit 28 on the Brussels–Liège motorway.

🚂 **Railway station**: west of the town. Trains go to Landen (change here for Brussels and Liège) and Hasselt.

USEFUL ADDRESSES AND INFORMATION

Postcode: 3800.
🖪 **Tourist office**: Stadhuis, Grote Markt. ☎ (011) 701818. Friendly, helpful staff. Tourist brochures are available, and, as in Tongeren, there's a clearly marked monument trail.

WHERE TO STAY

There are only two hotels in the centre of Sint Truiden, and they're a bit pricey. There are three others near the Brutsem air base, on the road to Liège, but unless you're a keen plane-spotter, stay somewhere else

WHERE TO EAT

There must be somewhere around the Grote Markt where you can eat well, but it did prove difficult to find anything of note. Your best bet is to find a straightforward café and plump for the daily special.

✕ **Eetcafe den Artist**: Ridderstraat, behind the church. ☎ (011) 696392. Closed Thursday evening. A typically Flemish place, with exposed bricks, a superb bar and engravings. On the menu: omelettes, toasted sandwiches and pasta.

WHERE TO GO FOR AN ICE-CREAM

♀ **Venise**: Grote Markt 12. Open 8.30am–10.30pm. Closed Tuesday. Connoisseurs say this is one of the best ice-cream parlours in Flanders. The menu offers no fewer than 80 different flavours, as well as a few savoury snacks. There's outside seating in summer.

WHERE TO GO FOR A DRINK

♀ **Café Op de Beek**: Beekstraat 52. Turn left up Zoutstraat, opposite the Stadhuis, then take the first turning on the right. Open every day from 10am, this is a pleasant traditional brown café, decorated with enamelled advertising signs and wallpaper made of old newspapers. A bay window in the main eating area overlooks the inner courtyard. As you leave, look out for the fine wood balcony of the 'artisans' house' opposite, built in 1507, and the stunning mural on a nearby wall.

♀ **Brouwerij Van Kerkom**: Naamsesteenweg 469 (outside the centre). ☎ (011) 682087. From April to mid-December, open from noon to 7pm on Saturday, Sunday and public holidays; otherwise by prior reservation. A 1900-style café in a farm-brewery that's typical of the region. They've been brewing Bink, a pale ale, for 100 years. Guided tours, including a beer, cost 85BEF.

WHAT TO SEE

★ Three towers on the Grote Markt crowd Sint Truiden's skyline: two tall and elegant, one fat and sturdy.

The graceful lines of the first are those of the 17th-century **belfry**, whose cheerful carillon cheers the Renaissance-baroque facade of the Stadhuis.

The neo-Gothic spire of **Onze Lieve Vrouwekerk**, most of which was built in the 14th and 15th centuries, rises behind the belfry. The treasury, which contains examples of religious art from the former Benedictine abbey, is open to visitors between 2pm and 4pm on Sunday.

The spireless tower of the Romanesque **abbey**, now a seminary, looms in the background. It was founded in the seventh century by St Trudo. A fine baroque porch in light-coloured stone can be seen just next to the tower. Pass through the doorway of the newest abbey buildings and you'll come to the main courtyard. To your left is a splendid imperial room with walls and ceilings covered in murals (admission free).

★ **Begijnhof**: north of the centre. Go along Plankstraat, and keep going in the same direction until you get to the ring road, then turn left. The Gothic church of St Agnes, in the middle of the complex, now houses the **Provincial Museum of Religious Art**. Open Tuesday to Friday from 10am–noon and 1.30–5pm; from the beginning of April to the end of October, also weekends 1.30–5pm. On Sunday, there's a guided tour at 4pm. Admission: free. Work on the early-Gothic structure began in 1258. In 1860, the removal of a layer of plaster revealed 38 murals painted between 1300 and the early 17th century. These have all been restored, and are now on show in this striking, austere setting. The vaulting, choir, tombstones and frescoes recall the Italian churches of Tuscany.

In a building to the left of the church, still in the Begijnhof, you'll find the **Studio Festraets**: ☎ (011) 688752. The big attraction here is a gigantic astronomical clock. Tours take place from April to the end of October, from Tuesday to Sunday at 1.45pm, 2.45pm, 4.45pm and 5.45pm.

★ **Brutsem Gate**: southeast of the centre. A remnant of the old fortifications, which were demolished by Louis XIV's armies. Enquire at the tourist office if you want to visit the labyrinthine underground passageways (open April to late September).

FESTIVAL

– **Orchard Festival**: every year on the last Sunday in April. This custom started out as a solemn blessing of flowering fruit trees. The aim was to ward off the last frosts sent by the so-called 'saints of ice' in mid May. These days, it's more of a party, with a concert, banquet and bucolic walks in the countryside around the village of Guvelingen and the Spoelhof castle. You may have to book to take part, so check with the tourist office.

IN THE AREA

★ This is a good base for a visit to Zoutleeuw (see 'Flemish Brabant'), which is just a couple of miles from Sint Truiden, en route to Tienen.

The countryside around the Maas (Maasland)

The Maas (Meuse in French) passes through Liège, then continues northwards. Beyond Vise and level with Maastricht, the river marks the frontier between Dutch and Belgian Limburg. You can drive through the valley on the Belgian side by taking the N78, although the road doesn't follow the river. Be warned, too, that the region is sometimes flooded. The landscape is dotted with a spattering of towns, the last and most interesting of which is Maaseik.

WHAT TO SEE IN THE AREA

You'll need your own transport to travel through the Maas valley, because there are plenty of riverside sites and monuments along the way.

LANAKEN

There are medieval ruins in the grounds of Merode Castle, in Pietersheim, which is now a recreation centre with fishing facilities and a children's farm. This is also the place to come if you fancy a boat trip on the Maas. Trips are of varying lengths and include a candle-lit evening excursion: organized by Rederij Stiphout, they can be booked through the local tourist office (Jan Rosierlaan 28: ☎ (089) 722467), where cyclists can hire bikes and tour itineraries.

REKEM

This was once an affluent mini principality, and even had its own army. All that's left is picturesque 'old Rekem', which is blissfully tourist-free. Stroll along its silent streets and admire the splendid, yellow-stone castle, with its Renaissance facade (built by the counts of Aspremont-Lynden). Also worth seeing are two more castles, an old pharmacy, the church museum and the local town and regional museum. The museums are open from 2–5pm, except Saturday, from May to October.

WHERE TO GO FOR A DRINK

❢ The old coaching inn, the **Posthuis**, is now a café with a decidedly local feel. It's worth trying to master a few words of Flemish before you venture inside.

MAASMECHELEN

This is where the Maas overflows when it floods, hence, perhaps, the name. The place is also named after the **Mechelse Heide** nature reserve, which consists of 388 hectares (950 acres) of heath – all that's left of the primitive vegetation of the Kempen.

WHERE TO EAT

✗ **Da Lidia**: Rijksweg 215, Maasmechelen 3630. ☎ (089) 764134. Closed Monday and Tuesday and from mid-July to mid-August. This is an excellent Italian restaurant with none of the kitsch, pseudo-Venetian furnishings and decoration that you so often find in Italian restaurants. Instead, the floor is tiled and there's a great bar with bistro-style tables and chairs. Good value.

VUCHT

A mining suburb of Eisden that would hardly be worth mentioning were it not for a twist of fate that could have changed the course of World War II. In January 1940, when Belgium was clinging to its 'neutral' position, a German Messerschmidt, lost in the fog, managed to land by the Albert Canal, in the middle of the Belgian defence lines. Despite their best endeavours, the Germans failed to destroy the documents they were carrying, which included plans to invade Belgium, the Netherlands and Luxembourg. The powers that be only half believed them . . . and we all know what happened next.

MAASEIK

This is the furthest-flung tourist town in the country, but it's well worth making the trek. The capital of Maasland and the birthplace of the Van Eyck brothers, it boasts several attractive buildings and serves as a base for boating and watersports. In the 19th century, it was famous for pipe manufacturing, with seven per cent of the population involved in making two million pipes a year. Today, there's a wild carnival in the middle of Lent.

GETTING THERE

– **By car**: motorway E314, exit 32, then N75 for 25 kilometres (15 miles). Alternatively, take the E25 from Liège via the Dutch side of the Maas and cross at Maaseik.

– **By bus**: from Leopoldsburg and Hasselt.

USEFUL ADDRESS AND INFORMATION

Postcode: 3680.
🛈 Tourist office: Stadhuis, Markt 1.
☎ (089) 566372. There's plenty of useful tourist information here.

WHERE TO STAY

☆☆☆ Expensive

🛏 Hotel Aldeneikerhof: Hamontweg 103. ☎ (089) 566777. Fax: (089) 566778. Closed in January. Double rooms 2,480BEF. This is our favourite hotel in the area. To get there, leave the town on the eastern side and follow the Noordering (N78) until you come to the tiny village of Aldeneik – look out for the church bell tower. The hotel stands immediately opposite the church's porch. Built in 1899, this is a large house with a high brick facade. There are only eight rooms, all of which are light, airy, and well appointed. The atmosphere is wonderfully calm, the rural setting is inspiring and the landlady, Lieve, is charming. You can eat in the hotel, chill out in its garden or hire a bike on the premises. There are watersports facilities 200 metres (200 yards) away.

☆☆☆☆ Splash Out

🛏 Kasteel Wurfeld: Kapelweg 60. ☎ (089) 568136. Fax: (089) 568789. Double rooms from 3,250BEF. An impressive, prosperous-looking manor house in an estate of woods and meadows – the perfect setting for top-class accommodation. The rooms are huge and tastefully furnished, and you won't hear a footfall along the lavishly carpeted corridors. It's all exceedingly comfortable, and there's an equally tasteful restaurant offering *haute cuisine* (set menus from 1,090BEF to 1,850BEF). If anything, the atmosphere is a touch oppressive.

WHERE TO EAT

There are some fairly standard inns around the Grote Markt.

✕ De Bokkerijder: Markt 26. A 'Burgundian' restaurant that offers a decent daily special and tourist menu. Everything else is either too expensive or desperately dull.

WHERE TO GO FOR A DRINK

❢ The traditional 'brown cafés', favoured by the local youth, are all on one street, the Kleinekerkstraat, which is next to the Markt and in the shadow of Sint Katharinakerk's green bell tower. They're called **De Vagant**, **De Sjuur**, **Den Olyfant** and **Het IJzerenbed** (there's also

PROVINCE OF LIMBURG

an *eetcafe* serving omelettes, pasta and snacks), and they're usually pretty vibrant.

Café De Beurs: Markt 7. ☎ (089) 564079. Closed Monday in winter. Light meals for about 350BEF. A smoky den with wood panelling, exposed beams, old engravings of the town and tables covered with rugs, worn down by the elbows of hundreds of guests. Try the Celis Pale Bock, a beer imported from America, where it's made by the (Belgian) former owner of the Hoegaarden brewery, who sold up and took the 'white beer' concept to Texas with some success. Waffles, ices and plum tarts galore, and the best shrimp croquettes in Belgium. Outdoor seating in summer.

Next door is **De Gekroonde Ei**, an ice-cream parlour that belongs to the same owner and sells home-made, additive-free ices. Open noon–10pm (closed from January to March).

WHAT TO SEE

★ There are 25 Mosan-style buildings dating from the 17th and 18th centuries, when they were built for canons and wealthy mariners. Many of them are on the Markt, a vast, attractive quadrangle planted with lime trees and with stone pumps at every corner. A statue of the Van Eyck brothers stands in the centre, while an attractive flight of steps leads up to the 18th-century Stadhuis. There's a market here on Wednesdays.

★ **Museactron**: Lekkerstraat 5. ☎ (089) 566890. In July and August, the Museactron is open every day 10am–5pm; in April, May, June and September, it's open every day except Monday from 10am–5pm; for the rest of the year, it's open only on Sunday, from 10am–noon and 2–5pm. Admission: 70BEF. Three museums for the price of one here: a museum of archaeology and local history, a bakery museum and the old pharmacy. By the entrance is a receptacle that was used for drawing lots to recruit conscripts before military service became compulsory. It featured in the film *De Loteling*, which was based on a novel by the Flemish author Hendrik Conscience. Audiovisual displays reveal the prehistoric composition of the area. In the pharmacy, you can see wooden, steel and Delft porcelain jars and remedy books with advice on how to cure a whitlow: mix mole's blood with honey, eggs and lily leaves. A herb garden completes the complex.

★ **Sint Katharinakerk**: a neo-Gothic edifice with a fascinating treasury. The highlight is the *Codex Eyckensis*, the oldest evangelical text in the Low Countries; there are also some precious reliquaries and valuable pieces of religious silver. Opening times and conditions are the same as those for the Museactron.

★ There's a stunning house, **De Gasper**, on Breumerstraat (No. 47), which leads down to the Maas. Note the grimacing, carnivalesque faces on the facade. The boundary bridge and customs buildings, empty since the Schengen agreement, are a little further down (*see* 'Customs and duty-free' in General Information' for more on the Schengen agreement).

★ **Van Eyck Exhibition**: Van Eyck Tentoonstelling, Minderbroedersklooster, Boomgaardstraat z/n. Same opening times and conditions as the Museactron. Set in a 17th-century cloister, this is a display of small-scale reproductions of every Van Eyck painting. An ideal prelude to a trip to Bruges or Ghent, or a handy stop-gap if you don't have time to see the real ones.

IN THE AREA

★ **Neeroeteren** and **Opoeteren** are wooded communes interspersed with heathland and ponds, and are great for horse-riding, hiking and cycling. The area, with its many idyllic paths, is sometimes called 'Little Switzerland'. There's water everywhere, from limpid brooks and lush areas of bog to the many resort ports that dot the Maas between Maaseik and Thorn (in the Netherlands). Yachts, motorboats and pleasure craft float around the river complex, which stretches right up to Roermond. Inexplicably, this area is largely overlooked.

Sint Lambertskerk: in Neeroeteren. Access through the side entrance. On the outside, it's a clumsy brick tower with a workaday chevel, but step inside and you'll be overwhelmed by the triple nave, with its 12 massive columns, the 16th-century Gothic vaulting, painted with intertwining plants, and the stunning collection of 16th-century wooden statues, including Christ on the Cross (beneath a fresco of the Last Judgement), Mary, St John and the 12 apostles, all standing on a horizontal beam. In the left-hand transept, St George and the dragon have lost their original colours. Eight statues of saints lean against the pillars of the nave, and there's a superb Marianum: a statue of Mary, with a face on either side, suspended from the vaulting. Note the delicacy of the craftsmanship and the way Mary tramples a repulsive serpent with a human face. There's only one other of its kind in Belgium, in Zoutleeuw. Finally, take a look at the church's old tombstones.

WHAT TO DO

★ **The windmill trail** is a signposted cycle trail through the neighbouring villages, passing the region's windmills.

North Limburg

This region stretches from Maaseik to Leopoldsburg, and is part of the Kempen plateau (which continues all the way to Antwerp). The soil is poor and mostly sandy, and the landscape consists of pine woods and peat bogs. It's a sparsely populated region, and the only buildings you are likely to come across here are farms and watermills. Ecotourism is taking off, however, and a few small towns are worth visiting.

BREE

An old fortified town that shows an obvious Dutch influence: everything's squeaky-clean and on a small scale. Take a look at the church, the lookout tower, the Stadhuis (which houses a small regional museum, open on the first Sunday of the month) and the *vrijthof*, which incorporates a former Augustine convent.

USEFUL ADDRESS

☎ Tourist office for the Kempen: Cobbestraat 3, Bree 3960. ☎ (089) 462514.

WHERE TO GO FOR AN ICE-CREAM

🍴 De Potter: Hoogstraat 12, Bree 3960. An elegant café with extremely tasteful decor. Good old-fashioned ice-cream.

BOCHOLT

A town on the Maastricht – 's Hertogenbosch canal. Several early-16th-century works of art can be seen in Sint Laurentiuskerk. In 1910, locals managed to move its 2,600-ton tower nine metres (30 feet).

USEFUL ADDRESS

☎ Tourist office: Gemeentehuis, Dorpstraat 16, Bocholt 3950. ☎ (089) 465034. They can suggest routes for cycling tours in the area.

WHAT TO SEE

★ Don't miss the **Brewing Museum** (funded by the local Martens brewery), which is a fine example of industrial archaeology. Unfortunately, you can only visit in groups, accompanied by a guide and by prior arrangement. If you can meet all these requirements, here is the number to contact: ☎ (089) 472980. Admission: 175BEF.

PEER

Once a major town in the county of Looz, Peer is now a mere village. It's dominated by the tall, 75-metre (246-foot) tower of Sint Truidenskerk, which is topped with a pear (*peer* in Dutch). Inside you'll find Our Lady of the Pear, while the village fountain is adorned with a 100-kilo (220-pound) pear. A lantern in the shape of, you've guessed it, adorns the roof of the Stadhuis. Given the recurring fruit theme, you might be surprised to learn that the name actually comes from *peere*, meaning 'protected place'.

USEFUL ADDRESS

☎ Tourist office: Oud Stadhuis, Markt, Peer 3990. ☎ (011) 634327.

WHAT TO SEE

★ **Museum of Ancient Instruments**: Oud Stadhuis, Markt. Open on weekdays from 10am–noon and 2–4pm. Some rare musical instruments, both genuine and reproductions.

FESTIVAL

– **Festival Belgium Rhythm 'n' Blues**: mid-July.

LOMMEL

The best time to visit Lommel and its acres of woodland is between mid-August and mid-September, when the heather turns purple. The Kattenbos military cemetery, which contains the graves of 40,000 German soldiers who died in World War II, lies on the outskirts of town, while the Gothic tower that greets you as you enter the town dates from the 14th century.

WHERE TO EAT

✕ **Koffiehuis In de Sociëteit**: Dorp 17, Lommel 3920. ☎ (011) 554308. This farmhouse, next to the museum, is the place to be on Wednesday (market day) when everyone rushes in to wolf down ample helpings of what they laughingly call 'light meals'. fish stew, chicory in béchamel sauce, *stoemp* and gargantuan omelettes, all of which are filling if not especially tasty. There's a New Orleans atmosphere, with waitresses in suitable attire, and a cosy-looking pair of slippers hang on the wall.

WHAT TO SEE

★ The tourist office and **Kempenland museum** are on the triangular main square (open Tuesday to Friday, 9am–noon and 2–5pm; weekends 2–5pm. Admission free). The museum traces the history of the Teuten, who lived in Lommel in the 17th and 18th centuries, but who were forced by grinding poverty to become travelling pedlars. They left for Alsace and Denmark in spring and returned in autumn, their purses full. They used dogs to pull their carts of merchandise, which carried copper, clay- and glassware, cloth and wigs. Another service offered by the pedlars was the castration of domestic animals. There were more than 300 of these salesmen in Lommel at the beginning of the 19th century, and there's a statue dedicated to them on the main square. The museum also has an archaeology section.

Fourons/Voeren

This region is a political hot potato, over which historians and journalists have pontificated endlessly over the last 30 years. Tucked between Liège and Limburg, this little enclave consists of six agricultural communes that have belonged to the Flemish province of Limburg since the linguistic boundaries were marked out in 1963. A large part of the population, however, refuses to accept Flemish local government, wishing instead to be part of Wallonia. Neighbouring cafés sport their respective banners of allegiance (visitors should be sure to take a neutral stance). There's nothing outstanding about this area, but the pretty valleys, where the Berwinne and Voer rivers flow through lush pastures, orchards and hills, are prime cycling territory.

USEFUL ADDRESS

🛈 Tourist office: De Voerstreek, Kerkplein 216, 's Gravenvoeren 3798. ☎ (04) 381 0736.

WHERE TO STAY

☒ Budget

🛏 Youth hostel De Veurs: Comberg 29B, Sint Martens Voeren 3790. ☎ (04) 381 1110. Fax: (04) 381 1313. Open from March to early November. Basic rate per night: 425BEF. This hostel sleeps 89 in dormitories and rooms with four or five beds, and has a sunny terrace, barbecues and a bike shed.

🛏 De Shetlandhoeve: Berg 5, Sint Martens Voeren 3790. ☎ (04) 381 0834. A peaceful little family hotel in an orchard, with four prettily decorated rooms and a pleasant breakfast room. Children will love the ponies.

WHAT TO SEE IN THE AREA

★ **Sint Pieters Voeren**: an impressive collection of buildings on the edge of a big pond that was once a commandery for the Teutonic Knights. It was founded in 1242, but the architecture is Mosan Renaissance. Trout are bred in the pond.

The Province of Antwerp (Provincie Antwerpen)

As you might expect, the metropolis has the lion's share of the sights in this province. But don't bypass Mechelen, an archbishopric and former capital of Burgundy with a fascinating history. There are several small towns that break the monotony of the endless Kempen plains: Lier, Hoogstraten, Turnhout, Herentals and Geel are all worth visiting.

ANTWERP (ANTWERPEN) 465,000 inhabitants

There's a mythical quality to this city, one that starts with its name. Much more than just the capital of the province, Antwerp is vital to Belgium's economic and cultural life. Ships departing from its vast port sail to northern France and Aachen, and bring back diamonds from South Africa and it has many of the characteristics of a seafaring town. For a start, it's a cosmopolitan metropolis where you can hear every imaginable language. The French writer Victor Hugo marvelled at this far-flung jewel among Belgian cities. He may have been a great romantic, but his impressions of Antwerp – a city of tipsy sailors, baroque gables, *waterzooi*, diamonds, Rubensesque odalisques and fruits from the Congo – were decidedly earthy. It's difficult not to be impressed. The city is bursting with powerful shipping magnates, captains of industry and affluent businessmen. First and fore-most, however, it's a place of artistic achievement with a history of tolerance – despite the alarming popularity of the far-right Vlaams Blok party.

Antwerp was home to Christopher Plantin (the Belgian answer to Caxton) and Rubens, who painted his baroque masterpieces here, and every forward-looking movement has flourished in the city. With such a heritage, you might expect it to rest on its laurels; but this dynamic city neither wallows in nostalgia nor neglects its heritage. European Cultural Capital in 1993, it continues to keep itself trim with new museums, important exhibitions and urban restoration programs, always with respect for the past and the city's soul. To find the spirit of Antwerp, head for its squares and parks, churches and guildhouses, or the old marble-tabled cafés, where you can try the local gin or get stuck into a simple dish of Flemish-style asparagus with an abbey beer. Thanks to a lifestyle that few other neighbouring ports can boast, the city radiates warmth.

The City of *Sinjoren*

A *sinjor* is quite simply, a *señor*, in the old sense of this Spanish word, which, roughly, means 'a gentleman'. The locals incorporated the word into their language as a result of the Spanish presence in the 17th century. They use it with this difference, however: a *señor* is touchy and totally useless, whereas the *sinjor* is a generous, cheerful businessman. Don't have any illusions about fitting in: to enter this club, both you and your parents must be natives of Antwerp.

Rubens's City

A European diplomat ahead of his time, Rubens successfully combined Italian painting with the Flemish style. Even today, he is Antwerp's best ambassador, drawing fans, some even claiming to be his descendants, from around the world. You can't escape him: Antwerp appears in many of his pictures, while you'll find his paintings everywhere. Sint Jacobskerk is where he was buried.

A Far-Right Stronghold

Antwerp woke up one morning to find that one in four of its inhabitants had voted for the Vlaams Blok, the extreme-Right Flemish national party. It's something of a stain on the city's tolerant character, but this step to the right predictably followed an influx of immigrants from North Africa and Turkey – and has been fired by the Blok's overtly racist campaigning techniques. Support for the party has shown no signs of diminishing in recent elections.

Humble Pleasures

Antwerp is a port, and a Flemish port, so it's definitely a place to have fun. Don't miss out on the Brueghelesque gatherings that continue to bring life to this city. Every weekend, the Dutch cross the border in droves to let their hair down in the streets of Antwerp – not that these weekend visitors are especially welcome, for the Dutch have never had much of a good press here.

There are bars and clubs a-plenty, but a fiesta in Antwerp is just as much about elderly ladies holding forth over a waffle in a tea-room, or office workers hanging out in their favourite *stampcafe* (bistro) over a *bolleke* of De Koninck beer.

NOT TO BE MISSED

– **Rubens and the Sinjoren:** see above.

– **Piet Pot:** a Dutchman who distributed *pains aux raisins* to condemned prisoners. It's not known if he hid a file in the buns, but he is remembered as a man whose heart was in the right place, and several streets are named after him. A baker in Korte Gasthuisstraat even makes the buns that Piet Pot used to distribute.

– **Lange Wapper:** you can see his statue on the Steen. Lange Wapper was a goblin who could shrink or grow to the size of a giant at will. His mission? To punish the wicked and tempt drunkards into looking for even more booze.

– **Statuettes of the Virgin Mary:** you'll see them on every street corner. The first appeared in 1585, put there by Jesuits after the fall of Antwerp. Rumour has it that the reason for their appearance was purely economic: if you had one on your own street, you didn't have to pay rates for lighting.

A SHORT HISTORY

Legendary Beginnings

Once upon a time, a giant called Druon Antigon imposed a heavy tax on ships rounding the bend of the Scheldt. If anyone complained, he cut off their hand. Silvius Brabo, a Roman soldier, decided to put an end to this unpleasant situation. He came, saw and conquered, killing the giant and cutting off his hand, which he hurled into the Scheldt. In Flemish, to throw a hand is '*hand werpen*', and tradition has it that this is how the city got its name. The sculptor Jef Lambeaux immortalized this heroic legionnaire with a statue that stands on the Grote Markt, although pedantic etymologists point out that Antwerp is more likely to come from '*aanwerp*' ('a place where the land juts out'), suggesting that the town jutted out into the River Scheldt.

A Strategic Point

The Franks settled on the Scheldt in the fourth and fifth centuries, long before they got to France. In the 10th century, the marquisate of Antwerp became part of the Holy Roman Empire. A century later, the *castellum* and Sint Walburgakerk arose out of the silt. Antwerp was annexed to the Duchy of Brabant in the 12th century, and grew rich thanks to the cloth industry.

The Golden Age

In the 15th century, Antwerp was the European centre for finance and trade, and merchants from every country rushed to open branches here. Fish, cereals and salt were the mainstays of the port, and they were traded in such quantity that Antwerp usurped Bruges as the region's trading capital, with the population jumping from 40,000 to 100,000. Silk, diamonds, glass,

---

■ Useful addresses

🛈 1 Tourist office
✉ Post office
🚆 Antwerpen Centraalstation
🚌 Coach station
  2 City Boutique
  3 Station bureau de change
  4 Thomas Cook
  5 Suikerrui 4
  6 Diamant metro station
  7 Groenplaats metro station
 10 Public telephone

🛏 Where to stay

 20 Scoutel
 21 International Seamen's House
 22 New International Youth Hotel
 23 Hotel Postiljon
 24 Pension Cammerpoorte
 25 Hotel Antigone
 26 Hotel Rubenshof
 27 Billard Palace Hotel
 28 Hotel Terminus
 29 Tourist Hotel
 30 Colombus Hotel
 31 Boomerang Youth Hostel

✕ Where to eat

 40 Mosselhuis
 41 Fouquets
 42 Did's Bistrot
 44 Hungry Henrietta
 45 Frituur No. 1
 46 Friture
 47 Dock's Café
 51 Restaurant Gistelein
 52 Sjalot en Schanul
 53 Hollywood Witloof
 54 Ulcke Van Zurich
 55 Pasta
 56 Zuidterras
 57 De Gulden Swaene and Facade
 58 Dagelinckx
 59 L'Entrepôt du Congo
 60 Den Angelot
 61 Del Rey

 62 Amadeus
 63 Huis de Colvenier

★ What to see

 90 Grote Markt and Stadhuis
 91 Cathedral and Quentin Metsys fountain
 92 Plantin-Moretus Museum
 93 Maagdenhuis (Orphanage)
 94 Mayer Van den Bergh Museum
 95 Vleeshuis (Butchers' House)
 96 National Scheepvaartmuseum (National Maritime Museum)
 97 Ethnografisch Museum (Ethnography Museum)
 98 Museum voor Volkskunde (Folklore Museum)
 99 Vlaeykensgang
100 Sint Pauluskerk
101 Dagbladenmuseum (Newspaper Museum)
102 Jordaenshuis
103 Rubenshuis
104 St Jakobskerk
105 Rockoxhuis
106 Sint Carolus Borromeuskerk
107 Handelsbeurs (stock exchange)
108 Torengebouw
109 Zoo
110 Centraalstation
111 Pelikaanstraat
112 Provinciaal Diamantmuseum (Diamond Museum)
113 Brouwershuis (Brewers' House)
114 Hessenhuis
115 Begijnhof
116 Museum voor Schone Kunsten (Fine Art Museum)
117 Museum voor Hedendaagse Kunst (Contemporary Art Museum)
118 Provinciaal Museum voor Fotografie
119 Mini-Antwerp
120 Lift down to the River Scheldt

NORTH

WAASLANDTUNNEL

Scheldt

★ 113
Brouwersvliet — Oude — Leeuwenr
Krieken str.
Van Meterenkaai
Sint Pieters Vliet
Leguit
Verversrui
FALCONPLEIN
Kommekens str.
★ 21
Falconrui
Klapdorp Paardenm
ST PAULUS PLAATS
Sint Paulusstr.
Klapdorp
Mutsaertstraat
★ 62
Nosestraat
Blindenstraat
★ 100
Zwartzusters str.
Minderbroedersrui
★ 47
Butchgracht
Zirkstr.
▲ 25
Zakstr.
★ 105
Keizerstraat
★ 96
Jordaenskaai
★ 95
Oude
Kuipersstr.
★ 52
Horistraat
Koepoort str.
Lange Koepoort str.
|●| 53
Beurs
Wolstraat
★ 57
Kipdorp
Borzestr.
★ 97
Suikerrui
★ 98
GROTE MARKT
★ 90
1 🏛
Kaasrui
★ 54
HENDRIK CONSCIENCE PLEIN
106
Melkmarkt
Koepoortstr.
★ 5
▲ 2
▲ 23
Blauwmoezelstr.
Kt. Nieuwstr.
Lange
Pieter Potstr.
P. Potstraat
★ 45
Oude Koornmarkt
91
Lijnwaadmarkt
★ 60
Sint Katelijne vest
★ 56
Vlasmarkt
★ 99
J. Blom str.
Sint Pieterstr.
7
Eiermarkt
★ 107
Lange Clara
Ernest Van Dijckkaai
★ 51
Zand
102
Begijnenstr.
55
GROEN PLAATS
108
Meirbrug
Meir
Reyndersstr.
★ 120
SINT JANS VLIET
92 ★ VRIJDAG MARKT
Hoog
Steenhouwersvest
Oever
✉
Schoenmarkt
★ 101
Lombardenvest
Jodenstr.
24
Nationalestraat
Kammenstr.
Augustijnenstr.
Klooster str.
St Andriesstr.
Lange Ridderstr.
✕ 46
Everdijstr.
Schuttershofstr.
Hukdevttersstr.
K. Gasthuisstr.
Komedie Pl.
GRAA MARK
63
St Antoniusstr.
Oudaan
Lange Gasthuisstr.
Arenbergst
★ 94
Schoytestraat
Bredestr.
Vleminckveld
Prekersstraat
Aalmoezenierstr.
Nationalestraat
Rosier
★ 93
Leopoldstraat
Sint Rochusstr.
Begijnenstr.
Schermers str.

ANTWERP

The district around the Koninklijk Museum voor Schone Kunsten and the Vlaamse Kaai district.
▲ 31
✕ 58, 59, ★ 116
43 ✕

★ 117, 118, 119

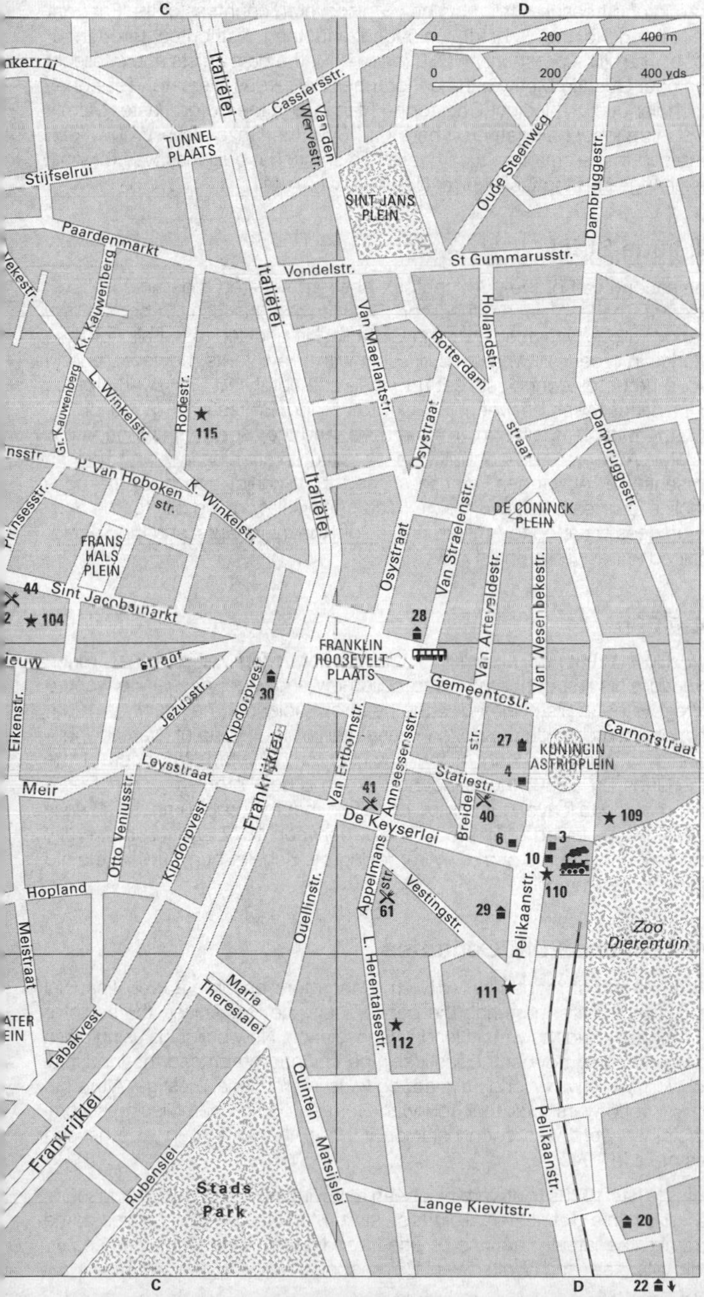
C
D
0 200 400 m
0 200 400 yds
1
2
3
4
Italiëlei
Cassiersstr.
Van den Wervestr.
TUNNEL PLAATS
Stijfselrui
SINT JANS PLEIN
Oude Steenweg
Dambruggestr.
Paardenmarkt
Vondelstr.
St Gummarusstr.
Kr. Kauwenberg
Van Maerlantstr.
Rotterdam
Hollandstr.
straat
Gr. Kauwenberg
L. Winkelstr.
Rodestr.
115
Osystraat
P. Van Hoboken str.
K. Winkelstr.
Van Straelenstr.
DE CONINCK PLEIN
Prinsesstr.
FRANS HALS PLEIN
44
Sint Jacobsmarkt
104
28
Van Arteveldestr.
Van Wesenbekestr.
FRANKLIN ROOSEVELT PLAATS
Kipdorpvest
30
Jezusstr.
Gemeentestr.
Eikenstr.
Van Ertbornstr.
Anneessensstr.
str.
27
KONINGIN ASTRIDPLEIN
Carnotstraat
Leysstraat
Frankrijklei
Statiestr.
4
Meir
41
Breidel
40
109
De Keyserlei
Otto Veniusstr.
Kipdorpvest
6
3
10
Appelmansstr.
110
Hopland
Vestingstr.
61
29
Quellinstr.
Pelikaanstr.
Zoo Dierentuin
Meistraat
L. Herentalsestr.
Maria Theresialei
111
Tabakvest
112
Quinten Matsijslei
Frankrijklei
Rubenslei
Stads Park
Pelikaanstr.
Lange Kievitstr.
20
22

porcelain and treasures from the newly discovered countries of the Far East were carried up the Scheldt, unloaded and then distributed throughout Europe. The city's prosperity was a magnet for the best artists and intellects of the age: Quentin Metsys, the geographer Gerhardus Mercator, Brueghel, the scholar Justus Lipsius, Christophe Plantin and the burgomaster Marnix van St Aldegonde, all gathered here. In 1559, the Onze Lieve Vrouwekerk was raised to the status of a cathedral. To show that business was thriving, an exchange and the Guildhall of Butchers were built.

Religious Strife

In the second half of the 16th century, Antwerp suffered a decline. Philip II, the son of Charles V, was rather more Spanish than his Flemish-born father, but above all, he was absolutist and Catholic. He decided to put his northern territories in order. Antwerp was bristling with Protestants, however, and in 1566, a group of iconoclasts set upon the cathedral and destroyed statues and paintings. War between the Catholics and Protestants raged on. In 1576, the King of Spain sent in his armies, and the 'Spanish fury' began. A year later, Antwerp rebelled, but it was recaptured after just a year. Philip II's representative, Alexander Farnese, closed the Scheldt and gave the non-Catholics four years to leave the city. This spelt isolation and ruin for the port. The refugees escaped to Amsterdam, as did the merchants, and the Scheldt remained unnavigable until 1795.

Napoleon

When Boney reached Antwerp in the all-conquering wake of the French Revolution, his first concern was to build new and wider docks. He wanted Antwerp to be 'a pistol aimed at the heart of England'. The year was 1803. Bonaparte's dream died a dozen years later on the plains of Waterloo, but Antwerp flourished as part of the newly created United Provinces of the Netherlands. In 1830, independence brought new problems. The Dutch were prepared to leave, but only on condition that they could impose a heavy tax, which they levied until 1863. Finally, between 1877 and 1885, the city spent serious amounts of money improving the Scheldt quays, while the old districts footed the bill.

The 19th and 20th Centuries

With the dawn of modernity, Antwerp once more became a lively financial and cultural centre, nurturing the painter Henri de Braekeleer, the sculptor Jef Lambeaux and the writer Hendrik Conscience. New buildings using glass and iron showed how enthusiastically the city had embraced the industrial revolution, while two World Fairs added to its international prestige. Although the two world wars took their toll, with German bombs demolishing several districts, Antwerp was soon back on its feet, thanks in part to American investment in 1945.

Since the late 1980s, Antwerp has been a thriving centre of designer fashion, specializing in a distinctive 'minimalist' style. Many followers of fashion come to admire the latest creations of Dries Van Noten, Anne Demeulemeester, Martin Margiela and Walter Van Beirendonck, while in the Vlaamse Kaai district, south of the centre, the mix of grungy fashion and contemporary art gives the area its own individuality.

GETTING THERE

By Train

From Brussels, there are five trains an hour for Antwerp Centraalstation via Mechelen and Berchem. There are fewer trains at the weekend. Don't get the following Antwerp stations muddled up:

🚆 **Antwerpen Centraalstation** (map D3): right in the middle of town. ☎ (03) 204 2040. The obvious place from which to set off on an excursion. All domestic services stop here, as do some trains from Amsterdam.

🚆 **Berchem station**: a couple of miles south of the town. ☎ (03) 272 0722. All international trains stop at Berchem, from which it's a 5-minute ride to Centraalstation.

By Bus

🚌 **Eurolines:** Van Stalenstraat 8 (map, D3). ☎ (03) 233 8662. Fax: (03) 232 6801.

By Car

The centre of town is well signposted, but traffic is heavy. It's much easier to leave your car in one of the many car parks in the town centre and use public transport (bus, tram and metro). Try the Groenplaats car park, which is central and open round the clock, or the Ernest-Van-Dijckkaai car park, opposite the Steen.

USEFUL ADDRESSES AND INFORMATION

Tourist Information

Postcodes: 2000, 2010, 2050.

🏢 **Tourist office** (map A2, **1**): Grote Markt 15. ☎ (03) 232 0103. Fax: (03) 231 1937. Email: toerisme@AntwerpCity.be. Website: www.dma.be. Open every day from 9am–5.30pm (4.30pm on Sundays and public holidays). Services include: literature on the town and province, accommodation listings and room reservations, reduced tickets for local museums and galleries, maps of the public transport system, information on what's on in town, guided walks, town trails, the port trail and where to eat. The only problem is that the office is usually mobbed. You'll save time by popping into the City Boutique across the road.

🏢 **City Boutique** (map A2, **2**): Grote Markt 40. ☎ (03) 220 8180. Open 10am–6pm. In theory it's closed on Sunday and Monday, but in practice you'll often find it open over long weekends. This is an offshoot of the tourist office, specializing in information on what's on and advance bookings. It sells books, catalogues and souvenirs, and offers information in English and a panoply of other languages. Ask for the Antwerpen City View, a marvellous 3-D map (though sadly it's not free).

🖪 Provincial Tourist Office (Toeristische Federatie van de Provincie Antwerpen): Koningin Elisabethlei 16, Antwerpen 2018. ☎ (03) 240 6373. Fax: (03) 240 6383. Open Monday to Friday, 8am–5.30pm.

Another place to get the information listed in the entries above.

– **Antwerp's cultural newspaper:** this large-format fold-out (in Flemish) is a mine of information about what's on in Antwerp, including cinema, exhibitions, festivals, plays, restaurants, shops and so on.

Money, Banks, Bureaux de Change

■ **Bureau de change at Antwerp Centraalstation** (map D3, **3**): open 8am–10pm.
■ **CGER** (map B2): Melkmarkt. Automatic currency exchange.
■ **Gemeentekrediet** (map A2): money dispenser for Visa cards.

■ **Thomas Cook** (map D3, **4**): Koningin Astridplein 33. Open Monday to Saturday, 9am–9pm.
■ **Suikerrui 4** (map A2, **5**): Suikerrui 36. Open 9am–9.30pm (10.30pm on Saturday). Booking service, information, and maps and phonecards on sale.

Phones and Post Offices

✉ **Post office** (map A3): Groenplaats 16. Open Monday to Friday, 9am–6pm, and Saturday 9am–noon.

■ **Public telephone** (map D3, **10**): on the ground floor of the Centraalstation. Open 6am–9.30pm.

GETTING AROUND

City Transport

The trams and buses are owned by De Lijn. There are 38 lines crossing Antwerp.

You can pick up maps of the network at the following information points:

■ **Diamant metro station** (map D3, **6**): open Monday to Friday, 8am–12.30pm and 1.30–4pm.
■ **Groenplaats metro station** (map A3, 7): Groenplaats. Lower ground floor. Same opening hours, also Saturday 9am–noon.
🚌 **Main coach station** (map D3): Franklin Rooseveltplaats 9. Open Monday to Friday, 7am–7pm , Saturday 8–11.30am and 12.30–4pm. Single tickets are pricey so a 10-journey card is a good investment. If

you're using the system a lot, you'll want the 110BEF day pass, or a pass for a longer period. You can get these at the offices above.
🚆 **Trains:** ☎ (03) 204 2111 (Centraalstation) and (03) 272 0722 (Berchem).
■ **Public transport:** bus, tram, metro. VVM-De Lijn. ☎ (078) 113883 or (03) 218 1411.
■ **Taxis:** ☎ (03) 238 9825.
⊕ **Deurne airport:** ☎ (03) 285 6500.

Bikes

Hiring a bike isn't easy in Antwerp. Nevertheless, here is an address:

■ **Fietsenverhuur Antwerpen Averechts** (map A4): Kronenburgstraat 34. ☎ (03) 248-15-77. Fax: (03) 248-50-11. Bus No. 1. Open every day 10am–2pm. Booking recommended. The office can also offer suggestions for trips around and outside the city.

City Tours

The tourist office has details of several tours with commentary. Here are some of the best:

– **Touristram:** ☎ (03) 480 9388. Between April and the end of September, tours start from the Groenplaats on the hour every hour between 11am and 4pm. The tram goes around the old town and the port on a 50-minute trip that's inexpensive (125BEF) and entertaining.

– **Rickshaw tours:** ATE Cars, ☎ (03) 324 3451. Tour the city in an environmentally friendly rickshaw powered by an electric motor. The 30-minute trip starts at the Grote Markt, and is available from July to September, 11am–6pm.

WHERE TO STAY

There are plenty of hotels in Antwerp, but most are a bit expensive (except around the station). It's well worth booking ahead, as the Dutch flock here on weekends. The tourist office on the Grote Markt can tell you which hotels offer weekend deals.

Youth Hostels

⌂ **Vlaamse Jeugdherberg Op Sinjoorke:** Éric Sasselaan 2, Antwerpen 2020. ☎ (03) 238 0273. Fax: (03) 248 1932. To get there, take tram No. 2 or bus No. 27 and get off at Bouwcentrum. Basic rate per night: 420BEF, and a bit more if you don't have a members' card. Closed from mid-December to early January. It's not exactly central, but it overlooks a pleasant green park. The hostel closes at midnight, but you can arrange to come back later. Rooms sleep between two and eight people, with 130 beds in all. The furnishings and furniture are a bit passé, but the food is good, plentiful and reasonably priced. Sheet hire is available.

⌂ **New International Youth Hostel** (off the map at D4, **22**): Provinciestraat 256, Antwerpen 2018. ☎ (03) 230 0522 and (03) 218 9430. Fax: (03) 281 0933. Email: niyh@pandora.be. Take tram No. 11 from Centraalstation (get off at the corner of Provinciestraat) or tram Nos. 2 or 15. Double rooms 1,490–1,870BEF. Only 10 minutes from Centraalstation and the zoo, this cheerful place provides well-maintained rooms, with or without showers, for the young and not so young. Rooms sleep one, two or four people; there's also a dormitory for eight, although you'll have to bring your own sheets. There's an open fire in the common room, while the landlady is happy to suggest ideas for your stay in the city. This place does a lot to liven up an otherwise slightly downbeat area. Meals are available, with a daily special at 350BEF.

🛏 **Boomerang Youth Hostel** (map A4, **31**): Volksstraat 49. ☎ (03) 238 4782. Breakfast included in the price. Bus No. 23 and tram No. 8 stop outside this former town house, with 60 beds for men and women in single-sex dormitories and showers and bathrooms on every mezzanine floor. Clean, cool and cost-effective, this place attracts a cosmopolitan clientele. No curfew.

🛏 **Globetrotter's Nest** (to the north of the city): Vlagstraat 25, Antwerpen 2060. ☎ (03) 236 9928. Take tram No. 3 or bus No. 23, and get off at Stuivenberg hospital. Double rooms cost 1,200BEF, or you can stay in dormitories from 400BEF. A cheap stop-over with nine-bed dormitories for singles, groups and families in a decent, largely immigrant neighbourhood. One room sleeps three people. As you may have worked out from the price, showers and toilets are communal, and you'll need to bring a sleeping bag, although sheet hire is available. There's a TV room, a kitchen, a library, plenty of tourist information and above all a good atmosphere, thanks to the couple who run it. You can hire bikes by the hour or by the day.

🛏 **Scoutel** (map D4, **20**): Stoomstraat 3, Antwerpen 2018. ☎ (03) 226 4606. A five-minute walk from Centraalstation and the Zoo. No curfew – you'll get your own key. This is a bit more expensive than your average youth hostel, but you'll get a discount if you're under 25. Rooms sleep two or three people, and are equipped with showers and toilets.

🛏 **Sleep Inn:** Bolivarplaats 1. ☎ (03) 237 3748. Fax: (03) 248 0248. In the Vlaamse Kaai district: take bus Nos. 1 or 23 and get off at Bolivarplaats (at the end of Amerikalei). Bargain-basement prices, with breakfast included. They'll give you the key so you can come back as late as you please.

🛏 **International Seamen's House** (map B1, **21**): Falconrui 21. ☎ (03) 227 5433. Fax: (03) 234 2603. Take bus No. 86. Double rooms with baths 1,720BEF, including breakfast. Often fully booked, so fax your reservation in advance. This unexciting tower block, built in 1954, is not simply for sailors, although landlubbers will pay slightly more. The clean rooms have showers and toilets, and the exotic array of guests should give you a flavour of Antwerp the port. The neighbourhood is lively, the food is cheap, there's no curfew, the staff are cheerful and the place sometimes hosts events – what more could you ask?

The District from the Port to the Grote Markt

The centre of the old town, with most of the nightlife.

☆☆ Moderate

🛏 **Hotel Postiljon** (map A2, **23**): Blaumoezelstraat 6. ☎ (03) 231 7575. Fax: (03) 226 8450. Expect to pay 2,000–2,600BEF, excluding breakfast. Right next to the cathedral, this is the hotel of your dreams, unless you can't stand the sound of bells. The clean and charming rooms have low ceilings: those at the back are quietest, especially when things hot up on summer evenings.

🛏 **Pension Cammerpoorte** (map A3, **24**): Steenhouwersvest 55. ☎ (03) 231 2836. Fax: (03) 226 2843. Get there by taking tram No. 8. Double rooms 2,450BEF. This is a hotel and guesthouse under the same sign: they're next door to each other, so pay attention or you could end up paying more than you expected. Sneaky guests stay in the guesthouse but use the hotel car park. The helpful, cheerful landlady will give you ideas about what to do in Antwerp while she serves breakfast. Prettily furnished, comfortable and keenly priced rooms. All in all, excellent value for money.

☆☆☆ Expensive

🛏 **Hotel Antigone** (map A2, **25**): Jordaenskaai 11-12. ☎ (03) 231 6677. Fax: (03) 231 3774. Get there on the No. 34 bus. A classic hotel near the Vleeshuis (Butchers' House). It's a bit pricey, but there are views of the Scheldt and the left bank. The rooms are cavernous, with the quietest at the back – you'll have to choose between a good night's rest and a room with a view. Avoid changing money here.

🛏 **Hotel Cammerpoorte** (map A3, **24**): Nationalestraat 38-40. ☎ (03) 231 9736. Fax: (03) 226 2968. Double rooms from 3,150BEF. Not to be confused with Pension Cammerpoorte (see above). An elegant hotel in the heart of the old town, slightly formulaic but not without charm. Generous breakfast buffet and private car park (250BEF a day).

Around the Vlaamse Kaai

☆ Budget

🛏 **Rubenshof** (off the map from B4, **26**): Amerikalei 115. ☎ (03) 237 0789. Fax: (03) 248 2591. Take tram No. 24 and bus No. 23. Double rooms 1,100–2,400BEF, depending on whether you want a sink, shower or bath. There are rooms for three or four. A first-class hotel that can't quite decide on its style – it's somewhere between art deco and the Roaring Twenties. The rooms have recently been done up, as has the rather loud yellow facade. The landlords are a cool Dutch couple who'll give you a friendly welcome, and the generous breakfasts are accompanied by the gentle strains of classical music. Plenty of parking space.

B&Bs

B&Bs are catching on in Flanders, and Antwerp offers numerous possibilities in this category. Here are some of the best:

🛏 **Maxi Matin, Greta Stevens:** Molenstraat 35, Antwerpen 2018 (between Britse Lei and Mechelsesteenweg). ☎ (03) 259 1590. Fax: (03) 259 1599. Email: fdj.greta@ wol.be. Three bedrooms with en suite shower and WC in a large town house that's been entirely renovated. A single room costs 1,250BEF, a double room 1,900BEF during the week and 2,400BEF at the weekend. The helpful landlords are fans of contemporary art and interior design, and there's plenty of useful tourist literature available. Strictly non-smoking. Breakfast is excellent, with hot dishes served in a light, pleasant dining room: home-cooked meals are also on offer. No credit cards. If they're full, Greta Stevens can help you book at other B&Bs.

🛏 **Lenaerts-Moelans:** Verschansingstraat 55 (near the B&B above, in a road leading to the Museum voor Schone Kunsten). ☎ and fax: (03) 248 0913. Double rooms

1,800BEF, with breakfast 200BEF. A handsome 1900s townhouse with two rooms. There's a flower shop on the ground floor, run by the landlady, whose sculptor husband has his studio here. A child's put-me-up is available, and you can use the bathroom and kitchenette. In summer, breakfast is served on the terrace in the garden. The family are friendly and environmentally aware.

☆☆☆ Expensive

♠ **Industrie:** Emiel Banningstraat 52. Near Lambermontplaats. ☎ (03) 238 6600. Fax: (03) 238 8688. A large town house with 13 well-equipped bedrooms decorated in pastel colours. Double rooms cost 3,000–3,200BEF, including en suite shower and bath: prices go down if you stay the whole weekend or more. A really cosy B&B where you'll get a warm welcome. Private car park.

The District around the Station and the Zoo

☆ Budget

♠ **Billard Palace Hotel** (map D3, **27**): Koningin Astridplein 40. ☎ (03) 233 4455. Fax: (03) 226 1426. Double rooms with sink and shower 1,400–1,800BEF. To the left of the Centraalstation. The area's a bit noisy and the reception borders on the unsavoury, but don't let that put you off. The first floor's a billiard hall, breakfast is served on the second and above are the rooms – and frankly, 'You pays your money, you takes your choice.' It's a hotel without pretensions, but you'll have everything you need for the night (including TV and phone), and the rooms are fairly clean. If you pile into them en masse, you'll pay even less. Fast-food restaurant on the ground floor.

☆☆ Moderate

♠ **Terminus** (map D2, **28**): Franklin Rooseveltplaats 9. ☎ (03) 231 4795. Fax: (03) 226 3240. Just above the coach station, so don't expect too much peace and quiet. A big, impersonal building with kitsch decor and a restaurant and bar in the evening. Ask for a room at the back. The apartments for four with kitchenette are a good option.

♠ **Tourist Hotel** (map D3, **29**): Pelikaanstraat 20, Antwerpen 2018. ☎ (03) 232 5870. Fax: (03) 231 6707. Double rooms with sink, shower or bath from 1,900BEF to 2,800BEF, with small weekend reductions. Right in the heart of the diamond district, this hotel offers good value for money, although you should give it a miss if you can't bear the rumble of night-time trains. Trainspotters, on the other hand, will love the views of the Centraalstation's stained glass. Generous breakfast.

☆☆☆☆ Splash Out

♠ **Colombus Hotel** (map C3, **30**): Frankrijklei 4. ☎ (03) 233 0390. Fax: (03) 226 0946. Website: www. colombushotel.com. Double rooms with en suite shower or bath and toilets from 3,300BEF to 3,975BEF. Opposite the opera house, this friendly, comfortable hotel piles on the attractions, which include a covered swimming pool and a central location. Paying car park nearby.

On the Outskirts

Campsites

– For information on campsites, call ☎ (014) 643 6111

🛏 **Molen:** Thonetlaan Sint Annastrand, Antwerpen Linkeroever 2050. ☎ (03) 219 6090. Near Sint Anna-plaats, with views of Antwerp (at least from the edge of the site). For 960BEF, you can rent a four-person *trekkershutte* (chalet) with cooking utensils. Book ahead if you want one: there aren't very many of them.

🛏 **Vogelzang**: Vogelzanglaan, Antwerpen 2020. ☎ (03) 238 5717. Take tram No. 2 or bus No. 27 and get off at Bouwcentrum. A city campsite with the same *trekkershutten* as the Molen.

B&Bs

🛏 **Het Drakenhof, Mr and Mrs Van Geertruyden:** Drakenhoflaan 194, Deurne 2100. ☎ and fax: (03) 321 2465. East of town, near Deurne airport: they'll fax you a map when you book. It's a 10-minute bus ride from Centraalstation: take bus No. 20 and get off at De Stampelaan, which is bang in front of the B&B's black gate. Rooms from 2,100BEF during the week, or 2,400BEF at the weekend. A bit out of the way, but this is a splendid place: a 17th-century manor set in a pretty park with a lake, away from the noise and traffic. As well as being peaceful, it's a model of hospitality, with charming hosts who take a real interest in their guests. There's a living room, a bar, a TV and dining room, with Flemish Renaissance-style furniture, a superb fireplace – and two magnificent double rooms with bathroom (one is separate from the room). Both are tastefully decorated: the white room is Japanese-style, while the blue room is Cambodian in style, with wicker furnishing. An 'art nouveau' room is under preparation. Smoking is not allowed, and you'll be asked to pad about on the splendid carpets in socks or slippers. Prices are high for an Antwerp B&B, but just think what you'd pay in a hotel with decor like this. No credit cards.

WHERE TO EAT

Or rather, how to choose? You'll find tourist-friendly restaurants galore on the Grote Markt, near the cathedral and in the port. Then there are themed restaurants (metallic, 18th-century, boats, religious, etc), which are very much the thing in Antwerp these days. The food is usually as stylish and ambitious as the setting, but all this refinement doesn't come cheap.

The District around the Centraalstation and the Zoo

☆ Budget

✗ **Beni Falafel** (off the map): Lange Leemstraat 188, Antwerpen 2018. ☎ (03) 218 8211. Open 11.30am–3pm and 5.30–11pm. Closed Friday and Saturday in summer. A vegetarian fast-food restaurant cum take-away in the heart of the Jewish quarter, where vegetable soup and falafels are the mainstays. Gets lively on Thursday evenings.

☆☆ Moderate

✗ **Fouquets** (map D3, **41**): De Keyserlei 17. ☎ (03) 233 9742. De Keyserlei is one of the locals' favourite spots for a promenade, and the advent of spring sees the tables come out at this two-room Parisian-style brasserie. There's an express menu if you don't fancy the full works. Interesting menu, indifferent service.

✗ **Mosselhuis** (map D3, **40**): Statiestraat 32, Antwerpen 2018. ☎ (03) 385 0291. Open 11am–11pm. Set menu 699BEF. For more than a century, the Mosselhuis has been dishing up juicy mussels and delicious eels for Antwerpers of every class and persuasion. The copper pots, porcelain dishes and red gingham tablecloths are reassuringly old-fashioned, and there are even children's portions of mussels if your little ones are so inclined. In summer, the tables spill out on to the pavement.

The District around Meirplaats

🏠 Budget

✗ **Did's Bistrot** (map C2, **42**): Sint Jacobstraat 21. ☎ (03) 231 7792. Open Monday to Friday 11.30am–2.30pm and 6–11pm, Saturday 3–11.30pm. Closed Sunday. Main courses about 300BEF. You can't miss it: there's a huge hand on the facade to point the way. Light-wood tables and chairs, and a decent menu with simple but filling dishes. Try the 'eat as much as you want' spaghetti or the fish lasagne, which you can wash down with a pitcher of house wine without breaking the bank.

🏠🏠🏠 Expensive

✗ **Hungry Henrietta** (map C2, **44**): Sint Jacobstraat 17. ☎ (03) 232 2928. Open 6.30–10pm. Closed at the weekend. Ease round the enormous bull to get into the huge dining room, where 'Henrietta salad' and steaks are served in an artsy atmosphere. It's not cheap, although the daily special's a bargain. In summer, you can eat in the garden.

Around the Grote Markt and the Port

Frituur (chip shops)

✗ **Frituur No. 1** (map A2, **45**): at the corner of Suikerrui and Hoogstraat. Open continuously, and known for miles around.

✗ **Friture** (map A3, **46**) Theodor Van Rijswijckplaats. Open every day till 7.30pm. Not far from the Hotel Cammerpoorte, this place fries the best chips in Antwerp.

🏠 Budget

✗ **De Gulden Swaene** (map B2, **57**): Hendrik Conscienceplein 15. ☎ (03) 233 1959. Open for lunch and dinner on weekdays and Saturday and Sunday afternoon. Closed Monday evening. About 350BEF for a full meal. A tiny *koffiehuis* in a 16th-century house near Sint Carolus-Borromeuskerk, with a mezzanine level overlooking the bar: old beams, wood panelling and lace complete the atmosphere. Very cheap pittas, quiches, salads and vegetarian dishes.

✗ **Restaurant Gistelein** (map A3, **51**): Zand 25-27. ☎ (03) 233 1366. Open from noon until late. Closed Tuesday. In a beautiful area, a stone's throw from the port, this comfortable place offers homemade vegetable quiches, served to the strains of Flemish singers.

✗ **Sjalot en Schanul** ('Shallot and Chives'); (map A2, **52**): Oude Beurs 12. ☎ (03) 233 8875. Open from breakfast time to 8pm. Full meals about 500BEF. Closed Wednesday. A good place to sample such Belgian classics as tomatoes stuffed with prawns and chicory in béchamel sauce. Veggies will go for the soups and salads, which you can eat in or take away. It's a real shame it's closed in the evening.

☆☆ Moderate

✗ **De Pottekijker** (map A2): Kaasrui 5. ☎ (03) 225 2197. Open every evening from 6pm. Booking recommended. In a street overlooking the Grote Markt, this restaurant's many charms include a bay window, darkwood panelling decorated with Burmese puppets, stencils on the walls, exposed brick, baroque mirrors and lights, a mezzanine and amazing furniture. They use seasonal produce to make soups the way grandma used to, and the menu's other highlights include a choice of salads, mouthwatering grilled meats and succulent cod cooked in tinfoil, all washed down with the cheeky house wine.

✗ **Den Angelot** (map A2, **60**): Lijnwaadmarkt 10-12. ☎ (03) 231 4757. Open noon–3pm and 6-11pm. Closed Tuesday in winter. A full meal costs about 650BEF. In the shadow of the cathedral, this restaurant looks like a kitsch, Gothic mock-up of a Flemish Primitive painting. The props all come from a church – confessionals, choir-stall lights, triptychs, effigies, pillars, and frescoes worthy of Bosch – and the toilets are adorned with a tombstone. Simple, earthy food, including mussels, rabbit, grilled fish and a filling hotpot (*hutsepot*). On fine days, you can eat in a little garden courtyard.

✗ **Hollywood Witloof** (map A2, **53**): Hofstraat 9. ☎ (03) 233 7331. Open from 6pm every evening except Monday (and Tuesday in summer). Set menu 750BEF, otherwise about 1,000BEF. 'Witloof' means chicory, although Belgium's national vegetable is not much in evidence

on the menu at this trendy restaurant in a 17th-century cellar. The decor's great, but the service is a bit slow.

✗ **Ulcke Van Zurich** (map A2, **54**): Oude Beurs 50. ☎ (03) 234 0494. Open every day from 6pm. A wood-panelled old town house where cheerful young Antwerpers tuck into chicken salad, spare ribs, chicken mousse with port and meat and fish dishes with plenty of twists. It's a great place, and booking is essential.

✗ **Pasta** (map A2-3, **55**): Oude Koornmarkt 32. (03) 223 1776. Open for lunch from noon and for dinner from 6pm. There's a refreshing absence of Venetian gondolas and Chianti bottles at this multilevel restaurant that certainly lives up to its name. The pasta on the ground floor is the priciest, but the fourth floor has magnificent views of the cathedral spire to whet the appetite.

✗ **Zuidterras** (map A3, **56**): Ernest Van Dijckkaai 37. ☎ (03) 234 1275. Open 9am–11pm. A ship-shaped structure right next to the Scheldt, this restaurant's main attraction is the astonishing decor, the work of the avant-garde architect Bob Van Reeth. Pop in for Sunday brunch or breakfast during the rest of the week. In season, regulars go for mussels, while scampi with asparagus and homemade chocolate mousse are year-round favourites.

☆☆☆ Expensive

✗ **Façade** (map B2, **57**): Conscienceplein 18. ☎ (03) 233 5931. About 900BEF for a full meal. Open for dinner on weekdays, and also for lunch on Saturday and Sunday. Façade is a favourite haunt of locals looking to inject a little romance into their lives. It's not cheap, but you're made to feel very welcome, the menu is fairly original, with an emphasis on vegetables, and portions are pretty generous. There's also a terrace.

☆☆☆☆ Splash Out

✕ **Huis De Colvenier** (map A3–4, **63**): Sint Antoniusstraat 8. ☎ (03) 226 6573. Open for lunch and dinner from Tuesday to Friday: dinner only on Saturday and lunch only on Sunday. Five- or seven-course menus 1,200–1,900BEF (excluding drinks), and worth every penny. Sip an aperitif in the wine cellars while you admire the *grand crû* wines in their alcoves, then head for the high-ceilinged dining room, which you enter via the kitchen, where the hyperrealist paintings on the wall are a surprisingly successful complement to the tasteful furniture and crockery, although in summer, the terrace in the winter garden is the place to sit. As for the cooking, it's sublime – simple but refined dishes inspired by market produce. Among the delights on offer are crayfish and lobster salad with pine nuts, chicken livers with new potatoes, melt-in-the-mouth lamb cutlets and pears steeped in Marie-Brizard liqueur. The wines that come with each course are chosen with aplomb. There's also a midday business lunch.

The District of the Old Port and the Maasland Tunnel

☆☆ Moderate

✕ **Amadeus** (map A1, **62**): Sint Paulusplaats 20. ☎ (03) 232 2587. Open every day from 7pm (6pm at the weekend) to midnight. Set menus start at 425BEF. An attractive, Ghent-style restaurant in the red-light district, with 1920s decor, coloured glass, bevelled mirrors on lacquered brick walls and red check tablecloths. You can stuff yourself with spare ribs for a fixed price, or tuck into traditional, homely cooking, washed down with full-bodied red wine. If you've not tried *carbonades*, a traditional Flemish dish, this is the place to do it.

☆☆☆ Expensive

✕ **Dock's Café** (map A1, **47**): Jordaenskaai 7. ☎ (03) 226 6330. Open noon–2pm and 6.30pm–midnight. Closed Saturday lunchtime. About 1,250BEF for a full meal. A trendy brasserie near the Steen, with postmodern decor that mixes wrought iron, marble, bronze and wood to stunning effect. The helpful staff rush around the mezzanine with a cornucopia of oyster bar/brasserie classics: lobster, shellfish, sophisticated *carpaccios* and the like. The bar is a great place to meet before you explore this lively area. Take a look at the toilets – they look as if they've come straight from the Empire State Building.

The District around the Koninklijk Museum voor Schone Kunsten

☆ Budget

✕ **L'Entrepôt du Congo** (off the map from A4, **59**): Vlaamse Kaai 42. ☎ (03) 238 9232. Open 8am–3am (food served until 10.30pm). An old warehouse that once stocked merchandise from the colonies. Now it's a trendy restaurant near the Fine Art and Photography museums, with a suitably intellectual atmosphere. Steaks, salads and vegetarian dishes are the top draws, as are the delicious cakes and whiskies.

✕ **Het Groene Paard**: Luikstraat 9 (on the corner of Waalse Kaai, between the Photography Museum and the Fine Art Museum). ☎ (03) 238 7750. Open from 10am. Closed Wednesday. This popular restaurant is ideal if you want a quick snack between museums, with an array of Flemish dishes, mussels and rabbit in De Koninck beer. The dining room is a jumble of bric-à-brac and indoor plants.

✕ **Finjan**: Graaf Van Hoornstraat 1. ☎ (03) 248 7714. Open from 11am. Next to the Fine Arts Museum, this unpretentious joint is another good spot for a snack when you've had your fill of art. Light-wood panelling, a huge round table for groups. The gallery is decorated with little cacti, and the menu has a Middle Eastern flavour, including pittas, *falafels*, *chawarmas*, kebabs and veggie dishes. The sauces are satisfyingly spicy.

☆☆ Moderate

✕ **Dagelinckx** (off the map from A4, **58**): Museumstraat 21. Between the Vlaamse Kaai and the Fine Arts Museum. ☎ (03) 238 7601. Open noon–3pm and 6pm–midnight. Closed Tuesday. About 800BEF for a full meal. The entrance to this brasserie is a spectacular homage to Phoebus, the sun god. Inside, things are slightly more restrained: the dining room is wonderfully light, with a circular bar and Chagall reproductions on the wall. In fine weather, you can sit out on the loud yellow decking. The menu, which changes according to the seasons, favours fish and salads, although the cooking is slightly humdrum. There's also a piano bar.

Tea-room

– **Del Rey** (map D3, **61**): Appelmansstraat 5, Antwerpen 2018. ☎ (03) 233 2937. Open 10am–6pm. Closed Sunday and early August. A tea room with Mediterranean decor and cakes that will break the resolve of the most devoted dieter. Light meals (a bit pricey) at lunchtime.

WHERE TO GO FOR A DRINK

Some of Antwerp's more celebrated watering holes are listed here, but the best place will be one you've found yourself, and with more than 2,000 bars to choose from, you can afford to be picky. On weekend evenings, the area around the cathedral, the port and the Stadhuis becomes a giant party, with beer, music and singing spilling onto the streets. So, decide on the kind of 'crawl' you want: there are literary cafés, beer bars and gin bars, as well as any number of clubs. Your only problem will be forcing your way through the crowds.

The District around Meirplaats and the Grote Markt

♟ **Via Via Reiscafé** (map B2): Wolstraat 43. ☎ (03) 226 4749. Open 2pm–2am. The place that unites hikers from Leuven, Barcelona, Dakar, Indonesia or Honduras, who sip exotic cocktails and South American wines as world music plays in the background. The safari-style decor is dominated by a huge planisphere, with ethnic objects hanging on the walls. The menu, chalked up on a blackboard, features dishes that, like the clientele, come from all four corners of the world (most about 300BEF). The bar also serves as a travel library and travel agent, with talks, screenings, a board advertising apartment exchanges and travel suggestions.

❡ De Foyer (map B3–4): Komedieplaats 18. ☎ (03) 233-55-17. Open from noon to midnight on weekdays, from 11am to midnight on Saturday and from 11am to 6pm on Sunday. Closed late July. The lavish bar of Antwerp's Bourlatheater offers drinks and light meals beneath an enormous frescoed dome. You don't have to be seeing a play to come here (handy, as they're all in Dutch). There's a fantastic brunch on Sunday, followed by a dessert buffet, which you'll need to book a few weeks in advance. It's worth it.

❡ Grand Café Poejskin (map B2): Sint Nicolasplaats 3. ☎ (03) 231 2270. Open from 11am. Closed Monday. The decor is medieval, but this is not your average Antwerp hangout. At the 'Pushkin', you can wet your whistle with a vodka or stuff yourself with *blinis* beneath statues of the poet and Peter the Great. As you might have guessed, the landlord is of Russian descent. In summer, tables spill out onto the square behind Sint Nikolaskerk, off Lange Nieuwstraat.

❡ 't Elfde Gebod (map A2): Torfbrug 10. ☎ (03) 232 3611. Closed Tuesday. The 'Eleventh Commandment', as shown on a sign on the ivy-covered facade, apparently consists of plentiful eating and drinking. It's not a hard one to honour, given the extensive beer list and the praiseworthy menu of Belgian specialities. The tavern is next to the cathedral, which bristles with gargoyles, and church music plays in the background.

❡ De Muze (map B2): Melkmarkt 15. ☎ (03) 226 0126. Open from noon. A jazz café, and what must be the last bastion of flower power in Flanders. It's a real 1960s time warp, but it's cool, and you can listen to John Lee Hooker, Memphis

Slim and Johnny Griffin as you drink. Free concerts every Tuesday, Wednesday and Thursday, and some other evenings. A monthly programme of events is available.

❡ De Negen Vaten (map A2): Zand 1. ☎ (03) 226 3983. In a passage next to the Beveren Café. Open Monday, Wednesday, Thursday and Friday from 6pm, and on weekends and holidays from 2pm. Negen Vaten means nine barrels (port, sangria, etc.), and you'll find them tucked at the back of a delightful courtyard in this bustling Spanish-style *bodega*. Foodwise, we're talking tapas, with the Gypsy Kings on the stereo and more than a hint of *fiesta* in the atmosphere.

❡ De Vagant (map A2): Reynderstraat 25. ☎ (03) 233 1538. Open from 11am to 2am on weekdays, and from 1pm at the weekend. Right by the Jordaenshuis, this bar offers a staggering choice of gin aperitifs – or *digestifs*. Take a look at the upstairs room, which is decorated with advertisements and has views of the cathedral. There's also a smart restaurant on the first floor. If you're into gin, visit the shop across the way, which sells dozens of varieties.

❡ Pelgrom (map A3): Pelgrimstraat 15. ☎ (03) 234 0809. Open from noon. Food available. A labyrinth of candle-lit medieval cellars, with huge tables and little alcoves for romantic evenings. There's always a festive atmosphere, but it's overrun with Dutch tourists at weekends, and best avoided. Next door is **De Grotte Ganz**, a medieval restaurant with waiters in period costume and plenty of other gimmicks.

❡ Beveren Café (map A3): Vlasmarkt 2. ☎ (03) 231 2225. Open from noon. Closed Tuesday. This is a great place to get a taste of the real Antwerp, as the locals are perfectly happy to mix with tourists and sailors. Sparks can fly, and the pandemonium is liable to spill out into the street, but that's Antwerp for you.

♥ Den Engel (map A2): Grote Markt 3. ☎ (03) 233 1252. Open from 9am. A veritable institution, much frequented by tourists but not without its regulars, including 90-year-old Fonske, who was chosen to advertise De Koninck beer. If you need some food with your *bolleke* of beer, tuck into the homemade vegetable soup with bread (a mere 70BEF). And if there isn't enough atmosphere, try next door's Den Bengel.

♥ De Groote Witte Arend (map A3): Reyndersstraat 18. Open 11am–1am (later on weekends). Closed Tuesday. A private chapel and quiet courtyard far from the madding crowd, once home to the Daughters of the Charity of St Vincent-de-Paul. A haven of tranquillity, complete with classical music, paintings on the walls and a superb wine list. There's a beautiful terrace for summer drinking.

♥ Mie Katoen (map A1): Kleine Kraaiwijk 8. ☎ (03) 226 9203. Open from 10am. Near the Veemarkt, this wonderful brown café on the edge of the lively southern district is housed in a barn at the back of a courtyard, which serves as a garden-terrace in summer. Inside, as well as the bar, you'll find a reading room and Dadaist sculpture, as well as computers for Internet access.

♥ De Faam (map A2): Grote Pieter Potstraat 12. ☎ (03) 234 0578. Open from 4pm. A 30-something (and more) café that'll never go out of fashion. Everyone crowds round the bar to chat to future travelling companions.

GOING OUT

Live Music

– If you like jazz, you'll need to seek out **De Muze** (*see above*) or make your way to Jordaenskaai, where you'll find **Jabeau** (Zakstraat 19: map A2), which has concerts on Sunday afternoon. Alternatively, head for the Vlaamse Kaai district and **Café Hopper** (Léopold De Waelstraat 2. ☎ (03) 248 4933. Open from 10.30am), where you can enjoy free concerts on Sunday afternoon and Monday and Wednesday evening as you sip a heady cocktail – outside if it's sunny.

Nightclubs

– **Café d'Anvers** (map B1): Verversrui 15, Antwerpen 2000. Entry: 300BEF. This former cinema, its colonnades and balconies decorated with drapes and candelabra, is packed on Fridays and Saturdays between 11pm and 7am, when the best DJs in town lay down house and techno grooves for a fashionable crowd. Along with Brussels's Fuse, the most famous club in Belgium.

Het Swingcafé (map A2): Suikerrui 13–15, Antwerpen 2000. ☎ (03) 233 7075. Open noon–4pm. Head for the port, and the sound of music will guide your footsteps: blues on Friday and jazz on Sunday afternoon and evening. There are several concerts a week, and it's usually heaving.

– **Pacific**: Jan Van Gentstraat 7, Antwerpen 2000. ☎ (03) 248 2877. Open every day from 6pm. This huge former warehouse in the Vlaamse Kaai district is a great after-dinner venue, where you can eat, drink and dance with what seems like the whole of Antwerp.

– **Zillion**: Jan Van Gentstraat 4, Antwerpen 2000. ☎ (03) 248 1516. Open Thursday to Saturday from 10pm. Right next to Pacific, Zillion hints at the state of clubs to come: three rooms, 10 bars, a 1,250,000-watt light show, lasers, videos, animated robots, a zero-gravity dancefloor, a cybercafé, a restaurant, a jungle-style bistro and buckets of perspiration every night.

Klein Afrika

Some areas of Antwerp are renowned for their lively atmosphere, by day as well as by night. But there's quite a difference between the Latin quarter (trendy cafés near the Bourlatheater and the Meir) and the Greek quarter (a rather dodgy area that stretches from Sint Pauluskerk to the old port). You'll know you're in the latter when you pass pink- and red-neon-lit windows displaying women of various ages and races like merchandise. A similarly seedy district lies between Centraalstation and the coach station, called Klein Afrika ('Little Africa'), as most of the women on show here are African. Although, like its counterpart in Amsterdam, it's always heaving with tourists, there's one important difference: in the Dutch capital, organized prostitution is overseen by the authorities and regulated by the girls themselves. In Antwerp, however, the red-light district is largely uncontrolled. Russian and Albanian mafias, for example, shamelessly exploit these women, many of whom entered prostitution in order to escape the poorest parts of the former Soviet Union, or were tricked into the profession. So, think twice before you encourage such degradation.

WHAT TO SEE

There's far too much to see in one go, and if you're only here for two or even four days, you'll have to content yourself with scratching the surface. Monuments and museums have been grouped by district; the tourist office sells themed itineraries, such as the Rubens trail, of 'famous women' or port walks; but you may well prefer simply to follow your nose and stumble by chance across something that's not listed in any guidebook. Whichever option you choose, it's worth picking up a combined ticket for any three of the city's public museums (200BEF).

The District around the Grote Markt

★ **The Grote Markt** (map A2, **90**) and **guildhouses**: the city's main square is dominated by Jef Lambeaux's monumental bronze fountain, which shows Silvius Brabo throwing Druon Antigon's hand into the river. The triangular square is surrounded by the Renaissance houses of the guilds: No. 5, now the café Den Bengel, was once the House of the Coopers, whose patron saint, Matthew, stands on the top, No. 7, topped by a statue of St George, was the meeting house of the Archers, while No. 38 belonged to the Drapers and Roodenborgh House (No. 40) was owned by the Tanners, the Shoemakers and then the Carpenters. You can see why everybody wanted it – the baroque facade is the finest on the square.

★ **Stadhuis** (map A2, **90**): there are several tours a week at 11am, 2pm and 5pm, except on Thursday and Sunday. For more information, ☎ (03) 231

1333. Plans for the town hall were drawn up in Gothic style, but as the town was under threat at the time of its construction, the money was used to strengthen the ramparts. Antwerp finally got a more-or-less Renaissance-style town hall in 1564, although the central section, burned down by the Spanish in 1576 and immediately rebuilt, is in Flemish style. Since money was in short supply, several doorways were built into the ground floor, in the hope that they could be rented out to traders.

The three alcoves on the facade all contain statues. The first holds the Virgin Mary (who usurped Brabo at the end of the 16th century); the other two house Justice and Peace, the two virtues necessary for good government. There are also three coats of arms: that of the duchy of Brabant on the left, with Philip II's in the middle and the marquisate of Antwerp's sigil on the right. An imposing stairway leads into the 19th-century interior. Most of the treasure here was looted by Napoleon's troops as they strove to wipe out the memory of 'former tyrants'.

★ **Onze Lieve Vrouwekathedraal** (map A2, **91**): open Monday to Friday 10am–5pm, Saturday 10am–3pm and Sunday and holidays 1–4pm. Admission 60BEF; no entry during services. This splendid building has become the symbol of Antwerp. Covering an area of one hectare (2.5 acres), it's the biggest Gothic church in the Low Countries. It took nearly 200 years to build (1352–1521), although the original plans had it three times as big – big enough to illustrate the city's prosperity. Like all its counterparts, Antwerp's cathedral has had its ups and downs, including the great fire of 1517, pillaging by Protestants between 1566 and 1581, and the equally tender ministrations of the French Revolutionary armies. On a happier note, the repairs that followed each destruction have actually improved the building, while between 1973 and 1993, the whole structure was restored, strengthened and cleaned. The crypt was also revamped, with all its treasures brought out for display.

Pick up a brochure at the entrance before you start your tour – it describes all the outstanding features. The cathedral consists of a seven-aisled nave and 125 pillars. Among the countless statues and paintings are four masterpieces by Rubens, in a style that could almost be dubbed baroque realism: *The Raising of the Cross* (1610), *The Resurrection* (1612), *The Descent from the Cross* (1612) and *The Assumption* (1625–1626). The colours are dazzling (Rubens used pigeon blood in the preparation of his paint). Balthasar Moretus, the son-in-law of the printer Christophe Plantin, commissioned *The Resurrection*, while the other three were painted for the guilds. Look, too, at the beautiful triptychs, *Our Lady Pietà* and *The Legend of St Barbara*, and at the spectacular recumbent statue of Isabella of Bourbon. Then there's the 123-metre (450-foot) tower, with its 47-bell carillon. Finally, at the crossing of the transept, you'll see the cupola, whose characteristic onion-dome can be seen from afar.

★ **Quentin Metsys's spring** (map A2, **91**): a stone well located to the right of the cathedral entrance. The young Metsys, so the story goes, was a blacksmith. He fell in love with the daughter of a painter, who refused to accept Metsys as his son-in-law. Every time he finished a work, the painter would head for town and treat himself to a girl, leaving his daughter alone at home. One evening, she opened the door to Quentin Metsys, who added a fly to her father's newly finished painting. The girl's father, when he finally returned, was convinced that it was real, and tried in vain to shoo it away. In recognition of Metsys's talent, he allowed him to marry his daughter. Hence the inscription above the well: '*De smidt die uit liefde schilder werd*', which translates as 'The blacksmith who became a painter out of love'.

★ **Plantin-Moretus museum** (map A3, **92**): Vrijdagmarkt 22. ☎ (03) 233 0294. Open 10am–5pm. Closed on Mondays and holidays. Admission: 100BEF. This splendid aristocratic residence, with an 18th-century facade, houses one of the city's best museums. The French-born printer, Christophe Plantin, a native of Tours, set up his printing business here in 1549. His son-in-law, Balthasar Moretus, continued the work, as did his descendants, who abandoned the firm only in 1876. For three centuries, the same family printed and exported vast numbers of Bibles, breviaries and missals. The house has now been turned into a remarkable printing museum with an impressive private library and cabinet of prints. The proofreading and casting rooms contain countless old characters, including examples of the Plantin and Garamond fonts, which are still in use today. If this sounds a bit technical, it's not – and there's an excellent English-language brochure. Also on display are some extremely rare manuscripts and illuminated manuscripts, including maps by Gerardus Mercator, an important *Biblia Regia* in five languages (Hebrew, Greek, Latin, Syrian and Chaldean) produced in 1572, and a superb Gutenberg Bible. Throughout the house, the austere, classically Flemish atmosphere is suitably austere: it's like walking into a 17th-century painting of a Dutch interior, an effect heightened by the distant ring of the carillon. The walls are covered in Cordoba leather and hung with tapestries from Oudenaarde and Brussels, and other noteworthy features include lacquered tables inset with ivory, creaking parquet flooring and Delft-tiled fireplaces.

★ **Maagdenhuis** (the old orphanage; map B4, **93**): Lange Gasthuisstraat 33. ☎ (03) 223 5610. Open 10am–5pm, weekends 1–5pm. Closed Tuesday. Admission: 100BEF. For several centuries, this building was a home for orphaned girls: it's now the local social-security office. There's a museum on the ground floor, where beautiful paintings are set against a superb tiled interior with large oak cupboards. *An Orphan at Work* is by Cornelius De Vos, and there are two majestic 16th-century *Saint Jeromes*: one by Antoon Van Dyck, the other by Maarten De Vos. The collection of ceramic bowls from Antwerp, on show in the chapel, dates from the same period.

★ **Mayer Van den Bergh Museum** (map B4, **94**): Lange Gasthuisstraat 19. ☎ (03) 232 4237. Take tram Nos. 7, 8, 12 and 24, or bus Nos. 1 and 23, and get off at Nationale Bank. Open 10am–4.45pm. Closed Monday (except at Easter and Pentecost. Admission: 100BEF. This is a monument to Fritz Mayer Van den Bergh (1858–1901), an assiduous collector who spent a lifetime accumulating official titles while also amassing a huge hoard of art (paintings, sculptures, *faïences*, porcelain and so on). He painstakingly researched the history of every object, and soon developed a reputation as an art expert. His dream was to bring his collections together in a museum, an ambition that led him to mark 'Museum' against certain purchases in his personal catalogue. He had already acquired the mantelpiece that was to have featured in this hypothetical museum, but he died too without ever realizing his dream. His mother, however, carried on her son's work, and, not content with establishing the museum, set herself up as its curator– a most unusual step for a woman at that time.

The collections comprise 3,098 *objets d'art* and 2,000 coins and medals. Among the statues are splendid triptychs of the *Passion* and the *Annunciation*. The finest of the paintings is *De Dulle Griet* (Mad Meg) by Pieter Brueghel the Elder – a masterly allegory of madness, vice and stupidity, and above all a denunciation of the horrors of the Inquisition – but there are other treasures by Pourbus, Van Orley, Hals, De Vos, Tenlers and Jordaens. In Room 4, there's a triptych of the *Calvary* by Quentin Metsys (he of the stone well).

★ **Vleeshuis** (Butchers' House; map A2, **95**): Vleeshouwerstraat 38–40. ☎ (03) 233 64 04. Open 10am–5pm. Closed Mondays and some holidays. Admission: 100BEF. Still known as the Old Butcher's Market, or Meat Market, this house belonged to the Butchers Guild between 1503 and 1795. Constructed in 1500, and typical of the late Middle Ages, it's a great example of late Gothic, with alternating layers of stone and brick known as *speklagen* (layers of bacon). It was built to help clean up a neighbourhood dubbed *bloedberg* ('mountain of blood') because of the streams of blood that flowed here after the slaughter of animals. Until the Napoleonic era, the guild's families married among themselves to keep their wealth and power 'in the family', hence the presence of a marriage room. There's splendid furniture on the first floor, as well as paintings describing the history of the city and a collection of musical instruments that includes 16th- and 17th-century harpsichords manufactured by the Rucklers family. Finally, wend your way to the second floor, where you can admire the timberwork in the attic.

★ **Nationaal Scheepvaartmuseum** (National Maritime Museum ; map A2, **96**): Steenplein. ☎ (03) 232 08 50. Open 10am–4.45pm. Closed on Monday and some holidays. Admission: 100BEF. The museum is in the Steen, on Jordaenskaai, near the Grote Markt; you can't miss it. The history of the Steen is inextricably linked to the history of Antwerp. During the Roman era, farmers settled on this site, but the *castrum* (castle) didn't appear until the ninth century, while the ramparts on the side of the square were built four centuries later, by which time the Steen had become a prison: there's a cross, once used for the condemned's final prayers, at the entrance. Thanks to its strategic position on the Scheldt, it also had a military function, guarding the border between French territory and that of the Holy Roman Empire. In the early 16th century, Charles V, the Holy Roman Emperor, spent the princely sum of 1,732 pounds on reinforcing its fortifications. His motto, inscribed above the door, reads: '*Plus Oultre*' ('always more').

There's a curious statuette above the castle door: a male fertility god known as Semini. Ladies used to kiss its member, until the horrified Jesuits removed the offending appendage. It was eventually restored – only to vanish again a few years ago, prompting a group of outraged Antwerp citizens to found the Semini Society with the aim of restoring the god's masculinity. Today, Semini's pride and joy is carefully covered to prevent it from harm, and it's only revealed on the first day of spring, during a festival in honour of the statuette.

The maritime museum, a showcase designed to boost the city's status as an international port, was created in the late 19th century, when the city's authorities acquired the Steen. You could easily spend hours here: the first few rooms are devoted to art and coastal life, and include beautiful images of ships on Delft tiles (the *Duke of Wellington* is one example) or porcelain dishes. This theme is developed in another room, where you can see three late-19th-century square masts, ships in bottles and even one in a light bulb. A room devoted to the life of the sailor contains a meerschaum pipe in the shape of a head, a graphometer and a snake's head carried as a good-luck symbol for safe passage. Fishing is the theme in room 6, which houses an extraordinary early-20th-century rowing boat from Ostend. Room 7 is devoted to sporting and leisure activities, with a late-18th-century 1:10 scale model of a yacht and an express 'steam yacht'. In room 8, you'll find a model of a mid-19th-century naval engineering works, complete with craftsmen clutching their tools. After this, the focus switches to the history of navigation, and there are also displays devoted to the colonial era, when people travelled by steamboat to Matadi and the Belgian Congo. Look out for the figure of Tintin leaning on the railings of the *Prince Baudouin*.

Every room contains paintings depicting the city and its port through the ages. You'll find the most memorable in the splendid 18th-century-style council room: *La Balade d'Anvers vue de la rive flamande* ('Antwerp walk seen from the Flemish bank'), by Jean-Baptiste Bonnecroye (1618–76). If this whets your appetite for all things maritime, you'll find life-size ships are in the maritime park next to the Steen. Check the opening hours at the Maritime Museum.

★ **Ethnografisch Museum** (Museum of Ethnography; map A2, **97**): Suikerrui 19. ☎ (03) 232 0882. Open 10am–5pm. Closed Monday. Admission: 100BEF. An excellent collection of objects from other cultures, which kicks off with a superb display of faces from different civilizations. Hikers nostalgic for Kathmandu will recognise the 54 mandalas used in Buddhist meditation, while even those without any wanderlust will admire the host of masks, statues and costumes from around the world, as well as the background music illustrating the traditions of each civilization. You'll find a delightful Eskimo child's kayak on the first floor, and a wooden mask painted red, white and blue on the ground floor – nothing to do with Great Britain or France, as these are the colours donned by the Yakas of Zaire to close initiation ceremonies.

★ **Museum voor Volkskunde** (Museum of Folklore; map A2, **98**): Gilde-kamersstraat 2–6. ☎ (03) 232 9409. Open 10am–5pm. Closed Monday. Admission: 100BEF. The museum takes up several former guildhouses behind the Stadhuis. The guilds who occupied them were: No. 2, *De Roose,* the Fishmongers; No. 4, *De Vier Winden* (1579), the Chamber of Boatmen; and No. 6, *De Swane* (the Swan), which belonged to the furniture-makers. This delightful museum, housed on three floors, traces the history of crafts in Flanders and offers an insight into the history of daily life and everyday objects. The ground floor is used for temporary exhibitions, but also has a section devoted to the history of local festivals. Legendary Antwerp figures are on display, among them Druon Antigon, who dominates the staircase, while the first floor is dedicated to 'rites of passage' with objects relating to school, marriage, death and superstitions. There's also a life-size reconstruction of an old apothecary's dispensary. The second floor consists of displays of craftsmen's tools.

★ **Vlaeykensgang** (map A2, **99**): off the Oude Koornmarkt (leave it at No. 16). Rows of spotless little white houses with green shutters line these narrow roads. In the 16th century, they were home to the cobblers and bell-ringers, and it's an ideal spot to listen to a carillon concert.

And, if you still have time

★ **Dagbladenmuseum** (Newspaper Museum; map A3, **101**): Lombardenvest 6. ☎ (03) 233 3299. Open Friday to Sunday from 10am–5pm. Admission: 100BEF. A whistle-stop tour of newspaper production.

★ **Jordaenshuis** (map A3, **102**): Reynderstraat 4. Behind the 'City Boutique' (*see* 'Useful addresses', *above*). Open only for temporary exhibitions. Although he spent much of his life in Rubens's shadow, Jacob Jordaens had become Flanders's most important painter, and his house reflects this pre-eminence. When you enter the courtyard, look out for the onion-shaped cupola.

★ **Around the Grote Markt**: the little streets in this neighbourhood are packed with typical Antwerp guildhouses. Suikerrui ('Sugar Street'), which runs from the Stadhuis to the Steen, was once a canal used for transporting molasses from the Canary islands. No. 5 is the Hanse House, one of the city's first 'office blocks': the facade, with allegorical figures depicting the rivers of Germany, was sculpted by Jef Lambeaux. On the side, the Rubensesque statue of a beautiful woman is the sculptor's muse; his studio was in the next street, so he saw plenty of her.

From the Cathedral to Centraalstation

★ **Rubenshuis** (map B3, **103**): Wapper 9–11. ☎ (03) 232 4747. Open 10am–5pm. Closed Mondays and some holidays. Admission: 100BEF. This museum is much more than an art gallery: it gives you a chance to discover Rubens the man. Born in 1577 near Cologne, where his family had sought refuge, Rubens arrived in Antwerp when he was 12 years old. His early attraction to art and antiquity played a huge part in shaping his future. Rubens had various teachers, the most famous of whom was Otto Venius. Like other artists, he travelled to Italy, an experience that significantly influenced his painting – as well as the architecture of his house. Hoping to discover the secrets of the old masters, Rubens painstakingly reproduced their work. In 1598, he became the master of the guild of painters, known as the Guild of St Luke. The high point of his career came under the reign of the Infanta Isabella, when his studio enjoyed such international renown that he was chosen to represent the town and made royal ambassador. In 1609, Archduke Albert made him court painter in Brussels. From 1622, Rubens the ambassador took to the roads of Europe on a mission to calm the Thirty Years War (1618–48). He died in Antwerp in 1640, and was buried in Sint Jakobskerk. Although they weren't his equal, his star pupils acquired lasting reputations in their own right: Jan 'Velvet' Brueghel, Jacob Jordaens and Antoon Van Dyck. During his lifetime, the painter is believed to have produced 2,500 paintings. Painters during the baroque era worked according to strict and efficient plans, which were almost as important as the finished product. Whereas the artist came up with each project, much of the painting was done by pupils.

Rubens moved into this house in about 1615, on his return from Italy. You can wander around and enjoy the charms of the studio, which is overlooked by a mezzanine from where visitors admired (and chose) the paintings. When he received a commission, Rubens would prepare a sketch according to what he was paid, then arrange for the work to be carried out in his studio, sometimes doing it himself and often putting in the final touches with his own hand. Rubens's sketches adorn a great number of European museums. Here, however, you can see a very fine *Annunciation*; as always, the composition is dynamic, the colours are vibrant and the faces are wonderfully expressive. In the dining room, he is immortalized in a self-portrait painted at the height of his success.

The house illustrates his nostalgia for Italy, with *trompe l'oeils*, Renaissance busts and works from the studio of Mantegna and Vasari. As befitted his status as a member of the Flemish bourgeoisie, Rubens was also a collector. The art room on the ground floor houses antiques, scientific instruments and books.

In one of the first-floor bedrooms is a portrait of Rubens's second wife, Helen Fourment, who gave him five children in addition to the three he had had with his first wife. Each room seems more beautiful than the last, with Cordoba and Mechelen leather on the walls and no shortage of precious objects.

★ **Sint Pauluskerk** (map A1, **100**): north of the Grote Markt; enter via Nosestraat, off Veemarkt. Open from May to the end of September from 2–5pm; otherwise, the church is open for daily mass (10am–noon) and for weekend mass. It's best to check the exact times. Ravaged by fire in 1968, the church was painstakingly restored, with work finishing in 1993. There's a strong 18th-century baroque influence in the stalls, although they're elegant rather than majestic, and in the detail of the confessionals. More masterly are three paintings by Rubens: *The Disputation on the Nature of the Holy Sacrament* (1609), *The Adoration of the Shepherd*, and *The Flagellation* (1617), which belong to the 15 panels of the *Fifteen Mysteries of the Rosary*. Sint Pauluskerk is thought to be the only place where paintings by Rubens, Van Dyck and Jordaens still hang in their original location. Miraculously, the Rubens works were saved from the great fire of 1968 by the district's prostitutes. Make sure you stroll through the garden and courtyard, home to a calvary with finely carved figures: it's especially evocative at twilight, when a ghostly light descends on the church.

★ **Sint Jacobskerk** (map C2, **104**): Lange Nieuwstraat 73. ☎ (03) 232 1032. Take tram No. 3. Open from 1 April to 31 October from 2–5pm, and in winter from 9am–noon. Closed during services. Admission: 70BEF. The treasury is open on Pentecost Monday and 15 August. This flamboyant Gothic church, built in the 15th and 16th centuries, was in Rubens's parish. He married here, and is buried inside. He also chose the work that was to decorate his chapel, *Our Lady Surrounded by the Saints* (1634). There's also a host of marble effigies and a Jordaens painting, *Saint Charles Borromeo Caring for those Stricken by the Plague* (1655).

★ **Rockoxhuis** (map B2, **105**): Keizerstraat 12. ☎ (03) 231 4710. Take tram No. 3. Open 10am–5pm. Closed Monday. Admission free. Nicolaas Rockox, one of Rubens's many influential friends, served seven terms as burgomaster of Antwerp. He lived in this spectacular mansion, where you can see one of the Rubens paintings he commissioned: *Virgin and Child*, modelled by Rockox's wife and son. As you wander through the rooms, you get a feel for his life and tastes. He liked fine furniture, for a start: there's a magnificent 17th-century Antwerp cabinet and, in the dining room, a portrait of Rockox in the style of Van Dyck. Take a look at the Gothic tapestry (made in Brussels or Tournai) in 't Groot Saleth (the Great Room), the *Proverbs* by Pieter Brueghel the Younger and the *Travellers en route* by Jan Brueghel (in room 6). The free English-language booklet is excellent.

★ **Sint Carolus Borromeuskerk** (map B2, **106**): Hendrik Conscienceplein 12. ☎ (03) 232 2742. Opening hours vary, so it's best to check in advance, although there's a fair chance it'll be open if you just turn up. Closed on Sundays. Admission free, with a guided tour on Thursday at 3pm. Built for the Jesuits between 1614 and 1621, the church was ravaged by fire in 1718, and has been a law court and a hospital as well as a house of God. Frescoes by Rubens once graced the ceiling: sadly, they perished in the flames, and the 39 original sketches are now in England. The only sections of the church that escaped the fire are the tower and two side-aisle chapels: three Rubens paintings also survived, but these are in Vienna (the Austrians 'bought' them at the end of the 18th century, when they outlawed the Jesuits). It's still well worth visiting, however, for the sculpted wood panels along the lower part of the side walls, the confessionals and the view as you look down on the church from the top of the stairs. You should also visit the museum and the catacombs. Beside the church is Antwerp's wonderful public library, which, combined with the church, makes Hendrik Conscienceplein one of the most romantic spots in the city.

Before you move on, there's a hidden curiosity at 37 Wolstraat: go through the open door and you'll find yourself in a delightful courtyard in the middle of a complex of workers' houses (**Bontwerkersplaats**).

★ **Handelsbeurs** (map B3, **107**): Twaalfmaandenstraat. ☎ (03) 232 4310. There are entrances on Lange Nieuwstraat and Meir. Open Monday–Friday from 7.30am to 7pm. This 16th-century building was used as a stock exchange: it's now closed for business, but hosts cultural events and exhibitions. After a fire in 1858, it was rebuilt at the junction of four roads, with four high porches, one at each entrance, and serves as a kind of crossroads linking the four districts that surround it. The Gothic-Renaissance arcades and beautiful interior gallery display a hint of Moorish influence.

★ **Torengebouw** (map B3, **108**): Schoenmarkt. Built between 1929 and 1932, this art-deco structure is often described as Europe's first skyscraper. It was conceived as the country's first peasant savings bank: it's now the headquarters of KBC, one of Belgium's biggest banking groups. The distinctive tower – 93.75 metres (309 feet) high – is as much a feature of the city's skyline as the cathedral.

The District around Centraalstation

This area is in the midst of massive changes, with sordid patches rubbing against decidedly *chic* areas. There's also a strong Asian presence, with Korean karaoke and Chinese grocers.

★ **Antwerp Zoo** (map D3, **109**): Koningin Astridplein. On your right as you leave the Centraalstation. ☎ (03) 202 4540. Open from 9am–6.15pm in July and August, until 5.15pm between mid-March and mid-October and until

4.30pm in winter. Admission: 460BEF, with discounts for under-11s and over-60s. Established in 1843 as a research centre for natural sciences, this is one of the oldest zoos in the world. It began as a collection of stuffed birds, and now offers an incredible assortment of species from all over the world, including many at risk of extinction, such as the okapi and the Grauer gorilla. The Nocturama (nocturnal birds' and animals' house) and the sea lions' feeding time are especially popular, and can get very busy, so get there well before dinner starts if you want a good view. Above the cages, signs in Dutch warn you not to feed the animals. The enclosures are as interesting as their inhabitants: the giraffes live in an Egyptian temple, the birds of prey are in a beautiful cage and there's even a 'dairy'. The man who dreamed up these temple-like houses, Charles Servais, appears to have been under the influence of the mania for things Egyptian, a fashion introduced by Napoleon's men when they visited the Mamelouks. The zoo takes up 10 hectares (24.7 acres), but is located right in the middle of the city centre: there's also a vast breeding park near Mechelen, called Planckendael, where the animals live in a more natural environment.

★ **Centraalstation** (map D3, **110**): this splendid neo-baroque terminus was built between 1895 and 1905 by the architect Louis de la Censerie. It offers passengers a spectacular welcome to Antwerp, and its stained glass and magnificent dome make it well worth a detour if you don't arrive by train. The main materials used in this steel construction, which Leopold II described as 'a railway cathedral' are iron and glass, which allow for a great mix of styles, and indeed it has been mistaken for a church by tourists in the past. Pop upstairs to the buffet, which has been redecorated.

The District around Pelikaanstraat

Turn left as you leave the station and you'll find yourself in the Jewish quarter. **Pelikaanstraat** (map D4, **111**) is the preserve of the jewellery companies, many of which have shops beneath the railway bridge. Hassidic Jews and Indians make up the 20,000-strong community here. The former are devoutly orthodox, as you'll see from their black gabardines, the fur hats, the yamulkahs and the long, curling locks around their ears. You could almost imagine you're in front of Jerusalem's Wailing Wall.

Many of the Hassidic Jews are employed in the diamond business, and this area deals with a significant slice of the world's diamond trade: it's home to four diamond markets, and 1,500 diamond companies have their head-quarters here. Nearly 85 per cent of the world's uncut diamonds pass through Antwerp, bringing the area's annual turnover to a staggering $20 billion, or 7 per cent of Belgium's export income.

★ **Diamant Museum** (map D4, **112**): Lange Herentalsestraat 31–33. ☎ (03) 202 48 90. Fax: (03) 202 4898. Tours between 10am and 5pm, with diamond-cutting demonstrations on Saturday. As in all the province's museums, admission is free, but you may have to pay to see temporary exhibitions. Plans and maps, often with a high level of detail, tell the story of *steenjes* (little stones) and the many places where they are found. Then you can see how the uncut stone becomes a polished jewel, then gawp at a display of diamonds fit for a princess.

The District around the Old Port

★ **Brouwershuis** (Brewers' House; map B1, **113**): Adriaan Brouwerstraat 20. ☎ (03) 232 6511. Take tram No. 7 or bus No. 9. Open 10am–4.30pm. Closed Monday. Admission: 100BEF. Gilbert Van Schoonbeke, a 16th-century town planner, designed a huge number of buildings in Antwerp, and his Vrijdagmarkt and Stadswaag districts definitively changed the face of the city. He planned to set up 22 breweries along the Brewers' Canal, but the waters of the Scheldt turned out to be unsuitable for use in the brewing process, so he had water from the Herentals Canal brought in instead. A hydraulic mechanism was created so that the Brewers' House could distribute water: not only to the breweries, but also to the local population, who used to drink beer when there was a shortage of water. Eventually, this building became the Guild of Brewers' headquarters. The machinery (pumps, tanks and cogs), was exceedingly sophisticated for its time, while the upper floors boast splendid examples of Mechelen leather on the walls of the guild's meeting room, immortalized in a painting by Henri de Braekeleer, and Delft tiling in the hallway.

★ **Hessenhuis** (map B1, **114**): Falconrui 53. German shipowners gathered in this regal building. It's only open to the public when there are exhibitions showing (details available at the tourist office), but the 16th-century exterior is striking.

★ **Begijnhof** (map C2, **115**): entrance on Rodestraat, off Ossenmarkt. Open 7am–7.30pm. The Beguines are thought to have arrived here in 1544. Besides the usual complex of small houses, these virtuous women also built a hospital. When they weren't tending the sick, they prayed or made lace. The houses have evocative names, like St Joseph or St Bernadette Soubirou, and all have delightful little courtyards. The cobbled street and old church (it's nearly always shut) radiate peace and serenity.

The District around the Koninklijk Museum voor Schone Kunsten

Between the Vlaamse Kaai and the old port, you'll find some fascinating modern buildings, best viewed on the 50-minute boat tour of the quays aboard the *Flandria*. At the corner of Sint Michielskaai are the black-and-white zebra stripes of a block designed by the city's most controversial architect, Bob Van Reeth. Muhka (Museum of Contemporary Art) is in line with the new architecture, dubbed 'naval'.

If you're into the avant-garde, the Vlaamse Kaal is the place to go. Trendy restaurants and cafés have sprung up in the recently restored warehouses, and the value of the chic warehouse conversions is rising fast.

★ **Koninklijk Museum voor Schone Kunsten** (Fine Art Museum; off the map from A4, **116**): Leopold De Waelplaats. ☎ (03) 238 7809. Open from 10am–5pm. Closed on Mondays and some holidays. Take trams Nos. 4, 8, 12 and 24, or buses Nos. 1 and 23. Admission: 150BEF; free for under-18s, and on Friday, although not for temporary shows. It's worth hiring a portable CD player at the entrance, as you'll get excellent commentaries on every painting. Built in 1884 to replace the old museum, which the collections had outgrown, this grandiose building, somewhere between neoclassical and neo-Gothic in style, is the biggest landmark in this district. There's too much on show to give full details, so the list of paintings below includes the unmissable works and those that feature Antwerp: the layout tends to get rather mixed up during temporary exhibitions, so don't be surprised if you can't find everything in its rightful place.

Your tour starts on the first floor, in the company of the Old Masters.

– Room B: Pieter Brueghel the Elder, Vranckx's *Traveller Attacked by Soldiers* and an interesting *Young Man* of 1655 by Erasmus Quellin and J. Fijt (it was fashionable at this period to dress little boys as little girls), with Antwerp in the background.

– Room C: Rubens painted the *Parable of the Prodigal Son* in 1618. The titular theme takes up only a small part of the canvas: the highly detailed farmhouse in the background is really the focus of the painting. There's also an idyllic *Virgin with Parrot*, again by Rubens.

– Room D: Antwerp's history comes under the spotlight in *Abraham Grapheus*, by Cornelis De Vos. Grapheus was the dean of the Guild of Painters, or Guild of St Luke. He left little to remember him by apart from this portrait, which isn't exactly flattering, but at least illustrates the trappings of his guild.

– Room E: look out for two works with a Flemish flavour. In *Pleasures of the Ice*, Jean Griffier (1645–1718) illustrates the fleeting nature of existence, with skaters against a backdrop of a town – throughout our lives, it implies, we're skating on thin ice. *Flemish Festival*, by David Vinckboons (1576–1632), depicts 17th-century village life and, in terms of the sheer volume of detail, can be likened to Breughel's paintings of such festivities. The village featured here is probably Hoboken, now a suburb of Antwerp. Beggars wear the letter 'L' on their hats, indicating that they're suffering from leprosy. Painters often depicted the traditional pleasures of Flemish life via fairs or markets, as in another painting in this room, the anonymous, 17th-century *Village Fair*.

– Room G: six Flemish proverbs, painted with a wealth of witty detail by Pieter Brueghel the Younger. 'If a blind man leads another, they'll fall in the same water'; 'The fool gets the trump card – luck favours the foolish'; 'It's too late to damn the spring when the bull has already drowned'; 'Who knows why geese go barefoot?'; 'Everything has a reason for being in this world'; 'Trickery comes back to its master'.

– Room H: Jacob Jordaens is the star attraction here. *The Fruit Seller*, a studio copy of a scene depicted in a Brussels tapestry, is a double painting: a candle-lit scene of a young woman holding a bunch of grapes, and two lovers at her window. It's an allegory of day and night, of the desire for love and satisfied love. *The Young Sing as the Old Play Pipes* illustrates the popular saying that the old should set a good example for the young, while the pious scenes depicted in *The Last Supper* and *St Yves* reminded Jordaens's contemporaries that it was impossible to think about the devil, or hell, or tackle issues such as guilt, without anxiety.

– Room I: Rubens. The figures in *The Adoration of the Magi*, and the horned satyr and winged Death in *Venus fregida* (1614), are frighteningly realistic. *The Doubting of Thomas*, a triptych, was painted as an epitaph for Nicolaas Rockox and his wife. They appear on the side panels, sporting fine buckles and buttons, and dressed in velvet clothing. Judging by the way Rockox is fervently clasping his hands to his chest, he probably believed he had a fair chance of entering Paradise.

– Room M: the Brueghels. *The Bride's Dance*, by Pieter Brueghel the Elder, depicts the dances of the day. Other highlights include *Census at Bethlehem*, by Jan Brueghel, and Pieter Brueghel the Younger's *Visit to the Farm*.

– Rooms N and Q: Primitives from all parts, including Lucas Cranach, Fra Angelico and François Clouet. *Portrait of the Artist and his Wife*, by the Master of Frankfurt, is one of the first double secular portraits produced by the Guild of St Luke. The Flemish are represented by Jan Memling's *Jan of Candida* and Rogier Van der Weyden's *The Seven Sacraments*, an expression of medieval theology in which each sacrament has its own colour and own angel.

– Room R: two major works by Quentin Metsys, *Peter Gilles* and *The Lamentation of Christ*. Metsys was clearly influenced by Dürer and Leonardo da Vinci.

– Room T: interiors by Adriaan Van Ostade (1610–85), Jan Steen's lively *Marriage Banquet* and works by Rembrandt and Frans Hals.

– The 30 rooms on the ground floor are devoted to more recent works, with paintings by the Impressionists, Symbolists, Expressionists, Fauvists and Surrealists. *The Man in the Chair*, by Antwerp artist Henri de Braekeleer (1840–88), shows a man ensconced in his seat in a room in Antwerp's Brewers' House, hung with Mechelen leather. *Le Marteleur* (the metal-worker), by the sculptor Constantin Meunier (1831–1905), shows the artist's obsession with physical power. The Flemish Expressionists of the schools of Sint-Martens-Latem, near Ghent, include Émile Claus, Henri Evenepoel (*Louise in Mourning;* 1897) and, most important, Constant Permeke. Take a close look at his *Fisherman's Wife* (1920) and *The Hour of Vespers*, which evokes Van Gogh's treatment of this theme.

There are several works by James Ensor (1860–1940), the master of Gothic fantasy, who used traditional carnival masks to evoke anxiety: *The Intrigue* and *Skeletons Arguing Over a Hanged Man* illustrate his love of sardonic caricature. Among other celebrities on this floor – Magritte, Modigliani, Pierre Alechinsky and Albert Servaes – look out for Rik Wouters, the best of the Brabant Fauvists, who favoured realistic depictions of daily life. He's represented by *Woman Ironing* and *Education*, painted in bold pastel colours on a white canvas.

★ **Museum van Hedendaagse Kunst Antwerpen** (Museum of Contemporary Art; off the map from A3, **117**): Leuvenstraat 16–30. ☎ (03) 238 5960. Take bus No. 23 and get off at Waalse Kaai. Open 10am–5pm. Closed Monday. Admission: 150BEF, with student reductions. This former grain repository is a sober, functional building with an apricot facade. The vast rooms inside, all painted a brilliant white, are used for themed exhibitions and retrospectives of work by contemporary artists. There's a wonderful sense of space – a single work can occupy a 100-square-metre (1,000-square-feet) room. If you want to see the museum's permanent collection (from 1970 to the present day), visit during the summer, when the exhibition season is over. If the art proves too puzzling, you can pause for thought at the cafeteria.

★ **Museum voor Fotografie**; off the map, from A3, **118**): Waalse Kaai 47. ☎ (03) 216 2211. Take the No. 23 bus. Open 10am–5pm. Closed Mondays. Admission: free. Connoisseurs of the camera consider this as one of the world's best photography museums. There are temporary exhibitions on the ground floor, with the museum's collection displayed on the second floor: August Sander, Man Ray (*Les Galets*), Berenice Abbott (*Lyric Theater 100 Third Avenue Manhattan*), Robert Doisneau (*Femmes de ménage au marché*), Henri Cartier-Bresson (*Valence 1933*), William Klein (the famous *Bikini*, taken in Moscow in 1959), Brassaï and many more.

The first and second floors explore the history of the camera, beginning with 18th-century silhouette machines and a 'miragioscope', a 19th-century gadget that is, in effect, a camera obscura. During your tour, you'll learn how Belgians succumbed to the Parisian fashion for printing visiting cards that bore the owner's portrait, how popular photo exchange markets became, and how amateur collectors swapped photographs of celebrities to stick in their albums. Other gadgets include the ancestors of James Bond's devices: cameras that looked like revolvers, walking sticks, fob watches or hats. Finally, there's a reconstruction of a life-size portrait studio with a dark room.

★ **Mini-Antwerp** (off the map, from A3, **119**): Hangar 15A, level with Cockerillkaai. ☎ (03) 237 0329. Open 10am–6pm. Admission: 160BEF, with discounts for children. As the name suggests, the whole of Antwerp is (or will be) reproduced in miniature. It's a masterpiece of its kind. The Stadhuis and Steen are especially lifelike. At the end of your visit, a miniature *son et lumière* tells the story of Antwerp. It's a delightful excursion, and one that should be even more fun when it's finished.

MARKETS AND FAIRS

– **Bird market**: Sunday 8.30am–noon, near the Bourlatheater and the Rubenshuis. Lots of plants and antiques.

– **Vrijdagmarkt**: Wednesday and Friday morning on the square in front of the Plantin-Moretus Museum. Antiques and attic clearance sales.

– **Antwerp** fair: a six-week-long fair, starting at Pentecost and held between the Waalse Kaai and the Vlaamse Kaai.

– **Rubens market**: a week-long fair in mid-August, in period costume and with events around the cathedral.

– **Brocante**: 15 August. In Rubens-era costume, on the Grote Markt.

WHAT TO SEE ON THE OUTSKIRTS

★ **Cogels Osylei**: take the train to Berchem from the Centraalstation. If you're driving, follow the route under the Guldenvliesstraat bridge. You can also catch buses Nos. 6, 9 and 34, which go from the centre via Berchem station, or tram No. 11.

This area in the Zurenborg district, not far from Berchem station, leapt to prominence towards the end of the 19th century, when it was an agricultural area. Édouard Osy and John Cogels, the descendants of the area's landlord (a banker named Jean Osy, who became a baron), decided to build a goods station to create an industrial zone along the Antwerp–Brussels railway. But Antwerp's rapid population growth in the 1880s persuaded them that it would be more profitable to build housing – and they were right. Every member of the well-heeled Catholic bourgeoisie dreamt of acquiring a beautiful villa in an area that soon became known as *Kalottenwijk* ('district of the sanctimonious'). The style of the villas varied according to fashion: some were Jugendstil, others art nouveau and some a world-weary eclecticism. For the *sinjoren*, appearances were everything: you'd do well to concentrate on the exteriors, as the interiors are pretty banal. Many of these houses are fine examples of art-nouveau architecture and some were designed by renowned architects such as Jos Bascourt, a pupil of Victor Horta.

★ **Silver Centre, Sterkshof provincial museum**: Hooftvunderlei 160, Deurne 2100. In a park in the eastern suburbs. Take trams Nos. 10 and 24, or bus Nos. 18, 33, 41 and 42. Open 10am–5pm. Closed Mondays. Admission free. This beautiful castle houses collections of Belgian jewellery from the 16th to the 20th century and shows the processes of silver production, starting with the extraction of the mineral.

★ **Linkeroever** (left bank of the River Scheldt): to get there by car, take one of the tunnels under the Scheldt: the Waaslandtunnel, which starts near the Italielei, or, more centrally, the Kennedy tunnel. If you take one of the trams that goes under the Scheldt (Nos. 2 and 15), get off at Frederik Van Eeden. By bike or motorbike, use the Sint Anna tunnel, which you reach via the Sint Jansvliet escalators or lift (map A3, **120**). This tunnel is 572 metres (1,887 feet) long, with a diameter of 4.74 metres (16 feet). If you're claustrophobic, avoid this trip, especially at night, although it's no worse than taking the Channel Tunnel.

Once you're over, you'll be rewarded with a spectacular panorama of central Antwerp. Architecturally, however, this area, the tunnel and the neighbouring beach, known as the Sint Anna district, leave something to be desired. You'd expect better, given that a 1933 competition invited architects to submit plans for a new town that was to house 50,000 people. Le Corbusier entered, but his project was deemed too ambitious. Nonetheless, the Antwerp locals like to come here to relax in the cafés and restaurants along the beach, from where they can enjoy the view.

★ **Openluchtmuseum voor Beeldhouwkunst St Middelheim Antwerpen** (open-air sculpture park): ☎ (03) 827 1534. Take buses Nos. 17, 27 and 32. From October to late March, open 10am–5pm; in April and September, 10am–7pm; in June and July, from 10am–9pm. Admission free, except during temporary exhibitions. You can pick up a map of the park and its sculptures at the ticket office next to the entrance (there's a lot of traffic on the Middelheimlaan, so take care crossing the road). The idea for this museum, established in 1950, grew out of a sculpture exhibition. The 20-hectare (50-acre) park, with a charming castle, provides the backdrop for 300 statues from around the world. The highlights are Henry Moore's *King and Queen*, Auguste Rodin's *Monument à Balzac* (1892–1897), Alexander

Calder's *Dog* (1958), which is best viewed from a distance, Ossip Zadkine's *Orpheus* (1956) and Pablo Gargallo's *Prophet* (1933). There are also pieces by Aristide Maillol, Hendrik Laurens and Rik Wouters. During special exhibitions, the park hosts works on loan from other galleries and museums. The most fragile statues are housed in a pavilion at the back of the park.

THE PORT OF ANTWERP

– **By car**: using a map (Havenroute, available at the tourist office), navigate your way here by following the signs to villages and industrial estates. It's not particularly easy, but it's well worth the effort. Antwerp's gigantic port is a surreal affair, with huge, lost-looking cranes rising up among the refineries, drawbridges suddenly appearing in your path, and even a little church set in a pleasant green space, a reminder that, in days gone by, the polders stretched into the distance as far as the eye could see.

– **By boat:** you can go on several excursions on the *Flandria* boats: Steenplein, 2000 Antwerpen. ☎ (03) 231 3100.

● *50-minute excursion*: from April to the end of October. The boat leaves from the quay next to the Steen every hour between 1pm and 4pm. Get your tickets when you embark (it's worth arriving a bit early in high season): you can also buy combined tickets for the boat trip and the zoo. During the excursion, you'll see the city's legendary docks, enjoy some fine views of the city and get a feeling for the architecture of Antwerp.

● *Three-hour excursion*: daily from the end of May to the end of August, at 2.30pm except on Wednesday in May and June; in April, September and October, weekends only, departing from Londenbrugkaai. Follow signs for *Flandria*, which you'll see on the quaysides.

● *Boat trip by candlelight*: Friday and Saturday evenings from July to the end of September, Saturday only in May and October. Book in advance for this three-hour dinner cruise. It's a bit pricey and a tad old-fashioned.

● *Day trip*: takes you right into Holland, or to the sea. Destinations Ostend, Vlissingen, Veere Goes and Delft. Details available at the *Flandria* offices. One option worth considering is a bargain ticket that includes the day cruise and a trip to the Zoo.

Although Antwerp is 88 metres (289 feet) above sea level, it is Europe's biggest port after Rotterdam, and is vital to the national economy. Napoleon did a lot to improve its prospects, hoping to create 'a pistol aimed at the heart of England': 2,000 workers shovelled away to construct the Bonapartedok and Willemdok, which formed his naval base. Two centuries have passed, and there's no more activity in these docks. It all goes on in the new sections of the port, which are still growing, spreading north towards the Dutch border, up the hill and towards the coast.

Massive locks have been built to provide access to ever bigger vessels. Berendrecht is the largest lock in the world: 500 metres (1,650 feet) long, 68 metres (224 feet) wide and 19.5 metres (64 feet) deep. Several polder villages made way for these extensions, and there have been many complaints about the construction of the new docks, with their towering industrial centres. But the industrial sector of the port, together with the docks, employs 70,000 people. It's a sprawling beast, with 127 kilometres (80 miles) of landing stages and 2,100 hectares (5200 acres) of docks, where 16,000 arrivals result in the loading and unloading of 110 million tons of merchandise ever year. Then there are the refineries, and the presence of the petrochemical and chemical industries – the latter provides Antwerp with one of the heaviest concentrations of companies in the world.

LILLO

This is the last of the polder villages in the port, happily unchanged. Turn left at the Royersluis lock and continue left along the Scheldt. You'll see Lillo on the left. It's a bit tricky to find, and there's no public transport, but the bell tower will help you get your bearings. There's something very poignant about this little port, which has stood firm against the rising tides of industry.

★ **Poldermuseum**: Tolhuisstraat 14–16. ☎ (03) 568 1600. Admission: 50BEF. Explains the history of the village and the surrounding area.

MECHELEN (MALINES)   76,000 inhabitants

Mechelen used to be the capital of the Low Countries, so it's no surprise that it has a host of historic buildings and a world-famous carillon. It's also famous for furniture, tapestries, asparagus, the *coucou de Malines* (chicken cooked in a clay oven), cauliflower and Gouden Carolus, the queen of brown beers. The city's most distinguished citizen is the Belgian Primate, Cardinal Daneels. You'll need plenty of time to see the city properly. The only disturbing thing about this place is that 30 per cent of its residents voted for the Vlaams Blok, the anti-democratic Flemish nationalist party, in the 1999 elections.

GETTING THERE

– **By train**: trains leave Antwerp every 30 minutes on the Amsterdam–Brussels–Charleroi line. From Brussels, take the same line.

– **By car**: take the Antwerp–Brussels E19. The Mechelen Noord (North) and Mechelen Zuid (South) exits will take you on to the bypass.

A Short History

Mechelen developed as a result of the cloth trade, and by the end of the Middle Ages, had become the capital of the 17 provinces of the Low Countries. In 1473, Charles the Bold established his Court of Accounts here, and 30 years later, the town was elected as the seat of the Grand Council, a governing body of the Low Countries. At the beginning of the 16th century, Margaret of Austria built her palace here, but when Maria of Hungary moved the court to Brussels in 1530, Mechelen's glory began to wane. The town never got over it, and suffered further during the 'Spanish Fury' of the late 16th century, after which it settled into prosperous provincialism The inhabitants are known as 'moon extinguishers' *(mane-blusser)*, a curious name that dates back to 1684. After a night on the tiles, a local was wending his way home when he thought he saw the tower of Sint

Rombouts Kathedraal on fire. Hearing his cries, the whole town turned out with buckets of water. Then the moon appeared above it, and everyone realised that the fire was nothing more than the orange glow that had framed the top of the tower.

USEFUL ADDRESSES AND INFORMATION

Postcode: 2800.
🛈 Tourist office: Stadhuis. ☎ (015) 297655. Fax: (015) 297653. Open 8am–6pm on weekdays and 9.30am–12.30pm and 1.30–5pm on weekends. There are guided tours in several languages at 2pm on weekends and daily in July and August. Look out for the curious information kiosk at the entrance.

✉ Post office: Grote Markt. Open 8am–6pm.
■ Public telephone: at the station.
■ Bike hire: in the Vrijbroekpark, a mile from the centre if you leave via Brussels' old gateway (Brusselspoort).

WHERE TO STAY

There are no cheap hotels in Mechelen, so your best bet is to find a B&B, a list of which can be obtained from the tourist office.

Youth Hostel

🛏 De Zandpoort: Zandpoortvest 70. ☎ (015) 278539. Fax: (015) 278540. This new hostel has 115 beds and prices range from 510–820BEF per person per night. Meals are also available, from 170–3,000BEF.

B&Bs

🛏 Masia del Viento: Beatrijsstraat 123, Sint Katelijne Waver 2860; 5 kilometres (about 3 miles) from Mechelen and 400 metres (400 yards) from the station). ☎ (015) 317222. From 1,700BEF for two, including a copious breakfast. Set menus between 500BEF and 900BEF. A small, Spanish/Flemish farmhouse in a peaceful village, with multi-lingual hosts, a family atmosphere and furniture that's an interesting mix of the rustic and modern. There are three pretty rooms, with a shared bathroom. A bit pricey, perhaps, but a bargain compared to any of Mechelen's hotels. Non-smoking.

Rented studios

🛏 Fran Van Buggenhout: Straatje Zonder Einde 3. ☎ (015) 209721. Email: fran.ronny@skynet.be. From 1,600BEF to 2,100BEF per night. Cosy, light and modern studios in a little street right in the centre opposite St Rombouts Kathedraal. A great place from which to enjoy the carillon concerts.

WHERE TO EAT

☆☆ Moderate

✕ Graspoort Eetcafé: Begijnenstraat 28. ☎ (015) 219710. A café-bar open every day from 11.30am. It's hard to decide between the daily specials (270BEF) and the set menus, which look good, especially dishes with prawns. You can sit outside in summer. An idyllic spot for listening to the Monday-evening carillon concert.

WHERE TO GO FOR A DRINK

❦ **De Gouden Vis**: Nauwstraat, near Vismarkt. This former fishmonger's, with a handsome art-nouveau facade and a small garden, has an attractive interior with carefully chosen lighting and bevelled mirrors behind the bar. The walls are adorned with posters advertising liqueurs.

❦ **Taverne Royal**: Grote Markt 29. ☎ (015) 206881. The viscous nature of Gouden Carolus makes it a nourishing and tasty aperitif. The locals drink it over a game of billiards at all hours of the day.

❦ **Borrel Babbel**: Sint Romboutshof (a little square behind the cathedral). Open Monday to Saturday from 11am until late into the night, and Sunday from 2pm. This café, Mechelen's smallest, specializes in gin. The terrace is a great place to sit in the evening, when you can soak up the lively atmosphere of the square, which is full of little cafés and restaurants.

WHAT TO SEE

★ **Grote Markt**: a square full of interesting architecture in a variety of styles, partly because the town decided to subsidize the replacement of wooden with stone houses to avoid the spread of fire. The resulting renovations took place over several centuries: the oldest building, now a Kredietbank, is Gothic. The baroque buildings are the easiest to identify, thanks to their scrolls and curls.

– **Stadhuis**: a former 14th-century cloth hall, which is a copy of the one in Bruges. The interior is worth a look, but you'll have to take a guided tour. The splendid wooden stalls are a reminder that Mechelen was a furniture-producing town.

– The 14th-century **burgomaster's house** (*steen*) lies south of the Grote Markt. It's been renovated, and was set to become a fine-art gallery when this guide went to press. Beyond lies the **Ijzerleen**, an elongated square lined with handsome bourgeois facades that was built when the canal underneath it was filled in. Metal balustrades are all that remain of the old waterway.

– **Statue of Margaret of Austria**: in the centre of the Grote Markt.

★ **Sint Romboutskathedraal**: also on the Grote Markt. Open 9am–noon and 1–5pm. Guided tours of the cathedral and tower at 2.15pm on weekends from Easter to the end of September, at 7pm on Monday from June to the end of September, and daily at 2.15pm in July and August. A splendid example of Brabant Gothic architecture, although its tower was never finished. Back in 1452, Mechelen planned to build a 167-metre (550-foot) tower that was to be the highest tower in the world. But the money ran out less than a century after work started, leaving the tower at a mere 97 metres (320 feet). During the turbulence that followed the Reformation, the Church had less cosmetic things on its mind. There's a model that shows what the tower would look like were it raised to its full height. In the 16th century, the warden lived in the upper gallery. From here, he could sound the alarm if there was an attack on the city, and alert the citizens to the risk of fire by holding up his lantern in the direction of the blaze. This tower does hold one world record, though: it houses a 49-bell carillon. Works of art in the cathedral include the *Martyrdom of Saint Sebastian*, by Michel Coxie.

Not far from the cathedral, near the Wollenmarkt, is the **Abdij van Sint Truiden**, where old, ivy-clad walls are reflected in the canal. There's a fine view from the bridge.

★ **The Carillon School**: Frederik de Merodestraat 63. Visits can be arranged at the tourist office. A charming, rococo-style building houses the only school of its kind in the world. Students from across the globe study here for six years, and as many as 60 sign up for the course each year. You may even be treated to a concert, but as pupils train on the carillons of the school, the museum and Sint Rombouts Kathedraal, it's pretty much impossible to avoid the sound of them practising. The tradition of attending carillon concerts began in Mechelen. In 1930, Monday-evening concerts attracted nearly 30,000 people, with people flocking from as far away as Paris on trains laid on for these events. The best place to listen to the carillon concerts is the Minderbroedersgang (to the right of Sint Rombouts Kathedraal). They take place every Monday at 8.30pm between June and mid-September (*see* 'Other Events').

City Walk

★ **Margaret of Austria's Palace**: Keizerstraat 20. The palace where Margaret of Austria lived during the regency of the early 16th century. It's not open to the public, but you can enter the splendid Gothic courtyard during office hours and on some weekends. The facade overlooking the street dates from the Renaissance, while Margaret lived on the first floor above the colonnades. The throne room (to the right as you come in from the street) now houses the Justitiepaleis (law courts).

★ **Sint Peter en Pauluskerk**: Keizerstraat. Open every day. In 1670, the Jesuits dedicated this church to one of their number, Saint François-Xavier. The oak pulpit represents the continents as they were then perceived, each symbolized by iconic characters and animals.

★ **Sint Janskerk**: Sint Jansstraat. Open Sunday afternoons in July and August. A Gothic church whose main attraction is Rubens's *Adoration of the Magi*, a triptych in which he painted his first wife, Isabella Brant, as the Virgin Mary.

★ **Groot en Klein Begijnhof**: on either side of the Sint Katelijnestraat, the road that leads to the cathedral. There's a pleasant signposted walk, during which you can pause to look at the pretty houses in Schrijnstraat, Twaalf Apostelenstraat and Krommestraat.

★ **Haverwerf** (Quay of Oats): don't miss three fantastic houses. The green one, Paradise House, is a Gothic building with a bas-relief on the front representing Adam and Eve's flight from Eden. The house on the left, The Little Devils, is in Renaissance style, while the third, the red house, is baroque. It dates from 1669, and is called Sint Jozef.

★ **Stedelijk Museum Hof Van Busleyden et Beiaardmuseum** (Commune and Carillon Museum): Frederik de Merodestraat 65–67. ☎ (015) 202004. Open 10am–noon and 2–5pm. Closed Mondays. The museum houses some interesting paintings displaying incidents in the history of the city, and Room 10 houses a wooden *mappa mundi* dated 1630. In Room 19, there's an anonymous late-17th-century painting illustrating the *Work of the Nuns of the Mechelen Begijnhof* in 46 little scenes. Bells of all shapes and sizes are on display in the other wing of the museum: church carillons, spherical bells, practice carillons, which show all the mechanisms, and so on.

★ **Onze Lieve Vrouw van Hanswijck**: a baroque church at the Leuven Gate, with a glass dome.

★ **Gaspard De Wit Royal Tapestry Factory** : Schoutetstraat 7. A five-minute walk from the Grote Markt and Sint Rombouts Kathedraal. Guided tour at 10.30am on Saturday, except in July and between Christmas and New Year. Pick up a timetable at the tourist office, or phone the factory: ☎ (015) 202905. Admission: 200BEF. This is the place to go if you want to learn how to distinguish an Amiens tapestry from a Brussels or Flemish one. You'll learn to guess the date, and even identify the workshops where they were made. The materials include silk and wool, with gold and silver threads, and you can see how the colours and size of the designs evolved over the centuries. Perhaps the most exceptional exhibit is *L'Allégorie du temps* (16th-century Tournai or northern France), which illustrates the maxim 'If you wish to win honours, you need to see the past and present, and foresee the future'. *L'Offrande d'Isaac*, after Simon Vouet, was probably made in Amiens in 1640. You finish on the second floor, among the contemporary works. In the workshops, meanwhile, you can watch a demonstration of tapestry-weaving and restoration.

★ **Speelgoed** Museum (Toy Museum): Nekkerspoelstraat 21. Leave Mechelen and head for Heist op den Berg: you'll see the museum next to Nekkerspoel station, after you've passed under the railway line. ☎ (015) 557075. Open 10am–5pm. Closed Mondays. Admission: 180BEF, with child discounts. Every toy from yesteryear is here to make today's children, not to mention grown-up collectors, wistful: dolls, teddy bears, mechanized toys, puppets, Meccano, puzzles, Monopoly and even King Leopold III's son's bicycle. Upstairs, there's a museum devoted to local folklore and agriculture.

★ **Museum of Deportation and Resistance**: de Stassartsraat 153. ☎ (015) 290660. Open 10am–5pm, Friday from 10am–1pm. Closed Saturday. The barracks that were used as an assembly point and transit camp for the deportation of Jews to Auschwitz now house poignant displays recalling the removal and extermination of Belgium's Jews by the Nazis.

★ **Technopolis**: Technologielaan. ☎ (015) 342020. Open every day from 10am–5pm. Admission: 290BEF. A new science and technology museum, with an interactive approach that should appeal to children and teenagers. You can fly a virtual plane, make a film, ride a bike on a high wire, build dams or electric circuits and so on.

OTHER EVENTS

– **Hanswijck Procession**: on the Sunday before Ascension Day. The oldest historical/religious procession in Belgium.

– **Carillon concert**: Monday at 8.30pm from June to September; otherwise Saturday at 11.30am, Sunday at 3pm and Monday at 11.30am.

WHAT TO SEE IN THE SURROUNDING AREA

★ **Dierenpark Planckendael**: Leuvensesteenweg 582, Muizen 2812. Located four kilometres (2.5 miles) southeast of Mechelen. ☎ (015) 414921. Fax: (015) 422935. Take the boat from Mechelen at Colomabrug, near the station: boats leave every 30 minutes between 9am and 6pm from April to mid-October. Open 9am–4.45pm in winter, and until 6.30pm in summer. Admission: 430BEF, with reductions for children and senior citizens. A vast park with a play area, used as a breeding ground for Antwerp Zoo.

LIER
32,000 inhabitants

Often nicknamed 'Little Bruges' or 'Lierke Plezierke' (Lier Little Pleasure), Lier is an essential detour when you leave Antwerp. The canals and Begijnhof are typical of Flemish towns, but the Zimmer Tower and the Grote Markt are delightfully unique. Indulge yourself with the local speciality, Lierse Vlaaikens: tasty tartlets based on a secret recipe

GETTING THERE

– **By car**: 17 kilometres (11 miles) from Antwerp on the Liège (Luik)–Hasselt motorway, the E313. Take exit No. 19, Massenhoven, then follow the signs for Lier. Use the Stadhuis car park.

– **By train**: trains leave Antwerp every hour and Brussels every 30 minutes. Change at Mechelen.

A Short History

The first mention of Lier occurs in the seventh century. According to legend, Saint Gummarus so loved the water that he established his hermitage here. Lier acquired town status in 1212, and has prospered ever since. Local heroes include the painter Isidore Opsomer, the writer Felix Timmermans and the clock-maker Louis Zimmer. When Lier's citizens were asked to choose between a university and a cattle market, they chose the latter, thereby earning the unflattering nickname of *Schappekopen* (sheep's heads).

USEFUL ADDRESSES AND INFORMATION

Postcode: 2500.
ℹ Tourist office: Stadhuis. ☎ (03) 488 3888. Fax: (03) 488 1276. Open 9am–12.30pm and 1.30–5pm.

Closed weekends in winter. List of B&Bs available.
■ Bike hire: at the railway station, Leopoldplein 32. ☎ (03) 480 0236.

WHERE TO STAY

🛏 Hof Van Aragon: Mosdijk 4. ☎ (03) 491 0800. Fax: (03) 491 0810. The town's only hotel is pleasantly situated beside a little canal. Ask for one of the refurbished rooms – they're a bit more expensive (2,200–3,150BEF), but more comfortable. Breakfast is an extra 400BEF.

WHERE TO STAY IN THE AREA

☆ Budget

🛏 Youth hostel 't Pannenhuis: Wijngardberg 42, Nijlen 2560, between Lier and Herentals. ☎ (03) 411 0733. Fax: (03) 411 0725. Closed between mid-November and mid-February. Basic rate per night: 420BEF. Take a train to Nijlen from Lier. Set in an attractive wooded area, this hostel offers 64 beds and three family rooms for grown-up hikers.

WHERE TO EAT

✗ Van Ouytsels Koffiehoekje: Rechstraat 27. ☎ (03) 480 2917. On the left-hand side of the main road leading from Grote Markt to Sint Gummaruskerk. Open 9am–7pm. Closed for lunch on Wednesday and Sunday. Light meals are served in this old coffee house, which still roasts its own beans. A great place for coffee and cakes.

✗ Tavern-restaurant De Fortuin: Felix Timmermansplein 7. ☎ (03) 480 2951. Open 11am–10pm. Closed Monday. Go for the tavern option, as it's much more expensive to dine in the restaurant (set menus from 850BEF). A great place for waterside eating in summer, with exceptionally pleasant staff who'll offer you a coffee or liqueur on the house.

WHAT TO SEE

★ **Grote Markt**: leave your car, as everything's within easy walking distance. Pause to admire the facades of the old guildhouses.

★ **Stadhuis**: a rococo building in the middle of the Grote Markt, on the site of an old grain market. The Gothic belfry, dated 1369, now houses exhibitions.

★ **Begijnhof**: free admission. You can arrange to see the church at the tourist office. Take Eikelstraat from the Grote Markt, passing Gevangenenpoort (Prisoners' Gate), then carry on until you come to Begijnhofstraat. Built in the 13th century, with 17th-century restorations, this is one of the finest Begijnhofs in the country. Start by looking at the Flemish baroque church, then stroll around the streets, where the old houses will give you some idea of the Begijnhof's golden age. Note the fine Calvary and Way of the Cross.

★ **Zimmer Tower**: on the Zimmerplein, between Grote Markt and the Begijnhof. In summer, open 9am–noon and 1–6pm; in winter, 10am–noon and 2–5pm (to 4pm between November and February). Admission: 60BEF. Eleven clock faces representing the earth and the moon adorn the facade, and automatic figures appear at noon on the right-hand side of the tower. The 'astronomic workshop' and planetarium are located inside, while the room next door, Zimmer's workshop, houses an astronomical clock. This is a fun place to visit, especially if you like scientific puzzles.

★ **Communal Museum**: Florent Van Cauwenberghstraat 14. Open 10am–noon and 1.30–5.30pm. Closed Monday, Friday and from November to March. The main draw is Pieter Brueghel the Younger's *Flemish Proverbs* (1607), which depicts 85 proverbs in one fell swoop. Jan Steen's *Vechtende boeren* (Brawling Peasants) and Constant Permeke's *Pilgrims* are more intimate, and, though painted centuries apart, are typical of northern Flemish art. Look out for works by Edgard Tytgat, Maurice De Vlaminck and Henri De Braekeleer, as well as furniture and an assortment of precious objects.

★ **Sint Gummaruskerk**: on the Grote Markt. Open 9am–5pm (to 4pm in winter). An excellent example of flamboyant Flemish Gothic (1425–1540). Note the lacy effect of the rood screen, delicately carved in pale sandstone, and admire the Way of the Cross and the beautifully preserved stained-glass windows.

FESTIVAL

– **Sint Gummarus procession**: usually takes place on the second Sunday in October.

HERENTALS   25,000 inhabitants

GETTING THERE

– **By car**: take the Antwerp Ring and join the E313 towards Liège, then take exit 20 or 22, Herentals. Head for the town centre and leave your car on the Grote Markt.

– **By train**: trains leave every hour from Antwerp.

USEFUL ADDRESS AND INFORMATION

Postcode: 2200.
🚉 **Railway station**: ☎ (014) 212-370.
🛈 **Tourist office**: Dienst Toerisme VVV, Grote Markt 41. ☎ (014) 219088.

WHERE TO EAT

✕ **Posterijen**: Grote Markt 13. Open 10am–1pm. Closed Tuesday. In summer, you can eat in the pleasant outdoor area. In season, the chef goes over the top with asparagus dishes.

WHAT TO SEE

★ **Grote Markt**: assuming that restoration works have finished, you can visit the delightful Stadhuis, once the headquarters of the Drapers' Guild. It has a 50-bell carillon.

★ **Waldetrudiskerk**: contact the tourist office if you want visit the interior of this Brabant Gothic church, which has a fine altarpiece by Pasquier Borremans, beautifully carved choir stalls and a 17th-century square tower.

★ **Begijnhof**: with your back to the post office, turn left out of the Grote Markt and take the fourth street on the right, Begijnenstraat. Dating from the 17th century, this is one of the oldest Begijnhofs in the Kempen region. The oldest houses are huddled around the Begijnhof church, which is often shut. The museum is open on weekends in July and August from 2–5pm.

GEEL   33,000 inhabitants

Geel has been famous for its care of the mentally ill since time immemorial. Saint Dimpna, the daughter of the King of Ireland, who had to flee to escape the advances of her own father, is its patron saint. The king caught up with her in Geel and cut off her head. The moral the simple folk of the area drew from this was that Dimpna had been attacked by a lunatic. They prudently resolved to care only for harmless patients, who are looked after in the community and live with local families.

GETTING THERE

– **By car**: take the Antwerp Ring and join the E313 towards Liège, then take exit 20 or 22, marked 'Herentals'. Follow the signs to the town centre.

– **By train**: Trains leave every hour from Antwerp, with a change at Herentals.

USEFUL ADDRESS

Postcode: 2440.
🖪 **Tourist office**: Stadhuis. ☎ (014) 570952. Open 8am–noon and 1– 3.30pm, from 10am–3pm at weekends.

WHERE TO STAY IN THE AREA

🛏 **Youth hostel Boswachterhuis**: Papendreef 1, Westerlo 2260, between Geel and Aarschot. ☎ and fax: (014) 547938. Closed from mid-November to the end of February. Basic rate per night: 420BEF. This hostel in the heart of the countryside has 80 beds. Bike hire is available.

WHAT TO SEE

★ **Sint Dimpnakerk, museum, and hospital**: Gasthuisstraat 3, opposite the museum on the Mol road. The church is rarely open, but if you get the chance, take a look at the magnificent retables of St Dimpna and the 12 apostles, and at the mausoleum of Jean III, the count of Mérode. The Renaissance-style room for the sick eventually proved too small, so the local population were asked to put them up.

– **Museum**: ☎ (014) 591443. Open from April to the end of September on Wednesdays, Thursdays and Sundays from 2pm to 5.30pm. Admission: 75BEF. On display are objects relating to Saint Dimpna and the old hospital, as well as daily life in the old infirmary. You can also see the church's treasures.

❢ There's a great tavern, **Gasthuishove**, in the old barn next to the hospital. It's open from 10am from Tuesday to Sunday.

TURNHOUT   38,000 inhabitants

The capital of the Kempen, northeast of Antwerp, is famous for playing cards, of which it turns out millions of decks a year.

USEFUL ADDRESS

Postcode: 2300.
🅱 **Tourist office**: Grote Markt 44. ☎ (014) 443355. Open 9am–4.30pm. You can pick up a useful brochure on camping in the Kempen.

WHERE TO STAY

☒ Budget

🛏 **Camping Balse Hei**: Roodhuisstraat 10. ☎ (014) 421931. Prices 490–650BEF, depending on the season. Only a couple of miles from the centre of Turnhout, this is an ideal spot for cyclists. It's an attractive site surrounded by fields and woods, and there's a lake where you can fish or swim. Meals are available, and there are four equipped cabins (*trekkershutten*).

WHERE TO EAT

✕ **Danina**: Bloemekensgang 8–12; Grote Markt 30. ☎ (014) 428246. About 795BEF for a set menu. A small place where the whole town gets together. On the menu: lamb chops, prawns and an interesting asparagus dish, *rauwkost met asperges en hesp*.

WHAT TO SEE

★ **Nationaal Museum van de Speelkaart**: Druivenstraat 18. ☎ (014) 415621. Open Tuesday–Friday from 2–5pm and Sunday from 11am–5pm. Admission: 70BEF. Tarot cards and playing cards from every country are mischievously displayed. They're oddly suggestive of national characteristics – Catalan and Castillian cards are delicate, Italian ones are elegant and so on. There's also a demonstration of card-making, the local speciality.

★ **Begijnhof**: leave the Grote Markt and take Begijnenstraat, then the first street on the left. This delightful place, built in the 14th century and rebuilt in the 16th century after a fire, is one of only 18 in Belgium. Don't miss the museum, especially if the learned, enthusiastic curator is on hand.

– **Museum**: open 2–5pm from Tuesday to Saturday, and 3–5pm on Sunday. Admission: 70BEF. The museum has benefitted from the edifying reputation of the Begijnhof, and a donation from a very wealthy curate. You can see Saxon and Brussels china, ancient books printed by Christophe Plantin, a fantastic model of the 1684 Saint Sepulcre, and an array of the delicate little objects that furnished the world of the Beguines, of whom there were 2000 here.

IN THE AREA

HOOGSTRATEN

★ **Sint Catharinakerk**: built between 1525 and 1550 in flamboyant late-Gothic style, the church tower rises to a height of 105 metres (345 feet). Completely destroyed by bombing in 1944, the church was rebuilt just four years later, using five million bricks of 50 types. It houses some beautiful 16th-century tapestries and has stunning choir stalls. The Begijnhof, open throughout the year, has a baroque church at its heart.

Walks in the Province of Antwerp

KEMPEN

This area of northeast Belgium occupies 75 per cent of the province of Antwerp. It's a fantastic spread of vast fields where cattle graze, conifer woods and flower gardens filled with azaleas and rhododendrons. Do take the time to go for a walk or cycle ride here once you've had your fill of city culture.

USEFUL ADDRESS

🅱 **Tourist office**: Grote Markt 1, Turnhout 2300. ☎ (014) 443355. They have a good selection of maps with signposted cycle tours.

WHERE TO STAY

☗ **Jeugdherberg Zoersel** (AJ): Gagelhoflaan 18, Zoersel 2980. ☎ and fax: (03) 385 1642. Open from June to the end of September, and at weekends during the school holidays. Basic rate per night: 360BEF. This 52-bed hostel lies in pleasant, wooded surroundings. Bike hire available.

☗ You can hire mini **chalets** for four people (minimally equipped) from Reserveringscentrale Trekkershutten, Pla TFPA Toerisme Kempen, Grote Markt 44, Turnhout 2300. ☎ (014) 43 6111.

WHAT TO SEE

★ **Kalmthoutse Heide** (dunes and heathland of Kalmthout): there's no bus, so take a train to Kalmthout and Heide. If you come by car, leave Antwerp in the direction of the Netherlands via Brasschaat (take a look at the sumptuous houses as you pass), and head for Kapellen. When you get to Kalmthout, head for Putte. A couple of miles further on, on the left, you'll see paths cutting across the heathland and sand dunes interspersed with small ponds. This is an area of outstanding natural beauty. If you don't trust your orienteering skills, free guided walks leave at 2.30pm on the second Sunday of the month. As you leave Kalmthout, stop off at the arboretum, which is also on the road to Putte.

KLEIN BRABANT

Klein Brabant ('Little Brabant') stretches along the Scheldt. Asparagus and eels are the things to sample here. As a post-prandial, try a bike ride to Bornem, Sint Amands, Puurs or Weert.

GETTING THERE

– **By car**: from the Antwerp-Ghent motorway, take exit 15 (Temse); then cross the Scheldt.

USEFUL ADDRESS

🛈 **Tourist office**: VVV Weert, Scheldestraat 18. ☎ (03) 889 0603. Open 10am–6pm, weekends from 1–6pm. You can hire bikes here, but it's a popular service, so make sure you book ahead. It's good value, too. The office also stocks plenty of maps. Cyclists should ask about the Aspergepad and Scheldekijkpad, two 40-kilometre (25-mile) circuits.

WHERE TO EAT AND DRINK

☒☒ Moderate

✕ **Gasthof de Veerman**: Kaai 26, Sint Amands 2890. ☎ (052) 333275. Closed Monday and Tuesday. Sit out in summer on the banks of the Scheldt and dine on young eels, which you can have plain or with cream, *maatjes* (herring) or a platter of fish.

WHAT TO SEE

★ **Verhaeren Museum**: Sint Amands, overlooking the Scheldt. From 1 July–15 September, open every day except Monday and Friday from noon–7pm, otherwise Saturday and Sunday from noon–7pm. Admission free. Through the windows of his tiny house (now a museum offering an exhaustive look at his life), the writer Émile Verhaeren drew endless inspiration from his native town and river, captured in his passionate texts: 'Scheldt, Scheldt, your strong, lush banks, your deep, slow flow are the image of [Flanders'] brilliant, deep-rooted nature.' He died a senseless death when he was hit by a train, and his remains are buried on the banks of the river.

★ **De Zilverreiger**: **Het Klein Brabantse Streekmuseum Weert**. Same address and opening times as the tourist office. This is the Museum of Fishermen and Scheldt Traditions. Its displays evoke the work of bygone days, such as clog-making, and the local fauna. End your tour with a sandwich and a beer in the courtyard.

WHAT TO SEE IN THE AREA

★ **Breendonk fort**: at Willebroek, between Antwerp and Brussels along the A12. Open 9am–6pm. Forbidding, but not to be missed. During World War II, the fort was used as a concentration camp: 4,000 prisoners were held here, and 200 were executed.

East Flanders (Oost-Vlaanderen)

The landlocked heart of Flanders, hemmed in by Flemish Brabant, by West Flanders, by the hills of Hainaut to the south and by the Dutch frontier to the north, which cuts this region off from the Scheldt estuary. Besides Ghent, the administrative capital of East Flanders and the spiritual capital of the whole region, there are four distinct areas in this province: Waas country, a densely populated area and the financial axis between Ghent and Antwerp, the area around the Scheldt and Dender rivers, whose population, like that of Dendermonde, Aalst and Grammont, depends mainly on Brussels for employment; the rolling landscape of the Flemish Ardennes, centred on the town of Oudenaarde; and Meetjesland, an agricultural area in which Eeklo is one of the principal towns.

GHENT (GENT)   230,000 inhabitants

Ghent is not just somewhere you'll visit, adore and leave without a second thought. The city goes out of its way to seduce you. You'll fall hopelessly in love with its enthusiasm, and leave consumed by an overwhelming sense of regret.

Ghent is a living city, fiercely proud of its past but never a museum-town. The industrial development of the 19th century has left it with indelible scars, but, rather than resort to major surgery, the *gentenaars* are slowly rehabilitating the city's ugliest patches. The result is a happy marriage of old and new: medieval buildings; sumptuous, shop-lined roads edged with handsome houses; striking civil and religious buildings that reflect 10 centuries of architecture; workers' districts, now filled with student digs; squares packed with café tables on fine evenings; quaysides where, during firework displays, the waters reflect the blue-green colours of exploding lights; dilapidated warehouses, where wayward vegetation appears in every nook and cranny; gardens descending to the canal; and neglected districts done up by artists and traders. The locals combine a sense of the dramatic with a simple, warm-hearted approach to life – a tradition that goes back to days of the guilds.

If you want to discover the real Ghent, you need to spend more than a day here. It takes some time to absorb its vibrant atmosphere, and you should opt for three days and two unforgettable nights. The ideal time to come is during the Gentse Feesten festival, when the town where Charles V was born comes alive with street theatre, stalls, dance displays and riotous behaviour. The festival takes place during the third week of July, and it's absolutely essential to book accommodation in advance.

GETTING THERE

– **By car**: Ghent is at the crossroads of two motorways – the E40 Brussels–Ostend, and the E17, Lille–Antwerp. Leave your car in a car park in the centre of town: the one on Vrijdagmarkt is the most central.

– **By train**: The station you're most likely to use is Gent Sint Pieters. It's quite a way from the old town, but not without interest: it was built in neo-Gothic style for the World Fair of 1913. From the station, take the tram or trolley bus, Nos. 1, 10, 11 or 12.

A Short History

Ghent's origins are modest. It began life as a *castellum* at the confluence of the Leie and the Scheldt. Around 630, St Armand appeared on the scene, converting the Franks to Christianity and founding the Abbey of Sint Peter. A second abbey was constructed, with a collection of settlements wedged between the two. Charlemagne built a port to accommodate his flotilla, but this didn't stop marauding Vikings from massacring the monks. Prudence dictated that a fortress be built – the future Gravensteen, while a humble chapel formed the origins of St Baafskathedraal.

Under the terms of the Treaty of Verdun in 843, Flanders fell to France and Ghent became a border town, with the Scheldt serving as the demarcation line. Early prosperity came as a result of the wool trade, with shipments from

England transformed into Flemish cloth and distributed to markets in the Champagne region. During this period, a small group of patrician cloth merchants were effectively in control, although technically the Count of Flanders held the reigns of power. This oligarchy was often at odds with the Count – and, even more frequently, with the workers of the deprived peasant community, many of whom worked in the textile industry. The living conditions of these weavers and dyers were dire, as the only concern of those in charge, apart from their profits, was to maintain good relations with England, which supplied the raw materials.

All that changed, however, after a dispute between Gui de Dampierre, Count of Flanders, and his sovereign, Philip the Fair. The Council of Patricians (whose sign was the lily, hence the name *Leliaerts*) sided with the king and against the count and the workers (who called themselves *Klauwaerts*, because they gathered beneath the banner of claws). The result was the battle of the Golden Spurs in 1302, which saw the French soundly thrashed, their allies in Ghent defeated and the proletariat permitted a hand in the government of the city. Ghent had taken its first step towards 'socialism' – a step that was to strongly colour its future.

In Ghent, the voice of the workers was, for the first time in Christendom, taken into consideration: they could at least vote for the city's rulers. Unfortunately, this early 'democratic' system was abused, and consequently deteriorated. The Hundred Years War did little for the city's economy. In the 14th century, Ghent was the most populous city in Europe after Paris. It stepped up protectionist measures against its neighbours, and did itself no favours when it killed off its greatest diplomat, Jacob Van Artevelde, the leader of the weavers, who met his end following an argument between guilds. An advocate of closer links with England in the name of Flemish economic interests, Van Artevelde had successfully avoided conflict with the English, and had even persuaded them to lift their blockade of the city. A child of the people, he was equally at home with kings, but finally it was the people who toppled him.

The 15th century saw the end of Ghent's liberties. The princes set themselves the task of eroding concessions made by their predecessors, and the Dukes of Burgundy suppressed the last revolts in bloody confrontation. Charles V, born in the city in 1500, subjugated Ghent once and for all when its inhabitants revolted against new taxation in 1540. Tamed by the rod of iron with which he ruled, they lost all their privileges.

Ghent was, once again, at the heart of conflict during the turbulence that followed the Reformation. The Treaty of Pacification, an agreement that united Catholics and Protestants against the common enemy, Philip II of Spain, was signed within its walls. The Calvinists took control, but a siege in 1584 forced Ghent to yield to Spanish troops under the Duke of Farnese and Catholicism was reinstated. Punishments, exile and famine halved the population, which fell to 30,000, and the city sank into lethargy for almost two centuries.

During the 17th and 18th centuries, Ghent was three times occupied by the French. In spite of a benevolent interim period under the Austrians, the city remained stifled by the persistent closure of the Scheldt. It was not until the French Revolution, and the arrival of Napoleon, that the economic situation began to improve. Encouraged by the Emperor, Lievin Bauwens smuggled a spinning jenny out of England. It was to revolutionize the textile industry. With the advent of Belgian independence in 1830, Ghent began to grow rich again. The university (then French-speaking) shaped the industrial bourgeoisie, and Ghent leapt to astonishing intellectual prominence, fostering numerous literary and artistic talents.

Meanwhile, industrialization was fast turning Ghent into a stronghold of socialism, spearheaded by the Vooruit ('Progress') movement. Edward Anseele, a native of the city, was the first Flemish Socialist member of parliament. The Flemish movement reacted against the French-speaking middle classes, and succeeded in getting Flemish instituted as the official language of the University in the 1930s. With the enlargement of the Ghent-Terneuzen canal and the construction of the port, Ghent developed an industrial belt that made it one of the most dynamic towns in the country. It also became internationally famous for flowers, with activity centred on nearby Lochristi. Every five years, the Floralies event attracts thousands of flower lovers, although the next one's not until 2004.

USEFUL ADDRESSES AND INFORMATION

Postcode: 9000.

🏠 **Provincial tourist office**: Woodrow Wilsonplein 3. ☎ (09) 267 7020. Fax: (09) 267 7199.

🏠 **Ghent tourist office** (map B2): Raadskelder, in the hall beneath the belfry, Botermarkt 17. ☎ (09) 266 5232. Fax: (09) 225 6288. Website: www.gent.be. Open 9.30am–6.30pm (9.30am–12.30pm and 1.15–4.30pm between November and April). Ask for the town map. They also take bookings for guided tours.

■ **Bureau de change**: Generale Bank (map C2), Belfortstraat 41.

✉ **Post office** (map B2): Korenmarkt 16, in the big neo-Gothic building opposite Sint Niklaaskerk.

■ **Taxistop** (map B2–3, **1**): Onderbergen 51. ☎ (09) 223 2310.

🚂 **Railway station** (off the map from B3): ☎ (09) 222 4444. Bike hire available. ☎ (09) 241 2223. Open 7am–8pm.

🚌 **Eurolines**: Koningelisabethlaan 73 (near the station). ☎ (09) 220 9024.

■ **Vélocité bike hire** (map B2): Hogpoort 22. ☎ (09) 234 0469.

GETTING AROUND

Ghent is pretty compact, so you'll be able to visit the most interesting parts on foot. The whole of the town centre is pedestrianized, but most of the car parks – even those near the university, the Fine Arts Museum and the station – are within a 20-minute walk from Sint Baafskathedraal. You can save time by hiring a bike, thereby joining 50 per cent of the city's population. If you're short of time, take trams or buses, which run between 6am and 11pm.

WHERE TO STAY

This can be a bit of a problem. Apart from a few chains (not usually listed in the guide), there aren't many hotels in the historic centre, so book in advance if you want to stay here. As a general rule, Ghent's hotels offer interesting weekend or long-stay bargains. These packages may include vouchers entitling you to discounts for museum entry. Brochures listing these deals are available at the tourist office, and you should get hold of this before you make your reservation.

☆ Budget

🛏 **Youth hostel De Draecke** (map B1, **11**): Sint Widostraat 11, next to the Gravensteen. ☎ (09) 233 7050. Fax: (09) 233 8001. Basic rate per night 495BEF. A double room costs 1,170BEF. A thoroughly modernized and well-maintained building with rooms for two, three, four or six people, and one dormitory: 106 beds in all. Lunch and evening meals are available.

GHENT

■ **Useful addresses**

🅸   Ghent tourist office
🚂   Railway station
1   Taxistop

🛏 **Where to stay**

10   Homes Universitaires
11   Youth Hostel De Draecke
12   Flandria Centrum
13   Brooderie
14   Eden Hotel
15   Erasmus
16   Sint Jorishof
17   B&B Huis Dael, Frank Pauwels

✕ **Where to eat, Where to go for an ice-cream**

32   De Zouten Inval
33   Het Blauwe Huis
34   Horta's Koffie en Eethuis
36   Avalon 1
37   Quicherie Patiron
38   Tap en Tepel
39   De Gekroonde Hoofden
40   Café-Brasserie des Arts
41   Amadeus
42   De Hel
43   Cur d'Artichaut
45   The Ghost
46   Stendhal
47   Vier Tafels
48   Brasserie Pakhuis
49   Le Tête-à-Tête
50   Veneziana

★ **What to see**

80   Sint Baafskathedraal

81   Lakenhalle and belfry
82   Stadhuis
83   Hoogpoort houses
84   Sint Niklaaskerk
85   St Michielsbrug
86   Korenlei
87   Graslei
88   Museum voor Sierkunst (Museum of Decorative Arts)
89   Gravensteen (Castle of the Counts)
90   Patershol
91   Museum voor Volkskunde (Folklore Museum)
92   Vrijdaagsmarkt
93   Korenmarkt
94   Vooruit
95   Abdij van Sint Pieter
96   Museum voor Schone Kunsten (Museum of Fine Art)
97   Oudheidkundig Museum Van de Bijloke (Museum of Archaeology)
98   Kouter
99   Museum voor Stenen Vorwerpen (Stone Museum)
100   Museum voor Industriele Archeologie en Textiel (Museum of Industrial Archaeology and Textiles)
101   Het Pand
102   Begijnhof
103   Rabot
104   Gerard Duivensteen (Castle of Gerard the Devil)
105   Kleine Begijnhof of Onze Lieve-Vrouw ter Hove
106   Museum Arnold Vander Haeghen

GHENT

≗ **Homes Universitaires** (off the map from C3, **10**): a good option in the summer (from 15 July to 24 September, except at weekends and on public holidays) if you have a student ID card. There are 1,000 single student rooms, with showers upstairs. Price: 600BEF, including breakfast. There are several halls of residence, all in the southeast of the city:

● **Home** Vermeylen : Stalhof 6. ☎ (09) 264 7100. Fax: (09) 264 7296.
● **Home Fabiola**: Stalhof 4. ☎ (09) 264 7204.
● **Home Boudewijn**: Harelbeekstraat 70. ☎ (09) 222 9721.
● **Home Astrid**: Krijglaan 250. ☎ (09) 222 9081.

≗ **Campsite Blaarmeersen** (off the map): Zuiderlaan 12. ☎ (09) 221 5399. Fax: (09) 222 4184. To the west of the city, out towards Drongen, beside the watersports centre and nature reserve. If you arrive by car, take exit 13; otherwise, your best bet is bus No. 38 from the centre of town. Open from March to mid-October. The facilities are excellent and you're guaranteed a warm welcome. Heated washrooms, a grocer's and a chip stand. Swimming, squash, table tennis and beach volleyball are available.

B&Bs

Ghent has some great B&Bs, where the hosts are locals who love their city and will happily help you get to know it. There are often only one or two rooms in each house. *Gilde der Gentse Gastenkamer*, a brochure available from the tourist office, lists 26 rooms with bathroom and breakfast included. For contacts and advance booking, contact Christine Dury, Tentoonstellinglaan 69. ☎ and fax: (09) 233 3099.

≗ **Jet Bogaerts**: Koningin Astridlaan 10. ☎ (09) 221 3432. Fax: (09) 221 5985. A double room costs 900BEF. A stone's throw from the station, with three rooms, a kitchenette and bathroom on the ground floor, and two upstairs rooms that can be altered to suit the number in your party (up to four people). Cooking and laundry facilities. Parking nearby.

≗ **Huis Dael, Frank Pauwels** (map D3, **17**): Visserij 169. ☎ (09) 224 0480. Double room 1,400BEF, including a generous breakfast, with discounts for stays of four or more nights. Three light, airy rooms are available in this art-deco house on an island between two 'arms' of the Scheldt, not far from the centre of town. There's a room on the lower ground floor for up to four people, a room for two or three upstairs and a room for two at the back, with a shared bathroom. Guests breakfast together and can sit in the garden or on the patio. Baby facilities available.

– You can get a list of 30 B&Bs in Ghent and the region through **Taxistop** (map B2–3, **1**): Onderbergen 51. ☎ (09) 223 2310.

☆–☆☆ Budget–Moderate

≗ **Flandria Centrum** (map C2, **12**): Barrestraat 3, behind Sint Baafskathedraal. ☎ (09) 223 0626. Fax: (09) 233 7789. Doubles 1,400–1,800BEF, including breakfast. Jo Boudry travelled extensively before taking over this 22-room hotel, where he and his wife have created a cool, well-maintained international meeting point. The focal point is the kitchen, where everyone gets a lunchtime meal. Jo's always good for suggesting places to visit in Ghent, and he'll go out of his way to help you get to know the town. He also has a real sense of family, so he lets out single rooms – with the option of sleeping five. Some rooms overlook the cathedral. Avoid the annexe in high season if comfort is a priority.

☆☆ Moderate

♨ Brooderie (map D2, **10**): Jan Breydelstraat 8. ☎ (09) 225 0623. Fax: (09) 329 5712. Double rooms from 2,500BEF, including breakfast. No credit cards. Somewhere between a hotel and a B&B, this establishment in the centre of town offers three rooms above a baker's and a café that sells organic bread. The rooms are large, light and unpretentious, with bathrooms and shared showers on the landing. Prices vary according to the season. At lunch time, there are vegetarian menus and a daily special (330BEF). If you arrive on a Monday, the shop is closed, so call before you get there.

♨ Adoma: Sint Denijslaan 19. ☎ (09) 222 6550. Fax: (09) 245 0937. Double rooms 1,900–2,100BEF. A recently renovated hotel near the station, with a large white facade. In the week, businesspeople occupy its 15 modern rooms, but it's worth keeping in mind if the hotels in the centre are booked up. There are two very reasonably priced en suite rooms if you want something a bit more luxurious.

☆☆ - ☆☆☆ Moderate– Expensive

♨ Ascona: Voskenslaan 105. ☎ (09) 221 2756. Fax: (09) 221 4701. Doubles 2,650–2,800BEF, including generous buffet breakfast, with weekend discounts. A modern-style concrete block between the station and the E40 motorway. The 37 rooms are comfortable but unremarkable, making it a useful fallback. There are flowers everywhere, adding a little charm.

♨ Eden Hotel (map C3, **14**): Zuidstationstraat 24, near the red light district. ☎ (09) 223 5151. Fax:

(09) 233 3457. Doubles 2,500–3,300BEF, including breakfast. There's nothing particularly charming about this place, but it offers a good quality:price ratio. The 30 rooms are extravagantly decorated and a bit on the heavy side, while the staff could be more attentive.

♨ Astoria: Achilles Musschestraat 39, near the station. ☎ (09) 222 8413. Fax: (09) 220 4787. Doubles 2,270–3,000BEF, including buffet breakfast. A modern hotel, not far from the Fine Art Museum, with 15 very comfortable rooms, the best of which overlook the garden. The decor is upmarket, and the service is impeccable.

☆☆☆ Expensive

♨ Erasmus (map A2, **15**): Poel 25. ☎ (09) 225 7591. Fax: (09) 233 4241. Closed in December. Doubles cost 3,850–4,200BEF, including breakfast. This charming hotel, in a tastefully decorated 16th-century house with exposed beams and choice furniture, is a stone's throw from the city centre. It's brimming with hospitality: there's a secluded garden where you can chill out after a busy day, while the vaulted cellar in the basement has been transformed into a library-bar. All in all, it's a credit to the humanist scholar whose name it bears, and while it's not exactly bargain-basement, it's of a rare standard. Make sure you book in advance, though, as the 12 rooms are much in demand.

♨ Sint Jorishof (map C2, **16**): Botermarkt 2 and Hoogpoort 75. ☎ (09) 224 2424. Fax: (09) 224 2640. Doubles 3,900–4,600BEF, including breakfast: four nights for the price of three in July, August, November, December and January. A very central hotel with two parts. The first, opposite the Stadhuis, purports to be the oldest hostelry in Europe (1228), with a guest list including the likes of Mary of Burgundy, Charles V and Napoleon. It serves as an *haute cuisine* restaurant and reception area, with neo-Gothic decor and a 15th-century fireplace. The rooms are on the other side of the street in two 18th-century family mansions. They're splendidly furnished with antiques, and offer every comfort. There's a private garage (extra charge). The restaurant (closed Sunday evening) is renowned for its fish dishes, and offers a candlelight supper every Friday evening. Expect to pay 1,500BEF per person.

â **Chamade**: Blankenbergestraat 2, near the station. ☎ (09) 220 1515. Fax: (09) 221 9766. Doubles cost 2,950–3,500BEF. Closed between Christmas and New Year. This businessperson's hotel offers reduced rate on weekends. The modern rooms are splendidly equipped, and buffet breakfast (included in the price) is laid on in the attic, from which you have a fine view of the spires of Ghent. It's a 20-minute walk to the centre.

WHERE TO EAT

While hotels are thin on the ground, there's no shortage of good restaurants in Ghent. A few tried-and-tested establishments are listed below, but you will no doubt find plenty of others. Just one word of advice: avoid restaurants and cafés around the main monuments, as the cooking tends to be very banal. Look for places with bikes parked outside, as this means they're frequented by the locals. Don't forget to try the famous Ghent *waterzooi*: chicken or fish stew cooked in a vegetable soup of carrots, leeks, celery and potatoes. If it's well done, it's a real feast. Some of the places listed in the 'Where to drink' section also offer inexpensive light meals.

✫ Budget

✕ **Tap en Tepel** (map B1, **38**): Gewad 7, near the Gravensteen. ☎ (09) 223 9000. Open from 7pm. Closed on Sunday, Monday, Tuesday and during school holidays. About 500BEF for a meal. A veritable Ghent institution, whose name means 'tap and nipple', this is a bohemian literary bar serving cheese and wine amid a delightful setting of ornaments and pot plants. House specialities include vegetarian quiche and *tarte tatin*. Get the landlord onto the subject of metaphysics and animal rights and he'll happily talk all night.

✕ **Horta's** Koffie en Eethuis (map B2, **34**): Zwartezusterstraat 32. ☎ (09) 234 1538. Open 8am–10pm (closed for lunch on Saturday and all day Sunday). Claudine, a descendant of the famous architect Victor Horta, concocts simple homemade dishes (moussaka, vegetable tarts, omelettes, pasta, lasagne and Flemish *carbonades*) at bargain prices: 175–375BEF. Breakfast, takeaway sandwiches and sweet crêpes are also available. The interior is delightful, and there's also a pleasant inner courtyard.

✕ **Avalon 1** (map B1, **36**): Geldmunt 32. ☎ (09) 224 3724. Open 11.45am–2pm. Daily special 260BEF. Closed Sunday and in July. Behind the Gravensteen, this is the perfect place for the brown-rice brigade, with vegetarian dishes served in a beautiful setting of palewood panelling at bargain-basement prices.

✕ **Café-Brasserie des Arts** (map B3, **40**): Schouwburgstraat 12, between the Kouter and the Justitiepalais. ☎ (09) 225 7906. A main course costs between 150BEF and 500BEF. It's a bit dark inside, with wood panelling, benches and dried hops on the wall, and the somewhat gracelessly served snacks are generous but slightly heavy: onion soup, omelettes, salads, spare ribs, local *hutsepot* (hotpot) and raclette. *Gentenaars* come here to fill a gap at midday or down a quick beer after work. Try some Hommelbier, from Poperinge, a pleasant refreshing beer.

☆☆ Moderate

✕ **De Gekroonde Hoofden** (map B1, **39**): Burgstraat 4. ☎ (09) 233 3774. Open 5pm–12.30am. Set menu 675BEF. Before you go inside, take a look at the facade. The carved heads all represent counts of Flanders. The pleasant interior has exposed beams, a huge fireplace and a monumental chandelier. You can eat as many spare ribs as you like here, or feast on salads and grilled meat. There's a good wine list. Whatever you get, it's always delicious, and whatever time of day it is, it's always crowded, so book in advance.

✕ **Quicherie Patiron** (map B1, **37**): Sluizeken 30, at the end of Oudburg. ☎ (09) 233 4587. Open 11.30am–6.30pm (to 8pm on Friday and Saturday). Closed Monday and the last two weeks of July. Main courses from 260BEF. A pleasant, light and airy space, this is the place to go if you like quiche – there are no fewer than 350 sorts on offer, including apple quiches, thyme and honey quiches, quiches with chicory, quiches with salmon and so on. Try the delicious courgette and Roquefort quiche.

✕ **Amadeus** (map B1, **41**): Plotersgracht 8. ☎ (09) 225 1385. Open 7–11.30pm and from noon on Sunday. Set menus 650BEF and 1,000BEF. A favourite with the locals in the

Patershol district, thanks to its lively atmosphere. Large tables draped with check cloths are set against a backdrop of wood panelling and art-nouveau stained glass. It smells a little greasy, but it's not surprising given that this is basically a grill room. Fingers, rather than forks, are the order of the day, and it's a great place to go if you're in a group. The service can be a little disappointing.

✕ **Cur d'Artichaut** (map B2, **43**): Onderbergen 6. ☎ (09) 225 3318. Open noon–2pm and 7–10pm. Closed Sunday and Monday. Main courses about 500BEF. This is a take-away that offers mouthwatering dishes and a retro-style brasserie with a varied, tasty menu featuring dishes such as carpaccio, lamb stew, tagliatelle and pâtés at more than acceptable prices. In fine weather, you can sit in the garden.

✕ **Stendhal** (map C3, **46**): Schepenvijverstraat 10. ☎ (09) 225 2173. Open 7pm–7am. Daily special 300BEF, with a set menu at 695BEF. Proof that Ghent really does have a nightlife. If a stint on the tiles has given you the munchies, you can sit in this restaurant near the Zuidstation and watch the sun rise. That's its only selling point, but it's good to know it's there.

☆☆☆ Expensive

✕ **Vier Tafels** (map B1, **47**): Plotersgracht 6, in the Patershol. ☎ (09) 225 0525. Open noon–2pm and 6.30–11pm. Closed from Christmas to New Year. Daily special 225BEF, with set menus at 500BEF and 1,100BEF. You've had world music, and now you can sample 'world cooking' – from Australia to Norway, from Japan to Zaire via Hungary, and even Belgium. To give you some idea: one little-known speciality on the menu is musk rat's feet with chicory and *gueuze* beer. Try it if you dare. You can concoct your own menu, so there's nothing to stop you washing down Cantonese-style rattlesnake with an Argentine wine, or antelope steak with sake. Take courage and tuck in! There's something to suit every budget and wine can be consumed by the centimetre – a gauge cunningly incorporated into the menu will tell you what you've spent on wine. The restaurant area is vast, with a veranda filled with pot plants linking it to **Virus** (entrance via Corduwanierstraat), a café that serves snacks on the same theme as the restaurant. To top it all, the service is quick and efficient.

✗ **De Hel** (map B1, **42**): Kraanlei 81. ☎ (09) 224 3240. Open noon–3pm and 6–11pm. Closed Tuesday and Thursday. Set menu 1,200BEF. A small house with a rococo facade on the quayside, not far from the Dulle Griet cannon. The eating area is a delicate bower, perfect for an intimate tête- à-tête, with a Chinese-themed decor and French cooking adapted to Belgian tastebuds. On the menu: stews, goat *cassoulet* and eels.

✗ **De Acht Zaligheden** (map B1, opposite **42**): Oudburg 4. ☎ (09) 224 3197. Open for lunch and dinner. Closed for lunch on Saturday, all day Monday and from mid-August to early September. Set menus at 850BEF and 1,000BEF. The 'Eight Beatitudes' lead you down the path to bliss in an art-nouveau setting on the edge of the Leie. The French cuisine majors in fish dishes and grills, with Belgian cheeses for dessert.

✗ **The Ghost** (map B2, **45**): Korenlei 24. ☎ (09) 225 8902. Open 11am–2.30pm and 6–10.30pm, and 'round the clock' in summer. Closed for lunch on Wednesday and Thursday. Set menus at 650BEF and 1,500BEF. Situated in Belgium's oldest crypt, this is the place for lovers of 'authentic settings'. The

vaulting in this beautiful cellar beneath Sint Michielsbrug, and the little tables for two, make this a cosy place to eat the fish and meat grills served here. House specials include eels in green sauce and the ubiquitous *waterzooî*. Be prepared for a jug of water to cost more than a beer.

✗ **Le Tête-à-Tête** (map B1, **49**): Jan Breydelstraat 32. ☎ (09) 233 9500. Open noon–2.30pm and 6.30–11pm. Closed for lunch on Monday and Tuesday. Set menus from 495BEF, with a full meal costing about 1,000BEF. In restaurant terms, this is about as good as it gets. The cooking is light and inspired (the *bouillabaisse* is splendid), and just reading the dessert menu will make your mouth water – and the setting is the only wooden house still standing in Ghent. The interior has been carefully decorated in wood and anthracite grey, while the zebra skin on the floor is a cheeky touch. The overall feel is 1940s, with photos by Robert Doisneau and Brassaï, and the lighting seems to have been specially designed to make your partner's eyes shine. There's a small eating area downstairs, and when the weather's good, you can sit beside the canal and gawp at the Gravensteen. The prices seem to have come down a bit recently, although the 'prestige' evening menu still costs a terrifying 2,990BEF.

✗ **De Zoeten Inval** (map C2, **32**): Kammerstraat 21. ☎ (09) 223 2488. Open for lunch and dinner, except Sunday evening, Monday and during September. Set menus from 795BEF to 1,395BEF. The ancient facade is gently succumbing to the ravages of wisteria, but inside, it's rustic and extraordinarily cosy, a great place to savour the simple things in life. The cheapest set menu offers oysters, pâté, Scottish salmon and melt-in-your-mouth beef.

✗ **Het Blauwe Huis** (map B2, **33**): Drabstraat 17. ☎ (09) 233 1005. Open noon–3pm and 7pm–midnight. Set menu at 1,100BEF. This place used to be called Diavolo. While the name has changed, it still sports the same electric-blue façade, and the decor is equally dazzling. The food, meanwhile, is well presented and extremely accomplished.

✗ **Pakhuis** (map B2, **48**): Schuurkenstraat 4, on a little street behind the Korenmarkt McDonalds. ☎ (09) 223 5555. Open noon–2.30pm and 6.30pm–midnight. Closed Sunday. Daily special 400BEF, with set menus at 750BEF and 1,050BEF. The hippest hangout in Ghent. Pakhuis was designed by Antonio Pinto, who also runs the Quincaillerie in Brussels and Antwerp's Dock's Café, and it's every bit as trendy as its sister establishments. It's a monumental canalside warehouse decorated with vast theatrical hangings, bronze-coloured metal girders, tall pot plants, bistrot tables, a 25-metre (80-foot) bar and shining copper pots and pans. This is complemented by efficient waiters and waitresses in traditional white aprons. The chic, expensive brasserie-style cuisine features fish, excellent daily specials, knuckle of ham with Tierenteyn mustard and wondrous *waterzooï*. There's an oyster bar, and an ordinary bar in the gallery overlooking the main eating area for those who simply want to see or be seen. The cheap lunch menu is worth checking out.

WHERE TO GO FOR AN ICE-CREAM

♀ **Veneziana** (map B1, **50**): Geldmunt 6. Open 11am–10pm. *Gentenaars* are unanimous in their belief that Veneziana, right next to the Gravensteen, is the best joint in town for ice-cream, *crêpes*, waffles and other sweet treats. The decor is reassuringly old-fashioned.

WHERE TO GO FOR A DRINK

You could easily devote a whole guidebook to Ghent's cafés. There are brown cafés, *kroegen* (bistros), cellar cafés, café-bars, rock cafés and places were beer or gin are frankly worshipped, and the town's 2,400-strong student community makes things even more lively. Bars are grouped by district in order to make your bar crawl easy to organize.

Sint Baafskathedraal and the Belfry

Good places to have a break during the day or to meet up with friends during the evening.

♀ **'t Vosken** (map C2): Sint Baafsplein 19. Open 8am–midnight. Thousands of visitors stop off here after their visit to St Baafskathedraal, desperate for a drink and for something that'll give them the strength to conquer the belfry. The place is much loved by locals, too, who come on Friday evenings and Sundays for an aperitif or to listen to a bit of piano music. Tasty snacks cost about 200BEF.

♀ **NTG Foyer** (map C2): Sint Baafsplein 17. Open from 9am. Closed Tuesday evening in winter. This upmarket first-floor brasserie in the city's main theatre, the Koninglijke Nederlandse Schouwburg, caters for actors, playgoers and anyone who fancies a copious breakfast beneath the coffered ceilings – or to drink in the stupendous views from the balcony, best enjoyed over a leisurely beer. A good place to escape the tourist hordes in the heart of the city.

Korenmarkt and Klein Turkije

This area is equally crowded by day and night, when people still mill about the place at two in the morning. You can sit outside on any of the many café terraces on the Korenmarkt.

❢ **Damberd** (map B2): Korenmarkt 19. This is an ideal place to get to know people, assuming you can find a chair among the chaotic jumble of tables and bikes that covers the terrace. There are whimsical pictures of Ghent on the walls, and world music plays in the background. If you aren't served, make your way to the bar and watch a game of chess. From October to March, there's live jazz on Tuesdays at 10pm.

There is a host of *muziek cafés* on Klein Turkije, which runs along the left side of Sint Niklaaskerk and leads to the Korenmarkt:
❢ **Icarus**: a fine vaulted cellar playing house music.
❢ **De Platte Beurs**: a neo-Gothic *kroeg* with a mixed clientele.
❢ **'t Vliegend Peert**: youthful atmosphere, with quiet corners where you can whisper sweet nothings in your companion's ear.

Towards Groentenmarkt

❢ **Het Galgenhuisje** (map B2): Groentenmarkt 5, at the end of the Groot Vleeshuis. Open noon–3am. This is Ghent's smallest tavern. It's tiny inside, with a tiny outdoor seating area and a tiny, touristy cellar restaurant, where you can have a daily special for 295BEF. Also visible here are the remnants of the old stocks, where debtors and women of ill repute were placed so that passers-by could splatter them with fruit and vegetables left over from the daily market. The name means 'Gallows House', a reference to the Groentenmarkt's former status as a place of execution.
❢ **Het Waterhuis aan de Bierkant** (map B1): right next to the Groentenmarkt. Open from 11am to 2am or later. This Ghent landmark, which has a terrace on the edge of the Leie, is unmissable. Just as well, since it's *the* place to go if you're into beer. There are more than 100 beers on the menu, some of them pretty rare, and they're all listed with intermittently humorous commentaries in several languages (including a delicious-sounding Ghent dialect): to the place's great credit, the jokes are different in each tongue. If you're feeling adventurous, try a Bush, but follow the menu's advice and make a note of the address of your hotel and room number first.
❢ **'t Dreupelkot** (map B1): next door to Het Waterhuis, but with no outdoor seating. Where there's a beer bar, tradition dictates that a gin bar should also be present, and this is a classic of its kind. Drinking takes place standing up around the bar or barrels, and for good reason: sit down and you may never get up. Cheek by jowl, everyone sips their gin in the time-honoured manner, from little frosted glasses that are filled to the brim. Whether you're drunk or sober, look out for trams

coming from the left as you make your way back to the bridge: it's a blind corner.

? Het Spijker (map B2, **86**): Graslei 10. ☎ (09) 234 0635. The oldest house in Ghent, with a Romanesque facade that leans dangerously over the canal. The high-tech interior is in slightly dubious taste, but it's worth coming for the amazing architecture. You can down a beer at the circular bar or have a snack or evening meal in the upstairs restaurant. There's also a splendid quayside terrace.

Patershol District (map B1, 90)

Cross the bridge and turn right along Kraanlei, and you'll enter the restored Patershol district. A bourgeois district in the 17th and 18th centuries, it was transformed by the arrival of textile-industry workers in the 19th century. In the last century, it was a neglected area populated largely by immigrant families, but it was saved from demolition and restored thanks to the local desire to preserve this unique complex of medieval dwellings. Today, it's been well and truly gentrified, and is the most desirable district for the city's trendy young things. In the triangle formed by Kraanlei-Oudburg, Lange Steenstraat and Goldmunt, you'll come across 20-odd restaurants (a bit trendy and expensive) and several spectacular bars. In the evening, the deserted streets take on a fairy-tale quality – except during the Patershol festivals, in mid-August, when they're heaving.

? Roccoco (map B1): Corduwa-nierstraat 57. ☎ (09) 224 3035. Open from 9pm. A pleasant, cosy oasis, frequented by artists who come here to find their muse, the fair Betty. The fires of the hearth and candelabra are reflected in melancholic eyes, and if inspiration strikes, Betty will move to the piano to sing a bewitching ballad.

? 't Velootje (map B1): Kalversteeg 10 (parallel with Oudburg). One of the most bizarre spots in town. It's a sort of shed inside, piled with odds and ends and old clothes, and hung with bikes. Liévin is the hermit who inhabits this den: he doubles as a bike mechanic and a secondhand clothes dealer. He's a bit fierce, and if you don't sit down, you won't get served. A sign formally forbids dancing in the establishment – although you'd have a job getting down amid all this clutter. Rumour has it that one of his bikes was used by the cycling regiments of Napoleon III, which he allegedly bought off the junkie son of a Ghent baron, who used the money to feed his habit. The Louvre in Paris is after it, but so far Liévin has refused its advances.

Vrijdagmarkt

Ghent's socialist leanings are immortalized on the Vrijdagmarkt in the statue of Jacob Van Artevelde, who used to harangue the crowds here. His voice was silenced long ago, but the crowds are still here in force, both on the square and in the numerous bars and at outdoor café tables.

? De Tempelier (map B1): Meerse-nierstraat 9. Cross the Leie on the side of the Dulle Griet cannon and carry on towards the Vrijdagmarkt. Closed Wednesday, according to the whim of the landlord and at the end of August. A tourist attraction and museum as much as a café, with a gruesome pseudo-medieval setting. You can drink from a glass in the shape of a *mammelokker* (a breast). All in the best possible taste . . .

♥ Herberg Dulle Griet (map B1): Vrijdagmarkt 50. Open noon–1am, Sunday 3–7pm and Monday at 4.30pm. *Dulle Griet* (Mad Meg), is the central character in one of Pieter Brueghel the Elder's most famous paintings. She represents war and its folly. This place however, represents beer, and its variety. As well as the usual suspects, there are a few specialities on offer, including Dulle Griet, which is 23 per cent proof. It's a bit like sitting in a museum, with displays of old glasses, bottles and enamelled advertisements, the best of which plugs Delirium Tremens, a beer with a pink elephant as its emblem.

♥ Pink Flamingo's (map C2): Onderstraat 55. Open noon–midnight or later on Thursday, Friday and Saturday. An outrageous temple to the art of kitsch, where the colours and wallpaper could give you a migraine. You've entered the realm of the handbag, plastic crocks, lace tablecloths, lights in the shape of exotic fruits and Barbie dolls, hunting trophies, a 1950s-style bamboo bar, cult objects from the Brussels World Fair of 1958, religious bric-à-brac, photos of Hollywood stars and so on. To cap it all, there's groovy 1960s music by Sonny and Cher, the Lovin' Spoonful, the Bee Gees and all your flower-power favourites.

Sint Jacobskerk

♥ Trollekekelder (map C1): Bij Sint Jacobs 17. Closed Monday. As soon as you enter, you'll be surrounded by leering trolls. Despite their threatening appearance, they're perfectly harmless, and if you pay them, they'll give you cheese, beer and concoctions from the chef's cauldron. They appear to like classical music, and have a penchant for unusual brews.

♥ Trefpunt (map C1): Bij Sint Jacobs 18. A 'meeting point for the promotion of street art', this brown café is one of the nerve centres for the preparation of July's Gentse Feesten. Throughout the year, it's a good place to catch some very good musicians.

Beyond Belfortstraat, the Vlasmarkt offers a few incredibly noisy 'young' cafés, where there's as much action on the street as there is in the smoky interiors. A few names to look out for: **Stax**, **Charlatan**, **Ambio**.

Botermarkt

♥ Lazy River Jazz Club (map B2): Stadhuissteeg 5, behind the Stadhuis. ☎ (09) 230 4139. A great place to round off an evening. The quality of live music on Fridays has been maintained over the 20 years it's been here.

Outside these Areas

♥ Cocteau (map C2): Jan Palfijnstraat 17, near the Flandria Centrum hotel. Open 5pm–1am, weekends noon–1am. Closed Monday and Tuesday. An elegant café-cum-art gallery in an old stable, with murals based on Jean Cocteau's drawings. Snacks available.

The nightlife is just as intense in the university district, to the southeast of the historic centre. There's a long line of student cafés from Sint Pietersnieuwstraat to the cinema complex, Decascoop, and around the Sint Pietersplein. A raucous atmosphere and bawdy songs are guaranteed – unless it's the weekend or during the holidays, when most of the students go home to Mum and Dad.

WHAT TO SEE

The Centre

Your tour of Ghent should begin at Sint Baafsplein, in the heart of the pedestrianized zone. You can prepare yourself for the rigours of the tour ahead at one of the cafés on the square, and study your *Guide* and town map (available at the tourist office, beneath the nearby Lakenhalle).

★ **Sint Baafskathedraal** (map C2, **80**): open 8.30am–6pm (to 5pm in winter). Closed during services (Sunday morning and public holidays). Along with the Lakenhalle and the Belfort, Sint Baafs is the pride and joy of Ghent. Although the dominant style is Gothic, the construction of the cathedral, which blends brick and white stone from Tournai, took several centuries, starting from the original church dedicated to St John the Baptist, where Charles V was baptized. It was renamed following the demolition of the Adbij Sint Baaf, again during the reign of Charles V. Charles's son Philip II made it into a cathedral and placed it in the hands of the first bishop of Ghent, Jansenius (who had nothing to do with Jansenism). The passing of the centuries brought constant alterations: the crypt is Romanesque, the choir is high Gothic and the tower, nave and transept are late Gothic. The 82-metre (270-foot) tower was originally topped with a spire, but this burned down in 1603.

St Baafs is like a museum, its status as a cathedral encouraging the well-heeled *gentenaars* to build chapels and tombs, or donate furniture and monumental paintings. The vaulting is intricate, and there's an obvious baroque influence, notably in the massive marble rood screen decorated with *grisailles*. The pulpit, by Laurent Delvaux, is in typical rococo style combining wood and marble (curiously, the trees are carved in marble). There are splendid choir stalls and candelabra bearing the arms of the Crown of England. Around the choir is the ambulatory, with chapels sponsored by important families (one of them is used to house the *Mystic Lamb*). In the first is *Jesus among the Doctors*, by Pieter Pourbus, with Charles V, Philip II and the Duke of Alba all represented. There are also several bishops' mausoleums: look out for that of Monsignor Triest, whose face seems to express the full tragedy of the human condition. The doors are richly carved, and there are some fine paintings, including, in the 10th chapel, a work by Rubens.

On the walls in the choir and transept, you'll see the coats of arms of great families from the days when the Burgundians and the Spanish governed the Low Countries. The 23rd and final meeting of the Order of the Golden Fleece took place in Ghent in 1559, and you can also see the arms of the counts of Egmont and Horn, both members of the Order, who were beheaded in Brussels in 1568 on the orders of another member, the Duke of Alba.

– **The crypt**: admission free. Built in 1150, its treasures include objects of veneration, reliquaries (including one of St Macaire) and tombstones. There's also a remarkable painting, *The Crucifixion of Christ*, by Justus van Gent, a Flemish artist who pursued his career in Italy with Piero della Francesca.

Unusually, the crypt was enlarged to make room for a choir and chapels. The Romanesque columns are adorned with 15th-century frescoes.

– The altarpiece known as the Adoration of the Mystic Lamb: on the left as you go in, in the old baptismal chapel. From April to the end of October, open 9.30–5pm, 1–5pm on Sunday; from November to the end of March, open 10.30am–noon and 2.30–4pm, 2–5pm on Sunday. Admission: 100BEF, which includes an audioguide.

This is one of the world's most important works of art. There's a vast body of literature about it, concerning its origins, how much it cost and its chequered history through the ages. The altarpiece was originally in the sixth chapel (the chapel of its donors), where light from the stained-glass windows shone on the clasp on the coat of the angel singing in the foreground. To the great chagrin of traditionalists, the powers that be decided to move it to protect it from vandalism and provide it with optimum conditions for its preservation. You now look at it through glass, and it has to be said that the lighting is not ideal. Try to avoid visiting when it's crowded, so that you can study this extraordinary work at your leisure.

Specialists have never been able to agree on who painted the *Mystic Lamb*. An inscription indicates that Hubert Van Eyck finished it in 1432, but it appears that Hubert died in 1426. There's some doubt as to whether Hubert even existed, and followers of this theory believe that his brother Jan carried out the work single-handedly. On the other hand, a tombstone testifies to the death of Hubert, and attributes the painting to him. It's a debate that will run and run.

The best way to get to grips with the altarpiece is to walk around it and look at the panels that appear when it is closed. This is how it was presented to the faithful on days other than festivals – it is a representation of the divine mystery, with the exterior of the altarpiece forming the prologue. In full regalia are the people who commissioned the painting: the rich magistrate Joost Vijdt and his wife, Isabel Borluut. He's all devotional dignity, while she doesn't look very pleased to be posing. They are praying to the statues of the two St Johns, the Baptist and the Evangelist. The statues look as though they really are carved stone. The middle part shows the tidings brought to the Virgin in a low-ceilinged room: through the windows, you can see street life going on outside, even down to the detail of people walking about. The words coming out of the mouths of the characters are back to front, which suggests that a mirror would allow you to read the text when the altarpiece is open. The characters above are the Sybils of Cumae and Eritrea (according to the Christian story, these oracles announced the coming of Christ), and the prophets Micah and Zacharias.

Now head to the front of the altarpiece to face the revelation of the Mystery of the Lamb. God, the Father or the Son, presides over the scene in all his magnificence. On his sceptre, you can see the play of light – whichever Van Eyck painted it, he had a total mastery of the laws of optics – and the detail in the clothing and jewellery is remarkable. If you crane your neck and screw your eyes up, you can make out the words in the book held by John the Baptist (he's in green). Every stone in the crown of the Virgin reflects the light that appears to be falling from the right, and the hairs have been painted one by one. The sumptuous brocades and intricacy of the floor tiling are equally impressive, while the cathedral's organ was recently rebuilt along the lines of the representation provided here, and is now in perfect working order.

A touchingly sincere Adam and Eve, surmounted by Cain and Abel in *grisaille*, are the first 'naturalist' representations of the human body in Western painting: you can even count the hairs on Adam's legs. This level of realism was unheard of at the time, and as late as 1781, it shocked Emperor Joseph II of Austria, who thought the figures indecent and had them replaced with 'dressed' figures. (You can see these at the entrance to the cathedral.) Eve is pregnant, the permanent state of women in those days, while Adam's right foot appears to be coming out of the frame.

The lower part unravels the mystery – the Lamb of Redemption is the key to understanding the mysticism of the age. Salvation came from the sacrifice of spilt blood to pay for original sin: here, the blood gushes out of the lamb's flank and waters the land via the Fountain of Life. A procession of the elect and (pregnant) virgins appears from the woods and converges on the altar surrounded by angels. In the foreground, to the left, are the prophets and patriarchs of the Old Testament (as well as the poet Virgil), with the apostles and confessors of the New Testament on the right. Each of them has been given specific attributes by which they can be readily identified if you know your Bible. In the background, the brilliant light of the Holy Spirit bathes the celestial city of Jerusalem, which is actually a complex of several famous cathedral towers, including Mainz, Cologne, Utrecht and Bruges. The plants depicted in the painting are astonishingly realistic. Botanists have peered through their magnifying glasses and made out 300 species, including fig trees, pomegranate trees, laurels, vines and palms, which, at the time they were painted, were little known in the northern hemisphere. It appears, however, that Jan Van Eyck spent some time in Portugal, and brought back sketches he made there.

The side panels illustrate the cardinal virtues. On the right, St Anthony leads hermits (signifying temperance) out of a ravine; behind them come pilgrims (representing prudence) guided by the giant St Christopher. Look out for the scallop shell of St John on the cap of the pilgrim from Compostela, and, at the back of the bunch, a weird and wonderful figure (who comes as a shock in this sober context) whom some have interpreted as the Devil.

On the left are the knights of Christ (strength) – St George, St Michael and St Sebastian – in full regalia, and behind them, emerging from the rocky gorge, are the famous Honest Judges (justice).

The final panel is only a copy: the original was stolen in 1934 by an unknown burglar who returned the back (St John the Baptist) to confirm that he was really the thief. The theft is a mystery as complex as that depicted in the painting. A police inquiry showed that the thief must have known the place extremely well, and concluded that the panel might even be hidden in the cathedral itself. The artist chosen to undertake the copy had great trouble finishing it: he was discouraged by the feeling that he could never aspire to the same degree of perfection as Jan Van Eyck. He's done a pretty good job, but you can't help noticing the difference in the luminous quality of the sky, and the absence of sharpness in the details.

The thieves of the *Honest Judges* are not the only ones to have coveted the altarpiece over the centuries. Philip II wanted to take it to Spain, the

Protestant iconoclasts wanted to burn it, and the *sans-culottes* transferred it to the Louvre. (It was returned after the fall of Napoleon.) While the bishop of Ghent was away, six panels were sold and ended up in the collection of an Englishman, after which they were purchased by the King of Prussia, who put them on display in Berlin. 'Indecent' Adam and Eve were bought by Brussels' Fine Arts Museum. The Berlin panels were sent back to Ghent in 1920 to make up for war damage caused by the Germans during World War I. In 1940, the altarpiece was transferred to Pau in a gesture of defiance, only to be swiped by Goering's special pillaging service. The panels turned up in a salt mine in Styria at the end of World War II, along with a mass of Nazi loot. From there, the altarpiece made its way back to Belgium and was placed in Sint Baafs without further adventure. At least for now.

★ **Lakenhalle and Belfort** (map B2, **81**): opposite Sint Baafskathedraal. The Belfort (belfry) is a defiant symbol of secular, as opposed to religious, power. At 91 metres (300 feet), it dominates the Lakenhalle and the Botermarkt, which stand out from the rest of the tightly packed town around them. In the course of time, the belfry has been significantly altered. The Lakenhalle was used in the 15th century as a business centre and cloth exchange, but became a training centre for the fencing guild. A double staircase leads you into a side entrance. It's open from mid-March to mid-November. You can go round on your own from 10am to 1pm and 2pm to 6pm (admission: 100BEF), or take a free guided tour: from Easter to the end of September at 2.10pm, 3.10pm and 4.10pm.

If you go up on foot, you pass a room where you can see traces of the old dragons and statues of knights. The 'secret room' contained the coffers, where the city's charters were jealously guarded. A lift takes you up to the gallery at the top, open to the sky, where the watch used to patrol and sound the alert in case of fire, a real problem in a town where houses were mainly made of wood. If you don't like heights, don't look down. The belfry houses a six-ton carillon of 53 bells: on the hour and the half-hour, you can see its mechanics in action, although you risk being deafened by the thunderous din.

As you go out, look at the corner of the Lakenhalle and the belfry: you'll see the old prison, at the top of which is a weird-looking frieze, the *Mamme-lokker*. An old Roman legend tells the story of old Cimon, who was imprisoned and had his teeth extracted so that he would die of hunger: his daughter visited him, and fed him through the bars of his prison from her own breast.

★ **Stadhuis** (map B2, **82**): from the Botermarkt, you can't miss this eclectic complex. The *gentenaars* were guilty of hubris when they conceived this structure: they wanted it to be the biggest town hall in Europe. In fact, it covers only 20 per cent of the area originally planned, and, as it took 400 years to finish, it ended up as something of a hybrid edifice. It was begun in 1518, in flowery Gothic style, as the House of the Squires of Keure, but building was interrupted by post-Reformation turbulence. Work was resumed under the Calvinists, using recycled materials (the Protestants were keen to use this style, called 'Reformation', as a reaction to the Gothic, which they saw as 'Papist'), and was completed with a Flemish baroque wing (where the warden lived) and a 'Poor Room'. The statues on the Gothic facade date from the 19th century. The Stadhuis saw the Catholics and

Protestants sign the Pacification of Ghent in 1576, a treaty that brought to an end the bloody religious conflict that had ravaged the Low Countries under the Spanish. The peace lasted only a few months, and the region was to suffer many more years of turbulence.

The interior is well worth seeing, but you can only go round the Stadhuis with a guide. A schedule of organized visits in the language of your choice is available from the tourist office. Admission: 100BEF.

★ **Hoogpoort houses** (map C2, **83**): on the oldest street in town are some very old houses. On the corner of Botermarkt is Sint Jorishof, built in 1476 and now a hotel. Then there is Grote Moor, followed by Zwarte Moor, and at No. 54, Grote Sikkel, which dates from the 14th century. On the corner of Nederpolder, over the road, is Kleine Sikkel, a Romanesque building constructed in 1200, and further along, on the corner of Biezekapelstraat, is the majestic Achtersikkel, which gives some idea of what a 15th-century patrician house would have looked like. If you happen to hear scales and arpeggios as you pass by, don't be surprised – this beautiful house is now a music academy.

Return to St Baafskathedraal and head for the panoply of towers beyond the belfry. Take a quick look at the bell called 'Triumphant' (which weighs in at a whopping 6,000 kilograms, or 13,200 pounds), which no longer hangs in the belfry; on your left is the bizarre Freemasons' House, where statues perched on little columns dance wildly in the wind.

★ **Sint Niklaaskerk** (map B2, **84**): go in via the entrance on the left as you approach the church from Sint Baafsplein. Open 10am–5pm (to 2pm on Monday), except during services. An imposing stone edifice in Scheldt Gothic that demands respect. It used to be the church of the Chamber of Rhetoric and several guilds. It's had its ups and downs over the years, perhaps the nadir being its stint as a stable during the French Revolution. A good deal of restoration was needed to make it what you see today. It's virtually empty, but this does nothing to detract from its grandeur. Opposite, on Kleine Turkije, the little houses were once the workplace of prostitutes.

★ **Sint Michielsbrug** (map B2, **85**): leaving the Korenmarkt and cafés on the right, make your way to the Sint Michielsbrug, on the left of the neo-Gothic post office. Like every other visitor here, you won't get all the way across: at the spot where St Michael stands atop a column, you'll turn round and see the dreaming spires of Ghent, famous the world over. From this point, on your right, you'll also see the Predikherenlei, the vast facade of Pand, the old Dominican convent, and, right beside it, Sint Michielskerk, with an unfinished tower that was to have been the highest in Belgium. It contains a *Christ on the Cross* by Van Dyck.

On your left is one of the finest cityscapes in Belgium: the Korenlei and the Graslei. The waters of the Leie reflect the facades and the Gravensteen (Castle of the Counts) in the background. You can take the steps that lead down onto the Graslei from the bridge, and from there stroll past nearly 10 centuries' worth of architectural styles.

★ On the **Graslei** (map B2, **86**), the old port of Ghent, the following houses can be seen, as well as the old post office (a neo-Gothic building, built for the World Fair in 1913, and not bad at all):

– **Gildehuis van de Vrije Schippers** (Guildhall of Free Boatmen), 1531: a late-Gothic building with curling gables that herald the fanciful twists and turns of baroque and a pretty decorative 14th-century sailing ship.

– **Coorenmetershuis** (Corn Measurers' House), 1698: a brick house in Flemish Renaissance style, with some baroque ornamentation.

– **Tolhuisje** (Toll House), 1682: the building where tolls were collected for the benefit of the town.

– The imposing **Spijker** (Staple House), 1200: a Romanesque building, and one of the oldest such edifices in Europe, this functional house was used to store grain, which was pulled up inside by ladders. Now a pub-restaurant (*see* 'Where to drink').

– The first **Coorenmetershuis** (Corn Measurers' House), 1435: a Flemish Renaissance building.

– **Masons' House**, 1527: a tall, elegant Gothic facade with gabling surmounted by pinnacles.

From Graslei, you can take a 35-minute **boat trip** that offers you the chance to see the Leie and Lieve from an unusual perspective, although the commentary is pretty dull. The trips that leave from Korenlei offer much more enlightening observations.

★ **Korenlei** (map B2, **87**): the town's more recent face, with baroque and Classical architecture, including the sweet little House of Free Boatmen, in yellow ochre and white, topped with a caravel (a Mediterranean sailing ship, as used by Columbus). There's also a three-storey fountain, where horses, humans and birds could drink.

Leave the quaysides and go along Jan Breydelstraat. At the confluence of the Leie and the Lieve Canal, you get your first glimpse of the brooding Gravensteen, or Castle of the Counts. At No. 5 is the Museum voor Sierkunst, in an 18th-century town house.

★ **Museum voor Sierkunst** (Museum of Decorative Art and Design; map B2, **88**): Jan Breydelstraat 5. ☎ (09) 267 9999. Open 9.30am–5pm. Closed Monday. Admission: 100BEF. Organized around a beautiful interior courtyard are rooms displaying furniture, ornaments, crockery and knick-knacks from the bourgeois homes of the 18th and 19th centuries. There's a large portrait of Louis XVIII, who lived here in exile during the Napoleonic era. One wing is taken up by 20th-century furniture, with an art-deco section and pieces by Victor Horta, Paul Hankar and Henry van de Velde; you can also see jewellery by Marcel Wolfers. Then you enter rooms exploring design between the 1960s and the 1980s.

– At the end of the street, on the corner of Burgstraat, is the restaurant De Gekroonde Hoofden (*see* 'Where to eat'), with carved medallion-portraits of all the counts of Flanders, including Philip II, the last of the line.

★ On the right as you cross the Lieve, take a look at the last wooden house in Ghent, now a restaurant (Le Tête-à-Tête; *see* 'Where to eat'), then enter **Sint Veerleplein**, the site of executions and the old fish market (not necessarily at the same time). You can still see the baroque gateway of the market, which depicts Neptune, the Leie and the Scheldt. On the right is the entrance to the Gravensteen.

★ **Gravensteen** (Castle of the Counts; map B1, **89**): open 9am–6pm (to 5pm from October to the end of March). Admission: 200BEF. Guided tours available. A splendid example of a medieval fortress, inspired by similar edifices discovered by the crusaders in Syria. It's not all as old as you might think, however: much of it was heavily restored at the beginning of the 20th century, which is obvious from the different-coloured stone used in the restoration. In the 19th century, the castle became a spinning mill, where the working conditions were pretty much Dickensian. Workers' hovels were even erected in the courtyard.

An early castle was replaced by Philip of Alsace in 1180. For 300 years, this served as the castle of the Counts of Flanders, who sat in this formidable, fortified structure to protect themselves from internal attack, as the *gentenaars* were apt to revolt against their liege lord. In 1353, however, they abandoned the uncomfortable fortress and its draughty halls, and moved out to the Prinsenhof, on the outskirts of town. The latter building is no longer there, but it was the birthplace of Charles V, the Holy Roman Emperor. The Gravensteen, meanwhile, was used as a prison and a mint.

The tour takes you around the ramparts and into the vast halls, then treats you to a spine-chilling encounter with the joys of medieval life in the torture chamber, where the instruments leave little to the imagination. You finish up in the armoury, with its collection of weapons and armour.

★ Now come back to the edge of the Leie, where you'll see the famous café **Waterhuis aan de Bierkant** (*see* 'Where to drink') at the point where the tram crosses the bridge. Opposite, you can admire the sombre 15th-century Vleeshuis (meat market) and, near the entrance to the Groetenmarkt, the vegetable market. Stay on the left bank of the Leie and go along the Kraanlei, which runs alongside the **Patershol district** (map B1, **90**). This is a popular spot for night owls and foodies (see 'Where to eat' and 'Where to drink'). No. 65 is the former **hospice for Alijn children**, which is now a museum. The district hosts a festival in mid-August.

★ **Museum voor Volkskunde** (Museum of Folklore; map B1, **91**): ☎ (09) 223 1336. Open 10am–12.30pm and 1.30–5pm. Closed Monday. Admission: 80BEF. Twenty-odd houses make up this charming complex, with a little garden at its heart. You won't need more than half an hour here, but it's well worth a visit. You'll get an insight into life at the end of the 19th and beginning of the 20th century thanks to a host of touching details. You can see the daily routines, middle-class interiors and craftsmen's workshops, the old crafts, the old-fashioned shops, lace-making and a puppet theatre. You get the impression, as you go round, that you've travelled back in time to the days your grandparents talked about as they dandled you on their knee. There's also a delightful tavern at the back of the courtyard.

★ **Kraanlei**: the 'Street of the Crane' gets its name from the crane that once stood here. It was fixed to a house and used to move heavy objects such as barrels, furniture or cannon. On either side were two wheels that were operated by local orphans. We know what such cranes looked like thanks to the paintings of Flemish Primitives where they sometimes appear in the background: perhaps the best example is Hans Memling's *Mystic Marriage of St Catherine*, which you can see in the Memling Museum in Bruges.

★ Level with the bridge over the Leie are two beautiful **baroque houses**, one of which is decorated with the Seven Misericords. If you count them, you'll find there's one missing: it symbolizes the burial of the dead, and is also absent from Saint Matthew's Gospel.

★ When you've crossed over (keeping the Dulle Griet cannon to your right), you'll come to the **Vrijdagmarkt** (map B1, **92**), which was the political heart of Ghent. Over the centuries, the square has seen tournaments, oaths and harangues from the Tanners House with its corner tower (*toreken*), and power struggles between members of the Cloth Guild, which led to the death of local hero Jacob Van Artevelde (his statue is still there). Little houses have been painted in colours that evoke the Caribbean as much as the waters of the Leie. In a corner of the square, with a vaguely art-nouveau facade, is **Ons Huis**, the headquarters of Ghent's all-powerful Socialist Party. On the left in Baudeloostraat is a remarkable row of houses: half Renaissance, half art nouveau.

– Cross the square diagonally and you'll find yourself in front of the Romanesque doorway of Sint Jakobskerk (which was started in 1200, took five centuries to complete and wound up being restored in neo-Gothic style). This is where the flea market takes place (*see* 'Markets').

– You can get back to the centre via Belfortstraat, but it's more scenic to enter Korenmarkt via Serpentstraat, Onderstraat and Lange Munt. This leads you back to **Groentenmarkt**, where a quick visit to the wonderful shop **Veuve Tierenteyn-Verlent** is a must. Here they make mustard in a huge vat to a secret recipe that was brought over by exiles from Dijon at the time of the Napoleonic wars. Another Ghent speciality to take back for your great-aunt is *gentse mokken*: dry, aniseed-flavoured biscuits. If you're in need of refreshment, the **Korenmarkt** (map B2, **93**) and its taverns await you.

Southern District

You can leave the Botermarkt via the city's main shopping streets, starting with Mageleinstraat. They're pedestrianized, and their baroque and neo-classical family mansions make them excellent strolling territory. Level with Bennesteeg, you'll come to a charming little square with benches and fountains: continue along Koestraat and you'll come to the university district.

★ On the left, at the beginning of Sint Pietersnieuwstraat, is the imposing facade of the **Vooruit** building (map C3, **94**), one of the flagship buildings of Ghent's Socialist Party and now the city's main venue for avant-garde dance, theatre and music performances. The huge function room is decorated with art-nouveau frescoes, while the rows of wooden tables are still used for union meetings. Students use the place to go over their work, and you can stop in the ground-floor *eetcafe* for a drink or a snack.

★ While we're on the subject of socialism, 100 metres further up Sint Pietersnieuwstraat, is a 'Soviet Constructivist'-style facade, all glass and steel, that dates from the 1920s. It used to be the offices of the *Vooruit* newspaper (which is no longer published), although it's unlikely to figure in any round-up of the city's great buildings.

★ A happier example of modern architecture in the area is the **tower of the University library**, designed by Henry van de Velde. It's an elegant mix of modernism and art deco.

★ Head south past the student cafés and you'll come out at a vast esplanade, Sint Pietersplein. You can't miss the majestic baroque facade and dome of Sint Pieterskerk (off the map, from C3, **95**), a church belonging to an abbey founded some time around AD 600. Vines are still grown on the slopes down to the Scheldt behind the abbey, just as they used to be when the monks were there. The grape harvest provides a good excuse for a festival each year. The abbey is now used for **temporary exhibitions**. If you take a peek in, you'll get some idea of the size of the cloister. The church is in classical Roman style, and was in the vanguard of the Counter-Reformation in Ghent. It's open to the public, and the crypt houses a permanent exhibition on the history of the abbey.

– Continue along Overpoortstraat and you'll come out at Citadelpark, where you can visit the Fine Art Museum.

★ **Museum voor Schone Kunsten** (Fine Art Museum, off the map from C3, **96**): Nicolas de Liemaeckereplein 3, in the Citadelpark. ☎ (09) 222 1703. Take buses Nos. 5, 50, 70, 71, 90 and 91. Open 9.30am–5pm. Closed Monday. Admission: 100BEF. One of Belgium's finest art museums, in a neoclassical building, with paintings and sculptures from the Middle Ages to the first half of the 20th century. Flemish art is presented alongside works from the rest of Europe, and all the works are excellently displayed.

Here is a suggested itinerary, as well as some of the best paintings.

To begin with, you'll come to a big room between the Ancients and Moderns, hung with Brussels tapestries. You need to head right to get to the old paintings.

– Room B, Flemish Primitives: *Saint Jerome at Prayer*, by Hieronymous Bosch, contrasts idyllic nature and the chaotic universe of temptation. *The Bearing of the Cross*, also by Bosch, is a wonderful painting. The canvas is crowded with nightmarish figures clustering round Christ and St Veronique, who are the only characters with their eyes closed, silent sorrow written on their faces.

– Room C: *Wedding Feast* and *Peasant Wedding*, by Pieter Brueghel the Younger (known as 'Hell Brueghel'), are copies of paintings by Brueghel Senior, although displaying rather less verve. The same artist is also responsible for a painting of considerable historical interest, *The Village Lawyer*, in which peasants are being maltreated by a shady lawyer.

– Room D: the most obvious influence of Italian art on Flemish painting is a new interest in human anatomy and a tendency to portray people in sophisticated poses. Martin Van Heemskerk's *Christ*, for example, looks as though he works out a lot.

– Room G: a superb family portrait by Cornelis de Vos shows that, even in those days, people had concern for the welfare of their toddlers – look at the way the baby's head is protected.

– Room K: the fashion for still lifes went far beyond a desire to reproduce fruit and flowers with 'photographic' realism. Cornelis De Heem's *Vanities* has a moralizing theme: the insects, snails, rodents and fruits and vegetables symbolize the human condition and the fragility of life.

– The museum also houses a rich collection of paintings by Pourbus, Rubens, Van Dyck, Jordaens, Hals, Tintoretto, Chardin, Hogarth, Reynolds and many others.

– Paintings from the 19th and early 20th century are displayed in the other wing. Many are by Belgians, especially James Ensor (while you're here, try to make a trip to his home town, Ostend – see our section on Ostend later in the book). Also well represented are Léon Frédéric (who was influenced by Courbet), Gustave Van de Woestijne, Edgard Tytgat, landscapes by Émile Claus and Henri Evenepoel, with his striking *Spaniard in Paris*. Neo-Impressionism gets a look-in, as do Théo Van Rysselberghe and the two schools of Sint-Martens-Latem, which are represented by Gustave De Smet, George Minne, Valerius De Saedeleer, Rik Wouters, Albert Servaes and Constant Permeke. French artists on show include Géricault, Daumier, Boudin, Millet, Rousseau and Corot.

★ **Stedelijk Museum voor Actuele Kunst** (Museum of Contemporary Art, or Smak): in the old casino opposite the Museum voor Schone Kunsten. ☎ (09) 221 1703. Email: museum.smak@gent.be. Open 9.30am–5pm. Closed Monday. Admission: 100BEF. This museum is the brainchild of maverick curator Jan Hoet, and its adventurous acquisition policy and innovative displays are just what you'd expect of a leading figure in the international art scene. The gallery shows art made after 1945: exhibitions are temporary, but you can usually see works by Magritte, Bacon, Panamarenko, Josef Beuys and Marcel Broodthaers.

To get back to the centre and the Museum Van Bijloke, go round Citadelpark to get into Kerkhovelaan, which becomes IJzerlaan. Cross the river and you'll come to an imposing complex of brick buildings.

★ **Oudheidkundig Museum Van de Bijloke** (off the map from B3, **97**): Godshuizenlaan 2. ☎ (09) 222 1106. Open Thursday 10am–1pm and 2–6pm, Sunday and public holidays 2–6pm. Admission: 100BEF. A wonderful collection of buildings that used to be a Cistercian abbey. They now house one of Ghent's most entertaining museums, although the place could be a bit more visitor-friendly. You're not made to feel welcome, the brochure is rather perfunctory, there are no signs to help you get your bearings, and the collections are incoherently arranged (prehistoric remains sit cheek by jowl with Masonic objects). The result is a bizarre telescoping of time and genre. That said, the place is a veritable Aladdin's cave, and armed with a little patience and curiosity, you can discover some amazing things: pewter, copper pots, weapons, pottery, costumes, enamels, porcelain, musical instruments, model ships, silverware, ironware and so on. The building is worth a look as well. The old refectory is monumental, with a beautiful wooden vaulted ceiling. There's a recumbent stone statue guarding the 14th-century frescoes, while a suite of rooms has been laid out in the style of *gentenaars'* houses. In the House of the Abbess, the Communal Souvenir Room displays artefacts in gold and silver, including the insignia of the town musicians.

You can get back to the town centre along the banks of the Leie until you get to the intersection with the Coupure Canal. Then plunge back into the bustle of the shopping district around the **Kouter** (map B3, **98**), taking in the fine collection of Classical buildings around this sizeable square. You'll see the Vlaamse Opera (Opera House) and the Justitiepalais (Law Courts) at the start of Veldstraat, the equivalent of London's Oxford Street. At No. 45, now a clothes shop, English and American diplomats signed an 1814 treaty that brought to an end the war of 1812, a post-independence conflict linked to Britain's struggle against Napoleon.

★ **Museum Arnold Vander Haeghen** (map B2, **106**): Veldstraat 82. Open Monday–Friday from 9.30am–noon and 2–4.30pm. Admission free. Behind a beautiful pale-green facade is the former library of Maurice Maeterlinck, a Symbolist French-language writer, who won the Nobel prize for literature and died a baron in 1949. Dubbed the 'new Shakespeare' by an over enthusiastic contemporary, he reached a wider audience by having one of his works, *Pelléas et Mélisande*, turned into an opera by Debussy. Curiously, however, he is best remembered for his scientific works, such as *The Life of Bees*, *The Life of Termites* and *The Life of Ants*, which are reprinted to this day.

Under the same roof is the office of Charles Doudelet and Victor Stuyvaert two illustrators and draughtsmen who were both members of Maeterlinck's circle. There are several marvellous *objets d'art*, including the 18th-century 'wallpaper' of painted silk in the Chinese Room.

If you still have time . . .

There are half a dozen more specialized museums in Ghent, and several on the outskirts of the city. Here is a selection of the best:

★ **Museum voor Stenen Voorwerpen** (Stone Museum; map D2, **99**): Gandastraat 7. Open Wednesday, Thursday, Friday and Sunday from 9.30am–5pm. Admission free. A must for frustrated archaeologists. On the grassy site of the ruined Abdij St Baaf, you'll find pieces of fresco and bas-reliefs, fragments of paving and the controversial tombstone of Hubert Van Eyck (*see* the description of the *Adoration of the Mystic Lamb*).

★ **Museum voor Industriële Archeologie en Textiel** (Museum of Industrial Archaeology and Textile, or Miat; map C1, **100**): Minnemeers 9. ☎ (09) 223 5969. Open 9.30am–5pm. Closed Monday. Admission: 100BEF. An old brick factory that now hosts fascinating temporary exhibitions about the city's industrial past. You can also see the Mule Jenny sewing machine that was smuggled from Manchester to Belgium in bits by Lievin Bauwens, kick-starting Ghent's economy. On machines like this, generations of working women ruined their hands in the name of industrial progress.

★ **Het Pand** (map B2, **101**): Onderbergen. The name means Great Building, and you'll recognize it from the huge slate roof on the quay of the Leie, next to St Niklaaskerk. A former Dominican convent, it now belongs to Ghent University, and houses a cultural centre, a restaurant and halls of residence. It's also home to the Museum of Stained Glass (visits on request).

Heading Northwest

★ **Sint Elisabeth Begijnhof** (map A1, **102**): from Michielsbrug, take Hoogstraat to Begijnhoflaan, then turn right. In the 15th century, the Begijnhof was a complex of thatched hovels: the brick houses are now

GHENT

being restored. There's a baroque church, and, on the right, a monument sculpted by George Minne in honour of Georges Rodenbach, a Symbolist poet, and fellow student of Maeterlinck, best known for his 1892 novel *Bruges la Morte*, who was drawn to this place of reverie and nostalgic melancholy. There's also a small museum devoted to the life of the Beguines.

★ **Rabot** (map A1, **103**): as you leave the Begijnhof, follow Rabotstraat for 100 metres. The Rabot is an old fortified sluice guarding the entrance to the Lieve. The two fat, round towers, with cones on top, are typical of the military architecture of the 15th century.

Heading Southeast

★ **Gerard Duivelsteen** (map C2, **104**): behind Sint Baafskathedraal, on the edge of the Scheldt. This was the frontier between France and the Holy Roman Empire in the Middle Ages. Gerard Duivel, nicknamed 'the Devil' in an unenlightened age because of the dark colour of his skin, ruled Ghent in 1216, and his castle is a forbidding place. It's now a repository for the state archives, and is not open to the public.

★ A stone's throw from here, near the old Zuidstation (now the Koning Albertpark), is the **red-light district**, where, in what was once a fine commercial street in the 19th century, Ghanean and Nigerian women sit and knit under the purple rays of the neon lights, as they wait for possible clients.

★ If you continue along Sint Annaplein and Lange Violettenstraat, you come to the **Klein Onze Lieve Vrouw Begijnhof** (map D3, **105**), founded in 1234 by Joan of Constantinople and rebuilt in 1600. A haven of peace, as it should be, where you can sit on the lawns and dream of the distant times when men went off on crusades, leaving their women to await their return, like Penelope, in piety, charity and the solidarity of deserted wives.

MARKETS

– **Antiques**: Friday and Saturday morning, on Bij Sint Jacob.

– **Flowers**: Saturday and Sunday morning on the Kouter.

– **Fruit and vegetables**: Monday to Saturday on Groentenmarkt.

– **Birds**: Sunday morning on Vrijdagmarkt.

– **Chickens and ducks**: Sunday morning on Oudebeestenmarkt.

– **Flea market**: Fridays, Saturday and Sunday morning on Bij Sint Jacob.

HITCH-HIKING OUT OF GHENT

Wherever you're heading (Antwerp, Brussels, Ostend or Lille, for example), get to the end of Franklin Rooseveltlaan (which goes round Koning Albertpark) before the point where the cars get into the fast lane leading to the motorway junctions. Don't forget to mark your destination clearly on a board.

Ghent countryside: around the Leie

Before it joins the Scheldt, the Leie meanders lazily through the Flemish plain, and its valley creates a particularly idyllic countryside. At the beginning of the 20th century, a colony of painters and sculptors invaded the area, descending on the villages of Deurle and Sint-Martens-Latem, which became a famous artistic centre. In their wake came the wealthy bourgeoisie, eager to commission their works. Nestling in the woods and pastures just a few miles from Ghent are some superb houses hidden behind hedges and fences.

WHERE TO STAY

The few hotels in these villages charge rates that correspond with the area's standing. It's better to base yourself outside the villages.

⌂⌂ – ⌂⌂⌂ Moderate–Expensive

🏠 **Charls Inn**: Autoweg Zuid 4, Gent 9051 (Afsnee). ☎ (09) 220 3093. Fax: (09) 221 2019. A couple of miles from the centre of Ghent, and about a kilometre from Sint-Martens-Latem. Doubles 2,100–3,000BEF. It's a bit complicated to explain how to get here, but it's well worth the effort. From the motorway: after exit 13, you'll see the sign Hotel painted on the roof; take exit 14, go under the tunnel towards Deinze, then take the second turning on the right for Sint Dionysiusstraat, then drive through the village and join a road parallel to the E40; the hotel is then on your left. If you're coming from Ghent, go along the Snepkaai, then Beukenlaan, under the E40 and turn right. When you finally arrive, you'll find a really delightful hotel with a family atmosphere, where you'll be offered a coffee as you sit in a big garden where ducks waddle about. The beautiful rooms are named after flowers; those with showers are a lot cheaper. The motorway is only 50 metres away, but double-glazing ensures that the rooms are soundproofed. Unfortunately, there's a stagnant pond in the vicinity – bring some insect repellent or ask for some flypaper. You can borrow a bike if you want to cycle along the Leie (free for one day).

WHAT TO SEE AND DO

– **Cruise down the Leie**: there are no roads along the Leie, so the best way of appreciating its charms in summer (apart from by bike) is to take one of the cruises that leave from Gordunakaai, in a western suburb of Ghent. There are several companies offering similar tours: the return trip takes between four and five hours, and the boat often stops next to a tavern, where you're given plenty of time to have a drink. For more information, contact the Ghent tourist office, ☎ (09) 266 5232.

– **Cycling tour of the villages along the Leie**: this is the best way of getting to know this very pretty area on your own. You can rent a bike for the day at Ghent and Deinze stations, and you'll get a discount if you've travelled to either by train. To book, call ☎ (09) 241 2223 or (09) 386 1110. The best place to start is on the edge of Waterspoortbaan, in Ghent, where rowing competitions take place. The best map is *Fietsroutes Oostvlaanderen (2)*,

Leierstreek en Denderstreek, which you can pick up at most bookshops. There's a signposted route that takes you through 40 kilometres (25 miles) of marsh, copses and undergrowth to the villages of Afsnee, Latem, Deurle, Bachte-Maria-Leerne and the Castle of Ooidonk: it's delightful, and not too taxing. On the way, you pass the opulent villas of the well-to-do, with their jetties and boathouses, golf courses, stud farms, lawns that look as though they've been cut with nail scissors and high-class cars in the garages. It's like Palm Beach, without the palm trees, and gives you an impression of how prosperous Flanders really is.

★ **Museums of the Artists of the School of Sint-Martens-Latem**: two movements developed out of this school. The first, which spans the period between 1899 and 1907, was led by the sculptor George Minne, and also included Gustave Van de Woestijne, Albijn Van den Abeele and Valerius De Saedeleer. The last-named sought inspiration in nature, and tended to the mystical, in reaction to what was called a 'superfluous Impressionism'. This movement was influenced by Symbolist poetry. The second wave came after 1918, and took these ideas further, beginning with Émile Claus' Luminist paintings and ending with an Expressionism influenced by Constant Permeke. Frits Van den Berghe, Albert Servaes and Gustave de Smet were the main exponents of this movement.

WHAT TO SEE IN THE AREA

DEURLE

★ **Dhondt-Dhaenens Museum**: Museumlaan 14, Deurle 9831. Open 2–6pm (5pm in winter), Saturday, Sunday and holidays. Closed from the end of December to the end of February. Admission: 70BEF. This is a wonderful collection showing the diversity of early-20th-century Flemish art. In addition to the painters already mentioned, you'll see works by Léon Spilliaert, Ensor, Henri Evenepoel, Eugène Laermans, Edgard Tytgat, Jan Brusselmans and the sculptor Constantin Meunier.

★ The brothers **Léon and Gustave de Smet** lived in Deurle. Fans can visit their two homes, mostly filled with memorabilia from their personal lives. You can get information about the houses at the Gemeentehuis (Dorp 3).

SINT-MARTENS-LATEM

★ **Gevaert-Minne Museum**: Kapitteldreef 45. From Easter to the end of September, open 2–6pm and 10am–noon on Sunday morning. Closed Monday and Tuesday. Admission: 50BEF. The works on display in this rather austere house are by George Minne, whose early career made him the sculptor who best represented art nouveau, although he later joined the ranks of the Naturalists. Edgard Gevaert, a painter, was Minne's son-in-law.

DEINZE

USEFUL ADDRESS

🛈 **Tourist office for the area along the Leie**: Stadhuis, Gentsepoortstraat 1, Deinze 9800. ☎ (09) 381 9501.

WHERE TO STAY

🛏 **Camping Groeneveld**: Groenevelddreef, Deinze 9800 (Bachte-Maria-Leerne). ☎ (09) 380 1014. Fax: (09) 380 1760. In a wooded area near Ooidonk. There are also five equipped cabins (*trekkershutten*).

WHAT TO SEE

★ **Museum van Deinze en Leiestreek**: Lucien Matthyslaan 3–5. Open 2–5.30pm on weekdays, and 10am–noon and 2–5pm at the weekend. Admission: 00BEF. An attractive museum in a beautiful, white, modern building in Deinze, the capital of the region of the Leie, which is famous for its fowl market. There are two sections: painters and sculptors of the Leie, with splendid post-Impressionist paintings by Émile Claus and Théo Van Rysselberghe, plenty of works from both schools of Sint-Martens-Latem, and works by the little-known sculptor Jozef Cantré. It's also a museum of daily life in the town, with objects recalling work, shops (including a spice counter) and so on. It's well organized and intelligently done: each example of daily life is accompanied by a picture relating to the objects on display. A scene in an 18th-century tavern by Frans Hals, for example, provides the context for a collection of pipes.

OOIDONK CASTLE

To reach the castle, pass through the village of **Bachte-Maria-Leerne**: it's at the end of an avenue of lime trees. ☎ (09) 282 6123. Open 2–5.30pm on Sunday and public holidays from Easter to 15 September; in July and August, also open on Saturday. Admission to the castle is 180BEF, but it's only 30BEF to get into the park. The brasserie on the left of the entrance is a good place to recharge your batteries if you're starting to flag. The Belgians call Ooidonk 'Little Chambord', after the French chateau on the Loire. You can see why – it's a princely residence in Flemish Renaissance style, and very picturesque. With its brick hunting lodges, moat, slate roof and corner towers with elegant onion bell towers, it's austere and intricate at the same time. It's still a private residence, although it's open to the public, and inside you can see plenty of Louis XV and Louis XVI furniture and imposing portraits, including one of Philippe de Montmorency, count of Hoorn. The oxbow lake, French-style gardens and pastures, and wooded plantations give the place a classy feel.

EAST FLANDERS

LAARNE CASTLE

This castle is 13 kilometres (nine miles) from Ghent. You can get there on the R4, coming off at exit 5. ☎ (09) 230 9155. From Easter to the end of October, open on Sunday from 2pm to 5.30pm; in July and August, open every afternoon except Monday and Friday. Admission: 200BEF. A 12th-century castle surrounded by a moat, with an entrance and loggia that were clearly tacked on some time afterwards. The huge corner towers have pointed roofs. A stone bridge leads you in. The central part of the castle houses beautiful Antwerp furniture, tapestries, paintings and a magnificent collection of jewellery and silverware.

Waasland

This area has gone down in medieval literature as the 'sweet country' ('doux pays'). It consists of the region between Dutch Zeeland, the Durme and the Scheldt, and is renowned for its flower industry. It's also highly industrialized, encompassing part of the ports of Antwerp as well as naval works and brick factories.

EAST FLANDERS

SINT NIKLAAS   24,000 inhabitants

The origins of the town stretch back to 1219, when local merchants obtained a large piece of land from Joan of Constantinople (who apparently spent her life giving away property). They established a trading town, and every Thursday since 1513, there's been a market here. According to our calculations, that makes more than 25,000 markets.

USEFUL ADDRESS

Postcode: 9100.

⌂ Tourist office: Grote Markt 45. ☎ (03) 777 2681.

WHERE TO STAY

≜ De Spiegel: Stationstraat 3, on the corner of a road leading into the Grote Markt. ☎ (03) 776 3437. Nothing to write home about, but useful in an emergency and perfectly comfortable. Prices vary depending on whether or not your room has a bath. There's a billiards hall on the first floor.

WHERE TO EAT AND GO FOR A DRINK

☆☆ Moderate

✗ Grand Café: Houtbriel 25. ☎ (03) 777 1115. Open from 10am. A lively brasserie with modern decor, parquet flooring, copper pots and pans and gallery upstairs. Quick service for quick meals, and sturdy salads.

✗ De Oud Rhétorica: Sint Niklaas-plein. A jolly brown café with two dining areas, both boasting quotations and maxims in neo-Gothic script in Flemish, Latin, French, English and German. The seats are attributed to Pliny, Corneille, Ovid, Rabelais and Shakespeare, and the shelves are lined with books for customers to look at. A sample of the pearls of wisdom on offer: 'The important thing is to love; it matters not who your mistress is!'

❣ 'Young' cafés and lively nocturnal haunts are concentrated around the Sint Niklaaskerk, and, as so often in smaller Flemish towns, they're unusual but very friendly.

WHAT TO SEE

Sint Niklaas is unlikely to bowl you over, but it's worth a visit on market day, if only to understand what the word 'crowd' really means. To accommodate everybody, the town built the biggest Grote Markt in the country – it covers an astonishing 3.2 hectares (nearly 8 acres). But this won't stop you getting your toes trampled on. In case the square looked a bit empty, a suitably gigantic neo-Gothic **Stadhuis** was built there, alongside an equally imposing **Onze Lieve Vrouwekerk**, with a gigantic gilt statue of the Virgin Mary at its summit. There are a few genuine **17th-century houses**: the Parochiehuis, Cipierage and Landhuis. In the **Sint Niklaaskerk** is a *Christ* attributed to Jérome Duquesnoy.

The emblem of the town and its region is a turnip, in memory of an enormous turnip that was given to Charles V when he visited. Honest.

There are also some interesting **communal museums**. They all have the same opening hours: 2–5pm from Tuesday to Saturday, and 10am–5pm on Sunday.

★ **Mercator Museum**: Zamanstraat 49. Admission: 100BEF. Dedicated to the great 16th-century cartographer, a native of nearby Rupelmonde. On display are an original edition of his *Atlas*, terrestrial and celestial globes from the period, and old and modern maps. Great if you like geography.

★ **Museum of History and Civilization**: Zwijgershoek. Closed October to end March. Admission: 50BEF. A grand title, and one that this curious museum wisely makes no effort to live up to: instead, it focuses on four specialized but intriguing themes. Barbierama explores the history of hairdressing and body care, with the highlight being sumptuous art-nouveau furniture that once graced a Belle Époque barber's shop; From Music Box to Gramophone includes old records, phonographs and various music-making machines; the International Centre for Ex-Libris is a unique collection of 120,000 ex-libris (the stamp on the inside front cover of a book, identifying its owner), with examples from as long ago as the 16th century, arranged by country, artist and theme; and in the final section, the Baudelozaal, you can see the remains of the Abbey of Boudelo, the floor of which has been reconstructed.

★ **Fine Art Museum**: Stationstraat 85. Admission: 50BEF. A handsome town house that displays the legacy of a local textile tycoon, and consists of furniture and porcelain fashioned between the 17th and 20th centuries, and paintings by Henri Evenepoel, Félicien Rops, Henri de Braekeleer and Louis Artan.

★ **Historic Museum of Pipes and Tobacco**: Regentiestraat 29. Open Sunday 10am–1pm (or by appointment). Admission: 60BEF. Among other things, you can see the biggest cigar in the world – six metres (nearly 20 feet) long and weighing 450 kilos (990 pounds).

FESTIVAL

– There's a fabulous **hot-air balloon meeting** on the first weekend in September.

Scheldt and Dender

The Dender flows gently north through the undulating hills of Hainaut province, rolling through Geraardsbergen, Ninove and Aalst before joining the Scheldt at Dendermonde, ('mouths of the Dender'). Here, the river is so wide that you'll sometimes see dolphins, carried from the sea by its flow.

GERAARDSBERGEN   30,000 inhabitants

This quirky town has become part of professional cycling folklore. Every year, the Tour of Flanders takes riders up the gruelling Wall of Grammont, the only section of the race where they have to ride over cobbles. Geraardsbergen (Grammont in French, which is the official language less than 5 kilometres/3 miles away) is on a slope at the foot of the 'mountain' that overhangs it and which rises to 111 metres (366 feet). It's also famous for its curd tart, which you can buy at any of the stalls around the Markt.

A Short History

Geraardsbergen had considerable strategic importance in the Middle Ages because of its position on the borders of Flanders, Brabant and Hainaut. It was also home to a Benedictine abbey (which disappeared long ago). It was overtaken by Oudenaarde and Aalst, however, and it wasn't until the 19th century that prosperity arrived, with the opening of a match factory.

USEFUL ADDRESS

Postcode: 9500.

🛈 **Tourist** office: Stadhuis, Markt 1. ☎ (054) 437290.

WHERE TO STAY

☒ Budget

⌂ **De Gavers**: a couple of miles northeast of town. ☎ (054) 416324. This is a leisure and watersports centre on the edge of the Dender, which also has a campsite and three wood cabins *(trekkershutten)*. Among the activities on offer are sailboarding, volleyball, tennis and fishing, and you can hire bikes and canoes.

⌂ **Youth hostel 't Schipke**: Kampstraat 59. ☎ (054) 416189. Fax: (054) 419461. Basic rate pre night: 300BEF, excluding breakfast, which costs an extra 120BEF. Closed between January and the end of March. In the same complex as De Gavers. Nearest station: Schendebeke. Two buildings on a 17th-century farm now offer 104 beds, with two family rooms. It's an ideal spot for a country holiday, Sheet-hire available. There's a dining area in the old stables, with main courses at about 300BEF.

☆☆ Moderate

🛏 **Hotel-restaurant Geraard**: Lessensestraat 36, near the station and the town centre. ☎ (054) 412073.

Fax: (054) 417199. Doubles 2,500BEF, excluding breakfast. This 19th-century town house offers three-star comfort at a bargain rate, though your bill will soar if you opt for breakfast. Go for the rooms overlooking the garden. There's also an *haute cuisine* restaurant in an incredible neo-Gothic dining room.

WHAT TO SEE

★ **Grote Markt**: Brussels does not have a monopoly on the Manneken-Pis. The midget outside the Stadhuis is actually older than his cousin in the capital: he was sculpted in the 15th century, as proved by his wardrobe in the nearby Communal Museum. Also near the Stadhuis is a fountain that looks like a stone stairway: it's known as Marbol and was carved in 1475.

★ **Sint Bartholomeuskerk**: this is worth a look to see the excesses of neo-Gothicism – outrageous friezes and kitsch altarpieces. Perhaps in another 500 years it'll be viewed as a masterpiece.

★ **Museum of the Abbey of Sint Adriaan**: Abdijstraat 10. From April to the end of September, open 2–4.30pm, Sunday 2–6pm. Admission: 30BEF. The former abbot's house is set in a park 200 metres from the Markt. Next to nothing remains of the abbey, which was demolished by French revolutionaries in 1789. There's a small area devoted to Chantilly lace (which is actually black, though you'd never guess it from name, chantilly cream being white), but most of the exhibition space is given over to furniture and bits and pieces from the commune. One section traces the history of the cigar from 1860 to the present day, and includes a pipe cabinet and a match museum.

FESTIVAL

– **Krakelingenstoet** and **Tonnekebrand**: on the last Sunday in February, there's a festival that has its origins in the Dark Ages. A procession mounts the Oudenberg (the local hill), and when it reaches the top, the local worthies have to drink wine from a silver goblet containing wriggling little fish. When this ritual has been accomplished, thousands of *craquelins* (little brioche-like cakes) are thrown into the crowd. One of them contains a gold coin. In the evening, everyone dances round a barrel of pitch amid flaming torches.

NINOVE   34,000 habitants

The road to Aalst passes through this town, which has little to offer the visitor apart from its majestic baroque church, the Onze Lieve Vrouwekerk. It's worth a detour if you want to understand the pretensions of Counter-Reformation architecture.

EAST FLANDERS

WHAT TO SEE

★ **Onze Lieve Vrouwekerk**: closed Sunday afternoon. The history of the town is closely linked to the Premonstratensian Abbey, founded in 1137. It closed down in 1796 and was demolished 30 years later. Apart from a few little buildings, all that's left is the 17th-century abbey church. Inspired by St Peter's in Rome, it's a vast, imposing pile, with a wealth of ornamentation. Inside, there's some wonderful woodwork: confessionals, choir stalls, panelling and an organ case. If you're in luck, you'll hear the organist bashing out a bit of Bach.

– The surrounding area has been excavated by archaeologists; you can see their finds in the Communal Museum.

AALST	77,000 inhabitants

Aalst is a small industrial and commercial town between Ghent and Brussels, with a remarkable number of architectural treasures for such a small place.

A Short History

Because of its position at the crossroads of the Dender and the trade route between Bruges and Cologne, Aalst became a centre of cloth production and a trading town. It was the capital of 'Imperial Flanders' (i.e. Flanders when it was part of the Holy Roman Empire: its arms juxtapose the Lion of Flanders with the Imperial two-headed eagle). There are two local heroes. The first was Dirk Martens (1446–1534), the first printer in the southern Low Countries and a friend of Erasmus. He published Thomas More's *Utopia* and Christopher Columbus's text on the discovery of the New World in 1493. You can see his likeness in the statue that adorns the Grote Markt. Then came Adolf Daens, a priest and defender of the working classes, whose untiring action in the late 19th century led to the formation of the Christian Socialist Party (the CVP), for much of the last century the main political group in Flanders. There's even a book and a film about him: Louis-Paul Boon, also from Aalst, wrote a novel on the life and work of Daens, which scandalized right-thinking folk by bringing to light the exploitation of the labouring masses; this was followed in 1991 by Stijn Coninx's highly successful film *Daens*, nominated for a best foreign film Oscar.

USEFUL ADDRESS

Postcode: 9300.
🖬 **Tourist** office: Grote Markt 3.

☎ (053) 732270. Beneath the belfry. Helpful, friendly staff.

WHERE TO EAT

☆☆ Moderate

✕ **Borse Van Amsterdam**: Grote Markt 26. ☎ (053) 211581. Closed Wednesday evening and Thursday.

Daily special: 350BEF. This is a great place to get to grips with the town. It's a vast old debating chamber, with four Flemish Renaissance-style gables. There's a heated terrace, so you can enjoy the magnificent buildings on the Grote Markt in all weathers. The snacks are pretty good, but you can also have something a bit more sophisticated, such as eels in green sauce or lamb chops.

✕ **Eet & Coffiehuis Rozemarijn**: Rozemarijnstraat 7, on a little street that comes out at Sint Martinuskerk. ☎ (053) 214401. Open 11am–6pm.

Closed Sunday. A real gem of a place, this old house with bricks and beams is full of delicate touches: carefully chosen knick-knacks, baskets, dried flowers and teddy bears on the scatter cushions. A Pekinese dozes in front of the oven. At lunchtime, they serve snacks and vegetarian lasagne. Or, if you're feeling sweet-toothed, try the homemade crêpes or a slice of apple tart.

WHAT TO SEE AND DO

On the Grote Markt, an array of fine buildings surrounds a statue of Dirk Martens: the belfry, the burgomaster's house, with a gatehouse (Gebiedshuisje) beautifully carved in Flamboyant Gothic style.

★ **Burgomaster's House**: this 13th-century early-Gothic house is one of the oldest in the Low Countries, and following a recent restoration, it's gleaming. Temporary exhibitions are held in the crypt. The adjoining belfry dates from the 15th century, and its lantern houses a 52-bell carillon. On its facade, next to a bas-relief depicting the warrior and the bourgeois, you can read the motto of Philip II: '*Nec spec, nec metu*' (neither by hope, nor by fear). His preferred method, as the Low Countries learnt to their cost, was force. The nearby Stadhuis is a Classical-style 19th-century structure with a rococo facade in the courtyard.

★ **Sint Martinuskerk**: an example of Brabant Gothic architecture, the church is unfinished – in spite of its 16 pillars, the nave is truncated. You enter through the right-hand transept. Inside, you can look at Rubens's *St Roch Receiving from Christ the Gift of Healing the Plague*, Dirk Martens's tombstone (with an epitaph by Erasmus) and a monumental tabernacle in black-and-white marble by Jérôme Duquesnoy the Elder.

★ **Oud Hospitaal**: Oude Vismarkt, just past the church. The Old Hospital was built in the 15th century on land given away by Joan of Constantinople. The chapel and cloister are now home to the local museum.

★ **Stedelijk Museum**: open Tuesday to Friday, 10am–noon and 2–5pm (to 7pm on Wednesday), weekends 2–5pm. Admission: free. A detailed look at the history and folklore of Aalst, with armour, the mayoral chains of the guilds, carnival masks and nine paintings by Valerius de Saedeleer, a native of Aalst who painted magnificent Flemish landscapes. He was a member of the first school of Sint-Martens-Latem.

FESTIVAL

– **Carnival**: on the Sunday before Mardi Gras, festivities begin with a procession of giants (including the 'Steed Bayard', the emblem of nearby Dendermonde) and floats of satirical displays. On Monday, onions are thrown from the top of the belfry, while the Tuesday sees the dance of the

Vuile Jeannette ('Dirty Jeannettes'), men dressed as women – you're guaranteed a good laugh. In the evening, there's dancing around a bonfire.

DENDERMONDE   43,000 inhabitants

At the confluence of the Dender and the Scheldt, Dendermonde is a big town with a thriving commercial life. It had its golden age under the Burgundians, as you can see from the splendid buildings on the Grote Markt is proof of this. The local emblem is the Steed Bayard, a mythical horse that was supposedly drowned in the Scheldt on the orders of Charlemagne.

GETTING THERE

– **By road**: from Brussels via the A12, then take the N17, which starts at Mechelen; from Ghent, take the E17, then the N47.

– **By train**: Dendermonde is on the Ghent–Mechelen line.

A Short History

Dendermonde is a fortified town, and was besieged in 1667 by Louis XIV, who all but drowned his army of 50,000 men by opening the sluice gates. He was forced to withdraw, exclaiming scornfully: 'I'd need an army of ducks to take you'. Dendermonde was less fortunate in 1914, when attempts to resist the Germans led to wholesale destruction.

USEFUL ADDRESS

🄸 **Tourist office**: Stadhuis, Grote Markt. ☎ (052) 213956.

WHERE TO GO FOR A DRINK

🛉 **Café Ahura**: Grote Markt 30, Dendermonde 9200. Open from 11.30am (4pm at the weekend) to 1am (later on Saturday). Closed Monday. Opposite the town hall, in a house with baroque gables and a sign displaying two swans, this *eetcafe* is decorated in orange and blue, with outdoor seating in summer and jazz playing in the background. It serves light meals at low prices.

WHAT TO SEE

★ The **Grote Markt** and surrounding roads are buzzing on a Monday (market day). The beautiful Stadhuis, used as a cloth hall in the 14th century, and the grey-stone belfry are decked out in huge, brightly coloured flags, a common sight in Flanders.

At the back, you can see the horizontal stripes of the Justitiepalais, a bizarre mix of quasi-medieval and art-deco architecture that's seen to best advantage from the riverside.

★ **Museum of Archaeology**: on the right-hand corner of the Grote Markt, at No. 32. From April to the end of October, open 9am–12.30pm and 1.30–6pm. Closed Monday. Once home to the butchers' guild, and boasting a dinky corner tower, this excellent museum displays objects relating to the town's history and fossils that have been dug out of the sediment layers along the Scheldt, as well as artefacts once used by the guilds and an arsenal of weapons (including crossbows).

Upstairs, you'll find the skeleton of a woolly mammoth, discovered in a polder, while the exhibits on the ground floor include a naive painting of a 17th-century fisherman harpooning what could either be a dolphin or a whale in the Scheldt. Go along Kerkstraat, and you'll come to the 14th-century **Onze Lieve Vrouwekerk**. Inside, look out for the Romanesque baptismal fonts in Tournai limestone and paintings by Teniers and Van Dyck. On weekends, there are guided tours from 2pm to 4.30pm.

★ You can also see the splendidly preserved **Begijnhof Sint Alexius**, which you enter through a gateway opposite Oude Vest. This is a vast, tranquil quadrangle where housemartins and swallows soar above the contemporary-art installations that are dotted across the lawn. The chrome carcasses of motorbikes are juxtaposed with an outrageously kitsch shrine to the Virgin Mary in a display that's never less than eye-catching. The **museum** (at No. 11 and No. 25; same opening hours as the Museum of Archaeology) offers a peep into the daily life of the Beguines (whose beds were tiny).

FESTIVAL

– **Reuzenommegang**: a historic procession with giants, held on the Thursday after the fourth Sunday in August. Every 10 years, they wheel out the Steed Bayard with its masters, the four brothers in armour, on top. It weighs 700 kilos (1,540 pounds) and measures nearly six metres (20 feet) high, and 34 men are needed to move him. The locals are justly proud of their talisman, but you'll have to wait till 2010 to see him again.

The Flemish Ardennes

The countryside in the south of the province consists of rolling hills where the Scheldt zigzags lazily from Tournai through a verdant landscape, scattered with old villages and winding roads. Here, the 'flat country' rises a little – the summit of the Kluisberg, near Ronse, is a towering 150 metres (nearly 500 feet) above sea level.

OUDENAARDE (AUDENARDE) 27,000 habitants

The area's 'capital' has had its day, but there are plenty of traces of its former glory. That said, the beautiful buildings around the Grote Markt could do with a bit of sprucing up. Oudenaarde is known for two main commercial activities, brewing and weaving.

EAST FLANDERS

GETTING THERE

– **By road**: if you're coming from Ghent, take the N60. From the south, you need to come via Tournai and Ronse.

– **By train**: on the Bruges–Brussels line; trains stop at Kortrijk, Oudenaarde and Zottegem.

– **By bus**: Oudenaarde is on the Ghent–Ronse line, which belongs to De Lijn.

A Short History

Following early settlement further north and the construction of an abbey in Ename, Oudenaarde grew up around a little port on the edge of the river. Ramparts were built to protect this border town, whose position between France and the Holy Roman Empire was somewhat precarious. In 1521, Charles V, on a campaign in French territory, fell under the spell of a local beauty, Jeanne Van der Ginst de Nukerke. He left her with a souvenir: a daughter who was to become Margaret of Parma, and the future ruler of the Low Countries between 1559 and 1568. Meanwhile, Henri IV head-hunted two weavers from Oudenaarde, and gave them the job of sorting out the Gobelins in Paris. During the 17th century, 20,000 locals were employed in the weaving trade. Alas, as happened all too often in Flanders, the town's prosperity was wrecked by war. The French took the town three times before they were routed by the Duke of Marlborough in 1708. Recaptured by the French in 1745, the town's fortifications were dismantled. Since then, the only time there's been any action is on Thursday, market day.

USEFUL ADDRESS

Postcode: 9700.
🛈 **Tourist** office: Stadhuis, Markt. ☎ (055) 317251. Fax: (055) 309-248. Email: toerisme@oudenaarde.be. Open 9am–5pm during the week and 10am–5pm at the weekend in summer. Open 9am–noon and 1.30pm–4pm during the week and 2pm–5pm on Saturday, closed on Sunday in winter.

WHERE TO STAY

☆ Budget

🛏 **Hotel Elnik**: Deinzestraat 55, beyond the railway and near an industrial estate. ☎ (055) 335031. Fax: (055) 335030. A functional hotel, a bit of a way from the centre, but cheap for the area.

☆☆☆ Expensive

🛏 **Hotel-restaurant De Zalm**: Hoogstraat 4. ☎ (055) 311314. Fax: (055) 318440. Closed 8–31 July. A 19th-century building with an appealing facade opposite the Stadhuis. There are seven comfortable rooms, and you can tuck into traditional fare at the restaurant on the ground floor (closed Sunday evening and Monday).

WHERE TO EAT

The restaurants around the Grote Markt offer something for everyone, and when the sun's out, there are plenty of terraces to choose from.

☆ Budget

✕ **Café-restaurant De Carillon**: Markt 49, in the shadow of Sint Walburgakerk. ☎ (055) 311409. Closed Monday. Two gabled, brick buildings with red-and-white shutters and typical Flemish interiors. Old photos of the town hang on the walls. The menu and the cooking are predictable but keenly priced.

☆☆ Moderate

Brasserie De Mouterij: Markt 42, opposite De Carillon. ☎ (055) 318898. Open 11am–11pm. Closed Monday. This former maltings house has been attractively converted into a restaurant and grill. The decor is delightful: tiled floors, brick vaulting, dried hops, studded leather benches, enamelled advertising signs, brewers' tools and old photos of brewing as it used to be done. The house specialities are kebabs and spare ribs, and there's a good choice of beers. A really great place.

WHAT TO SEE

★ **Stadhuis**: this alone makes a visit to Oudenaarde worthwhile. It was finished in 1537, and is a marvellous example of Brabant Gothic architecture. The level of detail in the carving is worthy of a silversmith. The belfry bears a gilt statue of Hanske de Krijger (John the Warrior, the town's protector), while you'll also see the Habsburg insignia, the double-headed eagle. The funds needed to finance this building would have paid for 35 bourgeois houses. The material used was Balegem stone, which is very porous and was corroded by carbon-monoxide pollution during the 20th century. Every damaged stone has now been replaced by more durable French sandstone. From April to the end of October, there are guided tours of the **Stadhuis** on the hour at 11am (weekdays only), 2pm and 3.30pm. Admission: 100BEF.

★ The roof of the 13th-century **Cloth Hall** is shaped like an upturned Viking ship. Inside, the walls are hung with blue-green Oudenaarde tapestries, most depicting biblical or bucolic themes. It took between four and five years to complete a tapestry, which would typically be commissioned and based on a prior sketch. If you want to impress your partner, the foolproof way to spot a tapestry that was made in Oudenaarde is the inclusion of a thistle in the scene.

In a corner of the burgomaster's room is a portrait of Louis XIV on horseback. (He paid for the dolphin fountain in front of the Stadhuis.) In the other state rooms, you'll find wonderful pieces of furniture, including a 17th-century marquetry cabinet, and paintings by the local artist Adriaen Brouwer, including peasant scenes and an allegorical rendering of the Five Senses. There are also paintings by Jan 'Velvet' Brueghel and Jan van Ruysdael. The museum area has a collection of covered metal pots, called *simarts*, that were given to distinguished guests, while silverware, porcelain and other treasures testify to the rich heritage of the town.

EAST FLANDERS

★ The gigantic **Markt** is surrounded by beautiful Renaissance houses, although it seems that the locals are satisfied with cosseting their Stadhuis, as everything else looks a little neglected. Sint Walburgakerk looks like an elephant on the way to its graveyard, while the house of Margaret of Parma needs a serious clean. The town council is apparently waiting for a generous donor with a spare 100 million BEF to come along.

★ **Sint Walburgakerk**: visits must be booked in advance, but in July, August and September, you can go round on your own on Tuesday and Saturday from 2.30–4.30pm and on Thursday from 10–11am. The building process must have been a bit chaotic, because from the outside it looks like two churches back-to-back. From the porch, there's a vertiginous view of the 90-metre (297-foot) tower, topped by a delightful baroque hat. Inside, the treasury has a wonderful collection of church silver.

★ **Onze Lieve Vrouw Hospitaal**: behind Sint Walburgakerk. This working hospital is a collection of buildings of several periods. Its fine Gothic cloister makes it an ideal place for quiet contemplation, while Oudenaarde tapestries depicting hunting scenes decorate the convent parlour. Group visits only.

★ Opposite the Stadhuis, take Burg then Kasteelstraat to get to the **Begijnhof**, which you enter through a baroque porch. Keep walking and you'll come to the river, which looks more like a canal here.

★ On the other side of the river is the melancholy **Onze Lieve Vrouwekerk of Pamele**, built by one Arnulf in the 13th century. It's a very pure example of Scheldt Gothic, with a brightly coloured choir. Recumbent statues of the Lords of Pamele lie on their tombs inside. For most of the year, you have to join a guided tour to see the church (they're afraid of theft, apparently), which take place every day. From July to September, however, you can go round on your own on Tuesday and Saturday from 2.30pm to 4.30pm.

★ **Lalainghuis**: Bourgondiëstraat 9, on the same side as the Onze Lieve Vrouwekerk of Pamele. Open 9am–noon and 1–5pm from Monday to Thursday (to 3pm on Friday). Closed at the weekend and on public holidays. This fine Renaissance building, with a rococo frieze on its facade, is a sort of tapestry hospital, where tapestries are restored. New ones are also manufactured, and there's a training centre for apprentices in the craft. A display of photos explains the process of restoration. On your way out, pop into the pretty garden at the back.

★ If you've had enough of tapestries, why not investigate Oudenaarde's other well-known product: beer? **Liefmans** produces a bittersweet red-brown beer at its brewery (Aalststraat 200; ☎ (055) 311391), which is just a few hundred metres from the centre of town on the right bank. A quick detour to sample a *kriek* or a raspberry beer is a must, and beer buffs will want to tour the brewing works as well (visits by appointment only).

FESTIVAL

– Oudenaarde organizes a **beer festival** on the last weekend in June, using the painter Adriaen Brouwer (and his peasant scenes) as an excuse for high-jinks with a historic flavour.

RONSE (RENAIX)   24,000 inhabitants

Ronse nestles at the foot of the Kluisberg (145 metres, or 480 feet). Life flows peacefully by, interrupted only by occasional folkloric festivities. You'll hear French and Flemish spoken here, as you're very near the linguistic boundary.

USEFUL ADDRESS

日 Tourist office: Hoge Mote, De Biesestraat 2. ☎ (055) 232816. Fax: (055) 232819. Open 9am–noon and 12.30–4.30pm, with longer hours on summer weekends. A fine collection of yellow buildings in Hospitalstraat.

WHAT TO SEE

★ **Sint Hermeskerk**: from Easter to mid-November, open Tuesday to Saturday from 10am to noon and 2pm to 5pm, and on Sunday from 10am to noon and 3pm to 6pm. The main reason to visit is to see the crypt, which houses the relics of the curiously named Saint Hermes. Since the Middle Ages, they have been said to cure the mentally ill, and sick pilgrims used to come here, drink at the spring for the miraculous powers of its waters, then return home cured. The proportions of the crypt are beautifully harmonious. Archaeological digs have brought to light ancient coins, now on display in the side chapels.

★ Ronse also has a **textile museum** and a **folklore museum**, under the same roof. They're open from Tuesday to Friday, 10am–noon and 1–5pm, weekends 10am–noon and 2.30–5.30pm. Admission: 40BEF.

FESTIVALS

– **Bommelsfeesten**: held on the Saturday after Epiphany. The star attractions are the masked people (called *Bonmoss*).

– **Fiertelommegang:** held on the Sunday after Trinity. This festival is folkloric and religious: Sint Hermes' relics are taken on a 33-kilometre (20-mile) walk in the Flemish and Walloon countryside, with walkers or riders bringing up the rear.

The Province of Western Flanders (West-Vlaanderen)

'Land of the lost canal'. Nobody has described the countryside of coastal Flanders better than Belgium's most famous *chansonnier*, Jacques Brel. It's a vast, flat plain, reclaimed from the sea over the centuries, where water, land and sky merge in the maritime mists. Sheltered from the wind, the land of the polders is a harsh place where people keep to themselves. For four years, foreigners from afar fought and died in terrible battles on these flooded plains, leaving nothing but ruins and heart-wrenching cemeteries. Along the dunes, tourism has created a new Atlantic wall, packed with hotels, but the dunes are also home to salt pastures and nature reserves where rare birds nest.

Bruges is a city that's just as varied as the landscape where it lies: there's 'Bruges the Dead', forgotten by history 100 years ago; 'Bruges the Beautiful', with its wonderful restored treasures; 'Bruges the Wealthy', with its innumerable visitors; and 'Bruges the Mysterious', with its lesser-known neighbourhoods and timeless mysticism.

BRUGES (BRUGGE)   117,000 inhabitants

Bruges, Belgium's number one tourist town, is a historical miracle. For four centuries, it was forgotten by the world and untouched by industrialization, but its magnificent buildings were thoughtfully renovated during the 19th century craze for the neo-Gothic. Not everything in Bruges is genuine, but you'll almost certainly feel that you've stepped back to its glory days, when the Dukes of Burgundy ruled in all their glory, and you might even uncover the city's secret romantic and mystical side.

Before visiting Bruges, it's essential to remember the following:

First, Bruges is one of the most romantic cities in the world, so come with your beloved. You'll forge lasting memories of walking hand-in-hand along the canals, even in the rain. The cosy restaurants and heartwarming cafés are perfect for intimate, night-time tête-à-têtes.

Second, the height of summer, when the city is swamped by tourists, is not the best time to come. Try to come for a spring weekend, when daffodils carpet the lawns of the Begijnhof, or visit in early autumn, when you can stroll unhassled along the quaysides, explore the antiques shops and stalls, and feast on Flemish painting.

Third, and this is absolutely vital, the city is absolutely not designed for traffic, so your best bet if you want to discover Bruges's hidden corners is to hire a bike and lose yourself in the small, winding streets. Simply cross a bridge and you'll come across a church that's off the tourist track, a bar where time seems to have stood still or the worthy Guild of Archers, out practising their shots. The only hills are the humpbacked stone bridges, and, at night, you can pedal lazily over the cobbles and lose yourself in an universe of ghostly shapes.

GETTING THERE

By road: Bruges is near the E40 Brussels–Ostend motorway, 100 kilometres (62 miles) from Brussels. An access road takes you into the centre, but vast car parks are located on the outskirts to dissuade you from driving into the centre. The best, with 1,200 spaces, is at Zand, Vrijdagsmarkt. It's closed from 12.45am to 6.45am unless you have a weekend package deal, and the railway station is nearby (bike hire available). There are other free car parks all around the city's ring road.

By train: direct trains from Brussels leave every two hours, and there are services from Lille and Ghent.

A Short History

Bruges owes its existence to the movement of the sands. A thousand years ago, the coast of the North Sea looked quite different from what we see today: equinoctial tides frequently broke the frail barrier of dunes, and the sea washed over the lower land, leaving sand banks and natural channels. The area's poor soil was peopled by early Christians, descended from the Morin and Menapian tribes, whom Caesar hadn't even bothered to civilize. Free peasants later settled on one of the natural jetties *(brygghia*, from where the city gets its name), which was a bit less precarious than the others, and fortified the place to protect it from Norman raids. Count Baldwin Iron Arm, a notorious ruffian, acquired these uncultivated lands as a dowry from King Charles the Bald, whose daughter he had kidnapped, adding 'Flanders' to Artois and Cambrésis, which were already in his possession. That's how the history of Flanders became entangled with that of France.

The miracle of the sea

The site was fortified, and trading with the northern ports soon developed. A city wall was built and, in 1134, the elements were suddenly unleashed, causing the channel that connected Bruges to the sea to swell. The result was the formation of the River Zwin – and, for Bruges, which maintained a constant draining programme to prevent the river silting up, three centuries of prosperity. By the time Philip of Alsace, the Count of Flanders, granted the city its charter in 1150, Bruges was already a leading trader with England and the Baltics, and was governed by prosperous merchants who were a law unto themselves.

Damme was founded in 1180 as an outer harbour from which merchandise could be transported in smaller loads. Its geographical position – between England and the trade fairs of Champagne and Lombardie, between southwest France and the Baltic, between the Rhine basin and Brittany – made Bruges the most important trading centre of the Middle Ages. The counts of Flanders reaped the benefits of this flourishing trade, and in return strove to preserve the city's security.

Free trade and capitalism were born in this city following the creation of the first exchange, or 'Beurs', named after Van der Beurze, an innkeeper and courtier who specialized in money changing. Merchants from all over Europe flocked to the city, but the citizens of Bruges reserved the right to sell retail and to make up English cloth using a hired and strictly regulated workforce.

Troubled times, however, came with the dawn of the 14th century. After being ruled by several successive counts, Flanders fell under the dominion of the King of France, Philip the Fair, whose attitude to Flanders was harsh. He sided with the city's worthies, or *Leliaerts* (whose emblem was the fleur de lys), and the skilled tradesmen revolted, as much against their exploited condition as against the power now pledged to the French. On the morning of 18 May 1302, the *Klauwaerts* (named after the claws of the heraldic Flemish lion) took up their swords and slaughtered anyone who, on waking, was unable to pronounce, with the correct guttural accent, the words *schild en vriend* (shield and friend, although it's more likely that the phrase was '*s gilden vriends*: 'friend of the guilds').

The French and the Francophiles were massacred, and a furious Philip the Fair sent his elite troops to subjugate the yokels.

The clash took place beneath the walls of Kortrijk on 11 July. The Flemish footsoldiers had no trouble unseating the French knights, who were hampered by the mud and weighed down, like their horses, by heavy armour. No prisoners were taken, and the spurs of the fallen French were carried off as trophies, a souvenir of the triumph of the small over the great and powerful.

Many equally brutal and important battles took place on Flemish soil, but the Battle of the Golden Spurs was the one adopted by the Flemish movement in the 19th century as an emblem of the struggle of the people against the oppression of the patricians. History can be handy when it comes to politics.

The rise . . .

In 1369, the marriage of Philip the Bold, Duke of Burgundy, to Margaret of Maele, heir to the county of Flanders, marked the beginning of Bruges' golden age, but also the start of its decline. The Zwin began to silt up, and Bruges had just one more glorious century in store. On an artistic level, the city rivalled Florence, with Memling, Van Eyck, Van der Goes and Gerard David producing masterpieces of the 15th-century Flemish school.

Every day, ships from Venice, Catalonia, Russia, Genoa, Biscay, Brittany, the Hanseatic League and Portugal unloaded their merchandise. As many as 150 boats at a time could be seen in the Minnewater harbour, unloading wine, carpets, oranges, furs, oil, leather, silks, metals, spices, wool, exotic animals, ivory and diamonds.

In 1429, Philip the Good established his court in the Prinsenhof, and his marriage to Isabel of Portugal was celebrated with the most sumptuous festivities. The town was hung with scarlet drapes, 800 merchants in full regalia were there to welcome the bride, and for the wedding feast, the crockery was made of gold, the hangings were woven with gold thread and the food was magnificent. Festivities continued the following day, with jousts and receptions, described, by contemporary reporters as unequalled in Christendom. To cap it all, Philip the Good created the Order of the Golden Fleece, with himself at the helm and 23 other members. It was to become the envy of neighbouring countries. Unfortunately, Philip committed the *faux pas* of failing to ask his king, Charles VII, for permission.

In 1468, the table was laid once more for the marriage of Charles the Bold and Margaret of York. But the new Duke of Burgundy was less popular. He raised taxes to finance his campaigns against, among others, Liège and Dinant. He died in 1477, during the siege of Nancy, leaving his daughter Marie (the idol of the citizens of Bruges) as heir to the duchy of Burgundy. When she married Archduke Maximilian of Austria, the duchy passed to the Habsburgs. Marie died in a hunting accident, and Maximilian made himself so unpopular that the people of Bruges took him prisoner. His chief adviser, Pieter Lanchals (Long Neck, as the Flemish called him), was decapitated under Maximilian's nose, and the Archduke, understandably perturbed, gave in to the demands of the locals – on condition that he be freed. The story goes that they honoured him with the job of looking after the long-necked swans – souvenirs of his beheaded adviser.

. . . and fall
Meanwhile, the River Zwin had finally silted up, and the city became ever more dependent on the harbours of Damme and Sluis. They stepped up protectionist measures and stringent controls, but their cloth production was no longer competitive: the English had learned to weave, and no longer needed to ship raw material to Flanders. As for Maximilian, the grudge he bore Bruges led him to favour the merchants' move to Antwerp, which was fast becoming a major international trading centre. When foreign residents left Bruges in the early 16th century, more than 5,000 houses were abandoned. In 1520, two Venetian ships dropped anchor in Sluis. The republic, also in decline, had come to pay its final respects to its sister city in the north. The religious turbulence that followed the Reformation did nothing to improve things, with many wealthy citizens preferring exile in the Netherlands to persecution by the Inquisition back home.

Over the next three centuries, Bruges lived in the hope, postponed a hundred times, that a canal would connect it to the sea. But the trade routes followed different paths, and Bruges's link with Ghent reduced its status to that of a regional port. It maintained a local lace industry, which just about sustained a small part of the population. The poor lived off charity, and landlords organized a system of almshouses and hospices to help the needy. Within the fortified city walls, there was room to grow crops. With Belgian independence (1830), Bruges became a provincial capital. Fourteen years later, famine caused the people to riot. Old plans to build a canal to the sea surfaced once again, and this time, thanks to the efforts of Leopold II, they came to fruition in 1907 with the Blankenberge–Heist canal, which was destroyed during World War II.

Rebirth
Bruges owes its renaissance to its past. In the second half of the 19th century, writers and English Romantic artists touring the Continent fell in love with the city, which was only too happy to satisfy their passion for all things medieval. They were joined by other Brits, who decided to move to Bruges for more practical reasons. Many were retired army officers from India, who could no longer afford the luxurious lifestyle they had enjoyed in Bengal or Punjab. Settling a short distance from England's white cliffs, they bought splendid mansions in Bruges for next to nothing, and staffed them with modestly paid employees. The new jet set formed a mini colony: friends and relatives visited them, and it wasn't long before an English school was set up, complete with boaters and uniforms. Bruges emerged from its torpor and began to restore its magnificent heritage and clean up the canals. New buildings went up, in imitation of medieval houses. Hotels and restaurants sprang up, and the rest is history – and is, indeed, why you are reading these words. In 1949, in recognition of its past as an international city, Bruges was chosen to train the future elite of the European Community in the College of Europe. The city is now gearing up for its stint as Cultural Capital of Europe in 2002.

GETTING AROUND

The historic centre of Bruges is an oval not much more than a couple of miles across, so you can get everywhere on foot or by bike. The one-way traffic system is designed to drive motorists mad, as is the speed limit of 30 kph (18mph). Bikes, however, can go both ways down many (but not all) of the streets.

As you leave the station, you'll see a De Lijn information point selling tickets for local buses (40BEF), all of which go to the central Markt. It's impossible to get lost in Bruges: you only have to look up and you'll see one of the city's three distinctive towers, all of which are useful orientation points. You'll soon learn to tell them apart.

If you've come by car, there's a big car park near the station. The town council is planning to offer all drivers who leave their vehicles here free bus tickets for the Markt. Price: 100BEF, which includes the bus ride. You may as well take the bus, since cars are not allowed into the Markt.

USEFUL ADDRESSES

Postcode: 8000.

⊞ Tourist office (map C2): main office, Burg 11. ☎ (050) 448686. Fax: (050) 448600. Email: toer isme@brugge.be. Website: www.brugge.be/brugge. From April to September, open Monday to Friday 9.30am–6pm, weekends 10am–noon and 2–6.30pm; the rest of the year, open Monday to Friday 9.30am–5pm, weekends 9.30am–1pm and 2–5.30pm. Bureau de change available. Combined tickets for Bruges's museums at discounted rates. Cassette guides for tours around the city: 300BEF, plus 1,000BEF deposit. These can be used by two people simultaneously. The tourist office also takes bookings for themed guided tours for groups; these last about two hours. In July and August, guided tours of the city leave the tourist office at 3pm, price 150BEF (free for children under 14).

⊞ Station tourist office: ☎ (050) 388083. Fax: (050) 381842. On your right, 50 metres further on as you come out of the station. Can make hotel bookings.

✉ Post office (map B2): Markt 5. ☎ (050) 331411.

■ Bureaux de change (map B2, **1**): all the cash machines marked Bancontact/Mister Cash will let you take out Belgian money with Eurocard, MasterCard, Visa and the main credit cards. There's a cash machine in the station.

🚆 Railway station (map A4): Stationsplein. ☎ (050) 382382.

🚌 Public transport: De Lijn. ☎ (059) 565353. A single ticket costs 40BEF.

■ Bike hire: on offer at some hotels.

– **Railway station**: ☎ (050) 302-329. Bike hire available near the left-luggage area (cheaper for ticket-holders): 325BEF per day.

– **'t Koffieboontje** (map B3, **2**): Hallestraat 4. ☎ (050) 338027. Bike hire by the hour, the half-day, the day (325BEF) and the week. Tandems and buggies can be hired. Special rates for students.

– **De Ketting** (map C3): Gentpoortstraat 23. ☎ (050) 344196. The cheapest in town: 150BEF per day.

– **Éric Popelier** (map B3, **2**): Hallestraat 14. ☎ (050) 343262. Bikes and scooters: 325BEF per day.

■ **Useful addresses**

- **ℹ**   Tourist Office
- **✉**   Post Office
- **🚂**   Railway station
- **1**   Bureau de change
- **2**   Koffie boontje and Éric Popelier bike hire

🛏 **Where to stay**

- **7**   Relais Oud Huis Amsterdam
- **8**   Hotel-restaurant De Barge
- **9**   B&B Marian Degraeve
- **10**   't Geerwyn, rooms from hosts Mr and Mrs De Loof
- **11**   Youth Hostel Europa
- **12**   Bauhaus International Youth Hostel
- **13**   De Passage
- **14**   Snuffel Travellers Inn
- **15**   Hotel Van Eyck
- **16**   Hotel Ensor
- **17**   Hotel Boterhuis
- **18**   Hotel Singe d'Or
- **19**   Hotel Lybeer
- **20**   Hotel Groeninge
- **21**   Hotel Lucca
- **22**   Hotel Asiris
- **23**   Hotel Jacobs
- **24**   Hotel Cavalier
- **25**   Hotel de Goezeput
- **26**   Hotel Fevery
- **27**   't Koffieboontje
- **28**   Hotel Adornès
- **29**   Hotel Impérial
- **30**   Hotel Botaniek
- **31**   Hotel Aarendhuis
- **32**   Hotel Ter Reien
- **33**   Hotel Ter Duinen
- **34**   Romantik Pand Hotel
- **35**   Hotel Die Swaene
- **36**   B&B Dieltiens Koen & Annemie
- **37**   Hotel De Pauw
- **38**   Hotel Karel De Stoute
- **39**   Hotel Malleberg

✕ **Where to eat**

- **40**   In 't Nieuwe Museum
- **41**   Tavern Oud Handbogenhof
- **42**   Gran Kaffee de Passage
- **43**   Tavern The Hobbit
- **44**   't Terrasje
- **45**   't Mozarthuis
- **46**   De Zilveren Pauw
- **47**   De Lotus
- **48**   Breydel-De Coninck
- **49**   De Koetse
- **50**   't Zonneke
- **51**   Den Eeckhoute
- **52**   De Stove
- **53**   De Mosselkelder
- **54**   Het Bargehuis
- **55**   Pannekoekenhuisje
- **56**   Den Dyver
- **58**   De Witte Poorte
- **59**   Tea-Room de Proeverie
- **60**   Soul Food

★ **What to see**

- **81**   Burg
- **82**   Stadhuis
- **83**   Heiligbloed Basiliek
- **84**   Groeninge Museum
- **85**   Brangwyn Museum
- **86**   Gruuthuse Museum
- **87**   Onze Lieve Vrouwekerk
- **88**   Sint Janshospitaal/Memling Museum
- **89**   Almshouses
- **90**   Straffe Hendrik brewery
- **91**   Prinselijk Begijnhof ten Wijngaarde
- **92**   Minnewater
- **93**   Sint Salvatorkathedraal
- **94**   Markt
- **95**   Belfry
- **96**   Sint Walburgakerk
- **97**   Sint Annakerk
- **98**   Stedelijk Museum voor Volkskunst
- **99**   Jeruzalemkerk
- **100**   Guild of St George
- **101**   Windmills
- **102**   Guido-Gezelle Museum
- **103**   Sint Sebastiaansgilde
- **104**   Engelsklooster
- **105**   Potterie Museum
- **106**   Sint Gilliskerk
- **107**   Tollhouse
- **108**   Huis ter Beurze
- **109**   Bladelin
- **110**   Sint Jacobskerk
- **111**   Diamond Museum

BRUGES

BRUGES

– **Bauhaus Bike Rental** (map D2): ☎ (050) 341093. A day's hire costs 250BEF.
– **Quasimodo**: Leenhofweg 7, Brugge 8310. ☎ (050) 370470. Fax: (050) 374960. Guided bike tours of Bruges and the surrounding area, to Damme or the Dutch border, from mid-March to late September. Price per person: 650BEF (550BEF for under-26s). Waterproofs, helmets and water bottles provided. Meet at the Burg. Phone ahead for departure times.
■ **Taxis**: ☎ (050) 334444.

WHERE TO STAY

One of the best things about Bruges is that there are 80 hotels in and around town, most of which are relatively inexpensive, given the hospitality and efficiency they offer. There are plenty of delightful establishments, and the only problem is making a choice.

Several hotels offer weekend and low-season bargains with extras, such as tickets to major exhibitions or religious processions. Inquire about these when you book – which you should do as early as possible. The hotels listed below are all popular, so it's essential to book well in advance. If you're stuck, head for nearby Ostend instead.

NB: the prices for the hotels below include breakfast unless otherwise stated.

Campsites

🛖 **Memling** (off the map from D2): Veltemweg 109, Sint-Kruis 8310. ☎ and fax: (050) 355845. A couple of miles east of town: take bus No. 11, which goes to the station. Expect to pay 350BEF to pitch a two-person tent. This campsite is shaded and well equipped, but a bit ordinary. There's a supplement if you want to use the showers. Restaurant on site. Bike hire available. A few wooden cabins (*trekkershutten*). Supermarket and covered swimming pool nearby.

🛖 **Sint-Michiel** (off the map from A4): Tillegomstraat 55, Sint Michiels 8200. ☎ (050) 380819. Fax: (050) 806824. Same prices as the Memling site. Small, cheap restaurant.

🖈 Budget

🛖 **Youth Hostel Europa** (map C4, **11**): Baron Ruzettelaan 143, Assebroek 8310. ☎ (50) 352679. Fax: (050) 353732. On the way out of town, towards Oostkamp. From the station, take bus No. 2 or No. 749, heading for Assebroek, then get off at Wantestraat. There's no reception between 10am and 1pm during the week and between 10am and 5pm on Sunday (cleaning day). Closed for three weeks from mid-December. There are 208 beds and 41 rooms, including 22 family rooms with shower and private toilet. Basic rate per night: 405BEF. The biggest youth hostel in the country, and ultramodern. There's no curfew, and they'll give you a decent town map. A lot of groups come here, so make sure you book well in advance.

🛖 **Youth Hostel Herdersbrug**: Louis Coiseaukaai 46, Brugge-Dudzele 8380. ☎ (050) 599321. Fax: (050) 599349. Next to the Bruges-Zeebrugge canal, 6 kilometres (4 miles) north of the city. Take bus No. 788 from the station and get off at Dudzele Dorp, from where it's a 15-minute walk. Closed mid-December to mid-January. A hostel with 19 rooms, nine of which are for families. Basic rate per night: 420BEF. Breakfast 120BEF. Free car park. Bike hire. Restaurant. Sheet hire available. Tennis court, rowing, canoeing.

♙ **Youth Hostel Die Loyale Maldegem**: Gentse Steenweg 1274, 9990 Maldegem. ☎ (050) 713121. Fax: (050) 719070. About 15 kilometres (10 miles) from Bruges. De Lijn buses run from Bruges, Damme and Gent (line No. 58). Closed between early November and mid-April. Basic rate per night: 495BEF, including breakfast. An elegant villa surrounded by a large garden, Die Loyale Maldegem has 66 beds and a brand new wing of light, well equipped chalets with four beds. Especially recommended for cyclists. Bike hire available.

♙ **Bauhaus International Youth Hostel** (map D2, **12**): Langestraat 133–137. ☎ (050) 341093. Fax: (050) 334180. From the station, take bus No. 6 or 16. Doubles 950BEF; dormitory beds 380BEF. This spacious hostel near one of the city's medieval gates has 112 beds in attractive rooms that sleep one to eight people. There's no curfew, it's clean, and shared shower facilities, duvets and showers are included in the price. There's also a laundry next door. The hostel can suggest a host of things to do in town, and you can hire a bike to get around; it also has a curious clock that tells the time backwards and the biggest selection of CDs in Bruges. The excellent bar-restaurant (open 6pm–midnight) serves salads, steaks, pizzas and vegetarian dishes for about 300BEF. All in all, it's a great place for hikers, although it can be a tad noisy. Bauhaus is a member of the Europe Famous 5 Hostels association, which represents 130 independent European youth hostels: a members' card (600BEF) entitles you to a discount.

An annex, **Bauhaus Twins Hotel**, is opening in a historic building next door (Langestraat 133; ☎ (050) 336175. It has 21 double or triple rooms with showers, and is in the 'moderate' price bracket: 1,300BEF for a double, with breakfast 60BEF. Needless to say, you get all the benefits of the Bauhaus atmosphere.

♙ **De Passage** (map B3, **13**): Dweerstraat 26. ☎ (050) 340232. Fax: (050) 340140. Take a bus towards the Markt from the station, and get off at Sint Salvatorkerk. Basic rate per night: 430BEF, including sheets and duvets. Breakfast for an extra 100BEF. Great location. Fifty beds, in double rooms or rooms for four, six and seven with bunk beds. Showers and toilets upstairs. Fairly well maintained. Doubles as a café-restaurant (*see* 'Where to eat'). Cool youth-hostel atmosphere, with prices to match. The restaurant's *plat du jour* costs an unbeatable 220BEF. They'll give you a handy foldout map that lists museum opening times. Next door, De Passage Hotel has simple, slightly more expensive rooms (*see below*).

♙ **Snuffel Travellers Inn** (map A-B2, **14**): Ezelstraat 47-49. ☎ (050) 333133. Fax: (050) 333250. Take bus No. 3 or 13 from the station and get off at Snuffel. Basic rate per night: 430BEF. Rooms sleep two, eight or 12, and there are 58 beds in all. All rooms have a sink, and some a shower, and there are lockable cupboards. The level of cleanliness depends on that of the occupants. Sheet hire available. Very good rates, with breakfast an extra 50BEF. Cooking facilities. Rock music in the café, where there's a special deal enabling you to sample five different beers. The charming manager goes out of his way to keep customers happy. Especially good for cyclists.

B&Bs

This option is highly recommended for your stay in Bruges, and some of these places are real gems. You'll have happy memories of your trip, and maybe even new friends, thanks to the warmth and consideration on offer.

There are at least 40 B&B options in Bruges, and we couldn't list them all. Look in the *Logiesbrochure*, where you'll find them all listed, with double or triple rooms; or visit the tourist office if you can stomach the queues.

≜ Dieltiens Koen & Annemie (map C2, **36**): Sint Walburgastraat 14. ☎ (050) 334294. Fax: (050) 335230. Email: koen.dieltjens@sky net.be. An establishment that's as enlightened as the era it was built in – the 18th century. Only 300 metres from the Markt, on a very quiet street. The hosts are a musician couple who let out three rooms for 1,600–1,900BEF. There's one big room with en suite bathroom that can take a family of four, while another has a cabin bed that kids will appreciate. Breakfast is an unforgettable experience (just look at the comments in the visitors' book), and you eat it together, so the topics of conversation are usually far-ranging. If they're full, they'll suggest other B&Bs in town. They also have a studio and flat for rent by the week or weekend. Non-smoking establishment.

≜ Gheeraert Paul & Roos (map C2): Ridderstraat 9. ☎ (050) 335627. Fax: (050) 345201. Email: paul.gheeraert@skynet.be. Double room 1,900BEF. On the second floor of a beautiful neoclassical building right in the centre, with three spacious, quiet rooms for two or three: double beds, en suite bathrooms and, at the back, views of the garden and Sint Walburgakerk. Reproductions on the walls and fine flooring. The landlady restores paintings and her husband is an architect. Across the street, they let out four apartments and studios for two to six people for weekends, midweek stays or by the week. They're self-contained, with kitchen facilities

and bathrooms, and are tastefully decorated. The best one is the attic, with its sloping ceiling directly under the roof. Prices from 7,000BEF to 11,000BEF for a weekend. From mid-November to early March (except at Christmas and New Year), there's a 20 per cent reduction. Non-smoking.

≜ 't Geerwyn, Mr and Mrs De Loof (map B2, **10**): Geerwijnstraat 14. ☎ and fax: (050) 340544. Website: www.sin.be/chris.deloof. Quiet street very near the centre of town, with three rooms for two: 1,900BEF. Shared kitchen facilities. The rooms are named after famous painters, decorated in Provençal style and furnished with the utmost taste by the polyglot couple who run it (the husband is a talented watercolourist). Your hosts are extremely attentive, and you can't fail to have happy memories of your stay. There's a car park nearby. Generous breakfasts.

≜ Het Wit Beertje, Mr Defour (off the map from A3: about 200 metres from the station, at the end of Smedenstraat): Witte Beerstraat 4. ☎ (050) 450888. Fax: (050) 450880. Email: jp.defour@worldonline.be. An unpretentious house outside the historic centre, but near the station. If you're coming by train, let them know, and they'll come and meet you. Run by a very kind local couple who let out three slightly kitsch rooms with TV, shower and en suite toilet at bargain prices: 1,600BEF, or 1,150BEF for a single. Breakfast is served in the garden or in your room. They don't take credit cards, but they do allow dogs, and can supply brochures about the city.

🛉 **Marian Degraeve** (map D3, **9**): Kazernevest 32. ☎ and fax: (050) 345711. Email: wimvandecappelle @worldonline.be. Near the outer canal. A grungy, artsy household where the decor's slightly crazy and verging on the kitsch, and where the owners are obviously into cinema. They offer two perfectly acceptable double rooms at 1,600BEF. Shared bathroom. Perfect for trendy young hikers, it also offers an excellent list of cheap restaurants and a beer that shares its name with the hotel.

🛉 **Mr and Mrs Goethals** (off the map from C1): Damse Vaart Zuid 14. ☎ and fax: (050) 350191. Website: bedandbreakfast@baeb.net. Closed January and February. Double rooms 1,700–1,800BEF. Right next to the start of the canal to Damme, this is a traditional Flemish building with a back garden that boasts some majestic rare trees. There are three good-sized rooms with timeless decor for two, three or four people, and the owners are friendly. The room for two has an en suite shower.

☆–☆☆ Budget–Moderate

🛉 **Bauhaus Twins Hotel**: annex of the Bauhaus International Youth Hotel (*see above*).

🛉 **Passage Hotel** (map B3, next to **13**): Dweersstraat 28. ☎ and reception: *see* De Passage, *above*. Almost the cheapest in town: 1,400–2,000BEF, including breakfast in the café next door. The annex of the youth hostel is a little house with a narrow stairway that has been modified to house 10 pretty rooms. They're all reasonably well decorated, each in a different colour: some have a sink, others shared bathrooms. It's clean but spartan, and not a good choice for basketball players.

🛉 **Hotel Ensor** (map A3, **16**): Speelmansrei 10. ☎ (050) 342589. Fax: (050) 342018. 200 metres from the Zand. From 2,200BEF to 2,400BEF. A huge brick house with geraniums in the window and 12 recently renovated rooms with bath or shower. Lovely owners. Lift and TV room. Fine views over the canal. Paying car park.

🛉 **Hotel Singe d'Or** (map A–B3, **18**): 't Zand 18. ☎ (050) 334848. Within walking distance of the station. If you like late nights and you're not afraid of the noise from the nearby funfair, this is the place for you. It's one of the cheapest options in Bruges: 1,600BEF, with a sink in every room. Rooms with shower and toilet cost 2,500BEF. On the ground floor, a neo-Gothic tavern offers light meals from 250BEF.

🛉 **Hotel Lybeer** (map B3, **19**): Korte Vulderstraat 31. ☎ and fax: (050) 334355. Email: lybeer@skynet.be. On a quiet street near the Zand. Double room from 1,650BEF to 1,950BEF. The 23 rooms in this hotel offer basic levels of comfort, although a little more effort in terms of general maintenance and welcome wouldn't go amiss. The prices reflect the social standing of the area. Bike hire available. Welcome drink on arrival.

🛉 **Hotel Groeninge** (map B3, **20**): Korte Vulderstraat 29. ☎ (050) 343255. Fax: (050) 340769. Closed January and the last two weeks of June. Eight rooms: doubles 2,800BEF. A bit dearer than the Lybeer, but rather more luxurious. Wonderful old-fashioned decor, with knick-knacks all over the place, and recently redecorated.

☆☆ Moderate

🛉 **Hotel De Pauw** (plan C1, **37**): Sint Gilliskerkhof 8. ☎ (050) 337118. Fax: (050) 345140. Email:

info@hoteldepauw.be. Closed January. Opposite Sint Gilliskerk. Eight well-kept rooms with toilets and sink or shower from 1,850BEF to 2,450BEF. A delightful hotel with flowers in the windows. Generous breakfast. The landlady is a model of kindness. Parking nearby.

♣ Hotel Lucca (map B2, **21**): Naaldenstraat 30. ☎ (050) 342067. Fax: (050) 333464. Light rooms with big, double-glazed windows and floral wallpaper: from 1,950BEF to 2,900BEF. Some rooms sleep four people, so they're ideal for families. This used to be the house of merchants from Lucca, in Tuscany; it was also once a Masonic lodge serving the area around Sint Jacobskerk. They now use the atmospheric 14th-century vaulted cellar as the reception area and breakfast room. Stay for two or more nights and you get a free canal tour or bike hire.

♣ Hotel Asiris (map C1, **22**): Lange Raamstraat 9. ☎ (050) 341724. Fax: (050) 347458. Email: hotel.asiris@skynet.be. An old patrician house in a quiet district around Sint Gilliskerk. Eleven rooms with bathrooms: from 2,100BEF to 2,500BEF. Family rooms for four are 4,000BEF. The smallest rooms are under the eaves. Special tariffs in low season, and weekend packages. Katie and Eric take their job as hoteliers very seriously, and will go to any lengths to satisfy their guests. Private paying car park.

♣ Hotel Jacobs (map C1, **23**): Baliestraat 1, in the same district as the Asiris. ☎ (050) 339831. Fax: (050) 335694. Email: hotel.jacobs@glo.be. Closed January. Doubles 2,500–2,850BEF, and cheaper if you only have a sink in your room. A beautiful corner house with window boxes, striking gabling and impeccable rooms with en suite bath or shower at very reasonable prices. The atmosphere is cosy, and

there's a friendly bar for a final drink and a chat before you sink into bed. Parking nearby.

♣ Hotel de Goezeput (map B3, **25**): Goezeputstraat 29. ☎ (050) 342694. Fax: (050) 342013. Closed mid-January to mid-February. A quiet establishment near the Zand, in a former abbey building. Big rooms with en suite shower and toilet at 2,800BEF. Good for families, with discounts for children under 10.

♣ 't Koffieboontje Restaurant-Tea-Room-Hotel (map B3, **27**): Hallestraat 4. ☎ (050) 338027. Fax: (050) 343904. Prices vary considerably: from 1,700BEF to 4,500BEF. It's hard to get more central than this hotel, right behind the Belfort. The 14 rooms are comfortable but standardized, and some have kitchen facilities. Prices plummet in winter. Rooms sleep four, apartments, six. Bike hire available.

♣ Hotel Fevery (map C1, **26**): Collaert Mansionstraat 3. ☎ (050) 331269. Fax: (050) 331791. Website: www.hotelfevery.be. In the shadow of Sint Gilliskerk. Rooms with en suite shower or bath from 2,000BEF to 2,600BEF. Closed February. Appearances can be deceptive: banal on the outside, this hotel has a welcoming, family feel inside, and has recently been redecorated. Peaceful nights guaranteed. If you're arriving by train after 11am, phone ahead and you'll be collected from the station. Car park nearby. Discounts for bike hire.

♣ Hotel Van Eyck (map B3, **15**): Korte Zilverstraat 7. ☎ (050) 335267. Fax: 050 349430. Email: vaneyck@unicall.be. Right by the Markt, in the middle of the shopping district, but on a quiet street. Eight recently decorated rooms, with varying levels of comfort: 2,200–2,700BEF. A big, white house with a decent, middle-class atmosphere. Pictures of the Belgian royal family greet you in the sitting room. There's an amazing spiral staircase, with a stained-glass window, leading to sober but pretty rooms. The buffet-style breakfast is served in a room painted in cheerful bright colours, with a reproduction of Manet's *Déjeuner sur l'herbe*. A dignified clientele seems to adore the slightly antiquated charm of this hotel, although the staff could do with improving their attitude a shade. Discount card available for Bruges's museums.

♠ Hotel Cavalier (map B2, **24**): Kuipersstraat 25. ☎ (050) 330-207. Fax: (050) 347199. Email: hotel.cavalier@skynet.be. Doubles 2,400BEF. A traditional house near the Markt, behind the municipal theatre. The walls in the main room are decorated with classical murals. The eight rooms offer varying degrees of comfort: none are brilliantly equipped, but all have toilets and baths. Only the best offer real value for money, so ask to have a look before you check in. The quietest are at the back. Reductions from mid-November to mid-December and January to mid-March.

☆☆–☆☆☆ Moderate–Expensive

♠ Hotel Impérial (map B3, **29**): Dweerstraat 24. ☎ (050) 339014. Fax: (050 (344306). Doubles 2,500–2,900BEF. A delightful hotel that's perfect for romantic couples, with stepped gabling and a delicately decorated hallway where flowers, ornaments and birds create a cosy, domestic setting. The nine light rooms have showers, lace curtains and king-size beds. Three family rooms and three small rooms (no TV, but who needs it in this city?). Two rooms sleep four. Breakfast is served in a room that looks onto the interior courtyard, arranged as a garden. No credit cards. Book in

advance to avoid disappointment. Car park available.

♠ Hotel Botaniek (map C3, **30**): Waalsestraat 23. ☎ (050) 341424. Fax: (050) 345939. Email: hotel-botaniek@ping.be. A 17th-century family mansion not far from Astridpark and the Burg down a quiet street. Nine very comfortable rooms, competitively priced: 2,500–3,000BEF. The decor is no-nonsense classy, and rooms under the eaves offer fantastic views over Bruges's dreaming spires. Buffet breakfast. Extra charge for use of the garage.

♠ Hotel Malleberg (map C2, **39**): Hoogstraat 7. ☎ (050) 344111. Fax: (050) 346769. In the centre of town, near the Burg. Doubles 2,900BEF. A small, chic hotel offering eight rooms with shower, some under the eaves, painted in warm colours with wood flooring and exposed beams. The street is noisy, so go for the rooms at the back or on the top floor. The restaurant serves such delights as eels in green sauce, a Belgian speciality.

♠ Hotel-Restaurant De Barge (map C4, **8**): Bargeweg. ☎ (050) 385150. Fax: (050) 38-21-25. Doubles 2,580–2,680BEF. Closed from mid-December to late January. Why not stay on a canal? As the name suggests, this is a barge, moored at the start of the Bruges–Ghent canal, not far from the station. It's been done up as a floating hotel, with 23 small but quiet rooms. The biggest are in the stern. Also on board is a restaurant serving decent food with a mostly maritime flavour, albeit seemingly tailored to suit coach-loads of visitors.

☆☆☆ Expensive

♠ Hotel Adornès (map C2, **28**): Sint Annarei 26. ☎ (050) 341336. Fax: (050) 342085. Closed January to mid–February. Doubles 2,900–3,700BEF. They treat you as a friend

BRUGES

at this hotel, a charming collection of three restored gabled houses at the confluence of three canals in the Sint Anna district, the most authentic in Bruges. It offers a handful of spick-and-span cream rooms with pine furniture, exposed beams and bathrooms decorated with plants. The best rooms are Nos. 15, 16 and 17, which overlook the canal. If possible, avoid the ones next to the lift. The ample buffet breakfast is served in a room with a beautiful fireplace. In the vaulted cellar, you'll find books of photos of Bruges in 1900. Free parking for cars and bikes. The hotel offers a card with reductions for the 10 main museums in town and a boat trip on the canals. In low season, you also get a free ticket for one of the city's museums if you stay for two or more nights. As you may have gathered, we really liked this place.

★ **Hotel Ter Reien** (map C2, **32**): Langestraat 1. ☎ (050) 349100. Fax: (050) 344048. Email: hotel.ter. Reien@online.be. Doubles 2,800–3,500BEF. Next to a canal, this modern building with 26 rooms offers reasonable value for money. The welcome is professional and cheerful, and the light, spacious rooms are functional and luxurious. Some are for three or four, at bargain prices. The most expensive look onto the canal, while the wedding suite has a four-poster bed. On fine days, you can eat breakfast in the little courtyard. Bar and fitness room. Parking on a side street.

★ **Hotel Karel De Stoute** (map B2, **38**): Moerstraat 23. ☎ (050) 343317. Fax: (050) 344472. Email: kareldestoute@itinera.be. In a quiet but central area near Sint Jacobskerk, with easy parking. Doubles 3,300BEF. A large white building on much older foundations, with a vaulted cellar and corner tower to prove it. Charles the Bold stayed here. The family rooms are spacious and comfortable, with shower and bath, but you'd expect a bit more individuality at these prices. No. 3 and No. 7 have bathrooms in the tower; No. 9 and No. 11 have views of the garden. Breakfast (homemade bread rolls) is served in a rustic room with beautiful baroque paintings. The staff are friendly, and the hotel is popular with musicians in July, when Bruges hosts the Flanders Festival.

★ **Hotel Aarendhuis** (map C2, **31**): Hoogstraat 18-20. ☎ (050) 337889. Fax: (050) 330816. Next to the Burg. Doubles 3,000–4,000BEF. This vast double house has a middle-class interior: the furniture's co-ordinated, but not in the best of taste, and it's a tad dusty. Good if you like four-posters, though, as you'll find them in six of the 20 rooms.

★ **Hotel Boterhuis** (map B2, **17**): Sint Jacobstraat, 38. ☎ (050) 341511. Fax: (050) 437089. In a cleverly renovated section of the town wall, this hotel has light, spacious rooms that are comfortable and decorated with restraint. The cheapest are at the front, overlooking a road that can be noisy. It's slightly pricey, but the rates improve if there are three or four of you. The best room, No. 8, is in a tower, and it's also the most expensive: 3,900BEF for two. There's a bar on the ground floor.

☆☆☆☆ Splash Out

★ **Hotel Ter Duinen** (map C1, **33**): Langerei 52. ☎ (050) 330437. Fax: (050) 344216. Email: info@ter duinenhotel.be. Closed January. Doubles 3,500–4,950BEF. An impressive white building on the edge of a wonderfully romantic canal, with 20 cosy and delightfully furnished rooms, and charming service. Try to get No. 28 or No. 34 – the view from the window is almost worth the money. A tad pricey, but it's a great place. There's park-ing nearby, and the breakfast (400BEF) is legendary. There's a 10 per cent discount if you pay by cash, except at the weekend (arriving Fri-day or Saturday) and on public holi-days.

Romantik Pand Hotel (map C3, **34**): Pandreitje 16. ☎ (050) 340666. Fax: (050) 340556. Email: info@ pandhotel.com. Doubles 4,890–7,490BEF. If money is no object, this refined hotel combines modern art, *ikebana* (floral Japanese art) and Anglo-Saxon comfort. The landlady personifies the city's tradition of hospitality: a polyglot and profes-sional guide, she'll keep you enter-tained for hours. The hotel is next to a canal-boat embarkation point.

Relais Oud Huis Amsterdam (map C2, **7**): Spiegelrei 3. ☎ (050) 341810. Fax: (050) 338891. Prices a bit above our usual range: 6,000–10,000BEF. All the luxury of the traditional hotels of the Hanse area: original 16th-century buildings, with wood flooring that creaks just en-ough to make you appreciate how thick the carpets are. Engravings and tapestries adorn the walls, while the extremely spacious rooms have period furniture and views over the canal. There's a cosy bar if you

fancy a nightcap, and a garden and terrace. Ample buffet breakfast.

Pure Self-Indulgence

Hotel Die Swaene (map C3, **35**): Steenhouwerdijk 1. ☎ (050) 342798. Fax: (050) 336674. Email: info@dieswaene-hotel.com. Beside the Groenerei and a stone's throw from the Burg. If you've got some-thing to celebrate, a potential con-quest to overwhelm or perhaps a surprise trip for your loved one, and you can't get a room at the Danieli in Venice, why not fall back on the Venice of the north and book a room at Die Swaene? You'll have the time of your life. This hotel came third in a survey of the most roman-tic hotels on the planet (behind two Italian hotels, needless to say), and to say it's luxurious would be doing it down. The furnishings have real class, the paintings are old masters and the food is clearly that of a star chef. You'll be treated like royalty, but what's truly amazing is that, apart from the really expensive suites, there are beautiful rooms for two at the relatively affordable price of 5,500–6,800BEF. What are you waiting for?

WHERE TO EAT

If you're feeling smug about how cheap your room is, you'll come down to earth with a bump when dinner time arrives. There's no shortage of good cooking in town, and some of the settings are delightful, but you'll need deep pockets to afford such delights. As so often in Belgium, the few places that don't cost a packet are unlikely to appeal to the taste buds, and tend to offer banal tourist food. A word of advice, therefore, for those who want to avoid the tourist track: with the odd exception, avoid the Markt unless you just want a beer.

☆ Budget

✕ **In 't Nieuwe Museum** (map D3, **40**): Hooistraat 42. ☎ (050) 331280. Closed Tuesday and Wed-nesday. Daily special 220BEF. A

regulars' bar on the corner of Gan-zestraat, in a quiet district, where the shine on the old wood panelling bears witness to the century that people have been coming here. It's all tiled flooring, sturdy tables, copper cauldrons and bunches of dried hops hanging from the ceiling beams, and there's a fireplace. Add to this all the trappings of the traditional Bruges tavern: piano, savings kitty, moulded bar, old cash register, moralizing engravings and a figure of Christ. Unpretentious, nourishing family-type cooking, if not exactly *haute cuisine*: the daily special with dessert is a steal, while steaks cost 400BEF.

✕ **Tavern Oud Handbogenhof** (map C1, **41**): Baliestraat 6. ☎ (050) 331945. Open 11am–2pm and 5.30pm–midnight; Sunday, afternoons only. Closed out of season, for lunch on Monday and Tuesday and the whole of January. Main course 400–800BEF. This old inn in the Sint Gilliskerk area has a typical rural Flemish interior. When the weather's good, you can sit outside beneath the lime trees and have a barbecue. Unpretentious cooking, including sides of pork, fried fish and Flemish-style hams.

✕ **Gran Kaffee de Passage** (map B3, **42**): Dweerstraat 26. ☎ (050) 340232. Also a youth hostel (*see* 'Where to stay'). A cross between a brown café and an *eetcafe,* where between 6pm and midnight, you can eat regional specialities for 300–400BEF: the menu includes *carbonade* (beef stewed in beer), *waterzooî,* lasagne, mussels cooked in white beer, *ribbetjes* and ratatouille. The tablecloths are Vichy lace and the decor is dark wood, jazzed up with old portraits. An old stove and a huge bar with brass fittings complete the picture. In the background you'll hear Eric Clapton, Van Morrison and other bluesy sounds. Excellent choice of beers. Great service and congenial atmosphere make this place a real find.

✕ **Tavern The Hobbit** (map B3, **43**): Kemelstraat 8. ☎ (050) 335520. Open 6pm–1am. Expect to pay about 600BEF for a meal. White gabling, big round tables with candelabra and pot plants, an open fire and dishes including spare ribs, spaghetti, lasagne and grilled meat. Young clientele. Dining room upstairs.

✕ **'t Terrastje** (map C2, **44**): Genthof 45. ☎ (050) 330919. Closed Monday and Tuesday. Full meal about 600BEF. A delightful 18th-century house opposite the Hotel Adornès: As the name suggests, there's a wonderful terrace where you can have a salad between boat trips down the canals, or grill your own steak on a super hot slab of volcanic stone. The famous *waterzooî* is also on the menu. The waiters sometimes seem rushed off their feet. Note that there's an extra charge if you pay by credit card.

✕ **'t Mozarthuis** (map C3, **45**): Huidenvettersplein 1. ☎ (050) 334-530. Open 11am–9pm. Closed Wednesday and throughout November. Extremely touristy, thanks to its position on the Huidenvettersplein, which is very much on the beaten track. What makes it special are the cheap snacks and steaks, which cost about 500BEF. As you eat, you'll be serenaded by sonatas and concertos by the maestro.

✕ **De Lotus** (map B-C2, **47**): Wapenmakerstraat 5. ☎ (050) 331078. Open for lunch and dinner. Closed Sunday. Daily special 350BEF. A vegetarian restaurant, as you might have guessed from the name, and a successful temple to the fruits of the earth. Good-value, sophisticated dishes. Seafood menu on Friday evenings. Divine chocolate pudding.

✕ **Soul Food** (map C2, **60**): Langestraat 15. ☎ (050) 334113. Dinner only. Closed Monday. A really nice, unostentatious place, where the locals come in droves. Blue and yellow facade, pot plants, terracotta and small wooden tables. Interesting, well-presented and often exotic dishes, including veggie options, from 250BEF to 300BEF, though portions are not overgenerous.

☆☆ Moderate

✗ **Breydel-De Coninck** (map B3, **48**): Breidelstraat 24. ☎ (050) 339746. Open noon–9.30pm. Closed Wednesday. Expect to pay around 1,000BEF per person. Children's menu 400BEF. This is a household name in Bruges, but you're unlikely to hear about it, presumably because the locals don't want it invaded by tourists on their way from Markt to Burg. The ordinary facade and unremarkable interior conceal a no-nonsense joint where you take your seat, place your order – and discover that your pot of mussels weighs a whopping 1.3 kilos (3 pounds), that the white wine they're stewed in could be drunk on its own, that the fish is mega fresh, the chips melt in your mouth, the eels in green sauce are delicious, and that the bill really isn't too steep (although prices have recently gone up). You can understand why the locals prefer to keep the secrets of this establishment under their hat. You'll probably feel inclined to do the same. Worth booking at the weekend.

✗ **De Koetse** (map B3, **49**): Oude Burg 31. ☎ (050) 337680. Open 10.30am–10pm. Closed Thursday. Menus start at 650BEF. A grand white house dating back to 1681, where the accent is on regional fare: eels, mussels, crayfish, prawn croquettes and grilled fish, all dished up with matching beers. Service is jolly and efficient, the atmosphere is friendly and prices are reasonable.

✗ **'t Zonneke** (map B2, **50**): Genthof 5. ☎ (050) 330781. Closed Sunday evening and Monday. Expect to pay 1,100BEF per person, excluding wine. This is a traditional restaurant in the Hanse district, frequented by the city's middle classes. Built in 1517, it used to be a lace shop. There are no surprises on the menu, just good, traditional Belgian food. At lunchtime, the special's a good bet, though you can't pay for it by credit card. The ambience is low-key, with *chansons* playing in the background. The cook will ask you what you thought of his creations. A lovely place, and good value for money. The name means 'little ray of sunshine', although the staff could lighten up a little and service is not the quickest.

✗ **De Stove** (map B3, **52**): Kleine Sint Amandstraat 4. ☎ (050) 337835. Closed Wednesday and Thursday, the second week in January and throughout August. Appealing menus from 1,450BEF. Booking recommended. The decor is simple and bright, with a wrought-iron stove in front of the fireplace, and the chef sets to with as much gusto for a quick snack as for a sophisticated dish. Fish stew is his speciality.

✗ **De Mosselkelder** (map C3, **53**): Huidevettersplein 1. ☎ (050) 342320. Open for lunch and dinner. Closed Tuesday. No prizes for guessing what's on the menu here: this is a temple to the national dish, mussels, for which you'll pay about 550BEF per portion. The fish market is right beside the restaurant, so quality is guaranteed. In fine weather, you can sit outside on the Huidevettersplein. On the down side, the service is a bit careless, and the restaurant is a bit touristy.

☆☆☆ Expensive

✗ **Den Dyver** (map C3, **56**): Dijver 5. ☎ (050) 336069. Open for lunch and dinner. Closed Wednesday and Thursday lunchtime. Menus from 1,400BEF, including drinks. Set lunch from 850BEF. Many dishes are cooked in beer: try salmon on a bed of spinach in Sint-Sixtus, lamb in Westmalle or eels in *gueuze*. The rustic Flemish decor matches the cuisine: dark leather chairs, massive beams, tapestries and dried flowers. Verging on perfection.

☆☆☆☆ Splash Out

✕ **De Lotteburg** (map B3, next to **25**): Goezeputstraat 43. ☎ (050) 337535. Open noon–2pm and 6.30–9.30pm. Closed Monday and Tuesday, and from the end of July to the beginning of August. Menus from 1,750BEF, including an aperitif and wine; monthly *haute cuisine* menu 1,950BEF. Booking essential. This typical Bruges street is a romantic setting for the city's best fish restaurant. Fish is brought in twice a day from Zeebrugge, so it's always fresh. Lobster and turbot fillet are the signature dishes, and it's also well worth considering the monkfish with leeks and a tomato zabaglione. Post-prandial liqueur on the house. An unforgettable experience.

✕ **De Witte Poorte** (map B2, **58**): Jan Van Eyckplein 6. ☎ (050) 330883. Open for lunch and dinner. Closed Sunday and Monday. Several set menus from 1,800BEF to 1,950BEF. Set lunch 1,200BEF. One of Bruges's top restaurants, De Witte Poorte is a former wine warehouse that's been done up in luxurious style: exposed brick vaults,

massive oak beams, high-backed chairs covered in fabric, yellow tablecloths and immaculate crockery and cutlery. *Waterzooî* of prawns, turbot, crayfish stew, pigeon with shallots and the generous sweet trolley are just a few of the marvels on offer. The wine list is as good as you'd expect at an establishment of this calibre, and the landlady manages the service to perfection.

✕ **De Zilveren Pauw** (map B3, **46**): Zilverstraat 41. ☎ (050) 335566. Closed Sunday and from the end of July to mid-August. Menus start at 1,100BEF, then head for the stratosphere. A magnificent Belle Époque building run by Patrick Devos, one of Belgium's most celebrated chefs. The neo-Gothic wood panelling is beautifully set off by the marble flooring and peach tablecloths, and there's a semi-wild interior garden. The set menus display infinite refinement, with fish taking pride of place, and the light cooking aims at harmony and subtlety, although there are plenty of audacious touches. Exceptional wine list, where the best labels remind one that France doesn't have the monopoly on great vintages. The desserts are to die for. To sum up, a grand occasion that you should enjoy without being vulgar and bothering about the bill (try to come as someone's guest!).

Something Sweet to Finish Up

✕ **Tea Room de Proeverie** (map B3, **59**): Katelijnestraat 5-6. ☎ (050) 330887. Open 9am–6pm. Don't be put off by the upmarket appearance: in a light and airy setting, coffee and tea are served with panache at modest prices, and come with little sweets. Baroque music plays in the background. Irresistible homemade cakes, so forget your diet.

✕ **Pannekoekenhuisje** (map B3, **55**): Helmstraat 3. ☎ (050) 340086. A small brick house that juts out, on a road in the shopping area. There's an old ice-cream cart and a terrace, and the facade is covered with flowers. This refined establishment is the place for sweet and savoury crêpes, best appreciated on a sunny afternoon. Lasagne and soups are also available, and a meal shouldn't set you back more than 400BEF.

WHERE TO GO FOR A DRINK

Compared with Ghent and Antwerp, Bruges' nightlife might strike you as tame. But if you know where to look, you'll find bistrots or *muziek cafés* where you can spend hours with the locals (a bit taciturn at first), discussing the merits of the local beer, legends of the past or the fortunes of the local football team, Club Bruges (the *Blauw-en-zwart*). So get on your bike and pedal off to explore Bruges's less famous corners.

While you're searching for evening entertainment, keep your ears open, as car-free Bruges offers a magical medley of sounds. There's the gentle trickle of water in the canals, the click of horseshoes, the ringing of bicycle bells, the distant rumble of mopeds on the ring road, the rustle of leaves in the sea breeze, the quacking of startled ducks, the crystal-clear notes of a nearby carillon . . .

Traditional Cafés

▪ **Craenenburg** (map B2): Markt 16. The locals' meeting place on the main square, with a terrace facing the post office. Filter coffee is served in silver cups. Maximilian of Austria was locked up in this house following a local uprising in 1488.

▪ **De Garre** (map B3): De Garre 1. Open noon–midnight. Closed Wednesday. Off the Breydelstraat, in a little cul de sac that used to be a firebreak, this little 16th-century house is a haven for beer fans, offering 127 types, five Trappist ales and the local brew, the formidable Triple Garre. With its bricks, beams and old wrought-iron stove, it's hard to find a more typically local venue. Get someone to translate the jokes on the menu for you. If, at around midnight, you hear the strains of Ravel's *Boléro*, this means it's closing time.

▪ **Vlissinghe** (map C2): Blekerstraat 2; behind the Hotel Adornès. Open from 11am. Closed Tuesday and Sunday evening. The people of Bruges like secrets – and this is one of them. On a little street in the Sint Anna district, parallel to Sint Annarei, this hostelry dates back to 1515. As soon as you enter, you can feel the history: there are old family photos on the walls, panelling stained by smoke from pipes, wooden tables worn by the elbows of card-players, a billiard table for regulars and a kitty with brass numbers (the original savings bank). Ask to see the book of photographs for an insight into daily life in Bruges in the 1900s. In summer, there's a pleasant courtyard with flowers and climbing roses.

Nocturnal Ports of Call

▪ **'t Brugs Beertje** (opposite the tavern *The Hobbit*, map B3, **43**): Kemelstraat 5. Open 4pm–1am. Closed Wednesday. A local institution as venerable as the swans on the Minnewater. The landlord, Jan De Bruyne, is a mine of information on all things beer related, so don't commit the *faux pas* of ordering a simple draught beer. Instead, admit your ignorance and drink in the man's words as you sip your brew – his life has been devoted to studying the world's beers, and he's regularly invited to the States as a consultant. The setting, as you might expect, is a veritable beer museum, with rare bottles, beer mats from every corner of the world, unusual glasses, advertisements and, for your drinking pleasure, more than 300 varieties. Two rarities are Pavé de l'Ours, brewed with honey, and the Rolls-Royce of barley beers, Westvleteren. You can even buy a poster with 26 witty dictums on beer and those who drink it.

't Dreupelhuisje (map B3): Kemelstraat 9. Next door to 't Brugs Beertje. Open 6pm–2am. Closed end of January. It's a Flemish tradition that next door to an alehouse, you'll find a joint that does *genever* (gin). Devotees never mix the two, but don't let that stop you. It's less fashionable to have an encyclopaedic knowledge of gins, probably because, even if you find 100 varieties of *witteke* (gin), expert analysis can start to get a little hazy after the fourth or fifth glass . . . Still, the jazz and blues music in this place is very pleasant, and the barflies are charming company. If you're after an offbeat souvenir, why not buy a T-shirt printed with a list of licences that used to regulate the sale of alcohol? New room now open upstairs.

Lokkedize (near the Hotel Lybeer; plan B3, **19**): Kortevuldersstraat 33. ☎ (050) 334450. Open 7pm–2am (3am at the weekend). Closed Monday. Near the Zand, this is a great place, with a fireplace, lively company and light meals. The music is Gregorian chants, rhythm 'n' blues and jazz, with French *chanson* on Saturday as well as live music at the weekend. They also hire out rooms and two furnished flats from 2,000 to 2,500BEF.

Vino Vino Blues & Tapas Bar (map B2): Grauwerkkerstraat 15. Open 6pm–2am. Closed Sunday and Monday. In the Sint Jacobskerk area, this café draws fans of the blues and Spanish wine. Try empanadas, tortillas, chorizo, cheeses and other tapas at the candle-lit tables. The landlord doesn't look particularly Spanish, and the atmosphere is definitely more Flemish than flamenco.

In den Wittenkop (near the Eiermarkt; map B2): Sint Jacobsstraat 14. Open until 3 or 4am. Closed Sunday and Monday. Not far from Vino Vino, this bar caters for hungry night owls, with satisfying dishes such as *bouillabaisse* (fish stew) and beef in beer available from 6.01–11.59pm. Although you'll be under the stern gaze of Michelangelo's *Moses*, it's a friendly place if you don't act the tourist, with jazz and blues in the background. Garden.

De Kluiver (map C2): Hoogstraat 12. Open 7pm–1am. Closed Wednesday and Thursday. An *eetcafe* for sailing buffs, judging by the sign of a three-masted ship, this place is perfect if you want to whisper sweet nothings to your beloved. In the evening they serve a variety of tempting snacks, from garlic bread or vegetable pâté to prawns or snails. Beneath the great sail on the ceiling, there's an entertaining collection of biscuit tins, all on a maritime theme.

L'Estaminet (map C3): Park 5. Open 11am–4am. Closed Monday evening and Thursday. Opposite Park Astrid, this huge glass-roofed terrace offers night owls the chance to slump into its cane chairs. The ice-creams and (depending on the time of day) the spaghetti have a good reputation, and it's always crammed with people meeting up to set off in search of adventure.

Du Phare: Sasplein 2. Closed Tuesday. It's a bit of an expedition to get to Dampoort (the start of the Damme canal) and this smoky, welcoming brown café, but it's easy enough to find: just follow the Langerei right to the end. Chicago blues and Delta blues lull conversation around the bar. If you're hungry, they'll rustle up some prawns or vegetarian fare for about 375BEF. Live concerts twice a month.

Musiek Cafés

♥ Marquies Carré and **Untitled**, Langestraat 145. Both belong to the Bauhaus International Youth Hotel (*see* 'Where to stay'), and attract handsome Italians and crazy Americans.

♥ Cactus (map B2): Sint Jacob-straat 36. ☎ (050) 332014. Open from 6.30pm–3am. Closed Sunday and Tuesday. A trendy café with well-maintained wood floors and art-deco furniture, the Cactus doubles as a theatre and attracts an intellectual clientele who debate world politics over the North African, Indonesian and Congolese menu. It's also one of Bruges's cultural hubs, and the home of the city's summer rock festival.

♥ Ma Rica Rokk (map A3): 't Zand 7-8. Open 11am till very late at the weekend. A permanent meeting place on Bruges's liveliest square. The large terrace is ideal for a bit of flirting (assuming you didn't come to Bruges with the love of your life . . .). They serve cocktails and aperitifs all day, although it's also a café in the afternoon. Happy hour is 6 7pm. Loud music, but at least you'll have an excuse to whisper in your neighbour's ear . . .

♥ Joey's Café (map B3): Zuidzand-straat 16. Closed Sunday. Entrance via the Zilverpand shopping centre. A long room with exposed brick walls; utterly calm some nights, totally wild on others. It doesn't matter how loud they play their music, as the surrounding shops are deserted. Light meals available.

♥ Pick (map B3): Eiermarkt 12. If you don't have time to traipse round in search of late-night venues, head behind the Markt, where you'll find four or five bars with dancing. People lurch from one to the other, drink in hand. There's rock and house music inside, while you can get your breath back in the cane chairs outside. Pick got in the guide because the go-go girls are a scream, though there's no guarantee they won't disappear next door after an hour.

♥ Cactus Club (map B3): Sint Jacobsstraat 33. Everyone gyrates to the throbbing techno music, all the rage with young Flemings.

♥ De Versteende Nacht (map C2): Langestraat 11. Open 7pm–2am. Closed Sunday and Monday. A relaxed place where a loyal clientele of blues fans listen devotedly to the groups that play here regularly. It's also an *eetcafe,* serving snacks and offering a good selection of beers.

♥ L'Obcédé (map A3): Zand 11. Admission fee on Saturdays. If there's nobody else around, the 1960s and 1970s relics will get up and dance on the podium to the music of the time. But not everyone here is a total square.

WHAT TO SEE

You can't possibly hope to see everything in one day. The suggested itinerary is split into two parts, and is more than enough for two days. If you follow it, you'll have done 90 per cent of the monuments and museums.

You can do the first tour on foot, while the second is best done by bike. Alternatively, you could just follow your nose: there's no better way to discover Bruges than by strolling around its streets and canals, leaving the discovery of its monuments to chance.

★ **Burg** (map C2, **81**): the home of the tourist office, in the former Justitiepalais (law court). The staff are cheerful and competent, and have the patience of saints. You can buy a combined ticket for the four main museums – Groeninge, Brangwyn, Gruuthuse and Memling – for 400BEF. There's a market on the Burg on Wednesday morning. The Burg used to be the embarkation point for barge trips, but has been usurped by the Markt. If you want to take one of these tours, the price is 1,000BEF for half an hour and five passengers.

The Burg is the site of the original *castrum*, the fort built by Baldwin Iron Arm in 879. The variety of architecture on the square is remarkable. The north side opens onto a square planted with lime trees, where St Donatian's church stood until it was razed by the French in 1799. During the construction of a large house, Romanesque foundations were revealed. You can see these remains in the basement of the building (guided tours available), along with a model of the Carolingian-style church. The paving in the square shows where the old walls used to be.

★ **Stadhuis** (map C3, **82**): from April to the end of September, open 9.30am–5pm. Admission: 150BEF, which includes entry to the Brugse Vrije. The Stadhuis is a jewel of Gothic architecture. Completed in 1421, it was the first of a series of prestigious communal buildings to be built in Flanders and Brabant, and marked an important shift of power from feudal counts to councillors. Unusually, it was built of stone rather than brick. Stone was expensive to transport and rare in this region, making it an ostentatiously extravagant material to use. The soaring vertical lines are reinforced by 48 statues of Flemish counts and countesses – all copies. The originals, painted by Jan Van Eyck, accidentally 'fell out' of their niches when the *sans-culottes* passed through. Note the coats of arms of the cities that formed the 'Liberty' of Bruges, including those of Bruges's vassal state, Dunkerque.

In the entrance hall, before you take the stairs on the left to the Gothic room, have a look at the vestibule: on the left, you'll see an enormous painting of Napoleon with the then burgomaster of Bruges. The latter commissioned this painting as a souvenir of the Emperor's visit: a glorious moment for him, as Napoleon bestowed on him the Légion d'honneur. But the tide of history changed, and the painting became something of an embarrassment to the burgomaster. When you look at it from different angles, you notice that the head has been cut out and replaced (by recent restoration). The burgomaster chose to have his head removed in a bid to prevent criticism from his political rivals. Other vast 19th-century canvases depict Marie of Burgundy's fatal riding accident (*see below*) and the death of her father, Charles the Bold.

The Gothic room is an entertaining introduction to the history of Bruges and Flanders. On the walls are depictions of the major events of the medieval period, when Bruges was at the height of its wealth and power. You'll need to follow the numbering of the paintings (there's an explanatory leaflet available at the entrance), because, apart from the fact that the neo-Gothic frescoes obscure historical fact, the story of Bruges told here doesn't conform to chronology. Notice the way it's illustrated – the return of the citizens from the Battle of the Golden Spurs is typical of a Romantic retelling of history. The vaulting in the room consists of magnificent oak decorated with medallions and carved keystones. In the annex are some fascinating old maps showing structures that no longer exist (the ramparts, for example, or St Donatian's), which give you a good idea of how the city once looked.

★ **Heilig Bloedbasiliek** (map C3, **83**): from April to the end of September, open 9.30am–noon and 2–6pm; otherwise 10am–noon and 2–4pm. This is an odd-looking building dedicated to St Basil, a Byzantine saint who enjoys the dubious distinction of having had four of his vertebrae brought back from a crusade. The basilica consists of a Romanesque church and a second, Gothic church, constructed on top of the first. They are linked by an exterior flight of Renaissance steps, at the corner that abuts the Stadhuis. It's so tucked away that a lot of people pass by without even noticing it. Seek it out, though, as the lower chapel is an example of the Romanesque style at its purest: huge thick walls, four massive round columns, a cramped choir and very little light.

On the right is a painted statue of the Virgin, typical of medieval statuary. The restoration of these statues has sometimes revealed surprises: some thought of as 'black virgins', for example, turned out to be painted in delicate colours. The blackness was due to the smoke from candles, as the cleaning process swiftly revealed. A wooden statue of Christ and a bas-relief representing the baptism of St Basil round off the list of the Romanesque treasures.

The upper chapel, of Romanesque origin, was rebuilt in Gothic style during the 15th century. It was demolished by the French during the Revolution, and rebuilt in the 19th century. On the right, on a rococo altar, is a reliquary revered by the locals since the 12th century. The story goes that, during the Second Crusade, Diederik of Alsace was given some drops of Christ's blood by the ruler of Jerusalem. The precious relic was kept in a crystal phial, brought back to Bruges with great ceremony and exposed for the veneration of the faithful. Tradition has it that it liquefies every Friday, thereby swelling the number of pilgrims. Every Friday, therefore, the phial is brought out and put on display. Each year on Ascension Thursday, the procession of the Holy Blood draws thousands of spectators to see the hundreds of statues that are brought out (*see* 'Festivals').

Museum of the Holy Blood: admission 40BEF. The big draw here is the reliquary of the Holy Blood, a marvel of craftsmanship that dates from the 17th century. It's surrounded by images of the honourable members of the Confraternity of the Holy Blood, painted by Pourbus in 1556.

★ **Brugse Vrije**: open 9.30am–12.30pm and 1.30–5pm. The combined ticket for the Brugse Vrije and Stadhuis (*see above*) includes an audio guide. the Vrije used to be the city's law court, but all that remains of the old building of 1525 is the south facade (which you can see from the Steenhouwerdijk) and the aldermen's hall, which houses a museum. The current buildings, in the Classical style, house administrative offices.

The most striking exhibit is the colossal Charles V mantelpiece, fashioned in 1531 by Lancelot Blondeel at the request of the city, which wished to celebrate the Emperor's victory over Francis I at the Battle of Pavia. The hearth is made of black marble, the frieze of alabaster and the upper section of oak. You'll also notice brass handles attached to the hood; these were to give the gentlemen something to hold on to while they dried their boots in the heat of the fire. Among the characters surrounding Charles V, you can make out Maximilian of Austria, Marie of Burgundy, Ferdinand of Aragon and Isabella of Castille.

★ Between the Brugse Vrije and the Stadhuis, under a delightful arcade, you'll enter the bizarrely named Blinde Ezelstraat, or 'Blind Donkey Street'. It leads to the **Reie**, from which boats could access the Markt. Note how shallow the water is. With the development of keels, it soon became clear that this canal was not deep enough for ships, and Damme became increasingly important as the place to load and unload merchandise.

★ There's a wonderful view from both sides of the bridge. The **Vismarkt**, or Fish Market, on the left, was a present from Napoleon.

★ The little **Huidevettersplein** (Tanners' Square), on the right, was used for trading skins. The column in the centre held a balance to weigh the hides; on the facade of the House of Burgundy (previously called De Koe, or 'The Cow'), friezes illustrate the different stages in the work of tanning leather.

★ Beyond the square and the unloading area for boats, you'll come to **Rozenhoedkaai**. From here, you can look back and admire the view of wooden houses (reconstructed), water, ivy, willows, the Belfort and the towers of the Stadhuis.

★ Continue along **Dijver** and along the canals, where you'll start to get a feel for the different types of houses denoting the city's social strata. There are patrician and merchant houses, identifiable by their jetties, gabled crafts-man's houses and little low houses on the edge of town, which belonged to less skilled trades. The College of Europe is on the Dijver, which is lined with antiques stalls on weekends.

★ **Groeninge Museum** (map C3, **84**): Dijver 12. Open 9.30am–5pm. Closed Tuesday out of season. Admission: 250BEF. At 400BEF, the combined ticket for the Groeninge, Gruuthuse, Brangwyn and Memling museums is good value. This museum is a must, even if you don't much care for painting; if you do, you need to allow at least an hour for a visit. There are 18 rooms, all beautifully arranged, with excellent explanatory notes that make the experience even more rewarding. You enter via a wonderful interior courtyard, enhanced by a fountain with a bronze dolphin.

The Flemish Primitives

The term 'Flemish Primitives' was coined at an exhibition in Bruges in 1902. It's a bit misleading, because there's nothing 'primitive' about this art, but 'southern Low Countries painting in the 15th century' is a bit of a mouthful. During this period, painting was treated very much as a trade or craft. Various materials were used to paint on, including cloth, furniture, walls, illuminated paper or coats of arms. Like other craftsmen, the painter worked to commission and had to work to a specific size, subject and colour. He carried out the order and was paid in return. He belonged to a guild, which taught him the techniques of his trade and regulated his work, and his works were anonymous and unsigned. His talent, assuming he had any, consisted in reproducing reality as exactly as possible; his craft, in finding new means to achieve this. Oil painting existed, but the technique was in its infancy.

The boom in painting was a direct result of the prevailing economic conditions. Prosperous merchants and city worthies loved to show off their wealth by funding private chapels and endowing them with paintings of religious subjects in which the donors also featured. They were sometimes shown at prayer, and always surrounded by fine things (especially if these were relevant to their lives) in domestic, urban or private settings. They could enjoy the good things in life, and they wanted to show it, demanding that their gold, carpets, brocades and all the luxuries of their position be represented. The painter's skill consisted in making the stones and enamels sparkle, the carpet so realistic that you could stretch out your hand and touch the threads, the faces so vivid that you could pick out every blemish. The whole was suffused with delicate nuances of colour, for the painter was in constant pursuit of perfection.

The nobles (dukes, princes and bishops) were less particular; they just wanted to have their portrait painted. It was a lucrative job for the artist, who would often be sent abroad to capture the likeness of a distant princess or a potential nobleman's wife. So, the painter had a dual mission: he was a portraitist working to commission, and an ambassador responsible for negotiating marriages. As such, it was impossible for him to remain anonymous, and this explains why Jan Van Eyck became so famous. From humble beginnings as Philip the Good's valet, he rose to become a secret ambassador who was sent to seek the hand of Isabel of Portugal. Following his success, painters gradually became known public figures.

The Tour

The first five rooms of the Groeninge Museum are devoted to the Flemish Primitives. Below are some of the highlights. All, thankfully, are accompanied by commentary in four languages.

– Room 1: in Jan Van Eyck's *Portrait of Margareta Van Eyck* (1439), the artist's wife, aged 33, there are no concessions to reality – and she's wearing a peculiar headdress. Take a look, too, at *Madonna with Canon George Van der Paele* (1436). The composition is superb, and the painting has been exceptionally well preserved. Note the imitation marble frame and the extraordinary detail of the cloth, weapons, carpet and the face of the poor canon, warts and all. Modern doctors have discussed the state of his health at the time he was painted, and their diagnosis has not been very positive. Still, he could have asked for a more flattering depiction if he had wanted one.

– Room 2: look out for Hugo Van der Goes's triptych of the *Martyrdom of St Hippolytus* (1475) and Rogier Van der Weyden's *St Luke Drawing the Virgin's Portrait* (around 1500), in which the background brilliantly captures the historical context.

– Room 3: the *Legend of St Ursula* (painted in 1482 by an anonymous artist known as The Master of the Ursula Legend) tells Ursula's story in a comic-strip style, with a dazzling array of costumes. The city of Bruges features in the background of *St Nicolas*, by the same anonymous artist as *The Legend of St Lucia* (1486). *Virgin with Child Crowned by Two Angels* is by an anonymous Brussels painter who placed an iris, chosen as the emblem of the modern Brussels Region, next to Mary's foot.

– Room 4: Hans Memling's *Moreel Triptych* (1484). Note the detail in the plants and humans.

– Room 5: Gerard David's *Baptism of Christ* (1495) is the masterpiece of the last of the Primitives, and shows perfection of composition and even a degree of naturalism. In the features of the mother and her daughters, family characteristics have been beautifully captured. *The Judgement of Cambyses* (1498), also by David, is an allegorical depiction of the punishment of a corrupt judge. The judge is clearly surprised. Further on, don't miss Hieronymous Bosch's *The Last Judgement*.

– Room 6: an overview of painting in Bruges after Gerard David.

– Room 7: painting in the southern Low Countries in the 16th century, including copies of works by Brueghel and paintings by Bernard van Orley.

– Rooms 8 and 9: the influence of Italian Classicism on Bruges's painters in the second half of the 16th century.

– Room 10: still lifes and 17th- and 18th-century landscapes, including works by Jacob van Oost, who came from Lille and painted in the style of Caravaggio.

– Room 11: upstairs, beyond the cafeteria, with attractive barrel vaulting, you'll find paintings by Jacques Louis David alongside Romantics, Naturalists and Symbolists, the last group chiefly represented by Fernand Khnopff.

– Rooms 12 to 14: Flemish Modernism is the theme, with an emphasis on the schools of Sint-Martens-Latem, including Albert Servaes, Constant Permeke and Gustave de Smet.

– Finally, you come to the section on contemporary art, with a room devoted to Marcel Broodthaers, master of the bizarre and heir of Dadaism.

★ **Brangwyn Museum, Arentshuis** (map B3, **85**): Dijver 16. Same opening times as the Groeninge Museum. Admission: 80BEF or on the combined ticket (see above). The museum is named after Sir Frank Brangwyn, an English architect and decorator who lived in Bruges in the 19th century and bequeathed his collections to the city.

This Victorian-style house holds a huge collection of lace. It's hard to say which deserves more admiration: the skill of the lacemakers, or the precision with which the artist has reproduced their work on the clothes of the painted figures. A majestic portrait of Maria-Theresa, Empress of Austria, dominates the room. Also on display are old views of Bruges and pottery, pewterware and porcelain. As you leave, look out for a glass case housing a collection of bygone means of transport, including sledges used when the canals were frozen, and a bizarre variation on the sedan chair.

★ **The Gruuthuse Museum** (map B3, **86**): Dijver 17. Admission: 130BEF or on the combined ticket (see above). Same opening times as the Groeninge Museum. *Gruut* was a mix of herbs and flowers that was added to barley to improve the flavour of beer. One family, the Van Brugges, had a monopoly on *gruut*. As a result, their workplace became known as Gruuthuse, and this eventually became the family's surname. In the 16th century, hops made the use of *gruut* unnecessary, and the Gruuthuse family converted their old warehouses into handsome mansions.

The most prominent member of the dynasty, Louis de Gruuthuse, was councillor to the three Dukes of Burgundy, a knight of the Golden Fleece and friend of King Edward IV of England, who made him Earl of Winchester. His contribution to the progress of humanity was the invention of the hollow cannonball, which is much more effective than its solid counterpart. Hence his motto: 'More is in you'.

When the dynasty died out, the Gruuthuse became a pawn shop and, eventually, a museum housing a vast collection of furniture, everyday objects, weapons, coins, tapestries (enhanced with proverbs in the form of comic-strip speech bubbles), musical instruments, kitchen and pharmaceutical utensils, implements of torture and even a guillotine. One of the most valuable items is a painted wooden bust of Charles V as an adolescent (Room 1). A pretty loggia with a balcony overlooking the garden of the Onze Lieve Vrouwekerk is in room 20. The family's oratory, which overlooks the choir of the church and was built so that they could attend Mass without leaving the house, is in room 17.

The Gruuthuse palace is next to the Onze Lieve Vrouwekerk, a soaring pile whose scale becomes apparent if you walk around it, keeping to the left-hand side, then stroll through the gardens filled with lime trees and a tiny bridge, under which boats pass on their way to the Begijnhof. The small wooden houses are replicas, although that doesn't make them any less pretty.

★ **Onze Lieve Vrouwekerk** (map B3, **87**): open 10–noon and 2–5pm; to 4pm on Saturday and 1.30pm in winter. Closed Sunday morning from October to the end of March. Admission to the mausolea: 70BEF.

The most striking thing about this 13th-century Scheldt Gothic church is its dizzying 122-metre (403-foot) tower, which makes the church the highest brick structure in the world. It is possible to build high with brick, but it cannot be carved, hence the building's rather severe appearance.

As you enter, your attention is drawn to a dark corner on the right, in front of the Chapel of Our Lady, and to the white marble *Virgin and Child*, one of Michelangelo's early works. It was commissioned by the Sienese Piccolomini family, but they never got round to paying for it, so the artist sold it to a local merchant, Jan Moscroen, who bequeathed it to the church.

In the choir are the two mausolea of Marie of Burgundy and her father, Charles the Bold. Charles, the last Duke of Burgundy, died in the siege of Nancy in 1477, leaving all his possessions to his only daughter, Marie. She married Archduke Maximilian of Austria. Bruges adored her: she had beauty, youth, two children, the whole shebang. She was the pin-up star of her day, but tragedy struck when she was 25. She fell off her horse during a hunt (see the painting on this subject in the Stadhuis). She didn't appear to be too badly hurt when she was helped up, but she died a week later, leaving her husband and two small children, the future Philip the Fair and Margareta of Austria, who were to have troubled lives. Before her death, Marie had expressed a wish to be buried in Bruges. A superb mausoleum was built for her, and legend has it that the knights of the Golden Fleece came to meditate upon it. On the orders of Charles V, her father's remains were brought from Nancy, where he had been buried, to join his daughter in her mausoleum. Recent archaeological excavations have revealed the cause of Marie's death. Aside from the fractures to her arms, she appears to have been kicked in the ribs by the horse's hoofs, puncturing her lung. And she was pregnant.

The craftsmanship of the mausoleum is superb: there's a touching grace about Marie, with her long, finely carved hands. Her father's mausoleum, built 70 years later in similar style to her own, shows a distinct Renaissance influence.

The sarcophagi in the crypt and in one of the chapels are those of 13th-century prelates. Art historians have long been fascinated by the frescoes on the inside. The designs were drawn on paper that was plastered onto the sides.

The church houses several artistic treasures, including the *Virgin of the Seven Pains* by Adriaen Isenbrant (1528), a *Christ on the Cross* by Van Dyck and paintings by Pourbus and Gerard David. Walk round the ambulatory (at the back of the choir) and you'll glimpse the private chapel of the Gruuthuse family above.

★ **Sint Janshospitaal** (map B3, **88**): Mariastraat 38. Open 9.30am–5pm. Closed Wednesday. Admission: 100BEF. The museum has recently been restored. This building houses the Memling Museum (*see below*). Opposite the Onze Lieve Vrouwekerk, this complex of brick buildings was the city hospital until 1876. Founded in the 12th century, it was originally a hostel where merchants could spend the night. The poor could also find shelter there for the night, but they were cast out into the world again during the day. It was some time before it became a place of care and benevolence.

The original building was altered throughout the centuries. Today, the sickrooms contain objects relating to hospital life, as well as a few works of art. The old pharmacy, which has a picturesque cloister and an interior courtyard with a pretty fountain and an odd-shaped conifer, is worth a detour. The mortars, scales and stone pots in the pharmacy indicate the former purpose of the place. Four centuries of pharmacists, some of them Spanish, stare down at you from the walls of the next-door meeting room.

The buildings at the back of the hospital date from the 19th century. They have been restored and rearranged for conferences and temporary exhibitions. It's well worth having a look at what's on. There's also a canal-side cafeteria, Promenade, where you can rest your feet and have a snack. It's an ideal spot from which to watch the passing boats and the many visitors on the roof of the nearby Straffe Hendrik brewery.

★ **Memling Museum** (map B3, **88**): in the hospital chapel. Memling was born in 1435 in Germany, and worked in Cologne and Brussels (with Rogier van der Weyden). He came to live in Bruges, and became a citizen of the town in 1465. His customers included prelates, the well-heeled middle classes and Italian merchants. He was blessed with a keen sense of colour, and although his compositions show the influence of past painters, they also herald the beginning of the Renaissance. The serenity of his figures contrasts with the Mannerism that characterizes the work of 16th-century painters. There are just six works on display, but they're all superb, and all are in the space for which they were originally conceived.

The Reliquary of St Ursula (1489): St Ursula is carved on a wooden box shaped like a Gothic chapel. She's on a pilgrimage to Rome, accompanied by her entourage of 11,000 virgins. They are also represented returning via Basel and being massacred by the pagans in Cologne. This legendary event is supposed to have happened in the first centuries of Christianity, but Memling's version sets the action in his own time: the protagonists wear contemporary clothes, and the spires of Cologne are clearly recognizable in the background.

Triptych of St John the Baptist and St John the Evangelist (1479): the central panel shows the mystic marriage of St Catherine; episodes from the lives of the two St Johns (patrons of the hospital) are evoked by a succession of scenes in the background. The Evangelist's vision of the Apocalypse in Patmos shows a wild imagination at work. Look out for the disdainful expressions of those watching John the Baptist's decapitation.

A small painting of the *Persian Sybil* (1480), in which the Sybil announces the coming of Christ, is on display in the chapel next door. The sense of perspective is accentuated by the ends of her fingers, which spill over onto the frame.

Diptych of Marteen Van Nieuwenhove (1487): the two figures are in the same room: look at the reflection of their backs in a round mirror behind the Virgin. Note the touching portrait of the donor.

★ **Almshouses** (map B3, **89**): as you leave Sint Janshospitaal, turn right along the bustling Katelijnestraat. On both sides, you'll see whitewashed passageways and, above them, a name and a date. These almshouses are a typical feature of social and urban Bruges. In the middle of the 19th century, Bruges was the poorest city in Belgium. The town had stopped developing in the 16th century, and vast areas within the ramparts remained empty. Poverty set in, and a whole section of the population ended up homeless. The guilds, which owned empty land (often just ends of gardens) were anxious about the fate of these waifs and strays, so they financed the construction of these small, low houses. Each consists of one room, one window and a skylight, but – and this was a luxury for the period – each had a supply of fresh water, a kitchen garden and toilets. The chapel next door is a reminder of the religious nature of this philanthropy. The wealthy citizens of Bruges have always been charitable, but the causes of poverty have never been eradicated. Today, the houses have been restored and are run by the Commission for Social Assistance, which allocates them to pensioners and those of modest means, but they retain an antiquated, doll's-house charm. There are a series of almshouses in the streets leading off Katelijnestraat. You can go in and have a look, but please respect the privacy of the tenants.

Continue along Stoofstraat, or 'Steamroom Road' – the site of a public baths in the Middle Ages, where men and women bathed together – until you reach Walplein, a shady spot that's home to one of the city's most popular tourist attractions.

★ **Straffe Hendrik Brewery** (map B4, **90**): 26 Walplein. Guided tours leave every hour between 10am and 5pm (11am–3pm in winter). Admission: 140BEF, including a beer. If you've never seen a brewery in action, this old malt factory is definitely worth visiting. The whole process is explained, and connoisseurs can enjoy the collections of glasses, beer cans and bottles. Workers who cleaned the tanks in the vat room had to wear masks to prevent them from getting drunk on the alcohol fumes. The coopers' workshop and turn-of-the-last-century tavern wind up the visit, which is a bit boring – mainly because the guide's drawn-out commentary is in four languages. The high point of the visit, however, is the fantastic view from the roof – and a glass of the tasty house beer of course!

★ **Diamond Museum** (map B3, **111**): Katelijnestraat 43. ☎ (050) 342056. Open 10.30am–5pm. Admission: 180BEF. More a commercial venture than a museum, this exhibition sets out to prove that diamonds have been cut in Bruges since the end of the 15th century – i.e. before Antwerp, the city's great economic rival. The annals tell of a certain Van Berquem, a gem-cutter who lived and worked in Bruges. Given the presence in the city of the court of the House of Burgundy, he must have had plenty of work. The displays cover every aspect of diamond-cutting, and you can also see the tools that were used. Panels explain the geology of the diamond and the diamond industry in modern times, including an indication of the enormous sums of money that change hands in this business. Cut diamonds in old and new settings are also on show, and demonstrations of diamond-cutting are held on request.

★ **Prinselijk Begijnhof ten Wijngaarde** (map B4, **91**): take Wijngaard-straat until you come to the Begijnhof, which is to Flanders what the Eiffel Tower is to France – a glorious photo opportunity. Along with the other Flemish Beguine houses, this is a UNESCO World Heritage Site. It's an exceptionally tranquil and poetic spot, with gently rustling poplar trees. In spring, when the lawn is dappled with sunlight and dotted with daffodils, it's almost like an Impressionist painting. Add to this the sight of a nun hurrying towards the chapel, and of red-and-white houses hidden behind the garden walls, and you've got one of the loveliest Begijnhofs in Belgium.

Founded in 1245 by Margaret of Constantinople, the complex was home to women who lived in a community but did not take vows, although they led a life that was both contemplative and active. They cared for the sick and washed wool destined for the loom. The latter occupation brought them into conflict with the cloth workers, but their case was judged by Philip the Good, who offered his protection. They were hounded by the Wars of Religion and the French Revolution; the last Beguine died in 1928. The place is now inhabited by a community of Benedictine nuns who wear the traditional black dress and white wimple.

The Beguines used to worship in the tiny Sint Elisabethkerk. Sneak in quietly and you can listen to the beautifully clear voices singing Vespers.

One of the houses has been arranged as a museum – it's on the left, near the entrance. Open every day in season (closed at lunchtime); closed Monday and Tuesday in winter. Admission: 60BEF. It offers an insight into the Beguines' daily lives.

★ **Minnewater** (map B4, **92**): yet another romantic spot. It once functioned as the city's main dock, but is now closed off by the lock-keeper's house. The large tower on the other side, part of the fortifications that once ringed the town, stands guard over the Bruges–Ghent canal.

– You've now reached the southernmost point of the walk. To get back to the centre, walk down Katelijnestraat until you come to the Onze Lieve Vrouwekerk. Continue along Heilige Geeststraat until you reach the foot of the church's soaring tower.

★ **Sint Salvatorkathedraal** (map B3, **93**): closed 11.30am–2pm (to 3pm on Sunday). A Romanesque church stood here in the ninth century. The vagaries of time took it from construction via fire and destruction to restoration, until the disappearance of St Donatian's, when it became a cathedral. Despite the lighter, neo-Romanesque summit, the solid tower is both austere and intimidating. Inside, however, you get a rather different impression. For once, the choir hasn't been overwhelmed by baroque flourishes, while the 18th-century rood screen was moved to the back of the church, beneath the organ, in 1935. The white marble statue of *God the Creator* bears the signature of Artus Quellin. Take a look at the coat of arms of the Knights of the Golden Fleece, who held their 13th chapter here in 1478. There's a *Christ on the Cross* in the chapel on the left. He looks as though he's about to kick someone: according to legend, he is supposed to have kicked down an iconoclast who tried to destroy him.

Cathedral Museum: open Monday to Friday 2–5pm, Sunday 3–5pm. In July and August, also open 10–11.30am. Admission: 60BEF. The museum contains some important works, including a series of brass funerary boards (a Bruges speciality, owing to the region's lack of stone), a 14th-century stone sarcophagus decorated with frescoes, an ivory St Maclou crosier and a handsome portrait of Charles V, aged 20. *The Martyrdom of St Hippolytus* by Dirk Bouts and Hugo Van der Goes, mentioned in the leaflet, is actually in the Groeninge Museum.

Wander down the shop-lined Steenstraat, which leads to the Markt.

★ **Markt** (map B2, **94**): this marks the end of the first walk and the start of the second. You can board a boat here, too. This square has been a marketplace since 958, and has witnessed festivals, revolts, tournaments, executions, marriages, burnings and military parades. Jan Breydel and Pieter De Coninck, whose statues are on the square, led the tradesmen when they massacred the French near Kortrijk in May 1302. This incarnation of the Markt spans six centuries, as you can see from two houses on either side of the entrance to Sint Amandstraat: on the left, there's a tall Gothic facade with a 15th-century weather vane, while the Café Craenenburg, on the right, dates back to the 14th century but has a reconstructed facade. Step-gabled 17th-century houses line the north side of the square. One is topped with a pretty golden basket, but despite its grand appearance, the facade is less than a hundred years old: it's pure neo-Gothic, although that hardly detracts from its elegance. The building how houses local-government offices and a post office.

The real attraction here, however, is the huge, proud Belfort (belfry), which dwarfs the hall below. There's something incongruous about this vast pile – you somehow expect to see another cylindrical tower emerging from the summit, as if it were a telescopic structure. Indeed, the belfry did have a spire, but it was destroyed by lightning in 1741. It probably looks less out of proportion when seen from a distance.

★ **Belfort** (map B3, **95**): open 9.30am–5pm (last entry at 4.15pm). Admission: 100BEF. If you're feeling athletic, you'll probably want to clamber up the 366 stairs that lead to the balcony at the top, (there are places to take a breather on the way up). The treasury, where the precious charters were kept behind iron grilles in coffers with multiple locks, is 55 steps up. The

BRUGES

burgomaster and eight aldermen each had a key, and all nine had to attend the grand ceremony of the opening of the boxes.

At step 112, you can pause and look at the view. At step 220, you can see a six-ton bell known as Victoria. The staircase is wooden until you reach step 333, where you can see the mechanism of the 47-bell carillon. The man who activates the carillon sits in a room 352 steps up. He rings it at dawn three times a week in summer. When you reach the top, a paltry 14 steps later, you'll be rewarded with splendid views of the city. Don't forget your camera – there's an orientation table on the balustrade. At the foot of the Belfry, meanwhile, there's a model of the whole structure, with explanations in Braille.

– **Carillon concerts**: in July, August and September, these take place on Monday, Wednesday and Saturday at 9pm, and Sunday at 2.15pm. Otherwise, they're on Wednesday, Saturday and Sunday at 2.15pm.

★ **The merchant halls**: these date back to the 13th century, and housed a covered market. Another hall, no longer standing, served as a warehouse. The Waterhalle (on the site of the local government offices) straddled the Reie, which allowed boats from the outer harbours to load and unload on its quays.

If you're going to do the rest of this itinerary by bike, you can hire one on Hallestraat, on the right of the Belfort. Watch out for the one-way streets, some of which apply to bicycles as well as cars, and look out for signs saying *Uitgezonderd*, which means 'except for'. If you're barred from entering a street, get off and walk – the local police are pleasant enough, but that doesn't mean they will let you get away with it.

– Leave the Markt by taking Philipstockstraat, on the right. Take the fourth left, Middleburg, and follow Sint Walburgastraat, which brings you to Sint Maartensplein.

★ **Sint Walburgakerk** (plan C2, **96**): this architecturally coherent church is in typical Jesuit style, and is the first in the world to have been dedicated to St Francis Xavier. Baroque but not frilly, it has a calm, harmonious feel, thanks to a series of Tuscan columns in the nave. The 'Victorian' confessionals are almost Egyptian in appearance. This church is strikingly different from most places of worship in Bruges. Every evening except Wednesday from Easter to the end of September, the dean organizes 'concerts' of recorded music (8–10pm). Hearing Bach or Gregorian chants while the light of the setting sun gilds the majestic nave can be truly uplifting.

★ **Sint Anna district**: walk around Sint Walburgakerk and take a right along Kandelaarstraat to Verversdijk, then turn left and cross a humpbacked bridge, which takes you to Sint Annakerk. This part of Bruges is pure chocolate-box. It was also once extremely poor. Today, the low houses look clean and pretty, and it's hard to believe that, until the 19th century, they housed a poverty-stricken population. It's a miracle that they're still standing.

★ **Sint Annakerk** (map C2, **97**): open from April to the end of September, 10am–noon and 2–4pm. Closed Saturday afternoon and Sunday. The exterior is nothing to write home about, but the incense-filled interior is a pleasant surprise. The mostly 17th-century decoration verges on the excessive, and it's unusually elaborate for a simple parish church, with a profusion of woodwork, brasses and vast paintings. Tokens for food and clothing were handed out at the *disbank*, to the right of the entrance, after Mass.

Leave the church and take the first right onto Rolweg.

★ **Stedelijk Museum voor Volkskunst** (Museum of Folk Art (map C2, **98**): open 9.30am–5pm. Admission: 80BEF. This delightful museum is housed in a row of eight old almshouses. The rooms take you through themed reconstructions of daily life 100 years ago. There's a typical sitting room, a sweet shop, a pharmacy, a costume room, a school room, a cobbler's, a milliner's, grocer's – even a room devoted to pipes and tobacco. The courtyard has been laid out like a garden, and is an ideal spot for a rest. There's a player-piano in the *Zwarte Kat* bar. Upstairs, you'll find artefacts relating to military service: lots were drawn to determine who joined up.

– Take Balstraat until you come to the exotic Jeruzalemkerk and the Lace Centre.

★ **Jeruzalemkerk** (map C2, **99**): open 10am–noon and 2–6pm during the week (to 5pm on Saturday). Closed Sunday. This was the private church of the Adornès family, wealthy Genoese merchants. It still belongs to their descendants. Around 1470, two of them, returning from a pilgrimage to the Holy Land, acquired papal authority to build a church similar to that of the Church of the Holy Sepulchre. This explains its odd appearance, and the fact that the beltry is topped with the cross and palm of St Catherine (from Mount Sinai). A sun and a crescent moon can be seen on the two turrets. The tombs of the Adornès family, their faces lit by sunlight during the summer solstice, lie inside: other members of the family are buried in the vault. There's a false crypt with a copy of the tomb of Christ in the chapel.

★ **Kantcentrum** (Lace Centre): open 10am–noon and 2–6pm during the week (to 5pm on Saturday). Closed Sunday. Admission: 60BEF. The almshouses behind the Adornès estate have been turned into a lace museum where, in the afternoon, you can see lacemakers at work. Actually, it's impossible to find lace that's made in Bruges. What you see in the shops is genuine in terms of technique and design, but much of it is made in workshops in the developing world.

★ From the Lace Centre, take Stijn Streuvelstraat until you come to a park used as a practice ground by the renowned crossbowmen of the **Guild of St George** (Sint Joris; map D2, **100**). Shooting takes place every Tuesday and Friday from 6pm. They have the added privilege of escorting the Holy Blood at the head of the annual procession, and are mighty proud of their traditions, which date back to the 14th century. If you ask, you can visit their guildhouse, where there's a collection of crossbows and related memorabilia. They are happy to receive visitors and to explain the subtleties of this noble art – the Swiss army still uses crossbows. If you're especially keen, you can also watch guild members shoot at vertical targets attached to the top of a 36-metre (119-foot) pole.

Continue along the same road until you reach the outer canal.

★ **Windmolen** (Windmills; map D1, **101**): in season, the working northern windmill (called Sint Jan) is open 9.30am–12.30pm and 1.30pm–5pm. Admission: 40BEF. In the 15th century, the sails of all 28 mills used to turn. The machinery is as impressive now as it must have been then.

The house of the famous Flemish priest and poet Guido Gezelle, now a museum, stands at the entrance to Rolweg, on the left.

★ **Guido Gezellemuseum** (map D1, **102**): open 9.30am–12.30pm and 1.30–5pm. Closed Tuesday in winter. Admission: 40BEF. A modest little house with a fine garden. In his day, Gezelle's work was translated into 17 languages, but you need to read it in Flemish to appreciate all its subtleties. The exhibits include personal memorabilia, documents and examples of his writing.

★ **Sint Sebastiaansgilde** (Museum of the Guild of Archers; map D1, **103**): Carmerstraat. Open Monday, Wednesday, Friday and Saturday, 10am–noon and 2–5pm. Admission: 60BEF. Ask for the excellent taped commentary. The elite archers of this guild, founded in 1302, received Charles II of England when he lived in exile in Bruges during Cromwell's Commonwealth. Since then, all English monarchs have been made honorary members. Members practise every Monday evening, in the garden or in a long covered gallery.

★ **Engels Klooster** (Church of the English Convent; map D1, **104**): Carmerstraat 85, not far from the archers' guild. Open 2–3.40pm and 4.15–5.15pm. Closed on the first Sunday of every month. Admission free. Ring the bell, and the sister/tour guide will let you in and hand you a brochure. This is the only church in Bruges with a cupola, a splendid example of Renaissance baroque. The radial two-coloured paving and the altar, made of 23 types of marble, are truly splendid.

– At the end of the street, turn right onto Speelmanstraat – if you're cycling, you'll find yourself zigzagging about a bit thanks to the one-way system. Exit at Potterierei, a peaceful, pretty canal that leads to the port of Damme, and keep to the right-hand side for 400 metres. If you see a swan swimming here, it's a good time to remember just how seriously the city of Bruges takes these birds. All of Bruges's swans have a 'B' (for Bruges) engraved on their beaks at birth.

★ **Potterie Museum** (map C1, **105**): Potterierei 79. Open 9.30am–12.30pm and 1.30–5pm; out of season, 9.30am–12.30pm and 2–5pm, closed Wednesday. Admission: 60BEF. An ancient charitable institution that still functions today. It was once a hospital, and the museum houses treasures relating to its past, including paintings by Jacob van Oost and Pieter Pourbus, religious art, books of hours and furniture. The baroque church, Onze Lieve Vrouw van de Potterie, is filled with shiny brasses and marble. Visitors are invited to kiss the reliquary of Saint Idesbald.

Leave the right quay and join the Langerei, which brings you back to the centre. Turn right at the crossroads with Sint Gilliskoorstraat.

★ **Sint Gilliskerk** (map C1, **106**): this church is worth a look for its hall-church architecture. Inside is an altarpiece by Pieter Pourbus, *The Adoration of the Magi*. Apart from this, it's a bit empty.

★ To leave this peaceful area, where time appears to have stood still, walk down Oostgistelhof, Spaansebrug and Spanjaardstraat until you reach Van Eyckplaats, which is graced with a statue of the famous painter. The impressive edifice on the corner of Academiestraat is the former **tollhouse** (Oude Tolhuis; map B2, **107**), built in 1478. Today, the building houses the Communal Library, which holds 130,000 books.

This square is the centre of the 'Hanseatic quarter', so named because of Bruges's association with the Baltic ports of the medieval Hansa League. All the foreign communities in Bruges had their own street, hostel and trading counter, as you can see from the street names in the area.

On a nearby corner, is the Burghers' Lodge, where, among other statues, you can see the bear of Bruges. According to legend, it was killed by Baldwin Iron Arm.

★ **Huis ter Beurze** (House of Van der Beurze; map B2, **108**): on the corner of Grauwwerkerstraat. The Van der Beurze family allowed commercial transactions and money exchanges to take place in their home. By extension, the word 'Beurs' came to mean the place where all such transactions happened: hence *bourse*, in French, meaning exchange.

★ **Hof Bladelin** (map B2, **109**): on Naaldenstraat. Pause to look at the decorative turrets of this house, which has had some famous occupants in its time, including Pieter Bladelin, the treasurer of the Order of the Golden Fleece, Lorenzo de Medici (whose bust adorns one of the niches) and the unfortunate Count of Egmont (who was executed in Brussels by the Duke of Alba). The courtyard is open 10am–noon and 2–7pm; 10am–noon only on Sunday.

Continue along the same road, turn down Boterhuis and you'll see the back of Sint Jacobskerk.

★ **Sint Jacobskerk** (map B2, **110**): this hall-church with three naves was much enhanced by the donations of the Dukes of Burgundy. The rich furnishing has long since disappeared, but there are still a few treasures on show. These include a fine rood screen, paintings by Lancelot Blondeel and Jacob van Oost, and a wonderful altarpiece, *The Legend of St Lucia of Syracuse*, attributed to the Master of St Lucia. Bruges is represented in the background.

– End this tour by returning to the Markt via Sint Jacobstraat. The tour is over, but there are plenty of hidden backwaters that you can explore at your leisure.

BOAT TRIP

A 30-minute boat trip is the perfect complement to your tour on foot or by bike. The commentary isn't great (they have to satisfy a large number of people in four or five languages), but you'll be able to tour parts of Bruges that are only accessible by water. There are five different routes, with no fixed times – they just wait until they've got a full boat. They run between 10am and 6pm except in winter, when it's weekends and school holidays only. Umbrellas are provided free of charge if it rains. Tickets: 190BEF per person; 95BEF for children.

If there's a nasty smell at any point during your trip, don't blame the city council, which does its best to keep the canals clean. The problem is that Bruges is a victim of its success. According to a development study carried out 15 years ago, the city was set to attract half a million tourists a year; by 1994, the actual figure was 4 million. So it's hardly surprising if the canals are, shall we say, fragrant.

MARKETS

– **'t Zand**: held on Saturday, a general market that floods the Beursplein. In July, August and September, there's a luxury flea market.

– **Vismarkt**: the fish market, held every morning except Sunday and Monday. The freshest fruits of the sea you could hope to find.

– **Markt**: a traditional market, held every Wednesday. Lots of market gardeners and florists. Surprisingly good.

– **Dijver**: held on Saturday and Sunday during the tourist season. A field day for those with video cameras, who can zoom in on the antiques stalls that line the canal as tourist-heavy boats churn through the water.

FESTIVALS

– **Heilig Bloedprocessie**: held every year on Ascension Thursday. Bruges decks itself out in all its finery for the traditional Procession of the Holy Blood. This is a religious festival attended by thousands of people, many of whom arrive early to secure their vantage point hours in advance. The floats in the procession present tableaux drawn from the Old and New Testaments. In their wake comes a procession of merchants and craftsmen from the Middle Ages, with Diederik of Alsace behind; his entourage carries the phial of Christ's blood that, according to legend, he brought back from Jerusalem. There's nothing carnivalesque about this pageant; it's more like primitive theatre, and bears some resemblance to the Mystery plays of medieval times. When the relic passes, carried by the Bishop, everyone stands up and crosses themselves. It's a silent, awe-inspiring ceremony.

– **Festival of Canals**: this touristy folkloric festival takes place every three years at the end of August. It's a nocturnal affair, where those involved dress up in glittering costumes, and there's dancing and sound and lighting effects all the way down the canals. The next one is due to take place in 2004.

– **Praalstroet van de Gouden Boum**: a similar sort of atmosphere is created by the festival commemorating the marriage of Charles the Bold to Margaret of York. It's the most brilliant commemoration of its sort in Bruges, and involves 90 groups. It takes place every five years; the next one is on 31 August and 1 September 2002.

– **Cactus Rock Festival**: second week in July.

Around Bruges

DAMME	11,000 inhabitants

Damme, which serves as Bruges's outer port, is a small town that's well worth a visit if you have any time left after exploring Bruges. It's an ideal starting point for a cycle tour of the polders, the flat region described by Jacques Brel.

GETTING THERE

– **On foot, by car or bike**: Damme is five kilometres (three miles) from Bruges, so it's easy to reach whatever your means of transport. It's also easy to find: from Dampoort, north of Bruges, follow the Damsevaart Canal until you get there.

– **By boat**: boats leave from Noorweegsekaai (map of Bruges, off from C1). The *Lamme Goedzak,* a tourist boat, offers trips between April and the end of September. The excursion takes 35 minutes, and boats leave from the Bruges end of the canal, on the left-hand side, every two hours between 10am and 6pm. Round-trip and one-way tickets are available. A one-way journey costs 190BEF, and there are reductions for children.

A Short History

Damme, you won't be surprised to learn, means 'dam', or 'dyke'. After the infamous storm of 1134, which created the River Zwin, the Frisians, early experts in the business, came here to build dams and drain the polders. A landing stage was built on the Zwin, and Damme, a fishing village, was founded at its far end. Linked to Bruges by a canal, the settlement soon acquired a monopoly over the imports of Bordeaux wine and Swedish herring. Bruges, meanwhile, was flourishing and several major buildings were built, among them Onze Lieve Vrouwekerk, the merchants' exchange halls and Sint Janshospitaal. The town was reduced to ashes in 1213. It was rebuilt, but the all-important River Zwin began to silt up in the 15th century. For Bruges, the connection with Damme was vital. It was here, in 1468, that Charles the Bold married Margaret of York. Over the next few centuries, Damme suffered as Bruges's trading importance dwindled and a succession of wars wreaked havoc and destruction.

The medieval walls were replaced with new fortifications in the 17th century, when Damme became an outpost in the war against the Low Countries. The Duke of Marlborough had the fortifications knocked down during the War of the Spanish Succession, while Napoleon, with scant regard for town planning, created a canal that led to the Scheldt, cutting the town in two. Fierce battles took place in the surrounding area during 1944.

USEFUL ADDRESSES AND INFORMATION

Postcode: 8340.
🄷 **Tourist Office**: Jacob Van Maerlandtstraat 3. ☎ (050) 353319.

■ **Bike hire**: Thyl et Nele, Jacob Van Maerlantstraat. ☎ (050) 357-192.

WHERE TO STAY

✉ Budget

🛏 **Camping Hoeke**: Damse Vaart Oost 10, Hoeke. ☎ (050) 500496. This canal-side site in beautiful countryside is a haven of tranquillity. Hot showers are available.

✉✉ Moderate

🛏 **'t Trompetje**: Kerkstraat 30. ☎ (050) 356430. Fax: (050) 357049. Doubles 1,600–2,000BEF, with breakfast included depending on the season. A café-restaurant

with a few small but decent rooms. The bathrooms are on the landing. It's a bit of a hike to get there, but the owners are most attentive.
🏠 **Hotel-restaurant De Gulden Kogge**: Damse Vaart Zuid 12. ☎ (050) 354217. On the edge of the Napoleon Canal. A few prettily arranged rooms, four of which have showers, at reasonable prices: 1,520–1,920BEF. The restaurant (closed Wednesday evening and Thursday) offers pricey *haute cuisine* set menus (about 1,500BEF).

WHERE TO EAT

You'll be spoilt for choice, although eating here doesn't come cheap. Flemish families traditionally flock here for Sunday lunch.

☆ Budget

✕ **Brasserie 't Hemeltje**: Kerkstraat 46. ☎ (050) 360707. Blue is the dominant colour here. There's outside seating in summer, and the unpretentious menu offers toasted sandwiches and omelettes. Good-value daily special.

WHAT TO SEE

The best way to get a historical perspective on Damme is to clamber up the 43-metre (142-foot) church tower (admission fee) and look down at the surrounding countryside. From this vantage point, you can see where the old fortifications lay, hemming in a town that was much bigger than it is today. Only a quarter of this shrunken town remains, and it's obviously seen better days, but there's still an upbeat, upmarket feel.

Below the church, the candelabra effect of the cut willows in the churchyard echoes the pillars of the ruined nave.

★ **Stadhuis**: open throughout the tourist season from 9am to noon and 2–6pm on weekdays, and until 10pm at the weekend. Dating from 1464 and topped with a vast roof, the Stadhuis is an excellent example of the Late Gothic style. In the niches between the windows are statues of the Flemish counts, while the south corner holds two punishment stones – gossiping women had to wear these cumbersome necklaces as a penance, and were forced to drag them to church to confess. The original clock is still in place, and there are some bizarre carvings illustrating Flemish proverbs in the museum.

★ The **statue** in the square is of a famous Fleming: the 13th-century writer Jacob Van Maerlant, recognized as the father of Dutch poetry. He was, above all, an observer of contemporary manners: Flemish schoolchildren are almost certain to have studied his works, as he was one of the first writers to use the people's vernacular, 'Diets'. His tombstone is in the church. It's sometimes mistakenly attributed to the mythical character Till Eulenspiegel, which is exactly the kind of confusion that this prankster would have revelled in.

★ **Sint Janshospitaal**: Kerkstraat 33. Open 11am–noon and 2–4.30pm (from 11am on Sundays). Admission: 40BEF. The hospital was founded by

Margaret of Constantinople in the 13th century, and funded by a special tax on wine, which involved measuring the capacity of Bordeaux wine barrels as they entered Damme. A small museum displays a collection of religious objects, furniture, tombstones and a statue of Christ by Jérôme Duquesnoy.

LISSEWEGE

A canal-side polder village. If you're coming from Bruges, take the N31 towards Zeebrugge.

WHAT TO SEE

★ The great tower of **Onze Lieve Vrouwekerk**, built in 1230, rises from a sea of small white houses with huge shutters and red roofs. A typical example of coastal architecture in this part of Flanders, the tower is used as a lighthouse to guide ships through the fog.

★ A short walk south will bring you to a bizarre 13th-century **Gothic barn**, a utilitarian building that has somehow managed to survive the rigours of time. It was originally part of the Ter Doest farm, which belonged to the Abbey of the Dunes in Koksijde; the farm was looted by iconoclasts in the late 16th century. Its proportions are awesome: 60 metres (nearly 200 feet) long, 25 metres (80 feet) wide and 20 metres (66 feet) high. Inside, huge sturdy pillars support a massive oak roof. A small museum explains the history of Lissewege and the surrounding area.

ZEEBRUGGE

Bruges waited centuries for this harbour, which consists of enormous port installations and terminals for oil tankers. A ferry service links Zeebrugge to Hull and Felixstowe. It's also a fishing port, where you can buy sea-fresh fish and seafood at daily auctions.

★ **Seafront**: ☎ (050) 551415. Open 10am–9pm in July and August, 10am–6pm in May, June, September and October, and 1–5pm the rest of the year. Admission: 390BEF; a combined ticket, including a boat trip around the harbour, costs 595BEF; child discounts available. Seafront is near the port installations at the end of the canal linking Bruges to the sea. There are several overrated attractions here, including a lightship, an old Russian submarine, a museum on marine archaeology and displays about the sea, the history of navigation and sea monsters as seen by painters. There are also a couple of seals on display.

★ **Festival**: from mid-August to mid-September, there's a spectacular festival of sand sculptures on the beach, in which all the exhibits must represent a given theme. Admission: 150BEF.

JABBEKE

Jabbeke is a village between Bruges and Ostend, most famous as the home of the Expressionist painter and sculptor Constant Permeke. His house has been turned into a museum.

WHAT TO SEE

★ **Constant Permeke Museum**: Gistelsesteenweg 341. Open 10am–12.30pm and 1.30–6pm (to 5pm in winter). Closed Monday. Admission: 100BEF. Permeke lived in this huge house, known as 'The Four Winds', from 1930 until his death in 1952, and the 150 works on display include most of his sculptures. Permeke was an active member of the first school of Sint-Martens-Latem, and fought in World War I. He was wounded and cared for in England, where he made clay figures inspired by the agricultural world.

On his return to Ostend, where he had spent his childhood, he incorporated the fishing community into his work, and painted endless pictures of the sea at different times of day and in different conditions. Once he was settled in his house in Jabbeke, he started work on monumental sculptures, although his trips to Brittany inspired him to return to landscape painting. A year before his death, an exhibition of Permeke's work in Antwerp presented him as the most important Belgian painter of the inter-war years.

What distinguishes him from the German Expressionists is his systematic use of materials: he would apply several layers of paint to his canvas to evoke clay deposits at the edge of rivers. Brown and green are the dominant colours, and the works show an instinctive understanding of geology. Permeke had little time for fancy theories about his work, saying that his art was simply Flemish and peasant. The emergence of the first Sint-Martens-Latem school coincided with the birth of the Flemish nationalist movement, which was anchored in earthy values.

The works are attractively displayed in this large, unadorned villa. *The Farewell, The Sower* and *Family*, his most famous paintings, are all on show here. There's also a fine series of drawings of nudes, clearly influenced by Modigliani. Recumbent nudes and a 'self-sculpture' in wood are on show in the sculpture studio and several pieces are scattered about the garden.

OSTEND (OOSTENDE)   69,000 inhabitants

Ostend, once dubbed 'the queen of beaches', was among the most fashionable resorts in Europe during the Belle Époque era, though you'd never believe it now. Leopold II's dream of transforming Ostend into a coastal centre with a coherent and harmonious town layout never fully materialized, and the place has suffered at the hands of property developers and unscrupulous government officers. Like its casino, which could do with a total makeover, Ostend has fallen into neglect, with shops boarded up and to let, empty buildings galore and pavements dug up or badly maintained. The town looks as if it's in crisis, and there can be little doubt that the Channel Tunnel has deprived Ostend of many of the British tourists who once passed through the port on the way to sunnier climes. As a first step towards rehabilitation, the dyke has been rebuilt. The best way to appreciate Ostend is to remember that it was a town before it became a beach, and enjoy its artistic creativity, tradition of self-mockery and buzzing nightlife.

HOW TO GET THERE

– **By car**: via the E40. Ostend is 120 kilometres (72 miles) from Brussels.

– **By train**: Ostend is about an hour from Brussels.

– **By boat**: there's a catamaran terminal for Hoverspeed crossings from Dover. Ostend is the central point through which the coastal tram passes; it covers all 67 kilometres (40 miles) of the Belgian coast. You can pay on board, and there are reductions for children. Ring the bell for your stop when you want to get off.

A Short History

At the beginning of the 17th century, Ostend was Protestant, and its port was used by the Dutch 'sea beggars'. Archduchess Isabel laid siege to the town, and vowed not to change her underwear until the town was captured. Unfortunately for her, the siege lasted three years. As a sign of reconciliation, the occupying forces financed the Ostend Company, designed to set up trading posts in India and on the African coast, but the Dutch and English soon put a stop to that.

After the Battle of Waterloo, the English discovered the pleasures of sea bathing, and built the first beach huts: even the future Queen Victoria took a

---

■ Useful addresses

🛈 Tourist Office
✉ Post Office
🚂 Railway station
🚍 De Lijn tram and bus stations
⛴ Hoverspeed terminal

🛏 Where to stay

1 Youth Hostel De Ploate
  Jeugdherberg
2 Hotel Thévenet
3 Hotel Polaris
4 Grand Hotel George V
5 Hotel Old Flanders
6 Strand Hotel
7 Hotel Pick's

✗ Where to eat

11 Sea Breeze

12 L'Enfant Terrible
13 Mosselbeurs
14 Old Inn
15 Lucullus
17 Villa Maritza

🍸 Where to go for a drink and Nightclubs

21 Jan's Café
22 Tavern Den Artist
24 Bier Co
25 The Switch
26 Le Dôme

★ What to see

31 Museum voor Moderne Kunst
32 Museum voor Schone Kunst
33 James Ensorhuis
34 Mercator
36 Fish market

OSTEND

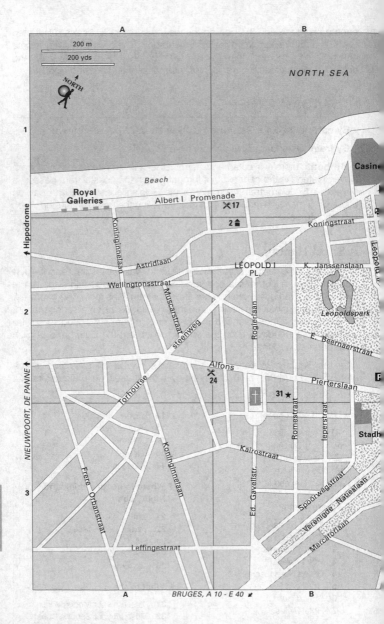

OSTEND

200 m
200 yds

NORTH

NORTH SEA

Casino

Beach

Royal
Galleries

Albert I Promenade

✕ 17

2 ▲

Koningstraat

Hippodrome

Koninginnelaan

Astridlaan

LÉOPOLD I
PL.

K. Janssenslaan

Wellingtonsstraat

Muscarstraat

Leopold

Leopoldspark

steenweg

Rogierlaan

E. Beernaerstraat

NIEUWPOORT, DE PANNE

Torhoutse

Alfons
✕ 24

31 ★

Pierterslaan

Romestraat

Jeperstraat

P

Stadh

Koninginnelaan

Kairostraat

Ed. Gavellstr.

Spoorwegsstraat

Frere-Orbanstraat

Verenigde Natieslaan

Mercatorlaan

Leffingestraat

A

BRUGES, A 10 - E 40

B

C

D

1

Beach

Albert I Promenade

Albert I Promenade

Iseghem

laan

Vlaanderenstraat

Kapucijnenstr.

Hofstr.

★ 33

P

14 ✕ 15

✕ 22

1 ⌂

✕ 11

Langestraat

4 ⌂

A. Buylstr.

WAPEN PL.

⌂ 7

P

12

✕

Nieuwstr.

St. Sebastlaanstr.

Museum voor Schone Kunsten ★ 22

GROENTEN-MARKT

3

13

VISSERS PL.

P

✕

Witte Nonnenstr.

Franciscusstr.

Oostetr.

P

Kaaistr.

Christinastr.

Kapellestraat

Sint-Paulustr.

Jozef II

Sint Petrus en Pauluskerk

Visserskaai

P

E. Beernaertlaan

straat

⌂ 5

⌂ 6

Vindictive

laan

34

★

Leopold III laan

Brandariskaai

G. de S. de Groentemarkt

ijndraaiersstr.

KNOKKE ↓ C

D

2

3

OSTEND

OSTEND

modest dip at Ostend in 1834. The waters were supposed to possess healing properties.

With the advent of the Brussels railway, the daily connection with England and the bourgeoisie's taste for casinos and horse racing, Ostend began to enjoy an international reputation on a par with Deauville or Monte Carlo. Leopold II had his finger firmly on the pulse, and tried his utmost to give the seafront a prestigious cachet. Behind the now disfigured dyke are several *fin-de-siècle* houses that blend seaside and art-nouveau styles.

World War I left destruction in its wake, while in World War II, the Germans razed the classic art-nouveau casino so they could build a gun emplacement. Today, the dunes are riddled with concrete bunkers – and matching hotels.

USEFUL ADDRESSES AND INFORMATION

– **Postcode**: 8400.

🛈 **Tourist office** (map B1): Monacoplein 2. ☎ (059) 701199. Fax: (059) 703477. Website: www.oostende.be. From June to the end of August, open 9am–7pm from Monday to Saturday and 10am–7pm on Sunday; otherwise 10am–6pm (to 5pm on Sunday).

✉ **Post office** (map C2): Hendrik Serruyslaan (at the edge of the Leopold Park).

🚂 **Railway station** (map D3): Natiënkaai 2. ☎ (059) 506284. Next to the Hoverspeed terminal.

🚌 **De Lijn tram and bus station** (map C3): Brandariskaai (100 metres from the station). For information: ☎ (059) 565353.

⚓ **Hoverspeed terminal** (map D2): quick crossings from Dover. ☎ (059) 559955.

WHERE TO STAY

Ostend's 68 hotels offer more than 5,000 beds, so you shouldn't have any trouble finding somewhere to stay, even though the town reaches saturation point in July and August. During the summer, there are plenty of rooms to let for one night, most of them above restaurants. If you do have any difficulties finding somewhere to stay, the Tourist Office will be happy to help. Prices are usually low, and Ostend is a useful base for visiting Bruges, which is only 20 kilometres (12 miles) away. That said, Ostend's hotels aren't much to write home about, as most cater for mass tourism.

☆ Budget

🛏 **Youth Hostel De Ploate Jeugdherberg** (map C1, **1**): Langestraat 82. ☎ (059) 805297. Fax: (059) 809274. Offers 102 beds in 21 rooms that sleep three to eight people. Basic rate per night: 480BEF. A bit dearer than the average Belgian youth hostel, this modern, comfortable and central establishment can get fairly lively in the evenings. It's squarely aimed at groups, with no double rooms.

🛏 **Hotel Thévenet** (map B2, **2**): Koningstraat 61. ☎ (059) 701035. Fax: (059) 809419. On a busy road, but 40 metres from the best bit of the beach. Doubles from 1,800BEF. A simple hotel offering clean rooms with showers, some for four. The rooms under the eaves are a bit cramped. It's not especially comfortable, and the welcome leaves something to be desired, but the breakfast room is convivial and there's a good selection of Belgian beers in the bar. Private car park (extra charge).

🛌 **Hotel Polaris** (map C2, **3**): Groentenmarkt 19. ☎ (059) 501-602. Fax: (059) 514001. Doubles 1,500–1,800BEF. The hotel's most notable features are the wide Classical facade and the fine sitting room on the ground floor. The wallpaper is floral, the decor Belle Époque and the comfort basic. Free bike hire.

☆☆ Moderate

🛌 **Grand Hotel George V** (map C1-2, **4**): Vlaanderenstraat 42. ☎ (059) 806556. Fax: (0590 804265, Email: hotelgeorgeV@oostende.net. Doubles 1,100–2,500BEF, including breakfast. A local institution in the heart of the shopping area, the George V has 52 rooms with sinks or showers and toilets at competitive prices, especially for families or groups. The owners take their job seriously, and are very welcoming. They're planning to add a sauna and a solarium in the near future. The restaurant offers decent grilled meats; a main course starts at 400BEF.

🛌 **Hotel Old Flanders** (map C2, **5**):

Josef II Straat 49. ☎ (059) 806603. Fax: (059) 801695. Doubles 2,300–2,800BEF. You're guaranteed a warm welcome at this family-style hotel in a fine brick house opposite the cathedral. The rooms are much of a muchness, apart from No. 12, which is also the biggest, but the breakfasts are generous. Paying car park.

🛌 **Hotel Pick's** (map C2, **7**): Wapenplein 13. ☎ (059) 702897. Fax: (059) 506862. Doubles 2,750BEF. In the centre of town, opposite the bandstand on the Wapenplein, this is an archetypal Ostend hotel offering the usual range of mod cons, although it's a bit slapdash. Half-board is available if you fancy the unexciting seafood restaurant (which is closed on Tuesday in winter).

🛌 **Strand Hotel** (map C2, **6**): Visserskaai 1. ☎ (059) 703383. Fax: (059) 803878. Closed January and February. Doubles 3,300BEF. A pricey three-star hotel, opposite the harbour, with a certain utilitarian charm. Modern and clinical, it's a good place to stay if you need to be up at dawn to catch the ferry, as breakfast is served from 5am. The crockery's stylish, but the cooking's a bit heavy and pretentious.

WHERE TO EAT

There are two main restaurant areas: the port or the dyke. If you choose the former, along Visserkaai, which locals call the 'longest restaurant in the world', you'll find mussels, eel and Ostend sole. Fish restaurants are as abundant as cod in a fishmonger's window, and all are worth trying. Their individuality lies in their decor, which tends towards the glitzy, given that most are competing for a clientele that wants something flashy for its money. The fish is always very fresh, although the cooking can be a bit heavy and excessive. If you're on a tight budget, the best thing to do is pick up some herring or a plate of excellent prawns from the stalls that line the harbour.

Opt for the dyke, between the casino and the royal villa, and you'll come across crowded restaurants with outside tables charging extortionate prices.

Prawn croquettes, for example, cost about the same as a steak. You get the feeling you're being made to pay for the privilege of watching the sun go down, so you really have to comb the menus to find a sensible price. If you don't want to be ripped off, stick to the centre, where cheap and cheerful greasy spoons serve excellent mussels.

☆ Budget

✕ **Sea Breeze** (map D1, **11**): Langestraat 103. ☎ (059) 707258. Open for lunch and dinner. Closed Wednesday. Near the port and good for tight budgets, this simple restaurant with a rather plastic-looking interior serves basic food: shrimp croquettes, prawns in garlic, mussels and a low-priced daily special, all for less than 400BEF. The owners also rent out basic rooms: 1,200–1,500BEF, with breakfast an extra 200BEF.

✕ **L'Enfant Terrible** (map D2, **12**): at the entrance to Nieuwstraat, on the same side as the port. ☎ (059) 802989. Closed Monday and Wednesday. This typical *eetcafe* rightly describes itself as 'attractive, small and pleasant', with green, spotlessly clean tables and simple, tasty, inexpensive dishes.

☆☆ Moderate

✕ **Old Inn** (map C1, **14**): Louisastraat 12. ☎ (059) 705060. Closed Tuesday evening and Wednesday. Ample helpings for 850BEF. This place has Parisian-style red shutters that open onto a prettily furnished restaurant with engravings on the walls. The house speciality: all sorts of steaks in all sorts of sauces done in all sorts of ways. Credit cards not accepted.

✕ **Mosselbeurs** (map C2, **13**): Dwarstraat 10. Near the vegetable market, this place does exactly what it says on the packet. The facade is encrusted with mussel shells, while the interior is all chequered tiling and tablecloths. The molluscs come in every imaginable form, and fish soup and eels are also on the menu. The mussels, sadly, are not always top-quality.

☆☆☆ Expensive

✕ **Lucullus** (map C1, **15**): Louisastraat 19. ☎ (059) 700928. Dinner only. Closed Sunday and Monday. Menus from 550BEF. Grilled meat and fish, with dishes cooked in beer a speciality. Nothing much to write home about, except perhaps the decor, which resembles a log cabin filled with pretty, lilac-coloured tables. Bike hire available.

☆☆☆☆ Splash Out

✕ **Villa Maritza** (map B1, **17**): Albert I Promenade 76. ☎ (059) 508808. Closed Sunday evening and the second fortnight in June. About 1,000BEF for lunch and 1,995BEF for a set dinner menu, which includes wine. A luxurious venue on the part of the restored part of the dyke: perfect if you've hit the jackpot in the casino. The facade is a wonderful example of Belle Époque architecture, tragically sandwiched between two blocks of concrete. Inside, there are high ceilings and Flemish Renaissance hangings and decoration. The light, imaginative cooking makes this one of the best restaurants in the country.

WHERE TO GO FOR A DRINK

Ostend's nightlife is one of its main attractions. Many Brits cross the Channel for it, and they can get pretty rowdy. Langestraat is where the action's at, and much of the booze downed in its bars ends up in the gutters. If you're planning to cut loose, watch out for prowling policemen.

❢ **Jan's Café** (map C1, **21**): Van Iseghemlaan 60. Open from 11.30am. Closed for lunch on Saturday and Sunday. A three-metre (10-foot) sea monster hangs over this famous bar, with blue and yellow decor, and arty photos on the walls. Conversation flows, as you'd expect in a bar where you never quite know who you might meet. Snacks and light meals served at lunchtime and until 11pm. Free coffee if you eat here.

❢ **Taverne Den Artist** (map C1, **22**): Kapucijnenstraat 13. Open 4pm–4am (later on Friday and Saturday). This art gallery-cum-tavern, a favourite with locals, has dark woodwork, a mezzanine with a carved balustrade and a buzzing atmosphere. Snacks, light meals and spare ribs are served until the wee hours, and there are blues and jazz concerts every first and third Tuesday of the month. Try a Hapkin, a delicious, strong blond beer.

❢ **Taverne 't Botteltje** (map C1, next door to **15**): Louisastraat 19. An Ostend institution that specializes in homemade beers and gin.

❢ **De Zeegeuzen** (Sea Beggars' Inn; map C1, opposite **22**): Kapucijnenstraat. Open 5pm–2am. A string of rooms where animated debate takes place around wheel-shaped tables. Souvenirs from the murky deep and the family tree of the Belgian royal family decorate the walls. The Spanish Inn, next door on the right, is one of the only surviving houses from the period of Spanish rule.

❢ **The Switch** (map C2, **25**): Cadzandstraat 12. Near the fish market, this is a typical bar full of life and smoke, where local youths drink beer and chat, and crowds spill out on to the pavement area. You can bring your own prawns and sandwiches.

NIGHTCLUBS

Langestraat is home to 300 metres of bars, karaoke clubs, leisure arcades, snack bars, pitta houses, topless bars and discos – all apparently competing to produce the highest number of decibels. In no particular order, **Brazzaville**, **Twilight**, **Manuscript**, **Road 99** and **Soul Store** attract Ostend's night owls.

– **Le Dôme** (map B1, **26**): Langestraat. The most popular club in town. There's a dancefloor on the ground floor and a gallery upstairs, from which you can watch the tightly packed dancers jigging down below. There's a cage of parrots in one corner, though goodness knows how they survive the noise.

– **Theatercafé-bistro Bier Co** (map A-B2, **24**): Alfons Pieterslaan 86. Open 11am–2am (later on the weekend). Closed Monday. This is where authentic Ostend hangs out. A co-operative has taken over the entire interior of a housing estate, now home to a baker's, an old-fashioned clothes shop, a salesroom, a street painter, a glass studio, a gin bar and Bier Co, which has a huge bar, porcelain tiling, metal beams and a stage for concerts. Katia and Dirk generate a good-humoured atmosphere that's reminiscent of English or Irish pubs. Themed evenings attract people of all ages, while the cooperative spirit is expressed in monthly beer promotions.

WHAT TO SEE

★ **Provinciaal Museum voor Moderne Kunst** (map B2, **31**): Romestraat 11. ☎ (059) 508118. Open 10am–6pm. Closed Monday. Admission: 100BEF. Dedicated exclusively to Belgian 20th-century art, with a few precursors, this museum is an essential stop-off for devotees of this period. The three levels contain permanent displays of drawings by Léon Spilliaert and paintings by the significant Belgian Symbolists and Expressionists, including Constant Permeke, Frits van den Berghe, Gustave de Smet, Edgard Tytgat and Albert Servaes. There are also sculptures by Oscar Jespers and Dadaist works by Paul Joostens.

CoBrA, Pop Art and more recent movements are represented by Panamarenko, Marcel Broodthaers and Roger Raveel. There's an amazing variation on the theme of the *Martyrdom of St Sebastian* by Frank Maieu, and wood sculptures by Vic Gentil. The museum ends with a display of works by a particularly unusual artist, Paul Van Hoeydonck. His *Chariot of Iris* is magical, but his chief claim to fame is that he is the only artist in the world to have shown on the moon. Yes, you did read that correctly – a small aluminium statue, *The Fallen Astronaut,* was placed there in 1971 by members of the Apollo XV team. There's a copy of it here with commentaries on the lunar installation. The temporary exhibitions are excellent, and there's a pleasant cafeteria upstairs.

★ **Museum voor Schone Kunsten** (map C2, **32**): Wapenplein. Open 10am–noon and 2–5pm. Closed Tuesday. Entry through the courtyard. Admission: 125BEF. A large part of this museum is devoted to Ostend's most famous son, James Ensor. Among the paintings on display are *Self-portrait in Flowered Hat* and *Christ Calming the Storm*, as well as satirical drawings depicting policemen and images of his parents on their deathbeds. His compatriot, Léon Spilliaert, whose paintings of the changing light of the North Sea are without peer, is also well represented. There's a bust of Ensor by Rik Wouters and an interesting collection of late 19th-century Belgian portraitists: Théo Van Rysselberghe is represented by his painting of bathers in a light-filled setting.

★ **Heemmuseum De Plate**: at the time of writing, this museum was due to move from Wapenplein to Langestraat so check with the tourist office before you set out. Admission: 50BEF. As usual in this type of bric-à-brac venue, some things are banal, some exciting. Many of the objects tell stories, such as the twinning of Ostend with Troy – both towns having been besieged. The jumble of artefacts on show includes a model of the glorious old casino, caricatures from the Belle Époque, a beached whale from 1826, a reconstruction of a bar, the saga of the Ostend–Dover mail, models of fishing boats – and an old chip-seller's barrow.

★ **James Ensorhuis** (map C1, **33**): Vlaanderenstraat 27. ☎ (059) 805335. From mid-June to mid-September and at Easter, open every day except

Tuesday, 10am–noon and 2–5pm; otherwise Saturdays and Sundays only, 2–5pm. It's sometimes closed because of lack of staff, so phone beforehand. Admission: 50BEF. Ensor inherited this house and souvenir and shell shop from his aunt in 1917. Even when he went bankrupt, he kept everything just as it was. He lived here until his death in 1949, and entertained friends, painters and critics within these walls. After his death, many of his paintings were sold, so the house is an attempt to replicate his universe, rather than a straight museum. The paintings are reproductions, but all the other objects in the house, many of which inspired his work, are authentic. Take a look at the tortoise shell, the sword fish, the stuffed swan and the carnival masks for which he is so famous.

A three-dimensional reconstruction of a painting that was lost when the Stadhuis burned down in 1940, *The Sick Pouilleux Warming Himself*, is on show on the mezzanine. Upstairs, you can see the studio-cum-sitting room where Ensor worked. His monumental compositions are reproduced here. The furniture and harmonium figure in some of his paintings

★ **Mercator** (map C3, **34**): berthed in the pleasure port on Vindictivelaan. January–March and October–December, open weekends 10am–1pm and 2pm–5pm; April–June and September, open 10am–1pm and 2–6pm; July and August, open 9am–6pm. Admission: 100BEF. The Belgian merchant navy's training ship was operational between 1932 and 1960. You can walk about the bridges and gangways, and get a feel for the spartan conditions endured by the cadets, who came here to train as naval officers. Commentaries in four languages describe how the sailing ship once brought back statues from Easter Island, as well as the remains of Father Damien, a priest from the village of Tremelo who was canonized by Pope Jean Paul II in June 1995 for his work with lepers.

What Else to See

★ **The western dyke and colonnades along the walkway**, which runs from the Royal Villa to the Wellington racecourse. The mathematical effects and perspectives recall the works of Giorgio de Chirico.

★ The **casino** (you have to play if you want to admire the Paul Delvaux mural inside) and, below the dyke, the **Stairs of Death**, where several hapless souls have drowned trying to get a closer look at the waves.

★ The **port**, **the wooden jetty** and the **fish auction** (map D2, **36**), when the fishing boats return with sole, plaice and prawns. The **North Sea Aquarium** is a bit of a bore: a few poor sea creatures languish dejectedly, presumably fed up with watching the odd visitor pass by. The stalls along the quaysides sell plates of deliciously fresh fish and prawns.

★ The neo-Gothic **Sint Petrus en Pauluskerk**, which has a marble mausoleum in memory of Louise-Marie, the first Queen of the Belgians.

WHAT TO DO

The principal activity for holidaymakers here is to walk along the dyke promenade or round the harbour. They come here for a peaceful holiday, renting apartments that, with a bit of luck, have sea views, and spend their

OSTEND

days sheltering behind colourful windbreaks on the beach, keeping a dozy eye on the children's sandcastles or pedalling '*cuistax*' (a go-kart with giant pedals) and eating waffles with ice-cream in the nearby tea-rooms.

It's hard to see the attraction of this flat coastline, packed with almost uninterrupted rows of concrete blocks. Yet hordes of French, German, English and Dutch tourists come here every year. In 1990, 35 million beds were calculated to have been occupied along the Belgian coast – an awesome figure that doesn't even include the many day-trippers who flock here. The real attraction is perhaps the seaside: the climate is pleasant, and the coast often gets the sunshine when the rest of the country is grey and cloudy. Then there's the North Sea itself, which has captured the imaginations of numerous painters and writers thanks to the subtle and inspiring play of light upon its waters, especially as the sun goes down.

– **Sea cruise**: from May to August, Seastar runs two-hour trips along the coast towards Nieuwpoort. ☎ (059) 232425.

FESTIVAL

– **First weekend in March:** on the Friday, there's the Procession of Candles, on Saturday, the Dead Rat's Ball and the Ball of the Prawn. It all winds up on Sunday with an outbreak of clog-throwing.

What to See in the Area

STENE

Before the tourist trade took over, little fishing villages were scattered along the coast, and the beach was the reserve of dunes and gulls. These villages have been swallowed up by urban sprawl, but a few hamlets, such as Stene, a mile from the concrete coastline, have survived. To get there, take Alfons Pieterlaan, turn right onto Torhoutesteenweg, then left onto Steensedijk for Stene Dorp (a brown sign points you in the right direction).

A group of low houses is clustered round the small Sint Mariakerk. There are eight restaurants and bars dotted along the 100-metre stretch. Ostenders come here on Sunday, hoping to experience a bit of authenticity. It's well worth the trip, as eating and drinking here is much cheaper than along the town's promenade.

WHERE TO EAT

☆☆ Moderate

✗ **De Vlasshaard**: Oudstrijdersplein 5, Stene 8400. ☎ (059) 803801. Closed Monday and Tuesday. Weekend set menu at 645BEF, with good-sized main dishes from 350BEF. The front of this establishment holds a bar and outdoor seating: the restaurant itself is at the back, with small tables, checked tablecloths, fireplaces, dark woodwork, brasses and porcelain. Imaginative cuisine and great food, plus attentive service and a good family atmosphere.

✗ The restaurants **Huize Gezelle**, **'t Pomptje**, **De Vier Torretjes**, **'t Vossenhof** and Molenaarshuis are in the same street.

RAVERSIJDE ESTATE

Among the dunes towards Middelkerke, west of Ostend: Duinenstraat 147. ☎ (059) 702285. Open April to early November. Admission: 100BEF.

Villa Goffinet: open 2–5pm. The former residence of Prince Charles, the brother of King Leopold III, who steered the country through the regency after World War II. It's now home to a display of historical bric-à-brac acquired by the old owner, a funny chap with a bit of a reputation as a womanizer and misanthropist, who dabbled with painting during his retirement.

Open-air museum of the Atlantic Wall: open 10.30am–6pm from July to mid-September and during public holidays in spring. Admission: 200BEF. Located in the bunkers and fortified trenches built by the Germans during the two world wars, this museum contains gun batteries, uniforms, and so on. Amateur historians will love it. Nearby, there's a park and an archaeological dig that shows the remains of a medieval village.

HITCH-HIKING FROM OSTEND

– **Heading for Knokke**: Graaf Desmet Denayerlaan, near the station.

– **Heading west or towards La Panne**: Koningin Astridlaan, near the racecourse.

– **Heading for Bruges and Brussels**: the Vuurkruisenplein roundabout, by the *Mercator*

The east coast, from Ostend to the Zwin

It's about 30 kilometres (18 miles) from Ostend to the Dutch border, with only the port of Zeebrugge and its industrial hinterland interrupting the relentless resorts and dunes. The Belgian coastline ends with a huge nature reserve, Het Zwin, which is a birdwatcher's paradise.

DE HAAN

This is a pleasant family resort east of Ostend, with a fine stretch of dunes and a wonderful early-1900s tram stop. Its name means 'The Cockerel' (French-speakers call it Le Coq). There's also a circular park with sporting facilities and a mini beach. The locals had the foresight to preserve the 1930s cottages (the only other place where they still stand is Het Zoute), with their little gardens, and they lend the place a certain charm. The Trammellant festival, when everyone dresses up in Belle Époque costumes, takes place in early August.

USEFUL ADDRESSES

🛈 **Tourist office**: you can't miss it, as it's like a huge pink cake in the middle of the resort. ☎ (059) 242135. Free hotel-reservation service.

■ **Bike hire**: Fietsen André, opposite the tourist office. Also stocks '*cuistax*' if you want to ride as a family.

WHERE TO STAY AND EAT

⌂ **B&B Stella Maris**: Memlinglaan 11. ☎ and fax: (059) 235669. Email: stellamaris@online.be. Three rooms for two at 1,800BEF, or 2,000BEF with shower, and one room for four at 2,400BEF, with sink and hot water; shared retro bathroom and toilets. Generous breakfast. An 1890s villa near the tram stop, with a distinctive red-and-black striped roof. They've given a lot of thought to the unusual decor: the all-wood interior has a faintly Russian feel, and there are some fine posters on the walls. It's reasonable value for money, and prices come down if you stay for more than two nights.

The landlords are charming folk, and offer tailor-made gastronomic/cultural evenings if you like that sort of thing. Otherwise, you can just enjoy the health-giving air of the North Sea. No smoking in the bedrooms.

✗ **Le Bienvenu**: Drifweg 14. You'll see it as you enter the village on a road running parallel to the tram lines. ☎ (059) 233254. Closed Tuesday and Wednesday lunchtime. Set menus from 790BEF. The house speciality is *bouillabaisse* (fish stew), concocted by a red-faced cook. They also offer *foie gras* in ginger and grilled turbot in a mustard sauce.

BLANKENBERGE

This is a popular seaside resort. The seafront's a mass of concrete blocks, but there are a few old-fashioned houses tucked away behind them. There's a pier with a funfair and a velodrome on the dyke, where children can ride funny-looking bikes with misshapen wheels, bikes without saddles and a host of other curious contraptions. Price: 45BEF for a short ride.

WHERE TO STAY AND EAT

⌂ **Youth Hostel De Wullok**: Ruitersstraat 9, Blankenberge 8370. ☎ (050) 415307. Fax: (050) 426014. Open year-round. Basic rate per night: 430BEF. A mile from the station between the sea and polders, with 66 beds. Most rooms are designed for six people. Lunch and evening meals served. Garden with barbecue.

✗ **Restaurant Oesterput**: Oude Wenduinesesteenweg 16, Blankenberge 8370. ☎ (050) 428677. Booking recommended. This former sheet-metal warehouse in the middle of the *jachthaven*, or pleasure port, is a local institution. It's an austere hangar with concrete flooring and hardly any decoration. The Canadian trout in the fish tank do their best to hide, as though they're aware of the fate that awaits them. You pay market prices for these beasts, so they're a bit expensive, but the other dishes (mussels, oysters and excellent soups) are perfectly affordable. The atmosphere is relaxed, with kids running about and dogs wagging their tails in expectation of the odd treat. The waiters sometimes struggle to cope with the crowds.

WHAT TO SEE

★ **Sea Life Centre**: Koning Albertlaan (bypassing the town). ☎ (050) 424200. Open 10am–6pm (to 9pm in July and August). Admission: 300BEF. A North Sea aquarium with a didactic and ecological mission.

Children receive a questionnaire to fill in, and hunt for the answers around the tanks, where they can also stroke the stingrays. There's also a centre for sick seals. The acoustics are a problem, and it's incredibly noisy, but at least the signs and captions are in four languages. Overall, this is a pretty impressive venture.

FESTIVAL

– **Carnival** takes place the weekend before Shrove Tuesday.

HEIST, DUINBERGEN, ALBERTSTRAND, KNOKKE-LE- ZOUTE

The Belgian coast gets more and more upmarket the closer you get to Het Zoute, with hotels, luxury shops, restaurants, bijou villas, casinos, art galleries, select nightclubs, Golf GTIs galore and a host of beautiful people parading through the squares. It's great fun to watch, but day-trippers are not made especially welcome. In an unusually heritage-conscious move by the local authorities, draconian regulations ensure that Het Zoute's white-washed, red-roofed cottages are preserved intact.

In Knokke, if you have money to throw around, go to the **casino**, where you can gamble beneath a 72-metre (240-foot) mural by Magritte, which includes a number of his favourite themes.

🛈 **Tourist Office**: Zeedijk 660. ☎ (050) 630380. Fax: (050) 630390.

HET ZOUTE

★ **Het Zwin nature reserve**: Ooievaarslaan 8, Het Zoute 8300. ☎ (050) 007000. From April to the end of September, open 0am–7pm; otherwise 9am–5pm. Closed Wednesday. Admission: 165BEF. Take bus No. 788 from Knokke station.

All that remains of the medieval estuary that brought in the ships from Bruges at high tide is a hole in the middle of the dunes that's submerged during equinoctial tides and violent northwest storms. Otherwise, there's nothing but salt flats. In this unique environment, 120 species of bird come to nest. Created in 1952, the reserve is divided into two sections: the first is a pine forest where white storks nest, dotted with ponds and cages for water birds, birds of prey, waders and web-footed birds; the second about 100 hectares (250 acres) of marshland, where you can brave the wind that whips around (wellington boots are a good idea) to squint through binoculars at migratory birds and salt-loving plants. The colours in spring and autumn are stunning. You can visit the area accompanied by expert guides: ring for more details.

The west coast, from Ostend to De Panne

As you follow the royal route towards the French border, the beaches get bigger and the dunes higher and thicker. The IJzer estuary forces the road to curve round. Beyond De Panne, there's another nature reserve which marks the end of Belgian territory.

WEST FLANDERS

NIEUWPOORT — 10,000 inhabitants

The fishing harbour of Nieuwpoort and its pleasure port, once the most important on the coast, were completely destroyed during World War I. The whole town was rebuilt according to original plans in a slightly sickly yellow brick.

USEFUL ADDRESS

Postcode: 8620.
🛈 Tourist office: Marktplein 7. ☎ (058) 224444. There's also an information kiosk at Hendrikaplein 11, near the dyke. Open at the weekend.

WHAT TO SEE AND DO

★ **King Albert Monument**: this marks the spot where, in 1914, Albert I decided to flood the IJzer plains in order to halt the German advance, a circular monument has been erected with a statue of the 'knight King' on horseback. There's a panoramic view from the top.

While Albert seems to have taken all the credit, the real hero of the hour was the lock-keeper who operated the sluice gates on a spot nicknamed Ganzepoot ('Goose foot'). The polders were immediately flooded, and the German troops were prevented from getting across for four years.

★ The **Markt** is a square with rather harsh yellow-brick facades, typical of this region. The arcades of the hall, complete with a belfry, are strikingly elegant. The building now houses a small ornithological museum, from which you can set off to explore the reserve of the IJzer channel.

★ **The landing stage**: most people come here for a breath of sea air and to watch the pleasure boats or fish using square nets, which are rented by the hour and hauled in with the help of pulleys. A good catch, however, is a rarity these days.

– **Boat trips**: in July and August, the *Jean-Bart III* sails from Nieuwpoort to Dixmuide between 2pm and 7pm. It's a great way to see the flat lands of the IJzer.

KOKSIJDE-OOSTDUINKERKE — 18,000 inhabitants

These two resorts gradually merged after the two communes were united. Note the 33-metre-high (110-foot) dunes, the fishing village and the wide beaches, which are ideal for sand-yachting.

USEFUL ADDRESS

🛈 Tourist office: Gemeentehuis, Zeelaan 24. ☎ (058) 533055. There's also an information office in the Koksijde casino.

WHERE TO STAY

⊠ Budget

⚑ **Jeugdherberg De Peerdevisser**: Dorpstraat 19, Koksijde 8670. ☎ (058) 512649. Fax: (058) 522880. Closed between mid-November and the beginning of March. Basic rate per night: 495BEF. A youth hostel on the dunes, where 135 beds, 12 double rooms and 24 family rooms bring seaside holidays to the masses. Bike hire available.

WHAT TO SEE

★ **Visserijmuseum** (Fishing Museum): Pastoor-Schmitzstraat 4, in Oostduinkerke. Open 10am–noon and 2–6pm. Closed Monday except in July and August. Admission: 80BEF. Oostduinkerke is perhaps the only village in the world where fishing is done on horseback. Now consigned to folk tradition, this practice was once taken very seriously: fishermen dressed in yellow oilskins and perched on sturdy Brabant horses, used to pull trawls for prawn fishing. The fisherman's skill consisted of guiding his steed through the waves and currents.

There's a display case devoted to the Guild of Prawn Fishermen in the museum, while a series of models explains the development of the techniques and tools used, including boats such as the hunter (a fast boat that supplied flotillas with empty barrels) and the boat on which herring were gutted and salted. River fishing also gets a look-in here, with a description of imports and exports on the Scheldt. The daily life of seafaring folk, and of their families, is catalogued in an array of documents, and there's a section on whale fishing, with details of the three unfortunate sperm whales that were grounded on Koksijde beach in 1994. There's a traditional inn at the exit.

★ **Abbey of the Dunes**: Koninklijke Prinslaan 8. From April to the end of September, open 10am–6pm; otherwise 9am–12.30pm and 1.30–5pm. This Cistercian abbey, which once owned 10,000 hectares (25,000 acres) of land, was one of the most powerful abbeys in Christendom during the 12th and 13th centuries, but its power declined during the wars between France and England. When it was pillaged by iconoclasts in 1566, the monks abandoned the abbey, which gradually sank into the sand. The museum offers an insight into the considerable power wielded by Europe's abbeys, in particular those run by the Benedictine order. Archaeological digs have uncovered 1,300 skeletons (98 per cent male, and therefore monks), which are on display here. It's hard to imagine what the buildings were like when you look at the silent ruins that remain. There's nothing more than two metres (seven feet) high, and you have to look at a plan of the abbey to identify the cloister, refectory, kitchens and monks' cells.

★ **Paul Delvaux Museum**: Paul Delvauxlaan 42. ☎ (050) 521229. From April to the end of September, open 10.30am–6.30pm, closed Monday; from October to the end of December, open Friday, Saturday and Sunday 10.30am–5.30pm. Closed January, February and March. Admission: 190BEF. Established well before the Surrealist painter's death in 1994, the home of the Delvaux Foundation is a magnificent museum, housed in an old farm and surrounded by gorgeous villas.

The world of Delvaux's dreamlike paintings is wonderfully re-created. You can see his workshop and the accessories he used to create his imaginary world – a collection of miniature trains, wooden tramways, a skeleton and models of Greek temples – as well as palettes spattered with paint and a replica of the artist's studio in Brussels. The plans for a frieze that he painted in the zoology lecture hall at the University of Liège resemble a comic strip, while photos of Delvaux, from his early childhood to his old age, show him dressed, as always, in an odd sleeveless shirt with a wide, open collar.

The blueish light of the dimly lit exhibition rooms provides an ideal setting for the seemingly petrified bodies of the beautiful, ethereal creatures in his paintings. People seem to meet by chance, their destinies cross, yet they never really come together. However implausible their juxtapositions, these dream-paintings are meticulously detailed, and there's an absurd humour about the men in bowler hats, the ghostly trains heading into temples from the moon and young women in hats and crinolines awaiting the arrival of sailing ships. Like Magritte and countless other Belgian artists, Delvaux was obsessed with the fantastical, and he was among the most gifted of them when it came to putting his vision on canvas.

DE PANNE   10,000 inhabitants

This seaside resort, popular with tourists from nearby Lille, shares a vast, breakwater-free beach with France. It's an ideal spot for sand-yachting. The Westhoek nature reserve is a beautiful area of unspoiled land, much coveted by developers but fiercely protected by environmentalists.

USEFUL ADDRESSES AND INFORMATION

Postcode: 8660.
🛈 Tourist office: Zeelaan 21. ☎ (058) 421818. Closed Sunday in winter.

🛈 Information kiosk: Albertplein. ☎ (058) 421819.
🚃 Railway station: in Adinkerke. Trains go to Ghent and Brussels.

WHERE TO STAY AND EAT

🛏 ✕ Au Filet de Sole: Nieuwpoortlaan 14. ☎ (058) 420360. Fax: (058) 411680. Closed November. Central location. Doubles 1,800–2,070BEF. A hotel with a family atmosphere, run by a good-humoured young couple. The 11 modern but cosy rooms have all mod cons, and the restaurant, done up in art-deco style, offers a dozen variations on the theme of sole, including sole soufflé with honey. Menus start at 650BEF. Half- and full-board available. In winter, you get one night and breakfast free.

WHAT TO SEE

★ The magnificent **monument to Leopold I**, who first set foot on Belgian soil here (a small step for man, but a giant step for Belgiankind), and the Westhoek nature reserve. The odd tower block hasn't managed to spoil this place.

★ **Westhoek**: the 340-hectare (85-acre) site belongs to the Flemish Region, which restricts access to it. In the middle of the dunes, constantly shifting thanks to the power of the sea and wind, there's a zone known as 'Little Sahara', where no vegetation grows. On hot days, you can almost believe it's the real thing. Beachgrass, privet, buckthorn, black elder and weeping willows help keep the dunes in place. Beneath the highest dunes lie deep depressions ('*pannes*'), which are flooded in winter and transformed into marshy areas where wild orchids and gentians grow.

You can visit the reserve throughout the year, following the well-signed paths, but the best way to see Westhoek is on a guided walk, details of which are available from the tourist office.

WHAT TO DO

Those in search of a thrill should try their hand at **sand-yachting**. When the tide is out, there's a vast expanse of beach, and you can get up a speed of 50kph (30mph) in a stiff breeze. But, be warned, it's a messy business. For details, contact SYCOD: ☎ (058) 513674.

VEURNE   12,000 inhabitants

This is a fascinating little town set in the coastal hinterland of Veurne-Ambacht. There's a heavy Spanish influence, not just in the architecture, but also in the traditions. The procession of Penitents is as good as you'd get in Seville.

A Short History

The cloth industry brought prosperity to Veurne (as it did to so many Flemish towns), whose wealth depended on relations between Flanders, England and France. The surrounding polders were drained during the reign of Archduke Albert and his wife, Isabel, and Veurne was home to a Spanish garrison, detailed to defend the town against the French, until the beginning of the 18th century

USEFUL ADDRESSES AND INFORMATION

Postcode: 8630.
🛈 **Tourist office**: Landhuis, Grote Markt 29. ☎ (058) 330531.
■ **Bike hire**: at the railway station on Statieplaats, to the east of the town. ☎ (058) 311299. This is the ideal way to visit Moerens (the drained marshes) and the region of Bachten de Kupe (in the IJzer hinterland).

WHERE TO EAT

☆☆ Moderate

✕ **Grill De Vette Os**: Zuidstraat 1. ☎ (058) 313110. Dinner only. Closed Sunday and Thursday. Main dishes 400BEF. Fine gabling, a yellow facade and massive beams, with steak and such at reasonable prices, plus scampi, mussels and the usual range of snacks and light meals. It can get quite lively.

☆☆☆ Expensive

✗ **Restaurant Onder den Toren**: Sint Niklaasplein 1. ☎ (058) 316566. Closed Monday evening and Tuesday. Set menus from 995BEF. At the foot of the great tower of Sint Niklaaskerk, this is an excellent restaurant where the food is adventurous and tasty: sophisticated salads at reasonable prices, fish gratins and trout. The high-tech decor is a bit too trendy, with shiny metal and light wood, but the young staff are efficient and cheerful.

WHERE TO GO FOR A DRINK

♟ **Pietje Pek Oud Veurne**: Appelmarkt 2. Open Friday, Saturday and Sunday; every evening in summer. The bar's in a spectacular vaulted cellar, and its clients come from far and wide.

WHAT TO SEE

★ **Grote Markt**: a harmonious collection of buildings, with a fine ensemble of Flemish Renaissance houses, each with its own distinct gable. The Landhuis, an old manor from which the surrounding communes were governed, and which later became the law court, is a Classical building; the belfry above is Gothic, while the pretty onion-domed tower tends towards the baroque. The carillon plays the *Ode to Joy*, from Beethoven's Ninth Symphony, now the anthem of the European Union.

Elsewhere on the square, the 15th-century **Spaans Paviljoen** (Spanish pavilion), on the left-hand corner of Ooststraat, used to be the headquarters for Spanish officers. Opposite this is the Vleeshuis (butchers' guild), with its prettily festooned gable, which is now a library. On the far side of the square, on the left, is a house with arcades where the night watchman was once based. A weather vane shaped like the lion of Flanders now mounts guard on the roof.

★ **Stadhuis**: squeezed into a corner beside the Landhuis, the Stadhuis has two facades, one of which is fronted by an elegant loggia with four columns. Behind this, there's a droplet-shaped cupola. The (variable) opening hours are posted on a board in front of the tourist office, and there are guided tours hourly from 11am, with the last at 4.30pm. Admission: 50BEF.

Inside, you'll find some wonderful relics of past eras, including a penitent's hair shirt. There's a portrait of the local hero who told the Allied forces how to flood the IJzer plains, and paintings of Archduke Albert and his wife, Isabel, Louis XIV and Joseph II and his brother Leopold. Several rooms are devoted to excellently preserved 17th- and 18th-century furniture. There's a splendid mantelpiece marked with the Spanish coat of arms and, in a chapel adjoining the public gallery of the old law courts, Paul Delvaux's *Young Girl from Veurne*. Splendid hangings adorn the walls: Mechelen leather in the council room, blue velvet with matching chair covers in the classroom, and embossed leather from Cordoba in a room that was used as Albert I's study. In here, the Belgian king received his English counterpart, George V.

★ **Sint Walburgakerk**: unfinished for hundreds of years, this church was completed at the beginning of the 20th century. In the nave to the right, you can see a reliquary containing a piece of the 'True Cross'. On the other side of the square are the ruins of the 14th-century nave and its porch. The little park next to the ruins is a delightful haven of peace, its hundred-year-old trees full of singing birds.

★ The massive square keep of **Sint Niklaaskerk**, which almost looks as if it has squashed the little houses beside it, stands on the other side of the square. The level of the original doorway gives you an idea of how much the ground level has risen since the 13th century, when the church was built. Sint Niklaas is a hall-church with some fine choir stalls, and there's a carving of the saint and his three children below the pulpit. You can climb the tower (10am–noon and 2–5pm).

SPECIALITIES

Veurne is known for its *babeluttes*, hard sweets made of sugar and butter that come wrapped in blue paper. They're a bit sickly, and you'll need to watch your fillings. The other local delicacy is *potjesvlèsch*, rillettes of rabbit, chicken or veal in jelly, eaten with rustic bread and Sint-Sixtus beer. Veurne dried ham is also excellent.

FESTIVAL

Boetprocessio (Procession of Penitents): last Sunday in July. Huge numbers of people take part, but at the centre of attention are 250 hooded 'penitents', who each carry a 40-kilogram (88-pound) Christ on a cross. The procession, which has been going since 1644, shows the extent of Spanish influence here, and the number of participants is actually on the rise.

WHAT TO SEE IN THE AREA

★ **Museum of Bakers and Confectioners**: Albert I-laan 2. ☎ (058) 313897. From April to September, open 10am–noon and 2–5pm, closed Friday, except in July and August, when it closes at 6pm; otherwise 10am–noon and 2–5pm, closed Friday and Saturday. Admission: 80BEF. This 17th-century farm near the junction of the E40 and A18 now houses a mouthwatering museum. One display examines the significance of bread in art; another is a 1900 bakery, complete with waffle and wafer irons, moulds, an old wooden oven, a 2.5-metre (eight-foot) bread shovel, sweet cylinders and a host of other objects for pastry cooking. You can admire masterpieces made of sugar, marzipan and chocolate, while an outside barn contains a display of old-fashioned delivery vans.

DIKSMUIDE   15,000 inhabitants

The locals call their town the 'pearl of the polders'. As the key strategic point on the IJzer plains, it was in the front line during World War I, and was ravaged as a result. After the war, it was designated a memorial town to the Flemish soldiers who died in the trenches, and a commemorative tower, the

IJzertoren, was built. There's an annual rally at the tower, which used to be a pacifist, international gathering, but is now dominated by the Flemish separatist movement.

The IJzertoren was blown up in 1946 in mysterious circumstances, and a bigger tower was built. A gateway dedicated to Peace, resembling a triumphal arch, was erected with the remains of the first tower. The tower looms over the region, forming a stern but impressive silhouette: in the eyes of many Flemings, it symbolizes the fight led by the people of Flanders to achieve autonomy. The motto written in a cross at the top of the tower is *AVV-VVK ('Alles voor Vlaanderen, Vlaanderen voor Kristus'* –'Everyone for Flanders, Flanders for Christ'), which underlines the strength of the nationalist and Catholic traditions in the Dutch-speaking part of Belgium.

If you want to form your own opinion, you should visit the war museum beneath the tower. Open mid-March until 11 November 10am–5pm (6pm at Easter and in September). Admission: 200BEF. A slogan is written around the tower in English, French, Dutch and German: 'No more war!'

A Short History

Diksmuide now lies 20 kilometres (12 miles) from the sea, but was once a port that traded with England via the IJzer, which once had an estuary. It was a cloth town, but was also famous for its butter. In 1914, German troops battled a stubborn Belgian defence line. The town was bombarded by artillery, and the defenders had to double back to the other side of the IJzer, where they stayed for four years. Diksmuide was reduced to rubble. After the war, the locals rebuilt the town according to the original plans.

USEFUL ADDRESSES AND INFORMATION

Postcode: 8600.
🛈 Tourist office: Bloemolens 57. ☎ (051) 519419.
🛈 Tourist information centre: Grote Markt 14. ☎ (051) 501321. Mrs Vuylsteke, a youthful octagenarian who recently made her first parachute jump, was born in the trenches. She'll be happy to tell you about her native town – and she's not short of stories.
🚆 Railway station: Bortierlaan, 300 metres from the Markt.

WHERE TO STAY AND EAT

🛏 ✕ Hotel De Vrede: Grote Markt 35. ☎ (051) 500038. Fax: (051) 510621. Restaurant closed on Wednesday. Doubles 2,200BEF. A comfortable family setting, with modern rooms at low prices and bourgeois cooking with no surprises.

🛏 Huize de Toren: IJzerdijk 71. ☎ (051) 500548. Rooms for two 1,600–2,200BEF. Farmhouse accommodation a couple of miles from the town, near the banks of the IJzer and Dodengang. The owners are friendly, and it's quiet, clean and fairly cheap. Generous breakfasts.

WHAT TO SEE

★ **Grote Markt**: Typically Flemish yellow-brick houses and a neo-Gothic Stadhuis, all rebuilt after 1918.

★ **Sint Niklaaskerk**: a faithful re-creation of the 14th-century design, this reconstructed church contains a *Way of the Cross* by the Belgian sculptor Georges Minne, while photographs of the destroyed town hang on its columns. Beyond the left-hand entrance to the church, there's a street that leads to the Vismarkt (Fish Market). Cross the canal and you'll come to the **Begijnhof**, a lovely, peaceful place arranged around a handsome lawn and chapel. It too has been rebuilt, which perhaps explains why it looks so clean and neat.

★ **Stedelijk Museum**: open from April to mid-September, 10am–noon and 2–5pm. Admission free. A small museum that deals with the local diamond trade, local history and folklore, pre-1914 art and art in the trenches. It's definitely worth a visit.

★ **Westoria**: open 9am–6pm (10am from October to March). Admission: 240BEF; discounts for under-16s. This old mill in the centre of town has been turned into an attraction with a historical theme. Follow the virtual miller and his cat on a tour through history from the time of the woolly mammoths to the carnage of World War I.

★ **Dodengang**: IJzerdijk 65. Open between April and the end of September, 10am–noon and 1–5pm. Admission free. A network of trenches meander for a mile along the left bank of the river, not far from the bridge over the IJzer. At this point, only 20 metres (66 feet) of river separated the Germans from the Belgians. Listening to the birds on the spot today, it's hard to imagine the persistent noise of gunfire and the appalling battles that took place. Occasionally, the soldiers from either camp could hear each other, and even began to get to know one another.

In the Area

WHERE TO STAY

☆ Budget

⚓ **Jeugdherberg De Sceure**: Veurnestraat 4, Vleteren 8640. ☎ (057) 400901. Fax: (057) 401-371. Closed the first fortnight in September. Basic rate per night: 405BEF. Vleteren is a village southwest of Diksmuide, near the IJzer, known for the Westvleteren Trappist beers. This hostel is a modern building beside the road, with 89 beds in rooms that sleep five or six, and two family rooms. Bike hire available.

☆☆ Moderate

✕ ⚓ **Kasteelhoeve Viconia**: Kasteelhoevestraat 2, Diksmuide-Stuivekenskerke 8600. ☎ (051) 555230. Fax: (051) 555506. Double rooms 2,200–2,600BEF. This Gothic-style brick farm and mansion north of Diksmuide, in the heart of the countryside, is a good base if you're touring the region. It has a lovely garden with sweeping lawns, and the rooms are comfortable, well equipped and good value for money. Well-judged regional cooking, too.

WHERE TO GO FOR A DRINK

⚑ In de Vrede: Donkerstraat 13, Westvleteren 8640. ☎ (057) 400377. Closed Friday. Right opposite the Abbey of Westvleteren, lost in the middle of the polders. The abbey is not open to the public, but it's still manages to pull in the tourists thanks to its status as one of Belgium's five genuine Trappist breweries. It's impossible to find Westvleteren beers on the super-market shelves, so hordes of connoisseurs descend on the adjoining shop to procure a bottle or several. This café is extremely ordinary, but you're here for the beers, full-bodied brown ales that come in three guises: Westvleteren 6, 8 and 12. The higher the number, the stronger the brew, though even the weakest one's no slouch, and you'll feel it the next morning if you knock back more than a couple in one go. Line your stomach with cheese and pâté made by the monks.

WHAT TO SEE

★ **The German cemetery of Praetbos-Vlasdo**: this is a large field to the east of Diksmuide, set in a peaceful wood. For more than 60 years, a magnificent group of sculpted figures has watched over the eternal rest of the 25,638 German soldiers who are buried here. Their names appear 20 at a time, engraved on simple flat stones. Many were students, among them Peter, the son of the German sculptor Käthe Kollwitz. As a tribute to him, and to all those who died during World War I, she gave the cemetery two poignant kneeling statues: a mother and father, bowed in silent grief. There's surely no better propaganda against war than the expression of despair on this couple's faces.

★ **Lo**: a charming little village where they make a delicious hard cheese. Stop here to look at the old pump and pond in the middle of the village, the proud old Stadhuis, the 16th-century belfry and the Westpoort, part of the medieval walls. Beside it stands an aged tree to which, according to legend, Julius Caesar once tethered his horse.

🛈 **Lo-Reninge tourist office**: Markt 17A, Lo-Reninge 8647. ☎ (058) 289166. Good tourist literature. Bike hire available.

★ **Bachten de Kupe open-air museum**: on Sint Mildredaplein in Izen-berge, to the west of Lo. From Easter to mid-November, open 1–5pm; 2–6pm at the weekend. Admission: 130BEF. This open-air museum is devoted to Westhoek rural life. You can wander round the farm, barn and stables, and admire the bread oven and a host of everyday objects used by simple country folk.

★ **Old Timer Museum Bossaert in Reninge**: Tempelaere 12, Reninge 8647. Open Monday to Friday 12.30–6.15pm (from 1.30pm on Monday). Admission: 140BEF. On the motorway from Veurne to Ieper, in a shopping centre between Oostvleteren and Woesten. A fantastic private collection of 100 old cars and motorbikes, displayed in an light and airy exhibition space. Wonderful for lovers of vintage vehicles.

IEPER (YPRES)   35,000 inhabitants

A victim of war if ever there was one, Ieper, or 'Wipers' as the British soldiers called it, has come to symbolize the folly of man – it even lent its name to a gas, 'yperite', otherwise known as mustard gas. For the British in particular, the town is a tragic reminder of the pointless loss of life, but it is also a model of courageous reconstruction. No visit to Flanders is complete without a visit. The destroyed monuments have been rebuilt with the kind of detail you'd find in a model, but the town itself is rather frosty. Don't miss the new museum, In Flanders Fields, where high-tech exhibits capture the horrors of the trenches to harrowing effect.

A Short History

In the Middle Ages, Ieper was one of the three great cities of Flanders, along with Bruges and Ghent. In the 13th century, it had a population of 40,000, most of whom were involved in the production of cloth sold throughout Europe: samples have been found as far away as Novgorod, in Russia. Like so many of its rivals, it suffered centuries of decline, which were hardly helped by the onset of the plague and a bloody conflict with France. The low point was an assault by the Duke of Parma, who massacred the population in 1584. The French repeatedly laid siege to Ieper during the following century, and finally won it thanks to the Treaty of Nijmegen in 1678. Transformed into a model fortified town, Ieper changed hands several times, falling to the Austrians in 1716, France again in 1792 and the Netherlands in 1815. Despite the violence it witnessed, the town managed to keep its architectural monuments intact – until they were blasted by German artillery.

In October 1914, with the flooded polders blocking the German advance to the north, the English kept up a vast offensive around Ieper, aided by the Canadians and French. Unfortunately, Ieper and its monuments were used for target practice by the German forces, who managed to reduce eight centuries of architecture to rubble.

For four years, this part of the Western front saw fighting and bloodshed on a scale unparalleled in European history. The nightmarish conditions and the devastating impact of machineguns and poison gas wiped out most of the coming generation in both camps. Defended by troops from across the British Empire, this particular corner of a foreign field cost nearly 450,000 lives. To this day, tens of thousands of the fallen have no official grave. Losses on the German side were even worse.

It took nearly 40 years to rebuild Ieper, and the town recalls the tragedy every day with the sounding of the Last Post.

GETTING THERE

– **By road**: from Lille and Kortrijk (E17), take the A19, which takes you to the edge of the town.

– **By train**: Trains run from Mechelen, Ghent and Kortrijk.

WEST FLANDERS

USEFUL ADDRESSES AND INFORMATION

Postcode: 8900.
🛈 **Tourist office**: Lakenhalle, Grote Markt 34. ☎ (057) 228584. Fax: (057) 228589. Brochures are available bike tours around the area and on the 1914–1918 trail. The tourist office is also the Regional Centre for Ieper and Westhoek.

🚆 **Railway station**: Colaertplein. ☎ (057) 200070. Bike hire available.

WHERE TO STAY

☆☆ Moderate

🛏 **Hotel-restaurant-café Sultan**: Grote Markt 33. ☎ (057) 228487. Fax: (057) 219537. Email: sultanyp@skynetbe. Closed for the last two weeks in December. Doubles 2,250–2,500BEF. Breakfast 250BEF. A traditional hotel, with nothing Sultanesque about the decor. The rooms are perfectly comfortable, and you'll get spectacular views of the Lakenhalle and chiming carillon concerts for no extra charge

WHERE TO EAT

Ieper's nightlife consists of a few establishments on and around the Markt that serve as café, bar and restaurant. The locals don't seem to go out much, so the only people you'll come across are groups of Brits on a pilgrimage to the area.

☆☆ Moderate

✗ **'t Ganzeke**: Vandepeereboomplein 5. ☎ (057) 200009. Closed Monday and mid-April to early May. A restaurant aimed squarely at coachloads of British tourists. The decor is unexceptional, but the old posters on the walls are worth a look. On the menu: huge kebabs, giant prawns and huge ribs. Don't come unless you're really hungry. You won't be disappointed if you are.

WHAT TO SEE

★ The huge, rather cold **Grote Markt**, the gigantic Gothic **Lakenhalle** (it's 125 metres – more than 400 feet – long) and the huge square **belfry** indicate the sheer volume of trade that was conducted here in the 13th century. Today, although the collection of reconstructive buildings is harmonious enough, their immense size feels somewhat over the top. The part-Gothic, part-Renaissance **Stadhuis** is smaller, and fits neatly into the surroundings.

★ **In Flanders Fields**: Lakenhalle, Grote Markt 34. ☎ (057) 228584. Open 10am–6pm from April to September; otherwise 10am–5pm. Closed for three weeks after Christmas and Monday out of season. Admission: 250BEF, which includes entrance to the town's other museums. Make sure you visit this museum. It's just a couple of years old, and they've done a superb job of evoking the horrors of World War I with all the latest technology. At the entrance, you're asked to choose an identity for yourself – man, woman or soldier – and you go around the museum as the person you've chosen.

You're also asked if you want to cross Ieper or not, and are issued with a ticket with a bar code that you use on your tour. A surprise greets you at the exit.

In the vast rooms, 18 sets have been designed using futuristic equipment, although the effect is far from gimmicky. Interactive screens in four languages, for example, allow you to find out more about particular themes or details. After a brief overview of the history of the town, which seems almost indecently peaceful in retrospect, you're plunged into the powder keg that was Europe in the summer of 1914. Kaiser Bill's invasion of Belgium is shown using a montage of period films. After a heady phase, during which British officers regarded the war as something of a picnic, Ieper's first battle is described, complete with the flooding of the plain and the building of trenches. The outdated, inappropriate equipment used in this war is illustrated with a quote from the French writer Céline, complaining of the noise made by his cavalryman's sabre as he gallops to the front.

During Christmas 1914, men in opposing camps began to suspect the pointlessness of the killings and tried to fraternize with each other, but their attempts at friendship were fiercely suppressed. In the Belgian army, Flemish conscripts, many poorly educated farm workers, complained that their officers gave orders in French (an apocryphal story claims that when a French-speaking soldier pointed out to his superior that many of the soldiers couldn't understand their orders, the latter shrugged and said: '*Et pour les flamands, la même chose.*'). Very soon, industrial centres began to contribute to the war effort, producing weapons that were to have decisive results. Heavy artillery, its accuracy bolstered by aerial observation, turned the countryside around Ieper into an area resembling a lunar landscape. Fake trees were constructed so that troops could hide behind them and spy on enemy lines. Mustard gas was a constant danger, with many soldiers reduced to urinating on their handkerchiefs to protect their faces. The use of masks became compulsory, and the Ieper bulge – or 'Salient' – became the antechamber to apocalypse. Going into one of the trenches, you find yourself in the worst imaginable hell, heightened by the effects of multimedia: in a cloud of gas and a sea of noise, you see disoriented British soldiers dismembered by German gunfire, while limbs emerge from the mud beneath the transparent flooring. In the agony of death, soldiers ask: 'Why?' Meanwhile, behind you, soldiers on leave try to forget the horrors of war before returning to the front; surgeons and nurses in provincial hospitals try to stitch up wounded faces and the stumps of missing limbs; and prisoners of war find that, in spite of their captivity, they've drawn the long straw. After four years, peace returns to Ieper, and its inhabitants come home and bravely start to rebuild the town. Tens of thousands of lines of crosses decorated with poppies appear in the area.

It's a poignant and captivating experience, heightened by the recollections of those who witnessed the horrors. You hope that, given the crowds who pass through every day, this museum may do something to dissuade future generations from going to war.

★ **Sint Maartenskathedraal**: the cathedral has benefitted from being rebuilt, as it acquired a new 102-metre (340-foot) spire. The impressive interior contains the tomb of the founder of Jansenism, Bishop Jansenius, along with that of Robert de Béthune, a Count of Flanders, in the chapel of the Holy Sacrament.

WEST FLANDERS

★ **Saint George's Memorial Church**: an English church near the Grote Markt. A notice by the entrance requests visitors to give money for the reconstruction of Dresden, bombed out of existence by Allied planes in 1944. It's a reassuring and moving detail.

★ **Walk around the ramparts**: from the Rijselsepoort (Lille Gate), leave the Grote Markt and go through the Vismarkt, where you'll see a wooden house, one of the 90 that stood in the town until 1914. The walk begins with the British cemetery, impeccably maintained, like all those in the area. It continues with the fortifications built by Louis XIV's architect Vauban (late 17th century), which overlook the moat, and end after the Menin Gate.

– **The Last Post**: at the Menin Gate. Every evening at 8pm, since 1928, this simple ceremony has taken place beneath the archway. Two members of the local fire service sound their post horns in memory of the 54,896 soldiers from the British Empire who were killed before 15 August 1917, and whose bodies were never found. After this date, another 34,984 disappeared. Their names are recorded at the **Tyne Cot Cemetery** in Passendale. Every nation of the Empire is recalled: it seems stupid and unjust that it was the Flemish sky the Australians, New Zealanders, Indians, Scottish, Welsh, Irish, Afghans, South Africans and Burmese saw for the last time. At least they have not been forgotten – over a hundred people regularly turn up to hear the Last Post.

WORLD WAR I LANDMARKS OUTSIDE IEPER

The area around Ieper is scattered with cemeteries, shell craters and small museums. Remains are uncovered every year. A brochure describing the **1914–18 route** is available from tourist offices around the region.

★ Head east along the Menin road when you leave the town and you'll come to **Hooge-Krater** (Meenseweg 467), where enormous holes bear witness to underground explosions. There's a chapel and a small museum.

★ **Langemark** is the biggest German cemetery, with more than 44,000 names engraved on bronze plaques, distinguished neither by age nor rank.

★ At **Poelkappelle**, where the N313 crosses the Forest of Houthust road at the spot where the liberating offensive began in 1918, there's a handsome monument in memory of Georges Guynemer, France's answer to the Red Baron: as the commander of the 'Stork' squadron, he downed 54 German planes before being killed in action on 11 September.

★ At **Zillebeke**, you'll find Hill 60 and Hill 62, their numbers relating to the height (in metres). Thousands of British soldiers died here, and their sacrifice is recalled by monuments to the Queen Victoria Rifles and the Australian sappers. There's also a small museum.

★ At **Zonnebeke**, Tyne Cot Cemetery is a reminder of the hell of Passendale, the section of the front most feared by British soldiers. More than 11,000 graves, mostly anonymous, are arranged across the hillside, while the names of more than 35,000 men whose bodies were never found are inscribed on the walls.

The **Streeksmuseum** (Kasteeldomein 5) is devoted to daily life in the surrounding villages during the Great War.

Other memorials and cemeteries in the area, surrounded by agricultural fields, are dedicated to the Canadians, Australians, New Zealanders, South Africans, Irish and many others who fought for the British Empire.

FESTIVAL

– **Festival of Cats**: in the Middle Ages, on a certain date, cats were flung from the top of Ieper's belfry. This politically incorrect tradition started the Festival of Cats, which takes place every year on the second Sunday in May. They use toy cats these days, and if you're hit by one, it's said to bring good luck.

A Procession of Cats, involving 2,400 'cats', takes place every three years. The next feline festivities are in 2003.

What to See south of Ieper

★ **Wervik**: a stone's throw from the French border, Wervik has a beautiful Brabant Gothic church. Otherwise, its main attraction is the **Tobacco Museum**, housed in an 18th-century windmill. Open March to October, every day except Wednesday 1.30–5.30pm. Admission: 70BEF. This area has always been a major producer of tobacco, and the border town provided smugglers with a base from which to carry out their activities.

What to See in the Area

POPERINGE

This little town to the west of Ieper gave its name to the material 'poplin', and is Belgium's hop capital. The surrounding countryside is spread with rank after rank of tall hop plants, almost like vineyards. In spring, you can sample a local dish based on hop shoots. There are a number of reasons to stop here, not least the charming town centre.

USEFUL ADDRESS

🏛 **Tourist office**: Stadhuis, Grote Markt 1, Poperinge 8970. ☎ (057) 346676. Helpful staff and good literature. Bike hire available at the railway station.

WHERE TO EAT

✗ **Brasserie 't Hommelhof**: Watouplein 17, 8978 Watou-Poperinge. ☎ (057) 388024. Closed Monday, Tuesday, Wednesday and Thursday evening, except in July and August. Gastronomic delights in the pretty village of Watou, within spitting distance of the French border. This Flemish-style inn, with dried hops above the bar, specializes in dishes cooked in beer, including chicken in white Watou beer and knuckle of ham stewed in beer. In season, try hop shoots with sole in Nantua sauce. It's good value for money, and you can sit outside when it's sunny.

WEST FLANDERS

WHAT TO SEE

Churches

– **Sint Bertinuskerk**, a hall-church with a massive square tower, stands near the Grote Markt. There's an unusual rood screen, an 18th-century canopy of the Holy Sacrament and a finely carved pulpit from Bruges.

– **Sint Janskerk**: topped by a delightful onion dome, this church was built in the 13th century, when the population had significantly expanded. Look out for the impressive organ pipes, the wrought-iron chandelier and a Renaissance altar with a fine statue of the Virgin Mary, which is wheeled out every year to commemorate a miracle of 1479, when a still-born child, unbaptized and buried in unconsecrated ground, was dug up and found to be alive. The baby's parents had prayed to the Virgin for three long days. The baby was hurriedly baptized, and passed away peacefully a few hours later. A host of pilgrims, overwhelmed by Mary's compassion, rushed to the church.

– **Onze Lieve Vrouwekerk**: another hall-church, with a pretty Renaissance porch, carved choir stalls and communion benches.

Other Sites of Interest

★ **National Hop Museum**: Gasthuisstraat 71, Poperinge 8970. Open Sundays in May and June, and every day from July to September, 2–6pm. Admission: 50BEF. Everything you ever wanted to know about making and flavouring beer with hops. An essential part of the brewing process, hops are related to the hemp plant and can grow to six metres (20 feet) in height. It's all a bit worthy, but there's an interesting old film about the folkloric aspects of hop-harvesting.

★ **Talbot House**: Gasthuisstraat 43. Open 9am–noon and 2–5pm. Thanks to its position near the front line during the World War I, Poperinge was used by the British as a centre for rest and recreation. An Anglican priest, 'Tubby' Clayton, made his house into a comfortable and friendly place for soldiers who had experienced the horrors of the battlefield. Rank and social status were left at the door – optimism and good old British humour were the order of the day. The attic was turned into a chapel. Its reputation spread fast, even reaching enemy lines, and Talbot House became a symbol of peace for everyone who had witnessed war. Reclaimed by its owners after the war, it continued to receive visitors. In 1940, the Gestapo tried to get hold of its archives, while in 1944, Talbot House became a centre for Polish soldiers during the Liberation.

Today, the tradition of hospitality continues, and young people from all over the world are put up here (25 beds: ☎ (057) 333228): there's no charge, but guests help maintain the cemeteries, and good humour is *de rigueur*.

KORTRIJK   76,000 inhabitants

Kortrijk was once the world capital of flax, thanks to the waters of the Lys, which are chalk-free and ideal for flax-retting. Today, it's an important financial centre, thanks in part to its proximity to Lille.

A Short History

The story of Kortrijk begins with a fortified castle, of which only the 13th-century Broeltoren remain. Philip the Fair's knights were slaughtered on the nearby plain of Groeninge on 11 July 1302 at the Battle of the Golden Spurs, an event fondly recalled by the Flemish to this day. They're less forthcoming, however, about the events of 1382, when the French torched the town. In the 15th century, Kortrijk was known throughout the Western world for its damask, and it's still a major producer of furnishing materials, carpets and interior decoration.

USEFUL ADDRESSES AND INFORMATION

Postcode: 8500.
🏢 Tourist office: Sint Michielsplein 5. ☎ (056) 239371. Fax: (056) 239372. List of B&Bs available.

🚃 Railway station: Stationplein, 300 metres from the Grote Markt.

WHERE TO STAY

☆ Budget

🛏 Jeugdherberg Groeningheem: Passionistenlaan 1A. ☎ (056) 201-442. Fax: (056) 204663. Basic rate per night: 420BEF. Closed from mid-December to mid-January. About a kilometre east of the station, next to the railway, this youth hostel has 96 beds and 20 rooms for couples. Sheet hire available.

☆☆ Moderate

🛏 Hotel Focus: Hovenierstraat 50. ☎ (056) 361571. Fax: (056) 212908. Double rooms 2,300BEF.

It's some way from the centre, but this is a pleasant hotel with four light, airy and well-appointed rooms (including one single and one triple), each decorated by different artists. The sitting room and break-fast room are both charming, and there are books and games for children. Half-board is available, and you can eat in the hotel's nearby restaurant. There are also four studio flats and two villas, which you can rent for between three nights and a month. Phone before arrival, as the reception is not permanently staffed.

WHERE TO EAT

☆☆ Moderate

✕ Restaurant Beethoven: Onze Lieve Vrouwstraat 8. ☎ (056) 225542. Closed Monday and Wednesday evening, and Saturday lunchtime. This cosy, if rather dark, restaurant offers a great variety of grills and tasty dishes. Try the excellent chicken in a saffron sauce or the homemade fondue. The daily special is usually generous, and costs a very reasonable 290BEF.

WHERE TO GO FOR A DRINK

❢ Bierhuis Brouwzaele: Kapucij-nenstraat 19–21. This temple of beer is opposite the Pentascoop cinema complex. The facade had to be stripped away to make room for the copper brewing tank, which serves as a bar. Unusual artefacts from breweries adorn the walls of this watering hole, which is much frequented by the local youth at the weekend.

❢ Sint Maarten Koffiehuis: on Sint Maartenskerkhof. There's an attractive tavern and tea-room upstairs, overlooking the magnificent church porch. The pale-yellow paintwork echoes the colour of the tower, the floorboards creak, the wind rustles in the trees and chimes sound every hour. Enjoy a low-priced daily special at tables with floral tablecloths, surrounded by tiny stuffed birds.

WHAT TO SEE

★ **Stadhuis**: a 16th-century building with a wonderful Gothic chimneypiece in the alderman's room, made of wood, stone and alabaster.

★ **Belfort**: this stands alone in the middle of the Markt, and is a remnant of the old cloth hall. With its five turrets and statue of Mercury, it is a symbol of local dynamism.

★ **Onze Lieve Vrouwekerk**: this 12th-century church had the dubious privilege of functioning as an exhibition room for the French spurs taken as trophies after the Battle of the Golden Spurs. They disappeared long ago, and those on show here are copies. The statue of Saint Catherine is a 14th-century masterpiece, and chief among the church's other treasures are the murals in the counts' chapel, portraits of the counts of Flanders and Van Dyck's *Raising of the Cross*.

★ **Sint Maartenskerk** is a 15th-century church with a splendid porch and a neo-Gothic interior.

★ The **Begijnhof**, not far from Sint Maartenskerk, is one of the most attractive in the country, with 31 little houses dating from the 17th century. A museum in the Mother Superior's house captures the atmosphere of bygone days.

★ **Stedelijk Museum**: Houtmarkt. Open 10am–noon and 2–5pm. Closed Monday. Admission free. The museum, housed in the buildings of Groeninge Abbey, traces the history of the town, with a predictable emphasis on the events of 1302. If you're not in martial mood, the main attractions are displays of objects produced by local craftsmen – samples of linen and damask, silverware, metalwork and pottery – and an entertaining collection of old pipes.

★ **Broelmuseum**: Broelkaai 4. ☎ (056) 257892. Near the embarkation point for trips on the Scheldt. Same opening times as the Stedelijk Museum. Admission free. This is the communal museum, and it deals with the artistic past of the town. The most notable figures are Roelandt Savery, a baroque landscape artist who worked in Kortrijk at the beginning of the 16th century, and Louis-Pierre Verwée, a 19th-century Realist and cattle-lover who painted animals. There's also a room devoted to ceramics, with a hugely detailed explanation of the production process.

★ **Nationaal Vlasmuseum**   (Flax and Lace Museum): E. Sabbelaan 4, south of the centre. ☎ (056) 210138. Open March to the end of November, 9.30am–12.30pm; 1.30–6pm and 2–6pm at the weekend. Admission: 100BEF per museum. Combined ticket: 170BEF. Two museums in one: you don't have to visit both, but they're both excellent. A series of tableaux describes the story of the unique farming of flax in the Lys region, and the surprisingly complex way in which it's produced. A new wing devoted to lace and linen has been added, and the objects on display really are works of art. There's a huge area devoted to the museum's collection of old lace, embroidery, sewing, and household damask and linen on the ground floor. Pause for a breather in the old tavern near the exit.

In the Area

ROESELAERE

A cheerful commercial centre, 20 kilometres (12 miles) northwest of Kortrijk, with a reputation for producing spies. In Roman times, Roeselaere was a centre for the cloth trade, like its neighbours. In the 19th century, a Flemish student movement, the Blauwvoeterie, was formed in the town's seminary. The town suffered extensive damage during World War I.

USEFUL ADDRESSES

– **Postcode**: 8800.
Tourist office: Zuidstraat 3-5.
☎ (051) 262450.

Railway station: 500 metres (500 yards) from the Grote Markt.

WHAT TO SEE

★ **Stadhuis**: Grote Markt. Designed in Louis XV style, although a new wing was added in 1925 in the style of the old halls and medieval belfry, which disappeared in the 18th century.

★ **Bicycle Museum**: Popelein 15. From April to the end of October, open Tuesday to Friday 2–5pm. Admission: 100BEF. The development of the bike, from the dandy horse to the mountain bike, is the focus here. There's also a section on the customs and costumes of cyclists.

★ **Church of the Augustinians**: built in 1735 in pure baroque style, this was the seminary where the poet and priest Guido Gezelle taught. The seminary's most celebrated pupils were the Rodenbach family – they were writers and brewers, who gave the world a unique ruby-coloured sour beer.

On the subject of which, you can visit the **Rodenbach Brewery**, but only in groups. Telephone ☎ (051) 223400 to arrange a tour.

Wallonia

Province of Walloon Brabant

When the old province of Brabant was carved up into political regions, French-speaking Walloon Brabant gained autonomy rather than any coherent cultural identity.

Wavre and the pleasantly green communes that surround it, for example, have now been more or less absorbed into the growing suburban spread of Brussels, while Nivelles has more in common with the towns across the border in Hainaut. As for Louvain-la-Neuve, it's a manufactured, concrete university town, created to house the French-speaking section of the University of Leuven when the French-speakers were kicked out of the historic Flemish university in the wake of the linguistic riots of the 1960s. So why bother coming? Well, the town that attracts visitors from all over the country and all over the world is Waterloo, where Napoleon met his.

WATERLOO	28,000 inhabitants

Over time, Waterloo has become something of a mythical place. Victor Hugo immortalized the town in his poetry and, in the 20th century, Waterloo was the name of the bouncy Eurovision song that launched the career of the Swedish pop group Abba. For some, the town is associated with victory; for others, it's a sorry symbol of defeat. On the edge of the Forêt de Soignes, about 35 kilometres (20 miles) south of Brussels, Waterloo makes an ideal day trip from the capital. The town itself, now home to thousands of Eurocrats, in particular French and Scandinavian expats, is nothing special. Surrounded by large, mainly modern villas, the centre consists of one traffic-heavy street lined with high-street shops and a few upmarket boutiques. But visitors don't come to shop; they come to see the famous battlefield, where British, Dutch, Belgian and German forces, commanded by Wellington and allied to Blücher's Prussian force, finally put an end to Napoleon's imperialist ambitions. Belgian loyalties were divided, so there were Belgian soldiers in both camps. Bizarrely, despite Boney's defeat, a cult of Napoleon has emerged in surrounding areas, especially in Hainaut, where annual religious processions involve participants parading in Napoleonic dress.

GETTING THERE

– **By car**: this is the best way to reach the three main sites at Waterloo, all of which lie on the same road out of Brussels: first, the Wellington museum, then the Butte de Lion, and finally the Maison du Caillou. They are all just a couple of miles apart. From the Brussels ring, take exit 21 and follow the signs for Waterloo.

– **By bus**: a bit complicated from Brussels, especially if you want to visit all three sites. Take bus W from Place Rouppe (near the Gare du Midi) to the Butte du Lion, and get off at the stop called Cosmos (*not* Waterloo). Buses leave every 30 minutes.

A Short History

'Waterloo, Waterloo, Waterloo, sorry field
Like an ocean wave, an unwilling captive in an overfilled urn,
In your circle of woods and hills and valleys,
Pale death made indistinguishable the dark battalions . . .'

(Victor Hugo)

It was an eerily quiet morning on Sunday, 18 June 1815. Rain had delayed the start of the battle, and fighting did not get underway until 11.30am. Two armies stood in the field: the allied forces – including Dutch and Belgian troops led by William-Frederick-Georges-Louis, Prince of Orange-Nassau, who was wounded during the conflict – commanded by Arthur Wellesley, Duke of Wellington, and allied to the Prussian forces led by Blücher; and opposing them, the army of the French Emperor, Napoleon Bonaparte.

On 14 June, Napoleon had advanced briskly. His plan was to fight the allied armies separately to prevent them joining forces, and on 16 June, the French army managed to defeat Blücher in Ligny. The following day, Napoleon arrived on the plain of Mont-Saint-Jean, near Waterloo, spending the night at the Caillou farm, while Wellington slept at his headquarters, located in an inn in the village of Waterloo. French Marshal Grouchy, meanwhile, had headed for Wavre in search of the Prussians.

The battle lasted all day. English and French armies began fighting at Hougoumont farm, where thousands of men met their death. At 1.30pm, the main French attack took shape and fighting was intensified, firstly at Haie-Sainte farm and then at Papelotte farm, but the French were forced to abandon their positions. Napoleon was still waiting for Marshal Grouchy, who was nowhere to be seen. The main attack began at 4pm. Two hours later, the news that the Prussian troops were approaching spread through both camps. Still waiting for Grouchy, Napoleon finally resorted to sending in the imperial guard. They advanced slowly, under murderous fire, but as soon as they broke through, they were attacked from the flanks. After several hours of bloody battle, the imperial guard collapsed. By nightfall, the French Emperor had to admit defeat, and 48,000 men lay dead on the battlefield.

USEFUL ADDRESSES

Postcode: 1410.
🛈 Fédération touristique de la Province du Brabant wallon: chaussée de Bruxelles 218, next to the Chapel Royal. ☎ (02) 504 0400. Open weekdays 9am–5pm.

🛈 Tourist office: chaussée de Bruxelles 149, next to the Musée Wellington. ☎ (02) 351 1200. Open 9.30am–6.30pm in summer, 10.30am–5pm in winter. List of local B&Bs available.

WHERE TO STAY

Waterloo is an upmarket town, and its hotels are rather pricey, so your best bet is to look for B&Bs in Waterloo or in the neighbouring *communes*.

WHERE TO EAT

☆☆ Moderate

✕ **L'Amusoir**: chaussée de Bruxelles 121. ☎ (02) 354 8233. Open noon–2.30pm and 6.30–11.30pm. *Plat du jour* 245BEF, with a full meal about 750BEF. There are plenty of restaurants in the area, but this is one of the best. Located in an 18th-century farmhouse, it has a rustic interior and a menu that's heavily weighted towards tender red meat (there are eight types of steaks) and salads, with an oyster bar in season. You can enjoy your meal with one of several full-bodied *vins de pays*. There's also a children's menu, as well as a playground, where parents can sip aperitifs beneath the trees and keep an eye on their kids.

☆☆☆ Expensive

✕ **La Sucrerie**: chaussée de Tervueren 198, 15 kilometres (10 miles) south of Brussels. ☎ (02) 352 1818. Open noon–2.30pm and 7–10.30pm. Closed Saturday and Sunday lunchtime. Set menus from 500BEF, or about 1,200BEF for an à la carte meal. Housed in an old industrial building with a spectacular interior of brick vaulting, this restaurant serves traditional, sophisticated brasserie-style cuisine. The lunch menu offers excellent value for money.

The restaurant is part of a four-star hotel complex, the **Grand Hôtel Waterloo**. ☎ (02) 352 1815 (of course!). Fax: (02) 352 1888. Doubles from 6,000BEF, including breakfast. It's expensive, but this is a great place to stay if you're want peace and pampering.

WHAT TO SEE

On the Battlefield, at Braine-l'Alleud

★ **Butte du Lion**: this famous mound, with a lion rampant at its summit, will be familiar to anyone who's been sent a postcard from Waterloo. The artificial hill, which marks the site of the famous battle, was built by the government of the United Provinces of the Netherlands as a 45-metre (150-foot) podium for the lion, the symbol of the house of Orange-Nassau. The lion faces France, symbolically protecting Belgium – or the Netherlands, of which Belgium was part in the aftermath of Napoleon's fall – from French invaders. A complex of museums and tacky souvenir shops has sprung up at the foot of the Butte.

TIP If all you want to do is climb the Butte, absorb the atmosphere of the battlefield and reflect on the significance of what happened, the best way to do it is to use the orientation table at the top of the hill (for French-speakers, the excellent, inexpensive Casterman guide will enhance the experience). If you'd rather get to grips with the history by visiting the town's museums, there are various money-saving deals, including a combined ticket for all the monuments and museums, valid for a year. There are also discounts for children, students, senior citizens and groups.

– **Scaling the Butte de Lion**: single admission costs 40 BEF or 20 BEF for children aged six to 12. From April to end October, open 9.30am–6.30pm; otherwise 10.30am–4pm. Access to the Butte is via the visitors' centre, which is stuffed with fantastically kitsch souvenirs (cuddly lions and the like). At the top of 226 steps, 28 tonnes of cast-iron lion rest on a brick column hidden by bushes. Nearly 300,000 cubic metres (10 million cubic feet) of earth was needed to raise the lion up to a level of 40 metres (132 feet).

– **Audiovisual show**: admission 300BEF, which includes access to the Butte de Lion. The main room houses an electronic model, complete with sound effects, that shows the movement of troops throughout the day, while a screen projects images of the different areas where particular events took place. The technology is rather outdated, but it'll help you visualize the battle. The second section offers a fictional montage in which children are depicted playing war on the battlefield amid a maëlstrom of terrifying images from Bondarchuk's film *Waterloo*.

– **Rotonde du Panorama**: admission is 110BEF or 80 BEF for students and senior citizens and 60 BEF for children. It's more than 100 years old, but you can't help but be impressed by the sheer size of this 360-degree, 110-metre (350-feet) mural, which captures the confusion of battle, the soldiers' determination to fight on and the distress of the dying. It's an amazing achievement, and far more effective than many high-tech museum displays.

– **Musée de Cire** (Wax Museum): opposite the visitor centre, at the back of a restaurant, *Le Bivouac de l'Empereur*. From April to the end of September, open 9.30am–6.30pm; otherwise weekends only, 10am–4.45pm. Admission: 60BEF. An outstanding collection of wax busts made by craftsmen from the Musée Grévin (Paris's answer to Madame Tussaud's) that will delight anyone interested in the Napoleonic era. The owner, whose ancestors include soldiers and restaurateurs, is extremely well informed. The restaurant, meanwhile, has been a hostelry and museum since 1818, when it was founded by sergeant-major Edward Cotton, a veteran of the battle. Queen Victoria once stayed here.

– **1815 trail**: the road on the right of the Butte leads to the Hougoumont farm, the scene of intense and bloody fighting during which 8,000 French soldiers were killed. You can still see traces of gunshot on the walls. Three huge trees are all that remain of the wood that stood here at the time of the battle. If you have time, the hour-long trail takes you to other important sites. Alternatively, try one of the reasonably priced Saturday or Sunday afternoon guided tours, organized by Guides 1815. The tourist office has details of these tours and sells the accompanying brochures.

The trail includes several commemorative monuments honouring English, French, Belgian, German and Prussian troops. There's even a memorial to Victor Hugo.

★ **Napoleon's last headquarters, Musée Provincial**: chaussée de Bruxelles 66, a couple of miles south of the Butte, on the left-hand side of the road to Genappe. ☎ (02) 384 2424. From early April to the end of October, open 10am–6.30pm; otherwise 1–5pm. Admission: 60BEF. Napoleon spent his last night as Emperor here in this rustic place, on 17 June, 1815. Exhibits include the Emperor's bed, a death mask, maps and the skeleton of a French hussar, discovered on the battlefield in 1910, as well as weapons, medals and souvenirs of the campaign. Dioramas of the campaign are on show in the final room. There's a small ossuary in the back garden.

In Waterloo

★ **Musée Wellington**: in the town centre, opposite the church, a couple of miles before you reach the Butte du Lion. From early April to the end of September, 9.30am–6.30pm; otherwise 10.30am–5pm. Admission: 60BEF, or as part of a combined ticket. This fascinating museum, filled with period items, is housed in Wellington's former headquarters, an old staging post. The excellent commentary gives you a real sense of the mood before the battle.

The first rooms are devoted to the Great European Alliance, and contain engravings and paintings. The following is a list of the museum's highlights:

– Room 4: Gordon's room, featuring the wooden leg of Lord Uxbridge, whose leg was shot off during the battle. It was later found on the battlefield, and buried at a macabre ceremony attended by Lord Uxbridge himself. You can read the letter of condolence Wellington sent to Gordon's brother.

– Room 6: this is where Wellington spent the night before the battle, and where he received confirmation that the Prussian armies were about to join him. The room contains furniture and some of the Iron Duke's personal effects.

– Room 8: engravings depicting Wellington's meeting with Blücher at the Belle Alliance farm, when the battle was won.

– Room 10: devoted to Napoleon and his generals. Engravings, paintings and watercolours recall his battles and transfer to St Helena; there's also a fine engraving of the Emperor on his deathbed.

– The last rooms chart the progress of the battle, via plans and other documents, all accompanied by informative captions. There's also a selection of weapons and uniforms.

The name Waterloo, by the way, became associated with the battle because it's where Wellington signed the communiqué declaring his victory on the evening of 18 June. The French used to refer to it as the Battle of Mont-Saint-Jean, while the Prussians talked of the Battle of Belle Alliance, in memory of the farm where Wellington and Blücher met after their victory. The Dutch and Belgians, meanwhile, named it the Battle of Quatre-Bras. Organized tourism began almost immediately after the battle, with a mail coach bringing visitors from Brussels for decades to come. The Duke of Wellington's heir comes once a year to inspect the 2,000 hectares (5,000 acres) that became his ancestor's property after the battle, and to collect his income from the tenant farmers.

★ **Royal Chapel**: this baroque structure opposite the Musée Wellington has a beautiful dome. It was built in the late 18th century by the Spanish governor of the Low Countries, who hoped, in vain, that it might help King Charles II to produce an heir. After 1815, the English turned it into a commemorative monument and financed the construction of the church.

There are several plaques engraved by the families of British and Dutch-Belgian regiments. Queen Elizabeth II was not amused to discover that a plaque in honour of Napoleon was recently erected here, in a chapel originally dedicated to his conquerors.

FESTIVAL

If you enjoyed your trip to Waterloo, you may want to return to see a re-enactment of the battle. It takes place every five years, and attracts thousands of participants from across Europe. Check out www.braine-lalleud.com/waterloo for details, or email info@waterloo1815.be. The next 'battle' is scheduled for 2005.

In the Area

ITTRE

This beautifully preserved country village lies in the very centre of Belgium, at the intersection of the Brussels Ring and the E19. Several traditional processions take place here, including the Assumption of the Virgin on 15 August. The surrounding wooded valleys make ideal walking country.

Postcode: 1460.

WHERE TO STAY AND EAT

☆ Budget

☗ **Campsite Ry-Ternel**: rue de Fauquez 10. ☎ (067) 646063. Tent site: 220BEF. Open from March to the end of November. A pleasant spot near Waterloo, with room for 50 tents.

☆☆ Moderate

✗ **L'Abreuvoir**: rue Basse 2. ☎ (067) 646706. Open noon–7pm and Monday and Thursday evenings. Closed Tuesday. Full meal about 800BEF. Housed in a spruce little floral house with brown shutters, the restaurant has a good-value set menu featuring farm ham with endives and veal kidneys with port.

WHAT TO SEE AND DO

★ **Musée de la Forge** and **Musée du Folklore**: rue Basse 11 and 14. From April to the end of October, open 2–6pm. Admission: 40BEF. These two small museums are located in a working forge, which also provides an unusual backdrop for wedding ceremonies. The blacksmith gives the newlyweds a horseshoe for good luck.

– If you've ever been tempted by the Romany lifestyle, you can spend a day or a weekend travelling through verdant countryside in a horse-drawn caravan. For information and bookings: SPRL Les Flocons, rue du Sart 45. ☎ (067) 646751.

BRAINE-LE-CHÂTEAU   8,500 inhabitants

A pretty Brabant village with several medieval monuments. It's on the River
Hain, about 18 kilometres (12 miles) southwest of Brussels. Take the E19
towards Mons, then exit 17 (Wauthier-Braine).

WHAT TO SEE

★ **Musée de la Meunerie** (Milling Museum): in a pretty stone-and-brick
riverfront windmill behind the castle. ☎ (02) 366 9691. From April to
September, open Saturday 2–6pm and Sunday 2–7pm. You can see the
two huge wheels that were used to work the four pairs of mills. Local
peasants were allowed to grind their corn here, for a fee of one bag of corn
per 22 bags ground.

★ The stocks on the Grand-Place have been there since the 16th century,
while an ancient yew tree still flourishes on the nearby rue des Contes-de-
Robiano. You can also see the tomb of Maximilian van Hoorn, Charles V's
chamberlain. The bailiff's house, with elegant stepped gabling, stands
opposite the castle, which is not open to the public.

FESTIVALS

– **Carnaval du Laetare**: three weeks before Easter.
– **Rencontres médiévales**: second weekend in September.

REBECQ

This village has a 14th-century hospice and several buildings with 16th-
century facades. Industrial-heritage buffs will find fascinating reminders of
the area's 18th-century development.

WHAT TO SEE

★ **Moulins d'Arenberg** (Arenberg Mills): rue du Docteur-Colson 6. ☎ (067)
638232. From May to September, open Saturday and Sunday 2–6pm. The
mills on the edge of the River Senne all belonged to the same business. Two
are still in working order: in the biggest, you can see the mechanisms that
keep it running, as well as an exhibition about the history of the quarries in
nearby Quenast. They produced porphyry, the stone used for pavements in
Paris, Berlin and even St Petersburg. The smaller mill houses a reconstructed forge, and grinds into motion every Sunday. Before you leave, try
the local Quenast beer in the small country tavern.

WHAT TO DO

– **Tourist train 'Le Bonheur'**: powered by a 1900 steam engine, the train takes you on a seven-kilometre (four-mile) round trip from Rebecq to Rognon via the Vallée des Oiseaux. Rides take place on Sunday afternoons between May and the end of September, and last for about an hour.

NIVELLES   24,000 inhabitants

A small, peaceful town that was heavily bombed by the Germans during World War II, Nivelles is famous for its splendidly restored Romanesque abbey and delicious Al'Djote tart. It's a 30-minute drive from the centre of Brussels.

GETTING THERE

– **By train**: Nivelles is on the Brussels–Charleroi line, with several trains a day from Brussels's Gare du Midi or Gare du Nord.

A Short History

In the seventh century, Nivelles abbey was founded by Itte, wife of Pépin the Elder. Their daughter, Gertrude, became the first abbess. The town gradually acquired a ring of walls, and the abbey became the luxurious residence of a series of well-connected canonesses. Traditionally a centre for linen and lace, Nivelles lost its importance with the collapse of the crafts market. The abbey fell into decline in the late 18th century, and in 1940, German artillery left the abbey and the town centre in ruins.

USEFUL ADDRESSES

Postcode: 1400.
🛈 **Tourist office**: rue des Brasseurs 38. ☎ (067) 215413. From April to September open Monday to Friday 9am–5pm, weekends 10am–4pm; from October to March open Monday to Friday 9am–5pm.
■ **Bank and post office**: next to Place Albert-Ier.

WHERE TO EAT

☆☆ Moderate

✕ **Le Prévert**: rue de Bruxelles 13, behind the Palais de Justice. ☎ (067) 211483. Open 11.45am–2.30pm and 6.30–10pm. Closed Sunday and Monday evenings. *Plat du jour* 295BEF, otherwise about 800BEF. It looks great, with ornate wooden panelling on the facade and a delightful orange interior, but the service is average and the food can be a bit heavy. Try the steak, prawn croquettes, fresh pasta or mussels with leeks. Credit cards not accepted.
✕ **Restaurant Les Arcades**: Grand-Place 5. This is one of the only restaurants in town to serve Al'Djote tart, which is made of cheese, chard, chopped onions and herbs and goes down a treat

with the local beer, Jean de Nivelles. The restaurant offers a take-away service, and has a pleasant outdoor terrace from which to admire the abbey.

✕ Several restaurants serve *doubles*: buckwheat pancakes with cheese. If you're after a quick snack, pick up a take-away *double* from the Marronniers or Jacquet pâtisseries on rue Sainte-Anne.

☆☆☆ Expensive

✕ **Le Clocheton**: rue de Namur 124 (on the way to the station). ☎ (067) 840120. Closed Saturday lunchtime, Sunday evening and Monday. This gastronomic restaurant has a pleasant interior decorated with green woodwork. The cuisine is French with a southwestern twist, and there's a generous lunchtime menu.

WHAT TO SEE

★ **Collégiale Sainte-Gertrude**: right in the centre of town. Open 9am–6pm (to 5pm in winter). Guided tours: during the tourist season, weekdays at 10.30am, 1.30pm, 3pm and 4.30pm (no 10.30am visit on Wednesday), weekends 2pm and 3.30pm; otherwise weekdays 2pm and weekends 2pm and 3.30pm. ☎ (067) 219358. The present cathedral is a replica of the medieval collegiate church, which was largely destroyed during World War II. It was rebuilt using compensation paid by Germany for war damage, after a referendum asking the citizens of Nivelles which architectural style they would prefer. Rhenish Romanesque won the local vote.

The original collegiate church was founded in 650, and building on this site began in the 11th century. Strictly speaking, it's an example of Ottonian architecture – named after the 10th-century Holy Roman Emperor, Otto the Great. The flat 'wooden' ceiling, typical of Ottonian architecture, is actually made of concrete. The most striking thing about the church is its 'double-headed' aspect, with choirs, transepts and chancels at either end. The east choir and chancel, above the crypt, were used for Mass, while the west end was used during feast days in the Christian calendar, such as Christmas, Easter and Pentecost. The west end symbolizes the authority of the Emperor, while the east end reflects Papal authority. The church is huge – 102 metres (115 yards) long – but the overall effect is of simplicity, another feature of the Ottonian style, and one heightened by the absence of ornamentation on the columns.

– You can see the remains of a 15th-century mural representing the martyred St Laurent at the back of the choir. Behind it is the reliquary of St Gertrude, a strikingly modern work; the original was destroyed during the German bombardment. Locals call it the 'sardine tin'. To the left of the west choir is a 15th-century wooden wagon, drawn by six horses, which carries the reliquary during the annual St Michael's Day procession. Saint Gertrude is supposed to protect the harvests from rodent invasions, which is why rats appear in paintings and sculptures of her: they are usually seen running about around her feet or over her crosier. A cardboard model of the old abbey church, complete with a Gothic spire and the small houses that once surrounded, is on show in the nave.

– The front tower, built in the 12th century, looks a bit like a chevet. It originally housed the west choir, and has been marvellously restored, with wonderful stone cupolas.

– The nave contains a beautiful pulpit carved by the 18th-century sculptor Laurent Delvaux, a native of Nivelles. The fine baroque statues of the apostles in the first chapel on the left are also his work. There's a graceful painted wooden statue of the Virgin, which dates from the 15th century and is a fine example of Brabant Gothic.

– If you join a guided tour, you'll be able to enter the gallery chapels at the front of the church and see the famous hole that links the wall with a column. It's a tiny passage through which, so the story goes, only the blessed could squeeze. This section was entirely rebuilt after the war.

If you climb the tower, you'll see the old abbey prisons and, at the top, the Imperial Room, where the abbess dealt out justice. It's now a museum that houses the remnants of the original reliquary of St Gertrude. The tower is topped with a gilt bell-ringer, Jean de Nivelles, who strikes the hour.

– You can only enter the crypt as part of a guided tour. Unusually, the crypt is not a cemetery but a place of prayer. Two square pillars mark the spot where the relics of St Gertrude were once placed on high; pilgrims could stand beneath them to be automatically blessed. The basement also contains several archaeological finds, including the remains of five successive churches that were built here between the 7th and 10th centuries. A number of skeletons have also been discovered, but they have not been identified. It's possible, however, that one of them was Charlemagne's grand-daughter Ermentrude, and that another may be Himeltrude, Charlemagne's presumed wife, who was an incredible 1.90 metres (more than 6 feet) tall.

– The cloister is another of the cathedral's unusual features: whereas the usual place for the cloister is on the south side, this one is on the north side. It was built in the 13th century, when Nivelles was an important merchant town, and the south side was taken up by the all-important market. Only one side of the cloister survived the bombings, and it is not open to the public.

★ **Musée Communal**: rue de Bruxelles 27. ☎ (007) 002200. Open every day except Tuesday 9.30am–noon and 2–5pm; Wednesday 9.30am–5pm. Admission is 40 BEF for adults and 20 BEF for children. Housed in an elegant 18th-century building, this slightly underwhelming museum contains several collections relating to the town's history. You start on the second floor, which is taken up by findings from local archaeological digs: flints, jewels and glassware. The first floor is devoted to musical instruments and local crafts, with a room devoted to studies by Laurent Delvaux, the official sculptor to the court of Charles de Lorraine, governor of the northern Low Countries. The highlight of this display is the study for the wondrous pulpit in the abbey church, and there's also a fine marble work called *L'Hiver et le Printemps* ('Winter and Spring').

The corridor is hung with five paintings that tell the story of Gertrude and her miracles, while engravings and drawings show the evolution of the abbey church over the centuries, and also depict the fire of 1859.

The ground floor contains paintings from Nivelles's churches, a fine tapestry depicting Noah's Ark and a coin collection, including some minted by the abbey in the 13th century.

The tour winds up with the church's masterpieces: four wonderfully graceful late Brabant Gothic statues from the old rood screen. Finally, you can see a fresco of St Gertrude that was rescued from the church.

★ The attractive neo-Gothic **Palais de Justice** is on the Grand-Place.

★ Take a quick stroll down some of the old streets around the centre and look out for the **tour Simone**, an old tower that was part of the 12th-century town wall.

★ **Parc de la Dodaine**: this attractive flower garden has walks and a lake for fishing.

FESTIVALS

– **Tour Sainte-Gertrude**: on the Sunday after 29 September. The central feature of this 10-kilometre (6-mile) procession through the surrounding fields is the horse-drawn wagon that bears the reliquary of St Gertrude.

– **Carnivals**: on the Sunday after Shrove Tuesday, continuing the following day with the Aclot Carnival and a night-time procession.

VILLERS-LA-VILLE ABBEY

The fame of Villers-la-Ville, renowned for its superb Gothic abbey ruins, is in inverse proportion to its size. It lies a few miles east of Nivelles and about 30 kilometres (20 miles) south of Brussels. Take the E19 towards Mons, leaving it at exit 19, and join the N93. You'll see a sign for Villers on the left.

OPENING HOURS

Between April and the end of October, the abbey is open Monday and Tuesday noon–6pm and Wednesday to Sunday 10am–6pm; otherwise Wednesday, Thursday and Friday 1–5pm, and 11am–5pm on Saturday, Sunday and holidays. Guided tours on Sunday at 3pm. Admission: 150 BEF; 100 BEF for under-18s. For information, contact the Tourist office, ☎ (071) 879898.

A Short History

Set in the beautiful Thyle valley, this Cistercian abbey was founded by St Bernard in the 12th century. It developed rapidly, and was destined to become the most important abbey in the Low Countries. By the time of its 100th anniversary, the abbey's fame had spread throughout Christendom. The monks owned huge areas of land, and oversaw a series of 'satellite' communities. The abbey was not fortified until the 16th century, and continued to grow until 1794, when the French looted the abbey following their victory at Fleurus. Thereafter, the abbey's importance began to wane; its stones were used to construct new buildings, and it was left to rot. The ruins that you see today, however, are extremely romantic, with an architectural coherence that's extraordinary given that it developed over six centuries.

The state bought the abbey in 1982 in order to restore it and open it to the public. You'll probably be able to recognize the most important buildings as you stroll through the ruins.

THE TOUR

★ **Abbey church**: an awesome 90 x 40 metres (300 x 130 feet) with vaulting 23 metres (75 feet) high. You can still make out a section of the nave, which was built in the 13th century in the shape of a cross, and was the first Gothic building in the province. It's fairly restrained for Gothic architecture.

★ **Cloister**: originally Romanesque, it was given a Gothic makeover. The tomb of the crusader-saint Gobert d'Aspremont, who died in Villers, stands in one corner, with a recumbent marble statue of its occupant on top.

★ **Refectory**: the sheer size of the place gives you some idea of how many monks once lived here. It's too late for Romanesque, but isn't quite Gothic, either. A series of fine ogive windows would have let the light stream in as the monks downed their tasty, home-brewed beer. You can still see the oven in the next-door kitchens.

★ **Brewery**: this wonderful Romanesque building, complete with vaulting and huge columns, stands at the back of the abbey. If size is anything to go by, they must have got through an awful lot of beer in the abbey's heyday. The local beer is still called Vieille Villers (Old Villers). There's another one known as Saint Bernard.

★ **Abbot's palace**: this 18th-century structure was the last addition to be made to the abbey before it was abandoned. It doesn't really fit in with the rest of the buildings, but it's still pretty impressive.

ALSO WORTH A VISIT

★ You can see the **Église Notre-Dame-de-la-Visitation**, which has two splendid 15th-century oak altarpieces, in the village of Villers-la-Ville. It's open on the first Sunday of each month, 3–5pm.

WHERE TO EAT NEAR THE ABBEY

✕ **Les Deux Marie**: rue de Suisse 5, Villers-la-Ville 1495, about a kilometre from the abbey. ☎ (071) 875358. From April to September, open every day except Monday, noon–10pm; otherwise, closed Monday and Tuesday, and open only for lunch and dinner. This friendly restaurant-cum-tea-room has a terrace and a garden from where you can admire the delightful surroundings.

FESTIVALS

The abbey provides a spectacular backdrop for various cultural events, including an Easter show, plays and concerts (in summer, during the Festival de Wallonie). A carnival procession winds through the town on the Sunday before Shrove Tuesday.

LOUVAIN-LA-NEUVE   24,000 inhabitants

This unusual town, which was tacked on to the commune of neighbouring Ottignies, sprang up like a mushroom in the 1970s following conflict between the Flemish and Walloon communities at Leuven University. When the French-speakers were forced out by the Flemings – a less extreme move than it might sound, given that for many years, Flemish students were required to work in French – they decided to create their own Louvain, a brand-new university town.

Louvain-la-Neuve, the youngest town in the region, was built on stilts, and looks a bit like a flying saucer poised for takeoff. Fortunately, the apprentice architects involved in the project had the sense to ensure that the dimensions of the town were human: it has a friendly, even cosy feel, although it could never be described as beautiful, being a predominantly concrete complex with the odd bit of brick and slate thrown in. On the plus side, it's entirely pedestrianized, with cars parked in an extensive network of underground parking lots beneath the stilts.

Arriving in the town can be rather disorienting. If you come by car, you'll end up going round and round in circles, wondering why the only signs you can see point to other car parks. Once you've parked your car and set out on foot, you'll find that the bridges, squares, residential areas, shops and the university are interlinked, as if to suggest that they are interdependent. It's quite difficult to tell the difference between the university and the residential areas.

Once you've got your bearings, you'll find that Louvain has a lively cultural and social life, a good museum, sculptures and frescoes dotted across town, and a theatre that attracts playgoers from Brussels. At first glance, it's a very youthful place. As you wander through the streets, however, you'll soon realize that Louvain-la-Neuve has its share of older people, who are drawn to its intellectual vibrancy, its libraries, its university and everything that goes with it. For them, Louvain-la-Neuve is an appealingly dynamic place.

Overall, Louvain-la-Neuve is a resounding success, and the town planners and architects who strove to create an urban community from scratch within just a few years are developing new plans for the town. Watch this space.

USEFUL ADDRESSES AND INFORMATION

Postcode: 1348.
🆑 Inforville accueil-info: place de l'Université 20. ☎ (010) 474747. Open 9am–5pm on weekdays and 11am–5pm on Saturday. It's not your average tourist office, but it does stock maps and the staff are usually helpful.

🚆 Railway station: under the pavement; entry via the rue des Wallons. Trains go to Wavre, Ottignies, Namur and Brussels. Take a look at the platforms: there's a pseudo-Renaissance mural by Thierry Bosquet, dedicated to Knowledge. Opposite are 25 reproductions of paintings by Paul Delvaux, who was made honorary stationmaster of Louvain-la-Neuve.

WHERE TO EAT

As you'd expect in a student town, there are numerous snack bars, watering holes and pitta and pizza joints scattered about.

☆ Budget

✗ **Onlywood**: place des Wallons 37. ☎ (010) 450361. Closed Saturday and Sunday lunchtime. Set menus from 250BEF. A cosy, American-style bistro with a light wood interior that serves tasty salads named after Hollywood stars: try a Kim Basinger, a Schwarzenegger or, for a little local flavour, a Jean-Claude Van Damme. Otherwise, the food is Tex-Mex, with a cheap *plat du jour*, and there's a good choice of cocktails and beers. Trendy students come here to top up their tans on the terrace.

✗ **Le Piano**: rue des Blancs chevaux, in the Hocaille district. ☎ (010) 450806. Open Monday to Friday 11.30am–4.30pm and 5.30pm–1am and 6pm–3am at weekends. Main courses about 220BEF. This cellar-restaurant serves simple, unpretentious food, such as hotpot or meatballs in tomato sauce.

WHAT TO SEE

★ **Musée de Louvain-la-Neuve**: place Blaise-Pascal 1. ☎ (010) 474841. Open Monday to Friday 10am–6pm and Sunday 2–6pm, closed on Saturday and public holidays and on weekends in July and August. This avant-garde museum is part of the university library. The collections include an unusual mixture of western religious art and African, Indian and Eskimo objects. The contemporary period is represented by Magritte, Delvaux and Jo Delahaut, and you'll also find some wash drawings by Picasso. One work that stands out is a sculpture jointly created by Tam, Paul Delvaux and the ceramist Max Vanderlinen.

FESTIVAL

– Annual **24 heures vélo** (24-hour bike ride): October.

WAVRE   29,000 inhabitants

Wavre is essentially a shopping centre in a verdant, refreshingly undulating region of hills and valleys. There isn't a lot to do here, but there are two decent local-history museums, and it's worth a detour to see the *Maca*, a comical bronze urchin who appears to be climbing a parapet. The best time to visit is on a Wednesday morning, when the town hosts a bustling weekly market, or in the middle of Lent, when the Carnival takes place.

WHERE TO STAY

⚓ **Ferme de l'Hosté B&B**: Drève de l'Hostellerie 101, about a kilometre from Wavre, near Walibi (*see* 'What to see in the area') and Louvain-la-Neuve. ☎ (010) 241569. Fax: (010) 242457. Email: debry@fermedelhoste.com.

Rooms for two and three 1,500–2,000BEF. This stately 18th-century working farm has five basic but comfortable rooms with sink, shower or bath. A home-cooked evening meal, usually featuring chicken, costs about 600BEF.

WHAT TO SEE IN THE AREA

★ **Domaine provincial Bois-des-Rêves**: in Ottignies. A large park and nature reserve, where squirrels, pheasants and 80 species of bird roam freely.

★ Fans of white-knuckle rides should not miss **Six Flags Belgium**, the country's biggest theme park. In July and August, open 10am–9pm; on weekends in October, open 10am–8am; from 28 April to the end of June, on weekends in September and from 29 October to 2 November, 10am–6pm. Admission costs 1,150BEF for adults, 975 BEF for senior citizens and 575 BEF for children; young children free. Previously known as Walibi, it was snapped up by American giant Six Flags in 2001, amid the usual moaning about American cultural imperialism: partly justified, as it's now peopled with Looney Tunes characters in place of national icons such as Lucky Luke. On the other hand, with 20 new rides already, including two new roller coasters, who's complaining? There's also a water park, Aqualibi, with slides, wave pools and so on.

CHÂTEAU DE RIXENSART

In the village of Rixensart, about 25 kilometres (15 miles) southeast of Brussels. From Easter to 1 October, open Sunday and on public holidays. Guided tours from 2pm; last tour 5.30pm. ☎ (02) 652 0110 or (02) 653 2132.

This splendidly simple brick-and-slate building, constructed in the 17th-century, is well worth a visit if you're staying in Brussels. It's a square castle, arranged around an interior courtyard, with a faintly introspective air, while the unusual lack of ornamentation makes the château particularly attractive. The Mérodes, whose motto is '*Plus d'honneur que d'honneurs*' ('Better to have honour than honours'), still live here.

Tour the château and you'll see rooms and galleries furnished with impeccable taste, mostly in 18th-century style. There's some particularly attractive 16th-century woodwork in the entrance hall, while other highlights include an unusual collection of 18th-century Arabic weaponry, tapestries, luxurious carpets and family portraits. Many of the 'exhibits' are drawn from the private collections of various family ancestors.

LAC DE GENVAL

If you're touring the area south of Brussels, make a point of visiting Genval. It's a favourite rural bolt hole for the *bruxellois*, especially on Sundays, when they stroll around the delightful lake, surrounded by handsome villas and dotted with watersports facilities. The French football team stayed at the swanky Château du Lac hotel during the Euro 2000 championships.

WHERE TO EAT

Most of Genval's restaurants are rather expensive, but it's hard to resist the pleasure of dining out on a waterfront terrace.

☆☆ Moderate

✕ **La Clef de Verre**: rue de la Station 39, Genval 1322. ☎ (02) 653 3526. Open for lunch and dinner. Closed Saturday and Sunday lunchtime, and Monday evening. This pleasant, straightforward bistro-brasserie is renowned for its popular terrace and live blues, jazz, country or *chanson* (Wednesday or Sunday evenings). The interior is plastered with vintage posters, and the menu offers classic Belgian fare: *tête pressée* with vinaigrette or knuckle of ham with mustard. The *plat du jour* is good value for money.

WHAT TO SEE

⋏ **Musée de l'Eau et de la Fontaine** (Water and Spring Museum): avenue Hoover 63, set back a little from the lake. ☎ (02) 654 1923. Open 10am–6pm on weekends and public holidays. Admission costs 100 BEF for adults, 50 BEF for children and 75 BEF for students and senior citizens. This appealingly eccentric museum is dedicated to the wells and fountains that have played such an important part in village life across the continent. There's an unusual fountain in front of the museum, with a Siren washed up on a rock.

WHAT TO SEE IN THE AREA

★ **Domaine de la Hulpe**: a splendid 22-hectare (550-acre) estate at the edge of the Forêt de Soignes, through which the tiny river Argentine flows. Once the property of the enlightened landowner and industrialist Ernest-John Solvay, it now belongs to the Walloon Region, and serves as another popular weekend escape for the *bruxellois*, who come in their droves to stroll through the sloping park, with its pretty ponds, lawns edged with azalea and rhododendron bushes, and rare trees. The château in the middle currently hosts temporary exhibitions, but is destined to house the works of the Belgian artist Jean-Michel Folon. It also provided the backdrop for Gérard *Farinelli* Corbiau's film *Le Maître de Musique*.

JODOIGNE   10,500 inhabitants

Set in an area of low, intensively farmed plains famed for the cultivation of sugar beet and grain, this is the principal town in Walloon Brabant. Known as the Hesbaye, the surrounding region is dotted with large farms, old mills, abbey lands and Romanesque church towers, so there's plenty to see. The delightful villages, all built in Gobertange stone, are a pleasure to explore. On the horizon, you'll see the bumps of old tumuli, a testament to the presence of ancient civilizations.

USEFUL ADDRESS

🛈 Tourist office: in the former Hôtel de Ville, Grand-Place 1. ☎ (010) 811515.

WHAT TO SEE

★ **Grand-Place**: a charming collection of buildings, including the Hôtel de Ville, the Viscountcy and the Chapelle de Notre-Dame-du-Marché, its stocky, square tower topped by a spiralling steeple. A Tree of Liberty from 1830, which commemorates local volunteers who went to Brussels to fight for Belgium's liberation from the United Netherlands, and an old pump complete this picturesque tableau. A spectacular animal fair takes place on Ascension Day.

★ **Église Saint-Médard**: this wonderful Gobertange stone building, part Romanesque, part Gothic, was built in the 13th and 14th centuries by the Order of the Hospitalers of Jerusalem. A silver reliquary containing Saint Médard's jawbone is on display in the treasury.

In the Area

ORP-LE-GRAND

The **Eglise St Martin**, which dates back to the 12th century, was destroyed in World War II and restored in keeping with its former Romanesque style. It was originally built on pre-Romanesque foundations, and an imposing crypt was discovered during the restoration works. Other finds are on show in the archaeological museum on the main square.

WHERE TO EAT

✕ **Restaurant Meys, chez Stéphane**: rue Jules-Hagnoul 42, Orp-le-Grand 1350. ☎ (019) 633167. Open every lunchtime and Friday evening. Set menus from 245BEF. You have to walk through a butcher's shop to enter this upbeat, locals' restaurant, where the sociable atmosphere more than compensates for the dull decor. On top of this, its set menu is almost certainly the cheapest in the land. During the week, it features ample helpings of soup, meat and vegetable dishes and dessert, which you can wash down with *bière de table*. Alternatively, you can opt for a fondue, which is the house speciality. The weekend menu, which features chicken dishes, is a bit more expensive, but still more than reasonable. Friendly and efficient service is guaranteed.

FOLX-LES-CAVES

Named after the caves that have been cut into the calcareous clay since time immemorial.

★ **Folx-les-Caves** (Racourt Caves): rue Auguste-Bacus 35. ☎ (081) 877366. Open weekends and public holidays 10am–6pm, as well as midweek in July and August. Admission costs 150 BEF or 120 BEF for senior citizens. The tour, which takes an hour, shows you how prehistoric man used stags' antlers to dig miles of galleries into the rock, some 17 metres (55 feet) beneath the surface, and explains the legends and myths associated with this mysterious place. Throughout history, the caves have been used as a refuge during troubled times. Today, they are used for mushroom-growing.

JAUCHELETTE

The abbey farm, which has an impressive courtyard and boasts Belgium's largest barn, was a branch of the famous Villers la Ville abbey.

HÉLÉCINE

This park lies just inside Walloon Brabant; the linguistic border is marked by a curtain of sugar beet.

★ An estate was created here amid the complex of buildings that made up the original Norbertine abbey, founded in 1129. Today, it's a cultural and exhibition centre. The 28-hectare (70-acre) park consists of a recreation area and nature reserve. It's open all year from dawn to dusk, and admission is free. ☎ (019) 655491.

★ **Musée Armand-Pellegrin**: rue du Moulin 15, on the same road as the estate, but a little closer to the village. ☎ (019) 656990. Open Tuesday to Sunday 9.30am–noon and 2–6pm. Closed Saturday and Monday, from 1–15 December and from January until mid-February. This museum, devoted to daily life in times past, is housed in a former school. You can learn how flax was worked, find out about other traditional crafts and see a reconstruction of a 1900s shop.

★ The charming valleys of the rivers Train and Nethen, which meander between the gentle green escarpments west of Jodoigne, are home to several much-coveted houses. It's also a great area for country walks, during which you can sample the local cuisine. People come from far and wide to taste the famous sweet tarts of **Chaumont-Gistoux**, where the Musée de la Ligne KW (rue Pré-Delcourt 1; open Sunday afternoon from May to the end of August) describes the phoney war of 1939–40, during which the Belgian army camped on a defence line that ran between Namur and Antwerp. During the Fête de la Saint-Georges (on the first Sunday after 23 April), crossbowmen and halberdiers in period dress parade about town in a long procession.

Crossing the magical country around Grez-Doiceau, you come to **Beau-vechain**, where the Musée de la Vie agricole (☎ (010) 866314) displays tractors and milking machines, then **Tourinnes-la-Grosse**, a beautiful village traditionally adored by artists. The Romanesque St Martin Church is an evocative setting for an annual Passion play, which takes place in November.

LIÈGE

The Province of Liège

Liège is a hospitable, outgoing and multifaceted province that combines the gentle woods and pastures of the Herve country (Belgium's answer to Normandy) with the wilder hills and almost tundra-like vegetation of the Fagnes, a source of inspiration for the French poet Apollinaire and a paradise for walkers, botanists and nature-lovers. It's also a region rich in industrial heritage, notably in the mining area of Blégny, which has an excellent eco-museum. Liège, however, is the jewel of the region, and shouldn't be missed on any account.

LIÈGE   200,000 inhabitants

Nicknamed the 'fiery city' or the 'Athens of the North', Liège is, after Brussels, the most northerly French-speaking city, and the last great Latin city of the north. It is fondly remembered by those who visit it as a hospitable, vibrant and cheerful city. The French love it because it celebrates 14 July (Bastille Day) with as much enthusiasm as the French. And the British? Well, they won't be disappointed either. The city may be in the throes of an economic crisis, but you feel its exuberance in the streets, the markets, the bars, in fact more or less everywhere you go. Liège also has a rich architectural heritage, with superb museums and distinct neighbourhoods, each with their own character, such as Outremeuse and Pierreuse. Despite the misguided efforts of property developers and the concrete eyesores that rub shoulders with handsome Renaissance masterpieces, this place has genuine urban charm.

Liège is a fairly compact city, so you can get almost everywhere on foot, which is by far the best way to appreciate the city's atmosphere and architecture. Above all, it's a human city, scarred by signs of degradation as a result of economic collapse and the consequent hardship suffered by the region.

A Short History

It all began one black day in 705, when St Lambert, the bishop of Tongeren and Maastricht, was killed while out collecting plants on the banks of the Légia. His successor, St Hubert, decided to build a chapel on the site of his assassination, and this soon became a popular spot for pilgrims. St Hubert eventually decided to transfer his bishopric (then at Tongeren) to the tiny village of Liège. The fledgling town grew further during the reign of Charlemagne, as it was a pleasant stopping-off point en route to Aachen. He even set up a mint there. The arrival of the Vikings saw Liège become a fiery city in a rather more literal manner than its citizens might have wanted: they torched the town in 881. But the city survived and flourished thanks to Bishop Notger, who was appointed by the Holy Roman Emperor Otto I in 972. Notger was a man with a mission, who built churches and palaces, and laid the foundations for a prosperous sovereign state – the Principality of Liège. A popular saying of the time was: 'Liège owes Notger to Christ and all the rest to Notger'.

A power struggle gives birth to democracy
Liège was essentially a clerical city, but it also became home to a secular society of merchants, craftsmen and liberal professionals. Bitter power struggles and tension split the bishop and his subordinates, and life in Liège became a tense round of revolts, negotiations and truces, until the bishop and the people's representative signed the Peace of Fexhe (1316). The founding charter of Liégeois democracy, it gave the people the right to intervene in the government of the state.

Democracy breeds envy
Many were those who wished to lay their hands on Liège: not least the Burgundians, whose expansionist ambitions were stymied by the stubborn principality. Louis XI, who was at loggerheads with the House of Burgundy, sided with the people of Liège, but let them down twice when the allegiance didn't suit his own plans. As a result of his first betrayal, Liège lost its ramparts and its privileges (and even its staircase of liberty, which was transported to Bruges), and they fared little better when he let them down again in 1468, as Charles the Bold demolished the town and most of the churches. He was a good prince, however, and immediately set about rebuilding the city.

The Renaissance and the rebirth of Liège
Under the reign of Érard de la Marck, Prince-Bishop between 1505 and 1538, Liège regained its importance and once again became a force to be reckoned with. Helped by the industrial potential of the coal and iron reserves in the nearby Ardennes, Liège became exceedingly wealthy, thanks in part to the manufacture of weapons and its support for Charles V, for which it was generously rewarded. It was an ideal environment for the Renaissance spirit to flourish, and scholars and artists gave the city a rich cultural and intellectual life.

The French Revolution
The ascent of Liège came to an abrupt end in 1789, when the town was set ablaze during the fallout of the French Revolution and the prince-bishops were cast out. In 1792, the Republican armies entered the city, much to the locals' dismay, and in 1795, the region became a French *département*, the department of the Ourthe, and soon became acquainted with the joys of centralization and bureaucracy. The occupiers also razed the Cathédrale Saint-Lambert – there's still a hole there today, although Place Saint Lambert has recently received a much-needed face-lift.

Industrial revolution, Belgian revolution
Napoleon needed cannon, and Liège was only too happy to produce them for him. After the battle of Waterloo, the British industrialist John Cockerill, impressed by the local appetite for heavy industry, set up a metal works in the city. In 1826, the Val St Lambert glassworks fired up its first oven, and the Herstal weapons factory was established in 1889. The surrounding country-side shuddered with the shock of industrialization, as vividly described by Victor Hugo: 'A whole valley is pitted with erupting craters. Some throw up clouds of star-studded scarlet steam; others create the lugubrious picture of blackened villages silhouetted against a red background . . . This may be peace, but it looks like war.'

In politics, too, things were moving at a considerable pace. The French were succeeded by the Dutch, but the new rulers found themselves distinctly unwelcome. Liège sided with Brussels during the revolution of 1830, and played a key role in the creation of Belgium. It was equally stubborn in resisting the advancing troops of Kaiser Wilhelm in 1914, earning member-shop of the Légion d'honneur in recognition of their heroic efforts.

Tchantchès and the Essence of Liège

According to legend, Tchantchès ('Francois' in Walloon) was born on 25 August, 760, in the Outremeuse district of Liège. Following a turbulent youth, he befriended Roland, Charlemagne's nephew, and became his companion in arms and counsellor to the emperor. He is often represented wearing a large smock, a tattered pair of trousers, a black silk cap, a red-check scarf and wooden clogs. He was a good drinker, preferring *peket* (Belgian gin) to milk, even when he was a baby, and married Nanesse, a woman with a great deal of character. He was strong-headed and quick-tempered, but blessed with a warm heart and oodles of common sense. The Tchantchès marionette, created in the 19th century, symbolizes the rebellious spirit and thirst for freedom that characterize the people of Liège.

Simenon, Native of Liège

Georges Simenon, born in Liège on 13 February, 1903, wrote several hundred novels, novellas, short stories and autobiographical works before his death in Lausanne on 4 September, 1989. No French-speaking author, other than Hergé, another Belgian, has had so many of his works translated into other languages. The creator of Maigret was born into a modest family in Outremeuse, a heavily populated district whose history and atmosphere had a profound effect on him. During his adolescence, he hung out in bookshops and displayed an instinct for detection.

At 16, he was taken on as a reporter by the local newspaper, the *Gazette de Liège*, where he wrote short pieces about run-over dogs and other bits of local news. When he was 18, he joined the 'Caque', a cultural and intellectual group with libertarian leanings that indulged in drunken poetry evenings and bohemian excitement. He soon drifted away from this dissolute set, and, like James Joyce, he headed for Paris, boarding the train one cold December day in 1922 with a one-way ticket. Later, he explained: 'It's like football, you have to choose which league you're going to play in – local, national or international.' Like Joyce, he rarely returned to his native soil, setting foot in Belgium only for a ceremony in his honour and when his mother was ill. In 1930, he launched the famous Maigret, whose motto was: 'Understand, don't judge.' Simenon's output was prodigious: he wrote more than 100 non-detective stories, as well as countless crime tales, and once finished an entire novel in a week.

Liège is proud of its popular, universal author, although this pride is tempered by the fact that Simenon showed so little attachment to his native land. Worse, he had his ashes scattered in Switzerland. No matter: Simenon will long remain associated with Liège. Indeed, the city features so frequently in his works that Maigret fans will experience a kind of *déjà vu* as they wander through the streets of Outremeuse.

Café Liégeois

This classic drink figures on all self-respecting bistro and brasserie menus. Until World War II, it was known as Viennese coffee, but that changed when the Germans invaded Belgium. The forts surrounding Liège resisted so strongly that the Kaiser's troops had to borrow Skoda howitzers from the Austrian army in order to break through their defences. Fired by Belgian

■ **Useful addresses**

1 Tourist office
2 Tourist information centres
3 Fédération du tourisme de la province de Liège
Main post office
Gare des Guillemins

Where to stay

10 Youth hostel Georges-Simenon
11 Pension des Nations
13 Hôtel Le Berger
14 Canal boat L'Embrun
15 Hôtel Simenon
16 Hôtel Univers
17 Le Cygne d'Argent
18 Passerelle Hôtel

✕ **Where to eat**

15 Le Bagne de Cayenne
23 La Feuille de Vigne
24 Amour, Maracas et Salami
25 L'Annexe 13
26 As Ouhès
28 Tavern Tchantchès et Nanesse
29 Café Lequet
30 Le Duc d'Anjou
32 Les Sabots d'Hélène
33 Mamé Vï Cou
34 Le Bourbonnais
35 Restaurant Robert Lesenne and Le Bistrot d'En Face
36 Au Vieux-Liège
37 Le Thème
38 Le Bal
40 L'Eureye
41 Amon Nanesse

★ **What to see**

45 Place Saint-Lambert
46 Palais des Princes-Évêques
47 Place du Marché
48 Hôtel de Ville
49 Musée de la Vie wallonne
50 Musée d'Art religieux et d'Art mosan
51 Escalier de la Montagne de Bueren
52 Impasses du Quartier Hors Château
53 Église Saint-Barthélemy
54 Musée Curtius
55 Musée d'Armes
56 Musée de l'Art wallon
57 Musée d'Ansembourg
58 Cathédrale Saint-Paul
59 Église Saint-Jean
60 Église Saint-Jacques
61 Théâtre Royal
62 Église Saint-Denis
63 Église Saint-Pholien and rue des Écoliers
64 Église Saint-Nicolas
65 Maison de Grétry
66 Musée Tchantchès
67 Aquarium, Musée de Zoologie et Maison des Sciences
68 Musée d'Art moderne et contemporain
69 Maison de la Métallurgie
70 Basilique Saint-Martin
71 Brocante d'Outremeuse
72 Marché de la Batte
73 Musée des Transports en commun
74 Le Carré

LIÈGE

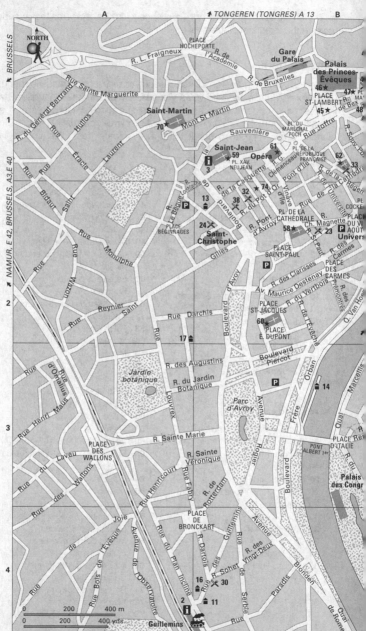

↑ *TONGEREN (TONGRES) A 13*

← BRUSSELS

NAMUR, E 42, BRUSSELS, A3, E 40

PLACE
HOCHEPORTE

R. L. Fraigneux

R. de
l'Académie

Gare
du Palais

R. de Bruxelles

Palais
des Princes-
Évêques

Rue Sainte Marguerite

46 ★
47 ★ PL.
MA
PLACE
ST-LAMBERT
45 ★   R. de Bex
48

R. du Général Bertrand

R. du

Hullos

Eracle

Saint

Laurent

Saint-Martin
70 ★   Mont St Martin

Sauvenière

PL. DU
MARÉCHAL
FOCH   Rue Joffre

R. Sauy-Par

Saint-Jean
59 ★   Opéra
61

PL. DE LA
RÉPUBLIQUE
FRANÇAISE

62

33

Bidaut

3 ★   PL. XAV.
NEUJEAN

Clemenceau   Pont d'Île

R. de la Régen

R. de la Casquette

R.
13
P

32 ★ 74
38   R. du Pot d'Or

Vinâve   R. de l'Univers

PL
COCKE

Rue   Monulphe

PLACE
BÉGUINNAGES

24 ★
Saint-
Christophe

Pont
d'Avroy

PL. DE LA
CATHÉDRALE

58 ★

Ch. Magnette   R.

23 ★   PLACE
DU VI
AOÛT

Univers

Reynier   Saint

Rue   Darchis

Gilles

P

R. des Clarisses

PLACE
SAINT-PAUL

PLACE
DES
CARMES

R. des
Prémontrés

Av.   Maurice Destenay

R. du Vertbois

O. Van Hoe

Boulevard   d'Avroy

PLACE
ST-JACQUES

60 ★   PLACE
É. DUPONT

17

Louvrex

R. des Augustins

R. du Jardin
Botanique

Boulevard
Piercot

Jardin
botanique

P

Orban

14

Rue   d'Omalius

Rue Henri   Maus

R. Sainte Marie

Parc
d'Avroy

Avenue

Frère

PLACE
DES
WALLONS

R. Sainte
Véronique

PONT
ALBERT 1er

PLACE Re
D'ITALIE

Quai   Marcellis

Laveu

Rue   du

Rue   des   Wallons

Rue Henricourt

R. Fabry

R. de
Rotterdam

Rotier

Boulevard

Palais
des Congr

Joie

de   l'Évêque

Avenue   de   l'Observatoire

Rue du Plan Incliné

PLACE
DE
BRONCKART

R. Dartois

R. des   Guillemins

R. des
Vingt-Deux

Avenue

Serbie

Blonden

Paradis

Quai
de Rome

16
2
i   11
30

Rue   Soher

Rue

0   200   400 m
0   200   400 yds

Guillemins

HUY, SERAING ↓

heroism and appalled at German brutality, Parisian café-owners decided to rename the famous coffee, as a way of showing solidarity.

USEFUL ADDRESSES

Postcode: 4000 and 4020.

🛈 Tourist office (map C1, **1**): En Féronstrée 92; soon to move to the Halle des Viandes (map C2), rue de la Boucherie 1. ☎ (04) 221 9221. Fax: (04) 221 9222. Open Monday to Friday 9am–6pm, Saturday 10am–4pm, Sunday and public holidays 10am–2.30pm. The staff are helpful, and there's excellent information about the town as well as details of what's on: ☎ (04) 222 1111. From April to October, there are several guided walks, mostly in the afternoon at 2pm: they cost 250BEF, and they're well worth taking.

🛈 Tourist information centre (map A4, **2**): place des Guillemins, in the station. ☎ (04) 252 4419. Between April and the end of September, open 9am–noon and 1–5.30pm, Sunday 10am–noon and 1–4pm; otherwise, open from Monday to Saturday, 10am–noon and 1–4pm.

🛈 Fédération du Tourisme de la Province de Liège (map B1, **3**): boulevard de la Sauvenière 77. ☎ (04) 232 6510. Fax: (04) 232 6511. Website: www.ftpl.be. Open 8.30am–5pm, Saturday 9am–1pm. Closed Sunday.

✉ Post office: Gare des Guillemins (map A-B4). The main post office (map B2) is on the corner of place Cockerill and rue de la Régence.

■ Telephone and fax: rue de l'Université 30.

🚌 Buses: Maison du TEC, place Saint-Lambert. ☎ (04) 619-444. Open 8.45am–6pm, Saturday 8.45am–12.30pm (until 6pm on the first Saturday in the month). Closed Sunday.

🚌 Eurolines: boulevard de la Sauvenière 26. ☎ (04) 222 3618.

🚆 Gare des Guillemins (map A-B4): ☎ (04) 252 9850. Information centre open 7am–10pm. Trains for Brussels, Bruges, Ostend, Verviers, Aachen, Cologne, Eupen, Louvain-la-Neuve, Arlon and Spa. You can also go to Huy, Namur, Charleroi, Mons, Tournai, Mouscron, Tongeren and Antwerp, as well as Luxembourg.

In 1998, work began on a new, futuristic station just 200 metres from the old one. This will consolidate Liège's role in Europe's 21st-century high-speed network.

➊ Liège-Bierset airport: ☎ (04) 234 8411.

WHERE TO STAY

☆ Budget

⚓ Youth hostel Georges-Simenon (map C2, **10**): rue Georges-Simenon 2, Liège 4020. ☎ (04) 344 5689. Fax: (04) 344 5687. E-mail: liege@laj.be. In Outremeuse. Access from the Gare des Guillemins: take bus No. 4 and get off at Congrès. Closed January. Basic rate per night 470–695BEF, including breakfast;

doubles 1,170BEF. Facilities for the disabled. This splendid four-floor brick construction with 204 beds, arranged around a cloister, is the Hilton of youth hostels. There's a vast paved courtyard, used for all types of entertainment (there's even a PA system), and the atmosphere really hots up in fine weather. Inside, there's a games room for trendy young things, a TV room and a kitchen. There's also a left-luggage area, a library and a games library. The dining room seats 100, and you don't have to wash up afterwards. Set menu and *plat du jour* (285BF). Reception is open until 1am, but there's an access code, so you can let yourself in as late as you like. Rooms, which sleep four to seven, are locked using individual magnetic cards: the largest ones, with mezzanine floors, are the most fun. Each room has a shower, toilet and lockable cupboards. There's a sheet- and towel-hire service, and four rooms are available for meetings and seminars. All in all, this is a great example of how to spend public money: the walls have even been treated with an anti-graffiti coating.

☆☆ Moderate

⚓ Hôtel Le Berger (map B2, **13**): rue des Urbanistes 10, in a street off the boulevard d'Avroy. ☎ (04) 223 0080. Fax: (04) 221 1948. Double rooms with sink or shower 1,400–1,800BEF; breakfast 200BEF. Paying showers on the landing if you plump for the cheaper rooms. Centrally situated with friendly staff, this hotel has the style and atmosphere of a pension. The furnishings are a bit hit-and-miss, but it's perfectly clean. There's a good-value room for four and a pleasant common room should you want a place to relax.

⚓ Pension des Nations (map B4, **11**): rue des Guillemins 139, near the station. ☎ (04) 252 4434. Rooms with sinks 1,400BEF. The cheapest place in Liège after the youth hostel is basic, bordering on spartan, but it's pretty clean and there's a restaurant on the ground floor.

⚓ L'Embrun (map B3, **14**): in the yacht harbour, level with Pont Albert-1er; you can only get there

from Place d'Italie or Quai Marcellis, on the other side of the harbour. ☎ (04) 221 1120 or (04) 343 8414. Fax: (04) 341 4878. Doubles 1,700–1,900BEF; breakfast 225BEF. Discounts for groups (up to 18 people). Ever wanted to spend a night on a barge? This is a splendid, beautifully maintained boat that lets its cabins by the night when it's not booked for a private function. It's pleasant and fairly comfortable, with one bathroom for every two cabins and one en suite 'room'. There's a fully equipped kitchen, a charming living room and friendly staff. Don't just turn up, however: you'll need to book in advance and agree on an arrival time.

☆☆–☆☆☆ Moderate–Expensive

⚓ Hôtel Le Simenon (map C2, **15**): boulevard de l'Est 16, Liège 4020 (place de l'Yser). ☎ (04) 342 8690. Fax: (04) 344 2669. Doubles 2,400–2,500BEF. Book in advance. This jewel of a hotel in the Outremeuse district offers the best value in town, with an ornate façade, comfortable rooms, stunning decor and a cosy atmosphere. As you might have guessed, each room bears the name of one of Georges Simenon's novels. If you want to splash out, plump for a suite (No. 32 has a jacuzzi). Honeymooners can even get a meal in their suite. There's a restaurant, Le Bagne de Cayenne, in the annex (*see* 'Where to eat').

⚓ Hôtel Univers (map B4, **16**): rue des Guillemins 116, opposite the station. ☎ (04) 254 5555. Fax: (04) 254 5500. Doubles 2,100BEF, with no reduction for single travellers; (small) discounts on weekends. A posh hotel with a paying car park, clean and functional but without any particular personality.

⚓ Le Cygne d'Argent (map A2, **17**): rue Beekman 49, on a quiet side street. ☎ (04) 223 7001. Fax: (04) 222 4966. Email: cygne@cybernet.be. Doubles 2,420–2,850BEF; breakfast 300BEF. A pleasant hotel with about 20 rooms, several recently redecorated, and a light, airy breakfast room. **Le Petit Cygne** (nearby, at 42 Rue des Augustins; same telephone number), owned by the same outfit, has gardens at the back and a room for four, but is best suited to long stays.

â **Hôtel La Passerelle** (map C1-2, **18**): chaussée des Prés 24, in Outremeuse, Liège 4020. ☎ (04) 341 2020. Fax: (04) 344 3643. Doubles 2,100–2,530BEF; breakfast 250BEF. A hotel beyond reproach, though some of the rooms are a bit on the small side – ask for Nos. 16 or 26.

Campsite near Liège

â **Provincial estate of Wégimont**: Soumagne 4630; on the Liège-Verviers road (bus Nos. 60 and 69, from rue Léopold). ☎ (04) 377 9902. Fax: (04) 377 9901. Closed January. You'll pay 400BEF for a tent site. A superior campsite on an estate that sprawls over 25 hectares (63 acres). Hot showers, entertainment, swimming pool, mini golf, fishing, boating and tennis. On-site snack bar.

WHERE TO EAT

☆ Budget

✗ **Amour, Maracas et Salami** (map B2, **24**): rue sur la Fontaine 78, near the Église Saint-Christophe. ☎ (04) 223 6586. Open for lunch from Monday to Friday and for dinner on Friday evening. This unpretentious place, which takes its name from a phrase in a novel by the French writer Georges Pérec, attracts local residents and employees from the neighbourhood. There are three rooms (the back one's next to a stained-glass window) and a mezzanine crumbling under the plants. Take a seat at one of the narrow tables and enjoy a *plat du jour* for 315BEF – often a filling, and tasty stew. Simpler still, try the soup of the day, a hearty sandwich, cheese or a salad, all served in a pleasantly bohemian atmosphere. Customers can play the piano and read the newspapers.

✗ **L'Annexe 13** (map C2, **25**): En Roture 13, in the Outremeuse district, Liège 4020. ☎ (075) 550104. Open every evening except Monday, public holidays and the three last weeks in July. *Plat du jour* 375BEF. This former wagon yard is at the end of a cul-de-sac on the left-hand side. The landlord's a well-known local personality (among other things, he's the mayor of the Free Commune of Roture) who has been the life and soul of this centre of Liégeois conviviality for 20 years. The menu changes 'according to the chef's whim', but there's never any change in the quality of the food, the size of the portions and the warm, cosy atmosphere. The regulars include a clutch of showbiz types and artists from the Saint-Pholien and Saint-Nicolas districts. As for the food, the chef concocts his own, delicious versions of regional dishes: black pudding, filleted pig's trotters and lentils, *beuchelle* (sweetbreads, ox tongue and kidneys), *fricadelle* (sausage) with grapes and *sirop de Liège*, and much more. Wash it down with the house wine – a highly drinkable and inexpensive *vin du Gard*. You can also purchase bottled specialities, such as *mitonnés d'Angèle*, a sort of stew with knuckle of veal.

✖ **La Feuille de Vigne** (map B2, **23**): rue des Surs-de-l'Hasque 12. ☎ (04) 222 2010. Open lunchtimes only from Monday to Saturday. *Plat du jour* 300BEF. This place stands out thanks to its large yellow facade, which overlooks a pedestrianized street near the cathedral. There's an organic grocers at the front and a brightly painted vegetarian restaurant in the conservatory at the back. On the menu: succulent, freshly made soups and vegetable omelettes, all eminently affordable.

☆–☆☆ Budget–Moderate

✖ **L'Eureye** (map B1, **40**): place du Marche 9, opposite the 'steps of liberty'. ☎ (04) 223 2813. Open noon–2pm and 6–9.30pm. Closed Sunday and public holidays. Full meals about 800BEF. Much-loved by local mover and shakers, this is a classic Liégeois tavern with exposed beams and a rustic appeal – ideal for stoking up on hearty local specialities without breaking the bank. The menu includes sweet herring salad, stuffed pigs' trotters, calf's head *garni* and the unparalleled brown-sugar tart.

✖ **Amon Nanesse** (map B1, **41**): rue du Stalon 1; behind the town hall. ☎ (04) 237 0592. Main courses about 300BEF. Open every day for lunch and dinner. This recent addition to the city's brasserie scene looks authentic enough, with a wrought-iron staircase and intimate rooms full of exposed brickwork, old street lamps from the boulevard D'Avroy, Delft tiles, blue-stone floor tiles, and lamp shades made out of galvanized buckets – not to mention the authentic well. It's also the place to go if you want traditional Liège cooking, such as onion soup, stews, kidneys, or port quiches. It's run by an exuberant Yugoslav woman who has given her adopted town a dose

of cheek and sauciness worthy of Tchantchès himself.

✖ **Le Bagne de Cayenne** (map C2, **15**): boulevard de l'Est 16. ☎ (04) 342 8690. Open for lunch and dinner from Tuesday to Saturday. Part of the Hôtel Le Simenon, with a predictably Maigret-inspired theme. The cuisine is functional: lamb with coriander, scampi with lemon and spare ribs with lavender honey, which you can wash down with a speciality beer (try a Guillotine).

☆☆–☆☆☆ Moderate–Expensive

✖ **Tavern Tchantchès et Nanesse** (map C2, **28**): rue Grande-Bêche 35, Liège 4020; tucked away down a small street in Out remeuse, parallel to boulevard Saucy. ☎ (04) 343 3931. Open for lunch and dinner. Closed Saturday lunchtime and Sunday. *Plat du jour* 350BEF; full meals about 1,000BEF. A 16th-century house hides one of Liège's best-kept secrets. It's the only sign of life in an otherwise unlit street, and the interior is warm and welcoming, with plenty of wood, brick and exposed beams. The walls are decorated with paintings of Walloon festivities, all by the landlord, and Liégeois puppets ornament the bar. It's a very friendly place, with a piano bar, and you can play *boules* on the terrace in summer. Have a snack at one of the tables in the bar, or have a full meal in the dining room, where generous helpings of traditional local and French cuisine are served. There's a good choice: *salade liégeoise*, grilled sausages, stew, homemade meatballs, quails, beef in beer, duck in *peket* (Belgian gin). After your meal, you'll be in the mood to meet the locals at the bar.

✖ **Café Lequet** (map B2, **29**): quai sur Meuse 17. ☎ (04) 222 2134.

Open noon–3pm and 6–9pm, Sunday 11.30am–5.30pm. The bar stays open until the last customer leaves. Set menus 320–545BEF. A deservedly popular bistro, a favourite of the Simenon family, attracts people from all walks of life, from postman to professor and comic-strip author, although there's a high concentration of the NPBU (*nouvelle petite bourgeoisie urbaine*, or yuppies). Try mouth-watering home-made meatballs or a hearty stew. The steak and chips are cooked to perfection. The best time to come is for Sunday lunch, when the place is filled with noisy crowds from the flea market.

✕ **As Ouhès** (map B1, **26**): place du Marché 19-21, opposite the 'steps of liberty'. ☎ (04) 223 3225. Open every day for lunch and dinner. *Plat du jour* 490BEF. A new venture from local celebrity, Robert Lesenne, who'll soon be feeding half the town, this vast brasserie in the bowels of the earth serves inventive regional cooking at reasonable prices. There's a bar on the left, cane chairs on the square and tasteful paintings and old engravings inside. Try meatballs in 'rabbit' sauce, pork kidneys in *peket* or *boukètes* (buckwheat pancakes), all served with speed and panache. If you can manage pudding, they do the world's best *café liégeois*.

✕ **Le Duc d'Anjou** (map B4, **30**): rue des Guillemins 127, near the station. ☎ (04) 252 2858. Open 11.30am–11.30pm. Full meal about 650BEF. It's an unpromising location for those in search of fine dining, but this place serves some of the best mussels in town in a big, pleasant, brasserie-style room with mirrors on the walls. There are round tables for groups, and the waiters are real pros. Start with prawn croquettes, then choose from 15 different mussel dishes – classic *moules marinières*, mussels with green pepper, *flambées*, *à la crème*, *au Ricard*, etc – served with as many chips as you can eat. Apart from this, the menu is as long as your arm. Highlights include rabbit *au sirop de Liège*, calf's head, steak *américain* (tartare), which is prepared in front of you, and Ostend sole. The beer's cheap, and wine by the glass or carafe isn't bad value either.

✕ **Le Bal** (map B2, **38**): boulevard de la Sauvenière 123, near the Carré. ☎ (04) 222 9075. Open Tuesday to Saturday noon–1.30pm and 7–11pm (later at the weekend). Set menus from 895BEF. This trendy restaurant has strawberry and apricot Palladian-style decor, with allegorical murals of plump cherubs on the walls. The vintage crockery has been chosen to match each dish, and smiling waiters and waitresses rush about to ensure the satisfaction of the young, slightly pretentious clientele. The cuisine is French with an Italian touch, and includes a good choice of elaborate salads and appetizing kidneys *à la liégeoise*. In summer, there's a fine terrace at the back that seats 100 people – a great place to see and be seen. The lunchtime *plat du jour* is cheap (265BEF), and attracts a more studenty clientele.

✕ **Le Piano Gourmand**: rue des Célestines 13. ☎ (04) 2230990. Open for lunch and dinner every day except Monday and lunchtime at the weekend. Full meals 500–600BEF. A 'music restaurant', where customers can bring their own instruments or borrow from a selection at their disposal. Things really get going at about 10pm, when the owner gives a signal to encourage amateur musicians to tune up and play. The menu offers tasty home cooking with an emphasis on regional specialities.

☆☆☆ Expensive

✕ **Mamé Vî Cou** (map B1, **33**): rue de la Wache 9. ☎ (04) 223 7181. Lunchtime *plat du jour* 400BEF. Pleasant rooms with Roman-style *trompe l'oeil* frescoes and exposed brickwork. The place has a certain charm and a long tradition of feeding the hungry: it's been a hostelry since the 16th century, and was a French café at the end of the 18th century. Today, it serves local specialities, and its menu is written in Walloon. For *entreyes tchafeyes* (hot main dishes), go for the *neûre tripe as Céline* (black pudding with cherries). If you'd rather try something more traditional, there's *pove al bîre* (chicken in blond beer) or *brotchèt à la crème* (pike with cream, white wine and tarragon). There's a good selection of *tchar* (meat), including *bokèt d'rognon* (kidneys) in gin, *cwève a r'moudou* (pork cutlets in cheese) and *robète as preunes* (rabbit with prunes).

✕ **Le Bourbonnais** (map C1, **34**): En Hors Château 64. ☎ (04) 223 0408. Open for lunch and dinner until 11pm (midnight on Saturday). Set menu at 695BEF. The restaurant, which is decorated with old toys, has all the charm of an old private house, and the French-Caribbean cuisine has an excellent reputation. At lunchtime, wage slaves flock here for the 295BEF *plat du jour* – it's always tasty, and will set you up for the afternoon. The set menu changes every day: so you might find homemade Liégeois meatballs with ham 'Fort des Halles', or a sliver of beef marinated in garlic and peppers, or breaded escalopes with mushrooms and cream sauce. If you're feeling flush, you can choose more sophisticated dishes from the à la carte menu. There's an excellent wine list, with some well-chosen suggestions.

Jazz and French *chanson* play in the background.

✕ **Les Sabots d'Hélène** (map B2, **32**): rue Saint-Jean-en-Île 18, in the heart of the Carré. ☎ (04) 223 4518. Open for dinner from Tuesday to Saturday. Behind a discreet facade, this good, if not especially original, restaurant, is ideal for a meal with friends. The tables are hollowed out to accommodate the massive shared grills, and there's a good old-fashioned barbecue with a hood to remove the smoke. There are various starters, then it's red meat or prawns, with *gratin dauphinois*, sauces and *crudités* (raw vegetables). The helpings are generous, but be warned: it's incredibly hot in here, so leave your coats in the cloakroom. There's an exhaustive wine list but you'll find that the bottle empties rather fast, thanks to the elevated temperature.

✕ **Restaurant Robert Lesenne** (map C1, **35**): rue de la Boucherie 9. ☎ (04) 222 0793. Open for lunch and dinner (until 10pm). Closed Saturday lunchtime, Sunday and from the end of July to mid-August. Set menu 1,495BEF. Another Robert Lesenne eatery. The celebrity chef is something of a household name in these parts and has plenty of admirers, although some people find his posing slightly irritating. After a few experiments elsewhere, he set up this restaurant, which offers a single menu that's pretty reasonable, considering the quality of what you get. This, perhaps, is the secret of his success. Don't even think of getting a table if you haven't booked – not even at the beginning of the week. This is an attractive place, with elegant, restrained decor, pastel colours, the odd pot plant and just the right number of paintings on the walls. Add to this professional, efficient service and a relaxed atmosphere, and you've got a restaurant that's a million miles from the chic

LIÈGE

and slightly uncomfortable restaurant you so often find in this category. It's popular with yuppies, who love being greeted by the affable patron in person. The cuisine is serious and inspired, featuring classic dishes with a twist and the unmistakable Lesenne touch: *marmite océane* (ocean stew), strudel of calf sweetbreads, veal kidneys in gin, thornback ray stuffed with crab, young rabbit tart and much more.

✗ **Robert Café** (map C1): rue de la Goffe 2. ☎ (04) 223 1407. Open for lunch and dinner (until 10pm). Closed Saturday lunchtime and Sunday. *Plat du jour* 490BEF. A newcomer to the Lesenne galaxy of restaurants, this chic, sensibly priced and glossily finished canteen caters for people in a hurry. The accomplished cuisine has a strong Italian flavour, with plenty of pasta, served with style but *non troppo caro*. You stand a fair chance of seeing the great Robert Lesenne himself – he often comes here to do a spot of 'public relations'.

✗ **Le Bistrot d'En Face** (map C1, **35**): rue de la Goffe 8. ☎ (04) 223 1584. Closed Saturday lunchtime and Monday. *Plat du jour* 490BEF, with à la carte meals about 1,100BEF. Yet another Robert Lesenne production, this time a bistro with all the traditional trimmings: exposed stone, Vichy lace, rustic ceiling, abstract paintings, hanging salamis, a parade of bottles along the bar and the odd reminder of rural life. The menu and prices are chalked up on the inevitable slate, and the cooking's earthier than in his restaurant: hot sausage with pistachio, prime cuts of beef, chicken and sauerkraut with four types of meat. It's always full, but

there's seating in the basement and on the first floor, which improves your chances of getting in.

✗ **Au Vieux-Liège** (map C1, **36**): quai de la Goffe 41. ☎ (04) 223 7748. Open for lunch and dinner (until 9.30pm). Closed Sunday, Wednesday evening, public holidays and from mid-July to mid-August. Set menus 900–1,800BEF A local classic in a converted 16th-century house, this charming restaurant has exposed beams and old-fashioned decor. The menu is suitably short on surprises, but makes a virtue of its traditional values. Highlights include duckling with lime, salmon stuffed with *fromage blanc*, *fricassée* of snails and quails and *biscuit tomaté* (cold baked custard with tomatoes) with asparagus. For dessert, what else but an authentic *café liégeois*?

✗ **Le Thème** (map C1, **37**): impasse de la Couronne 9, off rue En Hors Château. ☎ (04) 222 0202. Open for dinner (until 10pm). Closed Sunday. *Menu du marché* 750BEF, with a full set menu for 1,200BEF. Tucked away down a narrow passageway, this is another of the city's best-kept secrets. The owners are an innovative bunch who change the decor every season to suit the food on offer. It's quite expensive, and the atmosphere's quietly chic and discreet, bordering on the subdued, making it an ideal place to wine and dine a prospective partner. The dishes are carefully prepared but not overgenerous: veal sweetbreads with manzanilla, stuffed young guinea fowl with sherry or young turbot in cheese sauce. At lunchtime, the *menu du marché*, which includes two dishes and coffee, is a bargain.

NIGHTLIFE

The Carré

The Carré (map A-B2, **74**) is the heart of the city's nightlife. An unbelievably noisy pedestrianized zone, crammed with venues, cafés, clubs and plenty of atmosphere, it's the favourite haunt of young locals.

It's impossible to list all the fantastic places in the Carré, as it's in a constant state of flux. But it's always *the* place to be: there's something to suit every taste, and there's always a cacophony of music as the bars and clubs compete to pump out the highest decibels. Below are just a few of the countless fun hangouts.

L'Aquarelle: on the corner of rue de la Tête-de-Buf and rue du Pot-d'Or. This dark, smoky venue has a touch of class, and attracts a mix of bohemian artist types and trendy youngsters.

La Crèmerie: you'll see students dancing on the tables here. Jupiler flows freely at La Guimbarde. Le Spot plays driving hard rock amid piles of old barrels, enamelled plates, exposed brick and soft lighting.

On rue Saint-Jean-en-Île, you'll find L'Escalier (a whiskey bar), Le Barril, L'Aller Simple and many more. Tables in the street, numbingly loud music. Just take your pick.

Pepito mi Corazon: rue des Célestins. Closed Monday. A Mexican atmosphere, with tequila, mescal and sangria. If you've got the munchies, you can also get tapas, chilli, tacos or salads.

Le Bouldou: rue de la Tête-de-Buf 15. Open from 11am. The craziest decor in the area, and welcome relief from the relentless noise outside. Here you'll find hidden corners, bevelled mirrors, hangings and light fittings that look as though they've come from a provincial spinster's house. On the drinking front, you'll find tangos, mazout, half-and-half and other fancy cocktails. There's whiskey on tap, and all the country's newspapers are at your disposal. So why is it half empty? Perhaps it's too sane, although even here, they're not above making the walls shake with sound.

Doo be Doo (map B2): boulevard de la Sauvenière 182, off the place des Carmes. The main hangout for the scooter set. The atmosphere's great and it's jam-packed on weekends. From 10pm to dawn, it's sing-a-long a rock classic . . .

Le Vaudrée II (map A2): rue Saint-Gilles 149, just beyond place Saint-Christophe. ☎ (04) 223 1880. Open round the clock. The best beer bar in the world? Probably. Its looks aren't up to much, but it has the most amazing selection of beers, even by Belgian standards: 980 in bottles and 42 on tap. The owner is a connoisseur, who talks volubly on the subject and will happily suggest new things to try, describing every detail of the beer in question and offering critiques of the bouquet, flavour, texture, and so on. House specialities include Merveilleuse de Rochefort, brown Westvleteren, Superbe, *gueuze maracuja*, Kasteel and a host of beer cocktails. The menu also lists 'beers that have disappeared' (i.e. beers that are no longer in production: try the 15-year-old *gueuze* Saint-Job, Biss de Pipaix or Li Vi Bleu). If you want to line your stomach before some serious sampling, main courses here cost about 295BEF. The food's good and the portions are generous: the house speciality is meat cooked on a hot stone.

♣ Tavern Saint-Paul: rue Saint-Paul 8, near the cathedral. ☎ (04) 223 7217. Open until 1am on weekdays (later on weekends). A former coaching inn, where Trotsky once slept, this place is a spiritual cousin of the Flemish brown cafés. The charming rooms are all polished old wood and tiled flooring, with period decorative objects scattered about, and there's an excellent range of beers on tap, including white Hoegaarden and several Trappist brews. It's a lively place, and the barflies are usually good company.

LIVE MUSIC

– **La Notte**: rue de la Tête-de-Buf 10, in the Carré. ☎ (04) 223 0732. Open from 9pm. Closed Monday. This place keeps the Blue Note spirit alive in Liège. You'll hear good musicians of all types: funk, bebop, swing, cool and more. French *chansonniers* perform on Friday and Saturday. Phone ahead to find out what's on.

The Centre

♣ À Pilori (map B1): place du Marché 7, opposite the Hôtel de Ville. Open until 12.30am. Again, this place is a bit like a brown café. It's popular with solicitors and barristers from the nearby law courts, as well as businessmen, salesmen and tourists in search of atmosphere. There are good abbey beers on tap, and you can have a snack at lunchtime. Outdoor seating in fine weather.

♣ Les Olivettes (map B-C1): Pied-du-Pont-des-Arches 6, on a little street leading to the bridge. Open every day, but the best evenings are Friday and Saturday from 8pm and Sunday (10am–midnight). A Liégeois institution, with a good-humoured atmosphere where photographs of the regulars grace the walls and the old and not so old get up on stage to sing along with their favourite tunes. It's not so much fun when it's less crowded, and a knowledge of francophone pop would be a distinct advantage.

♣ Les Caves de Porto (map C1): En Feronstrée 144. ☎ (04) 223 2325. Closed Tuesday and Thursday. A *café chantant*, in the same vein as Les Olivettes. Reasonably priced drinks.

♣ There are a few bars in rue Souverain-Pont and rue de la Madeleine (map B1) for those who like a bit of spit and sawdust. Try Planète Interdite or Couleur Café, which is also a small restaurant with tasty food.

Outremeuse

♣ Le Tchantchès (map C2): rue Grande-Bêche 35 (*see* 'Where to eat'). As well as being an excellent restaurant, this is also a bar where you can discover the authentic spirit of Liège. The owner, Monsieur Ducroux, oversees a particularly sociable place that's also the headquarters of the *Confréries de la République libre d'Outremeuse* (Confraternities of the Free Republic of Outremeuse). Above the bar, regular customers have beer glasses marked with their names. Local puppets provide the decoration, along with the annual Tchantchès prizes, given to artists, illustrators, photographers and sportsmen. Try the Tchantchès and Nanesse beers. A real institution, this place is a must.

☛ Le Notger (Spirit Blues Bar; map C2): on the corner of rue des Berghes and rue Jean-d'Outremeuse. The tables are wooden and the benches are covered in imitation leather. Once a local neighbourhood bar, this place is now popular with trendy young things. There's a small stage for blues concerts (8pm Saturdays).

☛ Café Littéraire Wallon (map C2): rue Saint-Julien and rue Jean-d'Outremeuse. A slice of the district as it used to be, this is a tribute to Joseph Vrindts (1855–1940), who had a profound influence on the young Georges Simenon. Dubbed the 'Prince of Walloon Poets', he was a regular here.

WHAT TO SEE

Before setting out to explore, get hold of a map called *Liège, ville conviviale*, available at the tourist office. It's well illustrated and very useful. Liège, by the way, is definitely best visited on foot.

★ **Place Saint-Lambert** (map B1, **45**): this huge square is the core of the historic city. It's been undergoing excruciatingly slow restoration for 30 years, and has only recently begun to take shape. At least the long process, hampered by constant traffic, has thrown up some important archaeological finds.

One of the most impressive cathedrals in northern Europe was built on this square. After its destruction by Revolutionaries in 1793, the area spent 35 years as a vast quarry. You'll find a large model of the cathedral and exhaustive documentation of its history in the Musée d'Art religieux et d'Art mosan (*see below*). Excavation works revealed the foundations of the razed cathedral and of its predecessor, built during the reign of Prince-Bishop Notger, as well as remnants of a Gallo-Roman villa and traces of neolithic and even palaeolithic habitation. The task of overhauling the square fell to the sculptor-architect Claude Strebelle, who has made a pretty good job of it. The urban fabric has been sensitively stitched back together, with buildings that are very modern but don't clash with the Palais des Princes-Évêques. Buses run underground in the centre and come out beside the half-finished Archaeoforum (set to be the largest of its kind in Europe), where the results of the digs will be on show. Steel colonnades on a platform indicate where the nave of the old cathedral once stood. The different levels of the Romanesque, Ottonian and Gothic churches are marked in the tunnel that runs beneath the street, while the colours of the paving reveal how the cathedral was extended over time. The overall result is a successful compromise that offers the public a useful insight into the complexities of archaeology.

★ **Palais des Princes-Évêques** (map B1, **46**): this imposing palace, for centuries home to the prince-bishops, dominates place Saint-Lambert. This was the site of Notger's residence in the 10th century, but what you see today is a reconstruction of the palace of 1536, which suffered an enormous amount of pillaging, fires and war damage, although it somehow escaped the Revolutionary frenzy of 1793. Over the years, it has functioned as warehouse, prison and hospital.

The outer courtyard (admission free) shows Italian and Gothic influences, with beautifully arranged porticos and columns. The shape of the columns on each side varies, the better to match the rest of the building. The capitals and pedestals of each bear different motifs, such as flowers or laughing or grimacing masks. Bishop-Prince Érard de la Marck, a close friend of Erasmus, introduced elements from *In Praise of Folly* and other works by the great humanist: on column 28, you can see a madman having a stone taken out of his nose by a parrot. The sculptors were also inspired by the discovery of the Americas.

The Gothic vaulting is made of brick, while the facades, decorated with tall lattice windows, lacy balustrades and skylights with pinnacles, provide a sense of harmony and order. The fourth facade on the west side was built in the 19th century during the formation of the provincial government.

The reception and banqueting hall, which has splendid 18th-century decoration, is on the first floor. It's open only in exceptional circumstances (during the court of assizes for example), or by prior appointment. Ask at the tourist office.

★ **Place du Marché** (map B1, **47**): one of the oldest in town, this square provides a striking contrast to the dug-up place Saint-Lambert. Still surrounded by fine 18th-century buildings (constructed under Louis XIV, who razed those of earlier centuries), it's lined with cafés, restaurants and terraces, making it one of the most attractive spots to while away a summer evening. In the centre are the *perron* (steps) and fountain, symbols of the liberties granted to the commune. When Charles the Bold captured the town in 1467, they was taken to Bruges, where they stayed for 11 years. A pine cone, found on many similar steps throughout the province, tops the column. When closed, the fruit shows the people's solidarity; when it's open and spreading its seed, it's an expression of joy, openness to the world – and fertility.

★ **Hôtel de Ville** (map B1, **48**): an elegant edifice on the southern edge of place du Marché, which the locals call La Violette ('the Violet'). It's been the seat of communal power, counterbalancing the tyranny of the prince-bishops, since the 13th century. Originally a house. La Violette was replaced by the current Hôtel de Ville in 1718, after another round of mass demolition jobs (Louis XIV again). It's a restrained, Classical building, although the double staircase is adorned with pine cones. Note the curved and elegant pediments above the windows on the second floor, and the large pediment that bears the arms of the bishop-princes and of the two burgomasters who oversaw the construction of the building. Opposite stands the *cour d'honneur*, with two wings on either side. There's a memorial to policemen who died for their country, including Arnold Maigret, the inspiration for Simenon's famous detective – or so they say. Others claim that Maigret was the name of Simenon's neighbour, a doctor who lived on the place des Vosges, in Paris, with whom the author shared a passion for boats.

The Hôtel de Ville is open to the public. Inside, there's a vast hall with a pretty, painted ceiling and black granite columns. The carved oak Atlases supporting the gallery are by Jean Hans, a pupil of Jean del Cour whose sculpture of the *Three Graces* holds up the pine cones of the *perron*. On the first floor, you'll find the old marriage hall, which contains busts and paintings, and the communal council room, with its richly decorated stucco ceiling and the fine, 18th-century Brussels tapestry.

★ **District En Feronstrée and En Hors Château** (map C1): sandwiched between a hill and the Meuse, this area provided a natural northwards extension of the medieval town. It's well worth a visit, firstly because of its architectural interest but also, and perhaps more importantly, for the way it successfully blends modern architecture and innovative restorations. This district has many hidden charms, as well as five of the city's best museums.

Rue En Hors Château, constructed in the 11th century outside the town walls, is now home to some beautiful aristocratic and bourgeois houses. The Église Saint-Antoine, at the beginning of the street, was built in 1645 in Jesuit style, hence the highly decorative facade. Note the five floors of pilasters, capitals, wreaths, garlands and niches for statues. The church is due to be renovated, after which it will house collections of religious art.

★ **Musée de la Vie wallonne** (Museum of Walloon Life, map B1, **49**): cour des Mineurs, next to the Église Saint-Antoine. ☎ (04) 223 6094. Open 10am–5pm (to 4pm on Sunday). Closed Monday. Admission: 80BEF. Housed in an old monastery for apprentice monks, built in Renaissance Mosan style, this is the largest ethnographic museum in Wallonia. Note the wonderful brick facade, decorated with arms and mottos.

A comprehensive list of what's inside would take up most of this chapter, but here are a few of the main attractions:

– Religion: commemorative plaques, calvaries, memorabilia from pilgrimages, puppets, carnival rattles, 'May brides' and scenes of St George fighting the dragon in Mons.

– Witchcraft: ritual objects, including a 'tree with nails'. One such tree, which was known to have at least 70,000 nails in its trunk, was an easy target for lightning. There are also examples of witches' stones, which were fixed to stable doors to protect the animals.

– Gallery of house and shop signs: a picturesque collection of signs in carved stone, wood, steel, terracotta, paint and so on.

– Reconstruction of a typical Ardennes kitchen with domestic objects, among them bread moulds, old ovens and firebacks.

– Displays relating to old crafts and professions, including exhibits about merchants who sold 'brocales' (the first matches) or boiling water (available at any hour), and rabbit-killers, who kept the skins as payment. Other traditional professions in the area included pipe- and barrel-making, glass-blowing, slate-cutting and basket-weaving, and you can see perfectly executed examples of each.

– A gruesome *guillotine*, in use until 1824.

– Agricultural machinery: old ploughs, a wheelwright's workshop and hemp work.

– A large gallery of puppets: the *tchantchès* (puppets of Liège) and bronze ones from the Théâtre Lassaux, some weighing 20 kilos (more than 40 pounds). There are also collections of lace, porcelain and toys.

– A fine collection of sundials and astrolabes.

– 'The Stages of Life', or customs and traditions from birth to death: a fascinating display that includes the first 'school satchels', carved in wood. Other objects, including examples of traditional dress, relate to communion, education, marriages and mourning. One of the most interesting pieces in the museum is a terracotta market scene by Léopold Harzé, who knew all the characters he portrayed, including an especially expressive street singer and a 'boot girl' carrying a basket (appropriately, they often married cobblers).

– Finally, don't miss the age-old traditional puppet show (from the end of September to Easter, Wednesday at 2.30pm and Sunday at 10.30am). The performances are often based on historical subjects such as the Charlemagne epic *The Song of Roland*. You can get information at the museum.

★ **Musée d'Art religieux et d'Art mosan** (map C1, **50**): rue Mère-Dieu, not far from the Musée de la Vie wallonne. ☎ (04) 221 4225. Open 11am–6pm (to 4pm on Sunday). Closed Monday. Admission: 100BEF. A must for religious-art enthusiasts. Start at the top and work your way down.

– Third floor: the history of the Cathédrale Saint-Lambert, with documents about its destruction, engravings, decrees, a model (with a grandiose porch in front of the cathedral) and a plaque from the reliquary of St Lambert.

– Second floor: an engraved bone and ivory reliquary casket from the late 11th century, a processional cross and the original certificate for the institution of Corpus Christi (1252). There are also splendid 13th-century Latin Bibles, produced entirely by hand, books of hours and reliquary crosses. Among a superb collection of statues, look out for a beautiful enthroned wooden Christ (1240), 14th-century ivory crosses, a 16th-century Pietà from Limburg and a 15th-century reliquary of St Odile. Take the staircase up to Room 5, where you can see a fascinating domestic altarpiece and a bizarre item called the 'Lactation of St Bernard', dated 1480.

– First floor: processional banners, robes, religious jewellery and beautifully carved monstrances (shaped like turrets or suns). Reliquaries, candlesticks, cruets, busts and finely worked silver vessels are on display in a large showcase. The painted lime wood statues include a Virgin and Child (*Notre-Dame de Montaigu*), with wonderful flowing robes. There's also an ivory *Christ on the Cross* and an *Adoration of the Shepherds* from the school of Lambert Lombard.

The central display case contains a relaxed, graceful Virgin and Child, the *Vierge de Berselius* (1530), and some delightful little landscapes, like *Prédication de Saint Jean Baptiste* (1525) and *Montée au Calvaire*.

★ When you leave the museum, take a look at the handsome 18th-century houses on rue En Hors Château (map C1), especially Nos. 5, 9 and 13. At the end, there's an Antoinist temple, seat of the only religion of Belgian origin: there's also a branch in Paris, with others in French-speaking Belgium and northern France. An offshoot of spiritualism, Antoinism suggests that one can reach eternal happiness through reincarnation.

★ **Éscalier de la montagne de Bueren** (Bueren Mountain Stairway, map C1, **51**): With almost 400 steps, this bizarre, colossal staircase is one of the longest in Europe. It was built in 1880 to give the soldiers whose barracks lay at the top direct access to the city without having to pass through certain streets of ill-repute. The name was chosen in memory of the 600 Franchimontois and their captain, Vincent de Bueren, who made a heroic attempt to capture Charles the Bold, who had his headquarters at the top of the hill. You can tackle the climb to discover the areas that cling to the slopes of the hill (such as the Pierreuse district), but details are included in a later itinerary.

★ To the left of the Bueren stairway (map C1), take the delightful rue des Ursulines. This is the start of the hillside path, which leads to the remains of a well-restored Béguinage. In front of it stands a 17th-century coaching inn that was transported in its entirety up to this spot. Keep going until you come to the Tour des Vieux-Joncs, which has superb views of the town below, then take rue Pierreuse back to town.

★ Return to rue En Hors Château and look out for the impasses (map C1, **52**). These used to lead to the lodgings of staff employed in large private houses, and were then used by workers' families on modest incomes. Each looks a bit like an English mews, and they're now extremely popular among yuppies, who have fallen for these charms of these quiet pedestrianized streets. The houses have been tastefully restored, and there are flowers everywhere. Have a look at impasse Venta and impasse de la Couronne, which comes out into the impasse de l'Ange – there's a *potale* (little chapel) where they meet. Impasse de la Vignette, one of the prettiest, also has a *potale*.

★ Between rue En Hors Château and rue des Brasseurs, you'll come to cour Saint-Antoine, an example of the skilful restoration carried out in the 1970s under the auspices of the architect Charles Vandenhove. It's a harmonious blend of old buildings, modern additions and 'rehabilitations' (restored facades with new structures behind them). At one end are the remains of a half-timbered 16th-century brewery with brick tracery. At the other end, beyond the little red house, you can see the towers and belfries of the Église Saint-Barthélemy.

★ **Église Saint-Barthélemy** (map C1, **53**): open 10am–noon and 2–5pm. Closed Sunday morning. Admission: 50BEF. Consecrated in 1015, this is one of the oldest churches in Liège, and one of the few Romanesque collegiate churches in Europe not to receive a makeover during the Gothic period. It's a typical Romanesque structure, with weathered facades and well-worn arcades, although the vast porch is neoclassical. The elegant bevelled towers are diamond-shaped. The interior is decorated with 18th-century stucco, but the dark-sandstone narthex (an early-Christian vestibule), although renovated, gives you an idea of what the original interior must have looked like. The church is mainly known for its 12th-century baptismal font, which belonged to a church that was destroyed by French Revolutionaries. It's attributed to Renier de Huy, and is one of the finest in the country. The great bronze bowl weighs 500 kilos (more than 1,000 pounds) and rests on 10 oxen (originally there were 12); it's decorated with scenes of baptism, including that of Christ in Jordan, that of the Greek philosopher Crato and that of a Roman centurion called Cornelius. It's a real marvel of Mosan art, the work of a master craftsman at the height of his powers.

The church also contains carved wooden statues painted to look like marble in the classic blue-grey Liège colour. The 14th-century Christ in the sacristy has a Romanesque top and Gothic lower half – very rare for a sculpture.

NB: the Curtius, Armes, Verres and Ansembourg museums have been amalgamated to form the Ensemble muséal d'Art et d'Histoire du Pays de Liège. Watch out for renovation works or different layouts.

★ **Musée Curtius** (map C1, 54): quai de Maestricht 13. ☎ (04) 221 9440. Open 10am–1pm and 2–5pm; 10am–1pm on Sunday. Closed Tuesday and public holidays. Admission: 100BEF. One of the finest civic buildings in Liège, this palatial patrician mansion was built in 1610 for Jean de Corte, an arms merchant who adopted the Latin form of his surname. It's a typical example of Mosan architecture, built in limestone and red brick, with high, mullioned windows and a frieze depicting fables and biblical scenes. The tower on the side, once used as a lookout post for keeping an eye on boats travelling up and down the Meuse, and now home to the Musée d'Archéologie et d'Objets d'Art, which contains more than 100,000 items. The exhibition halls, in particular the vast Moxhon room, which has immense painted fireplaces, have retained their former magnificence.

– Start with the collections of prehistoric archaeology, Roman and Frankish archaeology, and medieval Mosan art from the 11th to 13th centuries. The most important item is Notger's evangelistary, with an ivory carving from the year 1000 in the centre of the binding. It depicts the prince-bishop himself, praying beneath a figure of Christ, who is seated on a throne with his feet resting on a globe. The symbols of the evangelists are visible in the corners. The room is lined with carved bronze plaques and 12th-century embossed enamels.

– On the first floor, you'll find splendidly carved wooden church doors and beautiful tapestries. These are a prelude to the Renaissance rooms, which house a vast collection of furniture, cabinets, carved sideboards and the like. On the painting front, the *Vierge de Don Rupert* (also called the *Vierge de Saint Laurent*) anticipates the Renaissance in its depiction of Mary's expression of loving kindness and the flowing lines of her clothes, but was painted almost two centuries earlier.

The rest of the collection consists of religious jewellery, silverware, ceramics, illuminated manuscripts, watches and clocks, old coins, weapons and intriguing *objets d'art*.

★ **Musée du Verre** (Glass Museum): an annex of the Musée Curtius, with the same address and opening hours. Here you can see thousands of old glass objects, some dating back to Greek and Roman times. The place positively overflows with beautiful glassware from Mediterranean, Byzantine and Islamic civilizations. There are fine examples of 16th-century Venetian glass, crystal goblets and floral-patterned vases, art-nouveau and art-deco works, coloured and subtly decorated goblets, chalices, glass baskets and crystal carvings.

★ **Musée d'Armes** (map C1, **55**): quai de Maestricht 8. ☎ (04) 221 9400. Same times as the Musée Curtius. Admission: 100 BEF. One of the world's best weaponry museums is housed in a neoclassical 18th-century mansion where Napoleon slept on two occasions with his legitimate partners:

Josephine, in 1803, and Marie-Louise, in 1811. During the Dutch occupation (1815–30), it was the governor's residence. The last owner was a wealthy arms manufacturer and collector who bequeathed the house to the town at the end of the 19th century. Even if you're not interested in weaponry, the rooms themselves are quite exquisite, and the objects on show are often so beautiful that you forget their original purpose. There's a fine portrait of Napoleon by Ingres, with a view of Liège and a fantasy depiction of cathedral ruins in the background. The museum contains swords and firearms for sport, hunting and war.

– The sumptuous *salon de musique*: a gilt setting, with pale-blue and white paintwork, exquisite ornamentation, a painted ceiling and medallion insets with images symbolizing art and science. Ancient pistols and powder horns are exhibited in the display cases.

– Even more sumptuous (and kitsch) is the *salon des glaces*, where vast mirrors are decorated with gilt palms intertwined with vines. A few items are displayed singly here, among them finely ornamented arms cases, caskets for 'Scottish' pistols and an ivory rifle butt.

– The Chambre de l'Empereur, which recalls the nights Napoleon spent in Liège, is followed by a room where you can see a reconstruction of a workshop and appreciate the artistry with which rifle butts were carved and engraved.

– Among the older firearms, look out for the splendidly decorated arquebuses (forerunners of the musket), including several with ivory trim. Other highlights include a beautiful 15th-century powder horn, made from an animal's shoulder blade and decorated with a finely engraved scene, and some marvellous 15th-century crossbows. Note the splendid work on the gauntlet dated 1585.

– In the rotunda are Venetian-style lamps, the work of craftsmen from Venice who used wood and coal from Liège to work their glass.

– The second floor is less interesting, and looks a bit too much like a barracks.

★ **Musée de l'Art wallon** (map C1, **56**): Îlot Saint-Georges, En Féronstrée 86. ☎ (04) 221 9231. Open 1–6pm, Sunday 11am–4.30pm. Closed Monday and public holidays. Admission: 100BEF. The concept and layout of this museum is stunning, so it's a shame that the hulking concrete exterior is so ugly. The inspiration for this venue was the rather more elegant Guggenheim, in New York. You start on the fourth floor and descend level by level, gradually discovering the rich output of Walloon artists on your way. Exhibits are arranged chronologically, from the 16th century to the present day. The pastel-coloured rooms are well lit, and it's a really good backdrop for the works on show. Here's a subjective selection of the best:

– Middle Ages: *Saint Denis refusant de sacrifier au dieu inconnu* (St Denis refusing to make a sacrifice to an unknown god), by Lambert Lombard. Wonderful *trompe-l'oeil* effects.

– 18th century: *Visit to a Tobacco Factory*, by Léonard de France, a painter who specialized in costume and interior details. Note the astonished expression of the children on seeing aristocratic women for the first time.

– *Joseph et le Taureau*, by Léon Mignon, Constantin Meunier's Socialist-Realist *La Coulée à Ougrée* and many other fine works on display here are barely known outside Belgium, although they all have something original and personal to say. There's Anto Carte, for example, with his lyrical, somewhat sorrowful *Aveugles* and *Archers de Saint Sébastien*. There are several paintings by Pierre Paulus, who specialized in industrial landscapes and depictions of working conditions in factories and mines. Auguste Mambour, a childhood friend of Simenon, is represented by *Nu de fer*, while there's a disturbing sensuality about Adrien de Witte's *La Femme au corset rouge*, painted in a style that recalls Degas.

– Next come the famous Belgians: Paul Delvaux's *L'Homme de la rue* depicts a diminutive stereotypical Englishman standing in the middle of a large road, and his *Christ au tombeau* is in similar Surrealist style. Magritte is represented by *La Forêt*. Finally, look out for paintings of local life and puppets by Joseph Zabeau, and a remarkable sculpture of a group of children by Mady Adrien, which beautifully captures their movements and expressions, playful and sublime.

★ **Musée d'Ansembourg** (map C1, **57**): En Féronstrée 114. ☎ (04) 221 9402. Open 1–6pm. Closed Monday and public holidays. Admission: 100BEF. Housed in a mansion built in 1738 for a wealthy banker, this museum is devoted to the decorative arts, as practised in 18th-century Liège. Short on display cases and long on atmosphere, it gives you the impression that the owner has invited you to pop in for a quick look round. You'll find pieces by Liège's finest craftsmen, including doors, panelling and furniture. There's a splendid music room, with a stucco ceiling, brightly coloured tapestries and carved wooden panelling, while the walls of the dining room are covered with gilt and polychrome Cordoba leather. Here, too, there are outstanding examples of carved wooden panelling.

★ **Maison du Jazz** (map C1, near **1**): rue Sur les Foulons 11, a narrow street near the Musée d'Art wallon. ☎ (04) 221 1011. Open Tuesday–Thursday 11am–5pm, Saturday 10am–2pm. Admission: free. A must if you like jazz, which almost everyone in Liège seems to. There are permanent exhibitions on the subject and extensive archives, but the main attraction is the library of thousands of records and videos, which you can watch or listen to for free. Nice . . .

★ **Îlot Saint-Georges** (map C1): There are several 17th- and 18th-century facades between the Musée de l'Art wallon and rue Sur les Foulons. Victims of 1970s property development, they were rescued and transported here for reconstruction. It's a sort of archaeological safe haven, and such a rarity that it's worth pointing out. The corner building, now the tourist office, is a good example of 17th-century Mosan Renaissance architecture, with alternating bands of brick and mullioned windows. The name rue En Féronstrée, incidentally, suggests that *férons* (metalworkers) once worked here.

Take a look at the 'Montefiore fountain', at the start of rue Sur les Foulons. There are several fountains in town, most bequeathed by philanthropists. This one has a bowl at the base where thirsty working dogs, which used to draw small wagons loaded with milk, could quench their thirst.

★ Other interesting buildings in the area include the 17th-century Maison Havart (map C1), on the corner of the quai de Maestricht and rue Potiérue, next to a vast car park. An eye-catching structure with slate-covered balconies jutting out on every floor, it's now a restaurant, Le Vieux-Liège (*see* 'Where to eat'). The Halle aux Viandes (Meat Hall), one of the oldest buildings in the city (1544) and soon to become the tourist office, stands on the other side of the car park, on rue de la Goffe.

There are several **17th- and 18th-century houses** on rue de la Goffe, whose name indicates the area's former function. La Goffe (literally 'gulf') indicates a place where boats could unload their merchandise. A popular flea market stretches along quai de la Goffe and quai de la Batte on Sunday morning (*see* 'Markets').

★ From the quays, turn back to place du Marché via rue de la Cité and rue Neuvice, an important thoroughfare linking the Meuse to the main squares. The 15th-century houses are still used for semi-skilled trades, and are decorated with old-fashioned metal signs with evocative names, such as the *Cerf fleuri* (leaping stag), *Lion vert* (green lion), or *al Manoie di Noûvice* (house of the novice). Rue du Carré, a tiny medieval thoroughfare where two people can barely walk abreast, is between Nos. 23 and 24.

Around the Island

Yes, there really is an 'island' in Liège. If you look at the map, you'll see a ring of boulevards created by boulevards de la Sauvenière and d'Avroy. These roads were once branches of the Meuse, but they were filled in the early 19th century. Look at the street signs and you'll see that quite a number recall this watery past: Pont-d'Isle, rue Pont-d'Avroy, Vinâve-d'Isle, rue Saint-Jean-en-Isle and so on. Today, the heavy traffic on boulevard de la Sauvenière and place de la République-Française make this area an 'island' for rather different reasons. Known as the Carré, its high concentration of bars and clubs make it a favourite night-time haunt for young locals. The pedestrianized area has plenty of shopping streets, but there are also some interesting churches and a few old houses worth taking a look at. But you won't see anything built before 1468, the year Charles the Bold had this part of town burned down.

★ **Cathédrale Saint-Paul** (map B2, **58**): closed noon–2pm. This former collegiate church was founded in the 10th century and rebuilt in Gothic style in the 14th century. It was somewhat insensitively restored by a local prelate after being upgraded to a cathedral in 1801, when it replaced the ruined Cathédrale Saint-Lambert, from which the new cathedral acquired various odds and ends, including a clock and a carillon. That said, while the tower and spire are obviously 19th-century, you can't help but be impressed by the rigorous layout and the great bays above the pinnacles.

The interior is thoroughly Gothic, with 13th-century vaulting above the nave, 15th-century vaulting over the aisles, and high windows and an apse (note the Germanic painting) from the same period. There's a marvellous *Pièta*, sculpted by Jean del Cour in 1696, when he was 65. It's clearly influenced by Bernini, but the draughtsmanship and emotional power are astounding. In death, Christ's face is sorrowful yet serene, and you can almost see the body move – not even marble can capture the stillness of death. Almost as marvellous is the 16th-century stained-glass window in the south transept. In the upper part, you'll see the Crowning of the Virgin by three members of the Holy Trinity; below is the conversion of St Paul.

The pulpit features a striking, almost attractive depiction of Satan – the horns are very discreet, but the hoofs and wings are a bit of a give away. There's also a fine carving on the canopy. To the right of the choir is an unusual Virgin and Child: Mary has no maternal contact with Jesus, and she presents him as though he were already a man. It's an elegant work and there are traces of early colour.

Be sure to take a turn round the little cloister, which has brick vaulting and a small garden. The Treasury is in the cloister's annex (access through the cathedral via rue Bonne-Fortune) Open every day except Monday 2–5pm. Guided tours every day at 3pm. Admission: 150BEF. Seven rooms of exhibits on three floors offer a summary of the history and artistic life of Liège. One noteworthy devotional object is the impressive reliquary bust of St Lambert. Prince-Bishop Érard de la Marck, who provided 5 kilos (11 pounds) of silver for its manufacture, is depicted kneeling before the pedestal, which is decorated with finely worked scenes showing the life of the saint. Another famous item is the St George reliquary, given by Charles the Bold (perhaps as an apology for torching the town). The rest of the exhibits include vessels, monstrances, crosses set with precious stones, crosiers and bishops' rings, period textiles, chalices and cruets, and incunabula, the last-named happily saved from the floods of 1926, when the water of the Meuse rose to 1.2 metres (4 feet).

★ Look out for the following old houses: there's a pretty 17th-century brick-and-limestone house at rue du Pot-d'Or 22 (map B2). Rue d'Amay 10 is reputedly the first house built after the destruction of the town by Charles the Bold in 1468, and is one of the finest buildings in the city, with an elegant Gothic-Renaissance facade and graceful mullioned windows with decorative supports. The house is now a café, and there's an 18th-century fireplace with Delft tiles and a painting above it. There are also several 18th-century buildings on rue Saint-Jean-en-Île. The most interesting are Nos. 8, 11, 23 (17th-century) and 30. If you've got time, have a peep at cour Saint-Rémy (access via rue Saint-Rémy, just by the Figaro hairdresser's), near the Église Saint-Jacques. It's full of higgledy-piggledy little houses that were once craftsmen's workshops. On place Vinâve-d'Île, the fountain features a fine Virgin and Child by Jean del Cour. Passage Lemonnier, built in 1839, was the first shopping arcade in Belgium.

★ **Église Saint-Jean** (map B1, **59**): open to the public from June to the end of September, 10am–noon and 2–5pm (6pm at the weekend). Closed Thursday and Saturday morning. A collegiate church founded in the 10th century, this charming, picturesque architectural hybrid has a square Romanesque tower flanked by two turrets, and an 18th-century rotunda separating the tower from the nave. Viewed from a distance and a certain angle, it looks a bit like a camel. The neoclassical rotunda has an attractive high cupola, which is surrounded by a gallery with several chapels. There's a wonderful statue of the Virgin, the 'Virgin of Miracles', dating from the early 18th century. The clothes are exceptionally realistic. Jesus sits on Mary's knee, a bit detached from his mother, who looks unmaternal and detached as she kicks a dragon.

★ **Église Saint-Jacques** (map B2, **60**): place Saint-Jacques. Open at Easter and from mid-June to mid-September, 10am–noon and 2–6pm; otherwise 8am–noon. Closed Sunday morning. This is the most beautiful church in Liège. Approach it from the south (on the side of the Meuse) to get the best view. On the left is the narthex, a huge, rustic-looking Romanesque building, enlarged by a Flamboyant Gothic nave. You'd expect a soaring spire, but there's only a curious little pinnacle. On the place Saint-Jacques side, you'll find an Italian Renaissance doorway dated 1558.

The first church was founded in 1016 by Baldéric II, Notger's successor, as an abbey church for a Benedictine monastery. Unusually, the abbots carried crosiers and wore mitres, and they were directly answerable to the Pope. It was here that the two burgomasters swore to defend the rights and liberties of the commune, and here that the commune and the prince-bishops discussed their differences. The Romanesque vaulting caved in at the beginning of the 16th century, and the Flamboyant Gothic nave was built in a record 25 years.

You have to go inside to appreciate the architectural splendour of the church, which is a fine example of Gothic at its most florid – like a final firework display before the onset of the Renaissance. The vaulting is stunning, and said to be the most intricate in the world. There's lots of fine ribbing and delicate patterns, while keystones abound – no less than 150, with portraits and painted motifs in between. Grey sandstone was used for the base of the columns; their tops are made of light volcanic rock.

Look around and you'll see that there are hardly any flat surfaces. It's all lacy stonework and festooned arches, while the surfaces between the triforium and the arcades are carved with arabesques and the heads of biblical characters. The nave is lined with monumental white statues that are made not of marble or alabaster, but painted wood (the work of the great Jean del Cour).

– Chapelle Saint-Rémy: skip the 19th-century reredos in the left transept and look instead at the gentle, sorrowful air of the 15th-century *Pietà* and the black funerary slab of a 16th-century abbot on the wall. You'd never guess that it was a copy of the original, which was stolen by French Revolutionaries. The boat carrying it off to Paris sank on the way to Charleville, and the slab remained at the bottom of the river for a century before being pulled ashore and displayed in the Louvre. Rather than reclaiming its rightful property, the city of Liège decided to demand a copy of it in 1925, and this was carried out by the Louvre itself. On the right of this chapel, there's a delightful *Virgin and Child*, in gilt wood, standing on a crescent moon (1523).

– Right transept: the 17th-century tombstone of Prince-Bishop Baldéric II is made of black marble from nearby Theux. There's a 16th-century polychrome *Entombment of Christ* (with mourners and Eastern figures in one of the chapels beside the choir – on the right and hidden behind the altar). Beside it, the 16th-century font shows the *Baptism of Christ* (note the fine carving of the clothes).

– If you've got 20/20 vision, binoculars or a zoom lens on your camera, you'll be able to pick out the detail on the vaulting. If so, you'll notice a rare image of the Virgin with two faces, symbols of the evangelists, St Michael fighting a dragon, and, in the centre of the choir, a statue of Christ on a hanging keystone.

The burgomasters' platform stands on the right of the choir.

– Choir stalls: these date from the end of the 14th century, and are well worth a closer look. Those bishops were not, perhaps, as straight-laced as you might have thought: the misericords (tip the seats up and you'll see them jutting out, so the choir could prop themselves up against them when standing) depict surprisingly satirical figures and grotesque images. No prizes for spotting the two figures answering a call of nature . . . (they're on the right).

– Take a look at the splendid 16th-century stained-glass windows. The one in the middle, which was donated by the abbot who built the church, shows Abraham preparing to sacrifice Isaac. The windows on either side were the gift of two great families, who agreed to forget their many differences for the occasion. On the left, you can see the Hoorns: Johann III is on his knees, while his two wives are depicted in the window opposite. To the right of the choir, you can see the La Marck family: the head of the family is kneeling before Christ, and his wife stands in the other window. Also on the right of the choir, there's an entertaining window donated by the commune, which shows 32 more contemporary professions – tailors, millers, tanners and so on.

★ **Théâtre Royal** (map B1, **61**): place de la République. This is a rare example of early-19th-century Liégeois architecture. It was built in 1818 with a seating capacity of 1600 by an architect who was influenced by the Paris Odéon. The theatre has a beautiful painted ceiling, while the triangular pediment was a later addition to satisfy the locals, who wanted their opera house to look a bit more sumptuous.

There are different architectural styles on either side of the building. On the left, you can see the shopping centre, with arcades echoing those of the opera house. The vast block on the right, forming part of the curve of the boulevard de la Sauvenière, belongs to Générale de Banque. Both were carefully designed to fit in with the opera house and the surrounding architecture.

A statue of André-Modeste Grétry, a famous Liégeois composer (whose house in Outremeuse is open to the public) stands in front of the opera house: an urn containing his heart sits within the pedestal.

Next, turn your attention to the streets and monuments of the Île neighbourhood.

★ **Église Saint-Denis** (map B1, **62**): place Saint-Denis. Open 9am–noon and 1.30–5pm during the week; 9–10am Sunday. One of the oldest churches in the city, Saint-Denis was founded by Bishop Notger towards the end of the 10th century. Several styles can be identified: the narthex and nave are Romanesque, the choir is Gothic and the interior of the narthex, which has been repainted in yellow, is 18th-century baroque. Look out for the rococo stucco in the side chapels, the handsome organ platform (1589) and, in the right-hand transept, the Gothic altarpiece, which has a wonderful, heavily peopled Passion scene. There are several 16th-century works by

Lambert Lombard in the aisles, including an *Ecce Homo* and *Baptême du Christ*.

★ **Rue Léopold** (map B1-C1): laid out and built in 1875 according to the tradition established in Paris by Baron Haussmann, this thoroughfare slices through the old Madeleine neighbourhood. Georges Simenon was born at No. 24, in a house above an old milliner's, on Friday, 13 February, 1903, at 10 minutes past midnight. His superstitious mother preferred to say that he had been born at 11.30pm. Baby Georges spent very little time here – the owners said his pram took up too much hallway space – so the Simenons moved out. They moved again in April 1905, this time across the river to the Outremeuse district.

★ The area between rue Léopold and rue de la Régence (map B1-C1), is a seedy neighbourhood where sex shops and girls are displayed in neon-lit windows (in particular along rues Florimont, Champion and de l'Agneau). The main reason to come here is to stroll down rue du Carré (it leads to rue Souverain-Pont), which is the narrowest street in Liège. In the early 20th century, it was lined with butcher's and tripe butcher's shops. Take the pont des Arches and continue towards Outremeuse.

Outremeuse

Beyond the Meuse, or 'Djus-d'là-Moûse' as they say in the local Walloon dialect, lies an area that to many is the home of the spirit of Liège. This is the birthplace of Tchantches, who perfectly represents the spirit of the city. Two 'cultural institutions', the République libre d'Outremeuse and the Commune libre de Saint-Pholien encapsulate the rebellious, independent-minded nature of the people of Outremeuse. The former represents the parish of Saint-Nicolas and its weavers, the latter the parish of Saint-Pholien and its tanners. In the words of Jean-Denys Boussard, Saint-Pholien's dynamic mayor, it is a matter of honour for the people of Outremeuse to defend their district and to preserve the Walloon language and the cultural traditions of Liège. There's a strong parochial feeling among them, which verges on the hostile. When people from Outremeuse cross over to the left bank, they say that they are 'going to town'. In two books, *Je me souviens* ('I Remember') and *Pedigree,* Georges Simenon describes how his grandmother referred to his mother as 'that foreign woman who's not from Outremeuse'.

The neighbourhood isn't exactly beautiful. Architecturally, it's a jumble of styles, mainly late-19th-century buildings and banal 20th-century tower blocks. Much has also disappeared, thanks in part to insensitive property developers. The canals and reaches of the Meuse where the tanners once worked have been filled in, and there are virtually no traces of their activity. Most of the picturesque roads and bridges are concentrated between Saint-Pholien and rue Puits-en-Sock. In the north, blasts of cold air sweep down boulevard de la Constitution, a former arm of the Meuse. This area is also home to the unattractive Fonck barracks, the fire station, the abandoned and partly demolished Bavière hospital and numerous wastelands, which are waiting for the developers to move in. One of the more attractive squares in Outremeuse is place du Congrès, which is surrounded by appealing residential streets. Wherever you go, though, there are cafés on virtually every street corner, proof of a resilient social spirit that can't be easily stamped out. Outremeuse is not suited to tourists rushed off their feet, but it's a great neighbourhood if you've got time to dawdle and home in on unusual architectural details, like the *potales* (street-corner shrines), or listen out for the wonderful Walloon dialect as you stroll down a back street or pause for refreshment in one of the many bars.

You can also explore Georges Simenon's haunts. 'We get most of our attributes during our childhood and adolescence,' he once wrote. 'At the age of 70, I still act, think and behave like a child of Outremeuse'. Later, when it became clear that many of his urban descriptions bore a strong resemblance to Outremeuse, he said: 'You'll find Liège all over my novels, even when the setting is Nantes or Charleroi.' *Le Pont des Arches* is the title of Simenon's first novel, written when he was just 16 and called himself 'Georges Sim'. The *passerelle* that leads to boulevard Saucy also appears in his writing: 'Acting as a boundary between the suburb and the centre of the city is the large wooden bridge called la Passerelle. It's shorter and better known than the Pont des Arches. La Passerelle somehow belongs to the inhabitants of Outremeuse; you certainly don't need to be wearing a hat to cross it.'

★ The **statue of Tchantchès**, the eternal symbol of Liège, stands at the corner of Surlet and boulevard Saucy (map C2). From here, take boulevard de l'Est and take a look at the row of 19th-century bourgeois town houses and the attractive facade of the Hôtel Simenon.

★ **Église Saint-Pholien** (map C1, **63**): boulevard de la Constitution 1. Rebuilt at the beginning of the 20th century to prevent it from collapsing, this is not an especially attractive church – the interior is a kitsch neo-Gothic affair – but it's something of a beacon for the Commune libre. The church provided the setting for the first Maigret novel, *Le Pendu de Saint-Pholien*: the plot was inspired by the death of one of Simenon's friends, Joseph Kleine, who was found hanged one morning from the handle of the right-hand entrance to the church. Kleine was a member of 'Caque', a secret society whose members, including Simenon himself, met to drink and to talk philosophy, art and literature into the small hours.

★ **Rue des Écoliers** (map C1, **63**): via impasse de la Houpe. This street doubles as the 'rue du Pot-au-Noir' in *Le Pendu de Saint-Pholien*. The Caque group used to meet on the first floor of No. 13, which was then an ironmonger's. Its members included artists, designers, young writers, poets and musicians, among them the painter August Mambour. It was an odd neo-Romantic set-up, with public readings of Nietzche's writings, poems by Laforgue and sacred Indian texts. Created in 1919, the group disbanded after Kleine's death in 1922.

★ **Boulevard de la Constitution** (map C1-D1): don't miss the Friday-morning antiques market that takes place here (*see* 'Markets and flea markets'). On the right, you'll see the Fonck barracks, where Simenon did most of his military service in 1922. The former Bavière hospital stands at the main crossroads. Today the chapel, along with the entrance, is one of the few surviving sections of the original building.

★ If you're on the trail of Georges Simenon, here are a few of his former homes: from 1905–11, he lived at rue Georges-Simenon 25 (formerly rue Pasteur), now a splendid new youth hostel; from 1911–17, at rue de la Loi 53; and from 1919–22, at rue de l'Enseignement 29, by which time he was already a young reporter on the *Gazette de Liège*, soon to head off to Paris.

On place du Congrès, there's a bust of the writer on the site where, as a small boy, he used to come and play. When he was 12, he used to stretch out on a bench here and watch the stars.

★ **Église Saint-Nicolas** (map C2, **64**): rue Fosse-aux-Raines. Open 9.30am–noon and 6–7pm, Sunday 10.30am–12.30pm. You're now in the République libre d'Outremeuse (the boundary with Saint-Pholien no longer exists). This is the oldest religious building in the area, built in 1710 and with a baroque facade. The furnishings inside are 18th-century. On the right, under glass, there's an early-16th-century wooden crucifix. An image of St Anthony graces the pulpit, while the saints of the Premonstratensians are represented in the choir. You can see the famous 'black Virgin', who's wheeled in for Assumption Day, in the transept on the left.

★ **Rue des Récollets**, one of the most characteristic Outremeuse streets, is directly opposite the church. It's lined with small, low houses, and looks pretty much as it did in Simenon's day, when his mother, Henriette, used to complain about dirty children from poor families playing in the street – not that you'll see many children playing here today.

★ **Maison de Grétry** (map C2, **65**): rue des Récollets 34 ☎ (04) 343 1610. Open Tuesday and Friday 2–6pm and Saturday 10am–noon (also by appointment). Admission: 60BEF. This half-timbered 18th-century house, once the residence of the great comic-opera composer, is now a museum. During one of his rare visits to Liège in 1952 (when he was accepted into the Académie Royale), Simenon was quite impressed by it: 'It still has greenish, bulls'-eye windows with leaded lights,' he wrote in his memoirs. 'It's the sort of house you find in chiaroscuro by the Flemish Masters . . . the sort of house I should have liked . . .'. It's quite charming inside, and still feels lived in. Everything's more or less as it was, including the period furniture and the composer's piano. Memorabilia and manuscripts are on display on the ground and first floors. Ask to see the facade that looks onto the courtyard, complete with an elegant, half-timbered turret enclosing a staircase.

★ **Rue Puits-en-Sock**: this is the shop-lined high street of the Outremeuse district, with plenty of narrow little roads running parallel, and it's well worth exploring. Simenon's father, Désiré, was born here, and his mother, Henriette, could still be spotted running about doing the shopping here in the 1960s. Chrétien, his grandfather, had a hat shop at No. 58, while Désiré, who worked at Guillemins, used to go and kiss his father 'good morning' every day. Little Georges visited his grandfather on Sundays. In 1918, a bit of a drama took place at the Simenons: Désiré was very ill, and Henriette asked Georges to drop his studies and help fend for the family. Simenon became an apprentice cake-maker, working at the *pâtisserie* Saint-Gérard, on the corner of Puits-en-Sock and Jean-d'Outremeuse, but his career only lasted a fortnight. He was too bookish, and ended up working as a salesman for a bookshop in the centre of town. Take a look at rue Porte-aux-Oies, a picturesque little street ending in an *arvô* (vaulted passage).

★ **En Roture** (map C2): level with rue Puits-en-Sock 44, there's another *arvô* leading to En Roture, which a few decades back was one of the most proletarian streets in the area. There's a bizarre double staggered gate at the entrance, known locally as the 'lion's cage', which was designed to stop over-enthusiastic children from rushing out of this small street. It probably saved more than one youngster from being knocked down by a passing tram. You can also see a figure of Christ and a fine *potale*. Traditional Liégeois puppet shows took place here until the 1920s. Today, En Roture is a hot spot for local nightlife, and there are numerous restaurants here and in the surrounding maze of tiny streets.

★ **Musée Tchantchès** (map C2, **66**): rue Surlet 56. ☎ (04) 342 7575. Open Tuesday and Thursday 2–4pm. Closed in July. Admission: 40BEF. The headquarters of the République libre d'Outremeuse contains an array of memorabilia about the local hero, including photographs, paintings, certificates and a superb collection of puppets. Every year, the museum, which once harboured the Théâtre Royal Ancien Impérial d'En Roture and its 129 string puppets, acquires more characters and costumes every year. Puppet shows take place on Wednesday afternoon and Sunday morning. The next-door **Maison des Métiers d'Art** hosts temporary exhibitions.

★ **Aquarium**, **Musée de Zoologie de l'université** and **Maison des Sciences** (map C2, 67): quai Van Beneden 22. ☎ (04) 366 5000. Open Monday to Friday 9am–5pm; also weekends from 10.30am to 6pm in the Easter holidays, July and August, and on public holidays. Admission: 150BEF, with student discounts. Whatever your age, you're bound to find something to interest you here, starting with the weird hermaphroditic figures in the huge mural by Paul Delvaux, a variation on the Genesis story. The Dubuisson Aquarium consists of several dozen pools with imitation natural environments that are home to 250 species from warm and cold seas; there's even a reproduction of a Walloon river. Don't miss the sharks, tropical fish (surgeons, angels, butterflies, morays and groupers, including one with spotted fins known as 'Grace Kelly'). There are turtles and crocodiles in the reptile house, and you'll find a fine display of madrepores (a reef-building tropical coral) from the coral reef in the Musée de Zoologie. Numerous specimens, including a dodo from the Mauritius Islands and a Tasmanian devil, both extinct today, are on show in the main hall, together with skeletons of large animals, such as a 20-metre-long (66-foot) whale.

Finally, budding young scientists are encouraged to perform experiments at the **Maison des Sciences**. Visitors can watch demonstrations of electric, optical and mechanical phenomena, including holograms of terrifying vampires and werewolves, Faraday's cage, Zénobe Gramme's dynamo (a Belgian invention), an Edison phonogram, the first TV sets and a spectacular experiment that shows the effects of vibration on suspension bridges. There's also a mineralogy department.

★ **Musée d'Art moderne et contemporain** (map C4, 68): parc de la Boverie 3, south of Outremeuse in a large park. ☎ (04) 343 0403. Open 1–6pm, Sunday 11am–4.30pm. Closed Monday. Admission: 100BEF. An oddly proportioned building, with a vast hall featuring stained-glass windows and white-and-gilt Corinthian pillars, built for the Liège World Fair in 1905 and renovated in 1993. The museum owes much of its excellent, largely 20th-century collection to the Nazi policy of removing 'degenerate art' from galleries: in 1938, a group of philanthropists from Liège snapped up works by Gauguin, Ensor, Picasso, Kokoschka and Chagall while attending an auction in Switzerland.

– The collection's highlights include Signac's *Château de Comblat*, *Bassin du Commerce* by Monet (as always, the morning light is beautifully rendered), *Woman in White* by Théo Van Rysselberghe, James Ensor's *Death Masks*, *Stripped Lights* and *Brussels Town Hall* (a beautiful cityscape) and *Le Sorcier d'Hiva-Hoa*, a minor Gauguin. Look out for an outstanding series by Boudin, small works by André Derain and Raoul Dufy, drawings by Matisse and Toulouse-Lautrec, a series of paintings by Corot and *Monte Carlo*, an unusual painting by Oskar Kokoschka. There are also works by Nicolas de Staël, Serge Poliakoff, Tapiès, Pierre Alechinsky, Hans Arp, Fernand Léger, Vasarely, Karel Appel and Kees Van Dongen.

– Finally, pause in front of several Symbolist works by Khnopff, especially *Isolation,* a splendid vaporous nude in pastels and charcoal, and his ravishing *Study of Women* (red chalk on paper).

– **Cabinet des estampes**: don't miss the fine displays of engravings on the lower ground floor. Same opening hours as the museum. ☎ (04) 342 3923. Admission: 100BEF. This venue hosts wonderful temporary exhibitions drawn from a collection of 26,000 works – enough for several decades' worth of shows.

★ **Parc de la Boverie** (map B-C4): a favourite spot for a quiet stroll, this park is laid out with French-style gardens, rose gardens, paths, pools and romantic little bridges. Works by various Walloon sculptors are scattered around the park, including the powerful *Faune mordu*. It's hard now to believe that, in 1905, this piece so scandalized the good people of Liège that it was withdrawn from the list of works accepted for display at the World Fair. Today, its soft eroticism is nothing more than vaguely entertaining.

★ **Maison de la Métallurgie** (map C3, **69**): boulevard Raymond-Poincaré 17, on the Route du Feu trail (iron trail). ☎ (04) 342 6563. Open 9am–5pm, weekends 2–6pm except between November and mid-March. Admission: 200 BEF. Located in an old factory, this museum is devoted to metal-working, once one of the most important activities in Liège. It contains a reconstruction of a 17th-century wooden coal oven and a forge with enormous bellows and anvil. A host of tools, firebacks and other instruments are also on display, as well as a peculiar clock powered by a battery created by Alessandro Volta. There's a room devoted to the modern steel industry, with different types of iron minerals, photographs and explanatory texts. The approach is a bit didactic, but there's some light relief in the bath specially made for Napoleon.

★ **Musée des Transports en commun** (Public Transport Museum, map C4, **73**): Richard-Heintz 9. ☎ (04) 361 9111. Open Monday to Friday 10am–noon and 2–5pm, weekends 2–6pm. Closed December to the end of February. Admission: 100BEF. Audio guide available. For those who like this sort of thing, this vast shed contains freshly painted old trams with polished wooden seats, and gives you a good picture of the history of transport in Liège. You can also watch some old films.

A FEW WALKS OFF THE BEATEN TRACK

For dedicated urban explorers who can spare the time, here are a few unusual tips for fascinating walks about town.

The Pierreuse District

★ This is the upper town (map B1), an old district where you need to be sensitive to your surroundings to appreciate its picturesque qualities. It used to be home to marginalized groups, such as recent immigrants, workers and craftsmen. It has retained some of that tradition today, in the form of political posters, charity shops for the developing world and environmental groups.

★ **Rue Pierreuse** starts behind the Palais des Princes-Évêques and leads to rue Hors-Château, from where it meanders up to the citadel – it's a tough climb. Places like Casa Nicaragua and the Cercle Culturel Italien betray the international character of the neighbourhood, which is sprinkled with low, brick 18th- and 19th-century buildings. Look out for the beaten copper sign, dated 1757, at No. 71, and the large figure of Christ at the crossroads of the cobbled rue Volière (once home to a cabaret) and cour des Minimes. On rue Volière itself, there's a 17th-century house with large mullioned windows at Nos. 29–31 and the delightful Saint-Roch chapel, with alternating bricks and bands of stone at the bend in the road. The whole neighbourhood has the atmosphere of a peaceful village.

– Cour des Minimes leads to the Tour des Vieux-Joncs. There's a small door on the right-hand side (open to the public 9am–6pm). The alley on the left-hand side has retained its primitive, medieval look, with idiosyncratic twists and turns, and houses with high walls and secret gardens. It seems a million miles from Liège. The Éscalier du Pery leads back to the Montagne de Bueren.

Continue along rue Pierreuse and, in an alcove on the right, you'll see a painted cross, Li grand bon Diu d'Piéreuse, which has been protecting the locals for several centuries.

Mont Saint-Martin

★ This is the **Publemont**, the oldest inhabited hill in Liège. It starts from Haute-Sauvenière (place de la République-Française). Behind the Église Saint-Martin is one of the city's most delightful neighbourhoods.

Starting from rue Haute-Sauvenière (map B1), look right and you'll see the Hôtel de Bocholtz, a beautifully restored 16th-century canonical house with Italian Renaissance and Mosan influences.

The first stop is Église Sainte-Croix: open 8am–6pm. It was founded by Bishop Notger in 979, but virtually nothing of the original building remains. The tower is 12th-century, while the choir and aisles are 14th-century. It's the only Belgian church with a Romanesque, as opposed to a Gothic, apse, and there are three aisles of the same height inside. The composer César Franck was baptized here in 1822. There's a heavy brass door in the nave on the right, dated 1700, that leads to the cloister, and a Renaissance-style mausoleum made of black Theux marble beneath the central window. In front are two statues by Jean del Cour, and a delightful 18th-century brass door. The best painting is Bertholet Flemale's 17th-century L'Invention de la Sainte-Croix.

In the sacristy, the Treasury contains two masterpieces: the 8th-century key of St Hubert and the astonishing 12th-century reliquary of the True Cross.

Two angels holding the relics stand in the middle and the 12 apostles, in embossed and carved gilt copper, stand at the sides. If you want to see the Treasury, contact the sacristan (in the cloister behind the chevet).

★ **Rue Saint-Pierre** (map B1): a cul-de-sac. No. 15 is the 16th-century Hôtel Torrentius, while No. 13 is the birthplace of César Franck. There's a delightful 'courtyard-road' by the chevet of Sainte-Croix. One of the houses in the cloister has two wonderful ribbed entrances. On the corner is the little church of Saint-Nicolas-aux-Mouches (not much more than a chapel). Today, it's a private house.

Leading to the Basilique Saint-Martin, rue Mont-Saint-Martin (map A-B1) has a fine 16th-century house with Flemish step gabling, the Hôtel de Selys-Longchamps, at No. 9. There are other interesting buildings all the way up to the basilica, while No. 23 has a pretty cobbled courtyard, complete with fountain and stone water nymphs.

★ **Basilique Saint-Martin** (map A1, **70**): at the end of rue Saint-Martin. ☎ (04) 223 2703. Open by appointment only. An outstanding piece of architecture – indeed, the basilica was once close to becoming the city's cathedral. The Cathédrale St Lambert was often the victim of flooding, so Notger's predecessor decided to build one on a hill. His plans foundered, however, on account of the opposition of the locals, who were determined to keep the cathedral on the site of St Lambert's martyrdom. The people revolted, sacked the bishop's residence, drank his wine and transformed the future Cathédrale St Lambert into the collegiate church Saint-Martin. Today, the whole thing has been restored.

Inside, you can see that the basilica is built in the traditional cross shape. It's not as big as Saint-Jacques (Place Saint-Jacques) or Saint-Paul (Place Saint-Paul), and it's squatter, but it still feels pretty monumental. The vaulting is in red brick, with colossal pillars, half sandstone, half limestone. Look up at the fine-ribbed vaulting over the choir. Dazzlingly colourful 16th-century stained-glass windows tell the story of the Virgin, and the carved oak pulpit is 18th-century. There's a beautiful 16th-century crowned and painted wooden statue of the Virgin Mary, while a dozen marble medallions by the sculptor Jean del Cour can be seen in the chapel of the Holy Sacrament. More recently, the church saw the funerals of Julie and Mélissa, two young girls who died in the basement of the alleged paedophile Marc Dutroux in 1996. Dutroux is currently awaiting trial for their murders, and for the killing of two other girls.

★ As you leave Saint-Martin, turn down degrés des Tisserands and cross rue Saint-Séverin to rue des Remparts. It's an old covered way, lined with ivy- or vine-covered houses with walled gardens, that meanders in romantic fashion towards place Hocheporte. Rue Hocheporte is home to some beautiful 17th- and 18th-century houses. Further up, you come to the picturesque, cobbled rue Naimette, with high walls and buttresses. The whole area has a delightfully rural feel.

Turn down boulevard de la Sauvenière via escalier des Bégards. It's archaeologically interesting (you can see the original ramparts), but local squatters have given the area a bit of a bad name.

MARKETS

– **Brocante d'Outremeuse** (Antiques Fair, map C1, **71**): every Friday morning, on boulevard de la Constitution. Success has led to its expansion, and it now goes right the way down to the old Bavière hospital. Dedicated antiques-hunters arrive at 7am to grab the best bargains. There's plenty of atmosphere in the nearby bars.

– **Marché de la Batte** (map C1, **72**): quai de la Batte (level with pont des Arches), every Sunday morning. A huge market, including antiques, with a huge crowd to match. Afterwards, everyone piles into the surrounding cafés and restaurants.

– **Petites Puces de Saint-Gilles** (Flea market, map A3): Saturday, 8am– 1pm. At the end of rue Saint-Gilles, on the other side of the A602. Bargains guaranteed.

FESTIVALS

– **Assumption of the Virgin, 15 August**: in Outremeuse. One of the liveliest festivals in Liège, this colourful three-day cultural event is organized by the République Libre d'Outremeuse.

14 August sees the erection of a massive metal structure representing the emblems of the old trades. Six metres (20 feet) high, it's decorated with flowers. In the afternoon, there's music, singing and Walloon folk dancing. Around 6pm, cannon are fired, and festivities ends with dancing until 2am in En Roture, rue Grande-Bêche. The weekend before the big day, there's an antiques market on place Del Cour.

15 August: the procession of the Black Virgin of Outremeuse, which begins at Église Sint-Nicolas (rue Fosse-aux-Raines), and snakes through rue Jean-d'Outremeuse and place Del Cour. There's Mass with a sermon in Walloon, traditional greasy-pole climbing, an exhibition of puppets at the Musée Tchantchès and a procession of giants. A puppet show takes place on Place de l'Yser at 2pm. The festival winds up with dancing in rue Grande-Bêche and on place Del Cour.

16 August: at 5pm, dancing in En Roture.

– **Christmas**: 'Market of the Star' in Outremeuse. A traditional crib with live animals moves around the district, stopping in front of the *potales* (street shrines) and leaving place Sainte-Barbe at 10pm. Try the little pancakes (*bouquètes*) and traditional Christmas sausage. The restaurants serve rabbit *à la liégeoise* (with prunes). Unlike in most parts of Europe, locals here go out instead of sitting at home. The Musée Tchantchès hosts a Nativity play on 24 and 25 December at about 8pm (rue Surlet 56).

– **Festival de Jazz de Liège**: end of April each year at the Palais des Congrès.

– **Saint-Pholien parish fête**: fourth Sunday in June. Great atmosphere, with dancing around the maypole.

– **14 July**: Liège has a republican tradition, so it celebrates Bastille Day with as much gusto as the French.

THEATRE

– **Théâtre des marionnettes de Liège** (Liège Puppet Theatre): Musée Tchantchès, rue Surlet 56. ☎ (04) 342 7575. Open Tuesday to Thursday 2–4pm. Shows at the Musée de la Vie wallonne, Wednesday at 2.30pm and Sunday at 10.30am. The stories are on historical themes, such as the Song of Roland.

WHAT TO SEE IN THE AREA

★ **La route du Feu**: quai Louva 21, Ougrée 4201. ☎ (04) 338 3830. This tourist trail takes you to the principal industrial-heritage sites in the Meuse-Vesdre basin, from the first flint and stone sparks of the earliest inhabitants of Ramioul to the blast furnaces that stand on the banks of the Meuse. En route, you can visit the coal mines of Blegny, explore the worlds of weavers and of glass-blowers at Val Saint-Lambert, see a centre for steam-driven machines and tour the machine collections of the Musée de la Métallurgie. The tour winds up at the Musée d'Armes and the Musée du Verre. You can buy a combined ticket to two sites of your choice for 500BEF (it's not much of a discount, but at least it saves you queuing). Phone first to book a place on an organized tour (the only way to see the Cockerill Sambre blast furnace and the TGV centre at Seraing).

★ **Préhistosite et la grotte de Ramioul** (Prehistoric site and caves): rue de la Grotte 128, Ivoz-Ramet. ☎ (04) 275 4975. Take bus No. 9 from the centre of Liège. Open 1.30–6.30pm at the weekend, on public holidays and from Easter to the beginning of November; every day during the school holidays; the rest of the year by appointment only. Admission: 290BEF, with child discounts. On the Route du Feu. The title of the guided tour, which starts at 2pm, translates as 'Unleash the primitive within you'. (Perhaps best to keep the kids in the dark on this one.) The prehistoric site focuses on the life of early man, with practical demonstrations of the great inventions of prehistory by enthusiastic members of staff. You can learn how to shape flint to make a tool; how to make a fire by setting dried mushrooms alight with marcasite, and how to make clothes with rudimentary sewing equipment. There's a replica of a prehistoric village, where you can learn how to build a hut, make a rope, throw a pot and so on. Suitably stirred kids can polish stones and learn to hurl spears. You will also be initiated into the secrets of Cro-Magnon man's cooking, with reindeer meat, bison and snails mainstays of the menu. Next come three floors of caves, with beautiful crystallized formations on the upper level. You will learn everything you ever wanted to know about the life of cave animals. All in all, this museum makes for a great, if disorienting, experience and might even make you question the meaning of modern-day life and its values.

★ **Manufacture de cristaux du Val Saint-Lambert**: rue du Val 245, Seraing 4100. ☎ (04) 330 3620. Take bus No. 9. Château: from April to September, open 10am–5pm; otherwise weekends and public holidays only. Admission: 200BEF. Part of the Route du Feu. This old Cistercian abbey was turned into a glassworks after the French Revolution. A competent but not hugely exciting multimedia display tells you more than you need to know about the history of the site, offers a virtual-reality look at a child's apprenticeship at a glassworks and chronicles the history of glass-making from the Babylonians and Ancient Rome to the master glaziers of cathedral windows. There's also a glass-blowers' workshop, where you can watch master craftsmen cutting and engraving glass. Buy a combined ticket (350 BEF) for both the glass works and the museum so you can look at some of the finest pieces produced by the factory and explore the inevitable souvenir shop.

✖ Refreshments are available in the cafeteria *La Manufacture*.

★ **Herstal**: famous for manufacturing arms and mopeds. The Musée communal is at place Licour, 25, Herstal 4040. ☎ (04) 240 6497. Open Wednesday and Saturday 2–4pm, and Sunday 10am–noon. Closed in July. To get there, take the Liège metro. It's an old house with a traditional bourgeois interior, and contains an exhibition on local folklore, archaeology and traditional trades.

Herve

Herve, which lies to the north and the east of Liège, is a lush, green region of woods and fields. Despite the encroachments of the city, there's still no shortage of villages that have kept their original character, including Soiron. Fourons/Voeren, the Dutch-speaking enclave that's part of Limburg (*see* 'Limburg' chapter), is in the far north.

BLEGNY MINE

This coal mine, 20 miles northeast of Liège, used to be one of the most important in Belgium. It was also the last in this area to close, in 1980, and is now a fascinating industrial museum. The mine was worked for centuries, first on the surface and then, in the 19th century, underground. It had eight levels, was 530 metres (1,750 feet) deep and employed 650 people at the peak of its production. Up to 1,000 tonnes of coal were extracted every day. You can visit the mine as well as the museum, which are both on the Route du Feu. Admission: 300BEF, with reductions for senior citizens and children. Guided visits take place in French, Dutch and German but are also available upon request in English,

PRACTICAL INFORMATION

– **Getting there**: from Liège (place Saint-Lambert), bus No. 67 to Trembleur. ☎ (04) 387 4333.

– **Opening hours**: mine open 10am–4.30pm (last tour departure) on weekends and public holidays from March to the end of November; also on weekdays from the beginning of May to mid-September and from the end of October to early November. ☎ (04) 387 4333. Fax: (04) 387 5850. Admission: 290BEF.

– **Musée du Puits-Marie**: same dates as the mine, but open 11am–6pm.

– **Length of tours**: 1 hour 30 minutes for the mine, and about the same for the museum. Single or combined tickets available.

– **Train rides**: weekends and public holidays from April to September. Every day during the Easter holidays, July and August. Departure times 2.30pm, 3.30pm and 4.30pm.

– **Musée rural Mortroux**: next door to the mine. Admission included on the mine ticket.

TOUR OF THE MINE

The best thing about this tour is that the guides themselves are retired miners who really know their stuff. They give you a real sense of what life in the mines was like.

– There's a film about the history of the mine.

– You can tour the surface to see the different means of transport used.

Descend in a traditional mine cage to 30 metres (nearly 100 feet) below ground, and visit a gallery where the machinery is still functioning. You'll learn the secrets of extracting coal, the buttressing of the galleries and the development of tools and techniques through the ages. You then descend another 60 metres (200 feet), where you will learn about the work of the miners, the harsh conditions that they endured – and the fact that silicosis (lung disease caused by inhaling dust from the mine) was recognized as an industrial disease only in 1964.

Sunday outings: 2 hour 30 minute tours through the area on the local Berwine train. Every Sunday from Easter to the end of August at 2.30pm. Price: 250BEF. Reductions available.

– **Fêtes de la Mine**: beginning of August.

MUSEUM TOURS

★ **Musée du Puits-Marie**: in one of the oldest mining buildings in Belgium (1816), this museum has more than 15 themed rooms. You can learn about the surface equipment used in the 19th and 20th centuries, as well as the techniques and processes of underground work in modern mines.

★ **Musée rural Mortroux:** chemin du Trimbleu 3, in the coaching inn at Berwinne. ☎ (04) 376 6297. Open every day from Easter to mid-September 11am–7pm, also weekends in March, October and November. Admission: 60BEF. This museum is devoted to regional rural life and includes an exhibition on the manufacture of traditional produce, such as the famous Herve cheese, *sirop de Liège*, butter and the like. You can also hire bikes here, or take a signposted walk.

★ **Recette and Triage-lavoir** (Income, Sorting and Sifting): this exhaustive history of coal, from the moment of its extraction to the finished product, winds up a visit to the mine. You can see where the wagons bearing the raw material arrived, and where slag was transferred to the slag heap. The sorting, sifting and stocking of the raw material were entirely automated processes. Guided visits take place in French, Dutch and German.

WHERE TO EAT IN THE AREA

✗ Cafeterias of the Mine and the Musée rural Mortroux: in the latter, you can try some regional specialities.

☆☆☆ Expensive

✗ **Jardins de Caroline**: rue Saivelette 8 Housse, 4671 Liège. ☎ (04) 387-42-11. Closed Monday, Tuesday and some holidays. Booking recommended. Set menus from 1,050BEF. A big, attractive restaurant with a rustic feel. The set menus are quite expensive, but the cheapest offers good value. The fine French cuisine includes excellent bass, turbot, prawns and crayfish stew, Peking duck, crispy shellfish, *roulade* of young rabbit and prawns, roast kangaroo with peppers and duck. There are outdoor tables in fine weather.

What to See in the Area

MORTIER

A few miles from Blegny, this village has two little museums that are well worth a visit.

★ **Musée de la Bouteille** (Bottle Museum): rue du Village 22. ☎ (04) 387 6742. Jacques Martin has been collecting old bottles for several years. He's accumulated 5,000, most of which are beer bottles, as well as a hoard of glasses by famous brand names, metal and porcelain tops, openers, cigarette-lighters, keyrings and the like. If you've a soft spot for beer and the bizarre, you'll love it. It's not hard to find – the facade is covered in enamel advertising signs.

★ **Musée de la Fourche** (Fork Museum): ☎ (04) 387-42-29. An agricultural museum with a large collection of forks (the garden, not the table, type), as well as tools for making hay and butter, threshing machines and other domestic objects.

DALHEM

A village that will intrigue sociologists and anyone interested in Belgium's rural traditions. Since time immemorial, Dalhem has been divided into two clans, the Reds and the Blues, each with its own cafés, festivals and so on. Nobody knows how this division, which is handed down from father to son, came about, but it certainly has nothing to do with class or politics. There was a time when it was fairly common for young people of either clan to end up fighting after a dance. You won't find much of the old antagonism today, however. Young people have got plenty of other things on their minds.

Good times to come to Dalhem include:

– June, for the Festival of Fanfares, when both clans honour the village's patron saint, St Louis. Great atmosphere.

– the first weekend in August, when Dalhem is swamped by thousands of merry-makers who come for the *Festival international des Bandas*. The atmosphere is crazy.

– the second Tuesday in October, when cacophonous music is accompanied by barrels of *peket* (gin).

VISÉ   17,000 inhabitants

Visé, 18 kilometres (11 miles) from Liège and a stone's throw from the Dutch border, has seen more than its fair share of wars. It was razed to the ground by Charles the Bold, had its ramparts knocked down by Louis XIV, who set up headquarters here when he laid siege to Maastricht, and was burned down in 1914 by the Germans. But it's worth a visit to see the splendid reliquary of St Hadelin and the small guild museums, and to sample the local speciality, goose.

USEFUL ADDRESS

☎ **Tourist office**: rue des Béguines 7. ☎ (04) 379 6263. Open Monday to Friday 10am–noon and 1.30–4.30pm.

WHAT TO SEE

★ **Collégiale de Saint-Martin**: place de la Collégiale. Only the 16th-century choir survived the fire of 1914. Look out for the 12th-century St Hadelin reliquary – the workmanship of the repoussé silver is superb.

★ **Musées des Guildes**: Visé continues the tradition of the guilds, which played a vital role in defending the liberties of its people. You can learn all about the history of the guilds and see memorabilia, archives, old weapons and much more at the following museums. Telephone in advance to arrange a visiting time.

– **Musée de la Guilde royale des Anciens Arbalétriers** (Museum of the Royal Guild of Old Crossbowmen): rue Haute 44. ☎ (04) 379 1434. Open by appointment only. Founded in 1310 this is the oldest guild in Visé. They hold a festival on the Sunday before 23 April (St Georges' Day), with a solemn mass followed by lots of jubilation and a procession.

– **Musée de la Guilde royale des Anciens Arquebusiers** (Museum of the Royal Guild of Old Arquebusiers): rue Haute 11. ☎ (04) 379 1264. Admission free. Open Sundays, May-September 11am–1pm. Their festival takes place on the last Sunday in June, with a traditional procession and firearm salutes.

– **Musée de la Guilde royale des Francs Arquebusiers** (Museum of the Royal Guild of Free Arquebusiers): rue Dodemont 3. ☎ (04) 379 5018. Open for their summer festival on the first Sunday in July, and also on the Sunday before 11 November.

– **Musée régional d'Archéologie et d'Histoire**: rue du Collège 31. ☎ (04) 379 0892. Open Wednesday and Saturday 3–5pm. Admission: 50BEF. Deals with the history of the town and displays the results of local digs.

In the Area

★ Intrepid explorers will be delighted to know that they're only a few minutes from the Dutch town of **Maastricht**, famous for its treaty, its carnival, its superb Romanesque churches and its lively pedestrianized streets. It's gone down in history as the place where the real d'Artagnan (of *Three Musketeers* fame) died while Louis XIV was besieging the town in 1673.

AUBEL

A little town in the Herve country, producing butter, *sirop* and cider. The Sunday and Tuesday markets attract people from nearby villages.

USEFUL ADDRESS

🔲 **Tourist Office**: Hôtel de Ville. ☎ (087) 687019. Pick up a *Route des Vergers* map, which details the area's beautiful hills and ancestral farms.

WHERE TO EAT AND DRINK

✕ ❢ **Le Vieil Aubel**: rue de Battice 2, Aubel 4880. Closed Monday evening and Wednesday. ☎ (087) 68-71-40. Main courses about 360BEF. Much cherished by the locals, this is a vintage 16th-century tavern with a suitably rustic interior. There's a selection of special beers to accompany such traditional dishes as rabbit with prunes and, in season, mussels and game.

WHAT TO SEE IN THE AREA

★ **Abbaye de Val-Dieu**: a few miles west of Aubel. ☎ (087) 687381. From Liège, take a train from Gare de Guillemins (line 37) and get off at Verviers, then take bus No. 38A (on Sundays). Founded in 1216, this Cistercian abbey is situated in a pretty valley, and its church and courtyard are open to the public. Most of the buildings date from the 17th and 18th centuries. The abbot's house was rebuilt in the 19th century, although part of the choir chevet, which has beautiful Renaissance stalls, was preserved. You can even get your car blessed here.

✕ There's a cafeteria (closed Tuesday) where you can sample good beers and local cheeses.

HERVE

The regional capital produces a famous, exceedingly pungent cheese. It's the smell, no doubt, that makes it so delicious.

🔲 **Tourist office:** rue de la Station 47, Herve 4650. ☎ (087) 679133. Open Monday to Friday 9am–noon and 2–4.30pm.

★ There are several 17th- and 18th-century houses in the centre of town, as well as the curious Six Fontaines, a huge public wash house built of brick in 1773. It consists of a gallery of arcades over six stone basins, each of which is fed by a spring.

– **Espace des Saveurs**: avenue Dewandre 36. Open every day in July and August from 2pm to 6.30pm. Admission: 50BEF for adults and 25BEF for children. An audiovisual display explains how cheese and apple and pear *sirop* are made.

– **Grand cavalcade**: Easter Monday.

CLERMONT-SUR-BERWINNE

This pretty village, east of Herve, has an unusual architectural coherence thanks to the 17th- and 18th-century houses that line the main square. None is more than two storeys high, and all have simple brick facades with elegantly aligned stone edging around the doors and windows. Note the Mosan Renaissance-style municipal building, complete with turret.

SOIRON

This is one of the most picturesque villages in rural Herve. It was an important crossroads in Roman times, with routes between Tongeren and Trier and Saint-Quentin and Cologne passing through. There's a beautiful architectural homogeneity, with old granite houses that surround the charming church nestling against the hillside.

WHERE TO EAT

✕ **Hostelry Vieux Soiron**: rue Principale 51, Soiron 4861. ☎ (087) 460355. Closed Monday and Tuesday. Set menus from 760BEF. Excellent traditional cooking served in a refined rustic setting where you're guaranteed a warm welcome. The menu features grilled meats and, in season, game, as well as fried eggs *Vieux Soiron* and Otero veal. Book if you want to come here for Sunday lunch.

WHAT TO SEE

★ **Église Saint-Roch**: a steeple and 11th-century defence tower. The interior decoration is extremely harmonious, with rich ornamentation on the tabernacle (showing Abraham's abortive sacrifice of Isaac) and delicately carved panels around the choir and on down the nave. The choir stalls, confessionals and benches are 18th-century, and are all the work of the same craftsman. In the choir, the central painting is an impressive copy of Raphael's *Transfiguration*.

★ In front of the church, on the right, are two houses built in Liège Renaissance style in 1663. The big corner house at No. 80 is the old village brewery. Other interesting buildings to look out for include the public drying area and the washing place.

★ The **Château de Soiron**, which is still inhabited (and not open to the public), lies on the edge of the village. The pediment on the facade is a good example of pure 18th-century Liégeois architecture.

In the Area

SOUMAGNE

Soumagne is five kilometres (three miles) west of Soiron, just off the Grande Route 563. Take a look at the Église Saint-Lambert, which has attractive furnishings spanning the 14th and 18th centuries and a beautiful ceiling (1710) adorned with the arms of local clerics and worthies.

★ **Petit Musée de la Vie populaire** (Museum of Ordinary Life): rue des Déportés 4, Soumagne 4630. ☎ (04) 377 1288. From early May to the end of September, open 9am–4pm, 3–6pm on Sunday and public holidays; otherwise Sunday and public holidays only, 3–5pm. Admission: 50BEF. Star exhibits are a replica of a 19th-century workman's house and a display of old craftsman's tools.

OLNE

South of Soumagne, this is another delightful village. There are fine sandstone houses scattered about the neighbouring hamlets. Towards Nessonvaux, the road meanders along a valley with lush, green hillsides on either side. You'll also pass several old mills.

WHERE TO EAT IN THE AREA

✖ **A Potche é Foure**: trou du Bois 30, Xhendelesse 4652. ☎ (087) 268139. Open for dinner from Thursday to Saturday and lunch on Sunday and public holidays; in July and August, open every day except Monday. Set menus from 690BEF. An intimate, friendly restaurant offering genuine local cuisine at good prices: fish soup, herring with apples, frogs' legs, crayfish, homemade meatballs, 'Abbey' steak (with Val-Dieu cheese), duck *confit* and various salads. There are mouthwatering seasonal dishes, and in fine weather you can eat on the terrace or in the sweeping garden.

WHAT TO SEE NEAR OLNE

★ **Chapelle Saint-Hadelin**: a couple of kilometres northwest of Olne, in the heart of the countryside, this cosy single-aisled chapel is well worth a quick detour. When the sun shines, it basks serenely in a halo of light. You can see the old boxes for the local squires, and benches engraved with the names of the families who used to come here. The last, dated 1750, is engraved with the name of the burgomaster. Outside, there's a lime tree that supposedly had the power to heal the sick if a nail was stuck into it. You can still see some imbedded in its trunk. One year, or so the story goes, there were so many nails in the tree that it was struck by lightning.

★ **Tancrémont**: south of Nessonvaux. The local chapel contains a magnificent piece of Mosan art: a 10th-century figure of Christ in painted wood. There's a wonderful serenity about his expression and pose, with none of the melancholy you often associate with such figures. Unusually, his body is wrapped in a vast tunic. In the café opposite, you can sample the local sweetbread tart and admire the amazing panorama.

★ **Banneux**: this was an important centre for the worship of the Virgin Mary, and it really took off in 1933 thanks to its canny ability to market religion. Its assets include a spring that works miracles and plenty of chapels dotted about among the pine woods, and it attracts an astonishing 400,000 pilgrims between May and October. Outside the tourist season, you can say here for next to nothing – and the surrounding countryside is beautiful. There's also a gypsy pilgrimage in July.

THEUX — 10,000 inhabitants

AROUND LIÈGE

This is a large, sprawling village in the Herve district, with some elegant buildings concentrated in the centre. Theux acquired the right to trade freely in the 15th century, and soon became an important centre for the metal and textile industries, as well as for the famous black Theux marble. For years, it was the headquarters of the Marquisat of Franchimont, the private property of the prince-bishops of Liège. In 1997, a gas explosion in the village killed two firemen.

USEFUL ADDRESS AND INFORMATION

Postcode: 4910.
🛈 **Tourist office**: rue chaussée 12.
☎ (087) 539212.

– **Train to Liège**: line 37.

WHERE TO EAT

☆☆☆ Expensive

✕ **Le Relais du Marquisat**: rue Hocheporte 13. ☎ (087) 542138. Closed Sunday evening, Monday and the second fortnight in July. The setting is elegant and the decor refined, with a fountain splashing outside, but this family-run restaurant has a relaxed atmosphere, with first-class service and not a hint of snobbery. The fine cuisine is French, and the gastronomic menu is excellent: try partridge supreme with cherries, bass fillet with green vegetables or plaice in cream and shrimp sauce, the 'mosaic' of asparagus with smoked salmon, monkfish braised in chicken juices or *waterzooï* of cod. There's a long wine list, which kicks off with an affordable Pinot Blanc and ends with a 1959 Château Lynch-Bages (Pauillac) for 9,900BEF.

WHAT TO SEE

★ **Place du Perron**: a harmonious collection of buildings dominated by an elegant 18th-century town hall with a double staircase and a fine wrought-iron balustrade. The distinctive old house next door is now an administrative building. The steps, complete with traditional pine cones, date from 1768. Other noteworthy buildings include No. 12 (the Générale de Banque, with mullioned windows, built in 1650), No. 22, with little wrought-iron balconies, and the typically 18th-century house at No. 42.

There are also some fine houses on the left as you head towards the church.

★ **Église Saint-Hermès et Alexandre**: open 10am–6pm (to 5pm from October to May). Shaped like a Romanesque *halle*, with three aisles and a stout keep-tower, this church is famous for its coffered ceiling, which is painted with characters and scenes from the life of Christ. Those over the nave are a bit dark, but they're easier to make out above the choir, where you can see the Nativity, the Three Kings, and the Flight into Egypt. There's a beautiful *Virgin and Child* in painted wood (1500) on the left. To the right of the choir is the Ascension of Christ, and to the left the Resurrection. The backs of the benches are engraved with the names of the families who sat there in the 17th and 18th centuries. There are funerary stones on the walls.

Nine signposted walks begin at the church.

FESTIVAL

– **Fête du Château**: every other year (odd numbers) on the third weekend in August. A medieval knees-up with period costumes and a variety of shows.

IN THE AREA

★ **Château de Franchimont**: a mile away from Theux. From April to the end of September, open every day from 9am–7pm; otherwise weekends only. ☎ (087) 741027. Admission: 60BEF. Guided tours on weekends in July and August, leaving at 10.30am and 2.30pm. If there's nobody in the kiosk at the entrance, buy your tickets in the cafeteria next door. This old fortified castle was once the seat of the prince-bishops. You can see the character-istic 16th-century 'shield', with two semicircular towers that frame a wall and protect the keep from gunfire. The top of the towers provided a splendid vantage point across two valleys, but its strategic importance diminished over the centuries. By the end of the 18th century, it was reduced to ruins, and the stones were used to construct other buildings.

Only a few steps remain of the spiral staircase that led to the covered way and the room at the top of the square tower, but there's a fine view of the two valleys. The central courtyard still contains remnants of rural buildings, including a spring, a kitchen and a communal oven.

Franchimont was the point of departure for 600 locals who made a brave attempt to rescue King Louis XI in 1468. The monarch had been taken prisoner by Charles the Bold, whose camp lay at the top of the Bueren mountain in Liège. The surprise raid took place at night, but the rescuers were outnumbered by the Burgundians, who massacred every one of them. Charles the Bold wreaked terrible vengeance, setting fire to Liège and Theux. This event is firmly anchored in the collective memory and history of Belgium.

★ **Polleur**: known for its stunning viaduct and for the congress held here between 1789 and 1791, which laid the foundations for the Declaration of the Rights of Man and put forward suggestions for a new democratic regime in the area of Liège.

There are a few half-timbered houses in the village, as well as a 15th-century church with a fine Romanesque tower and semi-spiralled roof.

– **Fête du Coucou**: every year (even numbers) on the last Sunday in July. Men from the village go hunting in the woods in search of the 'centaur woman' – all except the most recently married man, who is symbolically punished when the hunters return. It's really just an excuse for a lot of drinking and carousing.

★ **Sart**: an attractive little village with a square that's really square, a church, a small *perron* and stone houses. The village's oldest house, the doors and windows of which are enhanced with ornamental mouldings shaped like a brace, stands at the entrance to the square, which has a serene architectural unity.

★ **La Reid**: between Spa and Remouchamps, you'll find a game park covering 40 hectares (100 acres), where the wolf is the main theme of an educational display, and a charming village with three natural springs. There's a beautiful avenue of trees that form a sort of natural vault – it's 573 metres (600 yards) long, and makes for an attractive walk.

WHERE TO STAY AND EAT IN THE AREA

☆☆☆ Expensive

★ ✕ **Hôtel-Restaurant Le Menobu**: route du Menobu 546, La Reid 4910. ☎ and fax: (087) 376042. Doubles 2,200-3,200BEF. Set menus from 1,000BEF. This delightful hostelry is a member of Logis de Belgique. A haven of rural tranquillity, it offers very comfortable rooms and attractively presented French cuisine on a bright and airy veranda. There's also a respectable wine list. It's a favourite with newlyweds, who are always well looked after.

VERVIERS   55,000 inhabitants

A commercial and industrial town that rivalled Brussels in importance during the 18th century. In the Middle Ages, it was renowned for the quality of its cloth, but was better known for the treatment of wool by the 17th century. The Industrial Revolution helped Verviers become the most important wool centre in Wallonia. In the early 19th century, it was the first place on the continent to take up mechanized weaving, which was introduced into the area by the British engineer John Cockerill. The industry developed throughout the century, and after World War I, Verviers was the most flourishing wool manufacturing centre in Europe. Not surprisingly, it was also the site of workers' struggles for better conditions and salaries, and it consequently became one of the leading lights of European trade unionism.

Over the past 30 years, the crisis in the wool industry and cut-throat international competition have hit the town hard, and Verviers has found it difficult to adapt to other industries. The textile industry is not moribund, however, and there are still two firms in the wool business, one specializing in billiard-table covers, the other in cashmere.

Today, you can still see traces of the town's golden age. It's a pleasant place, with aristocratic houses, museums and small, picturesque neighbourhoods. The new Centre Touristique de la Laine et de la Mode (Wool and Fashion Centre) is a good introduction to the industry.

AROUND LIÈGE

Don't forget to sample La Ploquette, the local beer, which is fermented in the bottle.

USEFUL ADDRESSES AND INFORMATION

Postcode: 4800.

🚩 **Vesdre Tourist Office** (same site as the Centre Touristique de la Laine et de la Mode): rue de la Chapelle 24. ☎ (087) 307926. Fax: (087) 312095. Website: www.verviersima.be

🚩 **Provincial Tourist Office**: rue des Martyrs 1. ☎ (087) 350848. Fax: (087) 352857.

🚃 **Railway station**: ☎ (087) 331-614. Trains go to Liège, Eupen and Spa. Buses for the Fagnes leave from the station. ☎ (087) 619444.

WHERE TO STAY

🛏 **Hôtel des Ardennes**: place des Victoires 15, not far from the centre. ☎ (087) 223925. Fax: (087) 231-709. Doubles 1,600–2,000BEF. This well-maintained and completely renovated hotel is among the cheapest in town. The staff are friendly, and breakfast is served in a large room with benches and hunting trophies.

🛏 **Park Hôtel**: rue Xhavée 90, opposite the opera house. ☎ (087) 330972. Fax: (087) 316091. Doubles 1,800–2,400BEF. A thoroughly decent establishment that offers large rooms, although it's a bit less polished than the last place. There's a restaurant on the ground floor.

🛏 **Hostelry du Postay**: rue Mairlot 22, Wegnez 4860. ☎ (087) 461477. A mile outside Verviers: head for Pepinster, then Ensival and you'll see the rue du Purgatoire on the right, until you see signs for the hotel. Doubles 2,500BEF, including breakfast. An authentic farm on the Herve plateau, with fine views of pastures and cattle grazing from the outside terrace, which also offers views of the town. The place is riddled with intriguing nooks and crannies, and the rooms, some of which are under the sloping roof, are modern, bright and well furnished, with every comfort provided. There's also a splendid suite with a hearth. You can opt for half- or full-board – it's well worth choosing the latter, as the French cuisine, with a hint of Provence, is excellent. Lunch costs 450BEF, with a cheap *plat du jour* at 295BEF, and there's a barbecue on fine days. The whole package is great value for money.

WHERE TO EAT

🍴 **The Red Ball**: pont Saint-Laurent 10. ☎ (087) 333950. Meals are served until 10pm (bar open until midnight). Main courses from 250BEF. There's a friendly atmosphere at this little brasserie in the heart of town, a favourite with younger locals. Wood panelling, cosy nooks, colourful posters and excellent music add to the ambience, and the food is unpretentious and copious. Dishes include Provençal or Liégeois meatballs, homemade veal brawn, duck, steak and pasta. The affable landlord has put together an excellent list of beers, including Guillotine (which undergoes triple fermentation) and the powerful Delirium Tremens.

☆☆☆ Expensive

✗ **Le Patch**: chaussée de Heusy 173. ☎ (087) 224539. Open for lunch and dinner. Closed Saturday lunchtime and Sunday. Set menus from 365BEF; about 850BEF per head for a full meal. A charming little house above Verviers, with outdoor seating in summer. It's a pleasantly worn place, with hand-decorated wooden tables and an amazing collection of bird cages and assorted finds from the flea market, including a cash register. The landlady cooks tasty, regional dishes and serves them with a smile. There are good-sized hunks of meat that melt in the mouth and seasonal suggestions that depend on what's available at the market: veal kidneys, *coq au vin*, Liège-style meatballs or crispy monkfish. Well worth a visit, not only for the warm welcome of the owner, Laurence, but also for the '*chocolatine*' and the commitment to offering value for money.

WHERE TO GO FOR A DRINK

♥ **Le Saint Andrews**: rue du Marteau, off place des Martyrs. A warm little 'English' pub, with 1960s music, a decent choice of whiskies and plenty of board games.

WHAT TO SEE

★ **Verviersima-Centre de la Laine et de la Mode** (Wool and Fashion Centre): rue de la Chapelle 30. ☎ (087) 355703. Open 10am–6pm, to 5pm in winter. Closed Monday. The Vesdre Tourist Office is on the same site.

This is a relatively new museum (opened in 1999) with two display areas, one based on the wool industry and the other exploring the history of costume and fashion. The building is a renovated neoclassical edifice that belonged to a family of industrialists, the Dethiers, until 1970. There's an 18th-century steam engine in the courtyard, a symbol of the Industrial Revolution. The wool section explores the stages of wool production and the changing technology in its manufacture, taking you from Australian and Argentine sheep shearing to the haberdasher's or designer's workshop. In the costume area, 12 chronological exhibits place the costumes of different periods in their respective historical settings. Between each room are walkways with displays about the role of fashion in the history of Verviers, engravings and sketches of old costumes. The museum also has space for temporary exhibitions. It's very well designed, and should help to put Verviers back on the tourist map. A shop, bookshop, documentation centre and Fashion Café round off your visit. When you leave the centre, you can follow a recommended 90-minute walk around the town (approximately one hour 30 minutes) to complement what you've learned in the museum. The walk is called '*Je file en ville*', which means 'I go to town' and 'I spin in town'.

★ **Musée des Beaux-Arts et de la Céramique**: rue Renier 17. ☎ (087) 331695. Open Monday, Wednesday and Saturday 2–5pm and Sunday 3–6pm. The facade of this museum, formerly a hospice, is covered in funerary plaques, and has a doorway decorated with curling gables. Inside, you can see some fine collections of porcelain and paintings, including a beautiful *Virgin and Child* by Pietro Lorenzetti, enamels from Limousin, *The Punish-*

ment of Ananias and Saphira, by Pieter Pourbus the Elder, Gerrit Dou's *Adoration of the Magi* and Sir Joshua Reynolds's *Head of a Child.* A small room is devoted to engravings from Liège, and there are collections of 18th-century Chinese and Japanese porcelain.

In the modern section, you can see *Les Sirènes,* a work by one of Dali's disciples, Jean Ransy, and several fine landscapes. Look out for Fernand Khnopff's *Memory of Bruges,* Paul Delvaux's *Figures sur fond rouge* and a seascape by Gustave Courbet.

★ **Musée d'Archéologie et du Folklore**: rue des Raines 42. ☎ (087) 331695. Open Tuesday and Thursday 2–5pm, Saturday 9am–noon and Sunday 10am–1pm. Admission: 70BEF. This small communal museum is housed in an 18th-century town house. Inside are findings from archaeological digs in the area, and collections of weaponry, old furniture and Delftware. There are also rooms devoted to prehistory, the Ancient World, lace, boxes from Spa and other odds and ends.

A Stroll around Town

★ **Hôtel de Ville**: place du Marché. Take a look at this large, elegant grey-and-white building, a fine example of Classical 18th-century architecture. The motto on the pediment reads: 'Publicité Sauvegarde du Peuple'. Literally translated, it sounds a bit ambiguous – 'Advertising is the safeguard of the people' – but it's a piece of propaganda designed to keep legal proceedings public.

At the front are steps of the *perron,* the traditional symbol of the town's liberties. The main road, evocatively named rue de Crapaurue ('Toad Street') leads to place Verte, the heart and soul of the town. Note the fine mullioned windows, elegant mouldings and sign of a cow at rue de Crapaurue 37.

★ **Rue des Raines**: one of the town's most dignified streets, lined with bourgeois town houses, rue de Raines leads to the Église Saint-Remacle. Take a look at the elegant window frames of Nos. 42 and 50, and the charming, half-timbered brick houses at Nos. 11 and 13. The best time to see Saint-Remacle is at night, when it takes on an aura of peaceful mystery and appears a touch less forbidding.

★ Head down rue Renier and cross the bridge. The delightful promenade des Récollets, which goes over the hill through the trees and provides some fine views of the town, is on the right. There's a set of steps at the end of the promenade, where you can turn back into town or explore the old residential district around rue Spintay.

A miracle is attributed to the Black Virgin in the Église Notre-Dame des Récollets (on the corner of place des Martyrs). In 1692, during an earth-quake, the Madonna stretched out her left hand to seize the infant Jesus, whom she was carrying. According to the 4,000 people who witnessed the event, this action was to prevent him from falling; the clergy, however, claimed that it was to stop him punishing the locals for their sins.

LIMBOURG

Up on its hill, Limburg is one of Belgium's most attractive medieval towns. Until the end of the 18th century, it was an important defence town, and had a turbulent existence as a result of the religious wars following the Reformation, the Thirty Years War and so on. Louis XIV blew up the castle in 1675, but the town still has some fine remains, with great panoramic views from what's left of the old ramparts. The main square is truly delightful, with higgledy-piggledy cobbles, lime trees and pleasing uniform architecture. If you feel like a walk, follow chemin des Écureuils ('Squirrels' walk') along the side of the hill. At the bottom, you'll come to the 15th-century **Église Saint-Georges**, which has a fine porch with an oval decoration showing St George felling the dragon. The inside has fallen into disrepair, although you can still see a superb Gothic stone tabernacle, dated 1544, to the left of the choir, and a curious *Last Supper* where most of the apostles have their back to you. Next to this is a depiction of the *Descent from the Cross*. There's a 15th-century brass Virgin on a crescent moon above the railings, while lower down on the right, you'll see a beautifully carved 18th-century confessional and little altars with a painted baroque *Virgin and Child*. The baptistery is made of 16th-century blue stone.

WHERE TO EAT

✕ **Au Cheval Gourmand**: on the main square. Closed Monday and Tuesday. A café, snack bar and crêperie, with a pleasant outdoor seating area on fine days.

WHERE TO EAT IN THE AREA

✕ **Le Vieux Hêtre**: route la Fagne 18, Jalhay 4845, 8 kilometres (5 miles) south of Limbourg. ☎ (087) 647092. Fax: (087) 647854. Set menus from 850BEF. This enchanting house, surrounded by a park full of flowers and ponds, is the setting for one of the best restaurants in the region. It's an elegant, unpretentious place where you'll be warmly received. Ultra-professional and endlessly enthusiastic, Robert Dedouaire also writes excellent cookery books. He uses only the freshest produce in his highly innovative dishes, and the cheapest menu is fantastic value for money. Try pork with blueberries; filleted pig's trotter in a little pancake, lamb in Pauillac, or lobster sausage or crayfish with shrimps. On fine days, guests can dine in the lovely water garden. If you want to make a night of it, there are a dozen comfortable rooms (2,200–3,300BEF). They're often booked by golfers in the know, but it's worth a try. Half-board is also available.

WHAT TO SEE IN THE AREA

★ **Barrage and Lac de la Gileppe** (Gileppe Lake and Dam): the dam was started by Leopold II in 1878 to serve the textile industry in Verviers. It held back more than 25 million cubic metres (880 million cubic feet) of water on a surface of 130 hectares (325 acres). A majestic sandstone lion stands guard above the dam. Take a ride or a walk around the lake if you have time.

– **Mountain-bike hire**: Tonic Bike, at the bottom of the viewing tower. ☎ (087) 230344. Open 9am–7pm.

¶ Tour du Lac: route de la Gileppe 55A. Open 11am–8pm (to 6pm out of season). Closed Monday out of season. There's a modern brasserie at the top of the 77-metre (225-foot) tower, as well as the inevitable orientation table. Be prepared for a long climb.

EUPEN   17,500 inhabitants

This small town is the 'capital' of German-speaking Belgium (it's the headquarters of the council of the German-speaking community). During the Austrian occupation, it had the Gallic-sounding name of Néau, which doesn't quite suit a German town. Today, Eupen is a pleasant commercial and industrial town, perched on a hill at the edge of the Vesdre and on the boundary of the Herve plateau and the Ardennes. The town prospered in the 17th and 18th centuries, thanks to the textile and wool industries, and you can still see some attractive bourgeois houses from this period.

The dam on the Vesdre, which is a good starting point for tours around the Osthertogenwald (on the IGN map, Limbourg-Eupen 43/5-6), is 6 kilometres (4 miles) from Eupen.

USEFUL ADDRESSES AND INFORMATION

Postcode: 4700.
🛈 Tourist Office: Marktplatz 7. ☎ (087) 553450. Fax: (087) 556-639. Open Monday to Friday 9am–5pm and Saturday 10am–2pm. The tourist office organizes a two-hour walk around the town, the highlights of which are the Musée du Chocolat, which is free, and the Musée de la Forêt in Ternell, which costs 80BEF, with concessions for senior citizens and children.
🚂 Railway station: ☎ (087) 742-592. Trains go to Cologne, Liège, Leuven, Brussels, Ghent, Bruges and Ostend. The Vennbahn also leaves from here (*see* 'What to see and do').

WHERE TO STAY AND EAT

🛏 ✕ Campsite An der Hill: Hütte 46. ☎ (087) 744617. Open all year. A tent site costs 480BEF. A high-standard campsite with restaurant.
🛏 CBTJ Gîte d'étape (Jugend und Gästehaus): Judenstrasse 79, a couple of kilometres from the station and above the town; well sign-posted. ☎ (087) 553126. Fax: (087) 557903. Price: 385BEF for over-26s; under-26s pay 670BEF for half-board. Breakfast: 100BEF. This hospitable hostel is in a large house surrounded by fields, with fine views and fresh air. There are 102 beds in pleasant rooms with wood panelling or exposed brick. The bathrooms are beyond reproach, and they let you spread out a bit if there aren't many guests; couples, for example, can have their own room. Cheap meals are served in the restaurant, and there's an outside barbecue. You'll get all the advice you want on

the region (walks and rides in the Fagnes, sporting activities, skiing, etc).

🛏 **Zum Goldenen Anker** (Inge Rüben): Marktplatz 13, right in the centre on a lovely little square, opposite the church of St Nicholas. ☎ (087) 743997. Doubles 1,400–1,600BEF. This B&B has charming, cosy rooms (with or without shower), and offers hearty breakfasts. There's a bar on the ground floor.

✗ **Fiasko**: Bergstrasse 28, the main street. ☎ (087) 552550. Open for lunch and dinner (until 11pm). Full meal about 1,000 BEF. Booking essential at weekends. A lovely restaurant, where the staff are friendly and the service is extremely efficient. Try one of the tender, tasty meat dishes. The portions are plentiful, and the seasonal menu, which changes according to what's available, always features the freshest produce.

☆☆☆ Expensive

✗ **Alte Herrlicheit**: Gospertstrasse 104, just beyond the Stadtmuseum. ☎ (087) 552038. Open for lunch and dinner. Closed Tuesday. A large brick building, built in about 1900, with a turret-loggia topped by a bulbous dome. Inside, there are art-nouveau murals and high ceilings, beneath which you can enjoy good, bourgeois fare, including Ardennes ham with melon, salmon escalopes with tarragon or partridge supreme with orange.

WHAT TO SEE AND DO

★ **Église Saint-Nicolas**: Marktplatz. The church was built in 1724, but the two spires were added in the 19th century. Inside, there are three aisles of the same height, while the ornamentation is a masterpiece of rococo excess, especially the altar and the canopied alcoves, where statues of the Virgin and St Joseph stand in state. The pulpit is just as highly decorated, while the confessionals are beautifully carved. The benches are engraved with the names (sometimes in brass lettering) of the town's important families. In the first row, you find the legend 'Magistratus Eupensis', while on the left, the names of those who built the church are written in pretty lettering.

★ **Walk around the Oberstadt**: There are splendid aristocratic 18th-century residences on Marktplatz, Kirchstrasse and Bergstrasse. At Klotzerbahn 32, there's a fine building now used by the executive of the German-speaking community.

There are several affluent-looking houses on Gospertstrasse. Pause on Werthplatz to look at the 18th-century Grand-Ry house (No. 1) and at the chapel of St Lambert. The Rathaus, on Aachenerstrasse, is housed in a 17th-century convent. Beside it is the Church of the Immaculate Conception, which contains numerous 16th- and 17th-century statues.

★ **Eupener Stadtmuseum**: Gospertstrasse 52. ☎ (087) 740005. Open Tuesday to Friday 9.30am–noon and 1–4pm, and Saturday 2–5pm. Admission: 30BEF. A 17th-century bourgeois house with an elegant pediment. Inside, you'll find displays about the history of the town, including a history of the wool industry and local crafts, a wonderful collection of clocks, a reconstruction of a jeweller's workshop and displays of old clothes.

★ **Chocolaterie Jacques**: rue de l'Industrie 16. ☎ (087) 592967. Open Monday to Friday 9am–5pm and Saturday 11am–5pm. Admission free. This is one of the few famous brands of Belgian chocolate that has not been swallowed by a multinational. You can visit the factory (except in July, when production stops), where expert chocolate-makers work, and see the whole process, from cocoa-grinding to the wrapping and boxing. The museum explores the history of the brand, with exhibits such as old moulds, coloured lithographs, wrappings and old advertisements, before directing you to the shop, where you can buy marzipan, sweets and biscuits as well as the chocolate.

– **Vennbahn Railway**: ☎ (087) 858285. The line goes from Eupen to Bütgenbach or Trois-Ponts (the line divides at Sourbrodt), via Raeren, Monschau, Malmedy, Stavelot or Robertville. The trip costs between 140BEF and 340BEF depending where you get on and off and it's half price for children aged six to 12, and free for children under six. All in all, it's a great family outing. The line was built when the Eastern Cantons of Belgium belonged to Prussia. It fell into disuse, but was brought back into service along a route that straddles the German-Belgian border. A steam or diesel engine pulls the refurbished 1930s or East German carriages. Trains stop at 12 stations between May and the end of October, at weekends and on public holidays. The journey takes about three hours each way (there's one return trip per day) and takes you through the magnificent countryside of the Fagnes. That said, it drags on a little, especially if you haven't brought anything to entertain the kids. The best solution is to sample a section of the line: you can get on and off at any of the stations, and get someone to pick you up by car. You can also take your bike on the train, but you have to let them know beforehand.

FESTIVALS

– **Carnival**: one of the most captivating in the country, the Eupen carnival is in good Rhenish tradition. For years, the costumes in this textile town were made from colourful off-cuts. Eleven is the magic number in Eupen (as well as being the symbol of madmen and village idiots). The first session of the preparation takes place on the 11 November at 11.11am, when 11 laws are instituted by the Council of Eleven. On the Saturday before Shrove Tuesday, the Prince of the Carnival is fully empowered by the burgomaster. On Thursday, there's a procession of old women; on Sunday, it's the children's turn; and Monday sees another procession, during which sweets are thrown. It all ends on Tuesday evening with a dance.

– **Saint-Martin's Day**: 11 November. Fervently celebrated in Eupen, this festival winds up with a huge bonfire.

WHAT TO SEE IN THE AREA

★ **American cemetery of Henri-Chapelle**: take the N67 and turn left after Welckenraedt. Open every day; chapel and memorial museum open 8am–6pm (to 5pm in winter). The cemetery dominates the countryside, covering 23 hectares (58 acres) and containing the graves of 7,989 American soldiers who died in the Ardennes campaign, as well as the pilots who came down in the area. The layout of the cemetery is striking, with an imposing colonnade and a curving row of tombs resembling a vast, white wave.

★ If you have time, the delightful little German town of Monschau is on the other side of the border, 18 kilometres (11 miles) from Eupen via the N67, which crosses the Fagnes.

Hautes-Fagnes

This is an extraordinary place. A bit further south, the area around Torgny is Belgium's answer to Provence, but here in the Hautes-Fagnes, you're in tundra country. The region stretches from Eupen to Malmedy, and covers 4,000 hectares (10,000 acres). Most of it consists of damp, marshy country, heathland and peat bogs, with a few pine woods and copses. The summers are cool, the winters are long and rigorous, and it's often foggy. The annual average temperature is 7°C/45°F, August is the miniest month and frosts are possible from the end of September to April, and sometimes even May.

So, is this really the place to spend a holiday? Don't be put off: the conditions might not sound too promising, but they give rise to a wonderful ecosystem that supports all kinds of plants, some mountainous and some almost arctic: look out for molinia, cotton grass, myrtleberries, bilberries, orchids, daffodils and all sorts of mosses, heather and lichens. The fauna's no less varied: wild boar, stags and roe deer, as well as smaller animals such as foxes, weasels and stoats. About 160 species of bird have been listed, half of which live here throughout the year, including shrike, jay, thrush, warbler, cuckoo, lark, blue tit, lapwing, falcon, sparrowhawk, buzzard and that king of birds, the black grouse – of which there are only a few dozen left, so they're difficult to spot.

The area's geology is also interesting, in particular the great basins ('*pingos*'), depressions flooded with water and peat. They were formed when the ice-age glaciers melted, leaving these holes, which can be anything up to 50 metres (165 feet) wide.

How long this area will remain intact is uncertain. The ground has been drying out since the 19th century, and reforestation and extensive farming have combined to shrink the Fagnes. This harsh, dramatic landscape also attracts many nature-lovers and hikers, and although there are no restrictions, the volume of visitors poses a threat to the ecosystem. In 1957, it was turned into a national park, the Fagnes-Eifel, which straddles Belgium and Germany.

CENTRE NATURE DE BOTRANGE

On the Eupen-Robertville road. From Liège, take a train to Verviers, then bus No. 390. ☎ (080) 440300. Fax: (080) 444429. Open 10am–6pm. Admission: 100BEF. The centre is a light, wooden building that blends in beautifully with the surroundings. Texts and audio guides explain the history and geology of the Fagnes, and catalogue its flora and fauna. You can also learn about the previous inhabitants of the area, the bogs, *pingos*, the region's church and village architecture, the life of bees and much, much more. There's plenty of literature about the place and a good bookshop, as well as a complete schedule of events from April to November. These include bird-watching, bat-hunting and night-time walks in the winter forest. There are also various events for children, and exhibitions, nature films, guided walks and bike hire. Information about all of these is available at the centre.

IN THE AREA

★ **Botrange**: you've now reached the highest point in Belgium, at 694 metres (nearly 2,300 feet). If the weather's fine, you can enjoy the wonderful panorama over the Fagnes. You'll need to spend about an hour exploring the clearly marked trails. You'll also need to wear boots, although for much of the time, you are guided along paths made out of duckboards in an effort to protect the peat. The footpath starts on the other side of the road, across from the centre.

– There are other walks, too, such as the Croix des Fiancés, which starts at Baraque Michel. This one's about 2 kilometres (1 mile) long, and it's named after a young couple who perished in a snowstorm here in 1871.

– If you want a longer walk, try the **Fagne de Polleur** at Mont Rigi, which starts from the car park near the junction of the N68 and N676 (before it if you're coming from Eupen). It's about 8 kilometres (5 miles) long. Once again, make sure you've got sturdy footwear with you, either boots or waterproof shoes (the path consists of earth or peat). You must stick to the path, as the walk takes you through a protected zone. It's open from 10am to 6pm, and is closed for a few weeks from mid-November (you can get the exact dates from the Centre de Botrange). It's a fascinating walk, despite the strict restrictions. Don't forget to pick up map IGN 1/25 000 (50-1-2 Sart-Xhoffraix).

When you set off, you'll see a great yellow arrow and a board on the other side of the road from the car park, telling you to take the left-hand path. After a few metres, you come to the first duckboards. An icon showing a little man then directs you along the route. Various information boards tell you about the equipment for measuring the elements (weather stations, heliographs, anemometers, rain gauges and so on), the exploitation of peat from the 17th century to the 1960s, and the history of this asymmetrical valley. About halfway along, at the pont de Beleu, if you're wearing waterproof footwear, take the left-hand, asphalted path heading back to the Centre Nature de Botrange. After a few metres, take an earth path with wooden steps and you'll return to the centre through a beautiful forest on a track that runs parallel to the main path.

CHÂTEAU DE REINHARDSTEIN

Access is via Ovifat (it's well signposted) or through the wood from Robertville dam (about 800 metres/850 yards). ☎ (080) 446475 and (080) 446868. Guided tours every Sunday from mid-June to mid-September, and on Sundays at Easter and Pentecost; Tuesday, Thursday and Saturday from 1 July to 31 August at 3.30pm; the Thursday before Ascension Day, and 21 July and 15 August, every hour 2.15–5.15pm; and finally, the last Sunday of the year in a Christmas setting, at 2.15pm and 3.15pm. Admission: 200 BEF, with reductions for students and children.

The castle sits on a rocky spur in a narrow valley. In the Middle Ages, the site was fortified, and the four Aymon sons (who feature in *The Three Musketeers*) once sought refuge here. A new castle was built in 1354, and was home to various big-shot owners, including the Nassaus, the Schwarzenbergs and the Metternichs. The father of the famous Metternich (who played a key role in rearranging Europe at the Congress of Vienna in 1815) sold the castle, after which it was dismantled. It was eventually rebuilt on the same beautiful site in 1965, and it still looks pretty indestructible.

The new owner is a passionate collector, and has done a great job decorating and refurnishing the interior. Among the most outstanding items are: a majestic cathedral (bishop's seat), a rare 16th-century Italian suit of armour, a beautiful Oudenaarde tapestry, an Italian marriage trunk and a 15th-century wooden carving of Christ. They're all in the salle des Chevaliers. Elsewhere, there's a 17th-century statue of Charlemagne and a superb carving of David with his harp in the first room.

– There are several interesting statues in the chapel, including a 14th-century painted Rhenish school statue of the Virgin on the altar. Take a look at the 16th-century chasuble (robe worn by the priest while celebrating Mass), which bears the arms of the Order of the Golden Fleece, at the altarpiece panels with *grisaille* (a technique of painting in shades of grey) on one side and painted scenes on the other (a metaphor for religion as a source of light) and the 17th-century lectern.

– Finally, you pass through the beautifully furnished private apartments.

WHERE TO STAY AND EAT IN THE AREA

â Gîte d'étape: rue des Charmilles 69, in Ovifat (Robertville 4950). ☎ (080) 444677. Fax: (080) 444-762. On the edge of the nature reserve, this is a stout building with 30-odd rooms, all done up with en suite bathrooms and popular with hikers and cross-country skiers. There are a few rooms for couples, and the welcome is warm.

â ✗ Hôtel Le Fagna: rue Dessousmon-Jacques 12, Waimes 4950. ☎ (080) 446479. Fax: (080) 444942. Closed mid-June to mid-July. Double rooms including breakfast cost 2,200BEF. This pleasant, well-maintained hotel has a fantastic location – two steps from the Hautes-Fagnes nature reserve and right at the end of the road – so you can be sure of a peaceful stay. There's a restaurant, and given that you're in the middle of nowhere, you'd do well to stay half-board. The daily menu features knuckle of ham in gooseberry jelly, duck in honey and lemon, *fondue bourguignonne* and mushrooms stuffed with snails, with a full meal costing about 1,100BEF. Midweek, two nights' half-board will get you a third night free.

â Campsite and café Les Charmilles: in Ovifat (Robertville 4950). ☎ (080) 445864. Open from the end of June to the end of November and at weekends. A tent site costs 295BEF. High level of comfort, with meals available and cheese tasting.

â Other **campsites** can be found around the Lac de Robertville.

ROBERTVILLE

A popular holiday spot for those who enjoy watersports because of its artificial lake. Walkers and mountain-bikers will enjoy the 3,500 hectares (8,750 acres) of forest in the surrounding area. There's downhill and cross-country skiing (on the Ovifat piste) in winter.

🛈 **Tourist information centre**: rue de Botrange 133B, Robertville-Waimes. ☎ (080) 437400.

🛏 ✕ **Auberge du Lac**: rue du Lac 24, Robertville 4950. ☎ (080) 444-159. Fax: (080) 445820. Doubles 2,000BEF. This pleasant hotel, built of local stone in the village centre, has six tiny rooms with baths or showers. There's a sauna, a solarium and a cheap café-restaurant, where you can dine on game and mussels in season, or tuck into waffles and crêpes at teatime.

MALMEDY   10,500 inhabitants

In the beginning, there were two twinned abbeys, one at Stavelot, the other at Malmedy, both founded in 648 by St Remacle. While the Abbey of Stavelot was bigger, the Abbey of Malmedy became famous for its scriptorium and its school. Like many towns, Malmedy had its fair share of destruction – it was pillaged by the Vikings and Magyars in the ninth and 10th centuries, then wrecked by Louis XIV in 1689. Despite all its woes, however, the town prospered and grew rich on its tanneries, paper works and a textile industry. After the French Revolution, Malmedy was absorbed into the French *département* of Ourthe. Following the Congress of Vienna and the carving up of Europe, the town became German. It finally joined Belgium in 1925 after a referendum.

In December 1944, Malmedy found itself in a Catch 22-situation. Although it was occupied by the Americans, it was heavily and repeatedly bombarded by American planes. By the time the Americans had realized their mistake, the damage was done and the inhabitants set to work, rebuilding and improving their town.

Today, Malmedy is a major and very Walloon-minded commercial centre, with street signs sometimes appearing in French and Walloon. It's the biggest conglomeration near the Fagnes, and is therefore visited by a large number of tourists – not that this makes the accommodation any cheaper.

From Liège, take the train to Verviers, then bus No. 395 to Malmedy. Or take the train (line 43) to Trois-Ponts, then bus No. 450.

MALMEDY'S CARNIVAL: THE 'CWARMÊ'

This is one of the most picturesque carnivals in Belgium. For the four days (the 'Grantès Haguètes') before Shrove Tuesday, the town enjoys a non-stop party, with preparations made on the four Thursdays prior to the festivities. In principle, everyone attends in fancy dress, and the bizarre costumes and characters have equally bizarre names: *sôté* (the dwarf), the *djoupsène* (the Egyptian), the *véheû* (polecat), *Grosse-Police* (who opens the carnival), the *sâvadje* (the savage) and so on. It's led by the all-powerful *trouv'lé*, who reigns supreme throughout the festivities. The *longs-nés* ('long-noses') wander about in a *bâne corante* ('running band'), teasing people and imitating their gestures, and people often offer them a drink to get rid of them. The *haguète*, meanwhile, pounces on her victims and insists that they ask her pardon.

Monday is devoted to street theatre, with sketches recounting the town's, and the locals', misdemeanours, often in Walloon. Political events and politicians are often satirized – and the actors don't pull any punches. The *haguète* is finally burned on Tuesday evening. It's an intriguing event and one you should make the effort to see.

USEFUL ADDRESSES AND INFORMATION

Postcode: 4960.

ℝ Eastern Cantons Tourist Office: place Albert Ier, next door to the cathedral. ☎ (080) 330250. Fax: (080) 770588. Open 8.30am–noon and 1.30–5pm; 10am–noon and 2–4pm on Saturday, 10am–noon on Sunday. Good literature on the town and the region.

✉ **Post office**: rue J.-Steinbach 4.

🚌 **Bus terminal**: avenue de la Gare. Buses go to Eupen, Waimes, Ligneuville, Beurg-Reuland, Verviers, Trois-Ponts and Stavelot.

■ **Taxi**: ☎ (080) 330098 or (080) 330605.

■ **Bike and mountain-bike hire**: Cycles Roger Cornet, Mont Spinette. ☎ (080) 330620.

WHERE TO STAY AND EAT

🛏 ✗ **Youth hostel Hohes Venn**: Beverçé 8A, a mile or so from the centre on the Beverçé road. ☎ (080) 338380. Fax: (080) 770504. Email: malmedy@laj.be. To get here by bus, take No. 397 (Malmedy-Xhoffraix); there are four or five departures a day. Basic rate per night: 405BEF. Closed for three weeks in September and one week in December. This large, comfortable, modern youth hostel, near a public swimming pool, sleeps 178 and has 12 family rooms. Full- and half-board available.

🛏 **Taverne-hôtel de Rome**: place de Rome 23. ☎ (080) 339460. Doubles with sinks or showers 1,800BEF. This place has everything you need, and prices are among the lowest in town.

🛏 **Café-Hôtel La Forge**: rue Devant-les-Religieuses 31. ☎ (080) 799595. Fax: (080) 759599. Doubles 1,950BEF. A beautiful building on the way into town, with well-equipped rooms above a tavern.

🛏 There are a few inexpensive B&Bs and hotels in the surrounding area. For details, contact the tourist office.

🛏 **Campsite Mon Repos**: avenue de la Libération 3. ☎ (080) 338621.

🛏 **Campsite Au Moulin**: Village 26, Beverçé. ☎ (080) 799020. A tent site costs 320BEF. Open all year. High level of comfort.

✗ **Tavern A vî Mâmdi**: place Albert Ier 41. ☎ (080) 339636. Open every day. A pleasant establishment offering traditional Ardennais food in a rustic setting, with old photos on the walls. Specialities include meat cooked over a wood fire, fillet of lamb *gratin*, fried sausages, veal sweetbreads with asparagus, monkfish stew and grilled ham.

✗ **Le Chambertin**: Chemin-Rue 46. ☎ (080) 330314. Set menus from 450BEF. This centrally located, pseudo-rustic restaurant serves good, traditional food. The cheapest menu is good value, with seasonal dishes like country-style ham, knuckle of ham with mustard and roast fillet of lamb with thyme.

✗ **L'Hirondelle**: rue du Commerce 17. A small restaurant on two levels, with pictures of 18th-century uniforms on the walls. The menu features marinated herrings in apples and pork kidneys with mustard. Organic menus are also available.

WHAT TO SEE

★ **Cathédrale Saint-Pierre-Saint-Paul-et-Saint-Quirin**: a successor the old abbey, and the last remnant of it, this church became a cathedral between 1919 and 1925, when Malmedy was neither Belgian nor German. It was rebuilt in the 18th century after the great fire of 1689. The stone facade is quite restrained. Inside, the church has barrel vaulting and a single aisle, with a cupola at the crossing of the transept. It's a little austere, but the woodwork is interesting and there's a highly ornamented gilt pulpit with flowers and foliage

The bishop's seat, complete with canopy, stalls and carved doors, is in the choir. To the left, you can see the 18th-century sarcophagus-reliquary of St Quirin.

★ **Musée du Papier** and **musée du Carnaval**: place de Rome 11. ☎ (080) 337058. Open 2–5pm. Closed Monday, holidays and during the Carnival. Admission: 100BEF. The museums are housed in the Maison Cavens, a fine 19th-century building that used to be an orphanage.

– The first floor is devoted to the paper industry, once one of the most important industries in the region. You can learn all about the origins of different paper, from wasps gnawing away at wood fibres to paper made of Mexican bark, papyrus and parchment. The exhibits include paper from the Far East, paper made from the fibres of blackberry bushes, filigree paper from Taiwan and Arabic paper (made of rags). There are explanations of the manufacturing process, and models that visitors can operate.

– On the third floor, the Musée du Carnaval is a medley of documents, funny photos of past carnivals, models of floats, posters, newspaper cuttings, traditional costumes and carnival characters.

★ **A walk around town**: from Place de Rome, take rue Devant-les-Religieuses and head for the little bridge over the Warchenne, a tributary of the Warche, until you reach the 12th-century Chapelle Sainte-Madeleine (rebuilt between the 16th and 18th centuries). There's an old leper-house with several commemorative plaques.

Retrace your steps and take rue Ol'tchinrou to place Albert Ier. Next, head right to rue des Capucins, where you'll see a church with a beautiful 17th-century Virgin and Child above the porch. At the end of this street, turn left onto rue Podri les Mours ('Behind the Walls'), then walk along rue J.-Werson (the old seat of the Prussian government will be on your right) and take the first turning on the left, climbing the steps to route de Chôdes. The Maison Vinette, a half-timbered house with extraordinary windows, stands on the corner at No.1.

Next, head down rue Haute-Vaulx into old Malmedy, the district that escaped the bombardments of 1944. Here, you'll see houses with slate facades – it's one of the most attractive parts of town.

The 18th-century Chapelle de la Résurrection stands on place du Pont-Neuf. From the charming Rue la Vaulx (*o l'vâ* in Walloon), the first road on the right takes you to Gretedar (Old Hall), where you can see an old town gateway, the town hall and the prison. If you have the time and energy, round off your walk by ascending the Chemin du Calvaire (built in 1728).

WHERE TO STAY AND EAT IN THE AREA

≜ ✕ **Ferme Libert**: in Beverçé, a few miles north of Malmedy on the N68. It's well signposted. ☎ (080) 330247. Fax: (080) 339885. Set menus at a variety of prices: the midrange, 900BEF option is very good value. One of the region's oldest establishments, the Ferme Libert has a deservedly excellent reputation. It's a traditional rural building on the edge of the forest, and the roomy restaurant has a superb view over the valley. The setting is suitably rustic, with cloth tablecloths and napkins. The menu features generous helpings of classic country cooking, with game in season and, à la carte, a variety of meats, including bison, ostrich and springbok. The wines are sensibly priced, and all are chosen by the landlord. The rooms have everything you need, including sink, shower or bath, and start at 2,375BEF for a double. You can stay half-board, or plump for a full-board 'gastronomic' weekend.

≜ There are dozens of lodges and B&Bs in the area. Brochures detailing places to stay can be obtained at the tourist office.

≜ **Gîte, campsite and B&B at Ferme d'Arimont**: chemin de la Cense 22, a couple of miles from town. ☎ (080) 330068. Fax: (080) 770536. B&B rooms 1,940BEF for two, including breakfast, with a supplement if you stay for only one night. Open April to mid-November. A well-organized complex in the heart of the countryside. The campsite has bathrooms, but is quite small, so book ahead. The gîtes are attractively furnished and well equipped (four sleep two to six people, one sleeps 12), while the two B&B rooms in the barn are pleasantly rustic and sleep up to four people. There's a common room with a wood oven and kitchen-corner, and fresh farm eggs are served at breakfast. Cattle are raised on the farm and guests can take tractor rides in summer.

BÜTGENBACH

Another popular holiday resort with winter- and watersports facilities on the lake. Stags roam freely in the nearby Schwalm valley.

USEFUL ADDRESS

🛈 **Tourist Office**: Worriken-Center 1, Bütgenbach 4750, opposite the end of the Vennbahn. ☎ (080) 446358. Fax: (080) 447089. The charming and competent staff will provide information about pensions, B&Bs and other accommodation.

WHERE TO STAY

☆ Budget

🛏 **Campsite Worriken**: same address and telephone number as the tourist office. A two-man tent site costs 360BEF. Closed for four weeks from 11 November. An up-to-date setup by the lake, with fully equipped bathroom buildings (i.e. hot showers). Activities include swimming, fishing and windsurfing.

🛏 **B&B Eifelland**: Seestrasse 5, Bütgenbach 4750, on the edge of place du Marché. ☎ (080) 446670. Fax: (080) 445296. Doubles 1,850–2,250BEF, including breakfast. A fully equipped complex of apartments for two, all with baths, TV and telephone. Guests can use the sauna, solarium, table-tennis tables and winter garden. Half-board is available via an arrangement with local restaurants.

WHERE TO EAT

✗ **Café-restaurant Landhaus Küpper**: Krombachstrasse 1A, Berg 4750, on the other side of the lake. ☎ (080) 444539. Open every day in July and August; out of season, Friday to Sunday only. This old-style village tavern has a large garden, and a rustic interior with an open fire. The reasonably priced regional cooking blends Belgian and German cuisine. Try Ardennes-style open sandwiches, escalopes or trout.

FESTIVALS

– **Cortège des Vieilles Femmes** (procession of old women) on the Thursday, and **Rosenmontag** on the Monday, before Shrove Tuesday.

WHAT TO SEE NEARBY

★ **Hergesberg**: right on the border with Germany, this old customs house is now a commercial complex with various attractions. Open from noon (10am at the weekend) to 6pm.

– *Eurotecnica:* a huge model railway, with 60 miniature trains that run round 1,000 metres (3,300 feet) of track in a miniature replica of the countryside around Eifel. Kids (and a fair few fathers) will love it.

– *Krippana:* a display of Nativity crèches from all over Europe covering 2,500 square metres (3,000 square yards). It's quite magical. There's also a museum of religion.

SANKT VITH 9,000 habitants

Belgian since 1920, Sankt Vith is, after Eupen, the most important town in the German-speaking part of the country. It was completely destroyed by American bombers in 1944, but rebuilt to offer its population a pleasant setting in an environment of fields and woods. All that remains of the old town is the Büchel tower, a reminder of the 14th-century town walls.

USEFUL ADDRESS

Postcode: 4780.
🛈 Tourist office of the Eastern Cantons: Müllenbachstrasse 2.

☎ (080) 227664. Offers literature on the region.

WHERE TO STAY AND EAT

☆ Budget

🛏 ✗ Campsite Wiesembach: Wiesembachstrasse 65. ☎ (080) 221234. Ten sites 510BEF. Open all year. The site is 1 kilometre from the centre of Sankt-Vith, in the woods. There's a swimming pool and meals are available.

🛏 ✗ Youth Hostel Ardennen-Eifel: Rodterstrasse 13A, west of the town centre, about 500 metres (approximately 500 yards) from the coach station. ☎ (080) 229331. Fax: (080) 229332. Basic rate per night: 420BEF. Most rooms sleep three or four, with a total of 85 beds. Lunch and evening meals are available.

☆☆ Moderate

✗ 🛏 Hôtel-restaurant Zum Steineweiher: Rodterstrasse 32, in the woods on the edge of town. ☎ (080) 227270. Fax: (080) 229-153. Doubles from 2,500BEF. The restaurant is overloaded with rustic decorations, but it does have an open fire. The cooking is predominantly French, with a menu that's strong on game and victims from the trout farm on the grounds. There's an excellent wine cellar, and you can sit in a pleasant outdoor area if the weather's fine. The cosy rooms have baths or showers, and some have balconies.

WHAT TO SEE

★ **Heimatmuseum, Zwischen Venn und Schneifel** (Museum of Local Life): Schwarzerweg 6. ☎ (080) 229209. Open 2–4pm (to 5pm on Sunday). Admission: 40BEF. A former station-master's house now houses a collection devoted to local archaeology and popular traditions, as well as religious art. There's also a fine library.

★ **Forest Beer Museum**: in Rodt-Thommberg, west of Sankt Vith. ☎ (080) 226301. Open weekends and holidays 10am–6pm. Admission free. This collection includes no less than 2,500 different types of beer and matching glasses from all over the world. Drinkers' gadgets and collectors' items are also on display, and you can watch a video about brewing.

FESTIVAL

– **Carnival**: on the Sunday before Mardi Gras.

WHAT TO SEE IN THE AREA

★ **Burg-Reuland**: 12 kilometres (7 miles) south of Sankt-Vith. Open May to the end of September 11am–6pm. Admission free. Built at the foot of a fortified castle in the 11th century, this is one of the most impressive medieval buildings in the Ardennes. There's a magnificent view over the grey roofs of the village, and south to the Utf valley, from the top of the tower. A wooden model of the castle is on display in the pavilion in the interior courtyard. The church, which has a delightful onion dome, houses the black-marble mausoleum of the Lord of Reuland and his spouse, and is the venue for fantastic Rosenmontag and Shrove Tuesday celebrations.

🛏 ✕ **B&B-restaurant Burghof**: Wenzelbach 43. Burg-Reuland 4790 ☎ (080) 329801. Fax: (080) 420232. Doubles with showers 1,800–2,000BEF. Closed end of June and end of December. Set in peaceful, lakeside surroundings, this is a typical example of regional architecture, with a large wooden balcony. There's a Spanish-style restaurant serving seasonal game.

★ The **Our valley** snakes through the fields, becoming increasingly dramatic as it runs along the German border towards the Grand Duchy of Luxembourg, beyond Ouren. It's a paradise for fishermen.

🛏 **International campsite**: Dorf 14, Ouren. ☎ (080) 329291. Deep in the country, this place has an on-site store, restaurants and swimming and fishing facilities. You can also hire a mountain bike.

STAVELOT   6,500 inhabitants

The history of Stavelot is closely linked to that of its abbey, which once rivalled the abbey of Malmedy. In the Dark Ages, it was the seat of a small principality, governed by an abbot-prince. In 843, it was annexed by the Holy Roman Empire, although it retained a certain level of independence. The French Revolution put an end to this, and Stavelot was tacked on to the department of Ourthe in 1795. In 1815, the town was separated from Malmedy by the Congress of Vienna, and stayed within Belgium.

Today, Stavelot is an attractive, historic town that has preserved most of its architectural heritage, despite the vagaries of war. It's also an essential detour for fans of vintage cars.

In June 1998, part of the historic centre was destroyed by fire when the brakes of a lorry failed and it hurtled uncontrollably down Haute-Levée.

APOLLINAIRE IN STAVELOT

Stavelot played an important part in the life of the French poet Guillaume Apollinaire, and the town continues to honour him today with a museum that pays fitting tribute. Apollinaire was not his real name: he was born Wilhem de Kostrowitsky in Rome, on 26 August 1880, to an unknown father. It was the child's mother, a baroness called Olga-Angelica Kostrowitsky, who gave him the names Guillaume and Apollinaire. Together with Guillaume and his brother, she settled in Paris, but spent her holidays in Belgium. She was something of an old *rouée*, and her commitment to the gaming table was such that she attempted to set up a casino in Spa. Meanwhile, she placed the young Guillaume and his brother in the Pension Constant, at rue Neuve 12 (today it's a hotel – Ô Mal-Aimé – *see below*).

Young Guillaume spent his summers there, mixing with the town's literary types, rambling in the forest and, most importantly perhaps, embarking on a relationship with Maria Dubois, who became his muse. Maria was as pretty as she was spiritual.

Eventually, Apollinaire's gambling mother was thrown out of Spa and went to seek her fortune in Ostend, apparently forgetting all about her children. Guillaume wrote to her, and she wrote back with money for a train ticket to Paris. On the night of 5 October, the two brothers sneaked out of Stavelot, leaving behind a huge unpaid bill. The town was outraged: the family had seemed so respectable . . . Since then, Stavelot has been amply repaid.

USEFUL ADDRESSES AND INFORMATION

Postcode: 4970.
fi Tourist Office: in the old abbey. ☎ and fax: (080) 862706. Open every day from 10am–12.30pm and 2–5.30pm (to 4.30pm from November to the end of March). It can arrange guided tours of the old abbey, and provides maps for guided walks around town.
■ **Euro-Relais**: place Saint-Remacle 28. ☎ (080) 864242. A company that runs 450 holiday houses in the Ardennes. Free catalogue on request.
Railway station: there's a tourist train (Vennbahn; see 'Eupen') once or twice a month between May and October. Stavelot is on the Eupen-Trois-Ponts line. To get to Liège, take bus No. 44A or 45A for Trois-Ponts, then train line 35 or line 43.
■ **Bike and mountain-bike hire**: No Limits, rue Haute-Levée 8. ☎ (080) 862903.

WHERE TO STAY AND EAT

Campsites

Campsite l'Eau Rouge: Cheneux 25. Three kilometres (two miles) from the centre. ☎ (080) 863075. Tent site: 580BEF. Open all year.
Campsite de Challes: rue de Challes 5. ☎ (080) 862331. Tent site: 600BEF. Open April to the end of October. A couple of kilometres from the town centre. More family oriented – and basic – than l'Eau Rouge.
Campsite de la Cascade: chemin des Faravennes 5, in Coo, next door to a leisure park. ☎ (080) 684312. Tent site: 560BEF. Open April to the end of September.

☆ Budget

Gîte d'étape: rue Chaumont 9. ☎ (080) 863432. In an old brick building that used to be a brewery, this country lodge has 45 beds and takes group bookings.

Hôtel Ô Mal-Almé: rue Neuve 12. ☎ and fax: (080) 862001. Closed Monday and Tuesday. Doubles 1,800BEF. This is the inn from which Apollinaire made his guilty getaway, and it's full of memorabilia. The walls are decorated with poems by Desnos and Soupault, and various portraits. The rooms themselves are rather spartan, with showers on the landing, but they're the cheapest in town: There's a pleasant ground-floor café, and an attractive dining room with an intimate atmosphere and a funny menu designed for kids who've had enough of spelling tests. The set menu in the restaurant (closed Monday evening and Tuesday) is eminently affordable, and the cooking unobjectionable: quails à l'ancienne, lamb cutlets, steak, omelettes and so on. The three-course menu costs 695BEF. Half-board is virtually compulsory in high season.

☆☆ Moderate

♣ ✗ Auberge Saint-Remacle: avenue F.-Nicolay 9, opposite the abbey. ☎ and fax: (080) 862047. Rooms cost 2,000BEF per person, including breakfast. There are five bright, airy rooms for two at this hotel-brasserie, with a shared bathroom. There's also a room for four, with en suite bathroom, at the back. The hotel is well maintained and friendly, while the restaurant serves generous portions of local specialities such as monkfish with leeks and Ardennes-style trout. A full meal will cost about 600BEF.

♣ ✗ Hôtel d'Orange: devant les Capucins 8, in the centre of town. ☎ (080) 862005. Fax: (080) 864292. Website: www.users.skynetbe/hotel.orange. Doubles 2,700–3,300BEF. Weekends only from December to March. Tucked away down a quiet street, this charming hotel in an 18th-century coaching inn is run by a family who've been in the business since 1789, and they certainly know how to make guests feel welcome. The best hotel in this category, it was badly damaged in a fire that ravaged the district in 1998, but rose from the ashes at Easter 1999. There are cosy doubles and family rooms (Nos. 7 and 25 are the biggest), while the restaurant offers set menus for every budget, as well as a children's menu. Or sample Liège-style quails, fillet of lamb and chicken with tarragon from the à la carte menu (a full meal will cost about 1,000BEF). The overnight package including dinner and breakfast is a bargain.

♣ B&B 'Les Trois X': avenue F.-Nicolay 18, Luxen-Chauveheid. ☎ (080) 862303. Rooms 1,500BEF–1,800BEF, including breakfast. Four doubles and one room for three people, all on the second floor of a centrally located town house that dates from the turn of the last century. Guests share the shower and toilets, and have access to the kitchen and children's garden. Meals available on request.

✗ L'Âne Culotte: rue Haute 17. ☎ (080) 863438. Closed Wednesday out of season. Set menus from 295BEF, otherwise 800BEF for a full meal. A little house with a pleasant lounge and good cooking that includes pasta, *carbonades*, meatballs with *sauce chasseur*, cold cuts, croustade of mushrooms and steak with morels.

WHAT TO SEE

★ **The old abbey**: this abbey was bigger than the one at Malmedy, and it's obvious that St Remacle preferred it. All that remains of the original abbey church are the impressive tower, its immense bay, the 16th-century porch, with arms emblazoned over it, and the monastic buildings, rebuilt in brick in the 18th century. The huge courtyard in the centre is now home to the town hall. On the street side, you can see a beautiful brick porch with stone, mullioned windows and doors with accolades. The other buildings in the complex now house local-government offices, a library and the town's museums.

★ **Place Saint-Remacle**: a harmonious cobbled square lined with buildings full of character, in varying shades of grey. The 18th-century *perron*, complete with fountain, symbolizes communal liberties. There are some delightful winding streets off the square, with half-timbered or slate-fronted houses (rue Haute is especially charming).

★ **Église Saint-Sébastien**: open 9am–noon and 2–7pm in July and August and during the Easter holidays; otherwise by appointment only. This 18th-century church has recently been renovated. In the centre, there's an imitation-marble altar (1717), made of wood, along with a marvellous carved-oak pulpit, also early-18th-century, decorated with the four Doctors of the Church. Don't miss the 13th-century reliquary of St Remacle, a masterpiece of Mosan art that you can see in the choir, along with the relics of the abbey's founder. It's unusually long at 1.70 metres (5.5 feet), and the work of the jeweller is outstanding.

★ **Musée du Circuit-de-Spa-Francorchamps**: in the old abbey. ☎ (080) 862706. Admission: 160BEF; reductions available. This museum is a must if you like old racing vehicles and vintage motorbikes. A combined ticket for this museum and the two listed below costs 360BEF, with reductions for children, students and senior citizens.

Exhibits are shown in a splendid medieval brick vault, complete with 11th-century pillars rescued from the old abbey. Here are some of the highlights, including Formula 1 cars and prototypes (shown in a section called *Série et production*).

First come the products of the famous FN d'Herstal factory, starting with the first one-cylinder (133 cc) motorbike of 1902, called *la demoiselle d'Herstal*, and several other models. The first car built specifically for racing was the FN 1200. There are some fine Jaguars, including a 1954 Jaguar Cooper, and you can also see a Chevron B8 and racing motorbikes such as the Gillet de Herstal (1937). There's an awesome 1913 Rolls-Royce, and a superb 1930 Minerva Imperia. The collection also includes the Delage (1939), which competed in the 24-hour endurance race at Le Mans. Other specimens include the Cooper F1 (1959) and the Lotus 1 (1961), as well as a March Leyton (1980), which gives you an idea of how much these vehicles have changed over the years. There's a whole host of others to see, along with photographs and posters. Items from the collection are often on loan to other museums, so don't be surprised if some of the things listed above are not on display.

★ **Musée d'Art religieux**: on the ground floor of the building that houses the car museum. Admission: 222BEF; concessions available. The museum explores the history of the abbey and the principality, with portraits of abbots and a list of all those who served here from 648 to 1794, as well as a small archaeological section and a tribute to the Belgian Symbolist painter William de Gouve de Nuncques. Items on display include a limestone sarcophagus used for the Abbot of Odon in 836, and the tombstone of a monk with conspicuously large ears.

Wood carvings, relics (including one of the fictional St Philomena), chalices and a wrought-iron cemetery cross are on display in the chapel. On the statue front, look out for a painted-wood 18th-century Virgin, which was used in processions, and a graceful 16th-century Trinitarian St Anne in painted oak. There's also a splendid white silk robe, embroidered with gold thread.

★ **Musée Apollinaire**: situated in the abbey library. ☎ (080) 862124. Open 10am–12.30pm and 2–5.30pm in July and August. Admission: 120 BEF; reductions available. A must for fans of the French avant-garde poet, Apollinaire (1880–1918), and a good introduction for those not familiar with his work.

A series of rooms illustrates key stages in Apollinaire's life, with two devoted to his life and work and one to his stay in Stavelot. The documents, photos, manuscripts and memorabilia on display give you a vivid impression of his friends, who included Picasso, the evenings he spent in Paris, his travels and his experience of the Great War. You can see the bed he slept on when staying at the Pension Constant, the bed he died in and a raft of newspaper cuttings about his arrest in the wake of the theft of the *Mona Lisa*. There are also hundreds of picturesque and bizarre anecdotes, including that of his surreptitious departure from the Pension Constant.

FESTIVAL

– **Laetare**: the Carnaval du Laetare officially takes place on the Sunday three weeks before Easter (although it sprawls from Saturday evening to Monday evening). Hundreds of *Blancs Moussis*, dressed in white capes and hoods with long red noses, run about the town mingling with carnival floats and giants. It all began when an abbot-prince issued an edict forbidding monks to take part in the carnival. The locals got their own back on the killjoy abbot by dressing up as white-robed monks. 2002 marks the 500th anniversary of the event.

– **Festival de Musique de Stavelot**: this takes place in the abbey during the first three weeks of August.

– **Festival de Théâtre**: beginning of July, in the abbey. ☎ (04) 222 0696.

WHERE TO STAY IN THE AREA

🛏 **B&B**: Astrid-Delacroix 14, Monthouet 4987, near Stoumont, in the Valley de l'Amblève. ☎ (080) 785718. This old inn, built using local stone, has three rooms for two with sink, and one for three with an en suite bathroom. There's also a large garden with a splendid view. You can go mountain-biking, fishing and kayaking in the surrounding area, and there's skiing in winter. The prices, with or without breakfast, are reasonable.

WHAT TO SEE IN THE AREA

★ **Musée historique de Décembre 1944**: rue de l'Église 7, in La Gleize. ☎ (080) 785191. Open to groups throughout the year, if they book in advance. Open to individual visitors daily Easter–November and during Christmas holidays (except December 25 and January 1), 10am–6pm. Admission: 150BEF. In World War II, the German 'von Runstedt' offensive was defeated in this area, and this thorough museum examines the conflict through dioramas, photos, relief maps, uniforms, weapons, radio material and a reconstruction of a first-aid post. Collections of insignia and honours are on show on the first floor, and you can read contemporary newspaper reports declaring the failure of the offensive and the liberation of Belgium. One particularly touching item is an old bike used to save a wounded American soldier.

★ The **road from La Gleize to Spa** goes through Borgoumont, a village of sturdy houses and farms built with large chunks of stone. The road overlooks a wide, lush valley that's half woodland, half grassy meadow. Before you hit the forest road, you'll see the pretty village of Cour. You can visit the Musée de la Forêt (*see* 'Spa') en route.

★ **Coo**: a village renowned for its waterfall, and popular for canoeing on the Amblève and its touristy adventure park. ☎ (080) 684265. From the beginning of May to the end of October, open 10am–7pm; otherwise weekends and school holidays only.

– **Bike hire and outdoor activities**: Coo Bike Adventures, Petit Coo 4. ☎ (080) 689133. Caving, climbing, go-karting, microlites, archery, bungee-jumping, orienteering, quad-bike racing and skiing in winter.

★ **Ski resort at Mont des Brumes**: forget all the jokes about 'le plat pays'. This resort, between Francorchamps and La Gleize, is 530 metres (1,650 feet) above sea level, with a 1,000-metre (3,300-foot) piste and four ski lifts. Assuming there's enough snow, it's open from 11am–6pm (from 10am at weekends). Skis and boots are available for hire. There are also three cross-country pistes, which are 3, 5 and 6 kilometres long.

SPA   10,500 inhabitants

This is one of Europe's most famous thermal holiday resorts. It doesn't really attract backpackers, and this is hardly surprising: Spa is a faded, world-weary town, although it's still a great base for country walks and rides.

A Short History

The Romans were fully aware of the healing properties of the local waters here: the town's name comes from the Latin *sparsa*, meaning 'gushed forth'. But people didn't start bathing or taking the waters here until the 16th century. From then, Spa went from strength to strength, attracting such distinguished visitors as Marguerite de Valois, renowned for her many lovers, Queen Christina of Sweden, Peter the Great (who found the Berezina waters closer to home a touch too chilly), Emperor Joseph II, Charles II of England, Monteverdi, Victor Hugo and Meyerbeer. And those famous waters turned golden when the locals realized that the spa experience could be hugely enhanced by the addition of lucrative gaming tables. By the middle of the 18th century, Spa had earned the name of 'Café of Europe'.

During World War I, when Kaiser Wilhelm moved his headquarters here, the town was used as a place of rest and convalescence for 100,000 German soldiers.

USEFUL ADDRESSES AND INFORMATION

Postcode: 4900.
🛈 Tourist Office: place Royale 41. ☎ (087) 795353. Fax: (087) 795354. Website: www.colvert.be/spa. The office organizes guided walks, and provides a good list of B&Bs in the area.

🚃 Railway station: rue de la Gare. ☎ (087) 771036. Trains go to Liège (change at Verviers). There are about 15 every day. If you're coming from Liège, take train line 37 to Pepinster, then line 44.

■ **Bike and mountain-bike hire**: AB Bike, place Royale 31. ☎ (087) 775777. Scooters and kayaks are also available. You can hire bikes at the station.

WHERE TO STAY

⌂ **Hôtel-restaurant Le Relais**: place du Monument 22. ☎ (087) 771108. Fax: (087) 772593. Doubles 1,950–2,600BEF. This welcoming place with flowers in the windows could hardly be more central. Rooms are pleasant and comfortable, and the restaurant, tastefully decorated in yellow and green, is also worth trying. Lobsters and oysters splash about in blithe ignorance of their fate, while the French-style cuisine features Normandy quails and loin of piglet in thyme sauce. The three-course *repas gourmand* is good value at 750BEF.

⌂ **Campsite Parc des Sources**: rue de la Sauvenière 141. ☎ (087) 772311. Open from April to the end of October. There are 170 sites, each costing 395BEF for a two-person tent that sleeps two. All mod cons are available.

⌂ **B&B Mysotis**: rue G.-Beaupain 7F, Sart-lez-Spa 4845, 6 kilometres (four miles) from Spa. ☎ and fax: (087) 474822. Rooms 1,400–1,800BEF, with discounts for stays of more than one night. On the edge of the Fagnes, this is a peaceful base if you want to explore the countryside on foot. There are three rooms with en suite bathrooms, two for two people and one for three. Breakfast is generous, and guests can use the kitchenette for self-catering. There's also a garden with a barbecue, and you get a free aperitif on arrival.

WHERE TO EAT

✕ There are a few self-service cafeterias and brasseries, including **Euro-Taverne** (place Royale 4; closed Monday), which offers good, filling dishes and a cheap set menu.

✕ **Steak House Domino**: place Verte 80. ☎ (087) 771505. Closed Tuesday and Wednesday. A pleasant place that serves excellent meat dishes.

☆☆☆ Expensive

✕ **La Brasserie du Grand Maur**: rue Xhrouet 41. ☎ (087) 773616. Open for lunch and dinner (until 11.30pm). Closed Monday and Tuesday. Set menus 995–1,595BEF. A remarkably elegant old house, with polished wood flooring, prints on the walls and a fantastic fireplace with tiles and delicate stucco work. The refinement of the setting is echoed by classic, perfectly cooked dishes, and by the service. Try the excellent spicy fish soup, steak, kidneys or a tender noisette of lamb. All in all, excellent value for money.

WHAT TO SEE

★ **Musée de la Ville d'eau** (Museum of the Spa Town): avenue Reine-Astrid 77. ☎ (087) 774486. Open 2.30–5.30pm from 15 June to 15 September and during the school holidays; otherwise weekends and holidays only. Admission: 80BEF. Housed in Queen Marie-Henriette's former villa, this museum contains some of the finest examples of *jolités* (painted boxes), a speciality of Spa. The boxes are lacquered with between 12 and 16 layers, each sanded down and with the final layer polished to perfection. They're inlaid with mother of pearl or copper, decorated in Indian ink or adorned with mythological or rustic scenes. The boxes had various uses, such as trinket boxes, work boxes, boxes for toiletries, toy boxes, and so on. The prettiest are in yellow, with floral designs. Other highlights include miniatures on vellum and a decorated piano in burr maple.

★ **Musée spadois du Cheval** (Spa Horse Museum): in the old stables of Queen Marie Henriette's villa. Same opening hours as the Musée de la Ville d'eau. Admission: 100BEF. Carriages, weighing instruments, uniforms, engravings, miniatures and a blacksmith's forge are on show on the ground floor, with paintings, watercolours and old photographs one storey up.

Architectural Highlights

Most of Spa's buildings date from the 19th century, and the baths, springs and grand hotels evoke the town's heyday.

★ **Pouhon Pierre-le-Grand** (Peter the Great's Spring): rue Rogier, at the end of rue Royale). ☎ (087) 795353. Open 10am–noon and 2–5.30pm; out of season, 1.30–5pm, also 10am–noon at weekends and on public holidays. This is the most famous spring in town. It's a massive construction, with wrought-iron beams and a huge painting on the wall. The latter shows all the VIPs who have graced the town, including Peter the Great, who visited in 1717. The water comes out of a marble fountain: It's piquant and slightly acidic, rich in iron and salts – and doesn't taste too bad. Today, the building is used as an exhibition space.

In rue Gérardy, you can also see the Pouhon Prince-de-Condé.

★ **Établissement de bains** (The Baths): place Royale 2. Built in 1868, with a facade that's typical of its time.

★ Next door is the **casino**, which is the oldest in the world (1763), although the present building, with a semicircular rotunda and columns, dates from the beginning of the 20th century. The gaming rooms are in Louis XVI style, while the ballroom is reminiscent of the Queen's theatre at Versailles. The casino's theatre is 19th-century. If you're feeling lucky, you can place your first bet at 3pm.

★ **Galerie Léopold-II**: in parc des Sept-Heures. This is a long gallery with 160 gracefully worked wrought-iron columns linking the two small pavilions. It was originally designed so that visitors could take a little exercise during rainy weather. There's an antiques market every Sunday morning.

★ **Hôtel de Ville**: rue de l'Hôtel-de-Ville. Built in 1768, this is where distinguished guests used to stay. Note the traditional *perron*, symbolizing the town's communal liberties.

If You Have Time

★ **Musée de la Lessive** (Laundry Museum): rue Jean-Philippe-de-Limbourg 60. ☎ (087) 771418. Open Sunday 2–6pm; in July and August, open at the same times every day. Admission: 50BEF. Audio guides available. This unusual museum traces the evolution of washing and bleaching techniques from the time of Neanderthal man to today. You'll find a reconstruction of a washroom and an exhibition of antique washing machines, old soaps and so on.

★ **Musée de la Forêt** (Museum of the Forest): estate of Berinzenne, on the road to La Gleize. ☎ (087) 773320. Open 2–5pm every day except Friday at Easter and in July and August; otherwise open weekends and Wednesday at the same hours. Admission: 100BEF. Housed in an old farm, this museum tells you all about the ecosystem of the local woods.

SHOPPING

🔒 **Manufacture des jolités de Spa**: avenue Reine Astrid. ☎ (087) 770340. Free admission from Tuesday to Saturday, 2.30–5.30pm. A good selection of ornamental boxes.

🔒 **Centre d'artisanat local**: place Verte 8 (cour Body). ☎ (087) 772712. Open 9am–noon and 1.30–6pm. Closed Sunday. The centre for local crafts has exhibits all year. The distinctive Spa *jolités* and a host of other items are made here.

South of Liège

If you're heading for the province of Luxembourg (La Roche-en-Ardenne, Bastogne) or Namur, you may like to visit a few monuments and villages along the way.

HARZÉ

This attractive, architecturally uniform village is made up of small grey-stone houses.

★ The 17th-century **château**, which has been turned into a leisure centre, has a fine Renaissance gallery.

★ **Musée de la Meunerie et de la Boulangerie** (Museum of Milling and Baking): in the château's outbuildings. ☎ (086) 212033. In May, June, September and October (as well as Easter), open at the weekend and holidays from 1pm to 6pm; in July and August, open every day from 11am to 6pm. The reconstruction of a functioning water mill is the main attraction, but there's also an exhibition explaining how to make waffles, chocolate and marzipan.

– **Fête nationale du Fromage belge**: the 'national festival of Belgian cheese' takes place in August.

GROTTES DE SOUGNÉ-REMOUCHAMPS

From mid-March to the end of November, open 9am–6pm; otherwise, weekends only 10am–5pm. ☎ (04) 384 4682. Admission: 300BEF. The caves are famous for their stalagmites and stalactites. The 'cathedral room' is 100 metres long and 40 metres high (330 feet x 132 feet), and you can also see an underground river.

AYWAILLE

A major crossroads, known as the 'gateway to the Liégeois Ardennes'.

★ **Musée de la Seconde Guerre mondiale** (Museum of World War II): in a castle on the road to Dieupart. ☎ (04) 384 5972. Open 10am–noon and 2–6pm in July and August. A collection of weapons, uniforms, photographs, documents and posters. The complex also houses a campsite and a playground.

★ A pleasant footpath and cycle path takes you to **Remouchamps** along the Voie des Aulnes.

WHERE TO EAT IN THE AREA

✕ **Au Repos du Pêcheur**: rue de Fairon 9, Comblain-la-Tour. Hamoir 4180. ☎ (04) 369 1021. Open Wednesday evening to Monday, from noon for lunch and from 7pm for dinner. Closed in April and November. A slap-up feast will cost 1,200BEF. A restaurant in a private house with check tablecloths, an open fire and a family atmosphere. It has a solid local reputation, and the food is good and inexpensive. Try mutton stew, fresh grilled trout in butter or duck.

ANTHISNES

★ It's worth making a small detour between Comblain-la-Tour and Hody to see the imposing 13th-century keep, the **Avouerie**: avenue de l'Abbaye 19, Anthisnes 4160. ☎ (04) 383 6390. From April to the middle of September, open noon–6pm (to 5pm on Tuesday and Thursday); otherwise Monday to Friday 11am–5pm. Admission: 115BEF. The Avouerie is managed by a charity, and has the **Musée de la Bière et du Peket** (Beer and Gin Museum) on the ground floor. Note the fine staircase banisters. In the cellars, you can sample 'cervoise de l'Avouerie' and the Hauts-Voués beer, called after the name given to lawyers in this region during the 17th century.

SAINT-SÉVERIN-EN-CONDROZ

On the N63, just outside Neuville-en-Condroz.

★ Stop here to see a marvellous 12th-century **Romanesque church**. Set among old farm buildings, trees and a pond, the only French Romanesque church in the Mosan Valley is delightful. It has a beautiful octagonal tower with colonnaded windows and alternating round, square and fluted pillars inside. There's barrel vaulting above the transept crossing, and the decoration of the ogive crossing looks very primitive. The choir is shaped like a quarter sphere, flanked by two apses. Its main treasures are a 16th-century carved oak Christ in the transept on the right and an outstanding baptismal font supported on *colonnettes*; the coping is decorated with heads at the corners and lionesses.

JEHAY-AMAY

★ **Château de Jehay**: 20 kilometres (12 miles) southwest of Liège. ☎ (085) 311716. Open 11am–6pm on weekends and public holidays in July and August. Admission: 200BEF. This château, one of the most charming in the province of Liège, is a magnificent example of 16th-century Mosan Renaissance architecture. It was built on stilts, and has a chessboard appearance thanks to the alternating rubble and cut stone, which is unique in Belgium. It also houses a fabulous private museum.

The collections of objets d'art include pieces of old furniture, tapestries, silverware, an ivory *Christ* by Jean del Cour and some fine examples of lace, on show in the great hall. There's a painting by Jan Brueghel and *St John the Baptist* by Murillo. The vast dining room is furnished in Renaissance style, while the decoration and furnishing in the main salon is exceptionally refined. You'll also see priceless pieces of porcelain, a splendid Romanesque *Sedes Sapientiae* (a seated figure of the Virgin), a Gobelins tapestry, woven to a design by Teniers, works by Lambert Lombard, an 18th-century painted harpsichord, superb clocks and much more.

The cellars are devoted to archaeological finds, with about 22,000 items beautifully displayed beneath the splendid Gothic vaulting. They include flints, neolithic ceramics, jewels, Romanesque glassware, pots and weapons.

– The old Abbaye de la Paix-Dieu (17th–18th centuries) in **Jehay-Bodignée** is also worth a look.

HUY   18,500 inhabitants

This was one of Victor Hugo's favourite Belgian towns, and you can see why. It has a wonderful collegiate church and an old town centre where you can explore the tranquil, higgledy-piggledy streets and step back in time to the Middle Ages.

A Short History

Huy came to prominence thanks to its position at the confluence of the rivers Meuse and Hoyoux, halfway between Namur and Liège. In the 10th century, it was the biggest town in the principality bar Liège, and the busiest commercial centre. The town was part of the Province of Liège until the French Revolution.

Peter the Hermit came here to preach about the First Crusade in 1095, and is buried in the town.

Huy was also famous for its metalwork, and was home to such master craftsmen as Renier de Huy (who made the baptismal font in Liège's Église Saint-Barthélemy) and Godefroy de Huy (who made the reliquaries in the collegiate church).

Huy has seen its share of sieges and wars. In 1944, much of the town was destroyed, but the consequent reconstructions and restorations were more or less in keeping with the character of the old neighbourhoods. Don't miss the festival of Saint-Jean au mont Falise, featuring egg-throwing competitions and bonfires, which takes place on the last Saturday in June every year.

USEFUL ADDRESSES AND INFORMATION

Postcode: 4500.

🛈 Tourist Office: quai de Namur 1. ☎ (085) 212915. Fax: (085) 232944. Website: www.huy.be. Email: tourisme@huy.be. Housed in the old Hospice of Oultremont. The staff are friendly and efficient, and the office stocks some excellent literature.

🛈 Provincial Tourist Office: rue l'Apleit 10. ☎ (085) 254553. Fax: (085) 254554.

🚂 Train: line 125 for Liège-Guillemins. Also buses Nos. 9 and 85.

■ Bike hire: Vélos-Sport-Loisirs, place du Tilleul 6. ☎ (085) 211117.

AROUND LIÈGE

WHERE TO STAY

⚅ Budget

🛏 Campsite Mosan: rue de la Paix 3, Tihange 4500. ☎ (085) 234639. Tent site: 295BEF. Open from April to the end of September. You can fish, swim and shop for groceries on site.

☆☆ Moderate

🛏 Hôtel du Fort et la Réserve: chaussée Napoléon 6–9. ☎ (085) 212403. Fax: (085) 231842. Doubles 1,400–2,300BEF; breakfast 200BEF. Don't be put off by the fact that this well-maintained, welcoming family hotel overlooks a busy road on the banks of the Meuse: the windows are all triple-glazed. The cheapest rooms, with sinks, are above the restaurant; the en suite rooms in the annex are a bit more expensive, but still competitively priced, although the 1970s 'pop art' interior is a bit hard on the eye. The cuisine in the restaurant is a bit workaday, although the à la carte menu includes a few sophisticated dishes like trout in *pastis*. The wine list, on the other hand, is admirable – wine is the landlord's passion.

WHERE TO EAT AND DRINK

☆☆ Moderate

✕ La Tête de Chou: rue Vierset-Godin 8, on a little street near place Verte. ☎ (085) 235965. Open Tuesday to Sunday for lunch and dinner. Closed Saturday lunchtime. *Plat du jour* 360BEF. This place has a mauve facade and a cheerful yellow-and-blue interior. The well-balanced menu includes vegetable quiche, salmon steak with rosemary and duck *à l'écossaise* (with whiskey).

🍷 There's an excellent bar on the corner, Contre Vents et Marées.

LIVE MUSIC

– **Jazz Matazz**: Grand'Place 22. Open until very late at the weekend. This swinging café has tiles, wicker chairs – and a banana tree.

WHAT TO SEE

★ **Collégiale**: open 9am–noon and 2–5pm. The collegiate church was built between 1311 and 1536 on the site of several previous religious sanctuaries. The exterior is architecturally uniform, and the huge tower, a throwback to Romanesque style, gives it an imposing appearance. The tower lost its spire in a thunder storm in 1803, and now pretty much echoes the overall look of the building. The rose window was long considered one of the marvels of Huy (two other wonders disappeared – the bridge and the medieval castle) and is still one of the most beautiful in Belgium. When the afternoon sun shines through, the interior looks truly spectacular.

Inside, three aisles provide a sense of height and harmony. The choir windows are 20 metres (66 feet) high. The painted vaulting (1523) is pure Renaissance, while the crypt beneath the chevet dates from 1066 and has its original paving, as well as a fine 13th-century wooden Christ.

★ **Treasury**: closed Friday and during services. Admission: 50BEF. This is the real masterpiece of the church. The finest reliquaries in Belgium are on display: St Domitien's (1172), with characters in silver (their clothes are in gold); St Mark's (13th century), in gilt bronze and enamel, depicting scenes from the life of Christ (shepherds, Three Kings, Entry into Jerusalem, Descent from the Cross), and, on the other side, the Flight from Egypt, the Resurrection of Lazarus and so on; St Mengold's, adorned with three leopards; and the reliquary of Notre-Dame, attributed to the same craftsman who made the St Remacle reliquary in Stavelot, with fine engraving and filigree work depicting the 12 apostles in repoussé metal and precious stones. There's also a splendid statue of the Virgin Mary, watching the infant Jesus with a rapt expression. Other outstanding items include religious jewellery, a monstrance with turret, and a *Virgin and Child* by Jean del Cour. The next room contains a carved-oak, painted *Notre-Dame des Vignettes*, with a playful infant Jesus, Bishop Théodouin de Bavière's funerary cross (1075), St Domitien's shroud and the reliquary bust of St Odile.

★ Before leaving, wander down the side of the church to the **Portail de Bethléem**, which used to be the entrance to the cloister. It features a 14th-century Nativity scene with an ox and ass looking down on the swaddled Christ. The pillars are decorated with whimsical animals and grotesque figures.

★ **Musée Communal**: rue Vankeerberghen. ☎ (085) 232435. From April to the end of October, open 2–6pm. Admission: 100BEF. The museum is housed in an old convent and has a vast rococo portico and cloister, built in 1662 in pure Mosan style. It's an elegant blend of brick and limestone, with fine mullioned windows. The drawing room and dining room are typical of a 19th-century bourgeois interior.

– The archaeological section covers the prehistoric era, the Gallo-Roman and Merovingian periods and the Middle Ages, while more recent times are represented by cannon balls, keys and locks from various periods and a fine collection of prints, watches and coins. In the penultimate room, there's a decorative wrought-iron stove from 1880.

– The last room houses religious art and jewellery, travelling reliquaries and a 16th-century wooden sculpture of St John the Elder, who's wearing a large hat with shells. You then come to a real masterpiece: the *Beau Dieu* (1240), one of the biggest crucifixes in the country, with unusual detail on the folds of the loincloth.

– In the room to the right of the entrance, you'll find a bizarre collection of pipes, lamps, powder boxes, 19th-century clothing, objets d'art (including a wonderful carved-oak coffee-grinder), rural furniture and an 18th-century Walloon box bed ('*foume-éclose*' in Walloon). There's also a reconstruction of a peasant kitchen, with butter moulds in primitive designs.

★ **Fort**: 45 metres (nearly 150 feet) above the Meuse; you can get here by foot or cable car. From Easter to mid-October, open 10am–5pm (to 6pm at weekends). Built in 1818 on the site of the medieval castle, the fort was used as a prison in the 19th century, as a barracks in the 1920s and 1930s, and as a prison under the Nazis. Today, it houses the Musée de la Résistance et des Camps de Concentration.

Walk around the Town

★ As you leave the museum, you'll notice the **Octagonal Tower of Oultremont** (rue du Palais-de-Justice), a remnant of the 16th-century Count's Palace. The Maison du gouverneur (1535), which has a front courtyard, is just a stone's throw away. Follow the picturesque rue des Frères-Mineurs with its *arvô* (vaulted passage) and high walls, to get to the Église Saint-Mengold. Opposite is the beautiful **Maison de la Tour**, the oldest house in Huy (12th century), which has a five-sided tower. The Maison Nokin, with delightful windows with accolades, is on place Verte.

★ The **Hôtel de Ville** was built in 1766. It's a Classical structure with a carved triangular pediment built in blue stone and brick. The Bassinia, one of the wonders of Huy, stands in the middle of the Grand'Place. It's a 15th-century spring with a bronze basin that rests on four statuettes. The beautiful wrought-iron decoration with the two-headed Austrian eagle was added in 1733.

★ A severe, elegant building in alternating brick and local blue stone stands on the corner of Fouarges and Vierset-Godin. It has a huge mullioned window and a lacy cornice. At rue de l'Aplet 8, there's a solid-looking stone house with accolades on the door and windows.

★ Cross the pont Roi-Baudouin to see the Maison Batta, built in 1575 (rue de Batta), and the Hôtel de la Cloche (quai de Compiègne), a fine Mosan Renaissance building of 1606. A little further on, the Église Saint-Pierre has a 12th-century baptismal font.

– Take a look at the **vines** growing on the left bank of the Meuse above Huy. Vines were first grown in Huy in the Merovingian period, and viticulture here peaked in the 16th century. In a fit of jealousy, Louis XVI had the vines torn up, and the tradition of wine-growing went into decline – until 1963, when 20-odd vine-growers started producing decent plonk in keeping with the traditions of the vine-growing guild, the Confrérie du Briolet.

WHAT TO SEE IN THE AREA

★ **Amay**: 10 kilometres (6 miles) from Huy, by the Meuse. You can visit the splendid collegiate church of Sainte-Ode, where Odeou Chrodoara, a Merovingian noblewoman, was buried. Her sarcophagus is in the crypt.

★ **Château de Modave**: 15 kilometres (10 miles) southeast of Huy. ☎ (085) 411369. From the beginning of April to mid-November, open 9am–6pm; otherwise by appointment only. Guided tour every hour on the hour. Admission: 200BEF. Clinging to a rocky peak, the castle mostly dates from the 17th century, and is constructed in an elegant Classical combination of grey stone and brick. An ingenious Liège carpenter, who had managed to bring water from the river to the castle, was invited to Versailles by Louis XIV, who gave him the task of taking water to the fountains in the park. He invented the 'Marly' machine, which was used to take water from the Seine to Versailles. Louis XVI stayed here as a guest of the Count of Artois when he was forced to flee France. The decor is sumptuous, with wonderful ceilings, furniture, paintings and Brussels tapestries, and the gardens are no less impressive.

★ **Parc naturel des vallées de la Burdinale et de la Mehaigne**: Maison du Parc Naturel, ferme de la Grosse Tour, rue de la Burdinale 6, Burdinale 4210. ☎ (085) 712892. Fax: (085) 699167. Deep in the Haspengouw (Hesbaye) region, at the edge of the province of Namur and Walloon Brabant and west of the Meuse, this is an oasis of signposted walks and guided tours that take you through a fascinating natural area of heath and wetlands. The surrounding landscape consists of wooded farmland, with old farm buildings providing a remarkable monument to the area's agricultural heritage, and there are old villages like Huccorgne and the Oteppe and Fallais châteaux.

The Province of Luxembourg

This is the most densely wooded province in Belgium. No towns have encroached on the thick forests, and even the rivers seem reluctant to slice through them, flowing in never-ending meanders at the slightest obstacle. In one area, the River Ourthe goes through six meanders in the space of a few kilometres.

The Semois, meanwhile, is equally windy, cutting through an impressive landscape with features such as the 'giant's tomb'. The rivers, like the locals, take their time in this rolling country, where you'll come across any number of châteaux as well as painful reminders of the Battle of the Ardennes. Bastogne, the martyr town, will give you plenty of food for thought during your tour in the Gaume region.

LA ROCHE-EN-ARDENNE   4,000 inhabitants

Nestling in the valley of the Ourthe, La Roche-en-Ardenne is the dinky tourist capital of the northern part of the province. With its strategic position and escarpments, this area was long regarded as fine territory on which to build defensive forts. The Celts, the Romans and the Counts of Namur have all held sway here, followed by the Dukes of Luxembourg, the Burgundians, the Austrians, Charles V and Philip II. Louis XIV, finding that the aesthetics of the castle left a lot to be desired, made smart work of demolishing it and ordered a disciple of Vauban (the French military architect) to redo the whole thing. In December 1944, the Ardennes offensive brought terrible destruction to the town, but La Roche-en-Ardenne was courageously rebuilt. Today, nearly every house is a souvenir shop, and the hordes of tourists include thousands of Dutch and Flemish visitors eager to escape the flat monotony of their native lands and holiday among some hills.

USEFUL ADDRESSES AND INFORMATION

Postcode: 6980.

■ **Tourist Office**: place du Marché 15. ☎ (084) 411342. Fax: (084) 412343. Open 10am–noon and 2–5pm; 10am–6pm in July and August. Campers should ask for a brochure listing sites throughout the province.

■ **Fédération touristique du Luxembourg belge**: quai de l'Ourthe. ☎ (084) 411011. Fax: (084) 412439. Website: www.ftlb.be. Good literature.

■ **Hotel bookings**: Relobel, ☎ (084) 411011. Website: www. relobel.com. A free service provided by the Fédération touristique du Luxembourg belge.

■ **Mountain-bike hire**. Ardennes Aventures, rue du Hadja 1. ☎ (084) 411 900. You can also hire equipment for canoeing and rafting here.

■ **Open-air swimming pool**: Floréal Club, avenue de Villez. ☎ (084) 219411. Open 10.30am–noon and 2–6pm in July and August.

■ **Taxis**: ☎ (084) 412385.

WHERE TO STAY

Campsites

■ **Floréal 1**: route de Houffalize 18. ☎ (084) 219 467. Tent site: 500BEF for a two-person tent. It's a bit of a factory, but still a four-star campsite.

■ **Le Lohan**: just after Villez, right by the Ourthe. ☎ (084) 411545. Tent site: 370BEF.

■ **Le Bénélux**: rue de Harzé. ☎ (084) 411559. Tent site: 490BEF.

■ **Le Grillon**: rue de la Gare 10. ☎ (084) 412062. Tent site: 435BEF for a two-person tent. Open from Easter to the end of October. There's a small restaurant specializing in trout dishes.

■ **Les Nymphes**: ☎ (084) 411958. Tent site: 250BEF.

☆–☆☆ Budget–Moderate

■ ✕ **Hôtel Beau Rivage**: quai de l'Ourthe 26. ☎ (084) 411241. Fax: (084) 411242. Doubles 1,950–2,200BEF, with discounts available for stays of more than three nights out of season. A small, central hotel with views over the valley. The comfortable rooms come with sink or shower. Light meals are available.

■ ✕ **B&B Le Vieux Laroche**: rue du Chalet 45. ☎ and fax: (084) 412586. Email: LevieuxLaroche@online.be. Doubles 1,400–1,600BEF. A daintily restored house in typical Ardennes style near the centre, with five simple but attractive rooms with shower and a very hearty breakfast. When the sun's out, you can use the terrace and garden. Meals available on request.

⬧ ✕ **Hôtel Moulin de la Strument**: Petite Strument 62. ☎ (084) 411507. Fax: (084) 411080. Closed January. Double rooms 2,550BEF, plus 150BEF for a single-night stay. Half-board compulsory on weekends. It may be a little expensive, but this hotel is not lacking in charm: it's an old watermill in an idyllic valley 800 metres from town.

It's a hospitable place, and the bright, tasteful rooms are all well equipped. The restaurant, decorated in cheerful colours and local stone, offers generous helpings of fine, regional dishes.

⬧ There are several other B&B options: for information, ring the tourist office.

WHAT TO SEE

★ **The Château**: from April to June and in September, open 10am–noon and 2–5pm; in July and August, open 10am–7pm; otherwise 1.30–4.30pm on weekdays and 2–4pm at the weekend. Admission: 100BEF. The first castle was built in the 11th century, fortified by a succession of owners and dismantled in the 18th century by Joseph II. It has an imposing entrance, flanked on either side by towers. The castle is now a venue for various cultural events, while finds from archaeological excavations are on display in the Musée archéologique.

★ **Musée de la Bataille des Ardennes** (Museum of the Battle of the Ardennes): rue Châmont 5. ☎ (084) 411725. Open 10am–6pm. Closed Christmas and New Year's Day. Admission: 195BEF, half-price for children. One of the most interesting museums of its kind. Instead of the usual army of objects, the display consists of several impressive dioramas. Unusual items include: a 1942 Harley Davidson, old photographs of the town before the war, and photos of the devastation of 1945, when 70,000 shells were launched at it.

You can also see a reconstruction of a first-aid post (note the ingenious 'medical boiler'), a station for receiving and transmitting radio signals, a selection of trucks and jeeps, and an anti-aircraft half-track. There's also a scaled-down replica of an American B-17.

– First floor: dioramas on paratroopers, old posters, a weird escape bag, a reconstruction of 11 January 1945 (the second liberation of La Roche by the 4th Division of the US Infantry) and the clothes worn by the Belgian resistance. You can also see weapons, grenades, personal belongings found 45 years on and display cases devoted to English soldiers and pilots.

– Second floor: the German army. On show: a 1932 edition of *Mein Kampf* and an example of the 'Enigma' machine for encoding messages, which the English managed to get hold of and used to decode vital messages about German strategy.

★ **Les Grès de La Roche et le musée du Jambon d'Ardenne**: rue Rompré 28. ☎ (084) 411878. From March to end October 10am–noon and 1.30–5pm; during school and public holidays only in November and December. Closed Mondays, unless they fall on a public holiday, and in January and February. Admission: 130BEF. This museum is arranged around a rustic tavern where the waiters and waitresses wear traditional blue costumes and serve regional dishes. There's a pottery workshop, where you can see the whole process and admire the finished product. There's a small museum with a video displays and a reconstruction of an old kitchen. The real reason to visit, however, is to watch experts making Ardennes sausage, enjoy the delicious smells wafting around – and sample the results.

WHAT TO SEE IN THE AREA

★ **Belvédère des Six-Ourthes**: follow the beautiful Vallée de l'Ourthe (N860) to Nadrin. It's well signposted. The gazebo of this hotel has one of the finest views of the province – it has to be seen to be believed. The lazy River Ourthe appears in the landscape six times, meandering all over the place in search of the course of least resistance. The landscape is made up of large, forested undulations that have been broken up by wood-cutting and new plantations. As a result, conifers grow next to broad-leafed trees, and the whole area is a vast patchwork of greenery.

★ **Belvédère de Nisramont**: for more breathtaking views, head for Nisramont. Shortly after leaving Nadrin, you'll see another mesmerizing panorama of the Ourthe (the same you've just seen, but in reverse), complete with a lake and dam.

From here, there's a signposted path to the Rocher du Hérou. The landscape at its foot is especially picturesque. The GR57 road passes through this region.

WHERE TO STAY AND EAT IN THE AREA

🛏 ✕ **Hôtel-restaurant du Belvédère**: rue du Hérou 70, Nadrin 6660. ☎ (084) 444193. Fax: (084) 444511. Email: hotel@belvedere. be. Closed in January. Doubles 2,400BEF; breakfast 250BEF. The rooms are pleasant, and peace and quiet are guaranteed. There's also a panoramic view from the restaurant, which specializes in meats (wild-boar stew in season) and *fondue ardennaise*. Set menus 595–1,345BEF.

🛏 **Les Alisiers**: on route du Belvédère and route du Hérou. ☎ (084) 444544, (080) 418741. Fax: (084) 444604. Doubles 2,000BEF; breakfast 250BEF. This fine building with four B&B-type rooms is surrounded by a garden and overlooks the valley. It's peaceful and serene. You can book ahead for *Le Vieux Chêne* restaurant in Nadrin.

🛏 Next door is La Gentilhommière: a brick building with luxurious suite-style rooms at 3,250BEF for a double. You can book them in the swish Hôtel Le Cabri: route du Hérou 45. ☎ (084) 444185.

✕ **Restaurant Le Vieux Chêne**: in the centre of Nadrin. ☎ (084) 444114. Closed Tuesday. This restaurant has a good reputation and specializes in fish and regional dishes. Try *fondue ardennaise* or abbey trout. It's not too expensive, and there's an attractive veranda.

WHERE TO GO FOR A DRINK

🍷 **Brasserie d'Achouffe**: Achouffe 32A, Wibrin 6666. ☎ (061) 288147. A brewery near Houffalize that produces speciality beers. It produces several highly regarded brews, including 'MacChouffe', a sweet, strong brown ale.

The menu includes light meals and, if you're in need of something more substantial, rabbit cooked in La Chouffe beer.

VIELSALM   7,000 inhabitants

Vielsam is a little town 530 metres (1,650 feet) above sea level and surrounded by forests and rocky hills. Geologically, this is the most interesting area in Belgium. Watch out for the Sabbath of the 'Macrâlles' (witches) on July 20, a wild festival that's followed the next day by the Fête des Myrtilles.

USEFUL ADDRESSES AND INFORMATION

Postcode: 6690.
🖪 Val de Salm Tourist Office: rue des Chasseurs Ardennais 1. ☎ (080) 215052. Fax: (080) 217462.

■ **Bike hire**: Maison de l'Aventure, Bêche 40. ☎ (080) 786124.

WHAT TO SEE

★ **Archéoscope du pays de la Salm** (Archaeoscope of the Salm region): avenue de la Salm 50. ☎ (080) 216699. In July and August, open 11am–6pm; during school holidays and on public holidays, open 2–6pm (except Monday from April to the end of June and in September and October); from February to the end of March and in November and December, open Monday, Tuesday and Thursday; in January, open Sunday only. Admission: 180BEF, with discounts for children. The magic of multimedia takes you on an informative, inspiring journey through the region's heritage and the industry that thrived here thanks to the local geology. The audio guides provide an excellent 45-minute commentary. The sights and sounds of the forest are re-created in an introductory film, after which you plunge into the earth to discover the different types of shale that provided the population of the Val de Salm with a livelihood. You'll learn about the gold that was discovered here in the 19th century, when the region experienced a mini gold rush, see how slate was used and explore the traditions and working conditions of the miners and quarry workers. Touch screens and a story-telling session by the fireside of an Ardennes cottage reveal the wealth of the region's architectural heritage and folklore. Many of the spellbinding legends feature the Devil, who always gets his comeuppance in the end.

★ **Musée d'Histoire et de la Vie salmienne** (Museum of History and Life in the Salm region): Tienne Messe 3, near the church. ☎ (080) 216252. Open 10am–noon and 1–5pm, Sunday 2–5.30pm. Closed Monday. Admission: 60BEF. This 18th-century house contains exhibitions of local costumes and displays evoking the traditional Haute Ardennes house.

★ **Musée du Coticule**: Salmchateau. ☎ (080) 215768. From April to the end of October, open Tuesday to Saturday 10am–noon and 1–5pm, Sunday 2–5.30pm. Admission: 80BEF. Coticule is unique: it's such hard shale that it can blunt even the best steel instrument, which is why it's known as 'razor stone'. Indeed, it has even been used to make razor blades. In the 16th century, when coticule was first heavily exploited (the industry reached its peak in the 19th century), Vielsalm became the capital of razor stone, exporting its products all over the world.

Eventually, coticule was eclipsed by the disposable and electric razor, and the industry went into decline, with the first mines and workshops closing down in the 1950s. The last one shut down in 1982. This museum, housed in a former workshop, offers an entertaining insight into the industry that once nourished an entire region. On show are geological displays, documents, tools and working machines that give you a good idea of the manufacturing process.

HOUFFALIZE   4,500 inhabitants

The little town of Houffalize, tucked away on a bend of the Ourthe, was completely destroyed by bombardments in January 1945. A Panzer tank, fished out of the river after the German offensive, is displayed on one of the squares. It's a poignant reminder of a brutal episode in the town's otherwise peaceful history. The local authorities decided to build a memorial for a better future on the site of an old tannery where dozens of locals, including children, were buried. The educational and recreational centre, Houtopia, is the townspeople's attempt to convey a message of peace, with particular emphasis on the rights of children. It's an admirable enterprise. There are also a number of outdoor centres around Houffalize.

USEFUL ADDRESS

Postcode: 6660.
🛈 Tourist Office: place Janvier-45.
☎ (061) 288116. Open 9am–noon
and 12.30–4.30pm (later in July and August).

WHERE TO STAY AND EAT

🛏 ✕ Au Bon Accueil: rue du Pont 5, in the heart of town. ☎ (061) 288051. Closed Thursday out of season. Doubles 1,200–1,750BEF, including breakfast. This is an unpretentious family hotel with a tea-room and a restaurant serving Ardennes specialities: baked mushrooms, steak with wild mushrooms and game and trout in season. A full meal costs about 800BEF.

WHAT TO SEE

★ Houtopia: place de l'Église 17. ☎ (061) 289205. Open 11.30am–5pm, 10am–7pm in July and August. Admission: 185BEF, with small discounts for children and families. This is a recreational and educational centre designed for children under 12 and their parents. Kids can learn about their rights – and duties – through an excellent 20-minute multiscreen video presentation, narrated by Peter Ustinov. Short plays acted out by circus artists are interspersed with sometimes painful archive images, and the message is that children are the adults of tomorrow, and that the world can only evolve peacefully if their education and security is guaranteed. The films also highlight the harsh realities of child exploitation, whether through war, the perversion of adults, man-made environmental disasters or other evils of contemporary society. Visitors are encouraged to conclude that children have a right to know the truth, and that knowing the truth may make them better adults.

The main themes are developed through a series of games and interactive displays that help kids explore issues such as saving water, road safety, health and illness prevention, waste recycling, tolerance, racism and the migration of threatened species (in this case, the black swan). There are also picnic areas, a cafeteria and playground.

DURBUY   9,000 inhabitants

This little town nestles at the foot of a natural wall of rock (*La Falize*) in the shadow of a château. Until 1977, when it merged with other communes, it had only 400 inhabitants, even though it had acquired the title of 'town' in 1331 from Jean the Blind, Count of Luxembourg and King of Bohemia. Durbuy now markets itself as 'the smallest town in the world', and its winding medieval streets, old houses and picturesque setting (it's the first hilly landscape you come to after the polders), attract crowds of Dutch and Flemish tourists throughout the year, all looking for topographical and psychological relief. As you might have guessed, it's a bit of a tourist trap in season.

USEFUL ADDRESS

Postcode: 6940.

☐ Tourist Office: place aux Foires. ☎ (086) 212428. Fax: (086) 213681.

WHERE TO STAY

☎ Hôtel-restaurant de la Brasserie du Vieux Pont: place aux Foires 26. ☎ (086) 212808. Doubles with sink or shower 2,400–2,600BEF, breakfast included. A well-maintained establishment where you're guaranteed a warm welcome. The restaurant serves good, reasonably priced regional dishes, with set menus from 410BEF. Full-board is compulsory on weekends.

☎ Hôtel de la Falize: rue A.-Éloi, in the historic town centre. ☎ (086) 212666. You're guaranteed good value for money at this peaceful hotel, where the traditional rooms are carefully looked after and the staff are friendly. There's a shop selling regional produce on the ground floor.

☎ B&B Ninane Louis: rue Comte-d'Ursel 20. ☎ (086) 212712. Fax: (086) 214406. Rooms cost 1,700–2,100BEF, including breakfast, with a 10 per cent reduction in January and February. This place offers five rooms with private toilet, all above a shop in the heart of the old town.

☆☆☆ Expensive

☎ Hôtel du Prévot: rue des Récollectines. ☎ (086) 212300. Fax: (086) 212784. Doubles 2,500–2,950BEF. Tucked away down a quiet medieval street, this comfortable hotel also has a restaurant serving grilled meat, chicken and duck.

WHERE TO EAT

✕ **La Ferme au Chêne**: in the main street, just beyond Le Sanglier des Ardennes. ☎ (086) 211067. A friendly joint where you can tuck into a simple snack on the peaceful terrace and enjoy the view over the Ourthe. On the menu: crêpes, omelettes, waffles and *matoufé grand-mère* (a house speciality: grilled bacon and eggs beaten with flour), sandwiches and salads. Make sure you sample the home-made beer.

☆☆☆ Expensive

✕ **Le Moulin**: place aux Foires 17, ☎ (086) 212970. Closed Monday and Tuesday out of season. Several set menus, with the 895BEF option offering especially good value. This former mill, built in the 13th century, is a pleasant setting for a restaurant that majors in Provençal-style cuisine. The menu changes according to what's in season, and the dish of the day depends on what's available at the market: staples include shellfish soup with saffron, duck breast with honey and sherry, roast chicken, loin of lamb, monkfish and lobster couscous, and fillet of bass with slivers of Parma ham. The service is a bit slow. The restaurant also offers rooms for the night.

☆☆☆☆ Splash Out

✕ **Le Sanglier des Ardennes**: rue Comte-d'Ursel 14. ☎ (086) 213262. Closed on Thursdays (except public holidays), and in January. Set menus from 1,200BEF. This unmissable, solid-looking house on place aux Foires is home to one of the best restaurants in the province, with spectacular views of the River Ourthe and surrounding countryside. Service is a bit stiff (don't expect a smile), and the clientele tend towards the snooty, but the refined cuisine is truly outstanding, and standards are pretty consistent. The place is run with almost clockwork precision and professionalism. During the week, there's a fairly expensive lunch menu – although that pales in comparison with prices à la carte. Signature dishes include chicken cooked in sea salt and grilled trout, while sweet-toothed diners will love the wicked desserts: *assiette tout en chocolat, croustillant à la vanille*, stawberries *Romanoff* (with cream and vodka) and brown-sugar *crème brûlée*.

WHAT TO SEE AND DO

★ **Walk in the old centre**: the centre is small but architecturally uniform. Peep down rue des Récollectines, rue Éloi or rue de la Prévôté and you'll get a glimpse of delightful grey-stone buildings. The 16th-century corn hall on rue Comte-d'Ursel is one of the province's rare examples of half-timbered gabling. It was also the tithe barn, where tenant farmers used to come to pay taxes. The building was later used as a law court.

★ **Église Saint-Nicolas**: rue Comte-d'Ursel. This 1632 church has fine barrel vaulting and an impressive, frugally decorated wood altarpiece. The pulpit is a mass of carvings (including the four Evangelists), and there's a fine stone font dated 1588.

★ Don't miss the **view from La Falize**. If the private gazebo is open, there are splendid views from the top of the cliff, although houses have almost monopolized its edge.

★ **Parc des Topiaires**: on the other side of the Ourthe from the old town. Open 10am–6pm. Admission: 150BEF; free for children accompanied by an adult. This 1-hectare (2.5 acre) park is famed for its topiary, and you can see all kinds of shapes, including a crocodile and even a Manneken-Pis. You could be forgiven for admiring the uncut bushes instead – they demand less work, but perhaps deserve more attention.

FESTIVAL

– **Comic-strip festival**: beginning of October.

IN THE AREA

★ **Église Saint-Martin**: in Tohogne. This fine Romanesque church was constructed in the 11th century. The choir is panelled, and you can see the remains of old frescoes. The pulpit is emblazoned with the figures of the four Evangelists, and there's a superbly carved font with a frieze and four heads. Scenes in the surviving frescoes include Adam and Eve's abrupt departure from the Garden of Eden and the Annunciation. Unfortunately, many of the church's statues have been stolen.

★ **Domaine de Hottemme** (Hottemme Estate): in **Barvaux**. ☎ (086) 213011. Open throughout the year; phone to check the exact opening hours. Admission: 80BEF. Fifty dioramas depicting the local fauna are on show in one huge building. You can also take a walk in the lovely park.

★ **Labyrinthus**: rue Basse-Commène, Barvaux, a 10-minute walk from Barvaux station. ☎ (086) 219042. From early July to the end of August, open 10.30am–7.30pm. Admission: 265BEF, with discounts for children under 12. Each year, a 2-hectare (5-acre) field of maize is turned into a maze where children do their utmost to lose their parents. As you slog round in search of your little angels, you'll encounter all manner of characters in fancy dress.

★ **Grottes de Hotton** (Hotton Caves): south of Durbuy. ☎ (084) 466046. From the beginning of April to the end of October, open 10am–5pm (to 6pm in July and August). Admission: 250BEF. Discovered in the 1960s, these caves contain stalagmites and stalactites in every colour you can imagine. At one point during the tour, you look down on a chasm that's 30 metres (nearly 100 feet) deep.

★ If you have time, visit the **Moulin à eau Faber**, a working 18th-century watermill on the route d'Erezée. ☎ (084) 466122. Tours in July and August at 2.15pm, 3pm and 4pm. Admission: 80BEF.

| **MARCHE-EN-FAMENNE** | **16,000 inhabitants** |

This pleasant little town is one of the area's administrative and commercial hubs. Over the years, Marche-en-Famenne has gone to great lengths to make the most of its heritage, and the results are generally positive: the town centre has been thoughtfully restored, and it's lively without being hectic.

In 1577, the town witnessed the signing of the short-lived 'Perpetual Edict', which marked the confirmation of the Pacification of Ghent and the end of Spanish rule. The ramparts that once surrounded the town were destroyed by Louis XIV's army, and only one tower is still standing.

Until the end of the 19th century, the town's chief source of income was lace: at one time, 300 lace-makers were employed here, with about 800 in the region as a whole. A lace-making school is now trying to relaunch the industry.

USEFUL ADDRESS

Postcode: 6900.
Tourist Office: rue des Brasseurs 7. ☎ (084) 312135. Open 9am–12.15pm and 1.15–5.40pm in season; from June to September, also open Sunday 10am–12.30pm and 2–5pm. The building that houses it is one of the oldest in town, Le Pot d'Étain.

WHERE TO STAY AND EAT

☆–☆☆ Budget–Moderate

Hôtel Alfa: avenue Toison-d'Or 11. ☎ (084) 311793. Fax: (084) 321175. Doubles 1,450–2,400BEF. You'll be made to feel very welcome at this small, provincial hotel. The rooms are simple, but well maintained and inexpensive: the cheapest ones have sinks. The hotel restaurant is closed on Sunday evenings and Thursdays.

☆☆☆☆ Splash Out

Hôtel-restaurant Quartier Latin: rue des Brasseurs 2. ☎ (084) 321713. Fax: (084) 321712. Email: contact@quartier-latin.be. Doubles 3,000–4,800BEF. An elegant if rather commercial hotel complex built around an 18th-century Jesuit church. The ground floor houses conference facilities and a large shop on the ground floor, while guests get access to the gym, sauna and jacuzzi. There's also a classy restaurant with a brasserie-style menu that will set you back 1,000BEF. Free parking.

Aux Menus Plaisirs: rue du Manoir 2, in the Hôtel du Manoir. ☎ (084) 313871. Closed Sunday evening and Monday. A full meal costs about 1,400BEF, with set menus from 750BEF. This softly lit restaurant is in a spacious rotunda filled with indoor plants and the gentle strains of music in the background. The surroundings could hardly be more sophisticated, and the cuisine is suitably refined, although the service is perhaps a bit aloof. One menu is devoted to local produce, another is a fish and seafood menu that features such delicacies as lobster served with succulent, basil-flavoured lasagne. If you go à la carte, you'll be offered hot *terrine* of sole and lobster, roast lobster in thyme, veal kidneys in mustard, veal sweetbreads with spinach, *confit* of duck or loin of lamb.

WHAT TO SEE AND DO

★ **Musée de la Dentelle** (Lace Museum): rempart des Jésuites, off rue des Tanneurs, in the last surviving tower of the ramparts. ☎ (084) 312135. Open 9am–noon and 1.30–7.30pm. Closed Sunday and Monday out of season. Admission: 80BEF. The ground floor focuses on the changing use of lace in clothing between the 16th and the 20th centuries, with superb examples from Binche, Brussels, Bruges, Lille and Paris. One room is devoted to old lace from Famenne, bobbins and the school's efforts to kick-start the industry. The visit ends with a demonstration of lace-making tools and techniques.

★ **Musée de la Famenne**: rue du Commerce 17. ☎ (084) 327060. Open 10am–noon and 2–5pm in season. Closed Sunday (except in summer) and Monday. Admission: 100BEF. Housed in a pretty 18th-century brick building, this museum is devoted to crafts and local traditions, with displays exploring local ethnography and geology. Rare pieces include a pair of 14th-century shoes and an 18th-century Liège-style drawing room.

★ **Walk around the centre**: you can't miss the 14th-century Église Saint-Remacle, which is on the main square. It has a Gothic apse and a picturesque spire, and is surrounded by handsome 18th- and 19th-century houses with beautifully clean and polished facades. This neighbourhood has retained a certain stylish elegance. On rue des Dentellières, the low houses have steps leading up to the front doors.

★ **Hôtel de Ville**: a brick-and-stone building that dates from the 18th and 19th centuries.

★ There's a fine 17th-century building at rue du Manoir 2.

WHAT TO SEE IN THE AREA

★ **Église Saint-Étienne**: in Waha, 2 kilometres (1 mile) from Marche-en-Famenne. This is the oldest Romanesque church in Belgium. To the right of the choir, you can still see the consecration stone, dated 23 June 1050. The structure has a beautiful tower with bevelled roofs, arranged one above the other as if in accordance with some mathematical pattern. Inside, take a look at the vaulting and Romanesque bays, where the three aisles are delightfully simple. There are four pillars with arcades, four funerary slabs at the entrance, several old statues, and above the choir, a wonderful Gothic crucifix.

A venerable lime tree with a gnarled old trunk stands outside the church. People awaiting trial were tied to its trunk.

– **Carnival**: the high point of the year, with the election of the prince and a procession of giants.

– **Bird market**: 15 August.

– **Alsatian festival of Waha**: the main attraction is the creation of a massive bonfire, so big it's listed in the *Guinness Book of Records*.

FOURNEAU-SAINT-MICHEL

★ **Musée de la Vie rurale en Wallonie** (Museum of Rural Life in Wallonia): on the road from Nassogne to Saint-Hubert. From the N4, take exit Champlon, heading for Saint-Hubert. From the E411, take the Transinne exit. ☎ (084) 210613 and (084) 210890. From March to the end of November, open 9am–5pm (to 6pm in July and August). Admission: 100BEF or get a combined ticket to the Musée de Fer for 150BEF. Rural dwellings, farms and buildings from all over Wallonia have been moved to an area of more than 40 hectares (100 acres) in this stunning, peaceful valley. It's a delightful place, where you can stroll around and explore the Chapelle de Farnières, complete with its own enclosure and pretty tombstones, an old printworks, a school, a *sirop* factory, an Ardennais carthorse stables, barns and old workshops. There are two suggested walks, one of about 2 kilometres (1.5 miles), and a shorter one of 600 metres.

★ **Musée du Fer et de la Métallurgie ancienne** (Museum of Iron and the Old Metallurgy Industry): a couple of kilometres from the Musée de la Vie rurale, heading towards Saint-Hubert. It's well signposted. ☎ (084) 210613. From beginning of March to the end of the year, open 9am–5pm (to 6pm in July and August). Admission: 100BEF. Housed in a former blacksmith's house, this fascinating museum contains an old stove and little dioramas charting the progress of iron forging since 1400BC. You can see how the iron was moulded, and how cookers, firedogs, pots and railway tracks were manufactured. The beautiful stove in the middle of the main room has attractive ceramic and carved ornamentation.

– The first floor focuses on the history of the Fourneau Saint-Michel, with a model showing its various functions, examples of firebacks and statues of the patron saints, including a weathered statue of Notre-Dame de Luxembourg. You can also see a reconstruction of a traditional kitchen, a wrought-iron cemetery cross, waffle moulds and *rondeaux*, which were used to make communion wafers.

– On the second floor, you'll find a reconstruction of a forge, with a collection of pincers and pokers, blacksmith's implements, wrought-iron artwork, doors with nails, locks and old irons.

– The third-floor collection includes agrarian implements, ploughs, weights and measures, agricultural tools, tanners', wheelwrights' and coopers' tools, scythes and so on.

★ Outside, you can visit a section devoted to the history of the Ardennes Forest, which is housed in an old wooden coal barn. The timber industry was vital to metallurgy, and wood-cutting and carpentry are the main themes here. The display includes a tree planted at the time of Waterloo and felled in 1990, as well as implements and tools made of wood, including a weird poker that was apparently used to keep piglets in order. The awesome *maka*, or *martinet*, was an enormous refining hammer that weighed up to 200 kilos (880 pounds). Below is a blast furnace, dated 1771. The impressive bellows room, with its paddle wheel and casting centre, is still in perfect working order.

– A signed 3-kilometre (2-mile) walk leads you through the **Forêt de St-Michel**. There are information panels en route.

★ **Musée Redouté**: next door to the Musée du Fer. Open July to September, 2–6pm. Admission: 60BEF. A gallery of paintings by the Belgian flower painter Pierre-Joseph Redouté (1759–1840), who also painted Marie-Antoinette, the Empresses Joséphine and Marie-Louise, and Louise-Marie, the first Queen of the Belgians. One room displays nothing but his favourite subject: roses.

WHERE TO EAT AND DRINK

✕ ❢ **Bar A Pêle**: on a pleasant veranda on the first floor of the Musée Redouté. Open 10am–5pm; 10am–7pm in July and August, and on weekends. Closed Wednesday. Perfect if you're after light meals: soups, omelettes, local *matoufé,* potatoes with bacon, carrot soup, crêpes and ices. Wine is served by the glass.

SAINT-HUBERT — 6,000 inhabitants

Saint-Hubert is a small tourist resort surrounded by beautiful woodland. Named after St Hubert, a young, carefree seventh-century prince who liked hunting, it boasts a marvellous basilica and excellent restaurants. One Good Friday, the prince was about to dispatch a deer when a shining cross appeared among the trees. As a result, he entered a monastery and later became Prince-Bishop of Liège – and patron saint of hunters and butchers.

USEFUL ADDRESSES AND INFORMATION

Postcode: 6870.
🏠 **Tourist Office**: rue Saint-Gilles 12. ☎ (061) 613010. Fax: (061) 615444. Email: rsi.Saint-Hubert@swing.be; www.sthubert.be

■ **Bike hire**: Cycles Godfroid, route de Poix 11B. ☎ (061) 612810. Email: Godfroidsports@chez.com. You'll get a free drink when you return from your ride.

WHERE TO STAY AND EAT

🛏 ✕ **Hôtel du Luxembourg**: place du Marché 7. ☎ (061) 611093. Fax: (061) 613220. Closed Thursday out of season and for two weeks in mid-June. Doubles 1,200–2,500BEF, including a generous breakfast. This small, central hotel exudes a provincial charm. Guests can sample good, classic cooking in the friendly restaurant. There are several set

menus, while the à la carte options include Liège-style veal kidneys, noisettes of lamb and scallops, grilled turbot with cream and beetroot, wild boar stew and escalopes of veal with leeks and grapes.

🛏 **Campsite Europacamp**: rue de Martelange, 1.5 kilometres (1 mile) from the centre of the Saint-Hubert-Bastogne road. ☎ (061) 611269.

Tent site: 371BEF. Open all year. A family campsite covering 15 hectares (48 acres). The tents are spread out and surrounded by trees and bushes. There are decent washing facilities and children's activities.

✕ **L'Auberge du Prévôt**: in the Musée de la Vie rurale, Saint-Hubert 6870. ☎ (084) 210915. Closed Monday evening, Tuesday and from December to February. A full meal costs about 1,200BEF, with set menus from 650BEF. Booking is recommended, and essential on Sunday. This charming restaurant with a high, beamed ceiling is housed in a splendid 18th-century building. If you're looking for a snack or a salad, sit outside at one of the large wooden tables. Inside, the food is more sophisticated, with such elaborate dishes as homemade *jambon cru*, asparagus, salmon tartare and cutlets or *ragoût* of wild boar *au gratin*. The à la carte menu offers cream of celery with fillets of smoked eel, fish cooked in butter and *kriek* beer, pasta with squid, chicken supreme with a carrot *coulis*, duck *confit*, Ardennes trout with smoked bacon and veal kidneys.

WHERE TO STAY IN THE AREA

🛏 **Youth Hostel**: rue de la Gendarmerie 4, Champlon 6971. ☎ (084) 455294. Fax: (084) 457045. Email: champlon@laj.be. Closed in January and December, except during the Christmas holidays. Basic rate per night: 405BEF. This beautifully-renovated stone house enjoys a delightfully bucolic setting and offers a high level of comfort. The small dormitories sleep six, seven, eight or 15, and there's a room for two and a room for three. The kitchen is well equipped, and guests can also use the garden barbecue. Bike hire is available, and the hostel is 50 metres from the nearest bus stop.

WHAT TO SEE

★ **Basilique Saint-Pierre-Saint-Paul-Saint-Hubert**: open 9am–5pm. The basilica, which has one of the most complicated names of any church in Belgium, used to belong to the abbey. It was built in the 11th century and rebuilt in Gothic style in the 16th century, acquiring its rather large Classical facade and twin towers in 1700. Inside, it's wonderfully spacious, with five aisles, and involves an impressive variety of materials: the supports are in grey and pink stone, while the upper parts and parts of the triforium are white limestone. Look out for the superb brick vaulting and sandstone arches.

A 17th-century Renaissance-style tomb lies to the left of the entrance, and there's a typically over-the-top 19th-century mausoleum dedicated to St Hubert in the left-hand transept. The closed choir is made of marble, and the choir, dated 1733, has unusual carved panels devoted to lives of St Hubert and St Benoît, with detailed carving on the arms and misericords. The huge marble altar boasts a statue of the Virgin Mary from the school of Jean del Cour.

– The **ambulatory** (at the back of the choir) contains three stunning chapels and a 1589 tombstone. In the third chapel on the left, you can see an old treasury with Renaissance windows, while the first chapel on the right contains 24 painted Limoges enamels that were disfigured by the Huguenots.

– The **crypt** has original brick vaulting, which rests on two central supports, a marvellous black-marble tombstone and ancient terracotta tiling on the floor.

– In the **right transept**, there's a late-Renaissance altar to St Hubert, with a replica of the saint's stole. In front is a carved balustrade, while the altarpiece above depicts the legend of St Hubert and the Stag. The motifs on the fine Renaissance organ case echo those on the door.

★ **Old abbey buildings**: to the left of the basilica. The complex, which was rebuilt in 1729, houses a temporary exhibit. It has carved oak doors, marble mantlepieces, regal staircases and a fine wrought-iron banister.

★ **Église Saint-Gilles-au-Pré**: built in the 11th century. The sturdy square tower is all that remains of the original church. The 17th-century altar is in Louis XIII style.

★ **Museum-experience 'La légende de St Hubert'**: place du Marché 13. Open 10am–6pm. Admission: 180BEF. The saint who gave his name to the town is brought to life in *Le Grand Cerf blanc*, a comic-strip 'biography' by Pierre Glogowsky that captures the atmosphere of the Ardennes forest in the days of Charlemagne.

RELIGIOUS AND CULTURAL FESTIVALS

– **Saint-Hubert pilgrimage**: Pentecost Monday and 3 November.

– **Festival of the Butchers' Guild**: last Sunday in September.

– **Historic procession of hunters**: first Sunday in September at 2.30pm.

– **Juillet musical de Saint-Hubert**: concerts and recitals throughout July.

IN THE AREA

★ **Parc à gibier** (game park): 2 kilometres (about a mile) from Saint-Hubert on the Fourneau-Saint-Michel road. ☎ (061) 611715. Admission: 100BEF. A chance to see sheep, deer and boars in their natural habitat.

★ **Centrale hydraulique de Poix** (Poix Hydroelectric Plant): Scierie d'en Haut, Poix-Saint-Hubert, 100 metres from the railway station. ☎ (061) 613101. From May to October, open 1–7pm during school holidays and at weekends. Admission: 150BEF. A spectacular guided tour through a hydroelectric plant next to the River Lomme, which brought electricity to the region at the beginning of the 20th century. There are audiovisual displays and interactive exhibits.

REDU

To the west of Saint-Hubert lies a village that has been a book town since 1984. Inspired by Hay-on-Wye, in Britain, Redu (the 'village du livre') was the first such place in mainland Europe, and bookworms can browse for hours in the village's 25 bookshops of Redu. They all specialize in rare books, and are awash with tantalizing piles of second-hand books on any number of subjects. You can also see examples of the crafts associated with books – gilding, binding, engraving and paper-making – explore art galleries and admire the work of jewellers, weavers and blacksmiths. The project has proved a huge success, attracting more than 350,000 visitors annually, and the new Musée du Livre et de l'Imprimerie (Museum of the Book and Printing) should help to swell numbers even further.

Book-lovers gather over the Easter weekend and on the first weekend in August for the 'Night of the Book'.

WHERE TO STAY, EAT AND GO FOR A DRINK

☆☆ Moderate

🛏 There are several B&B options in Redu, but in high season, you should book in advance through the tourist office: ☎ (061) 656516.

🛏 ✕ **Cantine & Comptines**: rue Neuve 74, Redu 6890. ☎ (04951) 62034 or (04951) 63120 (both mobile numbers). A young couple run this traditional place, which has three rooms decorated with light wood panelling and stone. One is fairly large, with its own private bathroom (2,000BEF per night); the other two are under the eaves (1,500BEF). Both prices include breakfast. Guests can ask for a full home-cooked meal or try one of the (mainly vegetarian) light meals on offer, which include lasagne, *gratins*, quiches and omelettes, costing 200–300BEF. It's also an antiques shop, literary café and a calligraphy studio, so there's plenty to keep you occupied. Outside school holidays, there's a 10 per cent discount on rooms.

✕ ❢ **L'Escargon**: rue de la Prairie 36, Redu 6890. ☎ (061) 656327. Open Friday lunchtime to Sunday evening; every day at Easter and in July and August. A full meal costs about 750BEF. This pleasant, informal restaurant is a good place for a quick bite between bookshops. Less hurried visitors can dine on fillets of salmon trout, grilled ham in thyme and homemade tarts. There's also an entertaining literary menu, inspired by the classic authors, and a wine bar.

❢ **Café Diogène**: rue Neuve 77. ☎ (061) 688002. This place turns into a 'philosophy café' every Saturday at 7.30pm.

WHAT TO SEE IN THE AREA

★ **Musée de la Cloche** (Bell Museum): rue Grande 23, in Tellin. ☎ (061) 366007. In season, open from Tuesday to Saturday 10am–noon and 2–5pm, Sunday 2–6pm. Admission: 100BEF. If you've ever wanted to know how bells are made, you'll be able to lay your curiosity to rest. This museum explains the materials used in the foundry, the moulds, carillon mechanisms, electromechanical clocks and so on. Foundry tours can be booked in advance.

★ **Euro Space Center**: rue Devant-les-Hêtres 1, Transine-Libin 6890. ☎ (061) 656465. Website: www.ping.be/eurospace. Open April to November and during the school holidays, 10am–5pm. Admission: 395BEF; children aged 6–12 300BEF. This educational leisure centre has a suitably futuristic setting, and kids come in droves to marvel at the machines used in the conquest of space: the Mir station, Ariane, Hermès, the shuttle Discovery and so on. The Space Show, holorama and planetarium are particularly good. The centre also runs introductory courses on space engineering.

BASTOGNE   12,500 inhabitants

Bastogne is best known for its heroic resistance to the Germany army during the crucial Battle of the Bulge in 1944. The liberation of France and Belgium, which had begun on the Normandy beaches, finally ended here. The dominant features of the main square are a Sherman tank and a bust of the American general, McAuliffe, whose defiance helped save Bastogne. As well as a host of commemorative museums and monuments, the town has an outstanding old church, the Église Saint-Pierre, which has somehow managed to survive centuries of conflict.

A Short History

At dawn on 16 December 1944, the German army launched its last attack on Belgium. Its aim was to recapture Antwerp, isolate the Allied armies in the north and, if possible, force them to capitulate. It seemed the perfect time: the weather was poor, negating Allied Command's airpower, and the mobilization of men between 16 and 60 meant there were plenty of new infantry divisions: 240,000 men and 1,800 Tiger and Panzer tanks were sent into battle. It was a desperate gamble: this was Hitler's last operational reserve. The Allied frontline was held by only 120,000 men, 240 tanks – and a lot of inexperienced troops.

The Germans swept through southern Belgium, and Bastogne was soon surrounded. On 22 December, General McAuliffe, commander of the US 101st Airborne division, issued his now famous answer to the German demand for surrender: 'Nuts!' By chance, the fog lifted the next day, and supplies were dropped into Bastogne by air. There were constant attacks from the Panzers, continuous bombardments and terrible German air raids. By the time the Third Army, under Patton, launched an attack from the south to relieve Bastogne, only 1,000 people were left in the town, which was finally liberated on 26 December. The stubborn defence of Bastogne helped the Allies force the German army to withdraw, and was decisive in the failure of the offensive.

– There's a 60-kilometre (36-mile) tourist trail, with marker boards at the 14 most important points of resistance. Ask for the itinerary at the tourist office.

USEFUL ADDRESS AND INFORMATION

Postcode: 6600.
🄱 **Tourist Office**: place McAuliffe 24. ☎ (061) 212711. Fax: (061) 212725. Website: www.bastogne-tourisme.be. Email: info@bastogne-tourisme.be. Open 9.30am–12.30pm and 1–5.30pm.
🚆 **Railway station**: ☎ (061) 211108.

WHERE TO STAY IN THE AREA

☑ Budget

â **La Pommeraie**: Sprimont 41, Sainte-Ode 6680, 12 kilometres (7 miles) west of Bastogne. ☎ (061) 688611. Fax: (061) 688695. Email: contact@europaventures.be. Rooms cost 850BEF per person, including breakfast, with discounts for children aged 5–10. Home-cooked meals for guests about 600BEF. This old country house has a *gîte* (country lodge) for up to four people, and five comfortable, recently decorated rooms with sinks. Facilities include a garden and a sauna, and meals can be arranged in advance. Bike hire is also available. La Pommeraie is on the 'Transardennaise', a route linking La Roche to Bouillon. It takes several days to complete, and you can get more details at the hotel.

â **La Ferme des Bisons**: Foy-Recogne 6800, 5 kilometres (3 miles) north of Bastogne on the way to Houffalize. ☎ (061) 210640. Fax: (061) 210649. This splendid *gîte* sleeps between four and 13 people, and can be booked by the week or for a weekend. It's on the edge of the forest, in the outbuildings of an 18th-century farm, and has been sensitively done up to provide modern comforts while retaining the look and generous proportions of the original building. The *gîte* is fully equipped, with a microwave and a dishwasher in the kitchen, a bathroom, central heating, a wood fire, a TV, a washing machine, a barbecue and garden furniture. Kids will love it, especially when they discover that a 100-strong herd of American bison graze peacefully on the grass of a neighbouring field (*see* 'What to see in the area').

WHAT TO SEE

★ **Bastogne Historical Center:** 3 kilometres (1.5 miles) away from the centre, next to the memorial on the Mardasson hill. It's well signposted. ☎ (061) 211413. Open 9am–6pm in July and August; 9.30–5pm in May, June and September; 10am–4pm in March, April, October, November and December. Admission: 295BEF, with discounts for children. In this context, 'history' means the Battle of the Bulge, which is the sole focus of this museum. There are dioramas with models of the main protagonists: on the American side, you can see Bradley, Eisenhower and Patton, as well as a life-size photograph of General McAuliffe issuing orders from his Jeep. The Germans, meanwhile, are represented by weapons, campaign ambulances, newspapers, pamphlets and posters. An old red-and-yellow town plaque, riddled with bullet holes, hints at the civilian cost of the conflict. Don't miss the film of the battle, which contains some unique sequences.

★ **Mémorial**: next door to the museum. This huge construction, shaped like a five-pointed star, is a tribute from the Belgians to the American and Allied forces for the part they played in the liberation of Europe. The sentence in the middle is simple: '*Le peuple belge se souvient de ses libérateurs américains*' ('The people of Belgium remember their American liberators'). The walls are engraved with the names of all the units that took part in the Battle of the Ardennes. You can also go up to the memorial terrace.

★ **Église Saint-Pierre**: place Saint-Pierre. Don't miss this remarkable church as you wend your way to the memorial. The massive Romanesque

THE PROVINCE OF LUXEMBOURG

spire is 12th-century, while the nave was rebuilt in Flamboyant Gothic style in the 15th century. The most striking thing about the interior is the vaulting over the three aisles: a lattice of ivy, ribs and keystones springs from each pillar. The frescoes date from the time of Charles V and the furniture is stupendous, with a highly carved baroque pulpit and, behind the organ, a fantastic 16th-century wooden Laying in the Tomb. A sorrowful-looking Mary is supported by St John and other figures in period costume. The real masterpiece of the church, however, is the Romanesque baptismal font in carved stone (hidden behind the door at the back). Take a look at the primitive carved heads on the corners and the wonderful wrought-iron canopy.

★ **Porte de Trêves**: behind the church. This gateway is all that remains of the town ramparts, which were built by Jean l'Aveugle in the 16th century and demolished by Louis XIV.

If You Have the Time

★ **Musée En Piconrue**: place Saint-Pierre 24. ☎ (061) 215614. From mid-June to mid-October, open 1.30–6pm, weekends 10am–6pm. Closed Monday. Admission: 120BEF. This converted convent now houses religious art and exhibits relating to popular beliefs.

★ **Musée d'Histoire et d'Archéologie Unde Oreris**: maison Mathelin, rue G.-Delperdange 1, near the Porte de Trêves. ☎ (061) 211758. Open July and August only, 10am–noon and 1–5pm. Closed Monday. Admission: 100BEF. Located in a restored 18th-century house, this museum covers the history of Bastogne from its origins to 1944. The display includes original objects and documents, as well as spectacular dioramas.

★ **Animalaine**: 'La Source', Bizory 5. ☎ (061) 217508. From April to October, open every day 10am–4.30pm; otherwise weekends only, 2–6pm. Admission: 70BEF. This tiny eco-museum explains the manufacture of wool, from fleece to garment. Visitors can also watch a video about different shearing methods.

WHAT TO SEE IN THE AREA

★ **Ferme des Bisons** (Bison Farm): in Foy-Recogne (*see* 'Where to stay in the surrounding area'). ☎ (061) 210640. Admission: 80BEF, with discounts for children. A taste of the Wild West in the heart of the Ardennes. The farm has a herd of 100 large, peaceful bison, which you can view from a horse-drawn wagon. There's a fascinating museum explaining the daily life of native Americans in one of the farm buildings. A curator-guide takes you round, enthusing all the way about the life and ways of the Sioux, Creek and Dakota tribes. There's also a fantastic reconstruction of a teepee. From mid-April to mid-October, open Sundays and public holidays noon–7pm; from mid-July to mid-August, open every day except Monday. Admission to the exhibition: 150BEF, with discounts for children.

FESTIVAL

– **Nut Fair**: December.

ARLON   24,000 inhabitants

Arlon is the capital town of the province of Luxembourg. It's a quiet place in what used to be Belgian Lorraine, and, after Tongeren, it's thought to be the country's oldest town. Once an opulent, fortified Roman centre, Arlon succumbed to Barbarian and Frankish invasions. The French arrived in the guise of civilizers, but turned out to be just as barbarous as all the other invaders when they pillaged and sacked the town under the Duke of Guise and the Sun King.

USEFUL ADDRESSES AND INFORMATION

Postcode: 6700.
◨ Tourist Office: rue des Faubourgs 2. ☎ (063) 216360. Website: www.arlon.be

⊠ Post Office: rue de la Poste 1.
■ Taxis: ☎ (063) 221897.

WHERE TO STAY AND EAT

≜ Campsite: route de Bastogne 368. ☎ (063) 226582.

≜ ✕ Hôtel des Druides: rue de Neufchâteau. 108, 500 metres from the town centre. ☎ and fax: (063) 220489. Doubles 1,200–1,500BEF. This is an unobtrusive, well-maintained hotel. The rooms are not particularly charming, but they do have showers. Light meals are available, and there's a private car park.

≜ L'Écu de Bourgogne: place Léopold 9. ☎ (063) 220222. Fax: (063) 232754. Doubles 2,300–2,700BEF, including breakfast. A very central, classic hotel, where the comfortable rooms have en suite bathrooms. There's no restaurant.

✕ Le Dean: rue du Marché-au-Beurre 22, a stone's throw from the Grand-Place. ☎ (063) 223051. Open for lunch and dinner (until midnight). Closed Monday. Main courses about 300BEF. This place has a great atmosphere and modern decor, and is especially popular with young people. The restaurant serves generous helpings of freshly prepared dishes and specialities such as cutlets, knuckle of ham, mixed salads, spare ribs, chilli con carne and homemade hamburgers.

✕ Maison Knopes: Grand-Place 24. ☎ (063) 227407. Open 8am–1am. Closed Monday morning and Sunday morning. Nothing here costs more than 400BEF. A pleasant tea-room on a quiet square with outside seating. The light meals, grills and sweet and savoury delicacies are all recommended.

WHERE TO GO FOR A DRINK

The region's speciality is *maitrank*, which existed in Charlemagne's day. It's based on adding plants or fruit to white wine to make it less acidic, which is what monks in the region used to do. This custom has long since died out in most of Luxembourg, but not in Arlon, where families and inns continue this tradition. *Asperula odorantis* (woodruff) is added to the wine along with cognac, sugar and sometimes a slice of orange. As you might have gathered from the name, May is the month in which to drink this concoction.

¶ **Maison de la Knipchen**: on the corner of Saint-Donat and Vierge-Noire. A fairly average café that's worth mentioning for its pleasant terrace by the church. It also makes the best *maitrank* in town. The landlady's friendly, but tight-lipped when it comes to the secrets of her recipe. Light meals such as *salade niçoise* and spaghetti are available.

WHAT TO SEE AND DO

★ **Musée luxembourgeois**: rue des Martyrs 13. ☎ (063) 226192. Open 9am–noon and 1.30–6pm; from mid-April to mid-September, Sunday and holidays 2–6pm. Closed Monday. Admission: 100BEF. If you're into ancient history, this museum offers an excellent overview of the Roman occupation of the region, although the strong collection is displayed in a workaday, old-fashioned way. The most important items include: a beautiful first-century sculpture showing a Roman officer making a sacrifice; the funerary altar of Julius Maximinus; a striking stone tablet with a satyr; and a she-wolf feeding Romulus and Remus. There are also samples of pottery, which seem to have been stamped with seals, Roman glass (notably delicate perfume bottles) and oil lamps. You can also see bronze weapons, brooches, jewellery and a lead mould for forging coins and bronze statuettes of gods.

The first-floor displays concentrate on the Merovingian period, with fine belt buckles, jewellery and weapons. Carved furniture and painted statues illustrate the Middle Ages and the Renaissance.

★ **Parc archéologique**: rue des Thermes-Romains, south of the town. There are traces of the old basilica (which dates from the 4th century), the remains of the Roman baths and a Merovingian cemetery. They're not outstanding, but worth a look if you're interested.

★ **Église Saint-Donat**: built on a hill that was fortified by Vauban. You have to climb a flight of steps, flanked by a crucifix, to reach this eclectic-looking church. The choir, which sports some fine woodwork, has 18th-century doors, while the main altar is in rococo style. You can see the remains of 18th-century frescoes in the chapel on the left, which has an altar from the same period. There's also a Virgin and Child on a crescent moon.

From the terrace (check to see if the tower is open), you'll get a wonderful view of the town and the old quarter below the hill, which is now undergoing restoration. In fine weather, you'll be able to see Germany, the Grand Duchy of Luxembourg and France.

★ **Walk around the centre**: place Léopold. Buildings and monuments worthy of note in the centre include the former Palais de Justice, the neo-classical provincial government buildings of 1845 and an American Sherman tank. There's no shortage of cafés and brasseries with terraces should you want to pause for refreshment. Just around the corner in the cul-de-sac that leads from Café Alby, you can view the base of a Roman tower and the remains of the third-century ramparts (ask at the café if you want to have a look).

THE PROVINCE OF LUXEMBOURG

FESTIVALS AND FAIRS

– **Les Faaschtebounen** (Lent): a mid-Lent carnival with giants.

– **Maitrank festival**: in May. Information from the tourist office.

– **Antiques Fair**: first Sunday of each month, except in December, January and February.

WHAT TO SEE IN THE AREA

★ Nature-lovers should visit the **Marais de la Haute-Semois** (Haute-Semois marshes), between Arlon and Chantenelle. This is an outstanding natural area, ideal for observing local flora and fauna. In the old days, it was infamous for malaria, and was dried out in the 19th century. The marshes are now run by Les Réserves naturelles et ornithologiques de Belgique (see 'General information'), a voluntary organization that oversees the upkeep of Belgium's biotopes. They're always in need of support, so any contribution you can make will be much appreciated.

The Gaume

This is the southernmost point of Wallonia. The landscape, shaped by gently rolling hills and little villages with tiled roofs, is quite different from anything you see in the rest of the region. The area also benefits from a remarkable microclimate: within a few dozen kilometres, the temperature can go up by two or three degrees, making it much warmer than the Fagnes at the same time of year. Chimay, for example, a stone's throw away but at the door of the Ardennes, receives twice as much water as Torgny, which is in the Gaume.

The locals are anti-authoritarian and renowned for their 'southern' joviality. While Walloon is the language spoken in the Ardennes, Lorraine is spoken in the Gaume – all in all, it's quite an exotic place.

VIRTON   **11,000 inhabitants**

This pleasant town, built on a hill above the River Ton, is the capital of the Gaume, and has an excellent museum dedicated to the history and culture of the region.

USEFUL ADDRESS

Postcode: 6760.
🛈 **Gaume Tourist Office**: rue des Grasses-Oies. ☎ (063) 578904. Fax: (063) 577114. Open 9am–noon and 1.30–5pm.

WHERE TO STAY

🛏 **Campsite Vallée de Rabais**: rue de Bonlieu. ☎ (063) 571195. Open all year. A large, well-equipped campsite where you can swim, fish and play tennis. Bike hire available.

WHAT TO SEE

★ **Musée gaumais**: rue d'Arlon 38. ☎ (063) 570315. Open 9.30am–noon and 2–6pm. Closed from December to mid-March and Tuesday, except during the Christmas and carnival holidays. Admission: 100BEF. This well-presented, informative museum has superb displays and an attractive modern wing.

– The ground floor houses archaeological collections, with a bronze basin from Sainte-Marie-sur-Semois and finds from the Merovingian necropolis at Torgny. You can also see strings of beads made of molten glass, a beautiful gold disc-shaped brooch, splendid buckles and belt ornaments, and collections of porcelain. In the older part of the museum, you'll find displays of medieval objects, tombstones, a 16th-century stone tabernacle, huge mantlepieces, carved furniture, old stoves and wrought-iron objets d'art.

– Firebacks and old tombs are on display in the courtyard.

– On the first floor, you'll find a weaver's workshop and a *cabinet de curiosités* (Wunderkammer), a fine double dresser, the workshop of a saddler (in use until 1984), a reconstruction of the kitchen with a wonderful copper pump and an 18th-century box bed.

– The main exhibit on the second floor is a basket-weaver's workshop. Return to reception in order to continue your visit.

– The second floor of the modern wing explores customs, beliefs and religious practices. You can watch a video and see a commemorative plaque and a collection of chemists' drugs. This floor also houses several statues of the Virgin, used for pilgrimages and processions, including the beautiful, carved-wood Notre-Dame d'Orval, a fine painting under glass, an 18th-century ceramic cross that belonged to the priest Pierre Pierre and an 18th-century painting of the Assumption by Brother Abraham d'Orval. This section winds up with collections of religious jewellery, traditional crèches and irons used to make wafers for communion.

– On the first floor of the modern wing, the highlights are the log-maker's and cobbler's workshops. Peasant furniture and a box bed make up the rest of the exhibits.

★ **Église de Vieux-Virton**: built in the 11th century with Roman materials. There are some low-relief sculptures on the south wall plus 18th-century frescoes by Brother Abraham Gilson.

FESTIVAL

– **Lovers' Fair**: 26 December. A big festival involving D'Jean d'Mady and Djeanne, Virton's giants.

TORGNY

This is Belgium's southernmost village. The setting is wonderfully bucolic, and the climate rivals that of the French Midi. The houses have tiled roofs and are built of white limestone that turns honey and gold in the light of the setting sun. There's a 19th century wooden wash house on the village square. The lintels of many of the houses are centuries old.

Traditionally, Torgny is a vine-growing village that produces white wines: the Clos de la Zolette, of which the locals hope to produce up to 5,000 bottles annually, and the respectable Clos de Torgny. Not surprisingly, it was the Romans who brought viticulture here, and the tradition continued until the end of the 19th century. Torgny is well suited to vines thanks to its limestone soil, which warms up quickly in the sun, and the fact that it's well sheltered from the wind.

USEFUL ADDRESS

Postcode: 6767.
🛈 Tourist Office: at the top of the village near the church, beyond La

Grappe d'Or. ☎ (063) 579574 and (063) 578381.

WHERE TO STAY AND EAT

⛺ ✕ Campsite à la ferme: rue de Lamorteau 5. ☎ (063) 578387. Good tents. The river's 500 metres away. Light meals are available.
⛺ B&B L'Escoffiette: rue Escoffiette 7. ☎ (063) 577170. Fax: (063) 582589. Doubles 2,100–2,500BEF, with a 10 per cent discount for midweek stays at more than one night. A beautiful village house that used to be a girls' boarding school. It now has four fully equipped, distinctive rooms for two, and you're guaranteed a warm welcome and a good choice of food at breakfast.
✕ Taverne La Romanette: Rue Grande 3. ☎ (063) 577958. Fax: (063) 581922. Closed Wednesday out of season. A tavern serving light meals, and its terrace fills up fast in fine weather. There are four B&B-style rooms with shower costing 1,800BEF. Half-board available.

☆☆☆☆ Splash Out

⛺ ✕ La Grappe d'Or: rue de l'Ermitage 18, on a road leading to the church. ☎ (063) 577056. Fax: (063) 570344. Restaurant closed on Sunday evenings and for lunch on Mondays and Tuesdays during winter. Part of the Relais du Silence group, it has luxurious rooms, with doubles costing 3,800–4,200BEF, including an excellent breakfast. At 2,500BEF a head, the restaurant is hardly cheap, but its reputation precedes it. The menu includes veal sweetbreads in pig's trotters and foie gras, ravioli with duck foie gras and truffles and roast scallops *gratinées au champagne*. During the week, there's a set lunch for 1,050BEF.

WHAT TO SEE IN THE AREA

★ In the lovely hilltop village of Montquintin, you can visit the impressive ruins of the fortified château and the small Romanesque church. The **farm museum**, housed in an 18th-century building, is also worth exploring (open 2–6pm in July and August). You can visit the kitchen, bedroom and classroom, and learn about old farming methods.

ABBAYE D'ORVAL

The original abbey was founded on this splendid site in the 11th century, and quickly became one of the most affluent in Europe. The name supposedly comes from '*val d'or*' (golden valley), because the Duchess of Lorraine, the abbey's benefactor, once lost her treasured ring in a spring here. It was miraculously found, so the legend goes, by a trout. The abbey was destroyed several times over the years, first in the 14th century, then in 1637, when it was attacked by the Maréchal de Châtillon, and again in 1793, when it was bombarded by General Loison's troops. A new set of monks moved here in 1926, and a new church was built over the 18th-century cellars. Interestingly, the two neighbouring abbeys have managed to co-exist.

USEFUL INFORMATION

Postcode: Villers-devant-d'Orval 6823.
– **Opening hours**: from Easter to the end of September, open 9.30am–12.30pm and 1.30–6.30pm; otherwise 10.30am–12.30pm and 1.30–7.30pm. Admission: 120BEF.

WHAT TO SEE

– **Audiovisual tour**: history of the abbey, every hour from 2–5.30pm.

★ **Fontaine** Mathilde: this is where the famous gold ring was found.

★ **The ruins of the abbey church** have lost none of their grandeur, and are truly inspiring. There are several important ruins, including the rose window in the left-hand transept, the Romanesque and Gothic capitals, and the flat pillars where the stalls used to be (near the choir). You can enter the cloister on the right and also visit the fine chapterhouse.

★ The **museum**, in the magnificent 18th-century cellars, displays firebacks decorated with the abbot's arms, old paving and models of the old and new monasteries. It's a good overview of Cistercian abbeys.

★ Don't miss the **old pharmacy**: turn left on your way out and carry on until you come to the pharmacy. The display includes old bottles, mortars, painted drawers, retorts and a carved, 18th-century set of scales. The museum also hosts temporary exhibitions.

🔒 In the **shop**, you can buy the famous Trappist beer, the equally famous cheese and delicious small biscuits.

WHERE TO EAT

✕ **Auberge à l'Ange Gardien**: near the abbey. ☎ (061) 311886. This is an ideal place to stop before or after your visit to the abbey. You can have an open sandwich with Orval cheese, try the Gaumais pâté or soup, stoke up with 'touffaye' sauerkraut or simply opt for an omelette. Whatever you have, wash it down with Orval beer.

WHAT TO SEE IN THE AREA

★ **Relais Romain de Chameleux** (Roman Staging Post): south of Florenville. It's well signposted if you take the N88, which passes through beautiful woodland before reaching a pond-filled valley. It's a charming area, hence the number of luxurious dwellings and second homes. Look out for the first-century Roman staging post – you can still see remains of the warehouses and springs – and part of the embankment of the original Roman road.

If you have time, pop across the French border to visit the delightful, authentic village of **Williers**, with a pretty square-cum-street that runs along the length of the church. Pop into the village café if you're in need of refreshment.

WHERE TO EAT IN THE AREA

✕ **Le Chameleux**: next to the Roman staging post. ☎ (061) 311020. Closed on Tuesday evenings, Wednesdays and in September. *Plat du jour* 350BEF. Full marks to this small country inn, which has a relaxing terrace overlooking the valley, an affable landlord and good, unpretentious, generous dishes. Try the trout, a potato and bacon omelette or a plate of ham with raw vegetables. Pancakes are also served at lunchtime.

THE HAUTE SEMOIS

★ **Chiny-sur-Semois**: one of Wallonia's prettiest villages. It's on the edge of the lazy River Semois, just 4 kilometres (2 miles) from the commercial town of Florenville, where the tourist office stocks plenty of useful literature, as does the tourist kiosk on the main square. The village is full of 18th-century dwellings, and you can also see the remains of the old ramparts. Several nature walks start at the mill, the Moulin Cambier, and you can go canoeing or take a boat to Lacuisine in fine weather. Don't miss the ruins of the bridge, which was destroyed in 1940.

🏠 ✕ **Résidence Les Touristes**: rue du Millénaire 61, Chiny 6810. ☎ and fax: (061) 312910. Doubles 2,000BEF. Affordable B&B rooms, full of character, quiet and fully equipped, and a restaurant serving such unusual dishes as wild boar chops. The food is more expensive than the lodging: about 1,000BEF per head if you go à la carte. You can dine in the garden in fine weather. Half-board available.

🏠 ✕ **B&B Les Géraniums**: rue de la Goulette 1. 6810 Chiny. ☎ (061) 320708. Fax: (061) 320559. Closed January and February. Doubles 1,800BEF. This beautiful, bright and airy house in the heart of the village has five comfortable rooms. Guests can dine here if they arrange it in advance.

★ **Chassepierre**: another of the area's prettiest villages, especially lovely at sunset, when the old houses and the church are reflected in the river. There's an artists' and street-theatre festival on the first weekend after August 15.

★ **Herbeumont**: this impressive 12th-century château was destroyed by Louis XIV.

BOUILLON   5,500 inhabitants

Up on a dramatic ridge, above a huge bend in the Semois, stands one of Europe's most impressive fortresses. Bouillon was the capital of a duchy, the last heir of which was Godefroid, famous for his crusades to Jerusalem. Before taking Jerusalem by storm, however, he sold his castle to the Prince-Bishops of Liège. It passed to the Princes of La Marck, then once again to the Prince-Bishops, until, in 1676, Louis XIV gifted it to a family known as La Tour d'Auvergne. In 1795, the duchy was incorporated into the French Forests *département* in 1795 and finally became part of Belgian in 1830.

Today, Bouillon is one of the most popular tourist towns in Wallonia, attracting thousands of holiday-makers, weekend visitors and camper vans. Unsurprisingly, there are plenty of hotels to choose from.

USEFUL ADDRESSES AND INFORMATION

Postcode: 6830.

◻ Tourist office: by the entrance to the château. ☎ (061) 466257. Fax: (061) 468285. You can pick up a free brochure detailing walks in the Semois valley (Easter–November).

◻ Bureau de tourisme: this seasonal kiosk is at the entrance to the tunnel under the château. ☎ (061) 466289. Open from Easter to the end of September.

■ Bike hire: Moulin de la Falize, Vieille route de France 33. ☎ (061) 466200. Camping, swimming, sauna, bowling and canoeing are also available.

WHERE TO STAY

🛏 Hostel 'Sur la Hauteur': route du Christ 16, Bouillon 6830. ☎ (061) 468137. Fax: (061) 467818. Basic rate per night: 405BEF. Closed January and the first fortnight in December. Perched on the top of a ridge, this place has splendid views and 130 comfortable rooms sleeping four to 10 people.

🛏 B&B À la Cornette: route de Fays 32, Bouillon 6830. 10 kilometres (6 miles) from Bouillon. Take the road under the bridge at Fays-les-Veneurs towards Dohan and carry on for a few kilometres through the woods. ☎ and fax: (061) 413536. Doubles 2,000BEF, including breakfast. A haven of peace and tranquillity in the heart of the forest, with a little brook running through the garden. There are five modestly priced rooms for two, with shower and toilet, and supplementary beds

are available on request. There's also an apartment for four at 3,000BEF. Credit cards not accepted.

🛏 Hôtel Le Cordemoy: rue du Collège 44. ☎ (061) 466027. Fax: (061) 468192. Closed January. Doubles with shower 2,400–2,700BEF. This is a large, touristy hotel where the rooms have recently been renovated. The corner rooms are best. Half-board is compulsory in high season, so you'll be seeing plenty of the spectacular view from the first-floor restaurant. Snacks are served on the ground floor.

🛏 Hôtel La Villa d'Este: rue de la Maladrerie 17. ☎ (061) 467961. Fax: (061) 468557. Doubles 1,900–2,120BEF, including breakfast. Centrally situated and decidedly classy, this hotel offers bright, modern en

suite rooms with bath or shower.
Half-board available.

🛏 **L'Auberge d'Alsace**: faubourg de France 3, at the foot of the château. ☎ (061) 466588. Fax: (061) 468321. Closed January. Doubles from 2,360BEF, although you'll pay 3,560BEF for a room overlook-ing the Semois. Breakfast costs an extra 300BEF. Pleasant, cosy rooms above a rustic-style restaurant serving good traditional food. The menu features fish, Ardennes quail, chops, chicken with mushrooms and Alsatian guinea-fowl. Reasonably priced set menus.

WHERE TO EAT

✗ **Café-restaurant La Vieille Ardenne**: Grand-Rue 9. ☎ (061) 466277. On the corner of rue de l'Abreuvoir, below the château. Full meal about 750BEF. Closed Wednesday. One of the only places in town to resist the demands of mass tourism, this welcoming place is a genuine regulars' bar. An impressive collection of glasses hangs from the ceiling, and there's a good beer list. Simple meals incorporating local produce are concocted by the landlady. Try the omelette (it'll set you up for the day), Ardennes trout, seasonal game, salads or the cheese-filled escalope 'Val d'Or'.

WHERE TO GO FOR A DRINK

🍷 **The Saloon**: perched high on the old road to France. Open from 8pm. Closed Monday, Tuesday and Wednesday, except in high season. There are few obvious opportunities for meeting people in this town, but you could always try this Western-style saloon bar, complete with billiard table, cocktail bar, gallery, barrels for tables and even a mechanical bison for rodeo fanatics. The menu features chips and barbecues. It's an atmospheric place, with occasional live music and slightly risqué shows.

WHAT TO SEE

★ **Château**: ☎ (061) 466257. Open 9.30am–7pm in July and August; 10am–6pm in April, May, June and September; 10am–5pm in March, October and November; 1–5pm December and February (weekends 10am–5pm); 10am–5pm at the weekend in January. Last admission 45 minutes before closing time. Admission: 150BEF, with discounts for children and student; you can also buy a combined ticket for the château and the Musée ducal. Torchlight tours in July and August. The château, which consists of three forts defended by towers and drawbridges, was considerably altered in the 16th century, and again under Louis XIV's military architect, Vauban. The Dutch destroyed the medieval keep in 1824.

The 13th-century Godefroy de Bouillon room, which contains a display of waxworks and an exhibition about the château, can be reached via the main courtyard. You should also climb the Tour d'Autriche (1551), which stands at the end of the covered walkway, for fine views of the rest of the château, the town and the meandering Semois. Falconry displays take place between Easter and August.

★ **Musée ducal**: entrance in front of the château, next to the church. ☎ (061) 464189. From April to the end of September, open 10am–6pm;

10am–5pm in October, November and during the school holidays. Admission: 120BEF, with discounts for children and students. This imposing 18th-century monolith, formerly the seat of government, is now a museum devoted to local history and folklore. Exhibits include a reconstruction of an Ardennais hostelry, complete with kitchen and dining room, a weaver's workshop and memorabilia of the period when politically harassed French writers, among them Voltaire, Abbé Prévost, Mirabeau and Diderot, were forced by their homeland's censorship laws to publish their works abroad; many of them chose instead to publish in Bouillon. One room is dedicated to Godefroy de Bouillon and the crusades, and there's an impressive model of the château as it might have looked in the 12th century.

★ **Archéoscope Godefroy de Bouillon**: open from 10am to 4pm, 5pm or 6pm depending on the month. Closed on Monday between October and the end of February, and throughout January. Admission: 240BEF, with discounts for children. This superbly renovated former convent, which has also served as a blacksmith's forge, is one of contemporary Bouillon's most impressive achievements. The ultimate tourist attraction, Archéoscope takes you back to the glory days of the Duchy of Bouillon and the supposedly valiant Godefroy, Lord of Bouillon and first King of Jerusalem, which he conquered during the first crusade. A multimedia display offers a romanticized account of the pious and courageous duke, with spectacular *son et lumière* effects. Historical balance, meanwhile, comes in a section on the crusades as seen from an Arab perspective.

There's also an excellent exploration of frontiers and the concept of 'limes' (the Latin word for boundary), as well as a comparison of the fortresses in France and present-day Belgium. Another multimedia display, with a vast ground map and aerial videos, will give you a comprehensive grounding in the region's heritage. Your visit ends in the cells, where the nuns slept.

WHAT TO SEE IN THE AREA

CORBION

A typical Ardennes village, west of Bouillon in the thick of the forests, Corbion has a local hero: Sébastien de Corbion, the inventor of the pistol. Born in 1520, he was known as Sébastien 'Pistolet'.

WHERE TO STAY

☆☆ Moderate

⌂ **Hôtel Le Relais**: rue des Abattis 5, Corbion 6838, near the church. ☎ (061) 466613. Fax: (061) 468950. Closed July and August. Doubles 2,300–2,500BEF. A hotel with 11 recently decorated rooms with showers, a rustic-style sitting room and a family atmosphere: according to one reader, staying here is a bit like being at mum and dad's. It's excellent value for money, and an ideal base from which to explore the forest. Good weekend and midweek deals are available. The restaurant specializes in game (closed Tuesday; menus from 650BEF).

☆☆☆ Expensive

⌂ **Hôtel des Ardennes**: rue de la Hate 1, Corbion 6838. ☎ (061) 466621. Fax: (061) 467730. Website: www.hoteldesardennes.be. Doubles 2,950–3,800BEF. Closed January to the end of March. This peaceful, highly regarded establishment has classy, comfortable rooms and a pretty garden with a children's play area. Mountain-bike hire is available. The opulent restaurant tempts its upmarket clientele with an array of delicious specialities: duckling with baby onions, shoulder of spring lamb and pigeon stuffed with veal sweetbreads. There are affordable set menus.

ROCHEHAUT

The hilltop village of Rochehaut has fantastic views of the winding Semois, while the route here, via Corbion and Poupehan, is equally enchanting. A 1.5 kilometre (1 mile) hillside path takes you up to the small village of Frahan.

WHERE TO STAY AND EAT

⌂ **Hôtel Les Tonnelles**: place Marie-l lowet 5, Rochehaut 6830. ☎ (061) 464018. Fax: (061) 464-012. Double rooms: 2,100BEF. A traditional, well maintained hotel, where good bourgeois cuisine is served by the fire in winter and beneath the arbour in summer. The menu includes trout, game and Ardennes specialities. With a set menu at 800BEF, it's one of the cheaper restaurants in the area.

⌂ **Hôtel-restaurant Beau Séjour**: rue du Tabac 7, Frahan 6830. ☎ (061) 466521. Fax: (061) 467880. This large, half-timbered house on a curve of the Semois has pleasant en suite rooms at midrange prices, as well as a garden and decent cuisine. It's a good place to stay if you want to go walking in the area.

BOTASSART

This delightful village is near the river's most beautiful bend, known as the 'Giant's Tomb'. There's a grandeur and romance about the landscape here – it's a great place to come with a loved one.

– **Local shale church**: built in 1677, this pretty little church has a slate tower and a venerable old stove in the middle. There are beautiful tombstones on the walls, old benches and a wooden ceiling that looks a bit like an upturned boat.

– The surrounding area is fantastic walking territory.

– **Open-air museum**: Ucimont 12. Open all year 8am–10pm. Admission: free. You can see old washing houses and stoves.

WHERE TO STAY AND EAT

⌂ ✕ **Au Bon Accueil**: rue de Chateaumont 20, Botassart-sur-Semois 6833, not far from the Giant's Tomb. ☎ and fax: (061) 466771. Closed in January. Doubles 2,900BEF, half-board. You won't find anything much quieter than this unpretentious, likeable and well-maintained hotel, which has eight rooms with showers. The young owners really know how to make their guests feel welcome. Fresh vegetables from the garden are served in the restaurant, where the menu includes steak, leg of rabbit, noisettes of lamb and game in season, all accompanied by homemade bread. Set menus start at a very reasonable 700BEF. There's also a terrace with a veranda.

ALLE-SUR-SEMOIS

Without realizing it, you will cross into the Province of Namur here. This village, famous for its slate centre, is particularly popular with tourists visiting the Basse-Semois region. Campsites line the river banks, while the country-side is clogged with caravans. The Récréalle leisure centre doesn't help. The village has a pretty centre, with an onion-domed church and a little museum devoted to bees and honey (Musée de l'Abeille et du Miel).

WHERE TO STAY AND EAT

🛏 ✕ **Hôtel Au Central**: place Mongin 15, Alle-sur-Semois 5550. ☎ (061) 500323. Fax: (061) 466027. Doubles 2,100BEF; half-board compulsory in high season. Set menus from 395BEF. This rustic-style hotel has 15 en uite rooms (some at the front under the eaves). The restaurant special-izes in rabbit cooked in Trappist beer, duck and veal chops *à la grand-mère*.

WHAT TO SEE

★ **Ardoisalle**: rue de Reposseau 12. Guided tours every day in July and August at 10am, 11am, 2pm, 3pm, 4pm and 5pm (there are also night-time tours); no morning tours during school holidays. Otherwise, closed Monday and Tuesday from 1 May to 11 November, except during school holidays. Admission: 140BEF. You have to descend to the bowels of the earth to find out all about the slate industry, which has now died out. Down in the depths, you can wander through narrow corridors and flooded rooms, then find out more from a video and a small museum.

VRESSE-SUR-SEMOIS

The sister village of Alle-sur-Semois, Vresse is a holiday resort much frequented by painters, and was once a centre for tobacco production. In fact, the whole valley was once covered by tobacco plants. Now, the industry caters only for locals and tourists. The foundations of the bridge with three arches date from Roman times.

USEFUL ADDRESS

🆔 **Tourist Office**: rue Albert-Raty 112. ☎ (061) 500827. As well as offering literature about this region, the tourist office is a cultural centre, with a permanent exhibition featuring a reconstruction of the Belge (the first railway locomotive on the continent), a vast panorama depicting the painters of the school of the Semois, among them Albert Raty and Marie Howet, and a little Musée du Tabac, where they've accumulated objects concerning the use of tobacco: pipes, including one smoked by Georges

Simenon, boxes, roasters, spittoons and an oriental smoking room with a hookah.

PALISEUL

Once you've reached this charming village, you're back in the province of Luxembourg.

WHAT TO SEE IN THE AREA

★ **Au cur de l'ardoise** (Old Slate Mine): Morépire estate, rue du Babinay 1, Bertrix 6880. Take exit 25 on the E411. ☎ (061) 414521. From April to the end of September, open 10am–6pm. Admission: 250BEF for the guided tour, 150BEF to see the *son et lumière*, or 350BEF for a combined ticket. Discounts for children and senior citizens. A 1 hour 30 minute visit to an old slate mine takes you 45 metres (nearly 150 feet) below ground on a funicular. Once you're there, you can watch a 45-minute *son et lumière* illustrating the history and folklore of the region. NB: bring extra clothing to put on: it gets cold down there.

NEUFCHÂTEAU

WHERE TO EAT

✕ **La Ferme des Sanglochons**: Verlaine 29, Neufchâteau 6840, on the Recogne-Neufchâteau road. From the E411, take exit 26. ☎ (061) 222233. Closed Monday evening and Tuesday, except holidays, and from mid-January to mid-February. A full meal costs about 450BEF here. This handsome old stone building provides a pleasant setting for a delicious meal of local sausages, cold meats and the speciality, '*Sanglochon*' (a cross between a pig and a boar, which gives exceptionally flavoursome meat), as well as simpler snacks such as omelettes, Ardennes soup, lasagne and Ardennes ham on toast. You can also visit the steam room, drying room and smokery, and see how meat is salted in brine and then dry-cured.

WHAT TO SEE

★ **Musée la Remise**: Offaing, Neufchâteau 6840. ☎ (061) 278439. Open all year from 10am. Admission: 90BEF. This old farm is now a beautiful museum of rural life, with reconstructions of workshops and domestic interiors, such as a forge, a bistro and a peasant kitchen, as well as farming machines and domestic objects. There's also a 1900-style tavern.

WHAT TO SEE IN THE AREA

★ **Musée des Celtes** (Museum of Celtic Civilization): place Communale 1, Libramont 6800. Take exit 25 on the E411. ☎ (061) 224976. Open Tuesday to Friday 9.30am–5pm and Sunday 2–6pm. Closed Monday, Saturday and throughout January. Admission: 100BEF. Housed in an old presbytery, this museum explains the history of the Gauls, without the Asterix and Obelix clichés. The result is a thorough overview of a civilization that most of us know very little about. You can see a reconstruction of a funerary wagon, harnessing accessories, splendid jewels, weapons and the fruits of 30 years of archaeological digs in the Ardennes. There are also excellent dioramas that evoke the habitat and layout of Celtic villages.

Province of Namur

This green and pleasant province, which stretches down to the French border, has been shaped by the River Meuse, which cuts deep gullies into the countryside as it wends its way towards the Netherlands. Over time, this abundance of water has eroded the rock face, creating some impressive caves. The rugged landscape lends itself to all kinds of activities, so it's perfect for sporty types. The most popular pursuits are walking, cycling and climbing – on a Sunday, you'll even see queues of climbers waiting to clamber up the cliffs of the Meuse. For those of a more cultural disposition there are plenty of châteaux, stately homes, museums and churches to admire. Namur, the capital of the province, is the administrative capital of the Walloon Region, and the seat of the regional parliament.

NAMUR   105,000 inhabitants

If you found Liège a little hectic, you'll find the pace of life in Namur reassuringly laid-back. This compact, provincial place is easy to get around and refreshingly free of high-speed roads. The town nestles at the foot of a great cliff, and most of the sites are within walking distance of the historic centre. Namur has endured many a siege thanks to its strategically significant position between the Sambre and Meuse rivers, but has managed to keep much of its old centre intact. Property developers got away with murder during the 1970s and 1980s, but the locals have hit back. Recent years have seen an extensive restoration programme, and after much political wrangling, the Walloon parliament has settled into the Hôtel Saint-Gilles, below the citadel.

Namur sheds its reputation as a 'sensible' town during the wild Fêtes de Wallonie (on the third weekend in September), when there's music on every street corner and the gin flows freely. It's an ideal time to visit.

A Short History

Namur was originally a Gaulish fortress, which was occupied by the Romans at the time of Caesar. A small town took shape under Charlemagne, and fell victim to the usual raids, first by the Vikings and then by the Normans. The first Count of Namur was sworn in during the 10th century, but by 1421, his successor found himself in such straitened circumstances that he sold the town to Philip the Good, Duke of Burgundy. For the next five centuries, Namur was coveted by many an ambitious monarch and was consequently the object of many a siege. The long-suffering locals built their houses with tiled, rather than wooden, attics to prevent the spread of fire from red-hot cannonballs. You don't need to know the details of every siege to appreciate the town, but the following events were crucial in shaping its history.

The Burgundian dukes were succeeded by the Spanish, and Namur became the centre of Philip II's war machine for the Counter-Reformation. Louis XIV, well aware of the town's strategic importance, conquered Namur in 1692, but lost it to William of Orange in 1695. The French recaptured the town in 1701, but it was returned to the Dutch in 1715. The French took the town again in 1746, under Louis XV, only to be ousted by the Austrians, who destroyed the city's ramparts. In 1792, the armies of the French Revolution seized Namur and turned it into the *préfecture* of the Sambre-et-Meuse district, an 'honour' it held until 1814.

Namur slumbered away beneath its cliff throughout the 19th century, when the Industrial Revolution passed it by. Unlike so many Belgian towns, Namur emerged relatively unscathed from the two world wars, although it played a vital role in 1914, when its determined resistance gave the French Marshal Joffre enough time to hone his strategy and win the Battle of the Marne.

USEFUL ADDRESSES

❶ Tourist office (map C1): square Léopold 3. ☎ (081) 222859 and (081) 246449. Open 9.30am 6pm. You can hire audio guides for touring the old town. Themed guided tours are also available. Book in advance if you want to take part in 'Namur Nocturne' ('Namur By Night'), a nocturnal prowl about town, complete with theatrical entertainment in the historic neighbourhoods. The tour leaves at 8.30pm, and the price includes a free glass of *absinthe*.

❷ Bureau d'accueil (map C2): Grognon car park, at the confluence of the Sambre and Meuse. ☎ (081) 246449. Open from April to the end of September.

❸ Fédération du tourisme de la province de Namur: rue Pieds-d'Alouette 18, BP 2, on the Nannine industrial estate. ☎ (081) 408010. Fax: (081) 408020. Open Monday to Friday 8am–5pm. The service is excellent, and the office stocks plenty of literature on the region.

✉ Main post office (map B1): boulevard E.-Melot, next to the station. There's another post office at rue de la Monnaie 1.

🚌 Information on local buses: TEC, ☎ (081) 720840.

🚆 Railway station (map B1): place de la Station. ☎ (081) 252222.

■ Bike hire: at the station, ☎ (081) 223701.

■ Consulat de France: chemin du Pont-de-Briques 21. ☎ (081) 301586.

WHERE TO STAY

☆ Budget

⚓ Youth Hostel Félicien-Rops (off the map from B3, **12**): avenue Félicien-Rops 8. ☎ (081) 223688. Fax: (081) 224412. Basic rate per night: 405BEF. Closed in January. The hostel is in the La Plante district, about 3 kilometres (2 miles) from the city centre, heading for Wépion-Dinant. Take bus No. 3, which stops in front of the hostel, or No. 4 (get off at Les Marronniers stop) from the railway station. This old mansion on the edge of the Meuse has 80 beds in rooms that sleep four, five and six, as well as a couple of doubles. There's a kitchen and a garden with volleyball courts. Mountain-bike hire available.

🛏 **Campsite Les Trieux**: rue des Trys 99, Malonne 5020. ☎ (081) 445583. Fax: (081) 308023. Situated west of Namur. Tent site: 520BEF. Open from April to the end of October. Standards are high, and there's a shop on the site.

🛏 **B&B Namur-Citadelle**: route des Canons 6 *bis*, on the citadel estate, which is best reached by car. ☎ (081) 738821. Doubles 1,500BEF; 10 per cent discount if you stay for a week. Open June to September. There are three rooms on the first floor of this house, with a shared bathroom, and guests can use the garden, terrace and veranda.

☆☆–☆☆☆ Moderate– Expensive

🛏 **Hôtel Les Tanneurs de Namur** (map C2, **10**): rue des Tanneries 13. ☎ (081) 231999. Fax: (081) 261432. Email: info@tanneurs.com. Small doubles 2,000–2,500BEF, with larger rooms up to 8,500BEF. Breakfast 300BEF. This hotel is part of a 17th-century tanner's house, on a delightful street lined with historic buildings: the owner rescued the whole street from demolition by property developers. It has been beautifully restored, using the finest of materials, including marble, oak and quality fabrics. The result is a luxury establishment with splendid, individually furnished and decorated rooms, and the stairways and hidden nooks and crannies give it plenty of character. The smaller rooms are comfortable, tastefully decorated and surprisingly affordable: if you want to splash out, go

for broke and stay in the sumptuous duplex suite. The hotel has two restaurants: Le Grill des Tanneurs, which does an inexpensive *plat du jour*, and L'Espièglerie, which is decidedly upmarket (*see* 'Where to eat').

🛏 **Inn La Ferme du Quartier** (off the map, continuation of C1, **13**): place Sainte-Marguerite 4, Bouge 5004, in a suburb on the edge of the countryside, about a 10-minute drive from Namur. ☎ (081) 211105. Fax: (081) 215918. Doubles 1,450– 1,650BEF, including breakfast, with half- and full-board available. Restaurant open for lunch and dinner (until 9pm), lunch only on Sunday and public holidays. Closed in July. Leave Namur from place Léopold (near the station), take pont de Louvain and chaussée de Louvain, then turn right into rue Saint-Luc at the Shell garage; continue until you get to Bouge. The hotel is on the attractive main square. From the south of Namur, take avenue Albert-Ier, heading for Hannut; once you're level with the main square, turn left into rue de Balart, cross the level crossing and turn right into the road that leads to the centre of Bouge. From the Brussels–Luxembourg motorway, take exit 14 (Bouge). This hotel, once a farm, has 15 classic, comfortable rooms, and you're guaranteed a friendly welcome. The restaurant is more upmarket, with set menus from 950BEF, and has a very good reputation. Specialities include young rabbit with baby onions, quail with grapes, fish *waterzooî*, rustic *ragoût* of veal sweetbreads, guinea fowl *à l'ardennaise* and steak with mushrooms.

🛏 **Hôtel Opéra-Le Parisien** (map C1, **11**): rue Émile-Cuvelier 16. ☎ (081) 226379. Fax: (081) 231718. Doubles 2,050–2,250BEF. This central hotel has decent, if unremarkable, rooms. The café-brasserie on the ground floor offers a *plat du jour* for 290BEF.

☆☆☆ Expensive

⌂ **New Hôtel de Lives** (off the map from D1, **14**): chaussée de Liège 1178, Lives-sur-Meuse 5101. ☎ (081) 580513. Fax: (081) 581577. Doubles 2,800BEF. Off the beaten track, but easy to find: cross the pont de Jambes, take the Liège turning and, a few kilometres after the mo-

torway viaduct, you'll see a large building from the turn of the last century, with views of the cliffs and the Meuse. The staff are attentive, and there are 10 impeccable rooms, including two that would suit families, where you'll want for nothing. The hotel has a bar and an elegant, bourgeois dining room, where breakfast is served. The only drawback is that it's quite near the road, and lorries roar past early in the morning.

WHERE TO EAT

☆–☆☆ Budget–Moderate

✕ **La Cuve à Bière** (map B2, **19**): rue des Brasseurs 108. ☎ (081) 261363. Open 8am–midnight; food served noon–3pm and 6–10pm. Closed Sunday. A full meal will cost about 450BEF. This warm and welcoming tavern has a bar shaped like a beer vat. It's more of a bar than a restaurant, but it offers splendidly simple food: fish soup, Ardennais

soup, *salade liégeois*, meatballs in pepper sauce and other light dishes. There's a delightful courtyard, and a more expensive restaurant in the annex.

✕ **Le Grill des Tanneurs** (map C2, **10**): rue des Tanneries 13. ☎ (081) 240024. Closed Saturday lunchtime and Sunday evening. Lunchtime *plat du jour* 530BEF, including dessert. This first-floor restaurant serves decent food in an agreeable setting.

■ **Useful addresses**

- 🛈 Syndicat d'initiative
- 🛈 Bureau d'accueil
- ✉ Main post office
- 🚆 Railway station

⌂ **Where to stay**

- **10** Hôtel Les Tanneurs de Namur
- **11** Hôtel Opéra-Le Parisien
- **12** Youth Hostel Félicien-Rops
- **13** Inn La Ferme du Quartier
- **14** New Hôtel de Lives

✕ **Where to eat**

- **10** L'Espièglerie and Le Gril des Tanneurs
- **19** La Cuve à Bière
- **20** La Cava
- **22** La Maison des Desserts
- **23** Aux P'tits Brasseurs

- **24** Le Temps des Cerises
- **25** Restaurants on the square Chanoine-Descamps, Fenêtre sur Cour and La Petite Fugue
- **26** Brasserie Henry

🍷 **Where to go for a drink**

- **25** Extérieur-Nuit
- **27** Le Chapitre
- **30** Marché-aux-Légumes

★ **What to see**

- **30** Place du Marché-aux-Légumes and Église Saint-Jean-Baptiste
- **31** Musée Félicien-Rops
- **32** Musée diocésain
- **33** Musée de Groesbeeck de Croix
- **34** Musée des Arts anciens du Namurois
- **35** Trésor d'Hugo d'Oignies

NAMUR

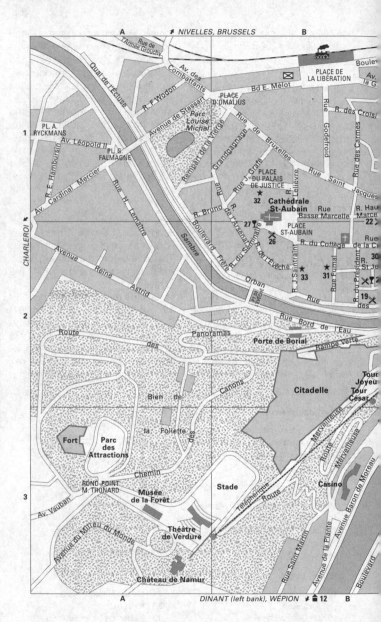

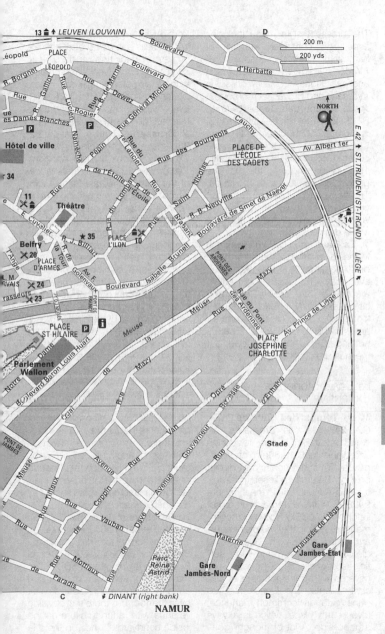

NORTH

E 42 → ST.TRUIDEN (ST.TRCND)

LIÈGE ↘

Boulevard
d'Herbatte

PLACE
LÉOPOLD

R. Borgnet
Gaillot
Rue
Rue Lucien
Rogier
Rue J. B. de Marne
Rue Dewez

Boulevard

Rue Général Michel

Cauchy

Av. Albert Ter

R. des Dames Blanches

Naméche

Pépin

Rue du
Lancier
R. de

Rue des Bourgeois

Nicolas

PLACE DE
L'ÉCOLE
DES CADETS

Hôtel de ville

34

R. de l'Étoile

R. de
l'Étoile

Salm

Brabant

B. B. Neuville

Boulevard de Smet de Naeyet

11

Théâtre

Rue du
Tombard

14

E. Cuvelier

R. J. Billiart

35

PLACE
L'ILON

10

Boulevard Isabelle Brunell

Rue des Ardennes

Mazy

Belfry

20

Via Tour de

PLACE
D'ARMES

Av. F.
Golenvaux

Boulevard Isabelle Brunell

Rue au Pont
des Ardennes

Av. Prince de Liège

GERVAIS

24

PONT DE
FRANCE

Meuse

Meuse

Rue

23

Range

Brasseur

Mazy

PLACE
ST HILAIRE

i

Meuse

la

Dame

PLACE
JOSÉPHINE
CHARLOTTE

Parlement
Wallon

Notre

Boulevard Baron Louis Huart

de

Mazy

Opré

Brasse

d'Enhaive

Crail

la

Rue

Van

Gouverneur

Rue

Stade

PONT DE
JAMBES

Meuse

Avenue

Rue

Avenue

Rue

NAMUR

Rue
Tilleux

Coppin

Dave

Rue
Mottiaux

Rue

Vauban

de

Materne

Chaussée de Liège

Gare
Jambes-État

de

Paradis

Parc
Reine
Astrid

Gare
Jambes-Nord

200 m
200 yds

The brasserie-style menu includes lamb with coriander, knuckle of ham with mustard, *cassoulet namurois* (with steak, sweetbreads and veal kidneys), mullet grilled in *tapenade* and Provençal fish soup.

✕ **La Maison des Desserts** (map B1-2, **22**): rue Haute-Marcelle 17. ☎ (081) 227451. Open until 7pm. Closed Monday. In the airy, glass-covered courtyard of an attractive 18th-century house, this is the perfect place for a light lunch. Try homemade *croque monsieur*, crêpes (Ardennais, Provençal or with leeks), quiche, salads and one of the delicious desserts.

✕ **La Cava** (map C2, **20**): rue de la Monnaie 20 (two steps from rue de l'Ange). ☎ (081) 230472. Open every day. This pizzeria-cum-grill in a splendid 15th-century Gothic cellar is extremely popular with the locals, who come for a good natter around the large tables. There's nothing special about the food, but the staff are cheerful and efficient.

☆☆–☆☆☆ Moderate–Expensive

✕ **Le Temps des Cerises** (map C2, **24**): rue des Brasseurs 22. ☎ (081) 225326. Open for lunch and dinner (until 10.30pm) on Wednesday, Thursday and Friday, dinner only on Saturday. Closed mid-July to mid-August. Full meal about 900BEF, with a three-course set lunch for 650BEF. Booking recommended. A typical *namurois* restaurant, with a relaxed, welcoming atmosphere. The red-and-white setting is spotless, and the walls are covered with the signatures of celebrity clients. The Oenology Club (wine club, in common parlance) favours this place, which is always a good sign. A lot of thought goes into the tasty dishes, which use the freshest ingredients. Try traditional dishes like *baekehoffe*, (a meat stew

from Alsace) *fricassée* of rabbit in wine, snails *à la namuroise*, knuckle of ham in beer and mustard, *cassoulet namurois* (veal sweetbreads, kidneys and steak in gin) and *crème brûlée au florange* (a fortified wine). Every two months, they produce a themed menu with matching wines.

✕ **Brasserie Henry** (map B2, **26**): place Saint-Aubin 3. ☎ (081) 220204. Open 8.30am–midnight. *Plat du jour* 290BEF. In the shadow of the vast Cathédrale Saint-Aubin, which looks like something out of Fellini's *Amarcord* when it's illuminated at night, this popular brasserie aspires to a little of the cathedral's grandeur, with cream walls, high, moulded ceilings, marble tables and green leatherette benches. There's so much space, however, that sound can get lost here, and the annoying acoustics can spoil your enjoyment of the classic brasserie cuisine. The menu includes calf's head in jelly, veal in cream and mushroom sauce, homemade sauerkraut and knuckle of ham, as well as a fine range of desserts. There's a good wine list.

✕ In fine weather, Place du Chanoine-Descamps (map B2, **25**) has plenty of **restaurants** with terraces, and there's a good range in terms of both price and cuisine. It's a bit touristy, but it's such a pleasant, upbeat square that it doesn't matter. Committed carnivores should try La Charbonnade d'Angus.

✕ **Fenêtre sur Cour** (map B2, **25**): rue du Président 35; there's also an entrance on place du Chanoine-Descamps. ☎ (081) 230908. Closed Sunday. *Plat du jour* 295BEF. The main dining area, with mirrors and an 18th-century mantelpiece, is a bit over the top, but there's a pleasing veranda with rattan furniture on the inside courtyard. Dishes on the à la carte menu vary depending on what's available, and can be a bit pricey.

NAMUR

✕ **Aux P'tits Brasseurs** (map C2, **23**): rue des Brasseurs 61. On the corner of the place Maurice-Servais. ☎ (081) 226697. Open noon–3pm and 7–10pm. Closed Sunday. One of the best-value restaurants in town, especially at lunchtime, it has a pleasant olive and daffodil-yellow interior and friendly staff. The innovative food includes duck with two sorts of pepper, quails in aspic and potato galettes.

☆☆☆ Expensive

✕ **La Petite Fugue** (map B2, **25**): place du Chanoine-Descamps 5. ☎ (081) 231320. Open for lunch and dinner (until 9.30pm). Closed Saturday lunchtime, Sunday evening and Monday. This highly regarded restaurant has two cosy, but not over elaborate, dining rooms, with wood flooring, engravings on the wall and world music playing in the background. The innovative French food includes truffles with *foie gras*, fillet of lamb in pie crust and spicy veal sweetbreads with snails. There's an affordable lunchtime set menu, but it's expensive in the evening, although you can keep the costs down by ordering the house wine by the glass. Credit cards not accepted.

✕ **L'Espièglerie** (map C2, **10**): rue des Tanneries 13. ☎ (081) 240024. Closed Saturday lunchtime and Sunday (except the first in the month) from mid-July to mid-August. A plush, comfortable eatery serving excellent French food, with the menu changing according to the season. Try quails stuffed with veal sweetbreads, chicken and lobster stew, *fricassée* of prawns in mushroom *pastilla*, roast duck with figs in red wine, fillet of beef stuffed with veal sweetbreads, fish lasagne or brill fillet in a mustard and tomato crust. The best way to sample everything is a 'discovery' menu, but those on a tight budget should try the set lunch, which comes with two glasses of wine.

WHERE TO EAT IN THE AREA

✕ **Le Val Mosan**: rue de Prémorel 29, Wépion 5150; take the Dinant road and turn left when you reach the centre of Wépion, just after the Burmah petrol station. ☎ (081) 460026. Open for lunch and dinner (until 10pm). Closed Monday out of season. Set menus from 595BEF, or about 1,000BEF for a full meal. The heated outdoor area offers views of the Meuse and the surrounding countryside. There's a good selection of Belgian beers, and the simple but sizeable snacks include veal kidneys, steak, *carbonades*, crayfish, *croque-monsieur* and excellent salads and pasta dishes.

WHERE TO GO FOR A DRINK

❢ Crowds flock to the **outdoor tables** on the Place du Marché-aux-Légumes (map B2, **30**) at the slightest hint of sunshine.

❢ **Extérieur-Nuit (map B2, 25)**: place Chanoine-Descamps 6. Open until 11pm on weekdays and 1am at the weekend. This spacious bar has a post-modern setting, with brick and metal walls, an aluminium bar and a video screen. There's also a pleasant outdoor seating area on the pedestrianized street.

❢ **Le Chapitre** (map B1-2, **27**): rue du Séminaire, on the corner of place Saint-Aubain. Open 11am–1am. Closed Sunday. The facade of this tavern is decorated with a humorous cat-and-dog mural, while inside the interior has exposed bricks and

NAMUR

beams, and cosy wooden tables. There's a good range of beers on tap, while the blackboard offers a selection of whiskies that could grace a Scottish pub.

♈ **Le Peanuts**: rue de l'Ouvrage 3, on the corner of rue Basse-Marcelle. Open until 2am. Closed Sunday. Namur has a reputation for being a bit sober, but this place fairly heaves with students on every night of the week. The exposed brick walls are decorated with African artwork, and there's a long bar where peanuts are dished out with the drinks (hence the name). On the mezzanine floor, you'll find cosy nooks that offer a bit of privacy. Light meals available.

♈ **Le Monde à l'Envers** (map B1): rue Lelièvre 26, next to the university. Open until late. This student hot spot

has table football, deafening techno tunes and decent sounds from other eras. You can also get a snack.

♈ **L'Éblouissant** (map A1): rue de l'Armée-Grouchy 27. Open noon–2pm and 6pm–midnight. This is an extremely cosy Irish pub, where guests ensconced in comfy old armchairs can sample a stout while poring over a map of the Belgian Congo. The decor's eclectic, and there's a long wooden bar where you can order one of the many speciality beers on offer. At lunchtime, the chef cooks soups and salads: the flavours depend on his mood, which also seems determine how much you'll pay for his creations.

♈ **Piano-bar** (map B-C2): place du Marché-aux-Légumes 10. Live jazz every Friday and Saturday evening.

WHAT TO SEE

Historic Centre

★ **Place du Marché-aux-Légumes** (map B2, **30**): dominated by the Église Saint-Jean and fringed with lime trees, this delightful square is home to the oldest tavern in town, the Ratin Tot (1616). Admire the handsome 18th-century residences – and the speed at which the well-behaved local youth flock to the terraces when the sun comes out.

★ **Église Saint-Jean-Baptiste** (map B2, **30**): this is Namur's oldest church, although most of what's visible now dates from the 16th century and the asymmetrical baroque spire is even more recent. The intimate interior is eclectic in style, with numerous additions from the 18th and 19th centuries: the carvings on the pulpit and organ loft, for example, are 18th-century. There are paintings on either side of the choir: the one on the left shows *Salome with the head of St John the Baptist*, while the picture on the right depicts a Rubensesque *Infant Jesus*.

★ Take a stroll down rues du Président, Ruplemont, Fumal and des Brasseurs (map B2). Many of the **old houses** (17th- and 18th-century) have been attractively restored. In 1704, an edict made it compulsory to replace half-timbered facades with brick and stone. The streets have 'broken corners', designed so that carriages and other vehicles can turn easily. On the corner of rue du Président and rue Saint-Jean, you'll see one of the oldest houses in Namur, with a 'tear cord' so that rain can trickle down in 'tears'.

At rue Ruplemont 20, there's a fine door, dated 1660, that leads to the École dominicale des pauvres. Rue des Brasseurs, which narrowly escaped the 1960s craze for property development, has retained a neat Classical regularity. One of the oldest houses in the neighbourhood is at No. 107, while No. 135 has an impressive baroque facade. Take a look, too at the lovely 18th-century gate that once provided access to the Sambre.

Outside the **Athénée royal**, on rue du Collège, you'll see the letters of the alphabet inscribed underneath the vaulting, so that they could be studied from the street. The emblem of the Dutch lion was placed here following the removal of the French in 1815.

★ **Musée Félicien-Rops** (map B2, **31**): rue Fumal 12. ☎ (081) 220110. Open 10am–6pm (to 5pm between All Saints Day and Easter). Closed Monday, except in July and August, and between Christmas and New Year. Admission: 100BEF. Housed in a handsome 18th-century house, this is a homage to the Belgian artist whom the French poet Charles Baudelaire described as: 'That frisky M. Rops, who may not have won the 'prix de Rome', but whose talent is as great as the pyramid at Kheops.'

The prolific Félicien Rops is little known outside his native country. Born in Namur in 1833, he died in Paris in 1898. As a student, he was much influenced by the satirists and libertarian trends of his day, and became a savagely sarcastic cartoonist of exceptional talent. He was a close friend of Baudelaire, and illustrated many of the poet's works. On his friend's advice, Rops moved to Paris, where he worked with Verlaine, Mallarmé, Maupassant, the Goncourt brothers and many others.

– First floor: drawings and oils by the artist's teacher, Ferdinand Marinus, as well as Rops's prints, cartoons and charcoal portraits. These include *L'Enterrement en pays wallon* (reminiscent of Honoré Daumier) and some wonderful drawings, such as the *Mort qui danse* and *Mort au bal*. Rops's paintings betray multiple influences. For example, there's a hint of Toulouse-Lautrec in *Les Deux Amies*, whilst *L'Incantation* is very much a product of Symbolism. There are some fine watercolours on display, but your attention will probably be diverted by the famously heretical *Pornocratès*, which hangs above the mantelpiece.

– Pause in front of *Dîner d'athées* (1874), an unusual drawing that Rops made for Barbey d'Aurevilly's *Les Diaboliques*: the light effects are stunning, and it has a disturbing sensuality about it.

– Second floor: the first section is dedicated to Rops's astonishing engravings. You can see one of his masterpieces, *Gandin ivre*, as well as a remarkable series devoted to the temptation of Saint Anthony and a rather unusual *Sainte Thérèse*. His *Ravissement de sur Marie* is equally arresting.

Next comes Rops the sketcher, with a fine display of charcoal portraits and travel sketches, followed by Rops the painter, whose work was predominantly sombre, although *Plage de Heist* is a notable exception. If you'd like to know more about the man, there's a one-hour video about his colourful life.

★ **Église Saint-Loup** (map B2): rue du Collège 1. Built in 1621, this is a magnificent example of Jesuit baroque, with a hint of Italian Renaissance. It's worth going inside to see the fantastic carved-sandstone ceiling. Coupled with the grey tones of the church and the ringed, red marble pillars, it makes for an unusually colourful place of worship. There's a beautiful communion bench, while the wildly baroque confessionals are covered in vines,

NAMUR

cherubim and cabled columns: the pulpit is equally exuberant. The church is sometimes used for concerts.

★ **Cathédrale Saint-Aubain** (map B1): built in 1751 by an Italian architect on the site of a Gothic church (he kept the 13th-century tower), this structure is predominantly Classical in style. There's an impressive transept crossing, with light streaming in through a glass cupola, and the decor is grandiose and ornamental. The huge, rather overwhelming pulpit, which dates from 1848, has an impressive double staircase. The confessionals are also oversized, in keeping with the massive proportions of the church. You can see paintings by a pupil of Rubens, Jacques Nicolaî, in the choir, while the Calvary on the left is attributed to Van Dyck. Behind the marble altar, the cenotaph contains the remains of Don John of Austria, the son of Charles V, who defeated the Turks at the Battle of Lepanto. There's also a fine 17th-century lectern shaped like an eagle and, in the right transept, an intriguing wrought-iron gate.

★ **Musée diocésain** (map B1, **32**): place du Chapitre, to the right of the cathedral. ☎ (081) 444285. From Easter to the end of October, open 10am–noon and 2.30–6pm; otherwise 2.30–4.30pm. Closed Sunday morning and Monday. Admission: 50BEF. The displays are a bit old-fashioned, and lighting is kept to a minimum, but there are several fascinating exhibits, including the Saint-Aubain treasury and the reliquary crown of the Saintes-Épines (1210), with a leather case and Limoges enamels. You can also see a host of reliquary arms, old wooden statues, some plain and some painted, and a splendid 11th-century altar, ornamented with walrus-tusk ivory figurines. Everyday period glassware, altar frontispieces, religious robes sewn with gold thread and *potales* (street-corner shrines) to the Virgin Mary make up much of the rest of the display, along with well-worn wooden statues from the 16th century. On the first stained-glass window, you'll see a Virgin Mary, with a book and an old man at her feet.

★ **Palais provincial**: opposite the cathedral. The bishop's palace was built in 1726. The old chapel, which is decorated with stucco work by Moretti, is used for meetings by the province's council.

★ **Musée de Groesbeeck de Croix** (map B2, **33**): rue Joseph-Saintraint 3. ☎ (081) 222139. Guided tours at 10am, 11am, 2pm, 3pm and 4pm. Closed Monday and between Christmas and New Year. Admission: 80BEF. This fascinating museum of decorative art is housed in a handsome, 18th-century aristocratic mansion. The carefully arranged salons and bedrooms evoke the main preoccupations of the aristos of the time: pleasure, ostentation and intimacy. There are some wonderful collections of objets d'art, and the following are just a few examples.

– On the ground floor, the spacious 18th-century rooms contain porcelain dishes, Venetian-glass mirrors, portraits of noblemen and aristocrats, period furniture and a clock decorated with marquetry. Several paintings depict Louis XIV's siege of Namur in 1695, in the presence of the Sun King himself. You can also see silverware, a Louis XIV ewer and a casket with a Namurois hallmark dated 1692.

– At the bottom of the stairs, look out for the marble clock, the huge coachman's boots and a sledge, as well as a painting attributed to Tiepolo, *The Triumph of Sicily*. There's also a delightful collection of terracotta statuettes and earthenware figurines, with a fine marriage trunk nearby. The exceedingly elegant stairwell has a carved banister leading up to a rotunda.

– In the music room, you'll find an old harp and a harpsichord dated 1640, paintings by the Namurois landscape painter Juppin and several Beauvais tapestries. Some rooms are decorated with gilt polychrome leather, patterned with hunting scenes. There's also an unusual 17th-century theology diploma, painted and printed on material.

– The vestibule houses some appealing portraits of everyday folk by Henri Michel.

– The alcove bedroom contains portraits of 17th-century aldermasters of Namur and a fantastic panorama of the town.

– Finally, you can enjoy a spot of peace and tranquillity in the small French gardens, and admire the building's rear facade.

★ **Musée des Arts anciens du Namurois** (map C1, **34**): rue de Fer 24. ☎ (081) 220065. Open 10am–6pm (to 5pm from All Saints Day until Easter). Closed Monday and from 24 December to 4 January. Admission: 50BEF. This wonderful museum is housed in an elegant 18th-century aristocratic house known as the Hôtel de Gaiffier d'Hestroy. You enter through the inner courtyard.

– On the ground floor, Mosan jewellery is beautifully displayed in a dimly lit, intimate setting that allows you to view the items close up. Visitors can pore over 12th-century phylacteries and a 13th century box for communion wafers, with Limousin ornamentation. You can also see a statue of the Virgin Mary, on which the Infant Jesus is depicted kicking aside a dragon (1250), an *Annunciation* and *Visitation*, painted panels from 1400 and a 13th-century cross of Lorraine (a double cross).

– The first floor is largely devoted to religious statuary, but there are several other splendours on show: a stone altarpiece, a chapel dedicated to Namur's invalids, a charming 16th-century oak altarpiece in Italian style, 16th-century chasuble crosses and a Virgin and Child in painted wood from the former Notre-Dame collegiate church.

One room houses a remarkable collection of statuary, including a St Peter, a fine *St Anthony* on painted wood, complete with altarpiece shutters, a *Crucifixion* with a wonderfully realistic weeping Virgin, and a finely chiselled *Resurrection* from the 15th century. Perhaps the finest piece, though, is the vibrant gilt and painted altarpiece, with several lively figures carved in a delightfully naive style. Start at the bottom and work your way up.

There's also some gold- and silverware, including a *Christ at Rest* from the 15th century. These were all the rage in religious communities during the Middle Ages, when nuns used to keep them in their cells.

– There's a pleasant garden at the back of the museum.

★ **Musée archéologique** (map C2): rue du Pont. ☎ (081) 231631. Open from 10am (10.40am at the weekend) to 5pm. Closed Monday and during the Christmas holidays. Admission: 80BEF. The museum is housed in the old 'halle al' Chair' (Meat Hall), a spectacular example of 16th-century civic architecture. You can see the arms of Philip II of Spain on the facade.

– In the prehistoric section, you'll find bronze torques (necklaces) dating from 1,350 BC, axes and Iron Age pots, delicate second-century glassware from Penteville, a first-century bronze vase, a well-preserved urn and a ribbed bowl from the Roman site of Seron, fragments of mosaic, and first-century Merovingian artefacts from tumuli and cemeteries.

There's also a scale model of 18th-century Namur, which gives you some idea of what the city looked like then before the property developers got their hands on it.

– The first floor displays objects found during a dig at Taviers, tools found in the Roman villa of Antheus, keys, carpenter's tools, oil lamps and a delightful collection of Roman brooches, jewels and enamelled pins. The quality and diversity of the artefacts from fifth-century Frankish cemeteries, including engraved bone combs and belt buckles, is particularly impressive.

– The second floor is devoted to the Merovingian period, with tombs, weapons, jewellery, necklaces and bone amulets on show. The exhibits are fantastically well preserved, and the accompanying texts are admirably to the point. There are beautiful glass vases from the cemetery of Devant-les-Monts, delicate sixth-century money-changer's scales and bronze and wood seals from the same period.

★ **Trésor d'Hugo d'Oignies** (map C2, **35**): rue J.-Billiart 17, in the Maison des Surs de Notre-Dame. ☎ (081) 230442. Open 10am–noon and 2–5pm. Closed Monday, Sunday morning, holidays and from 11–26 December. Admission: 50BEF. It's worth taking the 30-minute guided tour of this collection of religious treasures, considered by many as one of the seven wonders of Belgium. It's particularly strong on Mosan art, which reached its peak in the 13th century and was famed throughout Europe. Among the master jewellers of the time was Hugo d'Oignies, a craftsman of the same stature as Renier and Godefroy de Huy, the anonymous creator of the altar at Stavelot, and Nicolas de Verdun. Hugo reached the peak of his powers between 1228 and 1230. In the 13th century, the wars that ravaged the Low Countries led the religious authorities to hide Hugo's masterpieces in Namur. In 1794, they were walled up to prevent the French from seizing them, and remained hidden until 1818, when they were handed over to the Sisters of Notre-Dame of Namur, who kept them safe from the Germans during both world wars: even the notoriously acquisitive Goering couldn't get his hands on them. Today, the treasury is virtually complete, consisting of 40 wonderful items. Here are some of the highlights:

– The oak binding for a Book of Gospels, which is covered in silver leaf and gilt and decorated with an intricate pattern of leaves and *niello* work (a technique using black sulphur or lead to incize lines in gold). Hugo has represented himself on the bottom left. Christ enthroned sits on the left and the Crucifixion is depicted on the right.

– A superb Byzantine cross, with a double crosspiece.

– The rib-shaped reliquary containing a rib of St Peter.

– St Martin's phylactery, which sports some incredibly intricate filigree work.

– Some adorable ivory boxes.

– The chalice of Gilles de Walcourt (signed 'Hugo').

– A reliquary containing St Blaise's foot.

– A mitre embroidered with gold thread showing the martyrdom of Thomas à Becket.

– The most unusual reliquary is 'Lait de la Vierge', which is shaped like a dove. It contains, not the Virgin's milk, but galactite collected from the walls of the Cave of Milk in Bethlehem.

★ **A short walk in the area**: on the place d'Armes (map C2), you'll find the building that used to house the offices of the Walloon Region, which now holds court in the Hôtel Saint-Gilles. To the left, you can see the vaulted passage that leads to the belfry, the old tower of Saint Jacques and the 14th-century town gate. From here, you come to the Théâtre Royal, a magnificent early-19th-century pile that has been completely restored. Try to get a glimpse of the superb round room inside. When you get to rue de la Tour, take a look at the Marie-Spilar tower, another remnant of the 14th-century town wall. At rue de la Gravière 2, there's a 17th-century baroque porch.

Rue du Lombard and rue de l'Étoile are at the heart of the old quarter, which is currently undergoing renovation. For once, that doesn't mean wholesale demolition, so there should still be some historic buildings by the time you get there. Hopefully, those in charge of the restoration will follow the example set on Rue des Tanneries, where a series of 17th- and 18th-century buildings, mostly former tanneries or brothels, have been restored with respect for the original architecture and the appearance of the street as a whole.

The District Around the Citadel

Beyond the museum bridge, at the confluence of the Sambre and Meuse rivers, you come to the foot of the citadel, where a historic neighbourhood known as the 'Grognon' ('Grumpy') once stood. The area was razed in the 1970s by property developers, leaving a no-man's-land that the local authorities had earmarked as the site for headquarters of the Walloon Region. The project was the subject of much heated debate: some plans were blatantly ugly, while others were simply too grandiose and would have dwarfed the rest of this part of town. In the end, the pompous projects were dropped in favour of a discreet building and, to everyone's surprise, the Walloon parliament finally, and wisely, settled in the renovated Hôtel Saint-Gilles.

★ **Citadel** (map B2-3): a vast complex on the rocky spur. Since the town's beginnings, it has been a military base: a Gaulish *oppidum*, a Roman camp, the Château des Comtes and a Spanish citadel in the 15th century. It was fortified by Vauban in the 17th century, by which time it was one of the largest fortresses in Europe, and rebuilt by the Dutch in 1816. The rock, so the story goes, has been besieged 20 times in 20 centuries. Today, it's besieged by tourists.

– **Information: Comité Animation Citadelle**, route Merveilleuse 8. ☎ (081) 226829.

– Tour of the citadel: starts at route Merveilleuse 8. A tourist train takes you through eight hectares (20 acres) of woodland, or you can explore the citadel on foot. From April to the end of September, open 11am–5pm. Closed the first weekend in August. There's plenty to entertain visitors here: an audiovisual display; a tour of the Terra-Nova bastion; underground passages; displays of archaeological finds from the digs at Saint-Pierre; a perfume workshop; and a leisure park. There's also a cafeteria.

★ **Musée de la Forêt** (Museum of the Forest): route Merveilleuse 9. ☎ (081) 743894. From April to October, open 9am–noon and 2–5pm, closed Friday; from mid-June to mid-September and during the Easter holidays, open every day. Take bus No. 3. An exhaustive examination of Wallonia's forests, with fauna depicted in dioramas and displays about flora, the different uses of wood and other aspects of the forests.

WHAT ELSE TO SEE AND DO

★ **Musée africain** (map C1): rue du 1er-Lancier 1. ☎ (081) 231383. Open Tuesday, Thursday and Sunday, 2–5pm. Closed on public holidays. A host of ethnographic objects relating to the history of the Belgian Congo are displayed in a disused army barracks.

– **Boat trips on the Meuse**: ☎ (082) 222315. Fax: (082) 225322. Take a panoramic cruise on the Sambre and the Meuse. You can go from Namur to Wépion, or from Namur to Dinant and back, via a series of locks.

★ **Musée des Traditions namuroises** (off the map from A1): rue Salzinne-les-Moulins 200. ☎ (081) 738360. From Easter to the end of October, open Tuesday, Thursday, Saturday and Sunday, 2–5.30pm. This museum is devoted to folklore, festivals, popular games, local saints, crafts, clock-making and just about every other kind of popular tradition in the unhurried world of the Meuse valley.

★ **Musée de la Fraise et du Terroir wépionnais** (Strawberry and Rural Wépion Museum): chaussée de Dinant, Wépion 1037, a few kilometres south of Namur. ☎ (081) 460113. From mid-April to mid-September, open 3–6pm. Closed Monday. The hills above Namur produce 400 tons of strawberries a year, and are renowned throughout Belgium.

MARKET

– **Flea market**: every Sunday morning at Jambes, next to the Meuse. There are lots of stalls stretching out along the river on either side of the bridge. Get there early and you might well pick up a bargain.

FESTIVALS

– **Historic procession of the festivals of Wallonia**: ☎ (081) 222920. Held every year on the afternoon of the third weekend in September. The whole gamut of *namurois* folklore gets wheeled out for this procession, revealing the distant, deep-set roots of the town. It opens with the *Aurdjouwants* (giants), who are followed by several groups representing the Middle Ages, with period characters such as Blanche of Namur, Marie Spilar and the copper beaters, then groups evoking the Spanish occupation and Louis XIV's military campaign.

– **Strawberry Festival**: held in Wépion on the first weekend in September. A must for all strawberry addicts. ☎ (081) 460485.

– **Bouge**: at carnival time and during the feast of St John, huge bonfires are lit on the hills.

– **International Folklore Festival**: held in Jambes on the penultimate weekend in August. ☎ (081) 304446.

WHAT TO SEE IN THE AREA

★ Between Namur and Charleroi is the stunning **Abbey of Floreffe**, which stands high up on a rocky spur above the Sambre. This was the first Premonstratensian abbey in what is now Wallonia. Most of the buildings visible today are 18th-century, and the complex has a striking architectural harmony. The highlights are the beautiful choir stalls inside the church and the medieval annexes. You can watch a video about the abbey, or head straight for the brewery and mill, where you can sample the abbey's excellent beer. Guided tours: from Easter to the end of September, 1.30–7pm (10.30am–6pm in July and August). ☎ (081) 445303. Admission: 80BEF.

GEMBLOUX   **20,000 inhabitants**

Gembloux-sur-l'Orneau is spared the hordes of tourists that flock to Namur and the Porte des Ardennes, but it's not without charm. The town was founded by St Guibert, who also founded the Benedictine Abbey, and was once the centre of a flourishing cutlery industry. In May 1940, it was the site of a battle between German troops and Franco-Moroccan soldiers: it was the only French victory of World War II.

USEFUL ADDRESS

Postcode: 5030.

🛈 Tourist office: Château du Bailli, parc d'Épinal. ☎ (081) 626330.

WHERE TO EAT

☆☆ Moderate

✕ **L'Estaminet**: place Saint-Guibert 6, opposite the abbey entrance. ☎ (081) 615577. Open every day. L'Estaminet has a beautiful white facade and exposed bricks and beams inside, with a bar that adjoins the 12th-century town walls. The bottles above the bar are the empty shells of classic French *crus*, and the food is suitably bourgeois and rich. Regional specialities include Namur-style veal kidneys and mussels cooked in Gembloux beer. You can also pop in for coffee during the day.

WHERE TO GO FOR A DRINK

▼ Le Sun Club: place Saint-Jean 79. This place has an ochre facade and a California-themed interior with neon-lit depictions of Hollywood stars.

WHAT TO SEE

★ **Maison du Bailli**: now the Hôtel de Ville. This traditional 16th-century sandstone building with two corner towers is also home to the local history museum, which is chiefly dedicated to the cutlery industry. It's unexpectedly interesting: one display, for example, explains how a company called Le Paon (Peacock) made its money manufacturing machetes for the Congo. In one room, a model of old Gembloux shows you how little of the town's architectural heritage is still standing. There are also a few exhibits from the battle in 1940, and others relating to a battle that took place here in 1578, when Don John of Austria put an end to Protestant expansion in the Spanish Netherlands.

★ **Église Saint-Guibert**: the most striking thing about this old church is the Romanesque room beneath it, which is all that remains of the medieval abbey. It stands opposite a clock tower and an old belfry topped with an elegant onion dome, and is surrounded by picturesque winding streets and cul-de-sacs.

★ **Abbaye bénédictine**: open 9am–noon and 2–4pm. This neoclassical structure, designed by Laurent-Benoît Dewez, architect by appointment to the Austrian occupiers, is a fine example of the harmony and stunning perspectives that were typical of this style. The best way to appreciate the angles is to look from the keeper's porch to the four-columned porch of the abbey palace. A main courtyard and a series of old farm buildings complete this impressive complex. The original monks' quarters were built over a 12th century Romanesque cellar. The abbey became state property in 1860, and is now home to the faculty of Agricultural Sciences.

WHAT TO SEE IN THE AREA

★ **Corroy-le-Château**: 5 kilometres (3 miles) south of Gembloux. Guided tours from May to the end of September on weekends and public holidays, 10am–noon and 2–5pm. Admission: 150BEF. This wonderfully preserved château is a magnificent example of medieval military architecture. It's ringed by five sturdy cylindrical towers and has a gatehouse with a drawbridge and turrets on either side. The interior decor reflects the tastes of its owners, the Trazegnies family: rare marble, old paintings, furniture decorated with marquetry and a collection of dolls.

★ **Galerie Dieleman**: Château de Petit-Leez, rue de Petit-Leez 129, Grand-Leez 5031. Take exit 11 on the E411. ☎ (081) 640866. Open 10am–7pm. Closed Monday and Tuesday. Built in the 18th century, this château-cum-farm now houses superb indoor and open-air exhibitions of 19th- and 20th-century sculptures, including pieces by Magritte, Dali, Max Ernst and Henry Moore, many of them from the Dieleman family's superb private collection. Art-lovers come in their droves for the excellent temporary exhibitions organized by the owner's daughter. There is also an *haute cuisine* restaurant and a tasteful souvenir shop.

ANDENNE   24,000 inhabitants

The little Mosan town of Andenne, halfway between Namur and Huy, grew up around the seventh-century abbey, which was founded by St Begge, a descendent of Pépin of Heristal. Charles Martel, who halted Moorish expansion in Poitiers, was also born here. At first sight, the town looks like a long street of shops running at right angles to the river, but a closer look reveals several fine 17th- and 18th-century houses, as well as a well-preserved historic neighbourhood at the end of the valley, around the collegiate church of Sainte-Begge.

USEFUL ADDRESS

Postcode: 5300.
🛈 Tourist office: place des Tilleuls

48. ☎ (085) 849640. Fax: (085) 849031.

WHERE TO EAT

☆☆ Moderate

✗ **Le Barcelone**: rue Brun 14. ☎ (085) 843268. Open 9am–midnight on weekdays and 10.30am–1am at the weekend. Full meal about 800BEF. This tavern-restaurant, decked out in pseudo-Spanish style serves generous helpings of Belgian cuisine, such as veal kidneys *à la liégeoise* and knuckle of ham in mustard.

WHAT TO SEE

★ **Place des Tilleuls**: this square, dominated by the town hall and a bandstand, would be much more attractive without the car park.

★ At the end of rue Brun, bear left towards rue Lapierre. At No. 29, you'll find the **Musée communal de la Céramique**, which recalls Andenne's once-flourishing ceramics industry.

★ Rue Lapierre leads to **place du Chapitre**, which is fringed with aristocratic houses that haven't changed since the days of the Ancien Régime.

– The **Collégiale Sainte-Begge**, designed by the prolific Laurent-Benoît Dewez, is an impressive neoclassical pile with three aisles, a square tower and a curved roof. The facade is divided into Ionic and Corinthian levels, and topped with a triangular pediment. The fantastically light interior is filled with Louis XVI furnishings, Gothic and baroque statues; you can also see the tomb of St Begge, the patron saint of children's health.

– **Musée du Chapitre**: open Sunday 2–6.30pm from 15 July–15 August, and on the first Sunday in May. The best pieces are a silver gilt reliquary containing the relics of St Begge and a 16th-century silver bust-reliquary.

– The **Fontaine aux Poussins**, on the same square, is fed by the water that flows down from the hill. A bizarre notice declares that you are not allowed to wash your car here in freezing temperatures.

The slope behind the collegiate church leads up to a portico with a triangular pediment, a remnant of the old town walls. There's also a house dated 1622. It's well worth visiting this historic hillside neighbourhood, which is dotted with old buildings and former workers' cottages.

★ Pipe-smokers should drop into Andenne's excellent **Musée-piperie Léonard**, where they can learn about the art of creating clay pipes. Rue Cuvelier 5. Open Tuesday to Saturday morning; closed for lunch. ☎ (085) 841274.

FESTIVAL

– **Carnaval des Ours** (Bear Carnival): held on mid-Lent Sunday, the festival recalls a bear killed with a hammer by the nine-year-old Charles Martel. Teddy bears are hurled about during this somewhat eccentric event.

WHAT TO SEE IN THE AREA

★ **Vallée du Samson**: formed by the Samson, a tributary of the Meuse, this steep-sided, ramshackle valley lies upstream from Andenne, near Namè-che, and is riddled with caves. It runs to Gesves, 16 kilometres (10 miles) away, passing several charming hamlets where the houses are built of local stone.

★ In **Goyet**, you'll find caves that were once home to Cro-Magnon man and an assortment of our other ancestors. There are still digs in progress. The admission fee includes an interactive guided tour, with several fascinating reconstructions, as well as a museum. Open from March to the end of November 10am–5pm. Admission: 265BEF.

▲ The **campsites** at Faulx-les-Tombes, Mozet, Thon-Samson and Maizeret are particularly suited to nature-lovers and anglers.

THE MEUSE VALLEY

The area between Namur and Hastière, dotted with châteaux, splendid gardens and ancient little towns, offers some of the most captivating walks or rides in Wallonia. The tiny valleys of the Meuse tributaries lead to delightful monuments and settlements, such as the Château de Montaigle and the village of Crupet. Victor Hugo, a committed Belgophile, once deplored the fact that so few people had heard of this lovely region. He might think differently if he saw the hordes of tourists who flock here today.

USEFUL ADDRESSES

🛈 **Tourist office**: chaussée de Namur 2, Profondeville 5170. ☎ (081) 414037. Open June to September. You can hire boats to cross the Meuse and visit the caves.

■ **Bike hire**: Bill's Bike Évasion, chaussée de Namur 14, Profondeville 5170. ☎ and fax: (081) 414155. Open 8.30am–6.30pm. Mountain bikes, road bikes, maps and suggested itineraries are available.

WHERE TO STAY

☒ Budget

⛊ **Guest House Andrieux**: rue du Rivage 21, Annevoie 5537. ☎ (082) 611741. Fax: (082) 612467. Double and triple rooms 1,050–1,450BEF. Breakfast 160BEF. This sturdy-looking brick building in a rustic setting by the Meuse offers simple rooms with sinks. It's not the height of luxury, but at this price, you can't really complain. The restaurant serves wild boar stew *à la Maredsous* or trout from the gardens of Annevoie.

☒☒ Moderate

⛊ **B&B Beau Vallon**: chemin du Beau-Vallon 38, Wépion 5100. ☎ and fax: (081) 411591. Doubles 1,750–2,250BEF, including breakfast. Four rooms in a hillside farmchâteau above the Meuse, with views of the woods on one side and a formal garden on the other. There's a garage, a swimming pool, table-tennis table and a living room with TV. Cots and meals are available by prior arrangement.

WHAT TO SEE

Château and Gardens d'Annevoie-Rouillon

In the commune of Anhée, and well signposted. ☎ (082) 614747. Gardens open 9.30am–6.30pm from early April to the end of October; château open 9.30am–1pm and 1.30–6pm in July and August, weekends and public holidays only from mid-April to the end of June and in September. Guided tours of the gardens from 1 May to 31 August, and throughout the year for the château). Admission: 240BEF. Single tickets for the house or gardens are also available.

The château was built in the 17th and 18th centuries, and has belonged to the Montpellier family since 1696; work on the gardens began in 1758. The most striking thing about them is that the ponds, fountains and cascades are fed by a succession of springs that form a long canal at the top of the hill. The measurements of the canal have been carefully calculated to correspond with the division of time into years, weeks and days: it's 365 metres (1,200 feet) long, it's lined with 52 lime trees, and it's seven metres (23 feet) wide.

You can only explore the garden with a guide, which is a shame: the tour doesn't give you enough time to enjoy the gentle murmur of the water, or to admire the formal patterns of the French-style gardens (with hints of Italian and Romantic English influences).

Tour of the Château

If you look at the château from the gardens, you'll see that it has an almost imperceptible curve, to accommodate the shape of the hill. Apart from a few items of furniture, there's little of interest inside. You can visit the small rococo chapel, decorated by the Moretti brothers, who also designed the stucco work in the 'white room', or music room: it was inspired by mythology

PROVINCE OF NAMUR

and nature, as was then the fashion. There's a Chinese screen in the main entrance.

After your tour, you'll be taken around the gardens, which are far more interesting. The cascade and grotto to Neptune are particularly striking.

You have to go through the plant centre to reach the exit. This, and the fact that you're pointedly told that the guides rely on tips for their salary, suggest that the place is very much a tourist trap.

Château de Montaigle

At the end of the Vallée de la Molignée. In July and August, there are guided tours every day between 11am and 7pm; from March to the end of November, at the weekends and on public holidays. ☎ (082) 699585. Admission: 130BEF. The proud ruins of this 13th-century château, a Burgundian stronghold in the 15th century, are perched high on a hill. Henri II's army destroyed the château in 1554, but it was eventually restored with the aid of modern technology.

Sosoye

A village of solid blue-stone houses characteristic of this region. The church looks Romanesque, but was built in the 18th century, while the next-door barn, which has a double doorway, was constructed in 1646.

Track Cars of la Molignée

– **Tickets** can be bought at rue de Foy 21, Falaën. ☎ (082) 699079. Open 10am–6pm. A car holding four people costs 640BEF at the weekend, and 560BEF on weekdays. A ride through the wild, rocky landscape along the old railway line from Falaën to Maredsous. The 3-kilometre (2-mile) trip takes about 20 minutes. You can have a snack at the old station in Maredsous. It's all very touristy, but great fun for kids.

– Two kilometres (one mile) away, in Falaën, you can visit an 18th-century farm-château, which now houses the Musée des Confréries gastronomiques (the Museum of the Cooks' Guild).

Abbaye de Maredsous

It looks Gothic, but this impressive abbey was built in 1872, although that's hardly dented its magnetic effect on tourists. The delightful valley and surrounding countryside considerably enhance its romantic charm, as does the huge brasserie, which has a terrace where you can enjoy a beer and observe a broad cross section of the Belgian population at play.

✕ **Brasserie de Maredsous**: ☎ (082) 699396. Open 9am–6pm (to 8pm on Sunday). Try one of the three Maredsous beers on tap: they're not brewed at the abbey, but they have a distinctly rustic flavour. You can buy the bottled version as well, along with local delicacies like *Cochonou à la bière*, smoked ham, bread and a selection of honeys and cheeses.

Furnaux

It's worth coming here to see the recently restored 16th-century **Église Notre-Dame**, which has a splendid 12th-century Mosan-style baptismal font in the style of Renier de Huy. It's supported by four huge lions, and is decorated with a *Baptism of Christ*.

WHERE TO STAY AND EAT IN THE AREA

La Ferme des Oiseaux: rue Delcourt 5, 5520 Anthée; on the Dinant-Philippeville road, 10 kilometres (6 miles) west of Dinant. Doubles 1,800BEF, including breakfast, with a 100BEF supplement for a single-night stay. This hotel has four spacious rooms in a handsome old 19th-century farmhouse, although the staff could be a little friendlier.

Le Jardin d'En Bàs: rue d'En Bàs 1, 5537 Annevoie; in a little street beside the Meuse. ☎ (082) 613706. Closed Tuesday, Wednesday and Thursday. Set menus 800–1,000BEF; lunch menu 650BEF. This establishment has one of the most delightful garden-terraces imaginable, perfect for an hour or two of unadulterated bliss and tranquillity.

Inside, it's warm and cosy, with half-timbered walls and exposed beams. The menu offers plenty of local produce: fresh snail stew, salad of gizzards, *foie gras*, fish soup, goat's cheese and thyme tart, country omelette, farm chicken, duck with honey and leg of veal with herbs. On fine days, the outside tables are much in demand, so it's best to book well in advance. Credit cards are not accepted.

Gare de Maredsous: just before the abbey. The old station has been converted into a restaurant, and the platform is now a terrace. This is where the track cars pull up (*see above*). It's an ideal spot for a snack and drink. A few hot dishes are also available.

Crupet Valley

Return to the Meuse to discover this pretty valley and the towns of Crupet and Spontin.

★ **Musée des Bières belges** (Belgian Beer Museum): rue de la Gare 19, Lustin, on the right bank of the Meuse, near the station. ☎ (081) 411102. Open 11am–8pm on weekends and public holidays; every day in July and August. An Aladdin's cave of ale and all its associated paraphernalia: bottles, labels, beer mats, glasses, adverts and so on. It's a bit unwelcoming, but still well worth a visit. In May, there's a beer antiques market and a beer exchange; phone for details.

CRUPET

From Yvoir, beyond the stone quarries, the road meanders through a lush, green valley to the idyllic village of Crupet, where the houses are covered in flowers and plants.

WHERE TO STAY AND EAT

✕ **Inn Dol Besace**: rue Haute 11, Crupet 5532, opposite the church. ☎ (083) 699041. Closed Monday evening and Tuesday. Main courses about 350BEF. This warm and cosy inn sports a plaque saying 'Po riches et poves igna place!', a Walloon phrase meaning, 'Rich and poor alike are welcome here'. The atmosphere is relaxed, and the excellent local dishes include crêpes, *fromage blanc* on brown bread with salad, trout, wild boar soup, pheasant, *carbonade*, veal steak in mustard and marrowbone in sea salt.

☆☆☆☆ Splash Out

🛏 ✕ **Le Moulin des Ramiers**: rue Basse 31. ☎ (083) 699070. Fax: (083) 699868. Restaurant closed on Monday and Tuesday. Doubles 3,950–4,450BEF. A luxurious inn in an old stone riverside building. It's a magical, bucolic setting, the rooms are exceptionally comfortable and the cuisine is famous – but notorious might be a better word for the reception and service. The decor is elegant, and the atmosphere is pretty posh, as is the menu: ravioli, turbot and shellfish in a lobster *coulis*, medley of grilled fish in sorrel mousse and duck escalopes. The lunchtime *menu du marché* is significantly more affordable than the other menus. The restaurant also has a shaded outdoor seating area.

WHAT TO SEE

★ **Château**: below the village. This huge 13th-century keep acquired its turret, slate roof and brick and half-timbered structure in the 16th century. It can be reached via a small stone bridge. It's chocolate-box pretty – and, sadly, private property.

★ **Église Saint-Martin**: at the top end of the village. Enlarged in Gothic style, the church has a Romanesque tower, an 11th-century nave and original arcades and columns. The choir was expanded in the 18th century. There are some handsome old tombstones at the entrance to the dazzling white and mauve interior, which has a beautiful coffered ceiling, while the baptismal font dates from the 13th century.

The peculiar **grotte de l'abbé Jules Gérard** (Abbot Jules Gérard's cave), next door to the church, was built in the early 20th century, and is full of life-size painted statues of St Anthony, in ultra-kitsch scenes depicting episodes from his life. On the interior stairs, you can see St Anthony fighting off the Devil. Judging by the number of plaques and used candles, it's a popular place.

SPONTIN

Spontin is a large village famous for its mineral water and for the quality of the Mosan limestone used in its buildings. Its château is one of the most attractive in Wallonia.

PROVINCE OF NAMUR

USEFUL ADDRESS

🛈 **Tourist office**: rue des Rivières 7. ☎ (083) 699573.

WHERE TO STAY

🛏 **B&B and Gîte du Château de Spontin**: chaussée de Dinant 8, Spontin 5530. ☎ (083) 699055. Fax: (083) 699214. Doubles 1,500–3,500BEF, including breakfast. If you've ever wanted to stay in a castle, now's your chance. You'll get a warm welcome from the owner, M. Vermeersch, and the 15 mostly spacious rooms, in the château and a small annexe, possess considerable rural charm, although they're perhaps not as clean as they could be. Most are en suite, and there's an attractive arrangement for families (or two couples), where two rooms in the most attractive corner of the château share a bathroom. Dinner for guests (there's only one set menu) includes game in season.

🛏 **Gîte d'étape**: next door to the château, surrounded by trees. Same phone number as the B&B. This spacious residence has been divided up into *gîtes d'étape* (lodges). The small dormitories are well-maintained, with proper bathrooms and a common room. There's a garage for bikes.

WHAT TO SEE

★ **Château**: entry via the main courtyard. Open 10am–5pm. You can wander around unguided, consulting explanatory texts as you go. The château was built in the 11th century as a square keep, and was gradually enlarged, acquiring Renaissance windows in 1571 and its main facade in 1622. You can still see the old moat and the original drawbridge, which is flanked by tat, pepper-pot towers. The upper sections are brick, which makes for an appealing contrast to the local Spontin stone. The interior courtyard contains a splendid wrought-iron fountain, and there are some wonderful 15th-century Gothic fireplaces in the keep.

IN THE AREA

★ **Château de Poilvache**: return to the Meuse and, as you approach Houx, you'll see the castle ruins. In July and August, there are guided tours every day between 10.30am and 6.30pm; weekends only from April to June and in September and October. Admission: 50BEF. The château dates from the 12th century. According to legend, the four Aymon brothers came to this site after fleeing Charlemagne's wrath on the Steed Bayard. The château was fortified by Jean l'Aveugle, Count of Luxembourg and King of Bohemia, and then by Burgundian Philip the Good. It was dismantled in the 15th century by the Prince-Bishop of Liège.

PROVINCE OF NAMUR

BOUVIGNES-SUR-MEUSE

Just before you get to Dinant (to which it is now attached), you'll see a pretty little village that's less touristy than many in the area, although it's no less steeped in history: for the past 500 years, it's been a centre for the production of copperware. The place du Bailliage, with its fat cobblestones and splendid Spanish house, has real olde-worlde charm, and little seems to have changed since the Middle Ages. The town retains its old layout, with winding streets running parallel to the river.

Postcode: 5500.

WHAT TO SEE

★ **Musée de l'Éclairage** (Museum of Lighting): place du Bailliage 16, in the Maison espagnole. ☎ (082) 224910. From May to the first week in October, open 1–6pm. Closed Tuesday. The splendid 16th-century building is a rare example of fantastically preserved civic architecture, with an impressive brick-and-stone facade and an elegant pediment. The museum, which is a touch eccentric, has a section devoted to archaeology and history.

– The first room displays copperware and pottery, both traditional industries in the area, and finds from local digs, such as stone cannonballs, crossbows and 16th-century battleaxes.

– On the second floor, highlights include a reliquary cross containing a piece of the True Cross, robes embroidered with gold and silver thread, a silver St Lambert (1518) and a baroque monstrance (1645).

– The first floor offers an overview of how lighting methods have developed since the Dark Ages. You can learn all about wax whitening and the manufacture of candles, and study a fine collection of oil and paraffin lamps followed, in no apparent order, by a miscellany of mine lamps, safety lamps, acetylene car headlights, steam-engine lamps, lamps used on the railways, and many more. The collection also includes documents, photos and posters. Most illuminating . . .

★ **Église Saint-Lambert**: an unusual church with two choirs, one 13th-century and one 16th-century, which was added when the nave was rebuilt. Highlights include a beautiful pulpit and a stained-glass window dated 1562. Unfortunately, the church is currently closed. The last remains of the ramparts (1215) can be seen outside, next to the chevet.

IN THE AREA

★ **Château de Crève-Cur**: take the road that leads uphill from the church (it's well signposted) and continue until you reach a car park. There's also a small path from the church. A hundred metres below lie the ruins of what was once one of the most impressive strongholds in the region. Like Poilvache, it was built by the Counts of Luxembourg, and was dismantled in 1554 during the wars with Charles V. At sunset, you can enjoy beautiful views of the Meuse valley, including Dinant and medieval Bouvignes.

DINANT   13,000 inhabitants

This was the second-biggest town in the Principality of Liège. Wedged between cliffs and the Meuse, it was forced to expand lengthwise along the river. Its onion-domed collegiate church, cliff-top fortress and blue roofs make it one of the most distinctive, and best known, Walloon towns.

A Short History

The first people to recognize the security offered by Dinant's great rock were the Celts. The original settlement developed into a prosperous Gallo-Roman town. By the Middle Ages, it had become one of the region's most important ports, along with Liège and Namur. The copper industry grew in size and importance from the 12th century onwards: indeed, the town's name comes from the French for copperware ('dinanderie'). As part of the Principality of Liège, Dinant was a deadly rival of Bouvignes, which belonged to the Principality of Namur, and which also had a thriving copperware industry.

Dinant was besieged 17 times, and was stormed on several occasions. The Burgundians razed the town in 1466, when Dinant had sided with Louis XI against Charles the Bold. To teach the locals a lesson, Charles had 800 of them tied up in pairs and drowned in the Meuse. Since then, the locals have been known as 'copères', which loosely translates as 'another pair in the water'. In 1554, the French, then at war with Charles V, turned on the city, and Louis XIV seized it with minimal casualties in 1675. In 1789, the French Revolution caused considerable damage, but worse was to come during World War I, when German troops burned most of the town and massacred many of the inhabitants. Charles de Gaulle was wounded on the bridge. The town was rebuilt after 1918, providing the Luftwaffe's bombers with fresh targets when the Germans invaded in World War II. Despite this litany of crises, Dinant remains a lively, welcoming city.

The Town of Adolphe Sax

Dinant is particularly proud of its most famous son, Adolphe Sax, the inventor of the saxophone (1814–94). Sax's father was a manufacturer of musical instruments, and young Adolphe had developed a 24-key clarinet by the age of 20. In 1841, he unveiled the saxophone, which was applauded by Berlioz but derided by his rivals, who sabotaged the distribution of the instrument. Sax died in penury in Paris, a ruined man, but his invention was to inspire some of the best music of the 20th century, especially in the field of jazz. In 1994, Dinant commemorated the centenary of his death with a huge celebration.

A Few Local Specialities

Start with *flamiche*, a hot butter and cheese tart, then try a few *couques de Dinant*: hard little sweets made of flour and honey, which were invented when Charles the Bold was besieging the town in the 15th century. You can enjoy them with *copère*, the local beer (6°), which is also used in the preparation of several local dishes, including Meuse eels *à la copère*.

PROVINCE OF NAMUR

USEFUL ADDRESSES AND INFORMATION

Postcode: 5500.

🄷 **Haute-Meuse Tourist Office**: rue Grande 37. ☎ (082) 222870. Fax: (082) 227788. From Easter to All Saints Day, open 8.30am–6pm (to 7pm in July and August), with shorter opening hours from November to the end of March. You can get a combined ticket for the town's main attractions, including a 'treasure hunt in search of the secret of Bayard'.

■ **Mountain-bike hire**: Cyclos Adnet, rue Saint-Roch 17. ☎ (082) 223243.

WHERE TO STAY AND EAT

🛏 ✗ **Hôtel La Couronne**: rue Sax 1, near the collegiate church. ☎ (082) 222441. Fax: (082) 227031. Doubles 2,300–2,900BEF, including breakfast. This central hotel has classic, freshly decorated rooms. The cuisine in the restaurant (closed on Wednesday and Thursday out of season) changes according to the season, with set menus from 450BEF. You can dine outside in fine weather.

✗ **La Prune des Bois**: rue Sax 28. ☎ (082) 226642. Closed Sunday evening and Monday. Full meal about 850BEF. Unlike the sober decor, the cooking at this riverside restaurant is truly inspired, with several mouthwatering specials.

WHAT TO SEE AND DO

★ **Collégiale Notre-Dame**: the original Romanesque church was destroyed in 1227, when part of the cliff toppled onto it. It was rebuilt, but the vaults had to be restored after Charles the Bold's assault on the town, and the bulbous spire dates from 1566. A bricked-up doorway and a dilapidated Virgin and Child on the left-hand exterior wall are all that remain of the Romanesque church. Inside, the stone vaulting of the ogive nave makes for a spacious feel. On the right, you can see a little chapel in front of a 13th-century doorway, with a baptismal font designed in 1472. The pulpit is 18th-century, while the enormous confessionals date from the time of Louis XIV. Take a look at the ambulatory, behind the choir, and the curious statue of St Perpète behind the altar. The vast stained-glass window, one of the tallest in Europe, has fantastic shades of blue. A statue dated 1356 stands in the left-hand transept.

★ **Citadel**: Le Prieuré 25. ☎ (082) 222119. From April to September, open 10am–6pm; otherwise, open 10am–4.30pm, and closed on Friday and in January. If you're driving, take the Liège–Ciney road. If you're on foot, good luck – there are 408 steps. The most enjoyable way to reach the summit is to take a cable car from the Grand-Place (195BEF).

The first fortress on this site was built by the Prince-Bishops of Liège. It was demolished in 1466 by Charles the Bold, rebuilt, then altered by Louis XIV. The present citadel was erected by the Dutch in 1818 to help keep the French at bay. Inside, you'll find an arms museum and various dioramas explaining the military history of the region. You can also visit the prison, complete with torture room, and a reconstruction of a World War I shelter. The terrace has a superb view over the town and the valley.

★ **Musée du Cuivre et de la Dinanderie** (Museum of Copper and Copperware): route de Givet 27, by the Meuse, on the way to Givet. ☎ (082) 223017. Fax: (082) 227748. From Easter to October, open 1.30–6pm. Closed Monday, except on public holidays. The first section of the museum, in an old staging post for boatmen, houses an unexpectedly delightful display of church weathercocks. On the top floor, under the sloping roof, you'll find locally made copperware, including a sink, a water heater, an embossed copper cooking pot, 18th-century chandeliers, tobacco pots, a bronze oil jug and an assortment of chamber pots.

★ **Rocher Bayard**: about a kilometre (half a mile) south of Dinant, on the church side of the river. The 'Bayard Rock' is a spectacular 35-metre (116-feet) needle of stone that has become separated from the cliff with the explosives used by Louis XIV's men to blast a gap in the rock so that they could build a road.

– **Balades en bateau** offers a wide range of cruises on the Meuse. ☎ (082) 222315. Fax: (082) 225322.

● Dinant–Anseremme: a 45-minute round trip. Every 20 minutes from April to October.

● Dinant–Freyr: 1 hour 45 minutes there and back. In June, July, August, every day at 2.30pm.

● Dinant–Hastière: a three-hour round trip. Leaves at 2pm on Sunday in June and every day in July and August.

● Dinant–Namur: one-way; takes 3 hours 30 minutes. Leaves at 5.30pm on weekends in July and August.

– **Le Copère**: quay No. 9. ☎ (082) 222325. Same destinations as the preceding company. From early March to end October.

– **Bayard**: quay No. 10. ☎ (082) 223042. Same destinations, but sometimes on different days and at different times.

– **Steam train**: Dinant–Givet (France). See the Haute Meuse by steam train. For information and bookings: chaussée de Givet, 49, Mariembourg 5660. ☎ (060) 312440.

★ **Grottes de la Merveilleuse** (Merveilleuse Caves): 500 metres from the Citadel, on the road to Philippeville. From April to the end of November, open 11am–5pm, 10am–6pm in July and August. Admission: 190BEF. The visit takes about an hour. You can admire the wonderful stalactites and stalagmites, with the sound of rushing water cascading down in the background, and peer down into the murky depths of a great gulf, where you can make out a subterranean lake.

– **Take a kayak down the Lesse** from Houyet or Gendron to Anseremme, south of Dinant. A 4 hour 30 minute, 20 kilometre (12-mile) trip. Available from mid-March to the end of October. Kayaks Libert, quai de Meuse 1, Dinant 5500. ☎ (082) 226186.

PROVINCE OF NAMUR

CHÂTEAU DE FREŸR

Halfway between Dinant and Hastière. ☎ (082) 222200. From May to September, open Sunday 2–6pm, also Saturday in July and August. Admission: 220BEF. This château, in a majestic spot beside the Meuse, is one of the most elegant in the region, and its gardens are among the most attractive in Belgium. Work on the structure, built of brick and local blue stone in Mosan Renaissance style, began in 1571. A wing on the car-park side was demolished to provide views of the château from the front courtyard.

WHAT TO SEE

★ In the **vestibule**, there's a staircase with a remarkable carved balustrade.

★ **Chapel**: until 1951, this was the parish church. It's an atmospheric, intimate rococo structure, with stained-glass windows that softly filter the light. The 17th-century tabernacle is charming, the altar is made of red and black marble, and it's full of handsome 18th-century furniture.

★ The ceiling of the **Louis XIV salon** is decorated with garlands of roses and stucco work.

★ Several rooms have been restored following a fire in 1995, including the dining room and the Marie-Christine salon.

★ **Gardens**: this French garden laid out in 1760 is almost completely symmetrical, and makes the Meuse look like a large canal. You can wander among the flowerbeds, the ponds, the staggered rows of lime trees and, at the far end, the brick-vaulted orangeries. On fine days, the orange trees, some of which are 300 years old, are brought outside. Unusually, these orangeries are still used for their original purpose.

A new garden based on the theme of playing cards, with a fountain of Neptune at its centre, is currently under construction. It's decorated with statues of kings, queens and jacks, and has magnificent trees shaped like hearts, clubs, spades and diamonds.

The Frédéric Salle, a rotunda with a cupola and attractive stucco work by the Morettis, was built in 1774 for the visit of Austrian Empress Maria Theresa's daughter. The railway line was, of course, a later addition.

IN THE AREA

★ **Les rochers de Freÿr**: opposite the château, you can see the dizzying stretch of cliffs, much loved by local climbers and members of the Club alpin belge. At weekends, every cliff-face is a mass of ropes strung out in single file.

★ **Hastière-par-Delà**: this is one of the last villages before you reach the French border. The Romanesque abbey's church and its Benedictine convent are worth a look, although they've been almost over-restored. The Gothic choir is a recent addition, but the stalls, which date from 1443, are among the oldest in the land. Among its treasures are a 14th-century baptismal font and a fine sculpture of Mary and St John by Lambert Lombard. The crypt is open to the public.

CELLES

This charming little town narrowly escaped the bloodshed of the Battle of the Ardennes: the German advance was halted just outside Celles, and there's a tank on the outskirts of the town to prove it. The stone houses around the church are pleasingly uniform.

WHERE TO EAT

☆ Budget

✕ **Taverne l'Ardenna**: place de l'Église, Celles 5561, opposite the church tower. ☎ (082) 666858. Closed Wednesday. This fine tavern in the centre of the village serves simple but generous local dishes in a rustic setting. Try the Saint-Hadelin beer.

WHERE TO STAY AND EAT IN THE AREA

♨ ✕ **La Ferme des Belles Gourmandes**: rue du Camp-Romain 20, Celles 5500, about 7 kilometres (4 miles) away from Celles, in a farming village above the Lesse valley. It's well signposted. ☎ and fax: (082) 225525. Restaurant closed Sunday evening and Monday. Doubles 1,850BEF, including breakfast. High above Dinant, this is a lovely hotel in an attractively restored 17th-century farm. The restaurant seats 25, and the hotel annexe has four rooms, three apartments and a gym. It's exquisitely decorated and spacious, and rooms are fully equipped, although they don't have phones. The landlords, Michel and Céline, adore Tuscany and Umbria, and know how to make their guests feel right at home. The restaurant is decorated in blue and white, with matching straw chairs, natural pine and a tiled stove. The refined menus (from 950BEF) feature seasonal cuisine, and there's a superb wine list, right down to the house wine. For a small supplement, you can have brunch instead of breakfast.

WHAT TO SEE

★ **Église Saint-Hadelin**: the imposing square tower and two turrets with loopholes give the church a fortified look. The interior, which has been restored, contains several tombstones and, on the right of the choir, an enormous black marble slab supported by clowns. The vaulted crypt is open to the public.

IN THE AREA

★ **Château de Vêves**: in the Furfooz nature reserve. ☎ (082) 666395. From April to the end of October, open 10am–6pm. Closed Monday except in July and August. Admission: 190BEF; discounts available. This impossibly cute 15th-century château, with towers and pepper-pot turrets, is splendidly sited on a hill above a lush, green valley. Initially a fortified castle, it later became a rural retreat, and it hasn't lost any of its charm over the centuries.

A curved, fortified doorway, designed to enclose unwary attackers, leads into the courtyard, where there's a half-timbered double gallery. The oldest part of the château is the keep, which is 36 metres (nearly 120 feet) high. Inside, you'll find heraldic rooms and seals. There's some pretty 18th-century furniture in the Hilarion salon, while the bedroom is filled with Louis XVI furniture. The dining room is decorated with paintings of châteaux, and the ballroom houses a handsome ebony wall clock, inset with copper. You can also visit the kitchen, where there's a surprisingly banal-looking oven.

★ **Église de Foy-Notre-Dame**: a little village to the north of Celles. The discovery of a statue of the Virgin Mary in an old oak tree made Celles the object of a pilgrimage. It proved so popular that the locals founded a church in 1623. The exterior is rather plain, but the interior is considerably more ornate, with a fine coffered ceiling on which 145 panels relate the life of the Virgin and Child. The ceiling in the narthex, meanwhile, is decorated with the arms of noble families and bishops. The altars in the choir are superbly carved: the central one is made of marble, while those in the side aisles, with cabled columns, are made of sculpted wood. The main object of devotion here, as you might have guessed, is the miraculous statue of the Virgin, which is in the tabernacle. Throughout the church, you'll see outstanding woodwork, particularly the continuous band of oak panels that stretches along the walls. Other noteworthy features include the colossal confessionals, the high sandstone columns and the organ loft.

★ **Parc naturelle de Furfooz** (Furfooz nature reserve): entrance via the car park on rue du Camp-Romain, Furfooz. ☎ (082) 223477. From April to the end of October and during the Christmas holidays, open from 10am until the end of the afternoon (varies from 4.30pm to 6pm). Closed from January to the middle of February. Admission: 100BEF. Follow the beautiful, gentle walk along the Lesse valley and you'll see Roman and Merovingian remains, reconstructions of Roman baths and a fascinating series of caverns, caves and holes that were inhabited by prehistoric man. They open onto the Lesse, which flows under- and over-ground. Rare plants flourish on the limestone plains. The walk takes about two hours, and you can pause for refreshments halfway through.

Southeast Namur

CINEY   15,000 inhabitants

This small but lively commercial centre is the capital of the Condroz area. A seemingly endless series of wars have taken their toll, destroying much of the town's heritage. In the late 13th century, Ciney found itself embroiled in a two-year feudal conflict involving Liège and Namur, triggered by the theft of a cow and known to this day as the 'War of the Cow'. Ciney is also the headquarters of the Association of the Blanc bleu belge, a breed of cattle that's the pride and joy of the country's farmers, and much appreciated by

Belgian gourmets. The town has given its name to two beers, one brown, one blond.

USEFUL ADDRESS

🅸 **Tourist office**: rue du Centre 1. ☎ (083) 216565.

FESTIVAL

– **Antiques Fair**: on the closest weekend to 21 July.

WHAT TO SEE IN THE AREA

★ **Chevetogne**: a Byzantine church, richly decorated by Greek artists, a few kilometres south of Ciney. If you enjoy Gregorian chant, try to make it for one of the Sunday services.

– **Domaine provincial**: ☎ (083) 688821. Open from Easter to the end of September. Admission: 200BEF per car. This huge park is great for children – and parents, too. It's an area of outstanding natural beauty, with camera-friendly stags, deer, mouflons and wild boar. Water tobogganing, miniature trains, a swimming pool, horse riding and fishing are among the added diversions.

🛏 **Campsite**: a splendidly equipped, first-class campsite in the park. ☎ (083) 688821. You can also hire a chalet or a motel room. For information: ☎ (083) 687211. Fax: (083) 688677.

CHÂTEAU DE LAVAUX-SAINTE-ANNE

A splendid medieval château, built on flat land in the 12th century and altered in the 13th. Open 9am–7pm in July and August; otherwise 9am–6pm. Admission: 200BEF, with discounts for children and senior citizens. This château, surrounded by a moat, has two main parts: the towers and original keep, and the Renaissance-style courtyard. An exterior wall was knocked down to provide views of the countryside. The gallery has rounded columns with Tuscan capitals.

★ In the kitchen and the communal areas, there's a small **Musée Ethnographique**, with agricultural tools, children's toys, engravings and photographs. You can also visit the carpentry workshop and store room. The tower, which dates from 1500, once housed a prison.

★ **Musée de la Chasse**: this Hunting Museum isn't as bloodthirsty as it sounds, since it is as much about nature as hunting. There are vast marble fireplaces and curious pieces of furniture made of stag horns, including a chair, table, mirror and cupboard, while the keep houses a model of the medieval château. But it's the nature section that stands out, with a fine collection of small and large predatory animals and birds.

There's also an excellent, but extremely expensive, restaurant, with a magnificent terrace overlooking the château.

★ **Musée du Cyclisme**: rue de la Baronne Lemmonier 31. From July to the end of September, open 10am–noon and 2–6pm; otherwise weekends and public holidays only. Admission: 100BEF. A fascinating museum for fans of competitive cycling, with displays honouring cycling giants like Eddy Merckx and a selection of old bikes, winners' jerseys, cups, trophies and medals.

GROTTES DE HAN

Belgium's most famous caves are located in the commune of Han-sur-Lesse. Discovered in 1814 by four youths, who left a trail of flour to trace their way out, the caves have been a tourist attraction since1895. They get very crowded in high season.

★ **Domaine des Grottes de Han** (Estate of the Caves of Han): rue J.-Lamotte 2, Han-sur-Lesse 5580. ☎ (084) 377213. Fax: (084) 377712. Open 10am–6pm in July and August, with tours every 30 minutes; 10am–5pm (to 5.30pm on weekends) in May and June; 10am–4.30pm in April, September and October, with tours every hour; and 11.30am–4pm during the Carnival holidays, the second fortnight in March, 1–12 November and 23–31 December, with tours every two hours. Closed in January, at the beginning of February and from mid-November to Christmas. Tickets are sold in the reception area opposite the church. Admission: 360BEF, with discounts for children and senior citizens.

From the back of the reception area, a tram takes you on a 4-kilometre (nearly 3-mile) ride to the mouth of the cave. The average temperature down there is 13°C/55°F, so make sure you take a sweater. The exit is 500 metres from the village.

The Tour

Although speleologists have discovered more than 14 kilometres (8.5 miles) of cave, the tour covers only 3 kilometres (2 miles) of caves, galleries and halls. Highlights include the 'Salles des Mystérieuses', decorated with beautiful stalagmites and stalactites, the 50-metre-high 'Salle d'Armes', where you can see the River Lesse, and the stupendous 'Salle du Dôme', a staggering 129 metres (420 feet) high and 150 metres (500 feet) long, with a mini lake. You'll also see the so-called Minaret, a delightful stalagmite with a circumference of 20 metres (66 feet) that's justifiably nicknamed the 'Trophée'. You round up your trip with a boat trip along the underground river, and there's a surprise in store at the end.

WHERE TO STAY

🛏 **B&B**: with Mme Gillet, Grand-Hy 20, Han-sur-Lesse 5580. ☎ (084) 377289. This large, peaceful villa near the Lesse, complete with garden, has one single, one double and one triple room (1,100–1,400BEF, including breakfast), all comfortable and with enough room for an extra child's bed. On sunny mornings, you can have breakfast on the terrace.

ALSO WORTH SEEING

★ **Spéléothème**: on the Dry Hamptay farm. This 15-minute audiovisual display about the hidden wonders of the Grottes is an interesting complement to your tour. In July and August, open 11.30am–7.30pm; in April, May, June, September and October, open noon–6pm (to 7pm on September weekends), with shows every hour. Admission is free if you've bought a ticket for the caves.

★ **Musée du Monde souterrain** (Museum of the Underground World): near the church. ☎ (084) 377007. From mid-March to 11 November, open 11am–5pm (to 7pm in July and August). Admission: 120BEF. Finds from archaeological excavations in the caves and the surrounding area, including items from the Iron and Bronze ages.

★ **Réserve Naturelle des Animaux Sauvages** (Wild animal . nature reserve): wild boar, stags and deer, bison, brown bears, ibex, chamois and lynx roam freely in this 250-hectare (625-acre) park, which you can only visit on a 75-minute bus tour. Tickets are on sale in the reception area, from where the bus departs. There's one every 15 minutes in high season.

★ **Station de télécommunications Belgacom** (Belgacom Telecommunications Centre): in Lessive, on the Ave-et-Auffe road. ☎ (084) 377640. From May to the end of October, open 9.30am–5pm (to 5.30pm in July and August). Admission is a bit pricey. You can't fail to spot the centre's five huge satellite dishes, from which information is constantly beamed into space. Thousands of visitors flock here every year for the informative and entertaining guided tour, which offers an insight into the high-tech world of 21st-century communications.

ROCHEFORT   12,000 inhabitants

This popular holiday centre is the capital of the Famenne region. The French statesman La Fayette was arrested here by the Austrians in 1792. These days, it's besieged by Dutch and Belgian tourists as soon as there's a hint of fine weather, even though the town itself is not much to write home about: it once had an impressive château, but the ruins were sold off in the 19th century, and now all you can see is the keep. There is one world-class attraction, though – the astonishingly rich Trappist beers brewed at the Abbaye de Saint-Rémy – the strongest weighs in at a potent 11.3 per cent ABV. If French humour is your sort of thing, then try to come for the Festival du Rire (Laughter Festival).

PROVINCE
OF NAMUR

USEFUL ADDRESS

Postcode: 5580.
🛈 Tourist office: rue de Behogne 2. ☎ (084) 212537. Open 9am– 12.30pm and 1–6pm (to 5pm out of season). You can buy a tourist pass for any four of the town's attractions.

WHERE TO STAY AND EAT

♠ ✕ **Gîte d'étape Le Vieux Moulin**: rue du Hableau 25. ☎ and fax: (084) 214604. Basic price per night: 645–750BEF, half-board. Breakfast 100BEF. A well-maintained establishment with 80-odd beds, a restaurant, bar and wood fire. One child stays for free if accompanied by two adults.

♠ **Le Vieux Logis**: rue Jacquet 71. ☎ (084) 211024. Fax: (084) 221-230. Closed February and the end of September. Doubles 1,800–2,100BEF. This peaceful, intimate 10-room hotel feels more like a family-run B&B, with lovely old furniture and slightly quaint decor. The staff are a model of discretion, and guests can use the garden.

♠ ✕ **Hôtel Le Limbourg**: place Albert-ler 21, in the centre of town. ☎ (084) 211036. Fax: (084) 214423. Closed Wednesday out of season. Doubles 2,000BEF. This hotel has comfortable rooms decorated with pastel colours and floral prints. The restaurant specializes in lobster, with menus from 750BEF.

WHERE TO EAT IN THE AREA

✕ **Restaurant Le Plateau du Gerny**: rue d'Aye 3, Humain 6900, 7 kilometres (4 miles) northeast of Rochefort. ☎ (084) 221808. Open Friday, Saturday and Sunday; in the week, by reservation only. Booking recommended. Full meal about 750BEF. This delightful restaurant is opposite the church in the heart of a tiny village, surrounded by beautiful countryside, and has an outdoor seating area. There's also a studio-gîte that sleeps two. It's an incredibly low-key establishment, with a local clientele, but 'outsiders' are warmly received. You'll get generous portions of tasty, fresh regional cuisine, and the menu changes with the seasons. If only there were more restaurants like this in Wallonia . . .

WHAT TO SEE

★ **Musée archéologique du château**: in the ruins of the château. ☎ (084) 214409. Admission: 60BEF. From mid-May to the end of September, open 10am–6pm; from Easter to mid-May, open Sunday and on public holidays only. It may be in ruins, but the castle is still impressive, and there's an interesting view from the keep. The museum is in the east tower.

★ **Musée du Pays de Rochefort et de la Famenne** (Museum of the Rochefort and Famenne Region): avenue d'Alost 5. Open 2–6pm in July and August. Devoted to local customs and folklore.

★ **Grotte de Lorette-Rochefort** (Lorette-Rochefort cave): not far from the centre, near the Chapelle de Lorette. ☎ (084) 212080. In April, September, October and from 1 to 11 November, one-hour guided tours leave at 10am, 11.30am, 1.30pm, 3pm and 4.30pm; in May, June, July and August, there's one every 45 minutes from 10–11.30am and 12.30–5pm. Closed Wednesday, except in July and August. Admission: 200BEF; reductions available. Take some warm clothing with you, as the temperature inside is 8–10°C/45–50°F. You can watch an audiovisual display about the caves in the reception area.

This cave, discovered in 1865, has several galleries filled with stalagmites and stalactites, and vast halls with evocative names like Val d'Enfer (Valley of

Hell), Salle des Montagnards (Mountaineers' Room) and Glacier de la Cascade (Waterfall Glacier). The most dramatic hall is the Salle du Sabbat (Sabbath Room) – a vast opening that's 60 metres (nearly 200 feet) high. There's a tectonic research centre on the site.

★ **Malagne, Villa romaine et archéoparc**: Malagne 1, Rochefort 5580. ☎ (084) 222103. Admission: 150BEF. This is the site of one of the biggest Roman villas in Northern Gaul. There's a multimedia reconstruction of daily life in Gallo-Roman times, which focuses on animal breeding, crafts, crop-growing and cooking. The best times to visit are for the Gallo-Roman folklore weekend, at the end of July, and for the Saturnalia Festival, at the end of December.

Southwest Namur

Before heading off towards Hainaut province, it's worth making a short detour to **Viroinval**, a tiny town off the N99. When the European Union expanded to include 15 member states, its geographical centre moved from Saint-Clément, in the French region of Allier, to Viroinval, about a kilometre (half a mile) from the French border. If you're going to visit, do it soon: when the first eastern European states join the Union, the centre will be somewhere in Germany.

OIGNIES-EN-THIÉRACHE

While Viroinval is the main commune in the area, Oignies and Fumay-sur-Meuse are the 'real' centre of today's European Union. Fame has not turned the locals' heads, however, and you'll find that it's refreshingly free of souvenir shops and stereotypical *frites* stands. Instead, the local authorities have opted for a discreet signpost and a monument in the shape of a 15-pointed star: the length of the points varies, to represent the length of time each of the EU's 15 member states has been part of the union. A stone from each member country has been laid at each point. Finally, there's a glass structure that makes different sounds depending on the force of the prevailing wind. It was created by Bernard Tirtiaux, whose better known for his literary output.

It's hard to know whether this geographical fluke will kick-start the area's tourist industry, but one thing is certain: the beautiful countryside of the Viroin valley deserves a lot more attention, and you won't regret coming here.

WHERE TO STAY AND EAT IN THE CENTRE OF EUROPE

⚓ ✕ **Café-hôtel-restaurant L'Orée du Bois**: rue d'Olloy 43, 5670 Oignies-en-Thiérache. ☎ (060) 399525. Fax: (060) 390775. Doubles 2,000BEF–2,250BEF, with a 10 per cent discount midweek. Restaurant closed on Wednesdays. This large stone building, which looks like a Swiss chalet, lies in the heart of the countryside, with fishing and horse-riding facilities nearby. It's an ideal base for an activity holiday, or just for a walk in the forest. The rooms, some with brand-new furniture, have charmingly old-fashioned bathrooms, but no TV. The restaurant's a bit kitsch, but the food is good and cheap: the *plat du jour* is a mere 230BEF. Dishes include frogs' legs and local fish dishes.

🛏 ✕ **Le Sanglier des Ardennes**: rue Périquet 4. ☎ (060) 399089. An *haute cuisine* restaurant in the centre of the village, specializing in game. It also has affordable rooms (2,000–2,500BEF). Breakfast costs 400BEF.

IN THE AREA

🛏 **Campsite Le Try des Baudets**: rue de la Champagne, Olloy-sur-Viroin 5670, on the edge of the forest. ☎ and fax: (060) 390108. Closed November. Tent site: 225BEF.

★ **Viroinval**, **Vierves-sur-Viroin** and **Dourbes** are all built of limestone and slate, and share a rich history. Visitors can see prehistoric, Gallo-Roman and Frankish remains, explore châteaux ruins or use the area as a base for hiking, canoeing, climbing and caving.

★ **Nismes**: this 1,000-year-old village lies at the confluence of the rivers Eau Blanche and Eau Noire, and has long been a centre for clog-making. The regional museum is in the **Maison des Baillis** (☎ (060) 311635; open in July and August). The **Maison nature, culture et environnement** (rue Grande 2), organizes walks in the Viroin nature reserve, one of the best in the country, with several rare types of flower, including orchids, and spectacular geological formations known as 'foudrys'. These are natural limestone canyons, sometimes 20 metres (65 feet) deep, that were formed during the Ice Age and hollowed over the centuries by rain. Iron ore was mined here until the 19th century. Take great care if you want to explore the area, as it can be treacherous.

TREIGNES

This small village has a surprising number of attractions. For a start, it was home to the author Arthur Masson, who is best known for the fictional character Toine Culot, who typifies the comfortable, complacent Walloon – almost to the point of caricature – and winds up as mayor of the imaginary village of Trignolles.

WHAT TO SEE AND DO

★ **Musée du Chemin de fer à vapeur** (Museum of the Steam Engine): gare de Treignes. ☎ and fax: (060) 312440 and (060) 390948. Open every day in July and August 10am–6pm; otherwise, closed Monday from April to the end of October. Admission: 150BEF. The station is ridiculously large compared to the rest of the village, but it was once a linchpin for the country's railway network. Thanks to its proximity to the French border, it also served as a customs house. The museum opened in 1994 in a large warehouse, and houses splendid vintage locomotives, old wooden carriages, miniature train sets, postcards of stations and other railway memorabilia. You can wait for the trainspotter in your life at the cafeteria next door.

★ **Chemin de fer des Trois Vallées** (Three Valleys Railway Line): From Treignes, you can take a steam train to Mariembourg (250BEF), passing through some extremely pretty countryside. The line is open on weekends from April to October, and every day in July and August. Mariembourg was the last functioning engine shed in Belgium, and has an interesting selection of restored trains and engines. For information and bookings ☎ (060) 312440. You can ride in a steam engine or an old carriage: be sure to specify when you book.

★ **Écomusée de la Région du Viroin** (Ecological Museum of the Viroin Region): rue Eugène-Defraire 63, in the centre of the village, opposite the church. ☎ (060) 399624. From April to the end of October, open 9am–noon and 1–5pm; 1–5pm only on weekends and public holidays. Closed Monday. Admission: 120BEF. Housed in an old farm-château with a 16th-century tower, this museum examines the industries that brought wealth to the region, in particular clog-making. The collections are laid out in the old stables, with sections devoted to woodcutting, carpentry and basket-making. You can also see tools and machinery connected with the stone and iron industries.

★ **Musée du Machinisme agricole** (Museum of Agricultural Machinery): in the Écomusée. This display focuses on developments in farming technology between 1800 and 1950, and features some delightful old machines, including the famous double Brabant plough. You'll learn about the various means of powering machinery – human, horse and engine – and the social consequences of the industrial-agricultural revolution.

★ **Musée du Malgré-Tout**: rue de la Gare 28. ☎ (060) 390243. From mid-February to mid-December, open 9.30am–5.30pm (10.30am–6pm on Sunday and public holidays). Closed Wednesday. Admission: 120BEF. This private archaeological museum houses excellent temporary displays, and plans to offer permanent exhibitions focusing on local finds.

WHAT TO SEE IN THE AREA

★ **Gambrinus Drivers Museum**: Fontaine-Saint-Pierre 2a, Romedenne 5600, on the road from Philippeville to Givet. ☎ (082) 678348. From April to the end of October, open 11am–7pm. Admission: 170BEF, with discounts for children and senior citizens. This 19th-century malt factory now houses the only museum in Belgium devoted to lorries, in particular those used in the brewing industry. There's an exhibition of photographs, toys, documents and advertisements relating to one of the country's most famous industries, now in something of a decline as the big brewers squeeze the smaller firms out of the market.

PROVINCE OF NAMUR

COUVIN   13,000 inhabitants

A Short History

In 872, Charles the Bald ceded Couvin to the Abbey of Saint-Germain, founded in Paris by the son of Clovis. Couvin belonged to Hainaut for the next 100 years, until it was sold to the Bishop of Liège for 50 gold marks. It remained part of Liège until 1794, when the French incorporated it into the *départemente* of the Ardennes. Perched on an escarpment above the Eau Noire ('Black Water', so-called because of its shale deposits), this fortified town saw plenty of sieges and pillaging before the French dismantled its battlements in 1673. Metallurgy has been Couvin's main trade since the Middle Ages, and it was the proud owner of the first coke oven in Europe, built in 1824. The industry has all but died out now, and all that's left is the odd ruined workshop. The local archives, however, are full of information, including the details of the first recorded legal complaint about pollution. There are plans to open a Musée de la Poêlerie (Stove Museum), which will focus on the village's industrial heritage.

USEFUL ADDRESS AND INFORMATION

Postcode: 5660.
⋒ Tourist office: rue de la Falaise 3. ☎ (060) 347463. The staff are efficient, and there's plenty of good literature available.
🚃 Railway station: trains go to Charleroi.

WHERE TO STAY

B&B

🛏 Au Petit Chef: rue Dessus-de-la-Ville 6. ☎ (060) 347940. Fax: (060) 344175. Doubles 2,200BEF. This large, English-cottage-style villa has cheerful staff, smiling owners and five refined, comfortable rooms with pretty floral decor. One even has a four-poster bed (the house was apparently once a popular spot for clandestine meetings). Prices are about right for the level of comfort on offer. Breakfast is served in an elegant dining room.

WHERE TO EAT

Couvin's gastronomic speciality is *escavêche* – salt-water eels cooked in a white wine, beer and vegetable stock.

✫ Budget

✗ Tavern Le Prince d'Orange: faubourg Saint-Germain 16. ☎ (060) 345323. Closed Monday. Set menus from 450BEF. This 17th-century listed building has a period bar downstairs and a restaurant on the mezzanine. There's an olde-worlde feel, with exposed beams, bare stone walls, a blue-slate floor, a fireplace and a piano. The unpretentious, tasty dishes are made using whatever's available at the market that day. The *plat du jour* is an attractive option, and there's game in season. Specialities include rabbit cooked in Trappist beer.

✫✫ Moderate

✗ La Charlotte: rue du Bercet 9. ☎ (060) 347472. A gastronomic restaurant with an excellent reputation.

WHAT TO SEE AND DO

★ **Cavernes de l'Abîme** (Caverns of the Abyss): rue de la Falaise. ☎ (060) 311954. Open 10am–noon and 1.30–6pm from April to the end of September; also on weekends between Easter and mid-June and for the second fortnight of September. Admission: 160BEF. In the Tertiary period, the highest point of the Eau Noire was 16 metres (53 feet) higher than it is today The cliff-side Trou de l'Abîme (Hole of the Abyss) leads to caverns that were inhabited during the Palaeolithic era. A small museum and an audiovisual display examine the evolution of the human race.

★ **Grottes de Neptune** (Neptune's Caves): rue de l'Adugeoir 24. ☎ (060) 311954. In Pétigny, 3 kilometres (two miles) north of Couvin. Open 10am–6pm in July and August, and 10am–noon and 1.30–6pm from April to the end of September. Admission: 250BEF for the caves, and 360BEF if you buy a combined ticket for the Cavernes de l'Abîme. Visitors can enjoy two levels of marvellous stalagmites and stalactites, and take a boat-ride on the Eau Noire. The highlight of the tour is a *son et lumière* display with music by Vangelis.

– **Town trail**: ask the tourist office for the relevant brochure, and follow the signs (an icon representing the town's arms) that guide you to the town's oldest houses. It's an intelligent and informative initiative.

IN THE AREA

⌂ **Campsite Le Bailly**. rue du Bailli 1, Cul-des-Sarts, 11 kilometres (7 miles) south of Couvin. ☎ (060) 377366. Tent site: 274BEF. Open from March to the end of October. Fishing and swimming available nearby.

★ **Hitler's Bunker**: in Bruly-de-Pesche, south of Couvin. Open 10am–noon and 1–6pm from Easter to the end of September, weekends only in October. Admission: 100BEF. From 6 to 28 June 1940, the Führer stayed here while he oversaw his campaign against France. The museum-cum-monument has memorabilia from the period, and also documents local resistance to the Nazis.

★ **Musée de la Vie régionale** (Museum of Regional Life): rue de Rocroi 1, Cul-des-Sarts. Open from Easter to the end of September. Closed Monday, and Friday, Saturday and Sunday morning. Modest entrance fee. Housed in an 18th-century school with a thatched roof and cob walls, this museum is devoted to the customs and traditions of regional life.

★ North of Couvin, you can visit the village of **Walcourt**, dominated by the bulbous, pear-shaped spire and pinnacles of the Gothic Basilique Saint-Materne, which rise up above a rocky promontory in the old medieval quarter. The treasury contains a reliquary cross attributed to Hugo d'Oignies.

Province of Hainaut

Hainaut's not exactly on the beaten track, and at first glance, it's not hard to see why. Once a holiday resort favoured by the royals, it's been ruined by the ravages of the Industrial Revolution, when mining was its principal trade, and by the collapse of heavy industry. It's dotted with large villages and small towns, and the landscape is scarred by the constant presence of slag heaps.

Look again, though, and you're in for a surprise. The lively towns have sites and monuments a-plenty, as well as restaurants that stay open late and bars that buzz until the early hours. The villages are proud of their past and their traditions, and have gone to great lengths to preserve them. The countryside is clean and green, with picturesque hills and valleys where pretty black-and-white cattle graze, and there are châteaux galore. But the best thing about Hainaut is that the people are warm, welcoming, and fun-loving: it's the carnival capital of Belgium, symbolized for more than 500 years by the riotous festivities in Binche.

CHIMAY   10,000 inhabitants

This small town at the toe of the boot of Hainaut has a fantastically rich history. Jean Froissart, the chronicler of the Hundred Years War, was canon here, and the Trappist ales produced in its monastery have become the stuff of legend. The château and the collegiate church are both must-sees.

USEFUL ADDRESS

Postcode: 6460.
🛈 Tourist office: Vieille Tour, rue de Noailles 4. ☎ (060) 211846. Open 9am–noon and 1.30–5pm (to 10pm at the weekend).

WHERE TO STAY AND EAT

✫ Budget

⌂ Campsite of the commune of Chimay: allée des Princes 1. ☎ (060) 211843. Open from April to the end of October. Tent site: 300BEF. This is a good base if you're touring the region.

✫✫✫ Expensive

⌂ B&B Le Petit Chapitre: place du Chapitre 5, in the centre of town, east of the collegiate church. ☎ (060) 211042. Fax: (060) 214022. Email: brim@skynet.be. Doubles 2,600–2,950BEF, including breakfast. Booking recommended. This handsome old house, furnished with antiques, has five tastefully decorated en suite rooms, and there's a beautiful terrace.

✕ ⌂ Auberge de Poteaupré: rue de Poteaupré 5, Bourlers, 10 kilometres (6 miles) south of Chimay, and 800 metres from the Trappist Abbey of Scourmont. ☎ (060) 211433. Fax: (060) 214404. Email: poteaupre@chimay.be. Restaurant closed Monday out of season. Double rooms 2,000BEF out of season, otherwise 2,400BEF. A good-value three-course meal will cost about 1,000 BEF. The inn is a low building with an ochre facade, while the large dining room has varnished wooden floors and cloth-covered tables and chairs. The restaurant concentrates on local cuisine, with plenty of dishes cooked in beer, while other specialities include mullet fillets, Ardennes ham, roast chicken with vegetables and Chimay cheeses. There's a good wine cellar, too, with plenty of noteworthy vintages.

â **Hôtel de Franc-Bois**: rue Courtil-aux-Martias 18, Lompret 6463, 5 kilometres (3 miles) east of Chimay, beyond Virelles. ☎ (060) 214-475. Fax: (060) 215140. Doubles 2,800–3,000BEF. This charming hotel, in one of the most beautiful villages in the area, is housed in the wing of an old château that's linked to the keep. The rooms are light, well equipped and decorated in bright, cheerful colours that display a considerable amount of good taste. The breakfast room, meanwhile, is decked out in delicate pastel colours. A wonderful place to stay.

WHAT TO SEE

★ **Collégiale Saint-Pierre-et-Paul**: built in 1250, this brick-vaulted church has a flat chevet. The choir is original, while the three aisles, separated by arches and pillars, were added in the 16th century and the tower dates from 1732. The church's greatest treasure is the splendid tomb of Charles de Cröy, Charles V's private tutor, whose family owned the château until 1616 – on top is an effigy of the teacher, his feet resting gracefully on a lion – but the side chapels offer an unusually rich collection of important artefacts.

In the Notre-Dame-du-Rosaire chapel, the second chapel off the choir on the left, you'll find a painting of the *Virgin Mary of the Rosary*: attributed to Brueghel, it recalls the days when Christendom lived in fear of Turkish hegemony. In the fourth choir is the Chapelle de Saint-Jacques, where you can see a rare equestrian statue of the saint, known as the *matamore* ('killer of Moors'), alongside a bust of St Arnould, the patron saint of brewers, who carries a malt shovel. The next chapel is a confessional that dates from 1631.

On the right of the choir, the chapel of Saint-Sacrement contains two reliquary boxes; in the chapel next door, there's a beautiful statue of St Sebastian, and in the one after that, a statue and a painting show St George slaying the dragon. The penultimate chapel, the Chapelle Sainte-Anne-et-Joachim, contains a fine bas-relief framed by images of St Peter and St Paul. The baptismal font is made of marble, while the two large, exotic-looking shell shapes nearby were used for blessings.

★ **Château des princes de Chimay**: ☎ (060) 212823. Open from March to All Saints Day (late October/early November). Guided tours at 10.30am, 11.30am, 2.30pm, 3.30pm and 4.30pm (it's a good idea to go on one of these – the guide is great, and his talk, in French, completely enthralling). Admission: 200BEF. Built in the 14th century, the château has had a turbulent passage through history. It has gone up in flames eight times, most recently in 1935, when the interior, miraculously, survived. The grey stone facade is quite restrained, with mullioned windows, while the huge tower still has its original spire. In the early 19th century, it was the residence of Madame Tallien, whose story is worth telling. Born in Spain and blessed with a pretty face, she married a nobleman from Bordeaux, whom she divorced in 1793. She was condemned to death by the Revolutionary authorities, but was saved from the clutches of Madame Guillotine by the proconsul Jean Tallien. She became his mistress, then his wife, and according to legend, she persuaded Tallien to overthrow Robespierre. Under the Directoire, she launched her own fashion house, before divorcing yet again. In 1805, she married the Count of Caraman, Prince of Chimay, and spent the rest of her days in this château, where she died in 1835. She was a great fan of music, and all the great masters gave concerts in her home, among them La Malibran and Cherubini.

– The **chapel** is the oldest part of the house, and has strikingly thick walls. It served as the village law courts, and once housed the Turin shroud: the Bishop of Liège, who doubted its authenticity, sold it to the House of Savoy, which is how it came to be in Turin. You can also see an unusual portable altar.

– In the large **foyer**, there's a beautiful ceiling and attractive furniture, with drawers made of fossils. There's an *Odalisque* by Titian on the wall.

– The **Salle des Gardes** has a vaulted brick ceiling, ogive window, a vast mantelpiece and an unusual floor, with thousands of slate tiles arranged in star shapes.

– You'll find historic memorabilia in the **portrait room**, including a portrait of Madame Tallien by Baron Gérard, Tallien's cloak and clothes once worn by the King of Rome.

– The enchanting little **theatre**, built in 1863, is decorated in Italian style. It was used in Gérard Corbiau's film *Le Maître de Musique*, and has hosted informal concerts by legendary musicians such as Samson François, Mstislav Rostropovitch, Yehudi Menuhin and Byron Janis.

★ **Chimay Brewery**: at Scourmont abbey, a few kilometres from Chimay. You can learn how Trappist ales are concocted on a guided tour, although you may be disappointed to learn that the monks no longer do the brewing. If you're not familiar with the beers (they're available in Britain, and grace the shelves of most Belgian supermarkets), there are three types: the spicy, light-brown Rouge (7 per cent ABV), the blond, easy-drinking Blanche (8 per cent ABV) and the legendary Bleue (9 per cent ABV), a rich, dark brew that's one of the world's great ales.

WHAT TO SEE AND DO IN THE AREA

★ **Étangs de Virelles**: ☎ (071) 381761. Admission fee: 100BEF. Stretching over a wonderfully peaceful area of 80 hectares (200 acres), the Virelles reservoirs were dug in the 15th and 16th centuries to provide water for the metals industry. Over the years, they've gone back to nature, and are now used for hunting and fishing. Kites and buzzards hover overhead, while reed banks provide shelter for other birds, and are used for basket-making and thatching for roofs. Between May and September, you can hire a boat, which is a great way to appreciate the riches of the reserve. There are also excellent guided tours.

– **Lacs de l'Eau d'Heure** (L'Eau d'Heure lakes): a complex of 1,700 hectares (4,250 acres), which started with the construction of dams in the 1970s. From April to September the lakes are used for watersports.

CHARLEROI   210,000 inhabitants

The capital of the Pays Noir ('Black Country'), Charleroi is one of Belgium's biggest cities, and was once its industrial heartland. It's often dismissed by guidebooks, and it certainly can't compete with Bruges when it comes to obvious tourist attractions, but this gritty place is redeemed by its industrial heritage, its friendly inhabitants (Carolorégiens, or Carolos for short) and a surprisingly Latin atmosphere. It can be a bit bleak in winter, but when the sun shines on the place de l'Hôtel-de-Ville and all the café tables come out, it looks just like a Mediterranean town. The city's arts scene is flourishing, and there are several fascinating museums, while the surrounding landscape offers a rare insight into the rise and fall of heavy industry in Europe.

Still not sure that you want to visit? Then consider this: what other town do you know that has a statue of a cartoon character (Marsupilami – *see below*) on one of its most prominent squares? And he's not alone. Lucky Luke and Gaston Lagaffe are also honoured as distinguished local citizens. It's the kind of irreverence you'd expect from the town where René Magritte grew up.

You'll need to put a bit of effort in, but a trip to Charleroi can be just as rewarding as pottering round the canals in Bruges – and you won't spend the whole time jostling with other tourists.

A Short History

The Romans were the first people to settle on this spot. An officer named Marcius built himself a villa here, and called it the *Villa Marcianae* (the name gave rise to two neighbouring settlements, Marchienne and Marcinelle, now suburbs of Charleroi). Then came Carnoy, a tiny village named after a wood of hornbeam trees ('*charmes*'). The decisive moment in the city's history came in the 17th century, when the Spanish, forced to abandon several fortresses after losing the battle of Rocroi in 1643, chose Carnoy as the site for a garrison town. They built a new town in 1666 and called it Charleroi, in honour of King Charles II of Spain.

The paint had barely had time to dry before the town was seized by Louis XIV, who ordered the construction of the lower part of Charleroi. His architect, Vauban, beefed up the ramparts, but the whole thing fell to the Spanish again in 1679. Over the next century, Charleroi passed back and forth between the French, the Spanish, the Austrians and the Dutch, before being snapped up by the French again in 1794, when local support for the Revolution earned the town the grand name of Libre-sur-Sambre. Cossacks camped in front of Charleroi in 1814, and on 15 June, 1815, Napoleon stayed in the city on the way to Waterloo.

Capital of the Pays Noir

The Industrial Revolution saw Charleroi develop at an extraordinary pace, thanks to the presence of rich coal deposits around the town. Factories sprang up at breakneck pace, and the Pays Noir (Black Country) was born. Originally extracted at the surface, coal was later mined much deeper. Predictably, the workers saw little benefit from this economic expansion, although conditions improved after a violent general strike in 1886.

After World War II, the Belgian government offered Italy cheap coal in return for cheap labour, and thousands of Italians were shipped off to Charleroi (hence the city's Latin feel). Although this helped to slash labour costs, the mining industry soon fell into a terminal decline. The last mine closed in 1984, and the steel industry, Charleroi's other manufacturing staple, now seems to be on its last legs.

Charleroi was also the site of the country's worst mining accident, at Marcinelle on 8 August, 1956. More than half of the 262 victims were Italian.

A brush with fame

Charleroi's most illustrious son is the painter René Magritte, who grew up in one of the city's suburbs and first met his wife, Georgette, at the city's market. His mother, meanwhile, drowned in the River Sambre.

Equally famous, at least in France and Belgium, is the Marsupilami, a jolly yellow beast with black spots and a long tail who sits in the middle of the Grand-Place. He's the star creation of the cartoonist Jean Dupuis, who set up the Dupuis printing works in Charleroi and also created Spirou. Thanks to him, Charleroi became a haven for comic-strip artists.

USEFUL ADDRESSES AND INFORMATION

🛈 Tourist office: Maison Communale, avenue Mascaux 100, Marcinelle. ☎ (071) 866152. Fax: (071) 866157. Open weekdays 8am–noon and 12.30–5pm.

🛈 Bureau d'information touristique: opposite the south train station. ☎ (071) 318218. Open 9am–noon and 12.30–5.30pm. The staff are extremely helpful.

■ French Consulate: boulevard Tirou 11. ☎ (071) 271711.

■ TEC (public transport): place des Tramways 9. ☎ (071) 234111.

🚃 Gare du Sud: ☎ (071) 602294.

WHERE TO STAY AND EAT

🛏 Grand Hôtel Buisset: place Buisset, rue Léopold 1B. ☎ (071) 314588. Fax: (071) 313414. Doubles 2,000–2,300BEF This modern, well-maintained hotel, in a quiet spot in the heart of the Lower Town, has 25 decent rooms.

✗ Les Templiers: place du Manège 7, behind the Hôtel de Ville. ☎ (071) 321836. *Plat du jour* 450BEF. A regulars' tavern opposite the Palais des Beaux-Arts, this is also the headquarters of a Carnival troupe, the '*Récalcitrants*'. There's nothing special about the vaguely medieval decor, but it's a good-humoured place with a small restaurant serving steak, meatballs with tomato sauce, chitterlings or *esca-vèche de Virelles* (eels). There's also a good selection of beers.

✗ Chez Julot: avenue de l'Europe 6, in the Upper Town. ☎ (071) 309740. Open for lunch and dinner (until midnight, or 1 am on Friday and Saturday). Closed Saturday lunchtime and Sunday. This small, unpretentious and eccentrically decorated restaurant, with skeleton murals on the wall, has a cheerful, family atmosphere and serves excellent food with a strong Italian bias. The homemade pasta is simply fantastic, but it's also well worth trying house scampi, Venetian veal liver, grilled lamb with goat's cheese or *escalope Julot*. Wind up with a homemade *tiramisú*.

X **Le Trou Normand**: rue du Comptoir 12, in the Lower Town. ☎ (071) 325134. Open until 3am (to 4am at the weekend). Closed Monday. The waiters wear old-fashioned aprons at this old rustic-style inn, a good choice if you're looking for decent, reasonably priced traditional food. Meat is the main attraction, with *tête de veau*, duck, beef kebab and sirloin steaks on offer, but you can have monkfish with seaweed, or oysters or game in season.

X **La Machine**: rue du Grand-Central 16. ☎ (071) 307533. Closed Saturday lunchtime, Sunday evening and Monday. Innovative cuisine is the hallmark of this long, narrow restaurant, decorated with designer furniture, restrained wrought iron and a rather less restrained use of colour. There's a good lunch menu, and it's also a take-away.

X **La Digue**: rue du Grand-Central 37 (place de la Digue). ☎ (071) 325097. Open 11am–11pm (to 11.30pm on Friday and Saturday). Main courses 400–600BEF. This is the place to go if you're hankering after a large, steaming pot of succulent mussels. They are served in 29 ways, and come in two- or three-litre (four- or six-pint) bowls. The restaurant also offers a good choice of meat and fish.

WHERE TO GO FOR A DRINK

On a fine spring or summer evening, there are several café terraces on the place Charles II, where you can sip an aperitif. If it weren't for the lack of *pastis*, you could almost be sitting on the Côte d'Azur.

🍷 **Aux Mille Colonnes**: rue du Collège. This large bar in the Lower Town (at the entrance to the passage de la Bourse) looks like a 19th-century café and is appropriately placed next to a handsome 19th-century apartment block. It has a popular terrace and a good choice of beers.

🍷 **Cour des Miracles**: place de la Digue 42. Another Lower Town watering hole, this time with a lovely courtyard. It's open until late – 1am on weekdays and 3am on weekends – and has a wonderfully decadent baroque setting. The elaborate, dimly lit seating areas resemble a château done up by Roman Polanski: gold and red hangings, plaster statues, kitsch objects, furniture draped in cloth and plenty of intimate corners. It's known for its cocktails, which include an excellent 'cocktail for two'. Romantic couples can while away the evening in one of the four comfortable upstairs rooms, which you reach via a narrow staircase.

🍷 **Puits d'Orléans**: on the corner of rues Bassle et Orléans. You can't miss this Flemish-style brown café in the Upper Town, as the facade is covered in spectacular iron sculptures. Inside, it's pleasantly unrefined, with a wonderful carved bar, wooden benches and murals that years of cigarette smoke have turned a delicate shade of yellow. The music's usually blues and soul, and the regulars are trendy intellectuals.

🍷 **Faits Divers**: place Albert-ler. Trendy twenty- and thirty-somethings frequent this Lower Town bar, which is jam-packed on weekends.

🍷 **Bubble Gum**: avenue de l'Europe 11. If you like spit-and-sawdust joints, check out this Yankee-style bar in the Upper Town, which is decorated with vehicle registration plates and advertisements, and has high leatherette stools.

❢ Le Blues: avenue de l'Europe 5. A fairly anodyne-looking bistro that hots up with wild jam sessions on Saturday and Sunday evening.

❢ Le Louvois: rue de Turenne 11. A beer bar with a green facade. It also offers snacks.

❢ L'Impasse: in a cul-de-sac off rue de Dampremy 61. Another Lower Town bar with amazing decor, though it's less cosy than Cour des Miracles. There's an upstairs garden area, which is open from mid-June to the beginning of September.

WHAT TO SEE

As you'll have noticed from the descriptions of the establishments above, Charleroi's origins as a garrison town have left it with an Upper and Lower town. And a very steep road between the two.

Lower Town

A semicircle shaped by the River Sambre and boulevard Tirou, opposite the Gare du Sud, the Lower Town is surrounded by the ring road, which was once a branch of the Sambre. It's a lovely area, with a sprinkling of interesting buildings, and is home to lots of small restaurants and clubs, as well as most of the town's hotels.

★ **Rue du Collège**: there are several 19th-century apartment blocks on this street, some decorated with lace-like gabling and others with carved cornices. The most typical stands at the corner of rues du Collège and Marchienne, and has an elegant brick rotunda.

★ **Passage de la Bourse**: this was one of the first covered shopping arcades in Belgium. It has a long neoclassical interior, with Doric, Ionic and Corinthian effects. There are several bookshops in the arcade, but it has a slightly faded feel.

Next door is the **Église Saint-Antoine** (1837), which has a monumental neoclassical facade. To the left of the nave, there's a painting by François Joseph Navez, a follower of Jacques Louis David. Finally, have a look at the art-deco **pont de Sambre**, which is decorated with 'Socialist Realist' statues by Constantin Meunier.

★ **Place Albert-Ier**: the Hôtel des Postes is an odd mix of architectural styles. On Rue de Marcinelle, look out for the pretty 18th-century facade of the Institut Notre-Dame.

★ On the way to the upper town, pause for breath at place Saint-Fiacre, where you'll see the tiny, 17th-century **Chapelle Saint-Fiacre**. On the left are the low houses of place de la Digue, which is typical of 19th-century Charleroi, while the city's oldest street, rue Damprémy, now a pedestrianized shopping street, is on the right. The **Éscalier des Rames** – the remains of one of the roads that led to the ramparts – is level with No. 49. For centuries, weavers used to hang their wool out to dry on the trees. Don't miss the beautiful building at No. 67, dated 1694. As the climb steepens, rue Damprémy becomes rue de la Montagne, a pedestrianized street on which the buildings have plenty of art-nouveau flourishes.

Upper Town

If you look at a map of the town, you'll see that it was built along the lines of the old citadel, with straight roads leading out of the central square like the points of a star, creating a hexagon. Place Charles II, with its refreshing fountains, is the social hub of the area.

★ **Hôtel de Ville**: built in 1936 with a neoclassical facade that has pillars and an abundantly carved pediment. It even has its own belfry, a striking art-deco clock-tower at the back of the building that makes for an unusual contrast with the facade. UNESCO has designated all of Belgium's belfries listed buildings, so this stripling structure already benefits from its protection. Inside, you can visit the Musée des Beaux-Arts, where the art-deco interior, with elegant lines and an intelligent layout, is a superb setting for the works on show. The main foyer and the great staircase are outstanding.

★ **Musée des Beaux-Arts and Musée Jules-Destrée** (Museum of Fine Art and Jules Destrée Museum): on the second floor of the Hôtel de Ville. ☎ (071) 230294. Open 9am–5pm. Closed Sunday and Monday, except during temporary exhibitions. Admission: 50BEF; free for children under 12. The collection provides a good overview of local artists, with particularly strong Realist holdings. Look out for works by the populist painter Gustave Camus and by Constantin Meunier, who spent most of his career depicting the struggles, and dignity, of the working classes.

One of the most evocative paintings is Pierre Paulus's *La Cité industrielle*, which features belching chimneys, their sootiness emphasized by the light in the background. *Jeunesse*, by the same artist, depicts the downtrodden, with faces full of resignation; there's also a Paulus snow scene.

If all this grinding misery leaves you yearning for something more flamboyant, head for Jean Ransy's *Les Livres*, which is reminiscent of Dali, and the paintings of Gilberte Dumont, whose lyricism and eye for detail compare favourably with the Surrealist Paul Delvaux. There's also an extensive collection of works by the 19th-century portraitist François-Joseph Navez.

The star exhibits, though, are a Delvaux, *L'Annonciation*, and a superb Magritte, *Fée ignorante*. On the ground floor, there's an early Magritte, *Portrait de Pierre Bourgeois* (1920).

– **Musée Jules-Destrée**: this museum is devoted to the life of one of the city's most important figures. Destrée was a lawyer, teacher, journalist and writer, as well as an orator and statesman. It was he who invited the drunken Verlaine to lecture in Charleroi.

★ **Basilique Saint-Christophe**: this eclectic structure consists of a baroque facade and choir, and a concrete behemoth that was tacked on in 1956. Like the town hall, it's bizarre, but oddly endearing. The old nave is now a transept, and there's a beautiful mosaic inside.

★ **Place du Manège**: this square is home to the **Palais des Beaux-Arts**, built in the 1950s and a vibrant cultural centre with an international-quality contemporary-dance troupe, Charleroi/Danses. Continuing away from the centre, you'll come to boulevard Bertrand, where you can see the entrance hall of the early-20th-century **Institut supérieur industriel**, with art-nouveau stained-glass windows symbolizing the region's natural resources: coal, iron and glass.

★ Other buildings worth looking at include the apartment blocks on the southern side of **boulevard Audent**, where the bow windows have wrought-iron balconies or sculpted friezes, and the wonderful **Maison Dorée** (1899) on the corner of rue Tumelaire and boulevard Defontaine. Its brick facade is heavily decorated with art-nouveau motifs.

★ **Musée du Verre et Musée archéologique** (Museum of Glass and Archaeology Museum): boulevard Defontaine 10. ☎ (071) 310838. Same hours and prices as the Musée des Beaux-Arts. This rather faded museum explores the history of glass-making in chronological order. The main aspects covered are listed below.

The history of glass: a section devoted to manufacturing methods is followed by examples of ancient glassware, including Roman phials and Merovingian glass paste pearls. Next, items are displayed according to country, era and style: Byzantine, Islamic, Belgian Medieval, Venetian, 16th- and 17th-century Bohemian, Chinese, French, art nouveau and art deco. The art-nouveau pieces are gorgeous.

The uses of glass: this section covers chemistry, optics, physics, electricity and architecture. There are several decorative objects on show as well.

Glass-making: in the final section, you can see designs, models, moulds and machines, and learn the secrets of glass-blowing, glass-cutting, engraving, moulding and so on. There are glass-blowing demonstrations on Tuesday and Thursday.

– On the ground floor, you'll find a small **Musée archéologique**, where you can see the remains of an old Roman villa and a hypocaust (underground heating system), as well as a second-century marble urn, funerary pottery and examples of building materials and tools. There are fragments of a 'planetary vase', domestic objects and an alabaster *Angel of the Annunciation* – an outstanding example of 15th-century sculpture – as well as jewels, buckles, brooches and first- and fourth-century coins (including the famous *solidus*, which was legal tender for centuries, and gave its name to the French *sou*). The final exhibits include examples of damascening (silver or bronze thread encrusted in iron) and more jewellery.

★ **Musée des Chasseurs à pied** (Museum of Foot Soldiers): avenue du Général-Michel 1B. ☎ (071) 300748. Open Monday and Thursday 2–5pm, Saturday 10am–1pm. Admission: 50BEF. This small museum, located in a former barracks, is devoted to military history since 1830, when Belgium won its independence. The most interesting exhibits are documents, weapons and uniforms from the two world wars and the Liberation.

– The **Sunday Market**, which was started in 1709 and takes place on place Charles II, place du Manège and rue d'Orléans, is one of the oldest and most picturesque markets in Wallonia. It's a colourful, sociable affair that's become something of a local ritual, with Carolos turning up to meet friends as well as hunt for bargains. If you need a break, stop at Les Huit Heures, a café where workers met to discuss the fight for reduced working hours and better living conditions. The name, 'Eight Hours', is a tribute to their struggle.

FESTIVAL

– **Charleroi Carnival**: a procession of giants takes place on Shrove Tuesday. Children will love it. For the adults, there's a masked ball, the *bal masqué des Climbias,* on the Saturday after Shrove Tuesday.

A VISIT TO THE PAYS NOIR

Belgium's 'Black Country' begins in the working-class suburbs that fringe the city, including Marcinelle, Mont-sur-Marchienne, Marchienne-au-Pont, Montignies-sur-Sambre, Couillet, Jumet and Lodelinsart. It's not classic tourist territory, but it has its own kind of urban beauty, which you'll appreciate if you take a closer look at the architecture and the unusual use of space. You also find a sprinkling of old churches, handsome châteaux and some interesting museums.

Finally, the black slag heaps and depressed mining villages are a testament to nature's enduring vitality. The once grey heaps, now coated with grass, are home to bushes, trees and even orchids, and the lush, green hillsides make ideal playgrounds for kids. Birds nest here and, in some areas, such as Trazegnies, there are even vines growing. This reconversion has so successfully erased traces of the original mines and slag heaps that there's a movement lobbying for the preservation of the industrial past, in memory of a fascinating but tough era and as a homage to the men who worked and lost their lives in the mines.

MONT-SUR-MARCHIENNE

South of Charleroi: take the motorway interchange behind the Gare du Sud, then exit 29 on the ring road. It's well signposted.

★ **Musée de la Photographie**: avenue Paul-Pastur 11, on the edge of Charleroi, level with rue de la Villette. ☎ (071) 435810. Open 10am–6pm. Closed Monday and on public holidays. Admission: 150BEF, with discounts for children and groups of four or more. Housed in an impressive, neo-Gothic Carmelite monastery, this is a superb museum devoted to all things photographic. There's a wealth of original photos documenting nearly 150 years of history, while cameras from the daguerrotype to the disposable are displayed on the bright, white walls of the cloister that surrounds the interior courtyard. There are usually three temporary exhibitions on the go, and the museum also has a vast, international-quality permanent collection and a well-stocked reference library. Snappers of all abilities will love it.

MARCHIENNE-AU-PONT)

This extraordinary industrial landscape is just a stone's throw from the Lower Town. You can scramble up one of the slag heaps on the edge of town – it's at the beginning of rue de la Providence, on the way to Mons, and there's a metro station nearby – from where you can see the anachronistic Chapelle Saint-Ghislain, the Canal de Charleroi, the first houses built in Dampremy and the haunting silhouette of the Cockerill-Sambre steelworks. Marchienne is also home to the 17th-century Château Cartier (place Albert-Ier), which belonged to the family of the novelist Marguerite Yourcenar.

★ **Musée de l'Industrie**: rue de la Providence 134. ☎ (071) 237120/ 275610. Open Tuesday to Friday 9am–noon and 1–4pm, Saturday 2–5pm. Closed Sunday, Monday, December and late February. Admission: 50BEF. The museum is housed in the Forges de la Providence, a collection of old industrial buildings. You can visit a rolling mill, a forge and the machine workshops. The display includes some colossal steam engines and a print works, and there are demonstrations showing how the machines work.

★ **Musée Marchiennois**: place des Martyrs 38. ☎ (071) 362321/436363. Open Monday, Wednesday and Friday 5–7pm. A local-history museum, with documents, objects, photographs and a reconstruction of a primary-school classroom. It's worth phoning to check the opening hours.

MARCINELLE

This district will always be associated with the catastrophe of 1956, when 262 men lost their lives in the mines. The town's main square is dominated by the 15th-century Église Saint-Martin, which has a massive Romanesque tower. Go through Blanche Borne and you'll come to the mining area of Bois-du-Cazier, where the disaster occurred. Nothing has been touched since it happened, and the site is a moving memorial to the not so distant past.

FESTIVALS IN THE AREA

– **Brocante des Quais**: in June. This is a huge flea market, and it's *the* place to be each year.

– **International Folk Dance Festival**: on the weekend closest to 14 July.

– **Marche de la Madeleine**: in Jumet, on the Sunday closest to 22 July. A reconstruction of a Napoleonic military parade, with 2,000 participants and 200 horses.

– **Marche Saint-Louis**: in Marcinelle. Fourth Sunday in August.

– **Marche la tour Saint-Jean**: in Gosselies. Sunday closest to 24 June.

– **Comic strip salon**: in November.

WHAT TO SEE SOUTH OF CHARLEROI ALONG THE SAMBRE

★ **Gozée**: ruins of the Abbaye d'Aulne. From April to the end of September, tours every day except Monday. Admission: 40BEF. This Cistercian abbey, founded in the 12th century, was razed to the ground by the *sans-culottes* in 1794, along with a library of 40,000 books, including 5,000 ancient manuscripts. The lonely ruins, which nestle in a peaceful patch of green countryside, are a haunting reminder of the abbey's former grandeur.

★ **Thuin**: this old citadel town, once part of the Principality of Liège, is well worth a visit: riddled with cobbled streets and old houses, it's perilously perched above the Sambre, and the ramparts date from the 10th century. The belfry, built in 1639, is a UNESCO world heritage site, while the lower town still has an old boatman's quarter.

★ **Lobbes**: not far from Thuin, this is another small town perched high on a rocky peak. Its main attractions are the Église Saint-Ursmer, a glowering Carolingian church with a crypt containing the sarcophagi of two eighth-century saints, and the ruins of the Benedictine Abbey of Saint-Pierre.

BINCHE   33,000 inhabitants

Long ago, this depressed old mining town enjoyed a golden age. In 1544, Charles V gave the fortified town to his sister, Maria of Hungary. She built a palace, and lived a splendid life, receiving emperors and organizing huge banquets – until 1554, when Henri II of France seized the town and destroyed it. Following its brief spell of glory, Binche became a humble workers' village, although it kept its 12th- and 14th-century ramparts and 27 towers, and is the only surviving walled city in Belgium. When the area was plunged into economic crisis, Binche somehow managed to keep its head above water, although the signs of hardship are not hard to spot. The lasting legacy of Maria's reign is the spectacular Carnival, when groups of *Gilles* in padded costumes shuffle ritualistically through the streets, eventually joining forces for a mesmerizing dance on the Grand-Place.

THE CARNIVAL

The Binchois are justly proud of their Carnival, and go to great lengths to make it a success, sometimes saving throughout the year and forgoing holidays and other luxuries to pay for the insurance (thousands of oranges are hurled about the main square, and windows are often broken), costumes and copious amounts of drink. According to popular myth, the Carnival is based on the festivities held by Maria of Hungary in 1549, which celebrated the Spanish conquest of Peru, and the *Gilles*, who wear extravagant ostrich feather headdresses, are said to represent the South American Indians. Historians, however, dismiss this legend out of hand. What everyone agrees is that for centuries, Binche has held a festival at Lent, traditionally a time of fasting in the Christian calendar – hence the word 'carnival', which comes from the Latin 'carne', meaning meat, and 'levare' meaning to remove.

Today, the preparations for this annual event begin almost as soon as the last Carnival has ended, and are as much a ritual as the festival itself. Rehearsals take place every Sunday, starting in January, when processions wind through the streets, with fanfares and drum rolls echoing into the night, giving onlookers a taste of the big event several weeks in advance. The mad night of the 'Trouilles de Nouilles', when half the population roam the streets wearing masks, takes place on the Monday of the week before Shrove Tuesday. On the Sunday before Shrove Tuesday, numerous guilds take to the streets, each hoping to present the most original and innovative costumes. Monday is children's day, but the big day is Shrove Tuesday, when the *Gilles* take centre stage.

A *Gille*'s day begins at dawn, when he downs a glass of champagne and dons his costume: a straw-stuffed shirt and trousers decorated with heraldic lions, stars and arms. *Gille*-hood is a great honour in these parts – you have to be a man born within the city walls – and throughout the day, his gestures and actions are strictly dictated by immutable tradition. He carries a bundle of sticks and a string of bells, wears clogs on his feet and shuffle-dances to the beating of drum as he goes off in search of his friends. Wearing mustachioed wax masks, they gather in front of the Hôtel de Ville, joining the peasants, pierrots and harlequins who make up the other groups of the carnival ritual. There's more dancing before they pause for a lunch of oysters and champagne.

The *Gilles* continue dancing in the afternoon, but this time they wear hats with ostrich feathers, and bombard the crowd with oranges (never throw one back: it's a gift, and they take it very badly if you refuse it). Now you'll understand why all the windows are boarded up. The hammering of clogs on the cobbles holds the crowd enthralled, as they cluster around to watch. Next, everyone accompanies the groups to the Grand-Place, where the final dance begins. Illuminated by fireworks and Bengal lights, the festival goes on long into the night, always to the same ritualistic beating of drums, without which the *Gille* cannot continue on his shuffling way. Everyone collapses into bed in the early hours, and it's over for another year. By the way, a genuine *Gille* never leaves his native town. The *Gilles* paraded in other towns are but pale imitations of the real thing.

USEFUL ADDRESSES AND INFORMATION

Postcode: 7130.

🛈 **Tourist office**: in an annex of the Hôtel de Ville. Open 10am–noon and 2–6pm, 10am–6pm on Saturday and Sunday. ☎ (064) 336727.

✉ **Post office**: rue des Récollets, at the corner of ruelle Carlo-Mahy. Open 9am–5pm on weekdays, and 9am–noon on Saturday (except in August).

🚆 **Railway station**: place Derbaix. ☎ (064) 332870. A cathedral-style neo-Gothic structure; trains for Brussels leave every hour until 9pm. Special rates during Carnival.

■ **Bank**: Crédit Communal, avenue Charles-de-Liège 39. ☎ (064) 332164. Bureau de change and cash dispenser (Visa cards accepted).

WHERE TO STAY

There's virtually nowhere to stay in Binche, apart from the very pleasant campsite. Most visitors stay in Mons, Charleroi and La Louvière.

☆ Budget

🛏 **Campsite Aux Gloriettes**: rue de la Résistance 92, Waudrez. ☎ (064) 368269. Take rue des Récollets (heading for Charleroi), turn right at the *gendarmerie* and follow the signs for a kilometre (half a mile). Tent site for two adults, two children and one car: 500BEF. Open April to the end of October. Thousands of people pass through this clean and shady campsite, where little has changed since the 1950s (the bathrooms, thankfully, have been revamped). There's an adventure playground, mini golf, a mini zoo, a chip shop and a cafeteria (open in the afternoon during the week and on Friday and Saturday evening – sometimes even with dancing). The warm, welcoming atmosphere of the place is striking, even if you only stay for half a day and a bite to eat.

WHERE TO EAT

▣ Budget

✕ **Snack Chez Alex**: Avenue Wanderpepen 1, around the corner from the Grand-Place. ☎ (064) 341351. Open 11am–11pm (to 2am on Friday and Saturday). A big, slightly tacky chip shop. Not for the cholesterol-conscious, but other wise perfectly good.

☆☆ Moderate

✕ **L'Industrie**: Grand-Place 4, on the corner of rue de la Hure. ☎ (064) 331053. Open for lunch and evening meals until 9pm. Closed Monday and Tuesday evening, Wednesday and late August. *Plat du jour* 280BEF, main courses up to 600BEF. In 1935, five sisters each opened a restaurant with the same name, *Industrie*, in different towns within the region, thus launching Belgium's first restaurant chain. The Binche branch is the last of the chain to belong to the same family.

The landlady is charming, while the landlord tackles the cuisine, which features excellent meat cooked in beer. Try *tête de veau* (his speciality), baby eels or mussels (not served at lunchtime on Sunday), and you'll appreciate just how much he loves his work. Portions, especially of meat, are enormous, but try to save room for dessert (the crêpes are out of this world), and round off your meal in with a filter coffee, which is served in silver cups. The set menu of regional specialities, which includes beers from the local Brasserie La Binchoise, is also very reasonable. Or, if you really want to make the most of this deliciously old-fashioned, atmospheric restaurant, try a Binchoise *double*: a buckwheat crêpe filled with cheese. This is one of the only places that does them and, strange as it sounds, you need to order a day in advance.

WHAT TO SEE

★ **Musée international du Carnaval et du Masque** (International Museum of the Carnival and the Mask): rue Saint-Moustier 10, opposite the church, with a bronze statue of a *Gille* outside. ☎ (064) 335741. Open Sunday to Thursday 9.30am–12.30pm and 1.30–6pm. Closed Friday and Saturday morning. Admission fee, with discounts for students. Housed in a former Augustine college, the museum has an impressive array of masks and costumes from all over the world, from the swishing feathers of Rio de Janeiro to the terrifying witch costumes of Tyrolean carnivals and African tribal symbols. Gawp at devil faces and masks of conquistadors with huge moustaches, then wander into rooms of weird, sometimes scary-looking figures that can really freak you out, especially if you're the only one there. There's a large section on Walloon carnivals, with extensive displays on Binche and its *Gilles*. There are also displays about the manufacture of various costume parts, including a clog-making workshop that shows the process from wood to finished product, old posters, photographs and dioramas of *mam'zelles*, Eastern princes, harlequins, sailors and other characters who accompany the *Gilles* during their annual walkabout.

At the end, there's a slightly chaotic film about the Carnival, which does its best to explain (in French) what's going on. Every year, the museum hosts a temporary exhibition on one of the world's great carnivals.

★ **Collégiale Saint-Ursmer**: at the end of town, near the park and opposite the museum. You have to tiptoe in here during services: otherwise open Monday and Wednesday 10am–5pm, and Friday or Saturday 10am–1pm. Saint-Ursmer is an austere grey-stone church with a few 15th- and 16th-century religious statues, including a poignant figure of Christ. There's an evocative, if slightly dilapidated, painted stone representation of the *Entombment* behind the Renaissance rood screen. The statue of St Ursmer is paraded through town on 18 April.

★ **Hôtel de Ville**: Grand-Place. With foundations dating back to the 14th century, and a UNESCO-listed belfry, this used to be the Halle aux Viandes (Meat Hall). Inside are three attractive rooms, with an oak ceiling and a Renaissance mantelpiece.

★ Before you leave, take a look at the **rampart walls** that dominate the little park, and cast your eye over the **pharmacy** on avenue Charles-de-Liège (to your left if you're coming from the Grand-Place).

You won't be impressed by the total lack of respect some vandals have shown for the wonderful 19th-century tiled advertisements that decorate the facade, including one proclaiming the benefits of Scott emulsion, which 'cures ailments of the throat, lungs and blood'.

IN THE AREA

⊟ Syndicat d'initiative de la région du Centre: place Mansart 17-18, La Louvière 7100. ☎ (064) 215121.

⌂ Centre d'hébergement de la Cantine des Italiens: rue Tout-y-Faut, Houdeng-Goegnies 7110, 3 kilometres (2 miles) from La Louvière. ☎ (064) 662561. Open all year. This youth hostel has old riverside huts, originally built for Italian workers. There are 55 beds in clean, renovated rooms that sleep 11, each with shower and toilet. It's popular with school parties, so call in advance to check availability, and make sure you arrive before 8pm. The hosts are pleasant, and light meals and bike hire are available.

★ **Domaine and Musée royal de Mariemont**: 20 kilometres (12 miles) northeast of Binche. ☎ (064) 212193. Open every day 10am–6pm. Closed Monday, except on public holidays. Admission free. Mariemont is a magnificent 50-hectare (125-acre) park, laid out in the 19th century on land that originally belonged to Maria of Hungary. The garden and collections were bequeathed to the state in 1917.

Visitors to the park (its huge gates shut at 4pm in winter), can see several rare trees, some 300 years old, a rose garden and the romantic ruins of an 18th-century château that's overrun by plants. The undulating park is dotted with sculptures, including Rodin's *Burghers of Calais*, which stands in front of the ruins, and, near the rose garden, Constantin Meunier's *Semeur*.

The modern building that houses the museum was designed to incorporate the ruins of another château, which burnt down in 1960. Although the concrete block, in the shadow of a splendid Lebanon cedar, is not to everyone's taste, its light, airy exhibition spaces are perfect for the collections of Egyptian, Greek, Roman and Far Eastern artefacts. On the ground floor, there's a room devoted to local archaeology, in particular the Merovingian acropolis at Ciply, which was discovered during excavations for the phosphate industry.

The section on Tournai porcelain leads to a rather ugly cafeteria with views of the peacocks in the park. On the whole, this is a successful museum: the layout is a bit haphazard, but it has some fine collections, and hosts excellent temporary exhibitions.

★ **Canal du Centre**: between Mons and Charleroi. The Centre region enjoyed a golden age in the 19th century, thanks to the collieries. La Louvière, its capital, is an industrial city of limited charm. Much more interesting is the canal, which was dug to link the Meuse to the Escaut, providing the region's rapidly developing industry with improved transport links. The scheme posed one huge problem: the construction of locks that could level the 90-metre (300-foot) difference between the two rivers? Renowned for their engineering skills, the English came up with a system involving four huge hydraulic lifts that would enable the boats to pass from one river to the other. The resultant metal structures, built between 1882 and 1917, consist of a cross bar, stands and two tubs for holding the boats, which are lifted 15 metres (nearly 50 feet) by gigantic hydraulic pistons. They are now a UNESCO World Heritage Site. The method has proved its worth, and an enormous new elevator has been built in Strépy-Thieu (on a new canal, near the old one; there's a small exhibition devoted to these gigantic works).

– Visitors can take a short **cruise** on these lifts. Departures are in the morning, in season and on Sunday afternoon, from the Cantine des Italiens, rue Tout-y-Faut, in Houdeng-Goegnies. ☎ (064) 284337/662561. Phone to find out about times and boarding points. The Cantine des Italiens, a collection of huts built in the post-war years to house immigrant workers, is now a pleasant youth hostel (*see* 'In the area'), and has a small museum that you can explore while you wait for your trip.

★ **Écomusée de Bois-du-Luc**: rue Saint-Patrice 5, Houdeng-Aimeries, leaving the motorway at La Louvière West. ☎ (064) 225448. Open 9am–noon and 1–5pm. Admission fee; guided tours recommended. Apart from the courtyard, which is used to display disused engines and wagons, all the buildings, including the Saint-Emmanuel mine, the miner's house and the workshop, with working machinery that's activated by a single engine, are shut. Wherever they were, in the hospital, school or at home, the workers of Bois-du-Luc could never escape the sight of the pithead. Good luck to the ambitious team who are trying to transform this industrial wasteland into a museum. In the meantime, it's worth tagging along with a guide.

★ **Château de Seneffe**: rue L. Plasman, north of La Louvière. ☎ (069) 558492. Open 10am–6pm. Closed Monday. Admission: 150BEF. On Sunday at 3pm, there's a lecture tour. This holiday home was commissioned from the prolific architect Laurent-Benoît Dewez in 1763 by Julien Depestre, who made a fortune in the Indies and by selling supplies to the French armies. The resulting pile is the height of neo-Classicism, with pretensions to emulate Versailles. There's a pavilion on either side of the main courtyard, which has vast, enclosed colonnades. The main lodge, built in local blue stone, houses the new **Musée de l'Orfèvrerie de la Communauté française**, a jewellery museum with 800 items of silver from across Europe. They're displayed in salons enhanced with stucco, gilding and mirrors. The wood floors are so precious and delicate that you have to wear special slippers before entering. Outside, you can visit the orangerie, a mini theatre, an ice-house and a French-style terraced park with a café.

MONS   93,000 inhabitants

Behind its squeaky-clean, sober appearance, Mons is a capital city – the capital of the province of Hainaut – and has the rich history, administrative centres, university and ring roads that this status demands. Nearby are the headquarters of SHAPE, NATO's military arm, whose international employees add to the town's cosmopolitan atmosphere. You can spend hours wandering among the elegant houses on the small cobbled streets that lead up to the church, wandering around the Grand-Place and soaking up the lively evening atmosphere on the place du Marché-aux-Herbes. The students set the pace here, and seem to have enough free time to get involved in preparations for the folk fair ('Lumeçon'). In 1999, Mons organized a bus network to unclog the centre and it's proved a very successful enterprise.

A Short History

Back in the seventh century, on a hill that the Romans called Montes, a pious lady and good wife named Waudru founded a monastery. She was joined by the Counts of Hainaut, who fortified the town and made it their capital. Mons took off in the 16th century, thanks to a thriving textile industry. Sadly, its new-found prosperity was rudely disrupted by the religious conflicts that followed the Reformation. In 1691, a torrent of cannonballs fired by the troops of Louis XIV rained down on Mons. The Sun King rebuilt the city, which the French occupied and lost on several occasions over the following century. The last time it was captured was in 1792, at the Battle of Jemmapes, when the Revolutionary army took over. Mons was handed over to the new state of Belgium in 1831, and became the commercial centre of the mining region of the Borinage. During both world wars, the city was the scene of ferocious fighting.

Mons boasts a few famous names, among them the painter Jean Prévost (1472–1529) and the composer Orlando de Lassus (1531–94). Verlaine worked on his *Romances sans parole* here, while he was in prison for having tried to shoot his partner, Rimbaud.

The Ducasse

Every year, the Montois let rip in suitably crazy style at their traditional festivals, which are prepared long in advance and take place on Trinity Sunday (at the end of May or in early June). The first important event is the

Procession du Car d'Or (procession of the Golden Chariot), when the wagon in the collegiate church is wheeled out to parade the reliquary of St Waudru around town. The wagon is accompanied by 50 folk groups and the rest of the local population, who push the chariot up the steep slope to the church. It's considered bad luck for the town if the procession hesitates: legend has it that the last occasions when this happened were 1914 and 1939. The second event is the **Combat du Lumeçon**, in which a statue of St George on horseback is borne on the shoulders of the *chinchins*, figures dressed in tutus, who are teased and tormented by a band of devils. They fight a cardboard dragon while music plays in the background. The ritual always ends with the victory of the saint over the monster, and the spectators come forward to pull hairs out of the latter's long tail, which is supposed to bring them good luck. It ends just in time for lunch, when the Montois settle down to a splendid feast.

USEFUL ADDRESSES AND INFORMATION

Postcode: 7000.
⌂ Mons Tourist Office (map B2): Grand-Place 22. ☎ (065) 335580. Fax: (065) 356336. In summer, open Monday to Saturday 9am–6.30pm, Sunday 10am–6.30pm; otherwise, Monday to Saturday 9am–5pm, Sunday 10.30am–1.30pm.
⌂ Fédération touristique de la province du Hainaut (map A2, **3**): rue des Clercs 31. ☎ (065) 360464. Fax: (065) 335732.

✉ Post office (map B2): place du Marché-aux-Herbes.
🚂 Railway station (off the map from A2): place Léopold. ☎ (065) 322210. There are several trains for Brussels every day. Journey time about an hour.
▪ Bank: Crédit Communal (map B2, **1**), Rue des Clercs. Bureau de change and cash dispenser for Visa cards.

WHERE TO STAY

✿ Budget

The youth hostel, scheduled to open in 2002, is still a long way from completion, and the hotels around the station have a slightly dodgy reputation, so there's not much in the way of budget accommodation. The campsite, however, is pretty good.

⚓ Camping du Waux-Hall (off the map from B2, **11**): avenue Saint-Pierre 17, just outside the city. ☎ (065) 337923. Fax: (065) 363848. Open all year. Two-person tent site: 380BEF. This green and pleasant campsite is next to a large park that bears the same name. It's open all year and has clean bathrooms, electric sockets, a tennis court and well-equipped, modern tents and caravans.

✿✿ Moderate

⚓ Hôtel Saint-Georges (map A2, **10**): rue des Clercs 15, right beneath the belfry. ☎ (065) 311629. Fax: (065) 318671. Email: saintgeorges. mons@skynet.be. Doubles 1,290–2,350BEF; breakfast 185BEF. This small, friendly hotel in a white town house has an attractive reception and recently decorated rooms, from where you can hear the carillon play. There's also a paying car park.

WHERE TO STAY IN THE AREA

☆☆☆ Expensive

⚓ **Château de la Cense au Bois**: route d'Ath 135, in Nimy. ☎ (065) 316000. Fax: (065) 361155. If you're in a car, follow the Route d'Ath towards Nimy. Doubles 2,750–4,950BEF; breakfast 350BEF. Five kilometres (three miles) further on, on the right, you'll see the road that leads to the château, a large 19th-century structure in 15 hectares (38 acres) of parkland. It's been converted into a magnificent hotel with 10 delightful and sumptuous rooms, all individually decorated: those on the second floor cost only a little more than a room at the Saint-Georges. It's worth splashing out on a luxury stay here, especially if you like large beds, huge bathrooms (with dressing gowns) and views of the park. Breakfast is served in a small room flooded with sunlight (in fine weather, at any rate). The château is famous for its restaurant, the Oscièstre Gris (closed Sunday evening and Monday), which is expensive but excellent.

WHERE TO EAT

☆ Budget

✗ You can buy whelks at the **stall** on the Grand-Place, but it's only open on weekends and public holidays. If you want chips, try **Au Doudou** (*see* 'Where to eat').

✗ Like most student towns, Mons has its fair share of kebab vans.
✗ The pizzeria **Belvédère** (place Léopold, opposite the station) serves food until 6am or later.

■ **Useful addresses**
  🛈 Tourist office
  ✉ Post office
  🚃 Railway station
  1 Société Générale
  3 Fédération touristique de la province du Hainaut

⚓ **Where to stay**
  10 Hôtel Saint-Georges
  11 Camping du Waux-Hall

✗ **Where to eat**
  20 Le Pastissou
  21 Le Pain Quotidien
  22 La Coquille Saint-Jacques
  23 Chez Henry
  24 No Maison

🍷 **Where to go for a drink**
  30 Au Doudou

  31 L'Arnaque
  32 Le Chinchin
  33 L'Envers

★ **What to see**
  40 Collégiale Sainte-Waudru
  41 Belfry
  42 Grand-Place
  43 Hôtel de ville
  44 Musées du Centenaire
  45 Musée du Chanoine Puissant (Museum of Canon Puissant)
  46 Musée du Folklore et de la Vie montoise (Museum of Folklore and Life in Mons)
  47 Musée des Beaux-Arts (Museum of Fine Art)
  48 Église Saint-Nicolas-en-Havré
  49 Église Sainte-Élisabeth
  50 Place du Béguinage

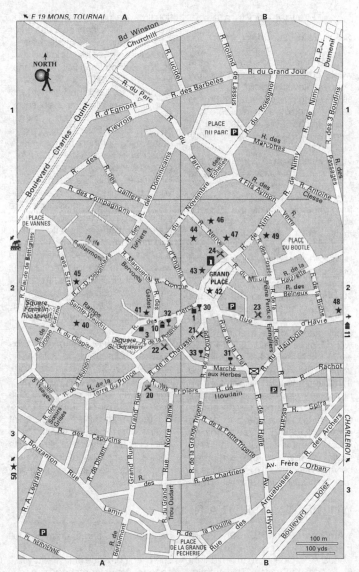

NORTH

Bd Winston Churchill

R. du Grand Jour

R. Lucidel

R. Roland de Lassus

R. des Barbelés

R. du Rossignol

R. de Nimy

R. des 3 Boudins

R. P. J. Dumenil

R. du Parc

R. d'Egmont

Kievrois

Boulevard — Charles — Quint

PLACE DU PARC

R. des Marcottes

R. du Parc

R. des Échelles

4 Fils Aymon

R. de Nimy

R. Antoine Clesse

R. des Passages

R. des Gaillers

R. des Compagnons

R. des Dominicains

R. des Telliers

R. du 11 Novembre

Nerve

R. des 4 Fils Aymon

verte

PLACE DE VANNES

★ 46

44 ★

47 ★

49 ★

PLACE DU BOOTLE

R. cfe

Benjamin

R. Marguerite

Bervois

R. d'Enghien

Cronque

24 ★

GRAND PLACE

R. de Nimy

R. des fossés

R. de la Raquette

R. des Belneux

R. de la Biche

45 ★

R. f. D. Chabolin

Gades

43 ★

42 ★

Peine Perdue

R. de

Minot

48 ★

Square Franklin Roosevelt

Rampe Sainte-Waudru

R. du Chapitre

41 ★

32 ★

Clercs

30

23

R. des Épingliers

R. du Hautbois

d'Havré

40 ★

Square St-Germain

10

3

21

22

33

31

Rue de la Clef

Rachot

Marché aux Herbes

R. de la Terre du Prince

20

Fripiers

R. de Houdain

R. des Sœurs Grises

Capucins

Grand Rue

Notre Dame

R. des

R. de la Grande Triperie

R. de la Halle

Lescarts

Spira

R. des Archers

R. A. Legrand

Rue

R. du Dinant

Grand Rue

R. des

R. des Chartriers

Av. Frère / Orban

CHARLEROI

★ 50

Lamir

R. de Berlaimont

R. du Grand Trou Oudart

Av. d'Hyon

Arquebusiers

Boulevard Dolez

PL. NERVIENNE

PLACE DE LA GRANDE PÊCHERIE

R. de la Trouille

des

Rue

100 m

100 yds

MONS

☆–☆☆ Budget–Moderate

✕ **Le Pain Quotidien** (map B2, **21**): rue de la Coupe 5. ☎ (065) 337138. The Montois branch of the wholesome breakfast bar that's now popular all over Belgium. Customers sit at a huge wooden tables in the centre, where they can feast on a huge variety of breakfasts, and, at lunchtime, healthy open sandwiches.

✕ **Le Pastissou** (map A3, **20**): rue des Fripiers 14. Closed Sunday and Monday. The main attraction of this unpretentious establishment, which has photographs of the Basque country on the walls, is the food, tasty, copious dishes from southwest France, including Bayonne ham, Landaise duck, *cassoulet* and duck *confit*. The *plat du jour* is really good value for money.

✕ **Chez Henry** (map B2, **23**): rue d'Havré 41. ☎ (065) 352306. Open 11.30am–8.30pm. Closed Sunday evening and Monday evening. Steak with chips and salad 250BEF; *plat du jour* about 250BEF; spaghetti or chips 120BEF. A popular lunchtime haunt for wage slaves, this is an unappealing-looking canteen that's only partly redeemed by the attractive old bricks, a fireplace and a pretty oak ceiling. There's nothing special about the food, but it's adequate, inexpensive and attractively served, with grilled meats, sauerkraut and salads in summer. Traditionally, you pay at the bar on the way out. Chez Henry now has a bar and brasserie on the Grand-Place, so business must be going well.

✕ **No Maison** (map B2, **24**): Grand-Place 21. ☎ (065) 347474. Open every day for lunch and dinner (until 11pm, or midnight at weekends). This large, old-fashioned brasserie on the Grand-Place is a bit of a tourist trap, but there's a reasonably priced set menu that includes four generous, good-quality courses. The lunchtime special is a real bargain. If you sit upstairs, you can enjoy the view whilst feasting on delicacies like pork chops 'al'Berdouille' (a local speciality with a tomato cream sauce and mustard), chicken breasts *à la Leffe* and mussels in season. The walls are decorated with cheerful paintings of local festivals, the property of a Walloon drama society that occasionally meets here. The restaurant frequently caters for groups, and can be very full.

✕ **La Coquille Saint-Jacques** (map A2, **22**): rue de la Poterie 27. ☎ (065) 843653. Open noon–7pm. Closed Sunday evening and Monday. Set menu 750BEF. If you're in search of sensible but refined cooking, fresh ingredients and a pleasant setting with exposed beams, this is a good option. Try roast salmon with apples, scampi, fillet of John Dory or roast lamb. The set menu is generous and tasty.

WHERE TO GO FOR A DRINK

♀ **Au Doudou** (map B2, **30**): Grand-Place 34, on the corner of rue de la Chaussée. Open 10am–midnight (from 4pm on Sunday). This authentic old bar, which still has decorations made from hops by customers in bygone days, makes a refreshing change from the workaday cafés and pizzerias on the Grand-Place. It's terribly small, with well-worn padded seats, and is crammed full of bric-à-brac. The service can seem a bit brusque at first, but you'll soon realize what a cheerful, good-humoured place this is. Ideal if you want to a plate of chips and a beer.

♀ **L'Arnaque** (map B2, **31**): place du Marché-aux-Herbes. Open every day until 3am (to 6am on Friday). This little square, just behind the main one, is the epicentre of the local nightlife. It's surrounded by noisy cafés, and the students drift happily from one terrace to the next. L'Arnaque is the nicest of the bars, with plain wood and enamelled plaques, and a real tree in the middle of the bar; in summer, they move all the tables outside, transforming the interior into a dancefloor. The music's pretty loud, especially on weekends.

♥ Le Chinchin (map A2, **32**): rue des Clercs 1, in the vaulted cellar of the Hôtel Saint-Georges. Open 10am–noon (and later at weekends). This cosy, intimate bar is a good place to start, or wind up, your evening. It's agreeably lively, but you don't have to shout to make yourself heard. The decor's more or less successful, with sophisticated lighting and plain chairs, but claustrophobics and non-smokers should probably give it a miss.

♥ L'Envers (map B2, **33**): rue de la Coupe 20. Night-owls flock to this well-designed, trendy café.

WHAT TO SEE

★ **Collégiale Sainte-Waudru** (map A2, **40**): side entrance in rue du Chapitre. The hilltop spot where Waudru founded her monastery became the site of a collegiate church, built by the canonesses of Waudru's religious community. Work began in 1450, starting with the choir, but stopped in 1686 when the nuns bowed to the impossibility of realizing their dream, which was to build a structure 90 metres (627 feet) high. Mathieu de Layens (who built Leuven's town hall) was one of the first architects to work on the building, and his successors continued in Brabant Gothic style. There's nothing outstanding about the exterior, but the overall cohesion is quite impressive.

The interior of the church, built in the shape of a Roman cross, is much more interesting. It's 110 metres (363 feet) long and 25 metres (83 feet) wide, and has 29 chapels, all dedicated to a guild or confraternity. You can see the Car d'Or ('Golden Chariot'), the 18th-century baroque wagonette used to carry the reliquary of St Waudru during the Ducasse, in the nave near the main door. It's covered in chubby cherubs. During the procession, the chariot is pushed uphill to the church – and woe betide the town if it pauses on its way. The 19th-century gilt copper reliquary dominates the altar. A bust of the saint's head rests on another reliquary, which you can see in the last chapel on the right of the nave.

The choir is decorated with seven white statues: the first four represent the cardinal virtues (Temperance, Strength, Justice and Prudence), while the others illustrate the theological virtues of Faith, Hope and Charity. They were originally part of the rood screen, created by a 16th-century Montois artist. The transept is adorned with bas-relief sculptures, which survived the two world wars. You can see a black-marble and alabaster altarpiece in the fourth chapel on the left of the ambulatory and sculptures of St Waudru (16th-century) and St Michael flooring the Devil (15th-century) in two of the chapels further round. Take a look at the 16th-century stained-glass windows in the transept and chevet, then head for the Treasury.

– **Treasury**: open from Easter 1.30–5pm. Closed Monday. Admission: 50BEF. The old chapter house, to the right of the nave, houses the church's treasury, where you can see paintings and a collection of gold and silver artefacts from the 13th to the 19th centuries. There are chalices, reliquaries and even a ring and brooch that supposedly belonged to St Waudru herself.

★ **Belfry** (map A2, **41**): Victor Hugo described the belfry as 'a vast coffee pot, with four slimmer teapots beneath its belly', and concluded in a letter to his wife that: 'It would be ugly if it weren't so big.' At 87 metres (nearly 290 feet) high, it is rather large, and it probably would be ugly if it were smaller, but the belfry dominates Mons and is an illustration of the city's importance. Built in the 17th century, the tower is undergoing apparently endless restoration, though work is scheduled to end in 2004. In the meantime, the belfry has been declared a UNESCO World Heritage Site. Although you can't visit the belfry, you can hear its 49-bell carillon chime in the hours.

★ **Grand-Place** (map B2, **42**): recently pedestrianized, and much the better for it, this huge, airy rectangle has been slightly defaced by new buildings constructed in the 1960s, but you can still see original old houses on the Hôtel de Ville side. Several date back to the 16th century, including the two gabled buildings on either side of the town hall. The café terraces on the square (all of which can be recommended) are ideal spots for watching the sun go down behind the buildings.

★ **Hôtel de Ville** (map B2, **43**): again designed by Mathieu de Layens, who was commissioned by Charles the Bold. Charles's death brought the project to an abrupt halt, but it got going again 100 years later. The 18th and 19th centuries brought several alterations, most notably the campanile, the slate roof and the neo-Gothic elements. Despite the length of time it took to complete it, the structure looks fairly coherent. It's basically Gothic in style, with stone cornices and broken arches over the doors and windows. Look out for the impressive-looking lock on one of the Dutch doors: it's a copy of the original, which was kept in the burgomaster's office. You can see a bizarre iron sculpture of a monkey to the left of the door. It's known as the '*Grand Garde*', and was the work of a 15th-century craftsman, but what it's doing here, nobody really knows. It may have been the sign of an inn, the profits of which helped swell the town coffers, but it's more likely that it was part of a pillory used for tying up naughty children.

To gain access to the Hôtel de Ville, you have to go through a very complicated procedure. That said, the doors are often unlocked. Gently push the one to the right of the coaching passage and you'll see if there's anyone around who's liable to throw you out. There are a few beautiful rooms to see, including the marriage room, which has an oak ceiling, and the Gothic room, with splendid flooring, impressive light fittings and a coffered ceiling. To the left of this room, behind a platform, you'll see a few steps that lead to the 'umbrella room', where you can admire the wonderful carved brick vaulting.

The Museums

Since 1998, the Montois museums have been in the throes of reorganization, and the consequent upheaval means that opening hours and arrangements may vary.

★ **Musées du Centenaire** (Museums of the Centenary) (map B2, **44**): jardin du Mayeur (entrance through the Hôtel de Ville). ☎ (065) 335213. Open noon–6pm. Closed Monday. Admission fee. Housed in an old pawn shop and other administrative buildings in the grounds of the Hôtel de Ville, this collection of slightly old-fashioned museums is scheduled to be rehoused in a former abattoir. In the meantime, you can see musty displays of cannon, uniforms and other paraphernalia from the two world wars. Other items include prehistoric objects, a few stray Greek urns and old coins, on show in an attractive, well-lit room with blue and yellow stained-glass windows.

★ **Musée du Chanoine Puissant** (Museum of Canon Puissant) (map A2, **45**): rue Notre-Dame-Débonnaire 22. ☎ (065) 336670. Same opening times as the Musées du Centenaire. Admission fee. When Canon Puissant died in 1934, he left the eclectic collections he had accumulated in his 16th century brick home to the city of Mons. A few years later, his house was turned into a museum and opened to the public. The higgledy-piggledy displays are the result of one man's obsessions and chance encounters. There's a small museum of stones in the courtyard, while the inside rooms are devoted to weaponry, engravings, everyday objects, religious artefacts, Renaissance furniture, work by blacksmiths and a piece of oak ceiling. It's a bit like wandering through a flea market.

★ **Musée du Folklore et de la Vie montoise** (Museum of Folklore and Life in Mons) (map B2, **46**): maison Jean-Lescarts, rue Neuve (follow the passage that goes around the Musée des Beaux Arts and it's on your left). ☎ (065) 314357. Same opening hours as the preceding museums. Admission fee. This 17th-century infirmary, at the back of a small garden, was converted into a museum in the 1980s. The displays include daily objects from past eras: shop signs, measuring instruments, furniture and the like. Upstairs, there's a room devoted to the origins of social welfare, with a cylindrical structure in which impoverished parents dumped children destined for the orphanage. One half of a picture bearing the name and baptism details of the child was left with him or her; the parents kept the other half as a testament of their parenthood, should they ever be in a position to reclaim their offspring. You can also see a poignant display of some of these cut-up pictures. The basement contains objects related to folklore, including the dragon used in the Combat du Lumeçon.

★ **Musée des Beaux-Arts** (Museum of Fine Art) (map B2, **47**): rue Neuve 8. ☎ (065) 405306. Open noon–6pm (from 10am on Sunday). Closed Monday. Admission fee. There's nothing elegant about this modern building, but it's an excellent display space for permanent and temporary exhibitions of paintings, sculpture and engravings from the 15th to the 20th centuries. There are no great names, but the collection is interesting, especially if you're interested in the Nervia group of Walloon Expressionists (1928–38). There's a bright and airy temporary exhibition space upstairs.

★ **Musée des Arts décoratifs François Duesberg** (map A2): square F.-Roosevelt 12. ☎ (065) 363164. Open 2–7pm on Tuesday, Thursday, Saturday and Sunday. Admission fee. This illustrious collection once belonged to a pair of philanthropists from Brussels. It includes clocks from around the world, including some shamelessly called 'au nègre' (negro's clocks), gilt bronzes, porcelain, pottery, jewellery, engravings and precious bindings.

MORE TO SEE AND DO

★ Don't miss the baroque **Église Saint-Nicolas-en-Havré** (map B2, **48**), built in the early 18th century, and the **Église Sainte-Élisabeth** (rue de Nimy; map B2, **49**), with its unusual bell tower.

– Every Sunday morning on place du Béguinage (off the map from A3, **50**), an **antiques market** is held near the fruit and vegetable market. It's a wonderfully eclectic affair, and people come from all over to rifle through the jumble of items on sale. Pause for refreshment at the Batia Moûrt Soü (Walloon for Drunken Boat), a haven run by an affable young man with a passion for unusual beers.

WHAT TO SEE IN THE AREA

★ **Site archéologique industriel du Grand-Hornu**: rue Sainte-Louise 82, 12 kilometres (8 miles) east of Mons. ☎ (065) 770712. Open 10am–6pm (to 4pm in winter). Closed Monday. Admission fee. The brainchild of a 19th-century businessman, Henry de Gorge, this complex of industrial and urban buildings is a splendid example of philanthropic paternalism. De Gorge, who was fired by a utopian vision, employed 2,500 workers here, including local miners, workmen and engineers who manufactured everything necessary for the smooth working of the mine and the life of the community in general, from steam engines to teaspoons. The site and mines functioned until 1954, and were saved from destruction by a local architect.

You enter via a square courtyard with a fountain by Pol Bury. To your right, the former electrical shop now houses a museum, which shows temporary exhibitions, and a pleasant cafeteria. In the vast main courtyard, an awe-inspiring elliptical structure designed by Bruno Renard, you can see an administrative building (on the right) that used to be the De Gorge family château; this is being transformed into a museum of contemporary art. The extraordinary brick ruins on the left look more like the remnants of an ancient abbey than a machine workshop, which they were originally part of. At the back of the courtyard, you can see the graves of the founder and his family. The 500 terraced workers' houses that surround the workshops are now private houses.

★ **Maison de Van Gogh**: rue du Pavillon, in **Cuesmes**. Open 10am–6pm. Closed Monday. Van Gogh lived in this modest dwelling from 1879 to 1880, while he was on a self-imposed mission to enlighten the miners in the region. Don't expect to see any original paintings; those on display are reproductions, accompanied by an interesting audiovisual display.

★ **Marais de Harchies-Pommeroel** (Harchies-Pommeroel marshes) This 200-hectare (50-acre) nature reserve lies 12 kilometres (7 miles) west of Mons, on the edge of the Bassin de la Haine. ☎ (069) 578784. The marshes were formed when the ground collapsed as a result of mining, and more than a third of the area – a unique environment for nesting and migrant birds – consists of water. You can follow a path around the reserve, but you'll need half a day if you want to tour the whole place and get a glimpse of all the visitors, which include herons, cormorants, bitterns, buzzards, egrets and grebes depending on the season.

★ The nature reserve is near **Bernissart**, where you can visit a small museum dedicated to the discovery of the famous iguanadons that are now on show in Brussels's Musée des Sciences Naturelles.

SOIGNIES   24,000 inhabitants

The pretty little village of Soignies acquired its wealth in the 14th century, thanks to the textile trade. Today, you can explore the network of winding cobbled streets that spreads out around the forbidding church of St Vincent. This saint, whose real name was Madelgaire, was the husband of Waudru (*see* 'Mons') and founded an abbey here in the seventh century. Every Monday at Pentecost, crowds flock to Soignies to see the procession of his reliquary. The Kermesse aux Célibataires (Bachelors' Fair) takes place on the same day, in the main square.

USEFUL ADDRESS

🚩 **Tourist office**: rue du Lombard 2. ☎ (067) 347310.

WHERE TO STAY IN THE AREA

🛏 **B&B La Fermette**: chemin du Bois-de-Steenkerke 2, Horrues 7060, on the Soignies–Enghien road (it's signposted). ☎ and fax: (067) 339672. Doubles 1,700BEF, with a 10 per cent discount if you stay for more than three nights. This delightful, tastefully renovated long farm has a garden, an orchard and a duck pond (fed by the River Senne). The hosts are eager to share their passion for the region, and will let you in on the secrets of making fruit wines or patchwork. There are three large, rustic-style rooms with pretty furniture and a shower and toilet.

There's a cot for babies, and meals using local organic produce cost 500BEF, including drinks.
🛏 **B&B La Japolinière**: chemin de Rognon 24, Petit-Rulx-lez-Braine 7090, about 8 kilometres (5 miles) along the Soignies–Enghien road. ☎ and fax: (067) 553921. Doubles 1,400–1,800BEF, including breakfast. In the middle of the countryside, this exquisite, exceptionally friendly little farmhouse is furnished with antiques-market finds. There are three fully equipped rooms with en suite bathrooms and toilets. Meals and bike hire available.

WHERE TO EAT

✕ **Le Modern**: rue de la Station 73, near the station. ☎ (067) 332221. Closed Saturday and in July. Full meal about 1,000BEF. The landlords of this magnificent art-nouveau brick building have had the sense not to change any of the original decor, so you can stare at the carved bar with floral stained glass and the wrought-iron mezzanine as you tuck into sirloin steaks, veal sweetbreads, veal kidneys and mussels in season.

WHERE TO EAT IN THE AREA

✕ **Le Pilori**: rue du Pilori 10, Ecaussinnes-Lalaing (*see below*), on a road near the château, with good signposting. ☎ (067) 442318. Closed Monday, Tuesday and Wednesday evening, as well as Saturday lunchtime. Full meal about 1,600BEF, with set menus from 840BEF. The young host will invite you to take a seat inside, where you can admire the brick walls and fine floor tiles, or on the verandah, which overlooks the garden. The excellent food includes scampi in creamy thyme sauce, cod with potatoes and olives, duck *foie gras à l'ancienne*, and elaborate desserts such as *liquorice crème brûlée* and fruit *gratin*. It's not cheap, but you can always plump for the *menu du jour*.

WHAT TO SEE

★ **Collégiale Saint-Vincent**: open 9am–5pm (7pm in summer). Such is the restrained elegance of this vast church, built between the 10th and 13th centuries, that even the rampaging French Revolutionaries stopped short of destroying it. It's an awesome pile, with two heavy towers and impressive proportions – 72 metres (238 feet) long and 34 metres (112 feet) high – and, like the cathedral at Tournai, is a fine example of the Romanesque Scheldt style. Inside, there's ancient vaulting over the side aisles and choir, although a 19th-century restoration has left the nave with a rather dull flat ceiling, and the elaborate choir contrasts with the prevailing simplicity. Look out for the Renaissance rood screen in black stone, marble and stucco, a moving, 14th-century representation of Mary feeding the Infant Jesus, the Gothic chapel of St Hubert and the expressive stone faces depicted on the 15th-century *Entombment* scene in the ambulatory. The reliquary of St Vincent is kept in the choir above the 17th-century stalls.

– The church's treasures are kept in the **Musée du Chapitre**, which recently opened in the west wing of the cloister. Open at the weekend from May to September 2–6pm.

★ **Old Cemetery**: in a little street off the left side of the church. There's a stone museum containing fragments of old tombstones and tablets. The **Musée du Cercle archéologique** (open on some Sundays: ☎ (067) 335421) has taken up residence in the graveyard's chapel.

★ The **Centre de Documentation de la Pierre bleue**, (Documentation Centre on Local Blue Stone) in the Centre d'Art et de Culture (admission free) offers a wealth of information about the local quarrying industry, mineralogy, fossils and the craft of stone-cutting.

WHAT TO SEE IN THE AREA

★ **Château d'Ecaussinnes-Lalaing**: rue de Seneffe 1. ☎ (067) 442490. Open 10am–noon and 2–6pm; from April to the end of June and in September to October, weekends and holidays only; in July and August open every day except Tuesday and Wednesday and on public holidays. Admission: 150BEF, with discounts for students. It's hard not to fall in love with the village of Ecaussinnes-Lalaing, what with its excellent restaurant, *Le*

Pilori (see 'Where to eat in the area'), and the château that dominates the place. The magic is partly due to the medieval origins of the château, and the way locals have enhanced its austerity by putting flowers in the red-shuttered windows, but it's helped by the domestic feel of the place, the fact that you can buy homemade jam here and, above all, by the château's delightful bric-à-brac museum.

Work on the château began in the 12th century, in grey stone. It was altered three centuries later, when the fourth wall in the courtyard was demolished. You enter via the square tower and go up to the first floor, where you'll see an iron grill, religious objects and a 16th-century shrine with a connecting door into a sickroom. Upstairs, there's a room devoted to the novelist Albert du Bois, which contains a 15th-century oak trunk. It used to contain the town archives, and seven aldermasters were responsible for unlocking its seven locks.

Downstairs, the drawing room is dominated by an impressive fireplace decorated with sculptures of Adam and Eve and other figures. In the Folklore room, you'll see a billiard table made by the lord of the manor, who went into hiding with a furniture-maker during the French Revolution. Alongside collections of medals, pottery, glassware, *michaulines* and *grands bis* – both predecessors of the bicycle – there's a bizarrely incongruous mummified cat.

The chapel, which contains several 14th-century statues, overlooks the prison (watch out for the steps), the magnificent kitchen and the adjoining laundry. Several ancient trunks, one on wheels for transporting war booty, are on display in the armoury. Finally, don't miss the *clepsydre*, a clock activated by water, which is wound up at midday when the angelus is rung.

– The **Kermesse aux Célibataires** (Bachelors' Fair), which features a wedding tea, takes place every Pentecost Monday on the main square.

★ **Plan incliné de Ronquières** (Ronquières incline): ☎ (065) 360464. Entrance at the tower. Open 1 April to 31 October, 10am–7pm. Combined ticket for the museum and boat trip: 330BEF. Rather than building several sluice gates on the River Senne, an ingenious engineer devised a two-kilometre (one-mile) incline so that fishing boats could access the different levels. A bold alternative to boat lifts, the incline was designed to save time – and lock tolls. Competition being what it is, however, road and rail freight firms companies slashed their prices, and the project was consigned to the annals of the 'GTIs' ('*grands travaux inutiles*', or white elephants). From miles away, you can see the 69-metre (230-foot) tower, which dominates the surrounding hills and valleys, and the extraordinary, slightly ridiculous incline.

– **Musée de la Batellerie** (Museum of the Boatmen's Guild): from April to the end of October, open 10am–7pm. Admission: 280BEF; reductions possible. You can explore a series of set scenes with an infrared audio guide. The special effects are a bit hackneyed.

★ **Enghien**: this attractive residential town lies 15 kilometres (9 miles) north of Soignies, on the edge of the Walloon-Flemish border, and its elegant 18th-century buildings and town houses make it an ideal place for a short stroll.

The grounds of the magnificent 185-hectare (460-acre) **park** contain several ponds, a Chinese pavilion, a 12th-century church in a tower and a cave. Open 1–8pm in summer; otherwise weekends only from 1pm to dusk. Admission fee.

Enghien is also home to a small **béguinage** and a **tapestry museum** in the Maison Jonathas, a 16th-century building on rue Montgomery. ☎ (02) 3955906. Open 2–5pm (to 7pm on weekends). Closed Monday.

🛈 **Tourist office**: Grand-Place 50. ☎ (02) 395 8360.

★ **Château du Roeulx**: 12 kilometres (8 miles) southeast of Soignies, on the way to Binche. You'll have to make do with admiring the beautiful 18th-century exterior: the park and château are in the midst of a thorough overhaul, and its collections (supposedly very interesting) are closed to the public.

ATH   25,000 inhabitants

A merchant town 20 kilometres (12 miles) northeast of Mons, Ath enjoyed the dubious privilege of being besieged by the Sun King in person in 1667. The town's fortifications were destroyed in a succession of wars, and all that remains today is the tower of Burbant, a massive square keep built in the 12th century by Baldwin the Builder, Count of Hainaut. The only other interesting monument is the 17th-century Hôtel de Ville, which dominates the Grand-Place and is best studied from one of the square's numerous cafés. It's not especially tempting for tourists, but it's worth visiting for the Fêtes de la Ducasse, during which 4-metre (13-foot) giants parade about the town. The festivities take place on the fourth Sunday in August, with a symbolic wedding ceremony the day before. Some of the giants fight each other on the Grand-Place.

Ath is the capital of the Ath region, a lush, green, agricultural area fed by two rivers, both called the Dendre, which meet at Ath. While the main town is a bit bland, there's plenty to do in the vicinity.

USEFUL ADDRESS

Postcode: 7800.
🛈 **Tourist Centre for the Region of Ath**: rue de Nazareth 2, Ath 7800. ☎ (068) 269230. From April to September, Monday to Saturday 2–5pm and 10am–noon on Thursday morning; in August, also Sunday 2–6pm; otherwise, you can get information at the Hôtel de Ville.

WHERE TO STAY IN THE AREA

🛏 **Gîte rural de la Brasserie**: rue de la Délivrance 13, Stambruges 7973, a couple of kilometres from the Château de Beloeil. ☎ (069) 578530. Fax: (069) 576269. From the E42 motorway, take the exit for Bernissart. Continue until you come to the church in Stambruges and then follow the signs. This *gîte* (country lodge), built in local stone, sleeps five to six people. There's also a fully equipped apartment for six, which you can hire by the weekend or the week, and a pristine B&B room that sleeps three and costs 1,200BEF a night. Meals (400BEF) are available on request, and there are even stables if you happen to be on horseback. Stay for two or more consecutive nights and you'll benefit from a 10 per cent discount.

WHAT TO SEE

★ There are three small museums in Ath: the **Musée d'Histoire et de Folklore**, rue de Bouchain 16; **Espace Gallo-romain**, rue de Nazareth 2; and the **Musée de la Pierre et le site des carriers** (Museum of Stone and Quarrymen), chaussée de Mons 419.

Ath Region

★ **Château de Beloeil**: rue du Château, Beloeil. ☎ (069) 689655. From Easter to the end of October, open 10am–6pm. Admission: 280BEF; discounts available. The dynasty of the Princes de Ligne, a family of diplomats and military men who were involved in Europe's most significant conflicts and alliances, was founded in the Middle Ages, and settled in Beloeil in the 14th century. The castle, complete with moat and four round towers, dates from the 16th and 17th centuries, but didn't acquire the residential aspect that you see today until the most famous de Ligne, Marshal Charles-Joseph, arrived on the scene. A warrior and aesthete, Charles-Joseph (1735–1814) created an English garden and sided with the Austrians in the wake of the French Revolution – not that this stopped this most European of men from declaring that 'every man has two homelands: his own and France'.

Charles-Joseph's descendants still live in the château, so you can only see about 10 rooms and bedrooms, all of which are richly decorated. You can't get too close to the Gobelin and Brussels tapestries or the priceless items of marquetry and old furniture on display: they're all cordoned off. You can see the family coat of arms in the drawing room, while the main object of interest in the bedroom, its walls decorated with 17th-century tapestries from Lille, is the sumptuous four-poster bed commissioned by Marie-Antoinette in Louis XVI style. In every room, you'll see paintings of the family and of the main events in its history, including several portraits of Charles-Joseph in the first bedroom and a stunning depiction of the siege of Kortrijk in the first-floor gallery.

The old library is home to more than 20,000 tomes, published between the 14th and 19th centuries, while the Salon des Maréchaux is dominated by a huge desk adorned with gilt bronze. After you've admired the brick vaulting in the chapel, you can relax in the pleasant café, in the old stables.

The park is sublime and really worth exploring: the English-style gardens are out of bounds, but you'll be more than satisfied by the French-style garden. It's arranged around a vast lake, and provides some wonderful vistas, especially from the Grande Vue, a wide avenue that's 5 kilometres (3 miles) long. This is Belgium's answer to Versailles: a superbly maintained place where you can stroll about freely for as long as you want.

★ **Château d'Attre**: avenue du Château 8, Attre. ☎ (068) 454460. From April to October, open 10am–noon and 2–6pm on Saturdays, Sunday and public holidays; in July and August, open every day except Wednesday. Admission: 150BEF, or 80BEF for the park. Guided tours in several languages: the 50-minute tours leave every 15 minutes.

Unlike Beloeil, which is laid out like a museum, the Château d'Attre seems much more lived-in, with photographs of children and papers and pens lying about. Even the cars parked anachronistically in the main courtyard of this fine 18th-century building, in front of pillars that once belonged to the Cambron-Casteau Abbey, remind you that this is a home as well as a tourist attraction. The visit is confined to the ground-floor rooms, and you'll be accompanied by one of the affable guides.

The entrance hall, where a cupboard hides a stunning chapel, leads to a series of rooms with views of the park, antique furniture, alcove beds, original wallpaper and splendid wooden floors. The Chinese room is decorated with *trompes l'oeil*, while others are decorated with compasses, a reminder of the fortunes brought back by the voyages of the Compagnie d'Ostende. The paintings on display include a portrait of Louis XIV by Mingnard and a pastel of Louis XV, attributed to Quentin de La Tour. Don't forget to tip the guide.

After the visit, you can explore the lavish park behind the château, where you'll stumble across a dovecote, a pillory, a handful of ruins, a shiny wooden chalet and some strange dark tunnels. The Dendre flows through the bushes, and 100-year-old trees continue to thrive. One of the tunnels leads to an artificial rockface, a bizarre structure of carefully positioned stones that was erected in the 18th century and used as a hunting observatory by the whimsical Maria-Christina of Saxe-Teschen.

★ **Parc Paradiso**: Cambron estate, Cambron-Casteau, between Mons and Ath. ☎ (068) 454653. From April to October, open 10am–6pm. Admission: 395BEF, with discounts for under-14s and senior citizens. On this site, in the 12th century, St Bernard founded the 55th 'daughter of Cîteaux', as the Cistercian abbeys were called. Several centuries of pious, hard-working lives later, the monks of the abbey had become rather rich, and had developed a taste for earthly pleasures. Rules slackened and several comfortable buildings were constructed. On the 18th-century staircase, which straddles the River Dendre and a Persian garden, Emperor Joseph II declared: 'This is one of the finest staircases in Europe, but I doubt that it leads to heaven.' All good things come to an end, and the decadent abbey was suppressed by the French authorities in 1797. The staircase is one of the few remaining traces of this Hainaut Xanadu.

Abandoned for several decades, the 55-hectare (137-acre) park and its splendid lakes were purchased by a rich family of bird-lovers, who turned it into a vast ornithological park. About 400 species live in semi-liberty among the stones, winding streams and undergrowth of the park, which has several 300-year-old trees. Waders hop about the water's edge, and birds of prey have their own area, but the most outstanding feature is undoubtedly the giant aviary, 15 metres (nearly 50 feet) high, with a detachable roof. You can walk through it, admiring the 150 birds from endangered species: they are raised here before being released into the wild. In the next cages, you'll see crested hornbills, chatty myna birds and a roadrunner. There's also a fine collection of orchids.

After your walk, stop off at the abbey farm, where you can have a drink on the château's 19th-century terrace and watch the ducks and chickens run around the yard. All in all, it's a fun outing, especially for families.

★ **Archéosite d'Aubechies**: rue de l'Abbaye 15, Aubechies-Belil. ☎ (068) 671116. Open Monday to Friday 9am–5pm; from Easter to the end of October, also Saturday, Sunday and public holidays, 2–6pm. Admission: 150BEF. The neighbouring village, Blicquy, was inhabited in the Stone Age, hence this reconstruction of a complex of houses from that epoch, with structures that span the neolithic age and the Gaulish period. You can see traditional cob walls and wooden frames, roofs made of straw, thatching or reed, and reproductions of everyday tools on the beaten-earth floors. In season and on weekends, the complex buzzes with tourists, as local craftsmen put on period costume and demonstrate everything from leather and copper work to cooking. The sight of a tribe of Gauls unloading equipment from their cars is unforgettable. There are also two museums with collections of Gallo-Roman objects (open by appointment only).

LESSINES   16,000 inhabitants

This small quarrying town nestles among the hills of the region. Despite its sleepy appearance, it has seen its share of conflicts down the centuries, with the Counts of Flanders and Hainaut involved in a long-running feud over the area. It's also the birthplace of the Surrealist artist René Magritte.

USEFUL ADDRESS

🔢 **Tourist office**: Grand Place 11. ☎ (068) 333690.

WHERE TO EAT IN THE AREA

✕ **Les Prés Bossus**: Bruyère-Seutine 18, Saint-Sauveur, 15 kilometres (9 miles) southwest of Ronse. ☎ (069) 769506. Closed Tuesday, Wednesday and Thursday. Full meal 1,000BEF. This white, rustic farmhouse on the edge of a wood offers tasty, creative dishes, such as warm salad with chicken livers in cider Aubel, grilled knuckle of ham in mustard and veal kidneys. It's popular, so book in advance.

WHAT TO SEE

★ **Hôpital Notre-Dame-à-la-Rose**: place Alix-de-Rosoit. ☎ (068) 332403. From April to the end of September, Sunday and public holidays 3–5pm; in July and August, every day except Saturday 2–5pm. Guided tour. Admission: 180BEF. Founded in 1242 by Alix de Rosoit, lady-in-waiting to Blanche of Castille, this hospital monastery was in use until 1980. Rebuilt from the 16th century onwards, it's a four-sided structure, enclosing a garden and surrounded by a cloister, with a step-gabled Flemish Renaissance facade. The baroque doorway was added later.

The museum displays everyday objects connected with religious life and the care of the sick, and has an extensive archive relating to both subjects. In the reconstructed sickroom, you'll learn that patients slept two to a bed in order to keep warm (preventing the spread of infection evidently wasn't a priority) and that the red curtains were chosen so that bloodstains wouldn't show up!

FESTIVAL

– The **Procession des Pénitents encagoulés** (Procession of Hooded Penitents) takes place on Good Friday. Penitents parade to the beat of drums.

WHAT TO SEE IN THE AREA

★ **Elezelles**: the Moulin du Cat Sauvage is a working windmill that's open to the public, to quote the plaque, 'when it's working'. The Sabbat de Sorcières (Witches' Sabbath) is held at the end of June.

★ **Écomusée du pays des Collines** (Ecological Museum of the Region of the Hills): Plada 3, La Hamaide 7890. From Easter to late October, open weekends only, 2–6pm; in July and August, open every day. The museum is devoted to 20th-century farming, with displays about rural life and craft workshops.

★ Near Leuze-en-Hainaut, in Pipaix, is the **brasserie à vapeur Dits** (Dits steam brewery): rue Maréchal 1, 7904. ☎ (069) 662047. Closed Thursday and Sunday afternoon. Tours and tastings on Sunday at 11am (or by appointment). Brewing takes place on the last Saturday of every month. It's a fascinating place where seasonal beers, originally designed to stay fresh for summer workers, are brewed according to traditional methods using steam power. In the 19th century, the steam machine was placed at the disposal of the next-door farm to give the agricultural workers something to do during the lean periods in winter. It still functions, and the man who works it, a retired history teacher, has a real talent for getting visitors interested in the brewing process. The beers – Vapeur Rousse, Vapeur Légère, Vapeur en Folie and Vapeur Cochonne (amber-coloured and sweet) – are exported to France, the US and Canada. Ask the owner to let you taste the 'esprit de Vapeur cochonne', a distillate of beer (somewhere between whisky, gin and calvados) that will blow your socks off.

TOURNAI   68,000 inhabitants

Tournai is less exuberant than Mons, partly because it doesn't have a university and partly because it's so near Lille. It feels a bit like a small provincial town that's had a glorious past but faces an uncertain future. But appearances can be deceptive: this unassuming town, one of Belgium's oldest, has attracted a never-ending stream of occupiers, from the Romans and Franks to the English, French and Austrians. And, while there's no university, the prestigious Saint-Luc school of art and architecture attracts around 4,000 students. Tournai doesn't flaunt its attractions, which include a fine belfry and a staggering cathedral, but with fine museums, excellent restaurants and lively cafés, you'll soon fall under its spell.

A Short History

Tournai was founded by the Romans, and became the capital of the Franks and Merovingians. Childéric died here in 481, and his son, Clovis, went to Soissons, leaving Tournai in the hands of the bishop. In the Middle Ages, the town was taken over by the French (the *fleur de lys* still adorns its arms), and enjoyed a golden age under Philippe Auguste, when the wool and stone industries kept the city's coffers full: the belfry and cathedral date from this prosperous period, After several attempts, the English, with Henry VIII at the helm, captured Tournai in 1513, but lost it to Charles V a few years later. Despite a heroic defence, the Spanish reduced it to ruins in the late 16th century. Louis XIV occupied the town in 1667, but was forced to hand it over to the Austrians after his defeat in the War of the Spanish Succession. Louis XV clawed the town back after the Battle of Fontenoy, and after the turbulence of the French Revolution, Tournai found itself attached to Hainaut.

The town was extensively damaged by German bombardments in 1940, but was rebuilt according to a set of original plans.

USEFUL ADDRESSES

🛈 **Tourist Office** (map A2): Vieux-Marché-aux-Poteries 14, at the foot of the belfry. ☎ (069) 222045. Fax: (069) 216221. Website: www.tournai.be. Open Monday to Friday 9am–7pm, Saturday 10am–1pm and 3–6pm, Sunday 10am–noon and 2–6pm. You can book guided tours and an art-nouveau walk around town.

🚂 **Railway station** (off the map from B1-2): place Crombez. ☎ (069) 866223. Trains leave Brussels every hour until at least 10pm.

✉ **Post office** (map A2): rue des Chapeliers 20. ☎ (069) 221025. Open Monday to Friday 9am–6pm, Saturday 9.30am–noon.

■ **Bank**: Crédit Communal (map A2, **1**), Grand-Place 63. ☎ (069) 214801. Open Monday to Friday 9am–12.30pm and 2–4pm (to 6pm on Friday), Saturday 9am–noon.

WHERE TO STAY

☆ Budget

🛏 **Tournai Youth Hostel** (map A3, **10**): rue Saint-Martin 64, a stone's throw from the Grand-Place. ☎ (069) 216136. Fax: (069) 216140. Email: tournai@laj.be. Closed January. Basic rate per night: 430BEF. Housed in the 18th-century Acadé-mie Royale de Musique, this is not your average youth hostel. The reading room has a gilt ceiling and a splendid floor, the function room is decorated with 18th-century tapestries from the school of Watteau, and the office was designed by the art-nouveau genius Victor Horta when he came to Tournai to build the Musée des Beaux-Arts. A 16th-century staircase leads to the 19 rooms, which are pretty much what you'd expect to find at a youth hostel, though they're all equipped with

TOURNAI

sinks. Most have four or six bunk beds, although if they're available (and if you're prepared to pay extra), you might get a double room. You're advised to bring your own sheets or sleeping bag, although it's possible to hire them. Bathrooms are on the landing, and showers are included in the price. The hostel closes at 11pm, but night-owls can ask for a key. This is a well-run, welcoming place with wheelchair access – for our money, the best accommodation in town.

🛖 **Camping de l'Orient**: Vieux-Chemin-de-Mons 8, 3 kilometres (2 miles) from the centre on the Mons-Brussels road; turn at the first set of lights then follow the signs. ☎ (069) 222635. Tent site: 480BEF. Open all year. Committed campers will appreciate the cleanliness and comfort of this campsite. There are also several caravans.

🛖 **Aux Armes de Tournai** (off the map, continuation of A2, **12**): place de Lille 24, near the Grand-Place. ☎ (069) 226723. Fax: (069) 227035. Doubles 1,400–1,600BEF. This establishment has a family feel and freshly decorated, well-maintained rooms.

🛖 **La Tour Saint-Georges** (map A2, **11**): place de Nédonchel, near the Grand-Place; access via the passage next to the Écu de France. ☎ (069) 225300. Doubles 1,100–1,580BEF. It's central and inexpensive, but to call the rooms and entrance hall depressing would be wildly generous. Still, it's a fallback if the youth hostel is full, which is often the case. The food's cheap, too, but staff could be a bit friendlier.

■ **Useful addresses**

  🛈 Tourist office
  ✉ Post office
  🚃 Railway station
  1 Crédit Communal

🛖 **Where to stay**

  10 Tournai Youth Hostel
  11 La Tour Saint-Georges
  12 Aux Armes de Tournai

✕ **Where to eat**

  20 A 'l Bonne Franquette
  21 Le Relais du Miroir
  22 Bistro de la Cathédrale
  23 Ô Pères au Quai
  24 Giverny
  25 Le Grand Jacques

🍵 **Tea-rooms and Where to go for a drink**

  30 Pâtisserie Quénoy
  31 Aux Amis Réunis
  32 La Mauvaise Herbe
  34 Les Trois Pommes d'Orange
  35 Le 747
  36 Le Tirwana

★ **What to see**

  40 Cathédrale Notre-Dame
  41 Belfry
  42 Grand-Place
  43 Musée des Beaux-Arts
  44 Hôtel de Ville, Musée d'Histoire Naturelle, Musée des Arts Décoratifs
  45 Musée de la Tapisserie
  46 Musée du Folklore
  47 Musée d'Archéologie
  48 Musée d'Armes et d'Histoire militaire
  49 Église Saint-Brice
  50 Pont des Trous

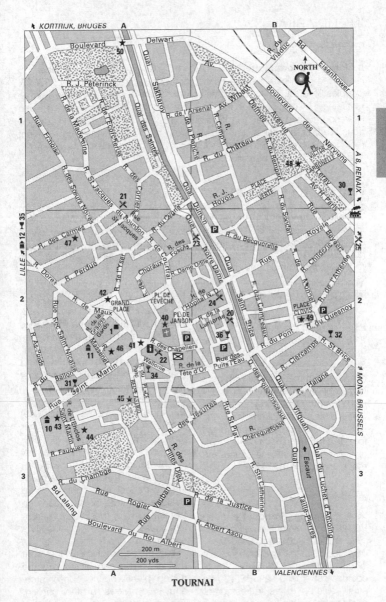

TOURNAI

IN THE AREA

☆☆☆ Expensive

🛌 **Floréal Panoramique**: place de la Trinité 2, Mont Saint-Aubert, 5 kilometres (3 miles) from the centre. ☎ (069) 891616. Fax: (069) 233323. Doubles 3,400BEF. On the slopes of Mont Saint-Aubert, this place lives up to its name by offering splendid views. The rooms resembles studio flats at a ski resort, with large bay windows and balconies as well as the usual mod cons. There's a small swimming pool and a solarium, while the excellent restaurant serves Belgian food, including *ragoût* of monkfish with vegetables and duck in Quintine beer.

WHERE TO EAT

Tournai is something of a gastronomic paradise, with everything from a *friterie* on the Grand-Place to classy restaurants. The French will tell you that the town's culinary prowess is the result of its proximity to the Hexagon. But rather than worrying about the reason, tuck into delicious rabbit *à la tournaisienne* (with grapes and prunes).

☆ Budget

✕ **Le Relais du Miroir** (map A1, **21**): rue Saint-Jacques 15. ☎ (069) 211079. Open 10.30am–4am on weekdays, Saturday 7pm–4am and Sunday 5pm–midnight. This late-night bar in a magnificent 16th-century gabled house has a fine oak ceiling and beautiful fireplaces, their lustre only slightly dimmed by the ugly tables and chairs. A good place for basic refuelling, with pasta, chicory with ham in cheese sauce and roast chicken on the menu.

☆☆ Moderate

✕ **A 'l Bonne Franquette** (map B2, **20**): quai Marché-aux-Poissons 13A. ☎ (069) 840196. Closed Monday lunchtime. Two-course set lunch and dinner 335BEF; four-course set menu 995BEF. This small, discreet riverside restaurant offers unbelievable value for money. The walls are primrose yellow and hung with tasteful paintings, and the short but well-balanced menu shows a slight Lyonnais influence – apart, of course, from the excellent 'américain préparé (raw steak served with spices) and the house speciality, rabbit *à la tournaisienne* (cooked in Bush beer). All the ingredients are fresh and tasty, and the delicious desserts prove that this is a serious establishment.

✕ **Ô Pères au Quai** (map A-B2, **23**): quai Notre-Dame 18. ☎ (069) 232922. Open for lunch and dinner (until 10.30pm). Closed Monday. *Plat du jour* 425BEF; weekday lunchtime set menus 1,245BEF, including wine. This large white building, with columns outside and designer furniture inside, stands on the left bank of the Escaut, near a few houses that survived Louis XIV's occupation of Tournai. Meat is grilled at the fireplace in the front room, or you can sit among the trailing plants of the conservatory and enjoy views of the garden. There's nothing very sophisticated about the cooking, but the steaks are good and come with as many chips as you can eat. There's also an *hors-d'oeuvre* buffet.

✕ **Bistro de la Cathédrale** (map A2, **22**): Vieux-Marché-aux-Poteries 15. ☎ (069) 210379. Open every day. *Plat du jour* 395BEF; main courses up to 575BEF. A good, unpretentious place where you can eat well. The service is efficient, so it's ideal if you're in a hurry, but the food is lovingly prepared, with rabbit *à la tournaisienne* and a variety of decent meat dishes on the menu.

✕ **Le Grand Jacques** (off the map from B2, **25**): boulevard des Déportés 62, opposite the station (although the staff will tell you the station is opposite Le Grand Jacques). ☎ (069) 847404. Closed Thursday. Weekday set lunch 395BEF. This heart-warming, brightly painted establishment is named after the great *chansonnier* Jacques Brel. The traditional French cuisine, based on fresh produce,

includes stews, tripe, trotters, cassoulet and veal kidneys, with excellent iced nougat in a summer-fruit syrup to follow. It's also a good place to sample regional dishes.

✶✶✶ Expensive

✕ **Giverny** (map B2, **24**): quai Marché-au-Poisson 6. ☎ (069) 224464. Closed Monday, Saturday lunchtime and Sunday evening. Weekday set menu 890BEF, including wine. Free children's menu. The decor of this magnificent riverside restaurant takes its cue from art nouveau as well as Claude Monet. The delightful landlords have arranged mirrors and frescoes around the walls in period style. Fish dishes are the speciality, although they're pretty expensive.

TEA-ROOM

– **Pâtisserie Quénoy** (map B1, **30**): place Combez 2. ☎ (069) 223923. Open 7.30am–7pm. Closed Wednesday. An original art nouveau building, this *pâtisserie* still makes the famous *ballons noirs* to the recipe patented by Émile Quénoy in the early 20th century. This highly successful family business is run by the third generation of Quénoys. You'll be greeted by the charming, chatty Madame Q, and by a fantastic array of wicked cakes.

WHERE TO GO FOR A DRINK AND LIVE MUSIC

♪ **Aux Amis Réunis** (map A2, **31**): rue Saint-Martin 89. Open 10am–10pm (later at the weekend). Closed Sunday. The proprietors of this establishment have had the sense not to change any of the decoration, which dates from 1911. From the old wrought-iron stove to the wooden benches and the carvings on the bar, everything is original. As is the *jeu de fer*, a variant of billiards: you use a cue to push a puck up a long slope (made slippery by marble powder) towards a metal arch. You only pay if you lose.

♪ **La Mauvaise Herbe** (map B2, **32**): rue Saint-Brice 16. Open Friday and Saturday evening. Tournai's wild bunch hang out at this candlelit club on the right bank of the Escaut. The furniture's second-hand, the music heavy rock. Concerts (monthly) start at about 10pm, and the atmosphere really hots up at weekends.

♪ **Le 747** (off the map from A2, **35**): place de Lille 7, underneath the Lindbergh restaurant. Open Friday, Saturday and Sunday. This is the most popular club in Tournai, with excellent DJs spinning house and techno tunes.

☏ **Le Tirwana** (map B2, **36**): place Saint-Pierre. Spartan decor, a wooden floor, and the place to be for all kinds of musical gatherings and associated events. The beer flows freely on weekends.

☏ **Les Trois Pommes d'Orange** (map A2, **34**): rue de Wallonie 28. This large centuries-old café suffered bomb damage during the war. The facade is pretty presentable these days, but it could do with some decent furniture.

WHAT TO SEE

Tournai has several museums, which very sensibly share the same opening hours: every day except Tuesday, 10am–noon and 2–5.30pm. Admission fees 40–120BEF.

★ **Cathédrale Notre-Dame** (map A2, **40**): open 9am–noon and 2–6pm (4pm in winter). Belgium's most beautiful cathedral, a soaring limestone edifice that's dominated by five square towers, the highest of which, at 83 metres (300 feet), rests on the pillars of the transept crossing and has been an inspiration for many a town church. It was built between the 13th (the nave) and 14th centuries (choir), and marks the transition from Romanesque Scheldt to the Gothic style. The two doorways in the facade are Romanesque, as is the false doorway, or large arch, that supports the passageway between the cathedral and the bishop's palace.

The cathedral is 130 metres (429 feet) long, and the first thing that strikes you as you go inside is its sheer size and elegance. Then you notice the difference between the pure Romanesque nave, with its six bays and four levels, the Gothic choir, which is richly decorated with frescoes, and the 19th-century stained-glass windows. A Renaissance rood screen by Cornelis Floris de Vriendt divides the two almost equal parts of the church, while the pillar capitals in the nave are decorated with floral, human and animal carvings. On the right, the Gothic chapel to St Louis is a late addition. There are several interesting items in the transept: an impressive 18th-century sculpture in wood by Nicolas Le Creux, which depicts fallen angels being chased by a rather disgruntled St Michael; a 12th-century mural painting showing the legend of St Margaret; several 15th-century stained-glass windows; and a painting on the theme of Purgatory by Rubens. You have to walk round the delicately built ambulatory to get to the Treasury.

– **Treasury**: open 10.15–11.45am and 2–5.45pm (to 3.45pm in winter). Closed Sunday morning and during services. Admission: 30BEF. There are three very different rooms. The first contains paintings, clothes and pieces of religious jewellery from the eighth to 18th centuries, including a Byzantine cross that supposedly contains a piece of the True Cross, 13th-century reliquaries containing the arm bones of various saints and a carved ivory diptych from the time of Charlemagne. One of the superbly carved 13th-century reliquaries, depicting small figures and decorated with precious stones, is the work of Nicolas de Verdun. Don't miss Charles V's sumptuous velvet cloak, woven with gold thread, or Quentin Metsys's *Ecce Homo*. Cross back in front of the entrance, from where some rather furious-looking angels glower down from their coat of arms, and you'll come to the second room, the Chapelle Saint-Esprit, hung with an Arras tapestry dated 1402. A series of 14 huge paintings illustrates the lives of St Piat and St Éleuthère. A narrow corridor leads to the chapter room – take a look at the 18th-century panelling, which once belonged to the Abbaye Saint-Ghislain.

★ **Belfry** (map A2, **41**): Belgium's oldest belfry, a UNESCO-listed World Heritage Site, was built towards the end of the 12th century, but has been embellished and restored many times over. The bell at the top of its square tower, which is supported by buttresses and topped with turrets, still signals the hour with the well-known Belgian tune 'Tournaisiens sont là' ('The people of Tournai are here').

★ **Grand-Place** (map A2, **42**): the belfry is the main feature on the triangular Grand-Place, which is decorated with wrought-iron street furniture, and surrounded by the cathedral, the 17th-century cloth hall and the Église Saint-Quentin. The square was partly destroyed by bombardments during World War II, after which replicas of some of the old houses, including the cloth hall, were painstakingly assembled. Christine de Lalaing, the town's heroine, sits in state in the centre of the square.

★ **Musée des Beaux-Arts** (Fine Arts Museum) (map A3, **43**): enclos Saint-Martin 1 (next door to the Hôtel de Ville). ☎ (069) 222043. Closed Tuesday. Admission: 120BEF; discounts available. Audio guide available. The most striking thing about this museum is Victor Horta's building, which has a beautiful, curving white facade, surmounted by a gigantic bronze statue. Inside, each of the rooms, all carefully designed so that natural light streams through their magnificent roof lights, leads off from the discreetly elegant central hall. The collection lives up to its home.

– On the ground floor, you'll find art from the 15th to the 19th centuries. Early paintings include a scary-looking bellows-mender, attributed to the studio of Bosch, and a *Winter Landscape* by Brueghel the Younger (a copy of his father's painting), as well as a *Virgin and Child*, a *Nativity* and the triptych *Salve Regina* by Rogier de la Pasture (aka Van der Weyden). There's also a permanent exhibition of photographic reproductions of Van der Weyden's entire output. Big names from the 17th and 18th centuries include Rubens, Watteau and Jacob Jordaens, but the 19th-century collection is more impressive, with a vast painting of a plague in Tournai by Louis Gallait, landscapes by Monet and Seurat, who's also represented by *Chez le père Lathuile* and *Couple d'Argenteuil*. You can also see the only two paintings by Manet in Belgium.

– From the **upper level**, you can survey the sculptures in the main hall, then explore works by contemporary painters, most of them local. Your visit ends with a display of drawings by Van Gogh and Toulouse-Lautrec.

★ **Hôtel de Ville** (map A3, **44**), **Musée d'Histoire naturelle** and **Musée des Arts décoratifs**. As you leave the museum above, take a look at the surrounding buildings, which used to be part of the Abbaye Saint-Martin. The main items of interest in the Hôtel de Ville (open 10am–noon and 2–5.30pm; closed Tuesday; admission free) are the 11th-century Romanesque crypt and the 15th-century cloister. The little Musée d'Histoire Naturelle (☎ (069) 233939) is the oldest in Belgium – and it shows – but the long gallery, with its display of naturalized fauna, is not without charm. Unfortunately, the collection of extinct animals is hidden away with the reserve stock. The pretty rooms in the Musée des Arts Décoratifs (☎ (069) 843795;

opening hours as above; admission 80BEF) contain displays of 18th-century porcelain, jewellery and 16th- and 17th-century coins.

★ **Musée de la Tapisserie** (Museum of Tapestry) (map A3, **45**): place de la Reine-Astrid 9. ☎ (069) 842073. Admission: 80BEF; discounts available. This homage to the art of tapestry-making, which brought prosperity to Tournai, is brand-new. You can see some splendid old tapestries, including the gruesome *Famine in Jerusalem*, where the mothers have been reduced to cooking their children on skewers. The upstairs area is devoted to contemporary works (made by the Somville-Dubrunfaut firm), some of which represent group scenes in quasi-Socialist Realist style. During the week, you can watch a weaver at work. It's pretty slow going, given that it takes a month to weave one square metre, but the technique is nonetheless interesting.

★ **Musée du Folklore** (map A2, **46**): réduit des Sions 36. ☎ (069) 224069. Admission: 100BEF; discounts available. A huge and extremely interesting museum devoted to the daily life and work of the guilds and semi-skilled professions of old. You can see a clog-maker's workshop, a cooper's workshop and reconstructions of a chapel, a convent, a classroom, a pharmacy and an inn. There's a simple and very informative tableau of tools and furniture and you can also see paintings and engravings by local artists.

★ **Musée d'Archéologie** (map A2, **47**): rue des Carmes 8. ☎ (069) 221672. Admission: 80BEF; discounts available. A tall, thin tower dominates this 17th-century building, which was one of Europe's first pawn shops. On the ground floor, you'll find Gallo-Roman objects, including a sixth-century lead sarcophagus that was discovered just a few streets away.

★ **Musée d'Armes et d'Histoire militaire** (map B1, **48**): rue des Remparts. ☎ (069) 223878. This is the vaulted room of a forbidding tower built by Henry VIII in 1513 to defend himself against the locals of Tournai, who were none too pleased to find themselves under English occupation (1513–18). In September 2000, the collections were transferred to Roc-Saint-Nicaise 59 (map A2).

★ **Église Saint-Brice** (map B2, **49**): place Clovis. Restored but not rebuilt, this church has a square tower and a triple *halle*. It stands next to two 12th-century Romanesque houses, one of them poised at a dangerous-looking angle, which are among the oldest in Europe.

★ Last but not least is the famous **pont des Trous** (map A1, **50**), which straddles the Escaut and has defended Tournai since the 13th century. It's all that's left of the old ramparts, and was raised by a couple of metres (7 feet) in 1948 to accommodate river traffic.

FESTIVALS

– **Mid-Lent Carnival**: on Friday and Saturday, you can watch the *nuit des intrigues* ('night of intrigue') and *pichou*-throwing ('*pichous*' are buns made with dried fruit). The king's enthronement is followed by a dance and a funeral march.

– **Comic Strip Festival**: in the cloth hall in mid-May.

Great Procession: since 1092, the locals have celebrated a lucky escape from an epidemic of the Black Death on the second Sunday in September.

WHAT TO SEE IN THE AREA

★ **Mont Sant-Aubert**: 6 kilometres (nearly 4 miles) from the town and well signposted from the centre, the hill provides a superb view of Tournai and the surrounding countryside. There's a good choice of restaurants and hotels (*see* 'Where to stay').

ANTOING

Antoing is a small town near Tournai. Just before you enter it, as you travel along the road that runs parallel to the River Escaut, you'll see the **fortified farm** where Louis XV celebrated his victory in the battle of Fontenoy in May 1745. Opposite the cemetery, you'll see an L-shaped building with a square tower, which was built in 1633. About 200 metres away, you'll find a path on the left that leads to the river. On the way is a structure that looks a bit like a crate of milk bottles: it's actually an oven, or *four Brébard*, once used for baking lime.

★ **Château d'Antoing**: open Sunday and public holidays from mid-May to mid-September. Tickets for guided tours (2.30pm, 3.30pm and 4pm) are on sale at the tourist office, place Barra 18. ☎ (069) 441729. Admission: 120BEF. Only a few rooms in the astonishing tower of this château are open to the public. The château was partially rebuilt in the 19th century and is still inhabited by the de Ligne family, from Beloeil. The tower leans against a keep, but one of the turrets of the keep is on the point of collapse, so you can't scale the tower. Apart from the *bolcwork*, a wall restored in the 15th century, you can also see a fine collection of tombstones in the chapel, especially that of Jean de Melun and his two wives. At the entrance to the château, a stone tablet recalls General de Gaulle's studies with the Jesuits of Antoing in 1907.

★ **Parc Naturel Transfrontalier du Hainaut** (Hainaut Cross-Border Nature Reserve): incorporating 52 French communes and six Belgian communes between Tournai, Beloeil, Valenciennes and Douai, the reserve tries to maintain an environmental balance between the countryside and mankind. The plains of the Scarpe and the Escaut are ideal for outings in the country; here you're in the wild, albeit a peaceful wild, and tourists are few and far between. The tourist office and Syndicat d'Initiative in Belil stock an excellent brochure with suggested itineraries for cyclists, walkers and horse riders.

WHERE TO STAY AND EAT

B&B Pays blanc: rue Baille-d'Orée 18, Antoing 7640, on the road to the château. ☎ (069) 443915. Email: masab@swing.be. Doubles 1,200BEF, including breakfast, with discounts for stays of two or more nights. This country house, which is typical of the area, stands in the middle of the Parc Transfrontalier. There are two unpretentious non-smoking rooms with a shared bathroom, while there's an orchard in the grounds. A fold-out bed is also available. Credit cards not accepted. Free parking.

🛏 **Gîte d'étape Moulin-Sart**: presqu'Île de l'Escaut 1, Péronnes 7460, next to an artificial lake. ☎ (069) 441729. Moulin-Sart is the French name for Marlinspike Hall, Captain Haddock's manor in Hergé's *Tintin* books, but that's where the similarity ends. This country lodge is a sluice operator's house, with 18 beds and three small chalets. Halfboard is available, and there are sport and watersports facilities nearby.

✕ **Le Médiéval**: place Barra, Antoing 7640. ☎ (069) 441331. Open 9.30am–9pm. Closed Monday. Main courses from 280BEF. An unpretentious tavern by the ramparts, where the unimaginative decor belies the highly imaginative cuisine. Try mussels with Roquefort or ox tongue with tagliatelle, and wash your meal down with a traditional beer. There's a stage for musicians, where accordion concerts give the place a Gallic feel: a reminder that France is just around the corner.

Index

Note: Page numbers in *italics* refer to maps

Aalst 306–8
Aarschot 198
Abîme, Cavernes de l' 551
accommodation 26–9
  see also individual places
  useful addresses 27
Adornès family 347
agriculture 67
air travel 13–21, 96
  from Australia and New
    Zealand 19–20
  from Britain 13–15
  from Canada 18–19
  from Ireland 15
  from S.Africa 21
  from USA 16–17
Alba, Duke of 59, 90
Albert I 62, 71, 170, 368,
  372
  statue 150, 368
Albert II 70, 72, 155
Albert, Archduke 147, 199
Albertstrand 367
Alden-Biesen Commandery
  213–14
Alexander I, Pope, reliquary
  172
Alle-sur-Semois 510
Amay 480
Ambiève valley 67
American cemetery of
  Henri-Chapelle 456–7
Andenne 529–30
Anneessens, François 91
Annevoie-Rouillon,
  Château and Gardens of
  531–2
Anseele, Edward 274
Anthisnes 475
Antoing, Château d' 593
ANTWERP 224–59, *228–9*
  accommodation 233–7
  bars and cafés 241–3
  Begijnhof 253
  boat trips 258
  Bontwerkersplaats 251
  Brouwershuis 253
  Centraalstation 252
  city tours 233
  Cogels Osylei 256–7
  Dagbladenmuseum 249
  Diamant Museum 252

eating places 237–41
Ethnografisch Museum
  248
fairs 256
getting around 232–3
getting there 231
Grote Markt 226, 244
guildhouses 244
Hessenhuis 253
history 58, 61, 226–31
Jordaenshuis 249
Klein Afrika 244
Koninklijk Museum voor
  Schone Kunsten
  253–5
Lillo 259
Linkeroever 257
live music 243
Maagdenhuis 246
markets 256
Mayer Van den Bergh
  Museum 246–7
Mini-Antwerp 256
Muhka (Museum of
  Contemporary Art) 253
Museum van
  Hedendaagse Kunst
  Antwerpen 255–6
Museum voor Fotografie
  256
Museum voor
  Volkskunde 248
name 226
Nationaal
  Scheepvaartmuseum
  247–8
nightclubs 243–4
Onze Lieve
  Vrouwekathedraal
  230, 245
Openluchtmuseum voor
  Beeldhouwkunst St
  Middelheim
  Antwerpen 257–8
Pelikaanstraat 252
Plantin-Moretus museum
  246
Poldermuseum 259
port 258–9
Quentin Metsys's spring
  245–6
red-light district 244

Rockoxhuis 250–1
Rubenshuis 249–50
Silver Centre 257
Sint Carolus
  Borromeuskerk 251
Sint Jacobskerk 225,
  250
Sint Pauluskerk 250
Stadhuis 244–5
Steen 247
Sterkshof provincial
  museum 257
Torengebouw 251
useful addresses and
  information 231–2
Virgin Mary statuettes
  226
Vlaamse Kaai 253
Vlaamse Kaai district
  230–1
Vlaeykensgang 248–9
Vleeshuis (Butchers'
  House) 247
Zoo 251–2
Antwerp province 224–71
Apollinaire, Guillaume 404,
  466–7
Archers, Guild of 314
  museum 348
architecture:
  art nouveau 134, 157–61
  Baroque 294
  Flemish baroque 135
  Gothic 135, 137, 311
  Ottonian 394
Ardennes 67, 271, 309
Ardennes, Battle of 63, 92,
  480, 541
  museum 482
Arlon 499–501
Armand, Saint 272
Arnould, Saint 553
art 58, 59, 62, 77, 78
  Flemish Primitives
    338–40
  School of Sint-Martens-
    Latem 300, 354
  Surrealism 80
art nouveau 134, 157–61
Artevelde, Jacob Van,
  statue 294
Artois 60

Aspremont, Gobert d' 397
asylum seekers 74
Ath 580–1
Atlantic Wall open-air
    museum 365
Atomium 92
Attre, Château d' 581–2
Aubechies, Archéosite d'
    583
Aubel 444
Aubert, Saint 138
Audenarde see
    Oudenaarde
Austrians 59, 60, 90, 91,
    273, 377, 481, 513, 555
Averbode Abbey 199
Aymon brothers 535
Aywaille 475

B&Bs 27, 28–9
    see also individual places
Bachte-Maria-Leerne 301
Bachten de Kupe open-air
    museum 376
Baels, Liliane 71
Balat, Alphonse 163
Baldéric, Prince-Bishop,
    tomb 429
Baldwin Iron Arm, Count
    315, 336
banks 47
Banneux 447
Barvaux 488
Bascourt, Jos 257
Basil, Saint 337
Bastogne 480, 496–8
Baudelaire, Charles 521
Baudouin I 63, 70, 72, 155,
    170
Bauwens, Lievin 273–4,
    297
Beatrix, Queen 195
beer 84–6, 175
    breweries 175, 312,
        343–4
    glasses 86
    museum 382
Beersel Castle 185
Begge, Saint 529
Beguines 193, 344
belfries, listed buildings 559
Belgian-Luxembourg
    Economic Union 62
Belgium 10–11
Beloeil, Château de 581
Benedictines 344
Benelux 62
Berchmans, Saint Jan 198

Beringen 209
Bernissart 577
Béthune, Robert de, tomb
    379
bicycles, hiring 53, 233,
    299
Bilzen 214
BINCHE 563–6
Bisons, Ferme des 498
Bladelin, Pieter 349
Blankenberge 366–7
Blankenberge-Heist canal
    317
Blégny 404
Blegny Mine 440–2
Blérot, Ernest 158, 161
Blondeel, Lancelot 337,
    349
Blücher, Gebhard
    Leberecht von 387, 390
boats 55
Bocholt 222
Bois-du-Luc, Ecomusée de
    567
Bokrijk 208–9
Bonnecroy, Jean-Baptiste
    166
Boon, Louis-Paul 306
Borgloon 214–15
Borgoumont 470
Borluut, Isabel 288
Borremans, Pasquier 267
Bosch, Hieronymus 295
Botassart 509–10
Botrange 458
Botrange, Centre Nature de
    457–8
Bouillon 506–8
Boussard, Jean-Denys 431
Bouts, Dirk 192
Bouvignes-sur-Meuse 536
Brabant, dukes of 89, 90,
    226
Brabant province 58, 60
    Flemish 69, 182–203
    Walloon 69, 386–403
Brabo, Silvius 226, 244
Bradley, General 497
Braekeleer, Henri de 230,
    253
Braine-l'Alleud 388–9
Braine-le-Château 392
Brangwyn, Sir Frank 340
Brant, Isabella 262
Bree 221–2
Breendonk fort 271
Brel, Jacques 75, 350
    evening with 145–6

breweries 175, 312, 343–4
Breydel, Jan, statue 345
Brouwer, Adriaen 311
Brueghel, Jan 'Velvet' 249,
    255
Brueghel, Pieter, the Elder
    75, 90, 137, 146, 166,
    230, 255
Brueghel, Pieter, the
    Younger 166, 254, 255,
    295
BRUGES 314–50, 320–1
    accommodation 322–9
    almshouses 343
    Arentshuis 340
    bars and cafés 333–5
    Begijnhof 314, 344
    Belfort 345–6
    boat trip 349
    Brangwyn Museum 340
    Brugse Vrije 337
    Burg 335–6
    Cathedral museum 345
    College of Europe 317,
        338
    Diamond Museum 344
    Dijver 338
    eating places 329–32
    Engels Klooster 348
    festivals 37, 337, 350
    getting around 318
    getting there 314–15
    Groeninge Museum
        338–40
    Gruuthuse Museum
        340–1
    Guido Gezellemuseum
        348
    Hanseatic quarter 349
    Heilig Bloedbasiliek 337
    history 58, 315–17
    Hof Bladelin 349
    Huidevettersplein 338
    Huis ter Beurze 349
    Jeruzalemkerk 347
    Kantcentrum (Lace
        Centre) 347
    markets 350
    Markt 345
    Memling Museum 342–3
    merchant halls 346
    Minnewater 344
    nightlife 333–5
    Onze Lieve Vrouwekerk
        341–2
    Potterie Museum 348
    Prinselijk Begijnhof ten
        Wijngaarde 314, 344

Reie 338
Rozenhoedkaai 338
Sint Anna district 346
Sint Annakerk 346–7
Sint Elisabethkerk 344
Sint Gilliskerk 348
Sint Jacobskerk 349
Sint Janshospitaal 342
Sint Salvatorkathedraal 345
Sint Sebastiaansgilde (Museum of the Guild of Archers) 348
Sint Walburgakerk 346
Stadhuis 336
Stedelijk Museum voor Volkskunst 347
Straffe Hendrik Brewery 343–4
swans 348
tollhouse 348
useful addresses 318, 322
Vismarkt 338
Windmolen 347
Bruly-de-Pesche, Hitler's Bunker 551
Brunfaut, Jules 160
BRUSSELS 89–181, *98–9, 102–3, 106–7, 159*
Abbaye de la Cambre 158
accommodation 110–17
Album 143–4
Atomium 92, 164
Autoworld 173
Avenue Louise 159–60
bars 125–31
Béguinage 175
Bibliothèque royale 150
Bois de la Cambre 161
La Bourse 142
Brigittines, Eglise des 157
La Brocante 156
La Brouette 138
Bruparck 164
Bruxella 1238 (museum) 142
Cantillon brewery 175
Cathédrale Saint-Michel 140–1
Centre belge de la bande dessinée 152, 169–70
La Chaloupe d'Or 138
la Chambrette de l'Amman 138

Chapelle, Eglise de la 146
comic-strip murals 152–4
Le Cornet 138
Le Cygne 139
eating places 117–25
economy 68
embassies 105
emblem 135
emergency phone numbers 108
entertainment listings 100
Etangs 158
L'Etoile 139
EU institutions 93–6, 162
European district 161–2
Falstaff 142
festivals 37, 90, 135, 139, 147, 179
Fondation Jacques-Brel 145–6
Galeries Saint-Hubert 91, 140
getting to 96–100
Grand'Place 60, 89, 91, 135–9
guided tours 104–5, 134
guildhouses 137–9
guilds 90, 135, 136
Halles Saint-Géry 140
L'Heaume 138
Heysel 163–5
history 58, 60, 61, 62, 63, 89–93, 154–6
Hospice Pachéco 152
Hôtel Hannon 160–1
Hôtel Otlet 160
Hôtel Ravenstein 150
Hôtel Saint-Cyr 162
Hôtel Solvay 160
Hôtel Tassel 160
Hôtel Van Eetvelde 162
Hôtel de Ville 135, 136, 139
Îlot Sacré 140–4
Impasse de la Cigogne 151
Ixelles 89, 157–61
Jardin Botanique 149
Jeanneke-Pis 145
Kinepolis 165
Koedelberg Basilica 162
Koninklijke Vlaamse Schouwburg 152
Laeken 92, 163
languages 69

leaving 180–1
live music 131
La Louve 138
Madeleine, Eglise de la 150
Magna Aula 148
Maison de la Bellone 151
Maison des Brasseurs 139
Maison des Ducs de Brabant 138
Maison d'Erasme 174
Maison du Paon 138
Maison du Peuple 92
Maison de la Radio Belge 157–8
Maison de Renard 137
Maison du Roi 90, 137
Mannekin-Pis 137, 144–5
markets 135, 139, 140, 179–80
Marolles district 89, 92, 148, 154–7
metro 94–5
Mini-Europe 164–5
La Monnaie, Théâtre royal de 61, 150–1
Mont des Arts 150
Mont-Thabor 158
Musée Antoine Wiertz 176–7
Musée d'Art Ancien (Fine Arts Museum) 75, 149, 165–7
Musée d'Art Moderne (Modern Art Museum) 76, 165, 167–8
Musée d'Art spontané 177
Musée de la Brasserie 139
Musée Bruxellois de la Gueuze 175
Musée du Cacao et du Chocolat 139
Musée Charlier 176
Musée du Cinéma 150
Musée Communal d'Ixelles 174
Musée Constantin Meunier 175–6
Musée du Costume et de la Dentelle 144, 175
Musée David and Alice Van Buuren 176
Musée de la Dynastie 149, 170

Musée Horta 170–1
Musée de l'Institut Royal des Sciences Naturelles 177
Musée des Instruments de Musique 149, 168–9
Musée du Jouet 174
Musée du Livre et de l'Imprimerie 150
Musée des Postes et Télécommunications 147
Musée Renée Magritte 162–3
Musée de la Résistance 173
Musée Royal de l'Afrique Centrale 178–9
Musée Royal de l'Armée et de l'Histoire Militaire 172–3
Musée du Transport Urbain Bruxellois 178
Musée de la Ville de Bruxelles 137
Musées Royaux d'Art et d'Histoire 171–2
Musées Royaux des Beaux-Arts 165–8
name 89, 135
nightclubs 132–3
Northwest 162–3
Notre-Dame de Laeken, Eglise 163
Notre-Dame-du-Sablon, Eglise 147
Océade 164
Old England 149
old port 150, 151
Palace of the Dukes of Burgundy 60
Palais des Beaux-Arts 150
Palais de Justice 91, 147–8
Palais de la Nation 149
Palais Stoclet 177
Palais du Vin 157
Palais-Royal district 144–50
Parc de Bruxelles 148–9
Parc du Cinquantenaire 91
museums 171–3
Pathé Palace 143
Pavillon Chinois 163

Pavillon des Passions Humaines 171
Pentagon district 90, 96, 135–9
Le Pigeon 138
Place de Brouckère 151
Place d'Espagne (Place de l'Agora) 140
Place du Grand-Sablon 146
Place du Jeu de Balle 156
Place des Martyrs 152
Place du Petit-Sablon 147
Place Royale 89, 91, 148
Place Saint-Géry 143
Place de la Vieille-Halle-aux-Blés 145
Porte de Hal 157
ramparts 89
La Rose 139
Le Roy d'Espagne 138
Royal Film Archives 150
Royal Palace 92, 148–9, 163
Rue Africaine 160
Rue des Bouchers 141
Rue Defacqz 160
Rue Faider 160
Rue Haute 156, 157
Rue Isabelle 148
Rue de Livourne 160
Rue de la Rasière 156
Rue des Renards 156
Rue de Rollebeek 146
Rue Van der Schrick 161
Sablon district 144–50
Le Sac 138
St Jacques-sur-Coudenberg 91, 148
Saint-Gilles 161
Saint-Jean-Baptiste-du-Béguinage, Eglise 151
Saint-Nicolas, Eglise 142
Sainte-Cathérine, Eglise 151
Scientastic 143
shops 133–4
shows 131–2
Société Générale 149
Square Ambiorix 162
Square Marie-Louise 162
La Taupe 138
Théâtre royal de la Monnaie 61, 150–1
Théâtre de Toone 141–2
Tour Anneessens 146

Tour Japonaise 163
tourist information 100–4
transport 109–10
Université Libre de Bruxelles (Free University) 91, 161
urbanization scheme 91
useful information 100–8
walks and tours 134, 159–61
companies for 104–5
World Trade Centre 92
Brussels Region 26, 69
budget 29
Bueren, Vincent de 423
Buls, Charles, statue 140
bureaux de change 47
Burg-Reuland 465–6
Burgundians 58, 90, 481
Burgundy, Dukes of 90, 314, 344, 349, 512–13
Bury, Pol 576
buses 54
Bütgenbach 463–4

Caesar, Julius 56, 315
cakes, sweets and biscuits 83–4
Calder, Alexander 149
campsites 26, 28
see also individual places
Cantillon brewery 175
carnivals 36, 460–1, 563–4
museum 565–6
cars 100
from Britain 24
driving 51–2
hire 51
lifts in 53
cashpoints 47
Catholic party 61
Catholicism 59, 90, 273
Céline, Louis-Ferdinand 379
Celles 541–2
Celts 481, 537
Centre, Canal du 567
Chameleux, Relais Romain de 505
Charlemagne 57, 75, 272
CHARLEROI 555–61
accommodation 556
bars and cafés 557–8
Basilique Saint-Christophe 559
Boulevard Audent 560
eating places 556–7
Escalier des Rames 558

festival 561
history 555–6
Hôtel de Ville 559
Institut supériur industriel 559
Lower town 558
Maison Dorée 560
Marchienne-au-Pont 561–2
Marcinelle 562
market 560
Mont-sur-Marchienne 561
Musée archéologique 560
Musée des Beaux-Arts 559
Musée des Chasseurs à pied 560
Musée Jules-Destrée 559
Musée du Verre 560
Palais des Beaux-Arts 559
Passage de la Bourse 558
Place Albert-1er 558
Place du Manège 559
Pont de Sambre 558
Rue du Collège 558
Saint-Antoine, Eglise 558
Saint-Fiacre, Chapelle 558
Upper town 559–60
useful addresses and information 556
Charles II of England 348, 471
Charles II of Spain 555
Charles, Prince (Regent) 365
Charles V 37, 59, 90, 135, 141, 148, 247, 272, 273, 287, 293, 310, 341, 405, 481, 537, 563, 585, 590
bust of 341
depicted in window 141
portrait 345
Charles VII 316
Charles the Bald 315, 549
Charles the Bold 59, 136, 316, 341, 350, 351, 405, 420, 428, 448, 537, 538, 574
Charles of Lower Lotharingia 89
Chassepierre 505
cheeses 83

Cherubini, Maria Luigi Carlo Zenobio Salvatore 554
Chevetogne 543
Childéric 585
Chimay 552–4
Chiny-sur-Semois 505
chocolate 84
Christian Socialists 64
Christianity 57
Christina, Queen of Sweden 471
Christmas 39
Ciney 542–3
Circle of Burgundy 59
Cistercians 369
Claes, Ernest, grave 199
Claus, Hugo 75, 79
Clermont-sur-Berwinne 445
Clijsters, Kim 64
climate 30
cloth production 272–3, 306
clothing, size conversion tables 32
Clovis 585
coach travel 24–5
coal/coal mining 66, 67, 551–2, 555–6, 561
Cobergher, Wenceslas 199
Cockerill, John 405, 449
Cocteau, Jean 135
coffee, café Liégeois 407
Cogels, John 257
colonisation 62
comic strips 80–1
communes 58, 69
communications 31, 67
Congo 62, 63, 71, 91
Coninck, Pieter de, statue 345
Coninx, Stijn 212, 306
Conscience, Hendrik 230
constitution 70
conversations 35–6
conversion tables 32
Coo 471
Corbion 508–9
Corroy-le-Château 528
Corte, Jean de 424
Coster, Charles de 80
Cosyn, Jean 151
Cotton, Edward 389
Couvin 549–51
crafts 49, 90
credit cards 47
Crève-Cur, Château de 536
Cro-Magnon man 530

crossbows, Guild of St George 347
Cröy, Charles de 553
Crupet 533–4
Crupet Valley 533
Cuesmes 576
cuisine 26, 81–4, 117, 537
vocabulary 82–4
customs regulations 34–5
cycling 47, 53, 299–300
Tour of Flanders 304

Daens, Adolf 306
Dalhem 442–3
Damien, Father 363
Damme 315, 317, 338, 350–3
David, Gerard 316, 339–40
De Haan 365–6
De Panne 370–1
Dedouaire, Robert 453
Deinze 301
del Cour, Jean 420, 427, 436
Delvaux, André 80
Delvaux, Laurent 287, 395
Delvaux, Paul 75, 80, 168, 434
museum 369–70
Demeulemeester, Anne 230
Dender, River 304
Dendermonde 308–9
Depestre, Julien 567
Destrée, Jules 559
Deurle 300
Devolution, War of 60
Dewez, Laurent-Benoit 528, 529, 567
diamond trade 252
Diederik of Alsace 337, 350
Dierenpark Planckendael 264
DIEST 195–8
accommodation 195–6
Begijnhof 197
café 196
eating places 196
Ezeldijkmolen 198
history 195
Lindenmolen 197
ramparts 197
Sint Sulpitiuskerk 197
Stadhuis 196
Tongerlo 197
useful addresses 195
Diksmuide 373–6
Dimpna, Saint 267, 268

Dinant 537–9
Doudelet, Charles 297
Dourbes 548
drinks 49
  beer 84–6, 175
Druon Antigon 226, 244, 248
Dubois, Maria 467
Ducasse 568–9
Duinbergen 367
Duivel, Gerard 298
Dumont, Gilberte 559
Dupuis, Jean 556
Duquesnoy, François 199
Duquesnoy, Jérôme 144, 353
Durbuy 486–8
Dutch 61, 225–6, 230, 513, 555
Dutroux, Marc 63–5
duty-free 34–5

East Flanders (Oost Vlaanderen) 271–313
eating out:
  see also individual places
  prices 29
Eau d'Heure, Lacs de l' 554
Ecaussinnes-Lalaing, Château d' 578–9
Ecomusée de Bois-du-Luc 567
Ecomusée du pays des Collines 584
economy 63, 64, 67–8
Edward IV of England 340
Egmont, Count of 90, 137, 147
Eisenhower, Dwight D. 497
elections 74
Elezelles 584
Elisabeth, Queen (Elisabeth of Bavaria) 71, 170
  statue 150
Elizabeth II of England 390
embassies 33–4, 105
emergencies, telephone numbers 31, 108
Enghien 579–80
English 273
Ensor, James 75, 80, 255, 362, 363
  house 362–3
entry formalities 34–5
Escaut river see Scheldt
Escher, M.C. 143
etiquette 35–6

EU (formerly European Economic Community) 63
  institutions 93–6
  Parliament 95–6
Eupen 62, 454–6
Euro 46–7
Euro Space Center 495–6
European Atomic Energy Commission 63
European Commission 93–4
European Convention on Human Rights 74
European Council of Ministers 94–5
European Economic Community 63
European Parliament 95–6
events 36–9
exports 62

Faber, Moulin à eau 488
Fabiola, Queen (Doña Fabiola de Mora y Aragón) 72
Fagne de Polleur 458
Fagnes, plateau des 66
Farnese, Alexander 230
federalism 68–9
festivals 36–9
  see also individual places
feudal system 58, 61
Fexhe, Peace of 405
fishing, on horseback 369
Flanders, Counts of 139, 293, 315
Flanders (Flemish Region) 26, 58, 60, 61, 68, 69, 271–385
Flanders, plain of 66
flax, museum 385
Flemish Ardennes 271, 309
Flemish Brabant 69, 182–203
Flemish Region see Flanders
Floreffe, Abbey of 527
folk music 87–8
folklore 36
Folx-les-Caves 402–3
Fontenoy, Battle of 585
food 26, 81–4, 117, 537
  shopping for 48
  vocabulary 82–4
Fourment, Helen 250
Fourneau-Saint-Michel 491–2

Fourons (Voeren) 223–4
Foy-Notre-Dame, Eglise de 542
Foy-Recogne 498
Franchimont, Château de 448
Francis Xavier, Saint 346
Franck, César 76, 437
Franks 57, 226, 585
French 60–1, 91, 273, 310, 315–16, 377, 513, 555, 585
French Revolution 60–1, 91, 273, 344, 405, 513, 537
Freÿr, Château de 540
Freÿr, rochers de 540
frites (fritures) 84, 117
Froissart, Jean 552
Furfooz, Parc naturelle de 542
Furnaux 533

Gaasbeek Castle 186–7
Gaulle, Charles de 537
Gaume 67, 501
Géal, José 141–2
Geel 267–8
Gembloux 527–9
Gent see Ghent
Geraardsbergen (Grammont) 304–5
Germans 62–3, 92, 377
geography 66–7
George V 372
Gertrude, Saint 394, 395
Gerval, Lac de 400–1
Gevaert, Edgard 300
Gezelle, Guido 348, 385
GHENT 272–99, 276–7
  accommodation 274–80
  bars and cafés 283–7
  Belfort 290
  Coorenmetershuis 292
  eating places 280–3
  festival 272
  De Gekroonde Hoofden 281, 292
  Gerard Duivelsteen 298
  getting around 274
  getting there 272
  Gildehuis van de Vrije Schippers 292
  Graslei 291–2
  Gravensteen 272, 293
  Groentenmarkt 294

guildhouses 292
Het Pand 297
history 58, 272–4
hitch-hiking out of 298
Hoogpoort houses 291
Hospice for Alijn children 293
ice creams and sweet treats 283
Klein Onze Lieve Vrouw Begijnhof 298
Korenlei 292
Korenmarkt 294
Kouter 297
Kraanlei 293
Lakenhalle 290
Masons' House 292
Museum Arnold Vander Haeghen 297
Museum voor Industriële Archeologie en Textiel 297
Museum voor Schone Kunsten 295–6
Museum voor Sierkunst 292
Museum voor Stenen Voorwerpen 297
Museum voor Volkskunde 293
Ons Huis 294
Oudheidkundig Museum Van de Bijloke 296
Patershol district 293
Rabot 298
red-light district 298
shopping 294
Sint Baafskathedraal 272, 287–90
Sint Elisabeth Begijnhof 297–8
Sint Jakobskerk 294
Sint Michielsbrug 291
Sint Niklaaskerk 291
Sint Pieterskerk 295
Sint Veerleplein 292
Spijker 292
Stadhuis 290–1
Stedelijk Museum voor Actuele Kunst 296
Toljuisje 292
University 62, 274, 297
University library tower 295
useful addresses and information 274
Vooruit 294
Vrijdagmarkt 294

giants 36
Gileppe, Barrage and lac de la 453–4
Girault, Charles 171, 178
gîtes 27, 28–9
gîtes d'étape 27, 28
glass and crystal 49
La Gleize 470
Godefroid de Bouillon 58, 506
Godefroy de Huy 476
Goering, Hermann 524
Golden Fleece, Order of 316, 341, 345
Golden Spurs, battle of 273, 316, 336, 384
Goncourt brothers 521
Gorge, Henry de 576
Goyet 530
Gozée 562
Grammont (Geraardsbergen) 304–5
Grand-Hornu 576
Grapheus, Abraham 254
Greens 64
Greignes 548–9
Grétry, André-Modeste 430
Grimbergen 188
Groenendaal 183
Grouchy, Marshal 387
Gudule, Saint 89, 140
guilds 58, 90, 135, 136
Gummarus, Saint 264, 266
Guynemer, Georges 380

Habsburgs 59, 60, 90–1
Hainaut, Parc Naturel Transfrontalier du 593
Hainaut province 60, 551–94
Hakendover 203
Halle (Hal) 183–5
Han, Grottes de 544–5
Hankar, Paul 158, 159, 160
Hannon, Edouard 161
Hans, Jean 420
Harchies-Pommerul, Marais de 576
Harpman, Jacqueline 80
Harzé 474
Haspengouw 209
HASSELT 204–8
accommodation 205
bars and cafés 206
Begijnhof 207
eating places 205–6
festivals 207, 208

Japanese Gardens 207
Museum Stellingwerff-Waerdenhof 207
Nationaal Jenevermuseum 207
Onze Lieve Vrouwekerk 206
Sint Quintus 206
Stedelijk Modemuseum 207
useful information and addresses 205
Hastière-par-Delà 540–1
Haute Semois 505
Haute-Semois, Marais de la 501
Hautes-Fagnes 457
health 39–40
Heist 367
Hélécine 403
Henin, Justine 64
Henri II 563
Henri IV 310
Henri-Chapelle, American cemetery of 456–7
Henry VIII 585
Herbeumont 505
Herentals 266–7
Hergé (Georges Rémi) 76, 80–1
Hergesberg 464
Hermes, Saint 313
Herve 440, 444–5
Het Zoute 367
Het Zwin nature reserve 365, 367
Heverlee 194
Heysel 163–5
history 56–66, 89–93, 154–6
  see also individual places
  dates of main events 64–6
hitch-hiking 52–3
Hitler, Adolf, Bunker 551
Hoegaarden 203
Hoeilaart 183
holidays, public 48
Holland, War of 60
Holsbeek 199
Hooge-Krater 380
Hoogstraten 269
Hoorn, Count of 90, 137, 147, 301
horse-riding 47
Horst castle 199
Horta, Victor 76, 91, 92, 150, 155, 158, 159, 160,

162, 163, 171, 176, 257,
591
museum 170–1
hotels 26
see also individual places
prices 29
Hottemme, Domaine de
488
Hotton, Grottes de 488
Houffalize 485–6
Hubert, Saint 404, 494
Hugo, Victor 135, 138, 224,
386, 387, 471, 479, 530
Huizingen 185
Hulpe, Domaine de la 401
human rights 73–4
Hundred Years War 273
HUY 475–9
accommodation 477
bar 477
Collégiale 478
eating places 477
Fort 479
history 476–7
Hôtel de Ville 479
live music 477
Maison de la Tour 479
Musée Communa
478–9
Tower of Oultremont 479
useful addresses and
information 477

Ickx, Jacky 76
IEPER (YPRES) 377–81
accommodation 378
eating places 378
festival 381
getting there 377
Grote Markt 378
history 58, 477
In Flanders Fields
museum 377, 378–9
Lakenhalle 378
Last Post ceremony 377,
380
Menin Gate 380
nightlife 378
ramparts 380
Saint George's Memorial
Church 380
Sint Maartenskathedraal
379
Stadhuis 378
useful addresses and
information 378
World War I landmarks in
region 380–1

IJzer, River 62, 367, 368
immigrants 73
independence 61–2
industry 63, 68, 91
Inquisition 59, 90, 317
insurance 39–40
invaders 57
Isabel of Portugal 339
depicted in window 141
Isabella, Archduchess 90,
199, 355
Ittre 391

Jabbeke 354
Jansenius, Bishop of Ghent
287
Jansenius, Bishop of Ieper,
tomb 379
Jauchelette 403
jazz 87
Jean l'Aveugle 535
Jeanneke-Pis 145
Jehay-Amay 476
Jemmapes 568
Jesuits 59, 226, 251
Jesus-Eik 183
jewellery 09
Jews 92, 252, 263
Joan of Constantinople
298, 307
Jodoigne 401–2
John of Austria 522, 528
Jordaens, Jacob 249,
254
Joseph II, Emperor of
Austria 60, 91, 289,
471, 582
Justus van Gent 287

Kempen 66, 269–70
Khnopff, Fernand 167
Klein Brabant 270–1
Knokke 367
Koksijde 368–70
Kollwitz, Käthe 376
KORTRIJK 382–5
accommodation 383
bars 384
Begijnhof 384
Belfort 384
Broelmuseum 384
eating places 383
history 383
Nationaal Vlasmuseum
385
Onze Lieve Vrouwkerk
384
Sint Maartenskerk 384

Stadhuis 384
Stedelijk Museum 384
useful addresses and
information 383
Kortrijk, battle of 316, 345

la Censerie, Louis de 252
Laarne Castle 302
Labour Party 61
lace 49, 90, 305, 317
museums 347, 385,
490
Laeken 92, 163
Lalaing, Christine de 591
Lambeaux, Jef 171, 193,
194, 226, 230, 244,
249
Lambert I ('the Bearded')
189
Lambert, Saint 404
Lanaken 217
Landen 203
Lange Wapper 226
Langemark 380
languages 35, 40–5, 57
official 62, 69, 170, 274
place names 52
vocabulary:
Belgian French 43–4
Bruxellois insults 44
Dutch 41–3
food 82–4
Walloon 45
Lassus, Orlando de 568
Lavaux-Sainte-Anne,
Château de 543–4
Layens, Mathieu (Mathys)
de 192, 573, 574
Le Corbusier 257
League of Augsburg, War
of 60
League of Nations 62
Leau (Zoutleeuw) 200–1
legal system 74
Leie, River 292, 296
cruise 299
villages of 299–301
Leopold I (Leopold of Saxe-
Coburg) 61, 70, 91, 163
monument 370
statue 149
Leopold II 62, 71, 91–2,
147–8, 162, 163, 171,
178, 252, 316, 358
Leopold III 62–3, 71–2, 92,
170
Lessines 583–4
festival 37

LEUVEN (LOUVAIN) 182, 188–94
accommodation 189–90, 194
bars and taverns 191
eating places 190
festival 194
Groot Begijnhof 193
Grote Markt 192
Heverlee 194
history 189
Klein Begijnhof 194
Museum Vander Kelen-Mertens 194
Naamsesstraat 193
Sint Pieterskerk 192
Stadhuis 192–3
University 58, 386, 398
useful information and addresses 189
Liberals 61, 64
Liefmans brewery 312
LIEGE 404–40, *408–9*
accommodation 410–12
Aquarium 434
Basilique Saint-Martin 437
Boulevard de la Constitution 432
Cathédrale Saint-Paul 427–8
eating places 412–17
En Roture 433–4
Escalier de la montagne de Bueren 422–3
festivals 438
Herstal 440
history 60, 404–6
Hôtel de Ville 420–1
Ilôt Saint-Georges 426
live music 418–19
Maison de Grétry 433
Maison Havart 426–7
Maison du Jazz 426
Maison de la Métallurgie 435
Maison des Métiers d'Art 434
Maison des Sciences 434
Manufacture de cristaux du Val Saint-Lambert 439–50
markets 438
Mont Saint-Martin 436–7
Musée d'Ansembourg 426
Musée d'Armes 424–5

Musée d'Art moderne et contemporain 434–5
Musée d'Art religieux et d'Art mosan 422
Musée de l'Art wallon 425–6
Musée Curtuis 424
Musée Tchantchès 434
Musée des Transports en commun 435
Musée du Verre 424
Musée de la Vie wallonne 421–2
Musée de Zoologie de l'université 434
nightlife 417–18
Outremeuse district 406, 431–5
Palais des Princes-Evêques 419–20
Parc de la Boverie 435
Pierreuse district 436
Place du Marché 420
Place Saint Lambert 405, 419
Préhistosite et la grotte de Ramioul 439
Publemont 436
Route du Feu 439
Rue des Ecoliers 432
Rue En Hors Château 421, 422, 423
Rue En Hors Château district 421
Rue En Hors Feronstrée district 421
Rue de la Goffe 427
Rue Léopold 431
Rue Pierreuse 436
Rue Puits-en-Sock 433
Rue des Récollets 433
Rue Saint-Pierre 437
Saint-Barthélemy, Eglise 423–4
Saint-Denis, Eglise 430–1
Saint-Jacques, Eglise 429–30
Saint-Jean, Eglise 428
Saint-Nicolas, Eglise 433
Saint-Pholien, Eglise 432
Sainte-Croix, Eglise 436–7
Tchantchès statue 432
theatre 439
Théâtre Royal 430
useful addresses 410
walks 435–8

Liège province 404–80
Lier 264–6
Lieve, River 292
Ligne, Marshal Charles-Joseph de 581
Lillo 259
Limbourg 453–4
Limburg, North 221
Limburg province 204–24
Lipsius, Justius 230
Lissewege 353
literature 79–80
Lobbes 563
Lochristi 274
Loison, General 504
Lommel 223
Lorette-Rochefort, Grotte de 546–7
Lorraine, Charles de 60, 91, 148, 182, 395
Louis XI 405, 537
Louis XIV 60, 91, 135, 200, 311, 420, 479, 481, 513, 522, 585
Louis XV 585, 593
Louise-Marie, Queen (Louise-Marie d'Orléans) 61, 70, 163
Louvain *see* Louven
Louvain-la-Neuve 386, 398–9
Low Countries 58, 59, 61
Lucky Luke 78
Lumière brothers 140
Luther, Martin 59
Luxembourg 61
Luxembourg, Dukes of 481
Luxembourg province 480–512

Maaseik 218–21
Maasland 217
Maasmechelen 218
Maastricht 444
McAuliffe, General 496, 497
Maeterlinck, Maurice 75, 80, 297
Magritte, René 76, 80, 168, 555, 556
museum 162–3
Maigret, Arnold 420
Malagne 547
Malibran, Maria 554
Mallarmé, Stéphane 521
Malmedy 62, 460–3
Mannekin-Pis 137, 144–5
Marais de Harchies Pommerul 576

Marais de la Haute-Semois 501
Marche-en-Famenne 489–91
Marchienne-au-Pont 561–2
Marcinelle 556, 562
Maredsous, Abbaye de 532
Margaret of Austria 262, 341
  statue 261
Margaret of Constantinople 344, 353
Margaret of Maele 316
Margaret of York 316, 350, 351
Margiela, Martin 230
Marguerite de Valois 471
Maria of Hungary 563
Marie of Burgundy 316, 341–2
Marie-Antoinette 581
Mariemont, Domaine and Musée royal de 566–7
Mariën, Marcel 80
markets 298
Marlborough, Duke of 310, 351
Marne, Battle of 513
Marshall Plan 63
Marsupilami (cartoon character) 555, 556
Martel, Charles 529, 530
Martens, Dirk 305, 307
Masson, Arthur 548
Maupassant, Guy de 521
Maximilian, Archduke of Austria 316, 341
Mayer Van den Bergh, Fritz 246
MECHELEN 259–64
  Abdij van Sint Truiden 262
  accommodation 260
  bars 261
  burgomaster's house 261
  Carillon School 262
  city walk 262–3
  Dierenpark Planckendael 264
  eating places 260–1
  events 264
  festival 37
  Gaspard De Wit Royal Tapestry Factory 263
  Groot en Klein Begijnhof 262
  Grote Markt 261

Haverwerf 262
history 58, 259–60
Ijzerleen 261
Margaret of Austria's Palace 262
Museum of Deportation and Resistance 263
Onze Lieve Vrouw van Hanswijck 263
Sint Janskerk 262
Sint Peter en Pauluskerk 262
Sint Romboutskathedraal 261–2
Speelgoed Museum (Toy Musum) 263
Stadhuis 261
Stedelijk Museum Hof Van Busleyden et Beiaardmuseum 263
Technopolis 263
useful addresses and information 260
media 45–6
meeting people 35
Meetjesland 271
Meise, National Botanic Gardens of 187–8
Memling, Hans 293, 316, 342–3
Menapian tribe 315
Mercator, Gerhardus 76–7, 147, 230, 246
  museum 303
Mercator (training ship) 363
merchant towns 58
Merckx, Eddy 77
Merovingians 585
Mertens, Pierre 80
Metsys, Quentin 230, 245–6, 255
Meunier, Constantin 146, 149, 193, 194, 558, 559
  museum 175–6
Meuse, River 427, 512, 567
Meuse valley 530–41
Meyerbeer, Giacomo 471
Michael, Saint 136, 140
Michaux, Henri 77, 80
Michelangelo Buonarroti 341
Minne, George 298, 300, 375
Mirabeau, Marquis de 508
Mobuto, President 64
Modave, Château de 480
money 46–7

MONS 568–76, 571
  accommodation 569–70
  bars 572–3
  belfry 574
  Collégiale Sainte-Waudru 573–4
  eating places 570–2
  festivals 37, 568–9
  Grand-Place 574
  history 568
  Hôtel de Ville 574
  market 576
  Musée des Arts décoratifs François Duesberg 575
  Musée des Beaux-Arts 575
  Musée du Chanoine Puissant 575
  Musée du Folklore et de la Vie montoise 575
  Musées du Centenaire 574–5
  Saint-Nicolas-en-Havré, Eglise 576
  Sainte-Elisabeth, Eglise 576
  useful addresses and information 569
Mont des Brumes 471
Mont-sur-Marchienne 561
Montaigle, Château de 532
Monteverdi, Claudio 471
Montquintin 503
Moreau, Marcel 80
Moretus, Balthasar 245, 246
Morin tribe 315
Mortier 442
Moscroen, Jan 341
motorways 51–2
Moulin à eau Faber 488
Museums of the Artists of the School of Sint-Martens-Latem 300
music 86–8

NAMUR 512–27, 516–17
  accommodation 513–15
  Athenée royal 521
  bars 519–20
  boat trips 526
  Cathédrale Saint-Abain 522
  Citadel 525–6
  eating places 515–19
  festivals 526–7
  historic centre 520–5

history 512–13
market 526
Musée africain 526
Musée archéologique 523–4
Musée des Arts anciens du Namurois 523
Musée diocésain 522
Musée Félicien-Rops 521
Musée de la Forêt 526
Musée de la Fraise et du Terroir wépionnais 526
Musée de Groesbeeck de Croix 522–3
Musée des Traditions namuroises 526
old houses 520–1
Palais provincial 522
Place du Marché-aux-Légumes 520
Saint-Jean-Baptiste, Eglise 520
Saint-Loup, Eglise 521–2
Trésor d'Hugo d'Oignies 524–5
useful addresses 513
Walloon parliament 525
Namur, Counts of 481, 512
Namur province 512–51
Napoleon 61, 91, 163, 230, 258, 273, 351, 386, 387, 389, 390, 391, 424–5, 555
Nationale Plantentuin (National Botanic Gardens of Meise) 187–8
NATO 568
Navez, François-Joseph 559
Nazis 63
Neeroeteren 221
Nemours, Duke of 61
Neptune, Grottes de 551
Neutchâteau 511–12
newspapers 46
Nicolas, St 39
Nieuwpoort 368
Nijmegen, Treaty of 377
Ninove 305–6
Nismes 548
Nisramont, Belvédère de 483
NIVELLES 386, 393–7
Collégiale Sainte-Gertrude 394–5
eating places 393–4

festivals 396
getting there 393
history 393
Musée Communal 395
Palais de Justice 396
Parc de la Dodaine 396
Tour Simone 396
useful addresses 393
Norbertine abbey 403
Normans 315, 512
Notger, Prince-Bishop 404, 419, 436
Nothomb, Amélie 80

Oignies, Hugo d' 524
Oignies-en-Thiérache 547–8
Olne 446
Ommegang 37, 90, 135, 139, 147
Ooidonk Castle 301
Oost Vlaanderen see East Flanders
Oostende see Ostend
Oostuinkerke 368–70
Opoerteren 221
Opsomer, Isidore 264
Orange-Nassau, William Frederick-Georges-Louis, Prince of 387
Orp-le-Grand 402
Ortelius, Abraham 147
Orval, Abbaye d' 504
OSTEND 354–64, 356–7
accommodation 358–9
bars 361
casino 363
dyke 363
eating places 359–60
festival 364
fish auction 363
getting there 355
Heenmuseum De Plate 362
history 71, 355–8
hitch-hiking from 365
James Ensorhuis 362–3
Little Paris 361–2
Mercator (training ship) 383
Museum voor Schone Kunsten 362
nightlife 361–2
North Sea Aquarium 363
port 363
Provinciaal Museum voor Moderne Kunst 362
sea cruise 364

Sint Petrus en Pauluskerk 363
Stairs of Death 363
useful addresses and information 358
Osy, Edouard 257
OUDENAARDE (AUDENARDE) 309–12
accommodation 310
Begijnhof 312
Cloth Hall 311
eating places 311
festival 312
getting there 310
history 310
Lalainghuis 312
Liefmans brewery 312
Markt 312
Onze Lieve Vrouw Hospitaal 312
Onze Lieve Vrouwekerk of Pamele 312
Sint Walburgskerk 312
Stadhuis 311
useful address 310
Ourthe, River 480, 483
Ourthe valley 67
outdoor activities 47–8
Overijse 183
Owen, Thomas 80

Pacification, Treaty of 273, 291
paedophiles 63–4, 74, 148
Paliseul 511
Paola, Queen 72
Paradiso, Parc 582–3
Parc naturel de Furfooz 542
Parc naturel des vallées de la Burdinale et de la Mehaigne 480
Parc Naturel Transfrontalier du Hainaut 593
Parc Paradiso 582–3
Parma, Duke of 377
Parma, Margaret of 310
passports 34
Patton, General George S. 496, 497
Paulus, Pierre 426, 559
Pays des Collines, Ecomusée du 594
Pays Noir 555, 561
Peer 222–3
people, meeting 35
Permeke, Constant, museum 354
Peter the Great 471

Peter the Hermit 476
Peyo (Pierre Culliford) 78–9
Philip of Alsace, Count of
    Flanders 293, 315
Philip the Bold 58, 316
Philip the Fair 315, 316,
    341
Philip the Good 58, 316,
    339, 344, 512, 535
Philip II 59, 90, 230, 273,
    287, 289, 307, 481, 513
Philippe, Crown Prince 64,
    72
Philippe Auguste 585
Pipaix 584
Plantin, Christopher 225,
    230, 246, 269
Plisner, Charles 80
Poelaert, Joseph 148, 150,
    151, 163
Poelkappelle 380
Poilvache, Château de 535
Poirot, Hercule 78
Poix, Centrale hydraulique
    de 494
politics 26, 61–2, 64
Polleur 448–9
Poperinge 381–2
population 73
post 31
Pot, Piet 226
Praetbos-Vlasdo, German
    cemetery 376
press 46
Prévost, Abbé 508
Prévost, Jean 568
processions 37–8
Protestantism 49, 273, 290
public holidays 48
Puissant, Canon 575
puppet theatre 39

Quellin, Artus 345

rail travel 21–2, 53–4,
    96–100
Ramioul, Préhistosite et la
    grotte de 439
Raversijde Estate 365
Rebecq 382–3
Redu 494–5
Reformation 59, 317
La Reid 449
Reinhardstein, Château de
    458–9
Rekem 218
Rémi, Georges see Hergé
Renard, Bruno 576

Renier de Huy 423, 476
Reninge 376
restaurants:
    see also individual places
    prices 29
Rimbaud, Arthur 140, 144,
    568
Rixensart, Château de 400
roads:
    motorways 51–2
    Roman 56
Robertville 460
La Roche-en-Ardenne
    480–4
Rochefort 545–7
Rochehaut 509
Rodenbach, Georges 80,
    298
Rodenbach family 385
Roeselaere 385
Roeulx, Château du 580
Romans 56, 471, 481
    staging post 505
Rome, treaty of 63
Romedenne 549
Ronquières, Plan incliné de
    579
Ronse 313
Rops, Félicien 521
royal family 62, 70–2
Rubens, Pieter Paul 59, 77,
    166, 225, 245, 249, 250,
    251, 254–5, 262
    house 249–50
Rwanda-Burundy 62

Saedeleer, Valerius de 307
Saint-Aubert, Mont 593
SaintGeorge, Guild of 347
Saint-Hubert 492–4
Saint-Michel, Forêt de 492
Saint-Séverin-en-Condroz
    475
Sambre, River 558
Sambre-et-Meuse district
    513
Samson, Vallée du 530
Sankt Vith 464–5
Sart 449
Savery, Roelandt 384
Sax, Adolphe 77, 537
Saxe-Coburg dynasty 62,
    70
Scheldt (Escaut), River 66,
    90, 226, 230, 253, 272,
    273, 304, 567
Scherpenheuvel 199
Schtroumpfs 78–9

Scifo, Enzo 77
sculpture 90
Scutenaire, Louis 80
sea travel 22–4
seasons 30
Semini 247
Semois, River 480
Semois valley 67
Seneffe, Château de 567–8
Senne, River 89, 91, 137
Senne Valley 143
Serclaes, Everard 't 90, 139
Serrurier-Bovy, Gustave
    158
Servais, Charles 252
sexual crimes 63–4
sgraffito 156–7
SHAPE 568
shopping 48–9
Simenon, Desiré 433
Simenon, Georges 77–8,
    80, 406–7, 431, 432–3
Simenon, Henriette 433
sinjoren 225
Sint Niklaas 302–4
Sint Pieters Voeren 224
Sint Truiden 215–17
Sint-Martens-Latem 300
Six Flags Belgium 400
Six-Ourthes, Belvédère des
    483
Sluis 317
Smet, Léon and Gustave
    de 300
smoking 49
Smurfs 78–9
snails 117
Socialist Party 64, 294
Soetkens, Beatrice 147
Soignes, Forêt de
    (Zoniënwoud) 182–3,
    386
Soignies 577–8
Soiron 445
Solvay, Ernest-John 401
Sosoye 532
Sougné-Remouchamps,
    Grottes de 474
Soumagne 446
SPA 471–4
    accommodation 472
    casino 473
    eating places 472
    Etablissement de bains
    473
    Galérie Léopold-II 473
    history 471
    Hôtel de Ville 473

Musée de la Forêt 474
Musée de la Lessive
  473–4
Musée spadois du
  Cheval 473
Musée de la Ville d'eau
  472–3
Pouhon Pierre-le-Grand
  473
shopping 474
useful addresses and
  information 471–2
Spanish 59, 90, 91, 230,
  555, 585
Spanish Succession, War
  of 60
Spilliaert, Léon 362
Spontin 534–5
sports, events 39
Stanley, H.M. 62
statistics 56
STAVELOT 466–71
  accommodation 467–8,
    470
  eating places 467–8
  festivals 470
  Musée Apollinaire
    469–70
  Musée d'Art religieux
    469
  Musée du Circuit-de-
    Spa Francorchamps
    469
  Musée hostorique de
    Décembre 1944 470
  museum 469–70
  old abbey 468
  Place Saint-Remacle 468
  Saint-Sébastien, Eglise
    468–9
  useful addresses and
    information 467
steel industry 556
Stene 364
Straffe Hendrik Brewery
  343–4
Strauven, Gustave 158,
  162
Strebelle, Claude 419
Streeksmuseum 380
Stroobants, Jacques 145
Stuyvaert, Victor 297
swans 348

Tallien, Madame 553–4
Tancrémont 446
tapestry 49, 90, 311
Taxistop 27, 29, 53

Tchantchès 406
  statue 432
telephones 31
  emergency numbers 31,
    108
television 45–6
tennis 64
Tervuren 177–9
Teuten 223
textile industry 272–3, 274
theatre, puppet 39
Theux 447–8
Thuin 562–3
Tienen (Tirlemont) 202–3
time 49
Timmermans, Felix 264
Tintin 76, 79, 80, 81
tipping 50
Tirlemont (Tienen) 202–3
Tohogne 488
TONGEREN 210–13
  accommodation 210–11
  Ambioriz 211
  Begijnhof 213
  eating places 211
  festivals 213
  Gallo-Roman Museum
    212
  getting there 210
  history 210
  Onze Lieve
    Vrouwebasiliek
    211–12
  ramparts 213
  Roman walls 213
  Stadhuis 212
  useful addresses and
    information 210
Tongerlo Abbey 197
Torgny 502–3
Tour of Flanders 304
tourist offices 50
TOURNAI 584–94, 587
  accommodation 585–8
  bars and cafés 589–90
  belfry 591
  Cathédrale Notre-Dame
    590–1
  eating places 588–9
  festivals 592–3
  Grand-Place 591
  history 585
  Hôtel de Ville 591
  live music 589–90
  Musée d'Archéologie
    592
  Musée d'Armes et
    d'Histoire militaire 592

Musée des Arts
  décoratifs 591–2
Musée des Beaux-Arts
  591
Musée du Folklore 592
Musée d'Histoire
  naturelle 591
Pont des Trous 592
Saint-Brice, Eglise 592
tea-room 589
useful addresses 585
traditions 36–9
trains 21–2, 53–4,
  96–100
transport 50–5
travel 13–25
travel agents 14–15, 17,
  18–19, 20, 21
Treignes 548–9
Trekkershutten 29
Turnhout 268–9
Tyne Cot Cemetery 380

United Belgian States 60
Ursula, Saint 339, 342–3
Utrecht, Treaty of 60, 91

Val-Dieu, Abbaye de 444
Van Artevelde, Jacob 273,
  294
  statue 294
Van Beurendonck, Walter
  230
Van Brugges family 340
Van Cutsem, Henri 176
Van Dam, José 78
Van de Velde, Henry 158,
  159, 295
Van den Beurze family 315,
  349
Van der Goes, Hugo 316
Van der Stappen, Charles
  149
Van der Weyden, Roger 90,
  192
Van Dormael, Jaco 78
Van Dyck, Antoon 249
Van Eyck, Hubert 78, 288
Van Eyck, Jan 78, 288,
  316, 339
  statue 348
Van Gogh, Vincent, house
  576
Van Maerlant, Jacob,
  statue 352
Van Noten, Dries 230
Van Oost, Jacob 349
Van Reeth, Bob 253

Van Rysselberghe, Octave 159, 160
Van St Aldegonde, Marnix 230
Van Schoonbeke, Gilbert 253
Vandenhove, Charles 423
Vauban, Sébastien, Marquis de 380, 481, 500
Vennbahn Railway 456
Verdun, Treaty of 57–8, 272
Verhaeren, Emile 271
Verlaine, Paul 140, 144, 521, 559, 568
Vernes, Henri 80
Versailles, Treaty of 62
VERVIERS 449–52
  accommodation 450
  eating places 450–1
  Hôtel de Ville 452
  Musée d'Archéologie et du Folklore 452
  Musée des Beaux-Arts et de la Céramique 451–2
  Rue des Raines 451
  useful addresses and information 450
  Verviersima-Centre de la Laine et de la Mode 451
Vésale, André (Vesalius) 78
Veurne 37, 371–3
Vêves, Château de 541–2
Victoria, Queen 355, 389
Viersalm 484–5
Vierves-sur-Viroin 548
Vijdt, Joost 288
Vikings 272, 404, 412
Villa Goffinet 365
Villers-la-Ville Abbey 396–7
Vinckboons, David 254
Virelles, Etangs de 554
Virgin Mary, statuettes 226
Viroinval 547, 548
visas 34
Visé 443
vital statistics 56

Vlaams Blok 64, 225, 259
Vlaams Brabant see Flemish Brabant
Voeren (Fourons) 223–4
Voltaire 60
Vooruit ('Progress') movement 274
Vresse-sur-Semois 510–11
Vucht 218

Waasland 271, 302
Waha 490–1
Walcourt 551
walking 47–8
Wallonia (Walloon Region) 26, 67–8, 69, 386–594
Walloon Brabant province 69, 386–403
Walloons 59
Wars of Religion 344
WATERLOO 61, 91, 386–91
  accommodation 387
  battlefield 388–90
  Butte di Lion 388–9
  eating places 388
  festival 391
  getting there 386
  history 387
  Musée de Cire 389
  Musée provincial 389–90
  Musée Wellington 390
  Rotonde du Panorama 389
  Royal Chapel 390–1
  useful addresses 387
Waterloo, Battle of 386, 387
watersports 47
Waudru 568
Wavre 386, 399–400
websites 55
weights and measures, size conversion tables 32
Wellington, Arthur Wellesley, Duke of 386, 387
  museum 390

Werchter 199
Wervik 381
Western Flanders (West-Vlaanderen) 313–85
Westhoek nature reserve 371
Wiertz, Antoine 176–7
Wilhelm, Kaiser 406
Willebroek, Breendonk fort 271
Willebroek Canal 90
William I (of Holland) 91
William of Nassau (the Silent) 195
William of Orange 59, 61, 90, 513
Williers 505
wine 479, 503
wool trade 272–3
World Fairs 62, 63, 92, 230, 291
World Heritage Sites 344, 567
World War I 62, 71, 92, 358, 373–4, 376, 377, 513, 524
  In Flanders Fields museum 377, 378–9
  landmarks 380–1
  Talbot House 382
World War II 62–3, 71, 92, 148, 155, 317, 358, 393, 481, 496, 513, 524
  museums 482, 497

Yourcenar, Marguerite 80
youth hostels 28
  see also individual places
Ypres see Ieper

Zaire 64
Zeebrugge 353
Zillebeke 380
Zimmer, Louis 264, 266
Zoniënwoud (Forêt de Soignes) 182–3, 386
Zonnebeke 380
Zoutleeuw (Leau) 200–1
Zwin, River 315, 316, 351